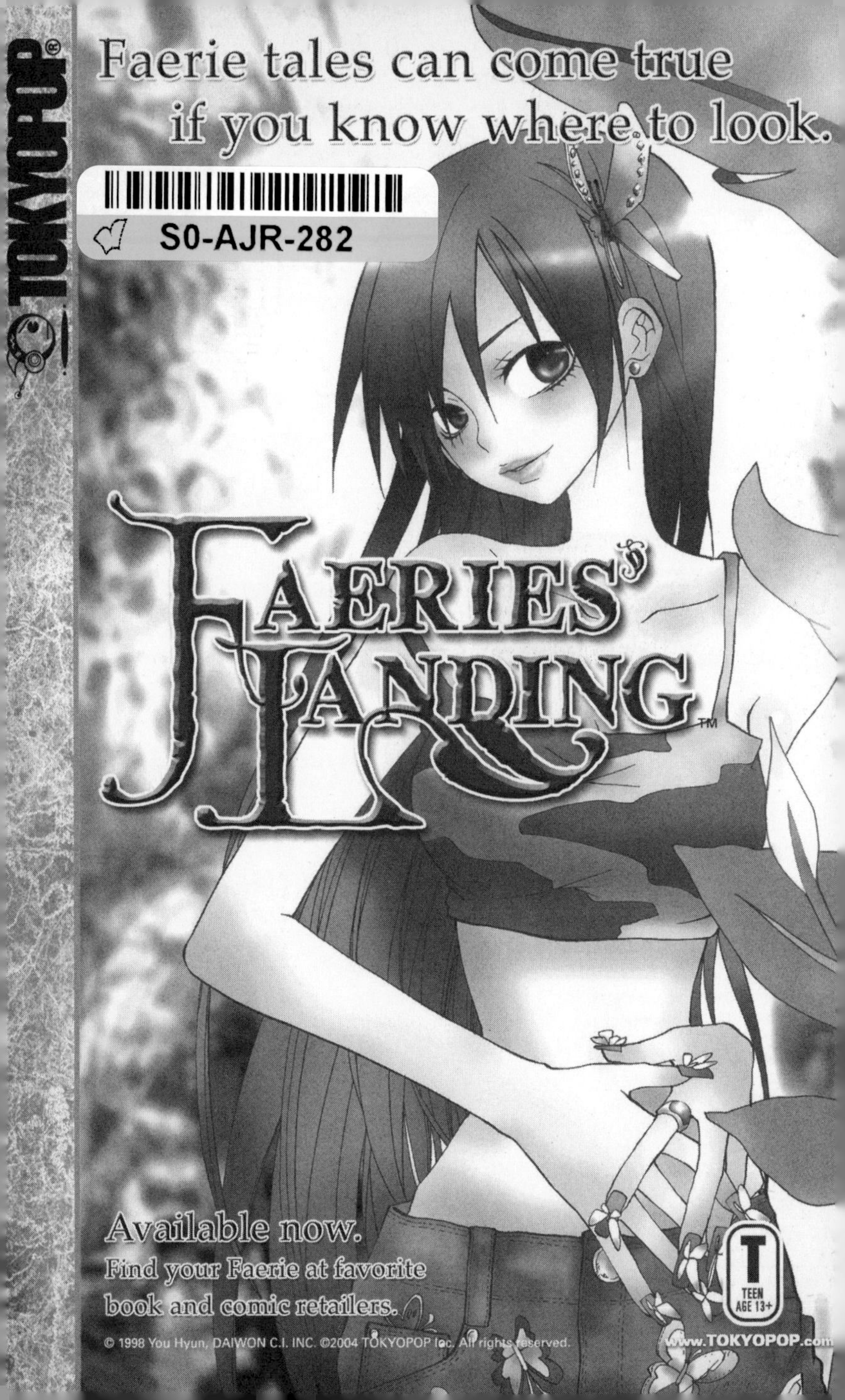
TOKYOPOP®
Faerie tales can come true
if you know where to look.
S0-AJR-282
FAERIES' LANDING™
Available now.
Find your Faerie at favorite
book and comic retailers.
T
TEEN
AGE 13+
© 1998 You Hyun, DAIWON C.I. INC. ©2004 TOKYOPOP Inc. All rights reserved.
www.TOKYOPOP.com

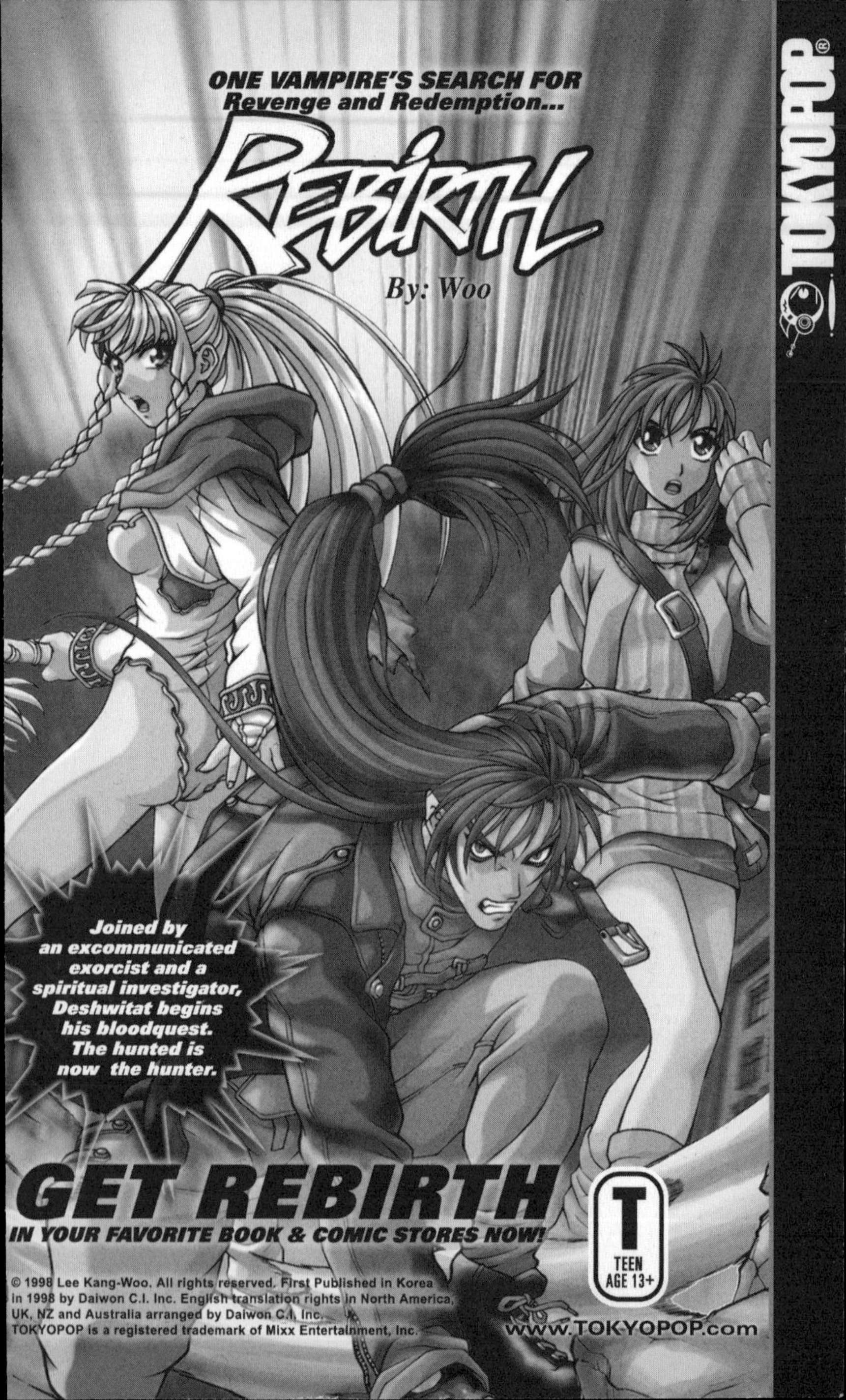

ONE VAMPIRE'S SEARCH FOR
Revenge and Redemption...
REBIRTH
By: Woo
Joined by an excommunicated exorcist and a spiritual investigator, Deshwitat begins his bloodquest. The hunted is now the hunter.
GET REBIRTH
IN YOUR FAVORITE BOOK & COMIC STORES NOW!
T TEEN AGE 13+
© 1998 Lee Kang-Woo. All rights reserved. First Published in Korea in 1998 by Daiwon C.I. Inc. English translation rights in North America, UK, NZ and Australia arranged by Daiwon C.I. Inc.
TOKYOPOP is a registered trademark of Mixx Entertainment, Inc.
www.TOKYOPOP.com
TOKYOPOP

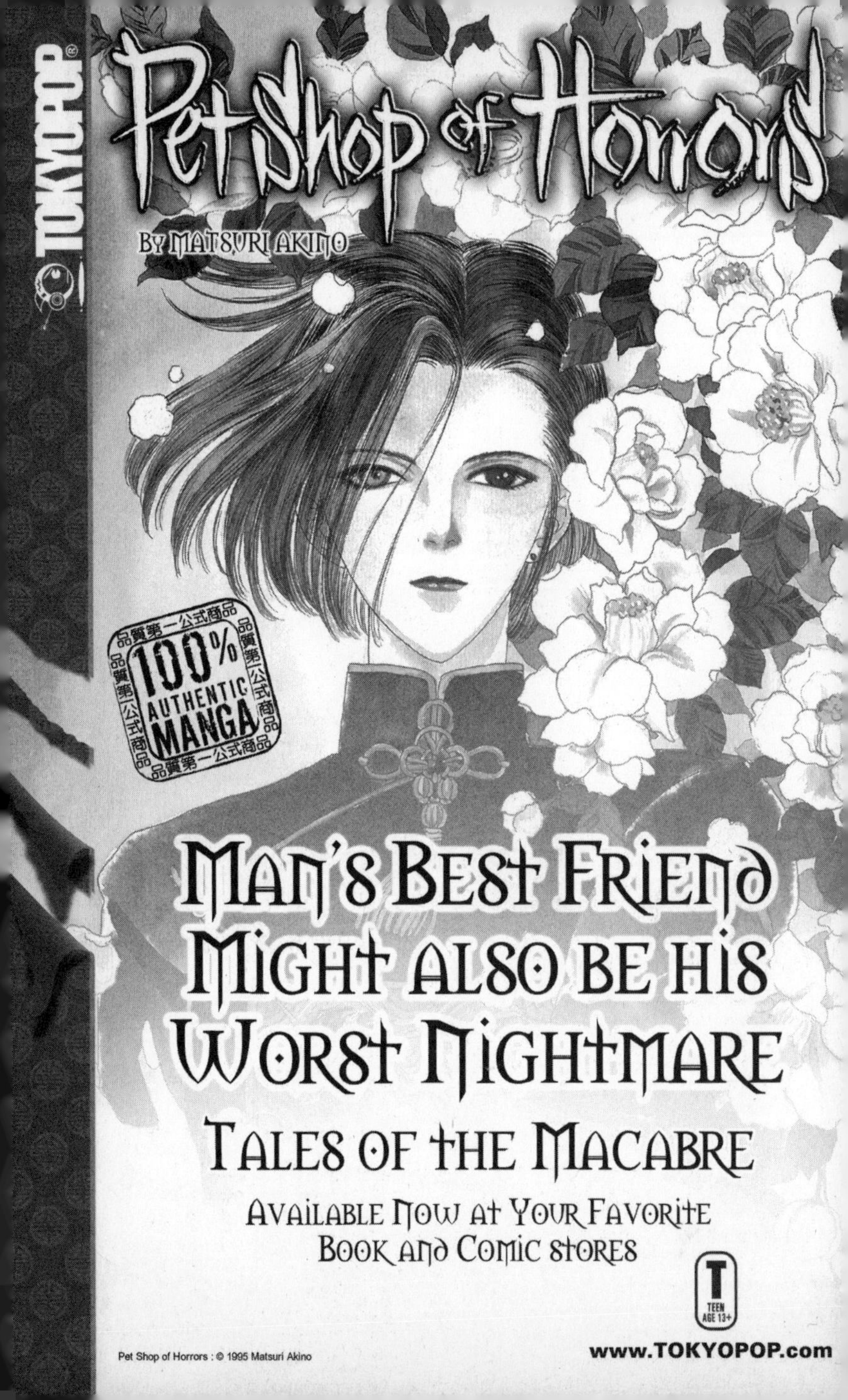
TOKYOPOP
Pet Shop of Horrors
BY MATSURI AKINO
100% AUTHENTIC MANGA
MAN'S BEST FRIEND MIGHT ALSO BE HIS WORST NIGHTMARE
TALES OF THE MACABRE
AVAILABLE NOW AT YOUR FAVORITE BOOK AND COMIC STORES
T TEEN AGE 13+
Pet Shop of Horrors : © 1995 Matsuri Akino
www.TOKYOPOP.com

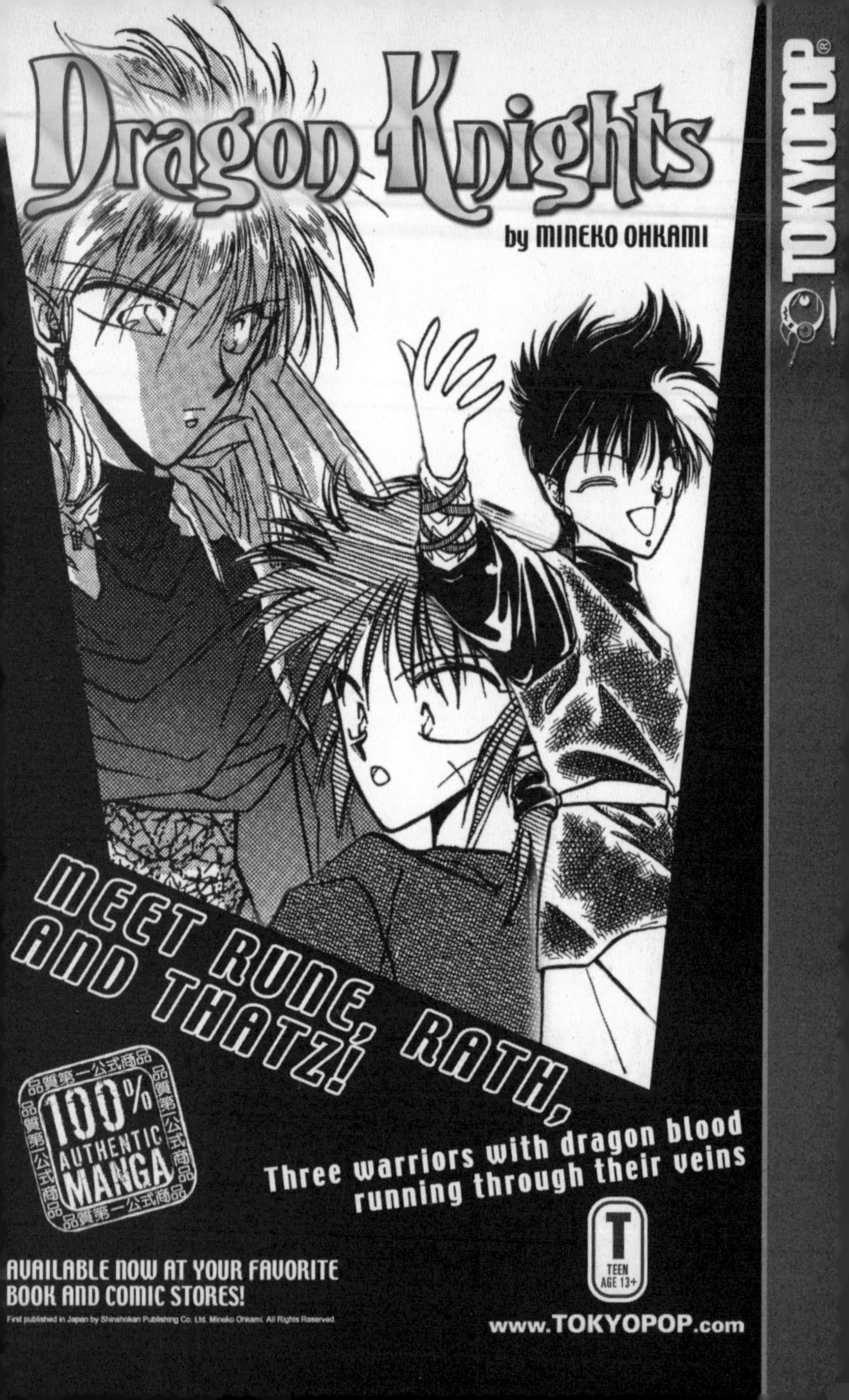
Dragon Knights
by MINEKO OHKAMI
MEET RUNE, RATH, AND THATZ!
Three warriors with dragon blood running through their veins
100% AUTHENTIC MANGA
T TEEN AGE 13+
AVAILABLE NOW AT YOUR FAVORITE BOOK AND COMIC STORES!
First published in Japan by Shinshokan Publishing Co. Ltd. Mineko Ohkami. All Rights Reserved.
www.TOKYOPOP.com
TOKYOPOP®

TOKYOPOP
Tired of the same old manga?
Try something refreshingly different.
Ai Yazawa's
PARADISE KISS
100% AUTHENTIC MANGA
品質第一公式商品
Where high fashion
and deep passion collide.
Available Now
www.TOKYOPOP.com

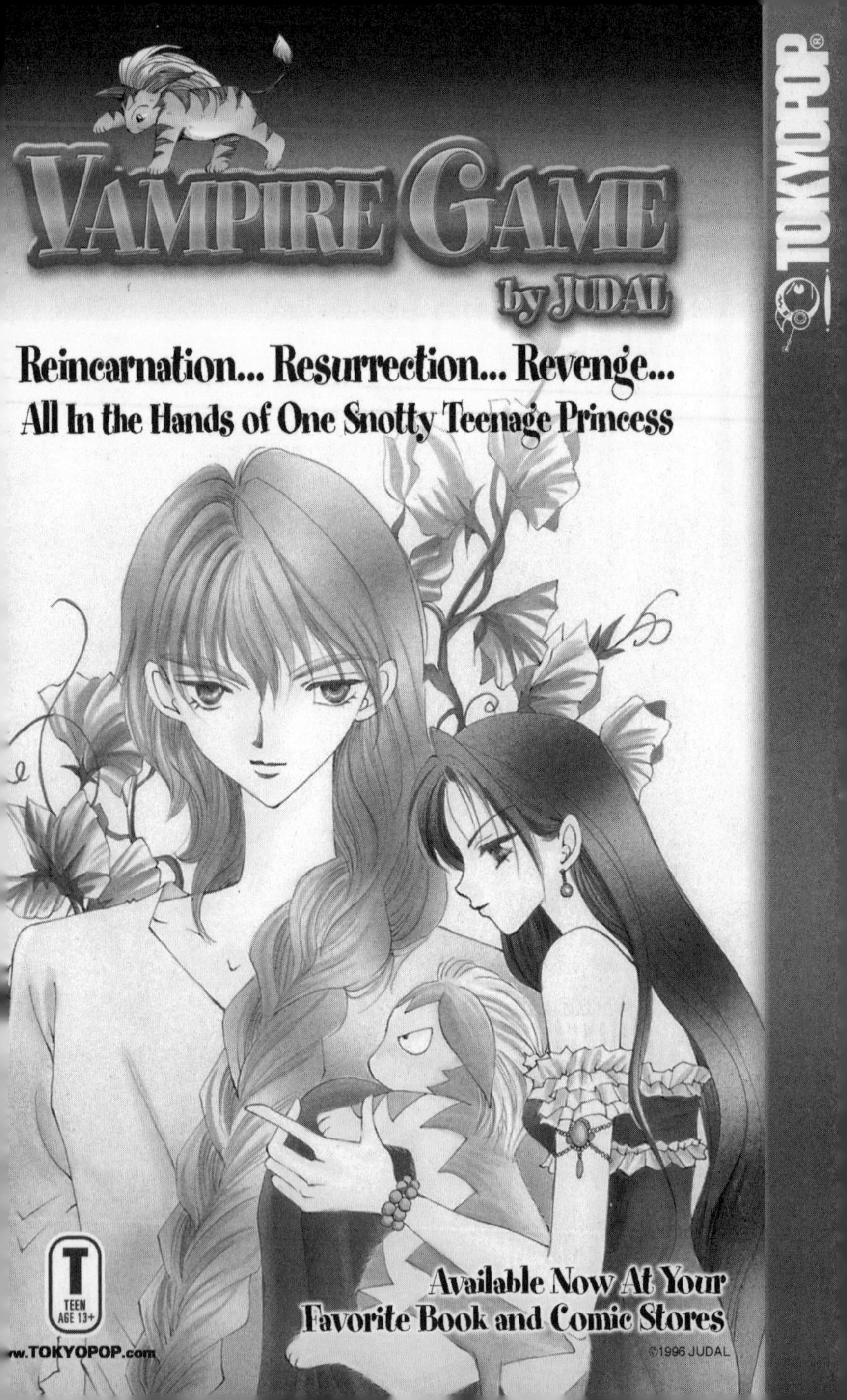
TOKYOPOP
VAMPIRE GAME
by JUDAL
Reincarnation... Resurrection... Revenge...
All In the Hands of One Snotty Teenage Princess
T
TEEN
AGE 13+
Available Now At Your
Favorite Book and Comic Stores
w.TOKYOPOP.com
©1996 JUDAL

ShutterBox

LIKE A
PHOTOGRAPH...
LOVE DEVELOPS
IN DARKNESS

NEW GOTHIC
SHOJO MANGA

COMING SOON TO YOUR FAVORITE
BOOK AND COMIC STORES.

TOKYOPOP

ShutterBox © 2003 Rosearik Rikki Simons and Tavisha
Wolfgarth Simons Copyright © 2003 TOKYOPOP Inc.
All rights reserved.

T
TEEN
AGE 13+

www.TOKYOPOP.com

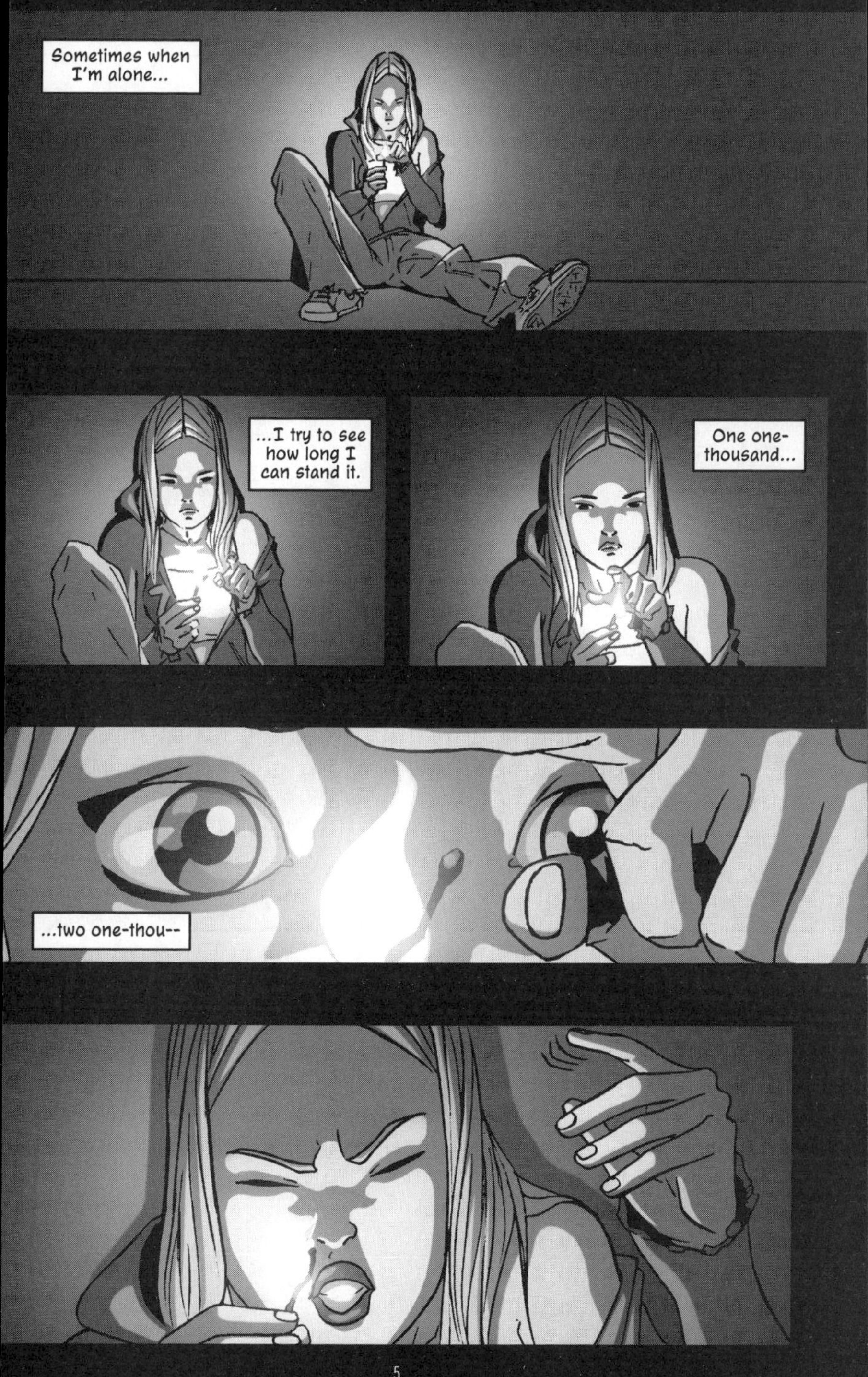
Sometimes when I'm alone...
...I try to see how long I can stand it.
One one-thousand...
...two one-thou--

BURNOUT

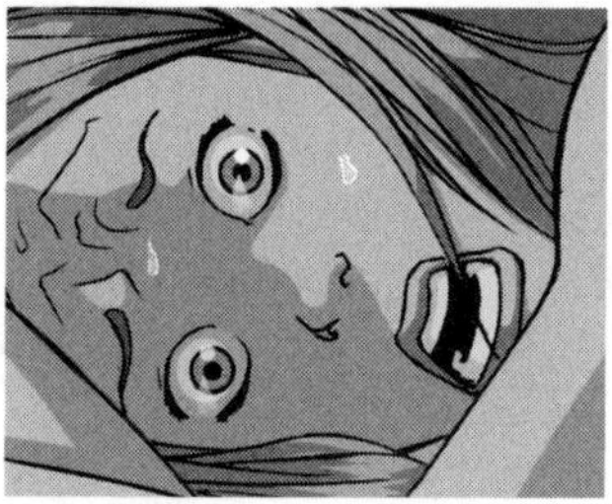

Written by Rebecca Donner

Illustrated by Inaki Miranda

Gray tones by Eva de la Cruz

Lettering by Jared K. Fletcher

minx

BURNOUT

Published by DC Comics, 1700 Broadway, New York, NY 10019.

Copyright © 2008 Rebecca Donner and Inaki Miranda.
All rights reserved. MINX and all characters featured in this book,
the distinctive likenesses thereof and related elements are
trademarks of DC COMICS.

The stories, characters and incidents mentioned in this book
are entirely fictional.

Printed in Canada.
DC Comics, a Warner Bros.Entertainment Company.

ISBN: 978-1-4012-1537-8

Cover by Inaki Miranda

Karen Berger Sr. VP-Executive Editor Shelly Bond, Editor Angela Rufino, Assistant Editor Robbin Brosterman, Sr. Art Director
Paul Levitz, President & Publisher Georg Brewer, VP-Design & DC Direct Creative Richard Bruning, Sr. VP-Creative Director
Patrick Caldon, Exec. VP-Finance & Operations Chris Caramalis, VP-Finance John Cunningham, VP-Marketing Terri Cunningham, VP-Managing Editor
Alison Gill, VP-Manufacturing Hank Kanalz, VP-General Manager, WildStorm Jim Lee, Editorial Director-WildStorm
Paula Lowitt, Sr. VP-Business & Legal Affairs MaryEllen McLaughlin, VP-Advertising & Custom Publishing John Nee, Sr. VP-Business Development
Gregory Noveck, Sr. VP-Creative Affairs Sue Pohja, VP-Book Trade Sales Steve Rotterdam, Sr. VP-Sales & Marketing Cheryl Rubin, Sr. VP-Brand Management
Jeff Trojan, VP-Business Development, DC Direct Bob Wayne, VP-Sales

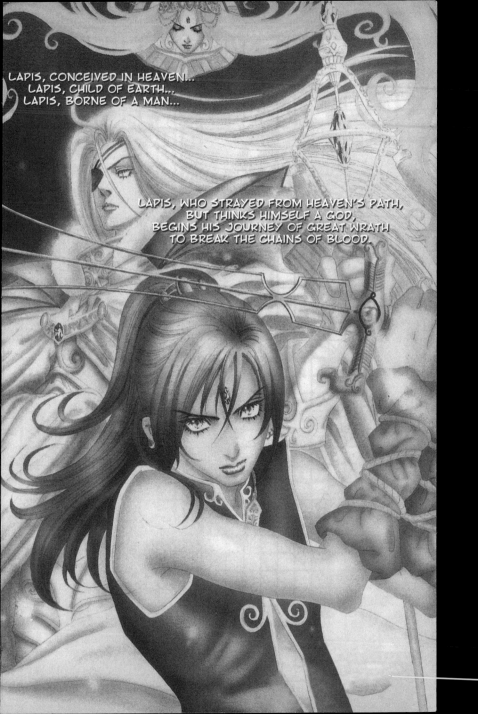

LAPIS, CONCEIVED IN HEAVEN...
LAPIS, CHILD OF EARTH...
LAPIS, BORNE OF A MAN...

LAPIS, WHO STRAYED FROM HEAVEN'S PATH,
BUT THINKS HIMSELF A GOD,
BEGINS HIS JOURNEY OF GREAT WRATH
TO BREAK THE CHAINS OF BLOOD.

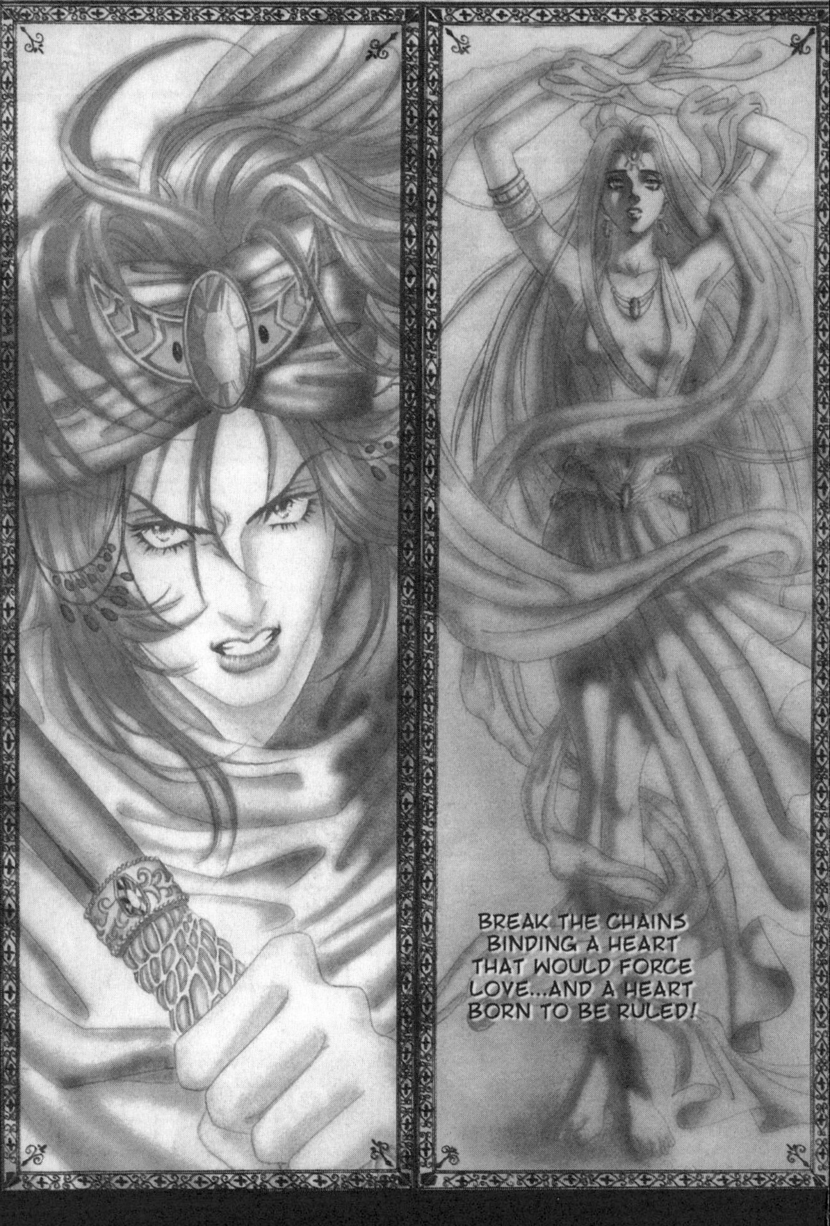
BREAK THE CHAINS
BINDING A HEART
THAT WOULD FORCE
LOVE...AND A HEART
BORN TO BE RULED!

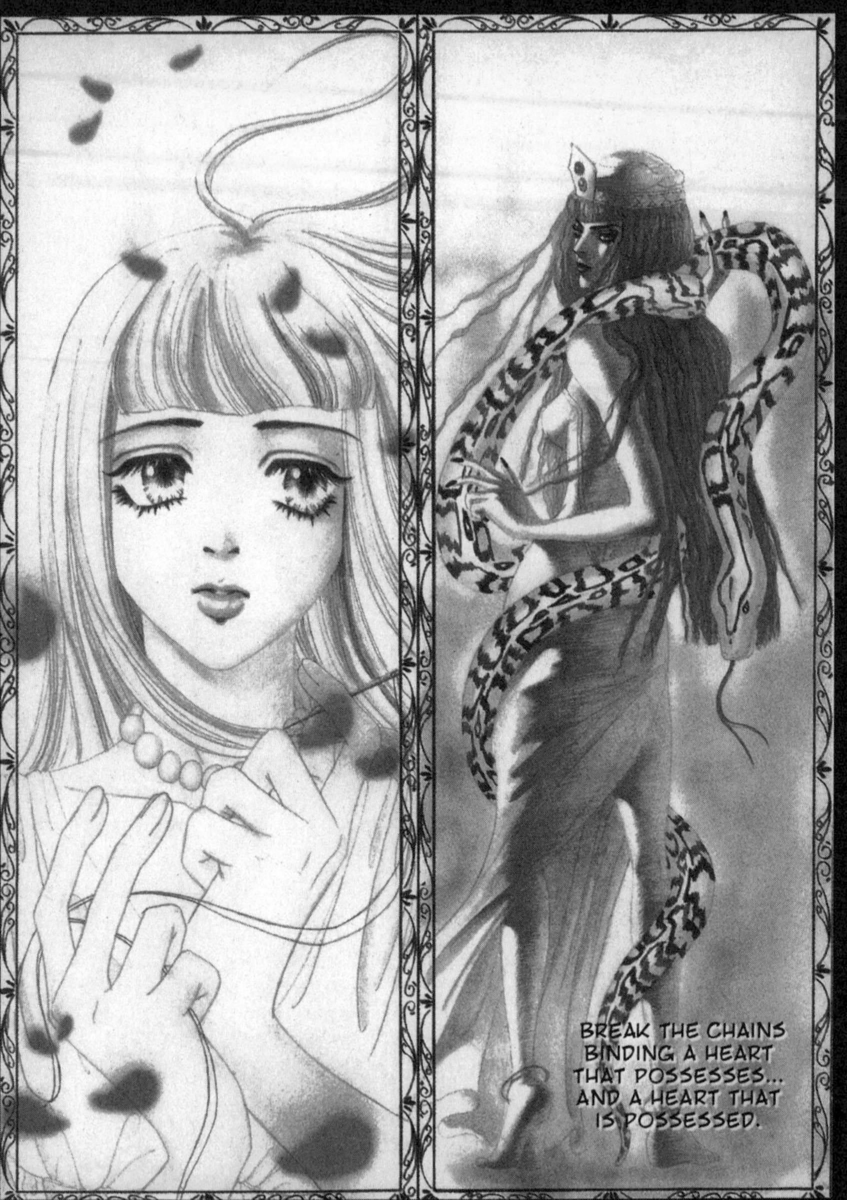
BREAK THE CHAINS BINDING A HEART THAT POSSESSES... AND A HEART THAT IS POSSESSED.

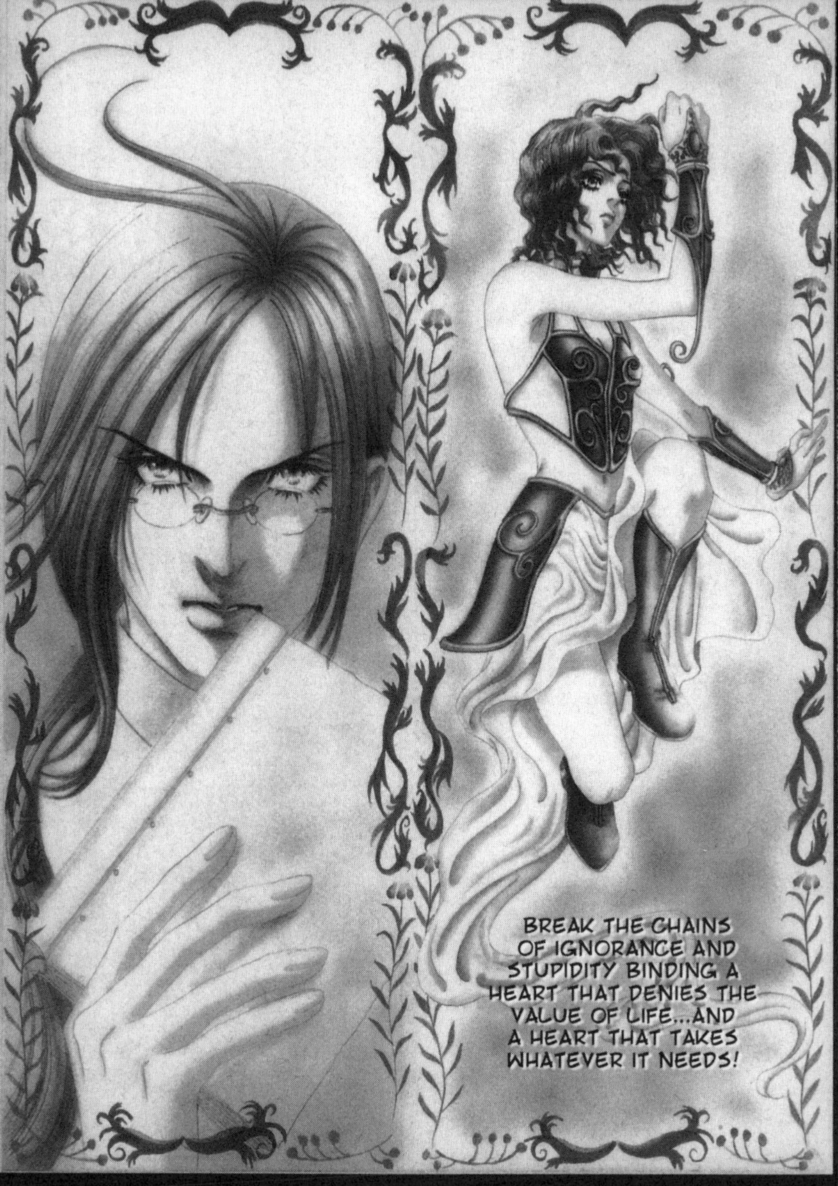
BREAK THE CHAINS OF IGNORANCE AND STUPIDITY BINDING A HEART THAT DENIES THE VALUE OF LIFE...AND A HEART THAT TAKES WHATEVER IT NEEDS!

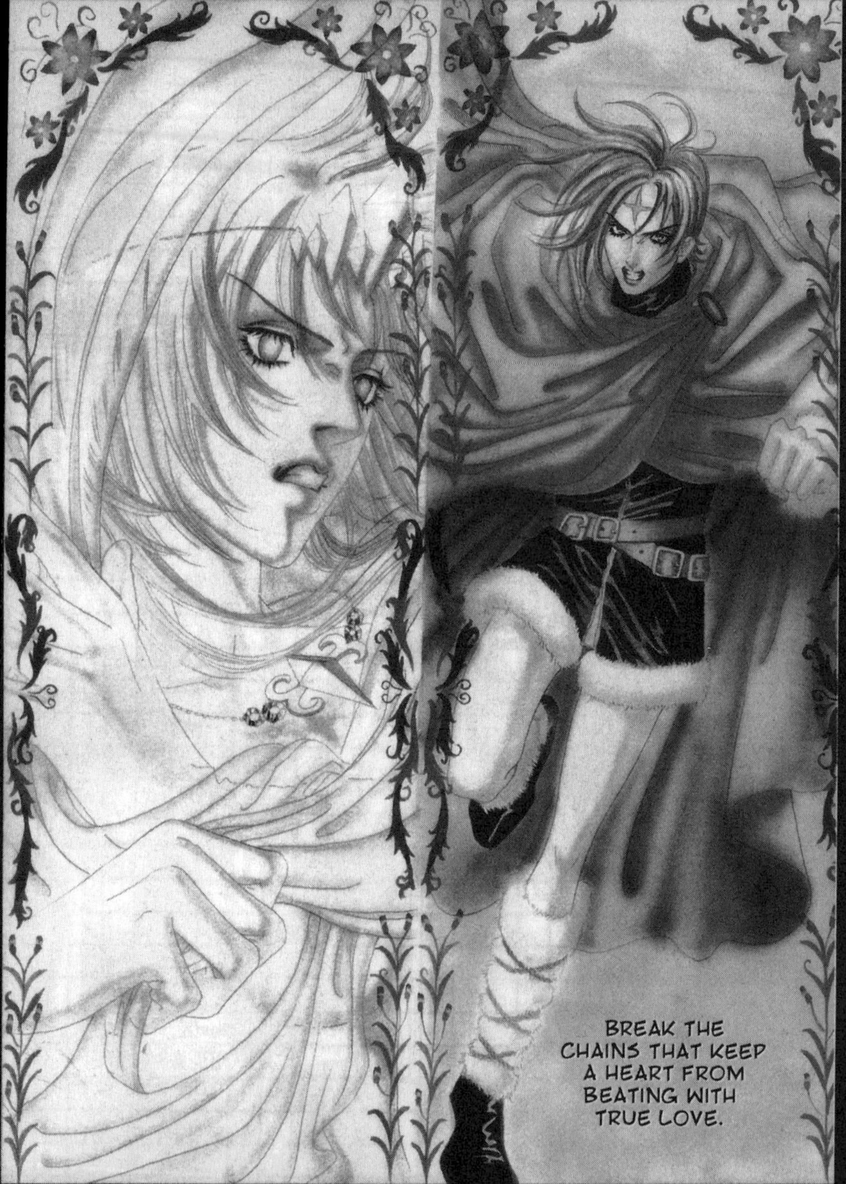
BREAK THE CHAINS THAT KEEP A HEART FROM BEATING WITH TRUE LOVE.

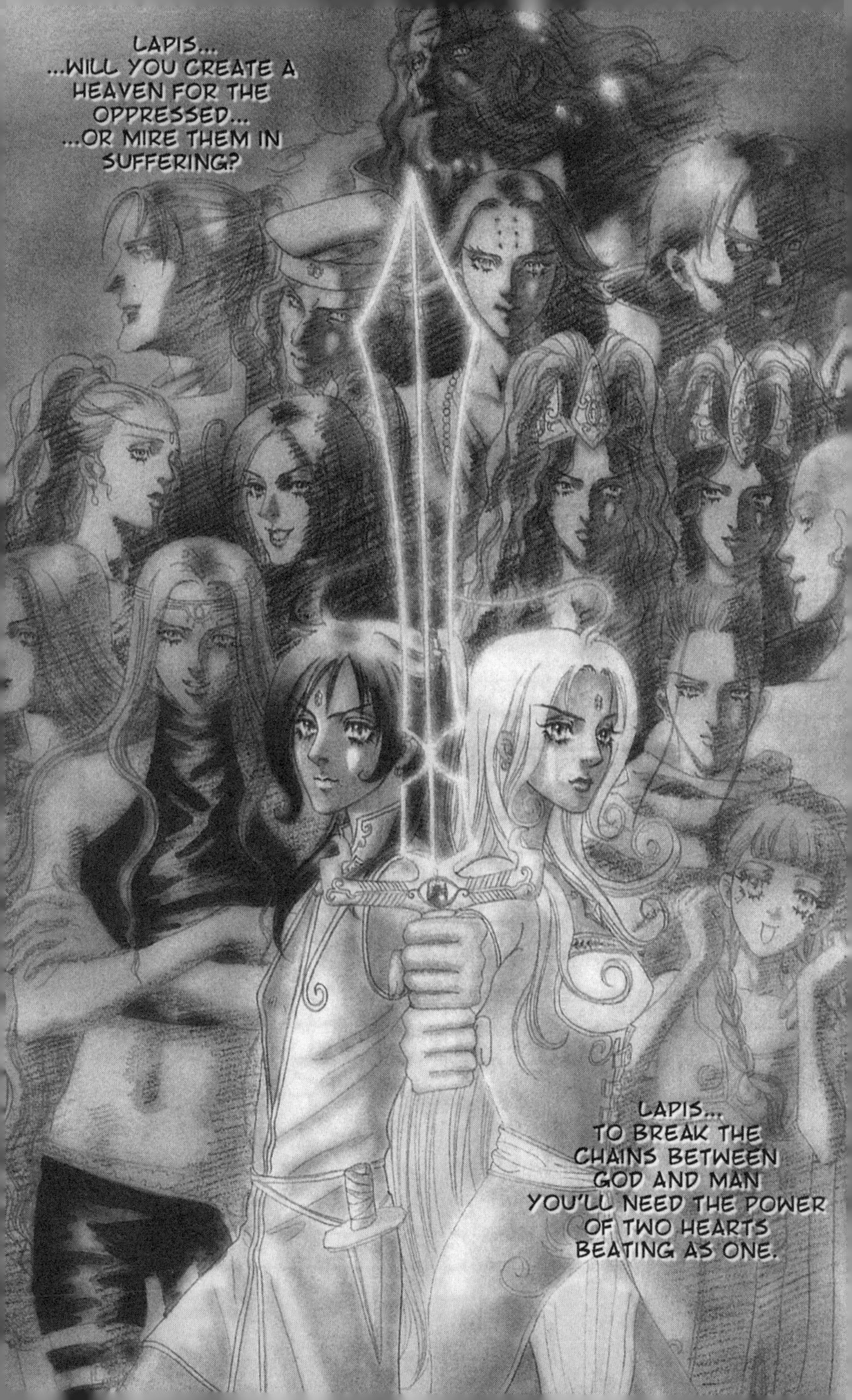
LAPIS... ...WILL YOU CREATE A HEAVEN FOR THE OPPRESSED... ...OR MIRE THEM IN SUFFERING?
LAPIS... TO BREAK THE CHAINS BETWEEN GOD AND MAN YOU'LL NEED THE POWER OF TWO HEARTS BEATING AS ONE.

Les Bijoux

Story by
Jo Eun-Ha

Art by
Park Sang-Sun

Volume 1

TOKYOPOP®
Los Angeles • Tokyo • London

Translator - Seung-Ah Lee
English Adaptation - Jason Deitrich
Retouch and Lettering - Caren McCaleb, Jose Macasocol, Jr.
Copy Editor - Aaron Sparrow
Cover Layout - Patrick Hook
Editor - Rob Tokar

Managing Editor - Jill Freshney
Production Coordinator - Antonio DePietro
Production Managers - Jennifer Miller, Mutsumi Miyazaki
Art Director - Matt Alford
Editorial Director - Jeremy Ross
VP of Production - Ron Klamert
President & C.O.O. - John Parker
Publisher & C.E.O. - Stuart Levy

Email: editor@TOKYOPOP.com
Come visit us online at www.TOKYOPOP.com

A  **TOKYOPOP**® Manga

TOKYOPOP Inc.
5900 Wilshire Blvd. Suite 2000
Los Angeles, CA 90036

Les Bijoux volume 1

Les Bijoux volume 1 is © 2000 Jo Eun-Ha & Park Sang-Sun, DAIWON C.I. INC. All rights reserved.
First published in Korea in 2000 by DAIWON C.I. INC.
English language translation rights in North America, UK, NZ,and Australia arranged by Daiwon C.I. Inc.
English text copyright ©2004 TOKYOPOP Inc.

All rights reserved. No portion of this book may be reproduced or transmitted
in any form or by any means without written permission from the copyright
holders. This manga is a work of fiction. Any resemblance to actual events
or locales or persons, living or dead, is entirely coincidental.

ISBN: 1-59182-690-X

First TOKYOPOP printing: Feburary 2004

10 9 8 7 6 5 4 3 2 1
Printed in the USA

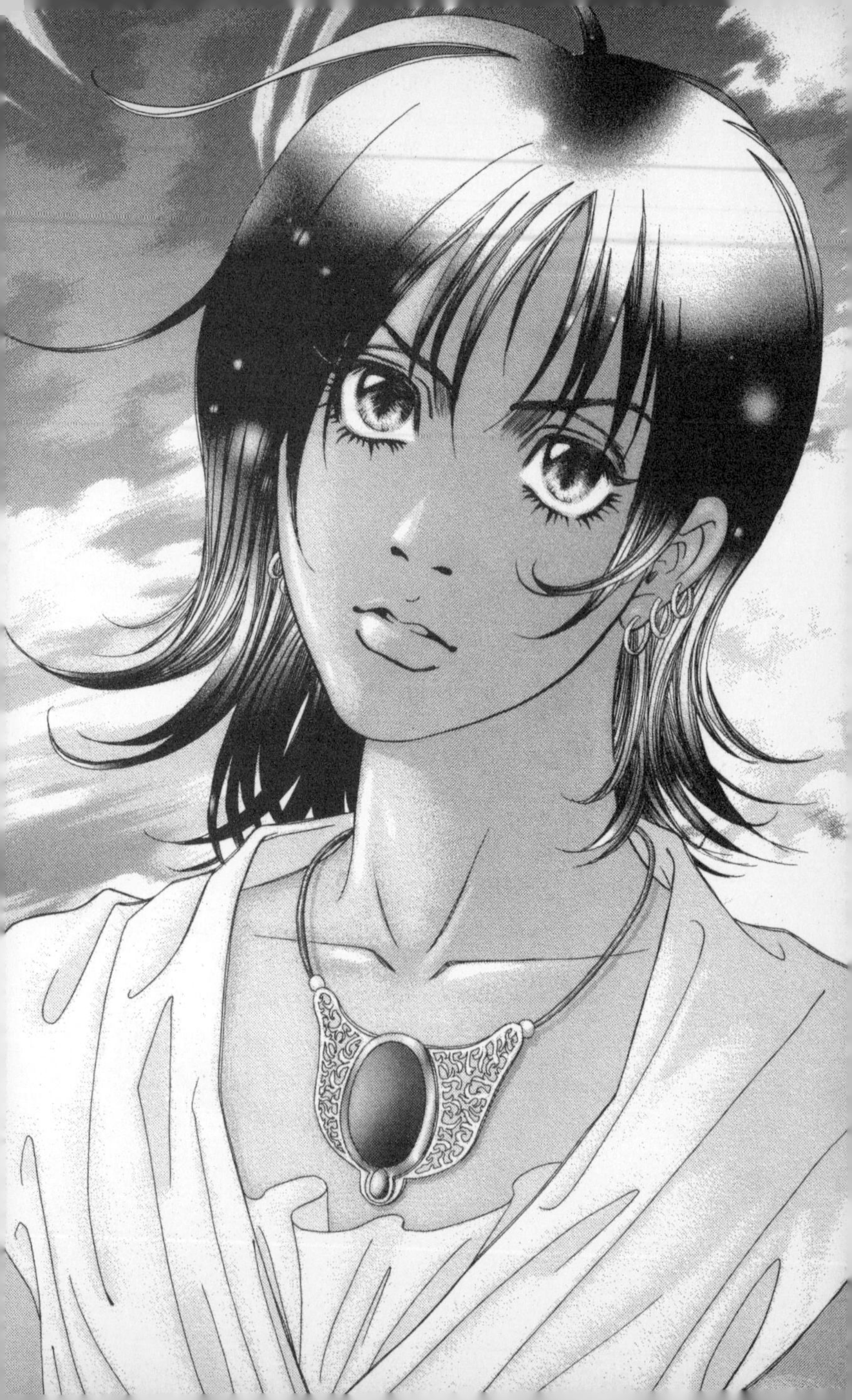

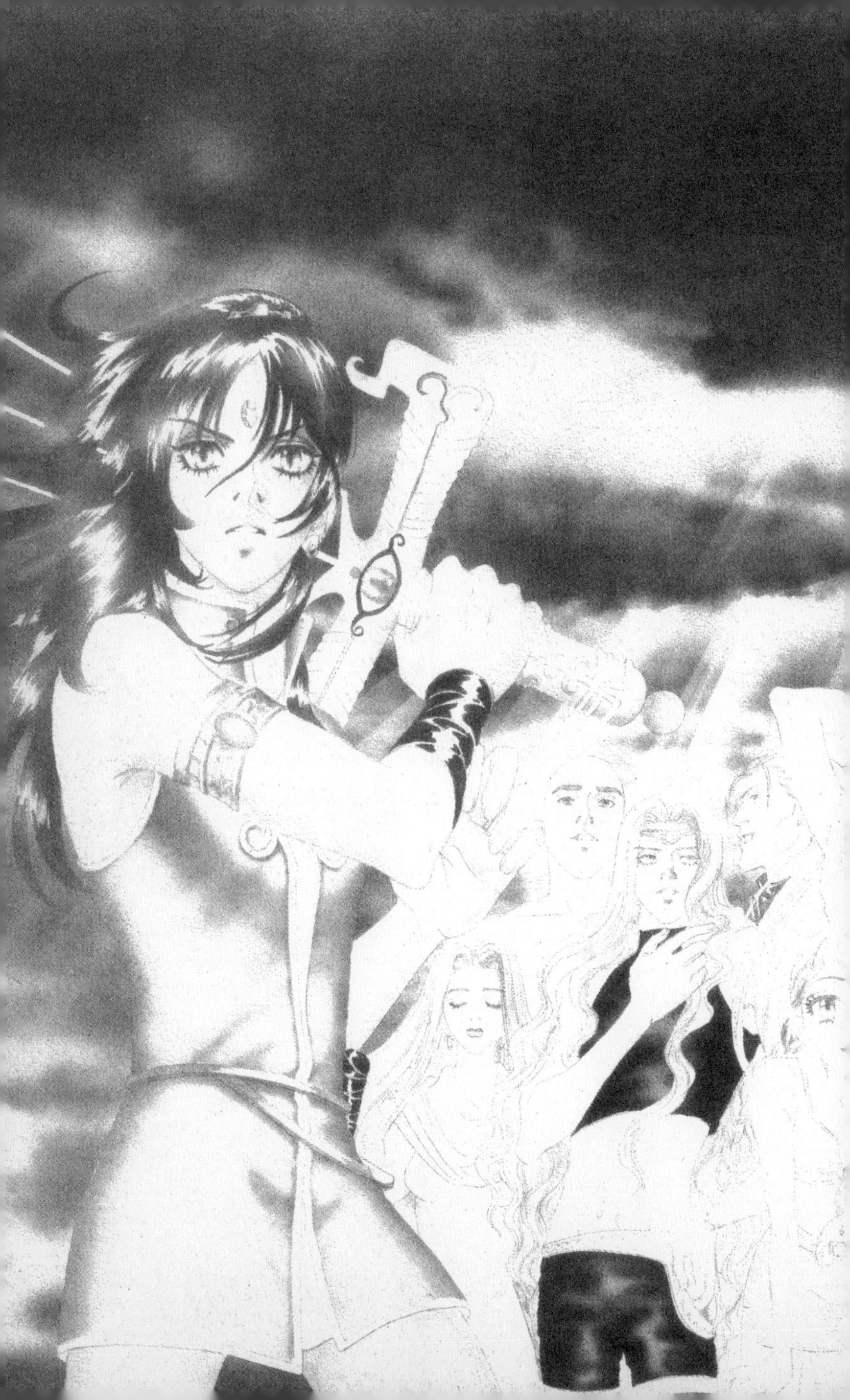

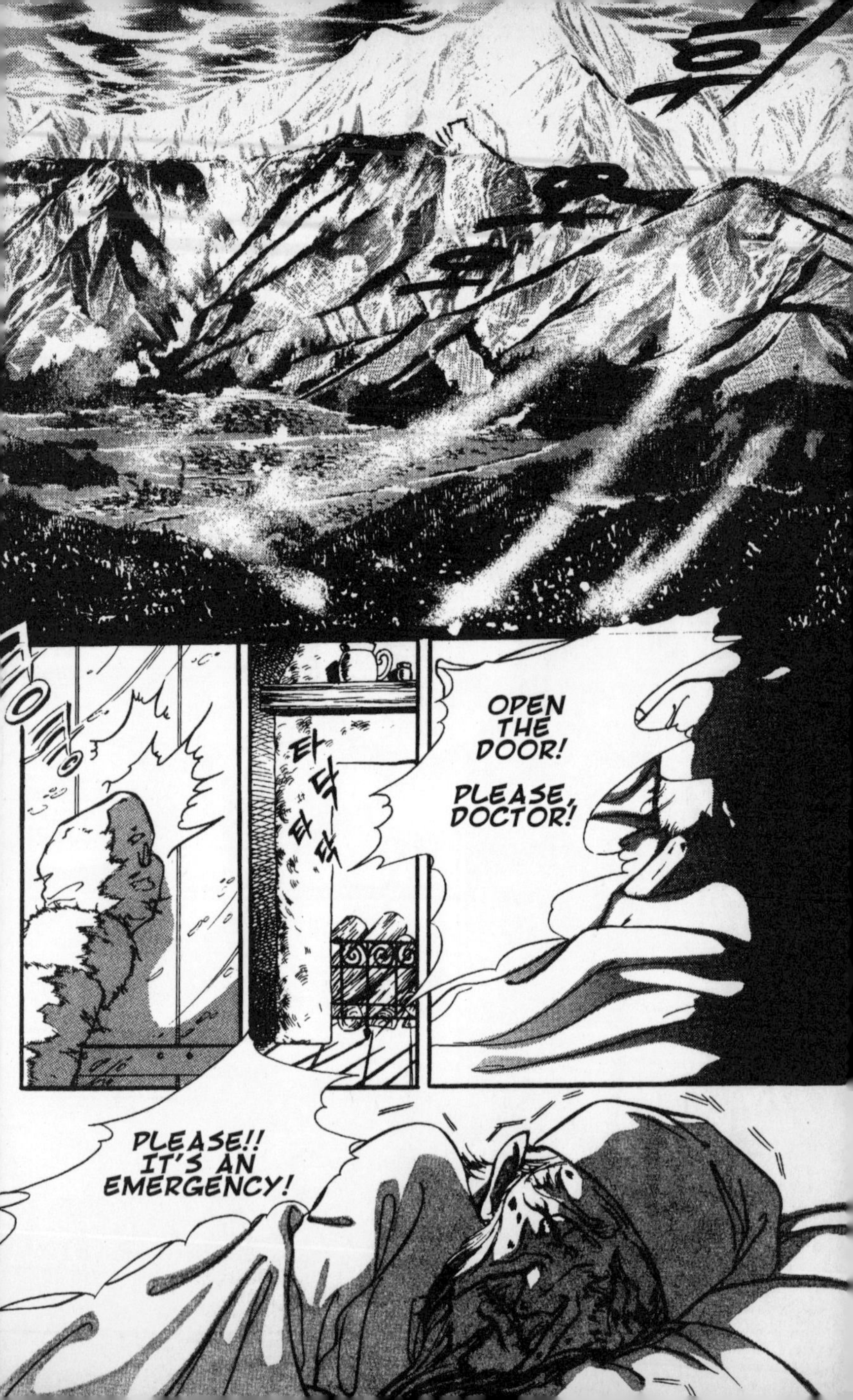
OPEN THE DOOR!
PLEASE, DOCTOR!
타닥 타닥
PLEASE!! IT'S AN EMERGENCY!

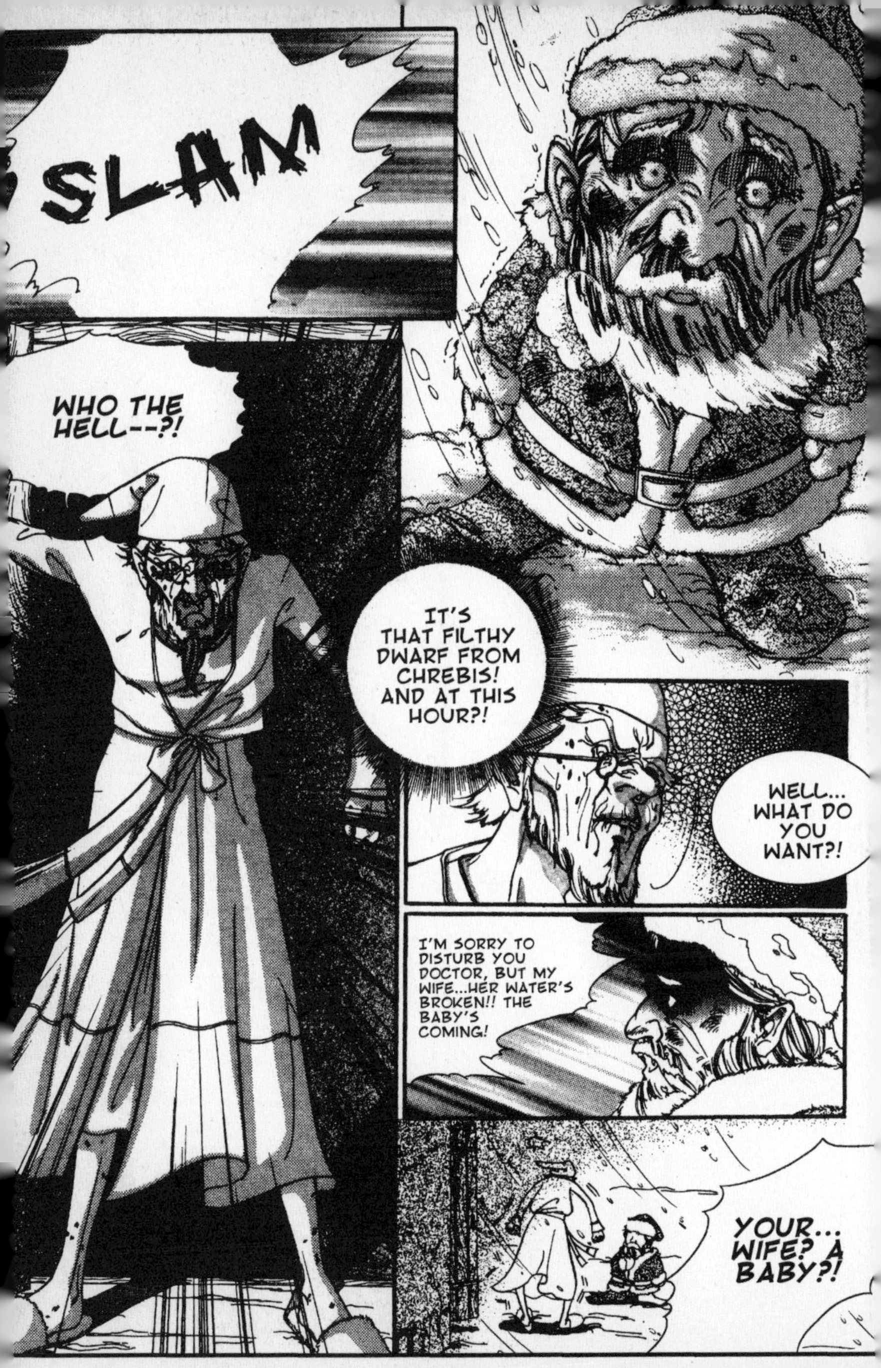
SLAM
WHO THE HELL--?!
IT'S THAT FILTHY DWARF FROM CHREBIS! AND AT THIS HOUR?!
WELL... WHAT DO YOU WANT?!
I'M SORRY TO DISTURB YOU DOCTOR, BUT MY WIFE...HER WATER'S BROKEN!! THE BABY'S COMING!
YOUR... WIFE? A BABY?!

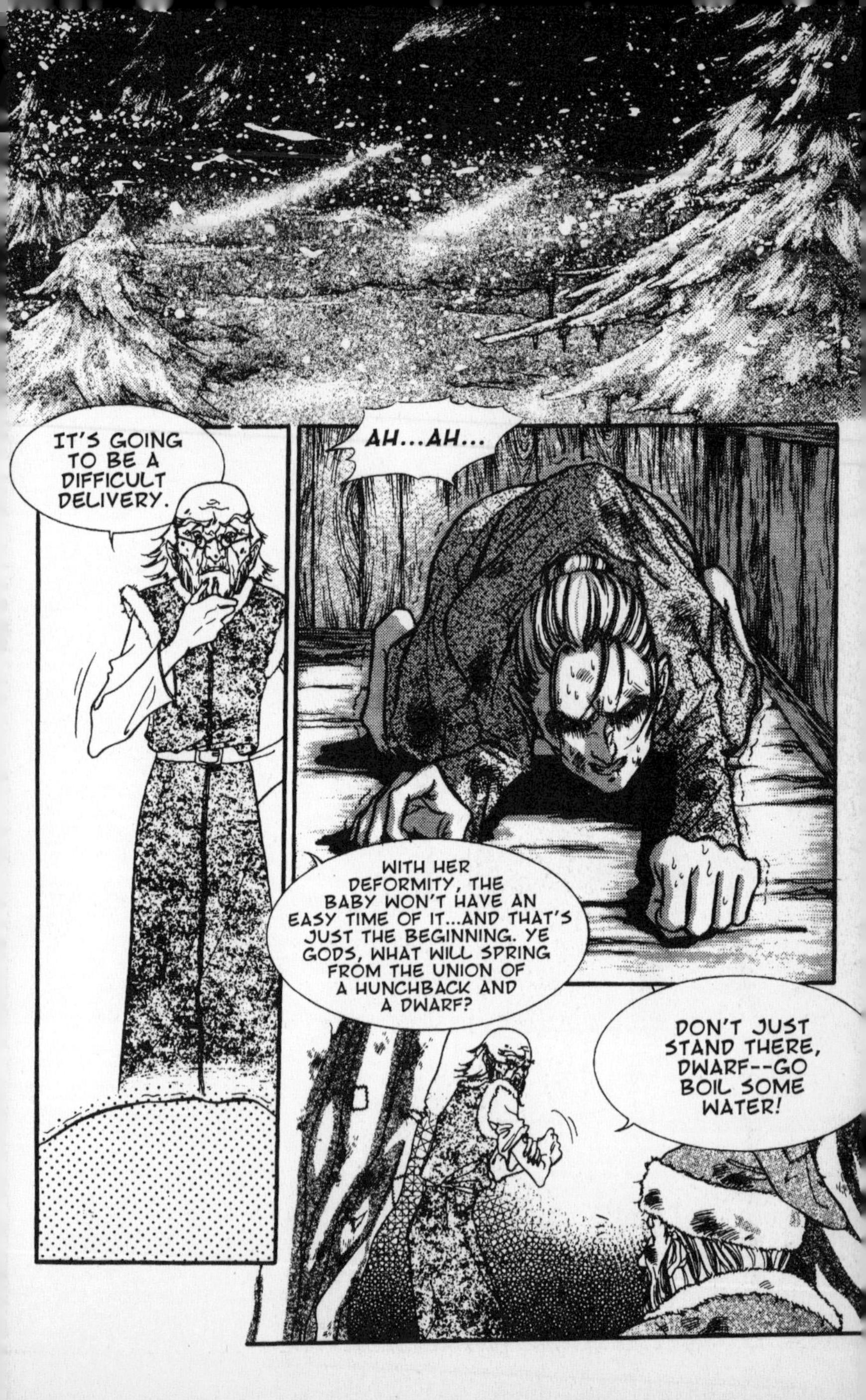
IT'S GOING TO BE A DIFFICULT DELIVERY.
AH...AH...
WITH HER DEFORMITY, THE BABY WON'T HAVE AN EASY TIME OF IT...AND THAT'S JUST THE BEGINNING. YE GODS, WHAT WILL SPRING FROM THE UNION OF A HUNCHBACK AND A DWARF?
DON'T JUST STAND THERE, DWARF--GO BOIL SOME WATER!

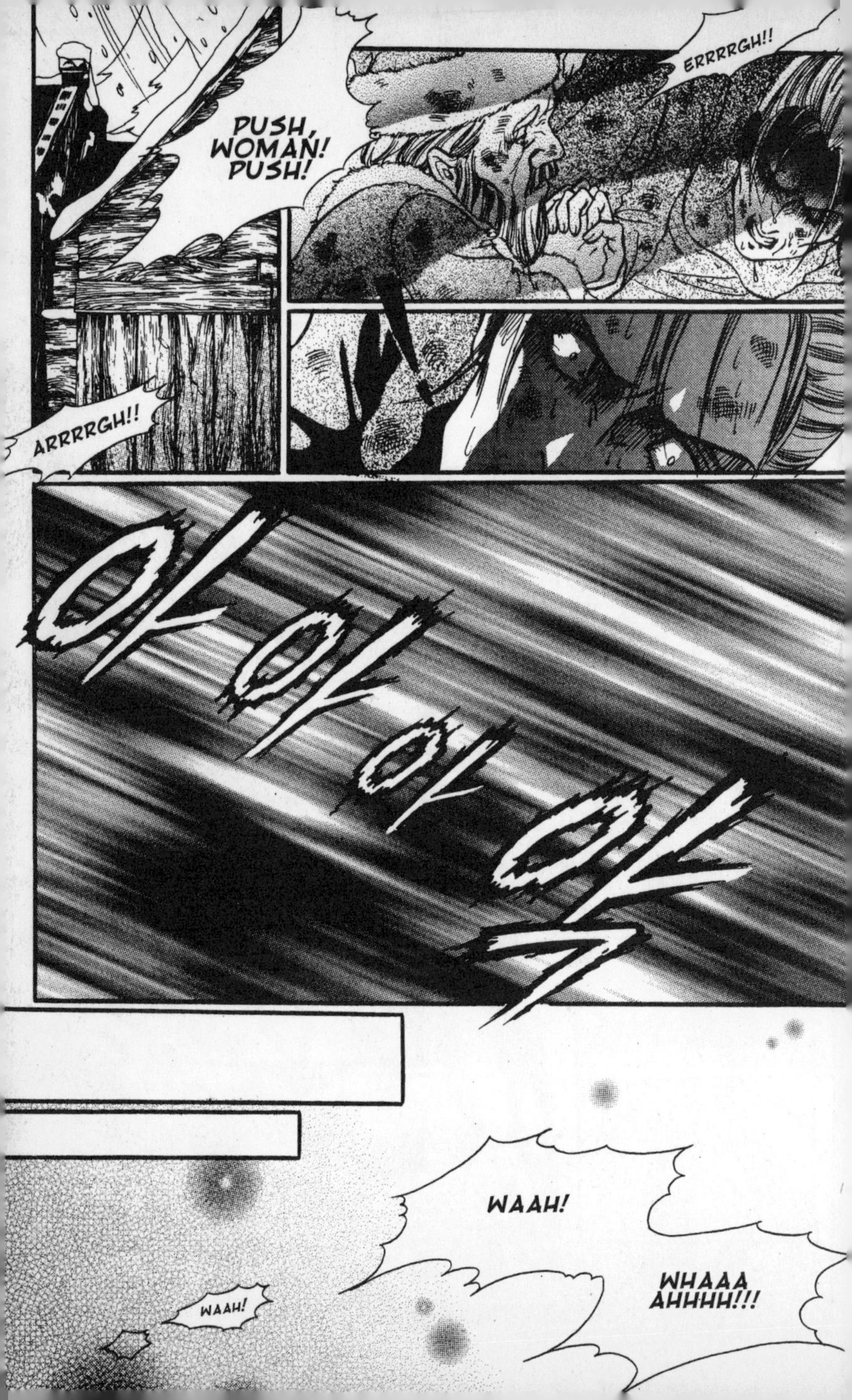
PUSH, WOMAN! PUSH!
ERRRRGH!!
ARRRRGH!!
아아아악
WAAH!
WHAAA AHHHH!!!
WAAH!

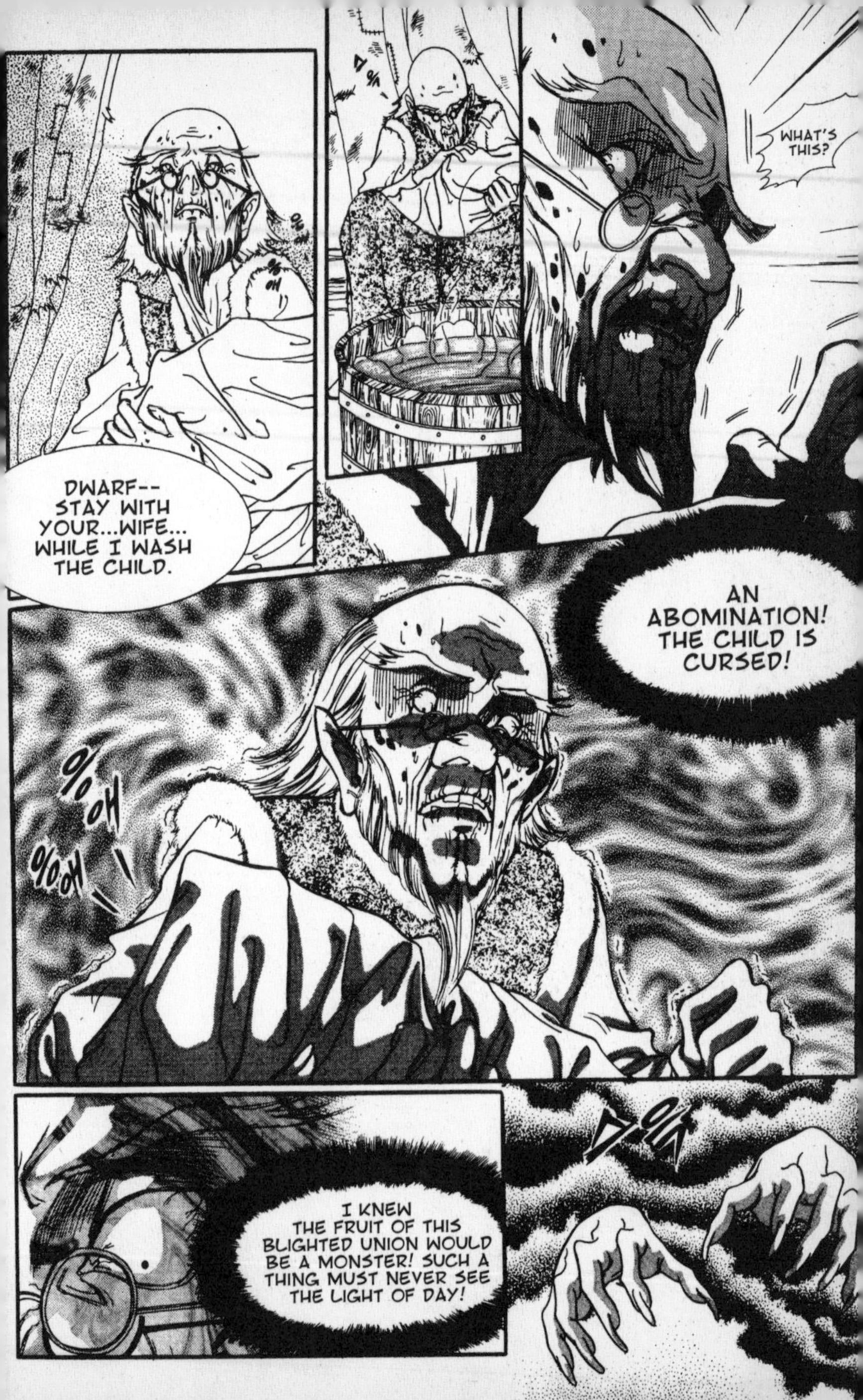
DWARF-- STAY WITH YOUR...WIFE... WHILE I WASH THE CHILD.
WHAT'S THIS?
AN ABOMINATION! THE CHILD IS CURSED!
I KNEW THE FRUIT OF THIS BLIGHTED UNION WOULD BE A MONSTER! SUCH A THING MUST NEVER SEE THE LIGHT OF DAY!

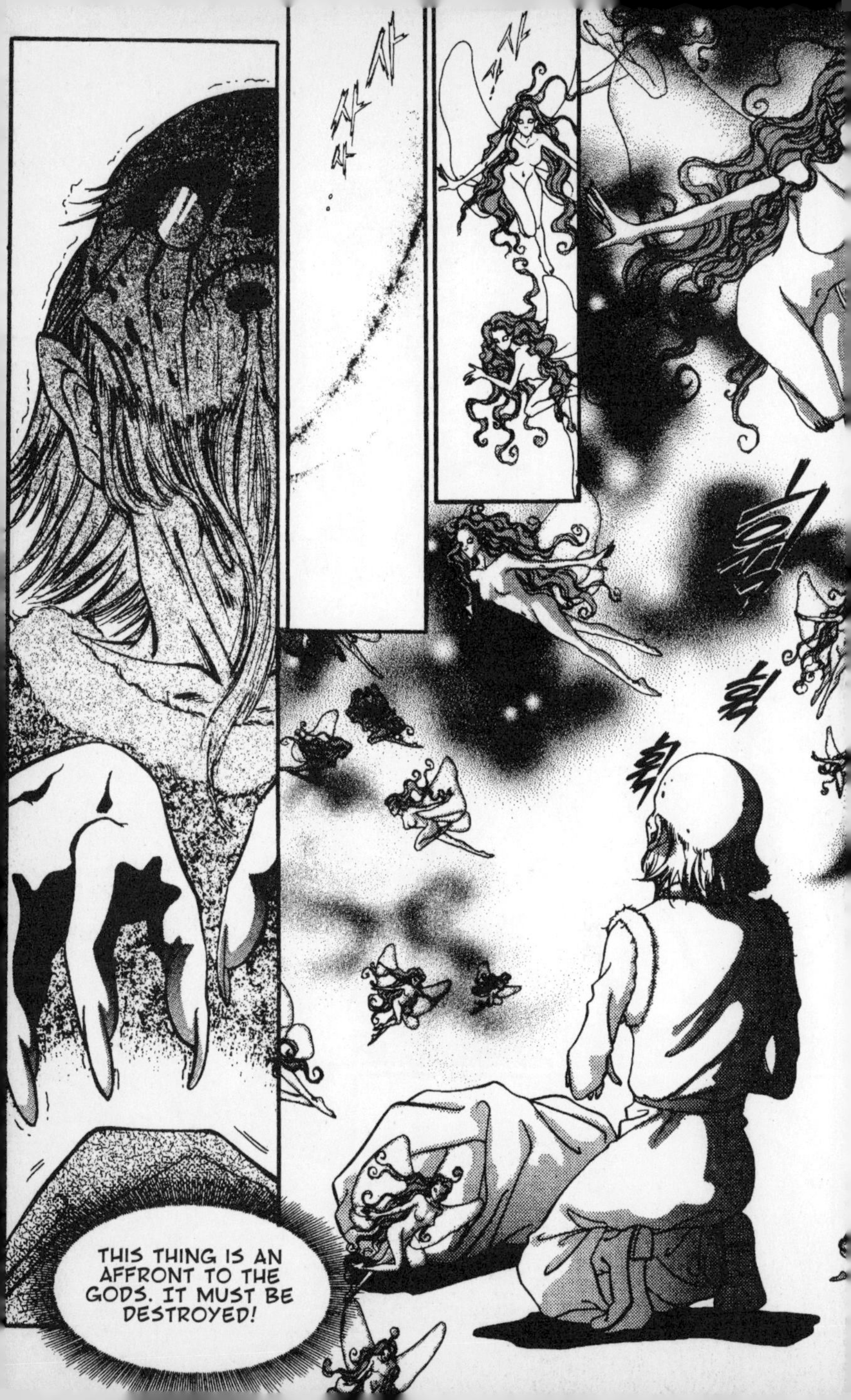
사사!
사사사..
휙
휙
휙
THIS THING IS AN AFFRONT TO THE GODS. IT MUST BE DESTROYED!

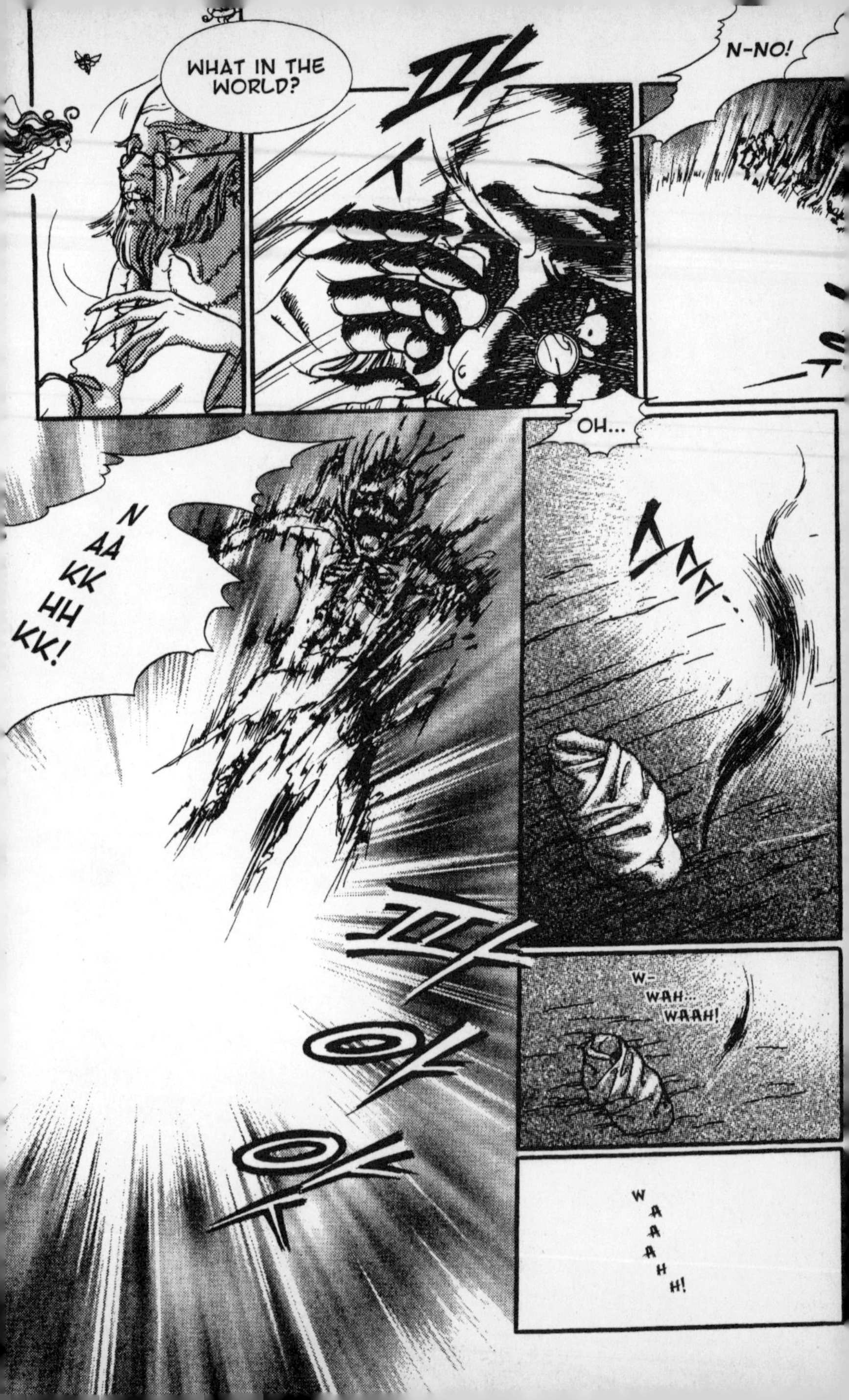
N-NO!
WHAT IN THE WORLD?
OH...
N AA KK HH KK!
W- WAH... WAAH!
W A A A H H!

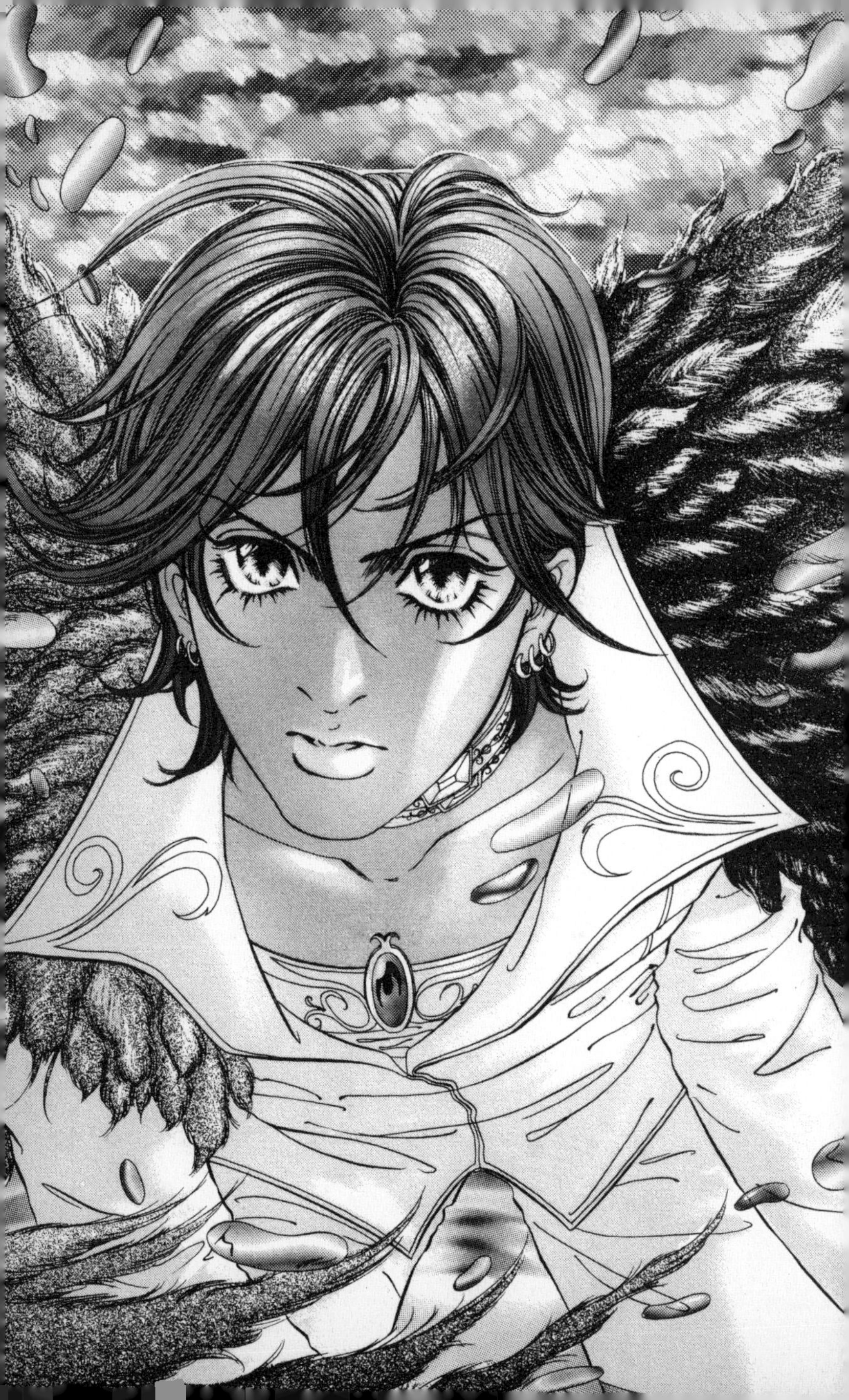

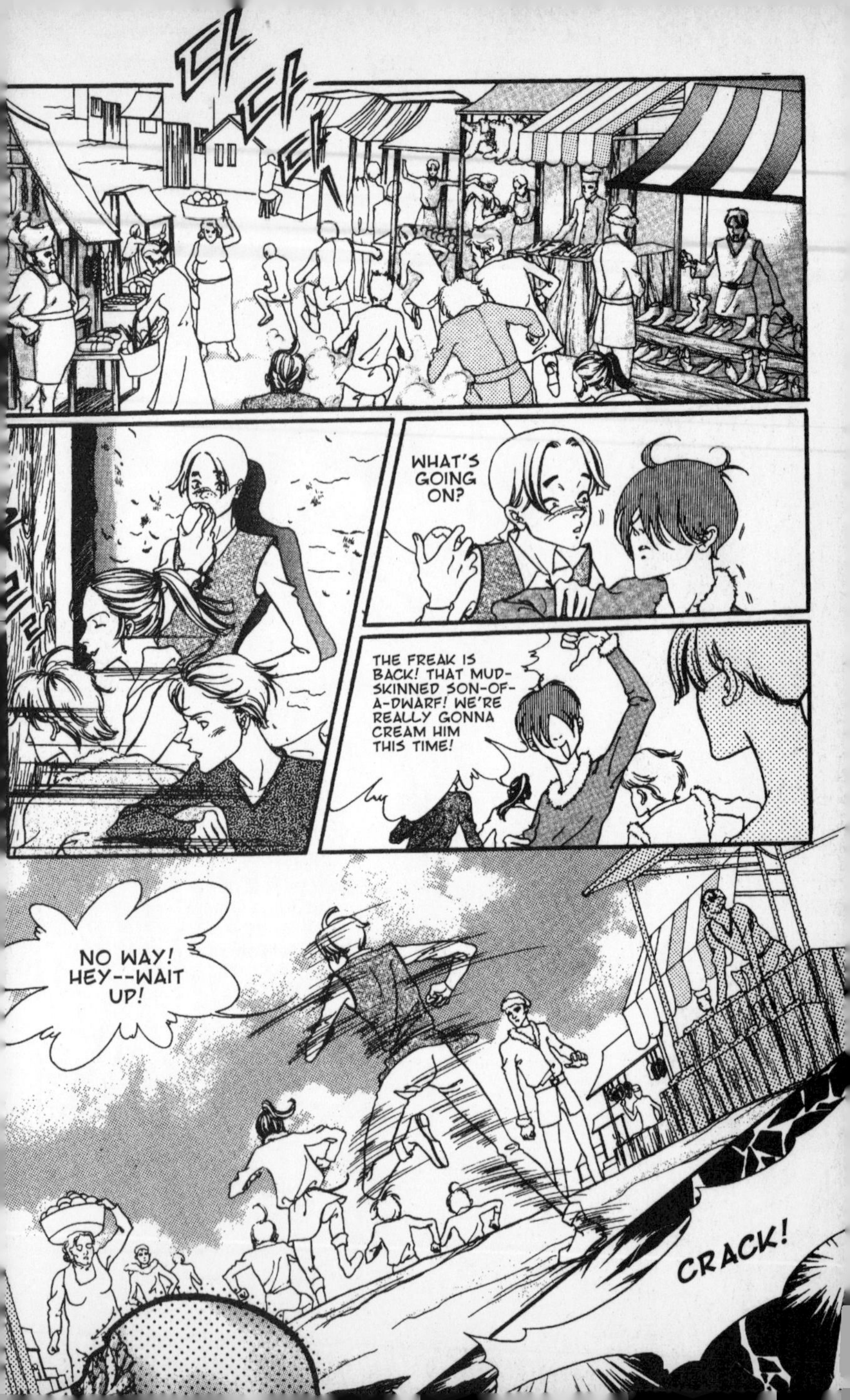
WHAT'S GOING ON?
THE FREAK IS BACK! THAT MUD-SKINNED SON-OF-A-DWARF! WE'RE REALLY GONNA CREAM HIM THIS TIME!
NO WAY! HEY--WAIT UP!
CRACK!

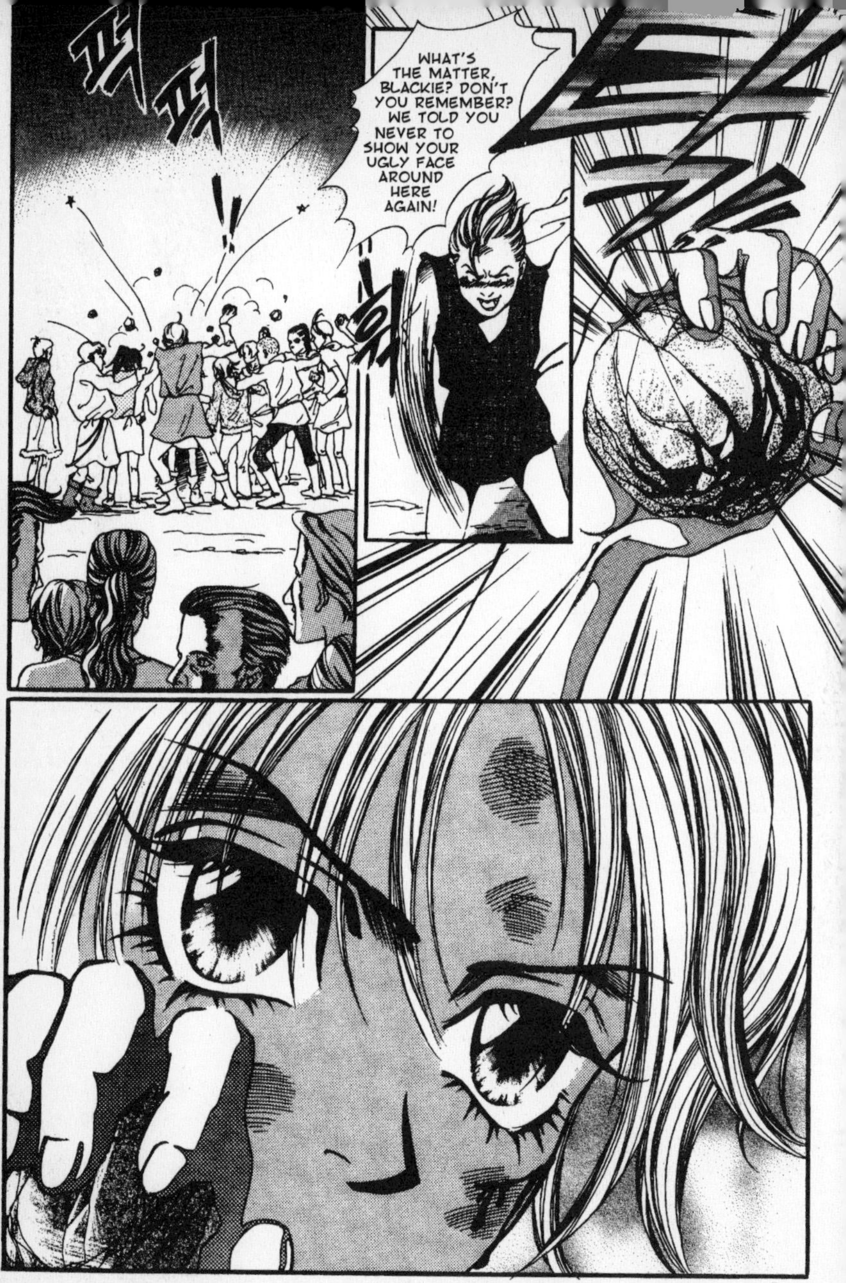
퍽
퍽
WHAT'S THE MATTER, BLACKIE? DON'T YOU REMEMBER? WE TOLD YOU NEVER TO SHOW YOUR UGLY FACE AROUND HERE AGAIN!

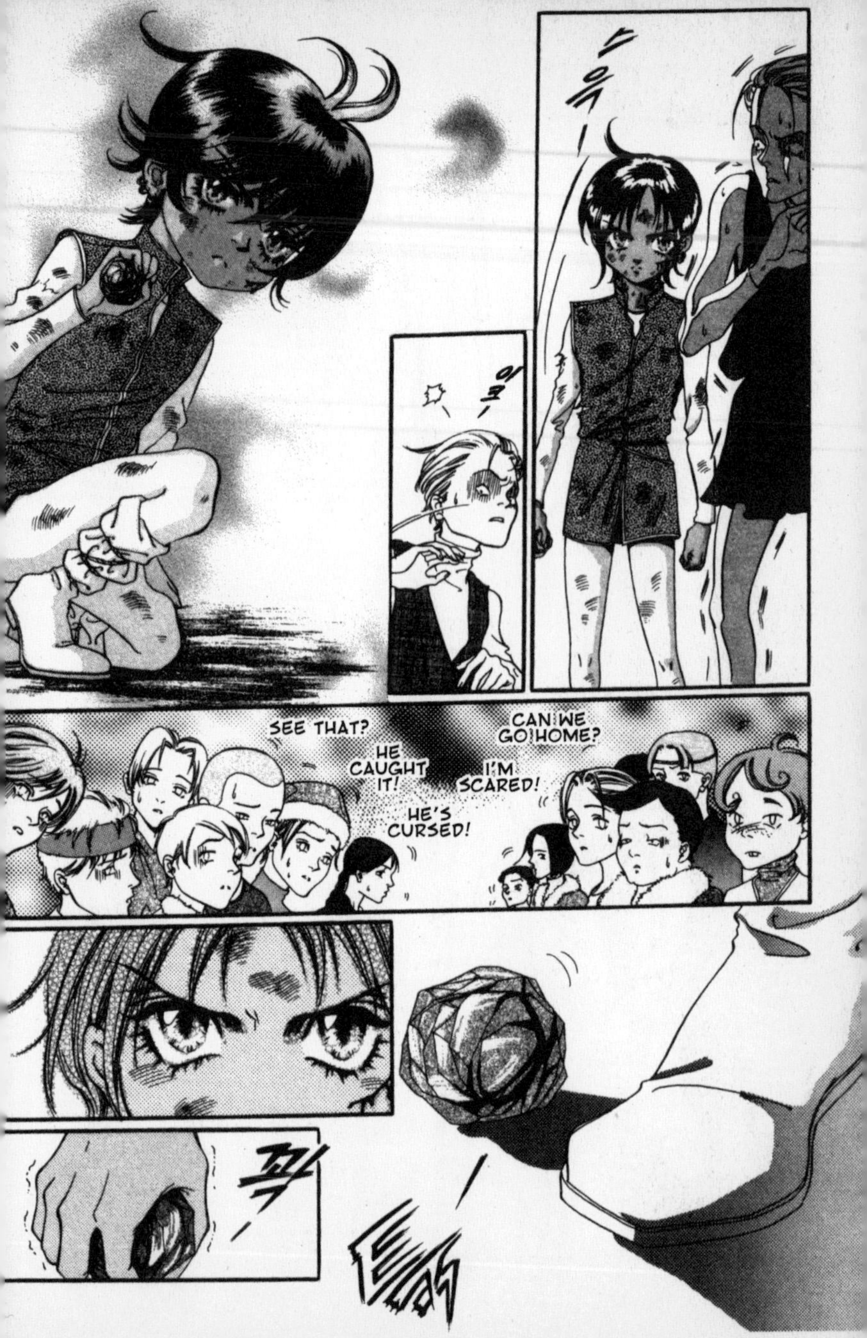
SEE THAT?
HE CAUGHT IT!
HE'S CURSED!
CAN WE GO HOME?
I'M SCARED!

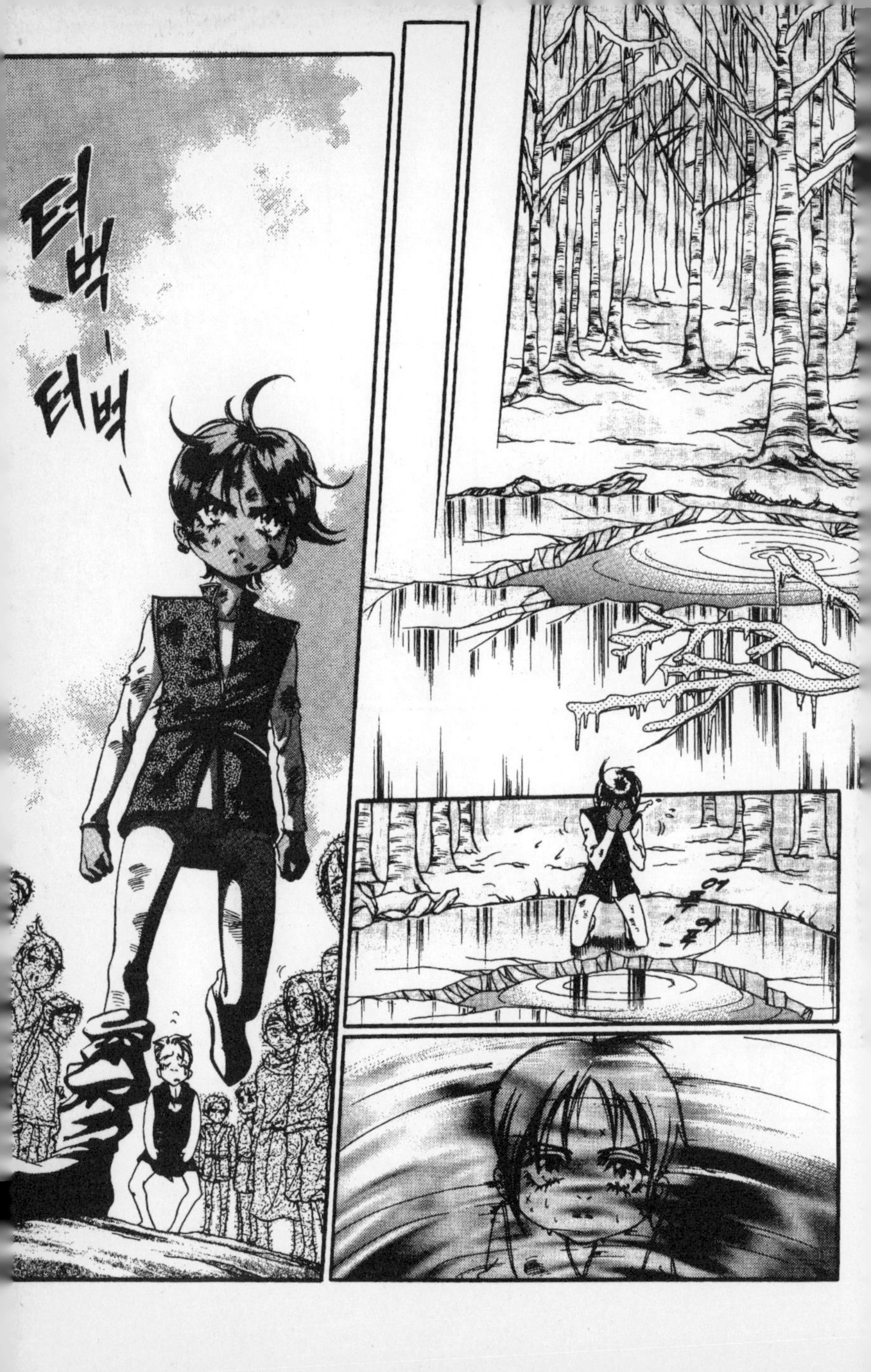
터벅 터벅
흐어 흐어

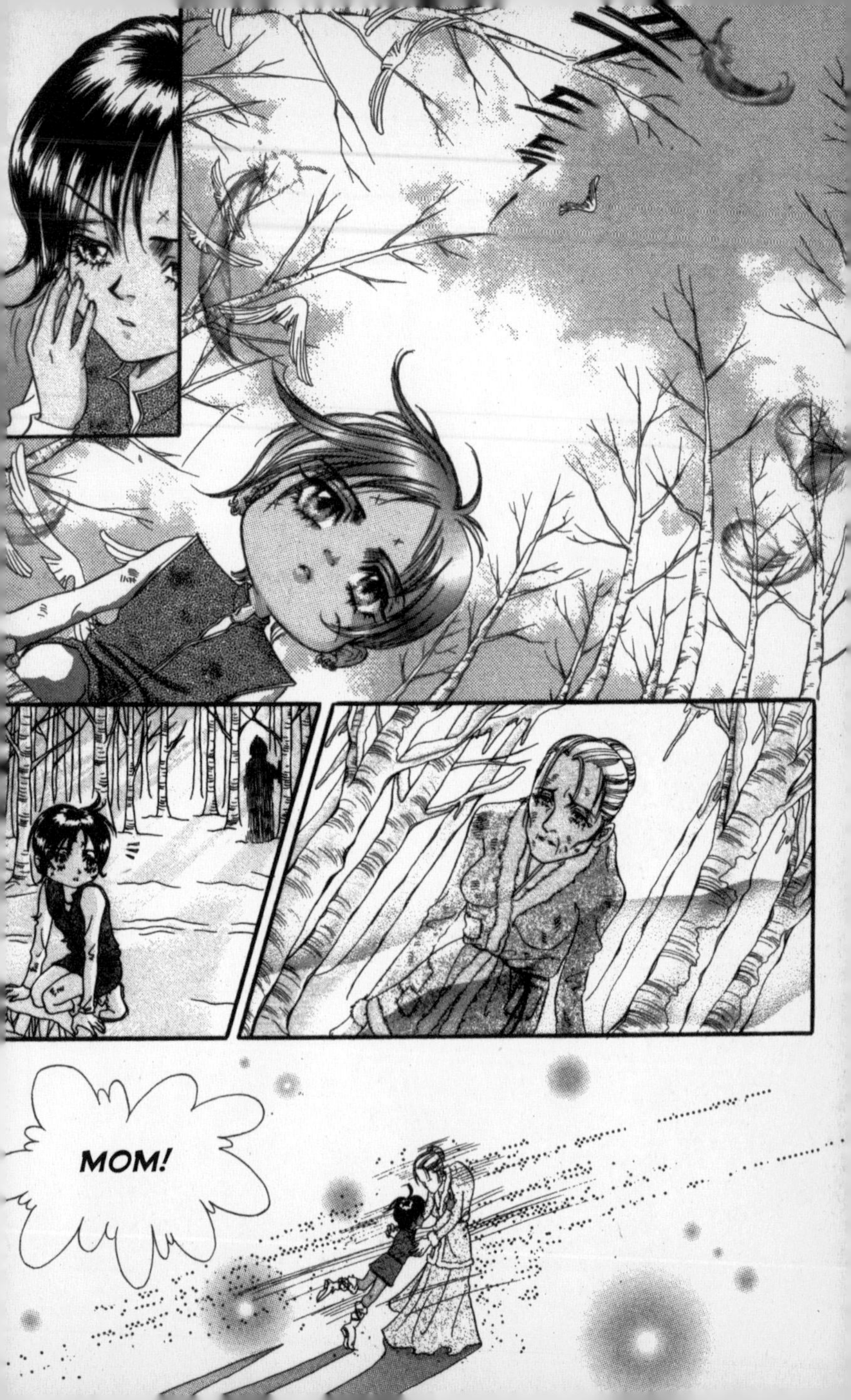
MOM!

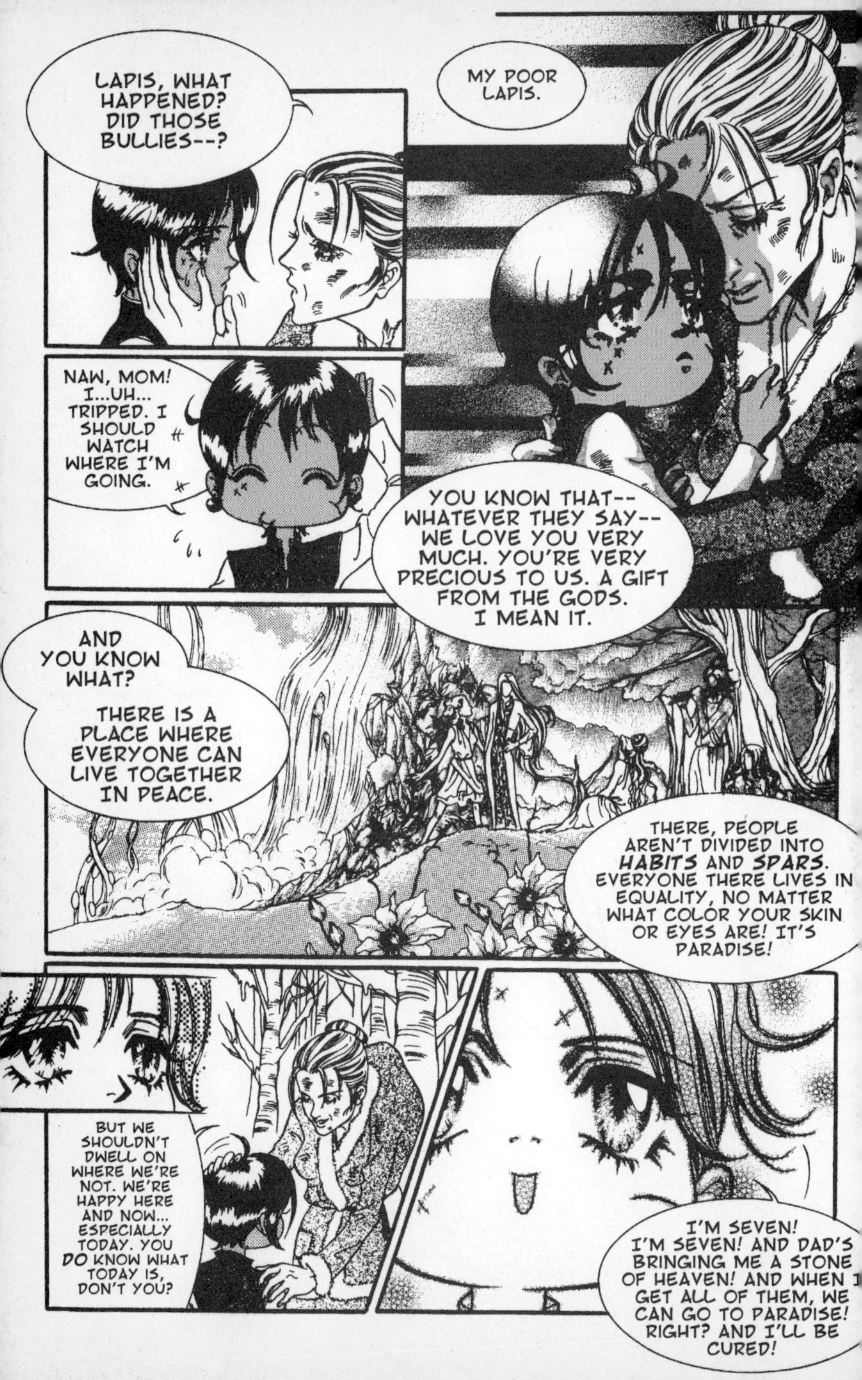

LAPIS, WHAT HAPPENED? DID THOSE BULLIES--?
NAW, MOM! I...UH... TRIPPED. I SHOULD WATCH WHERE I'M GOING.
MY POOR LAPIS.
YOU KNOW THAT--WHATEVER THEY SAY--WE LOVE YOU VERY MUCH. YOU'RE VERY PRECIOUS TO US. A GIFT FROM THE GODS. I MEAN IT.
AND YOU KNOW WHAT?
THERE IS A PLACE WHERE EVERYONE CAN LIVE TOGETHER IN PEACE.
THERE, PEOPLE AREN'T DIVIDED INTO *HABITS* AND *SPARS*. EVERYONE THERE LIVES IN EQUALITY, NO MATTER WHAT COLOR YOUR SKIN OR EYES ARE! IT'S PARADISE!
BUT WE SHOULDN'T DWELL ON WHERE WE'RE NOT. WE'RE HAPPY HERE AND NOW... ESPECIALLY TODAY. YOU *DO* KNOW WHAT TODAY IS, DON'T YOU?
I'M SEVEN! I'M SEVEN! AND DAD'S BRINGING ME A STONE OF HEAVEN! AND WHEN GET ALL OF THEM, WE CAN GO TO PARADISE! RIGHT? AND I'LL BE CURED!

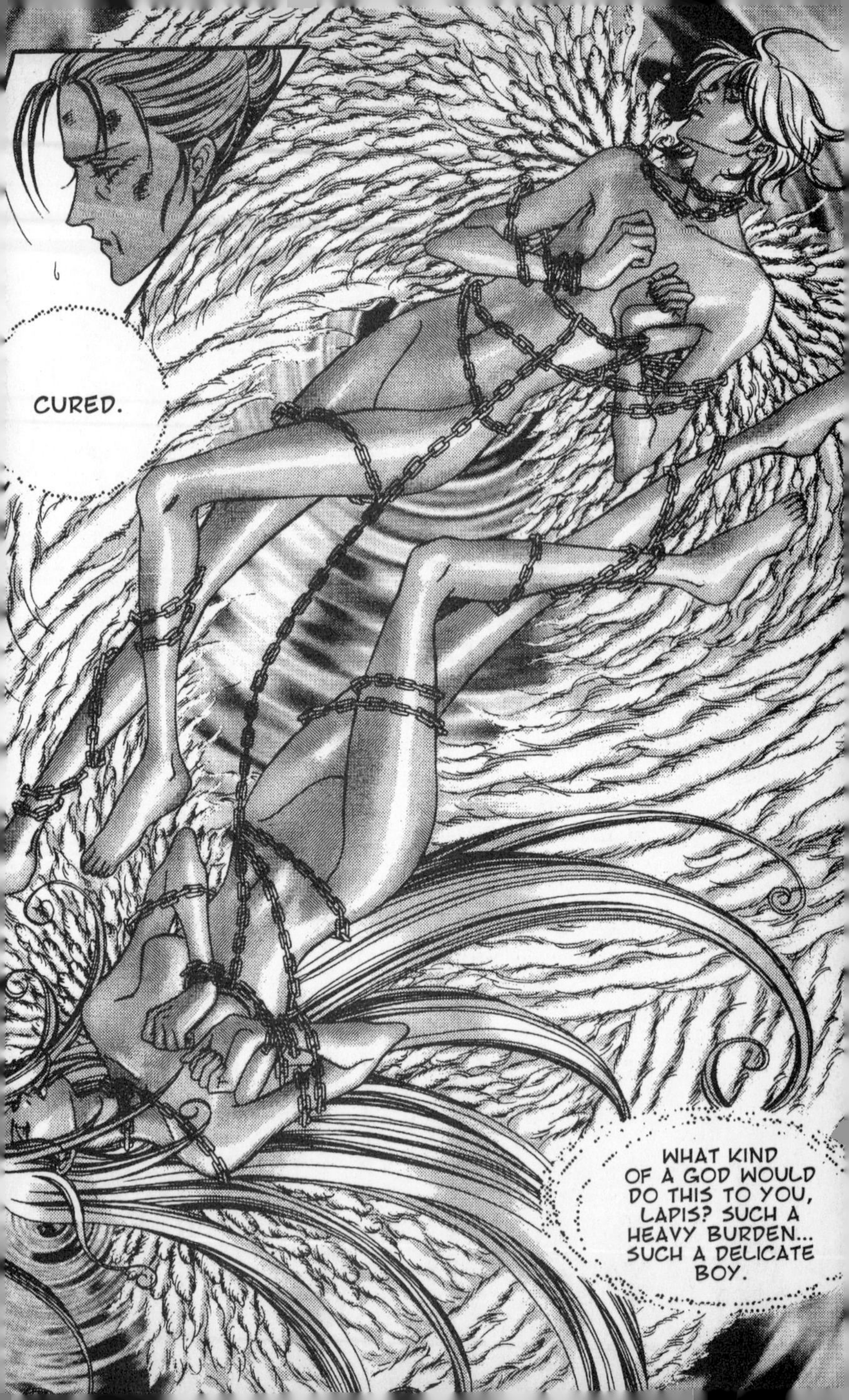
CURED.
WHAT KIND OF A GOD WOULD DO THIS TO YOU, LAPIS? SUCH A HEAVY BURDEN... SUCH A DELICATE BOY.

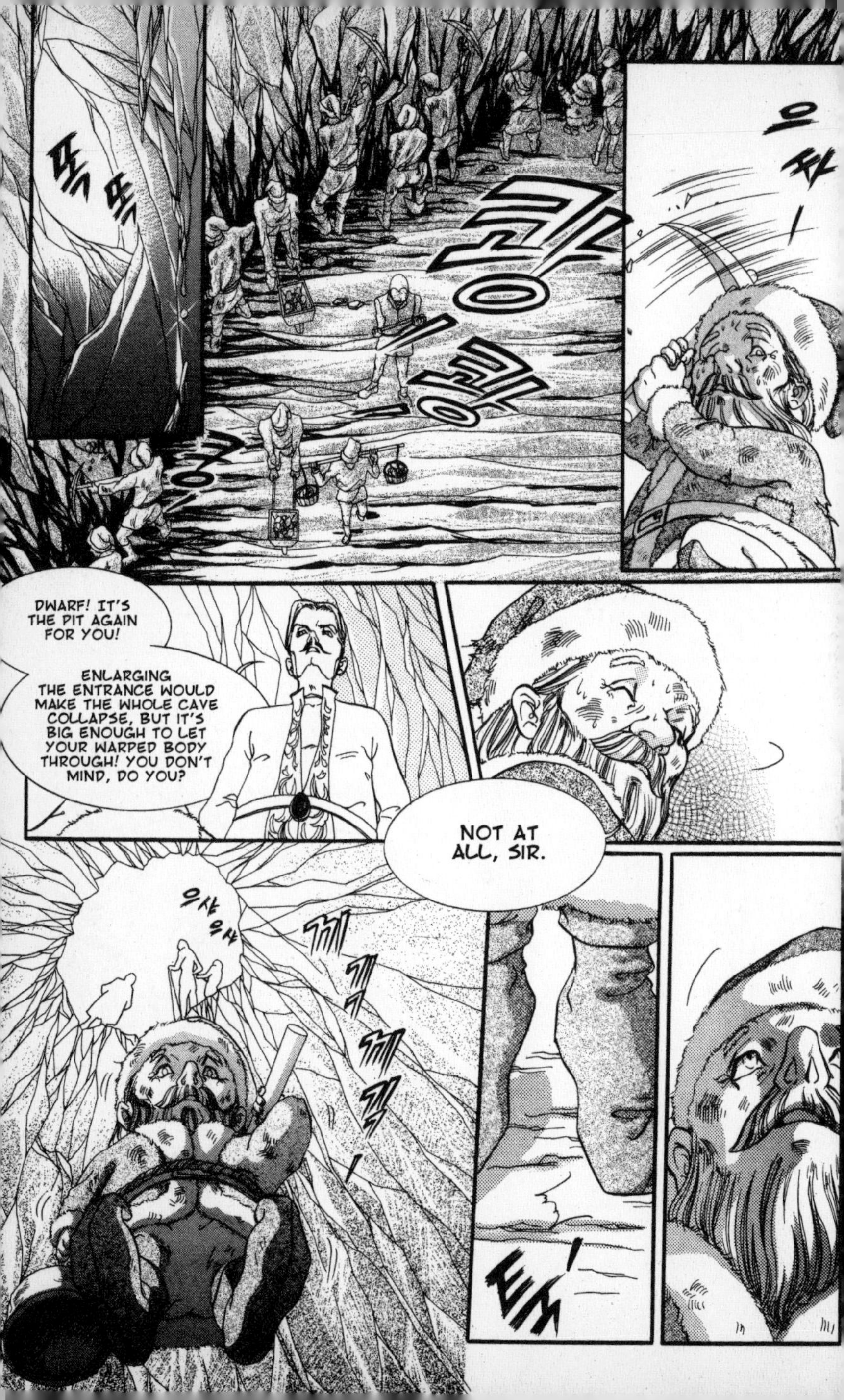
DWARF! IT'S THE PIT AGAIN FOR YOU!
ENLARGING THE ENTRANCE WOULD MAKE THE WHOLE CAVE COLLAPSE, BUT IT'S BIG ENOUGH TO LET YOUR WARPED BODY THROUGH! YOU DON'T MIND, DO YOU?
NOT AT ALL, SIR.

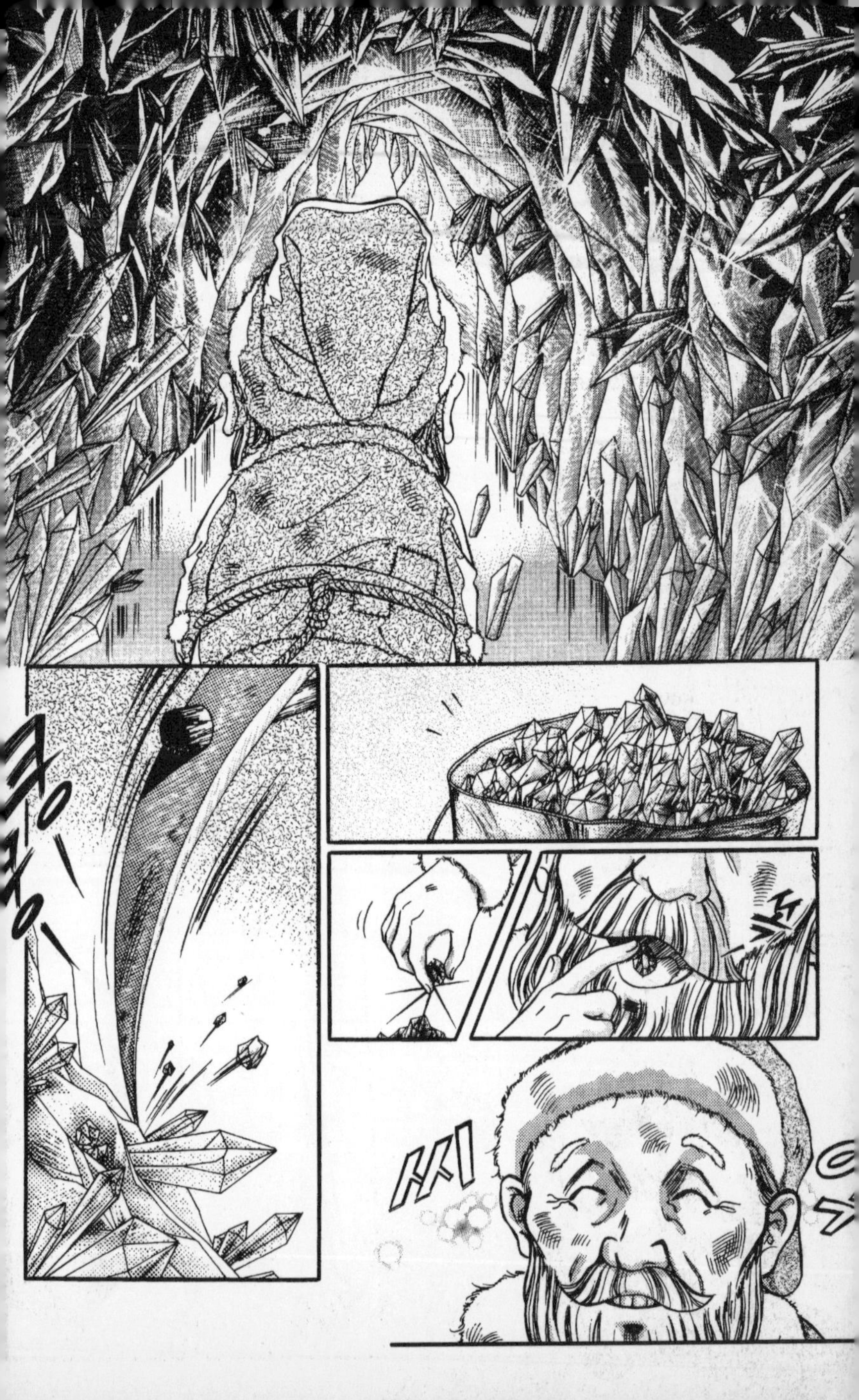

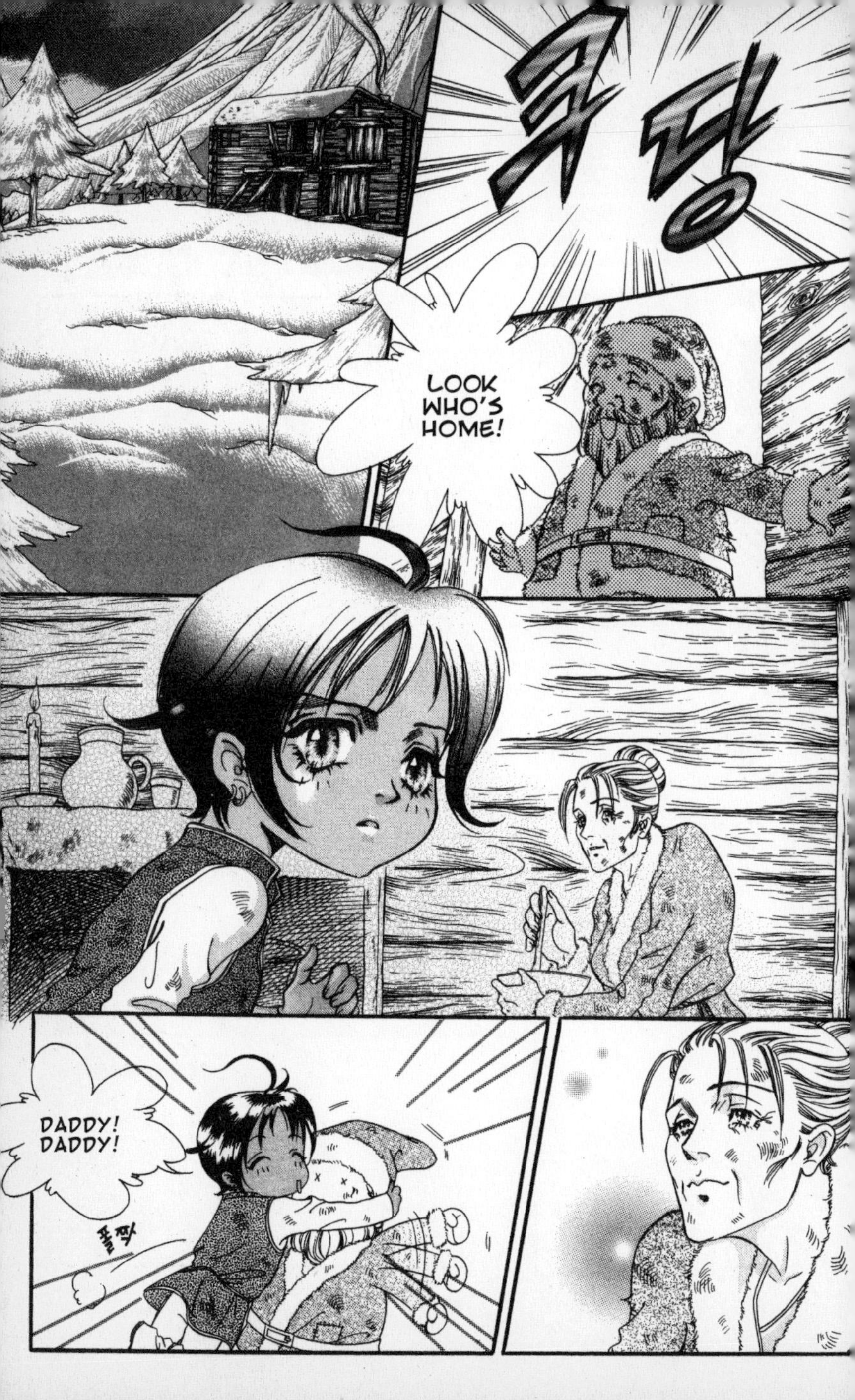
쿠당
LOOK WHO'S HOME!
DADDY! DADDY!
폴짝

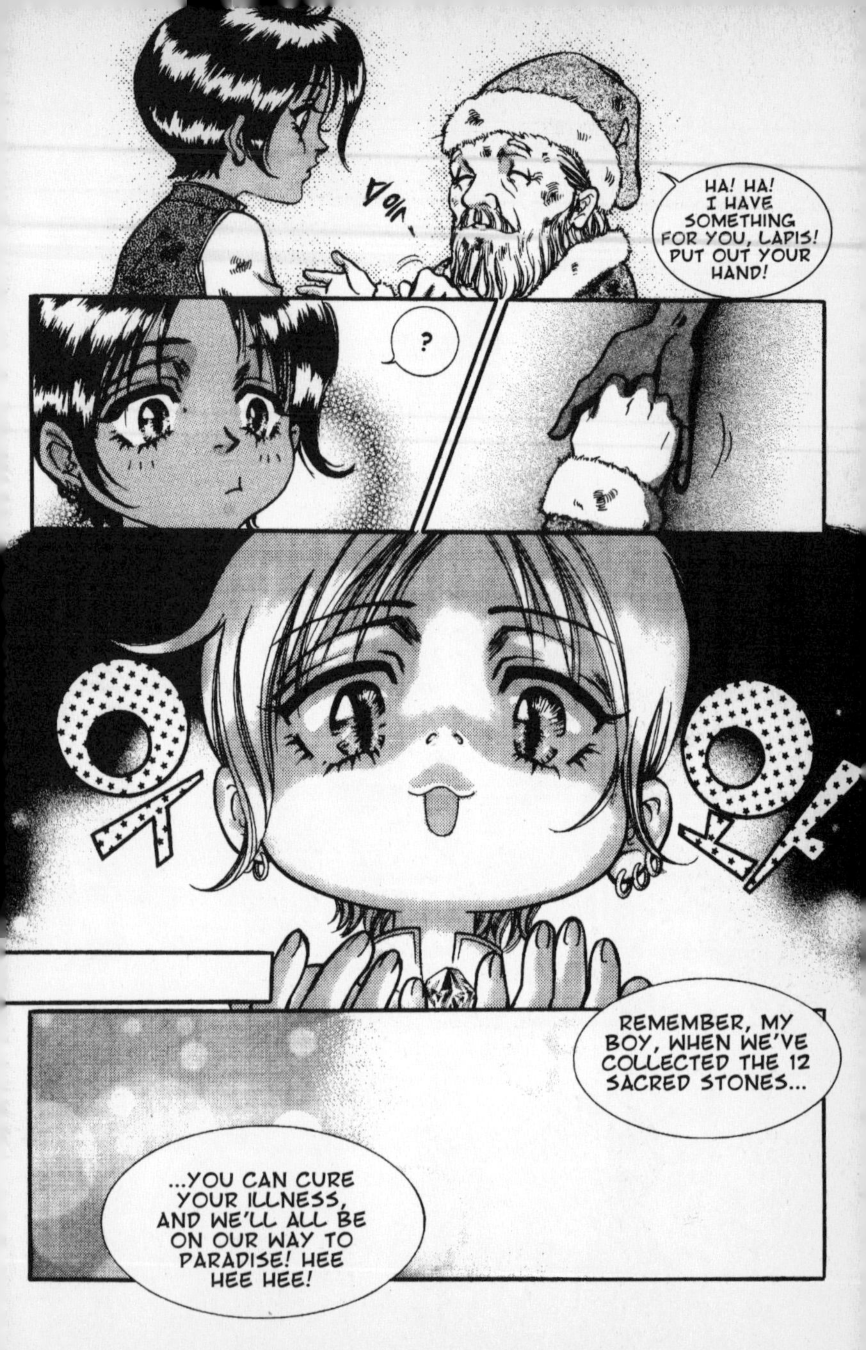
HA! HA! I HAVE SOMETHING FOR YOU, LAPIS! PUT OUT YOUR HAND!
?
REMEMBER, MY BOY, WHEN WE'VE COLLECTED THE 12 SACRED STONES...
...YOU CAN CURE YOUR ILLNESS, AND WE'LL ALL BE ON OUR WAY TO PARADISE! HEE HEE HEE!

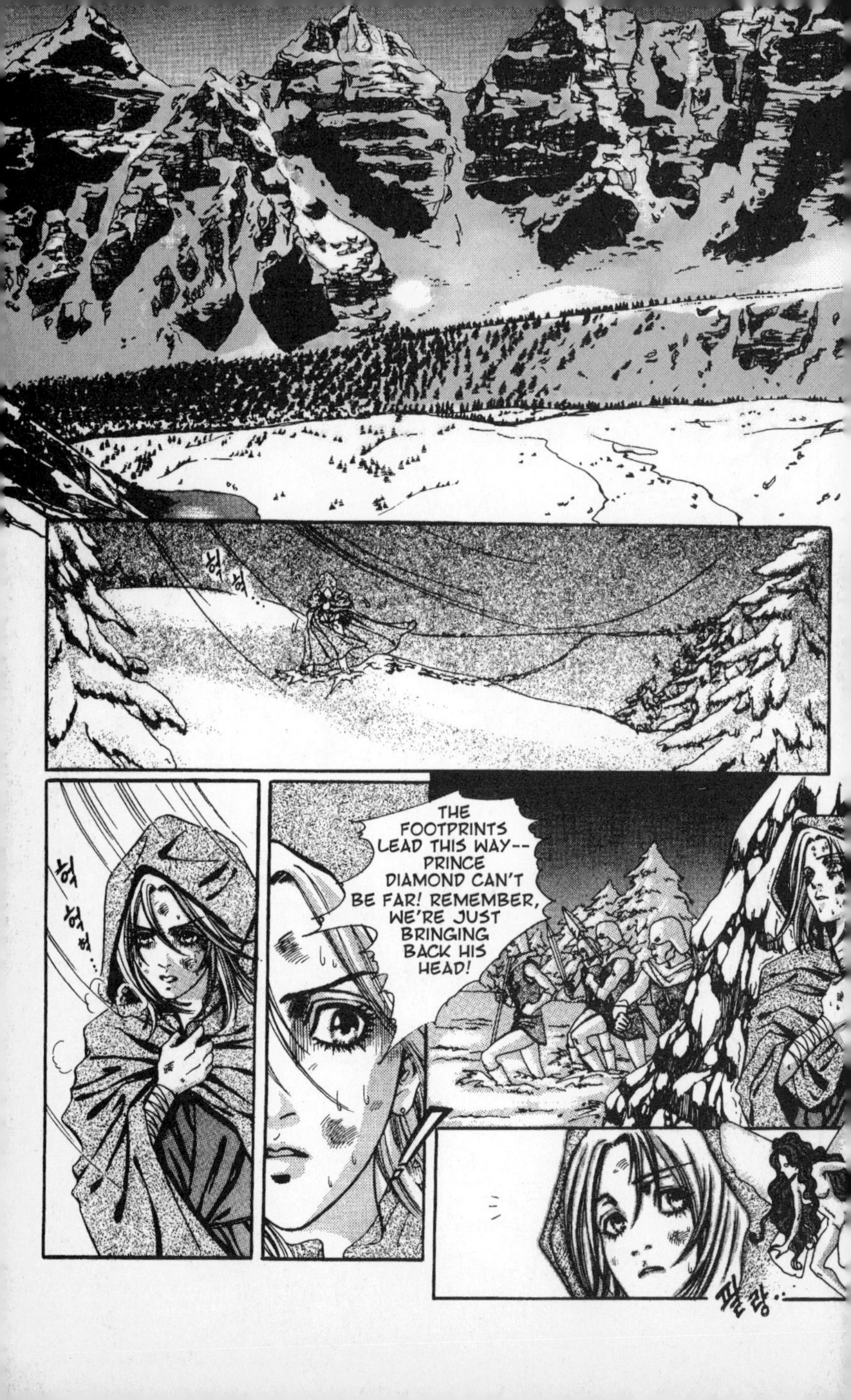
헉 헉...
헉 헉헉...
THE FOOTPRINTS LEAD THIS WAY-- PRINCE DIAMOND CAN'T BE FAR! REMEMBER, WE'RE JUST BRINGING BACK HIS HEAD!
팔랑..

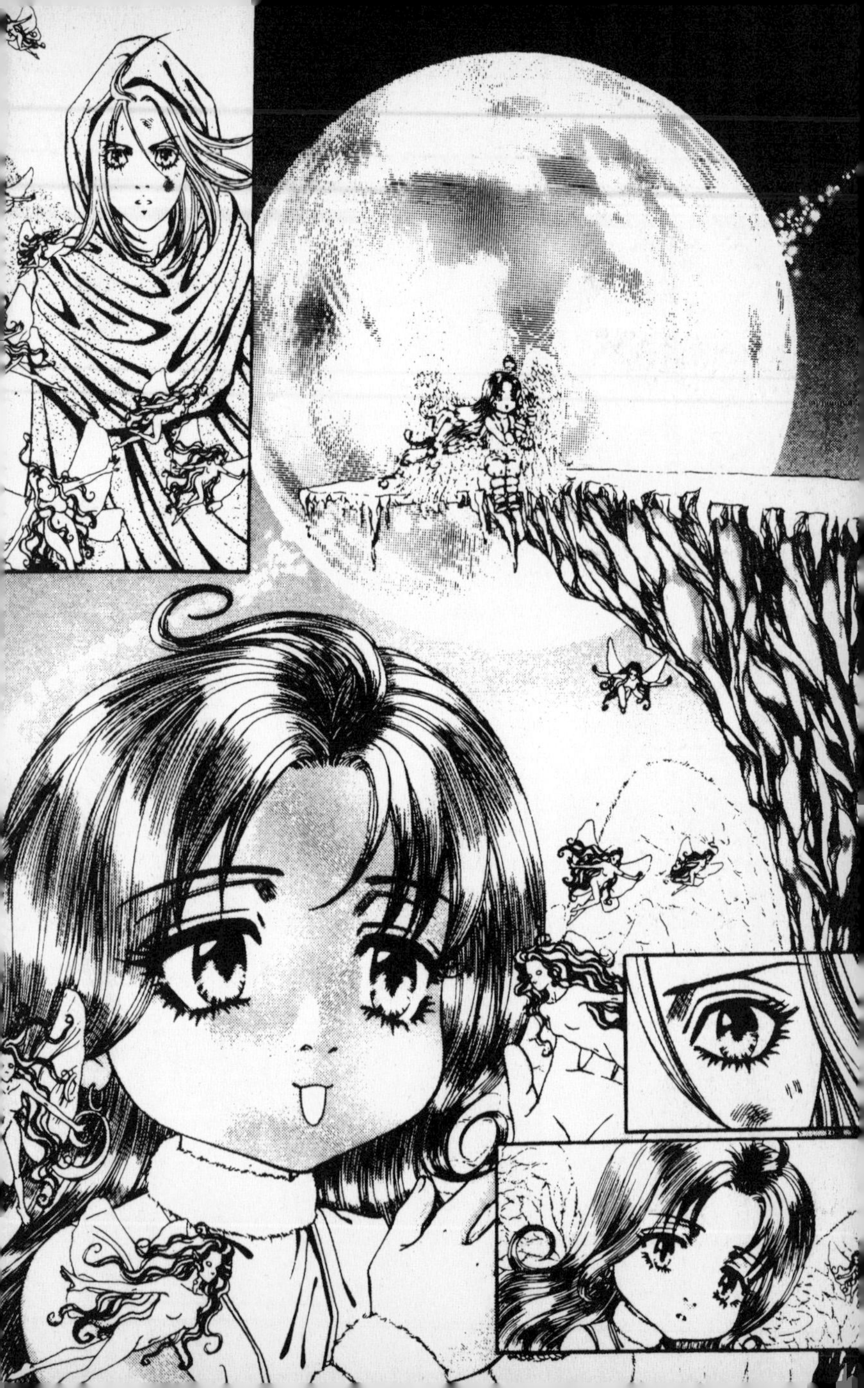

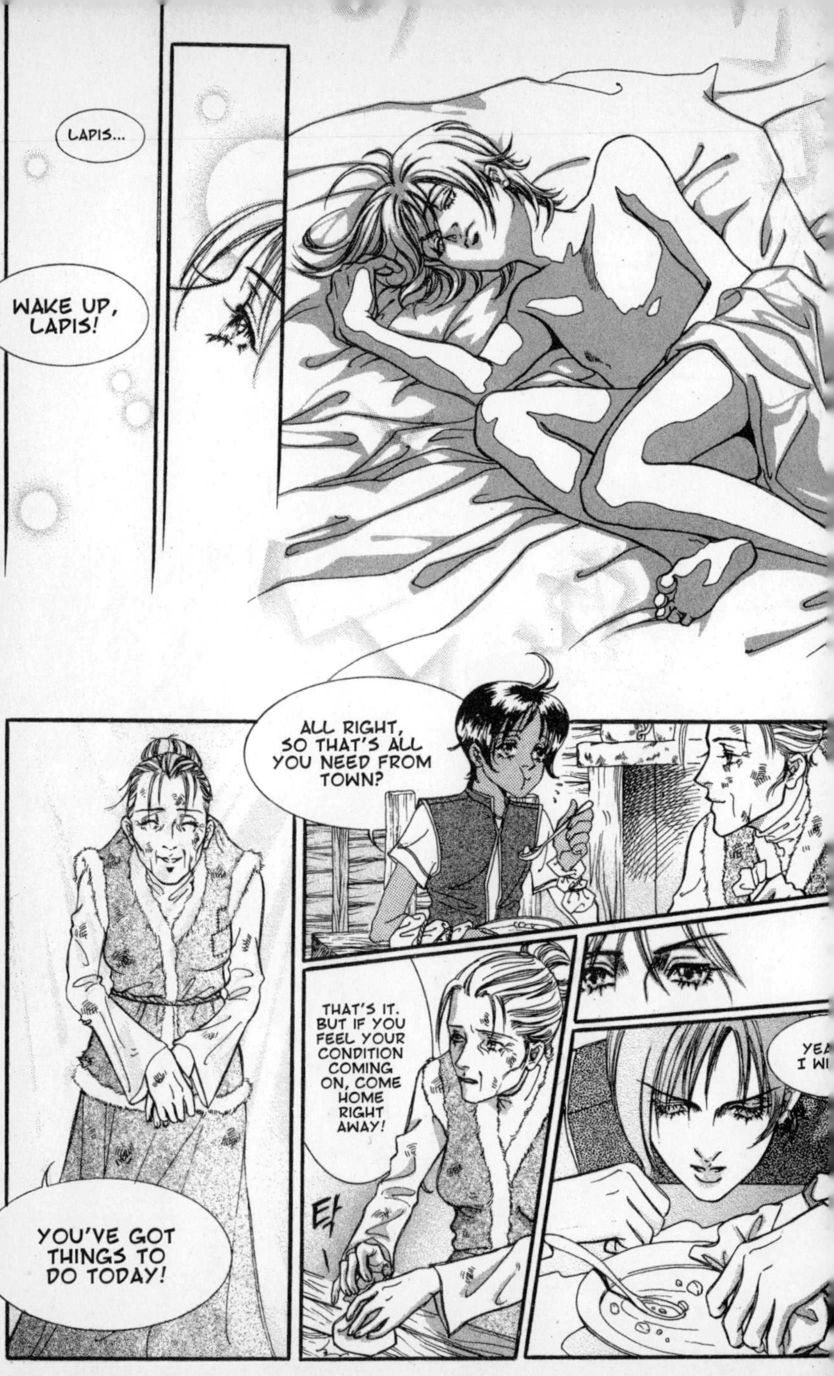
LAPIS...
WAKE UP, LAPIS!
YOU'VE GOT THINGS TO DO TODAY!
ALL RIGHT, SO THAT'S ALL YOU NEED FROM TOWN?
THAT'S IT. BUT IF YOU FEEL YOUR CONDITION COMING ON, COME HOME RIGHT AWAY!

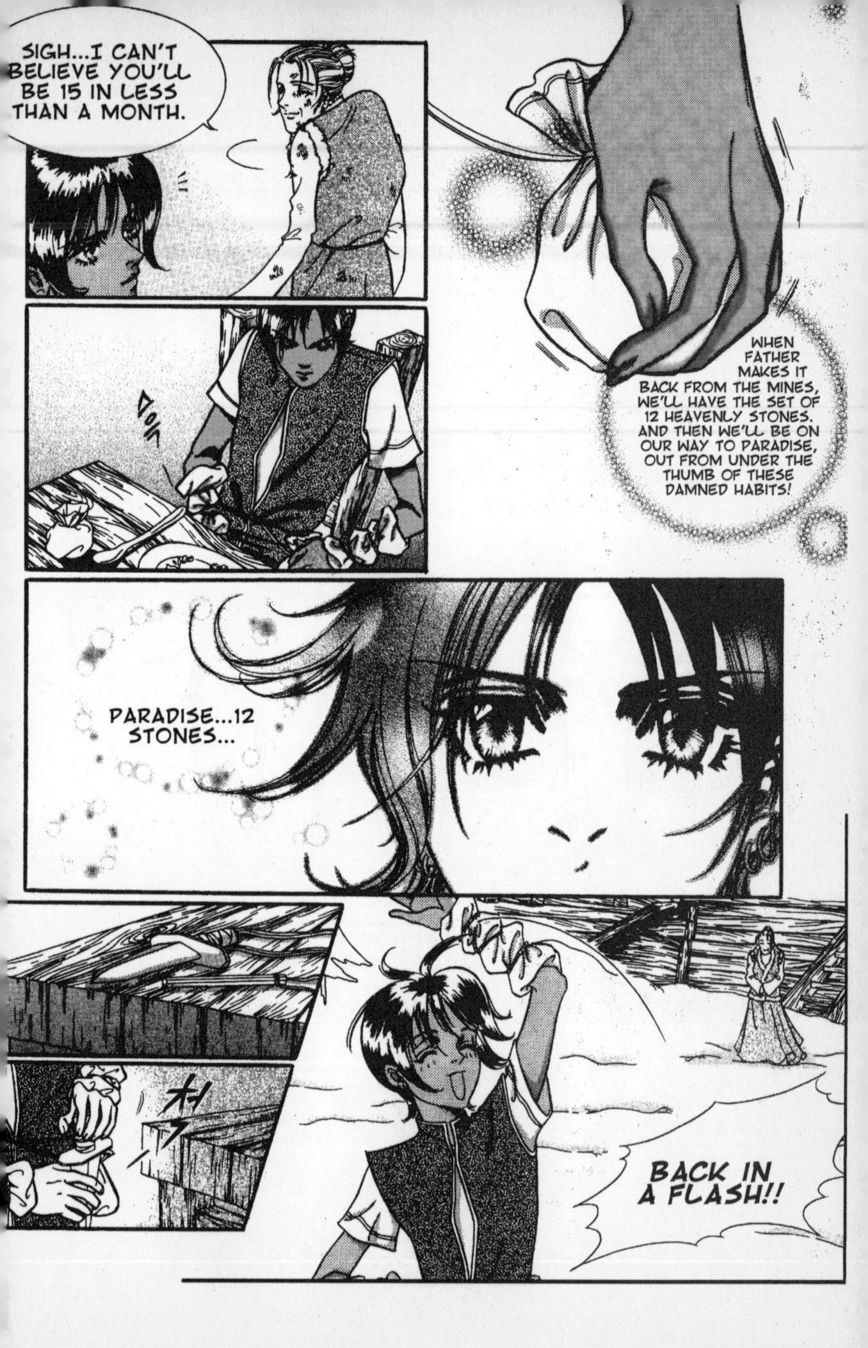
SIGH...I CAN'T BELIEVE YOU'LL BE 15 IN LESS THAN A MONTH.
WHEN FATHER MAKES IT BACK FROM THE MINES, WE'LL HAVE THE SET OF 12 HEAVENLY STONES. AND THEN WE'LL BE ON OUR WAY TO PARADISE, OUT FROM UNDER THE THUMB OF THESE DAMNED HABITS!
PARADISE...12 STONES...
BACK IN A FLASH!!

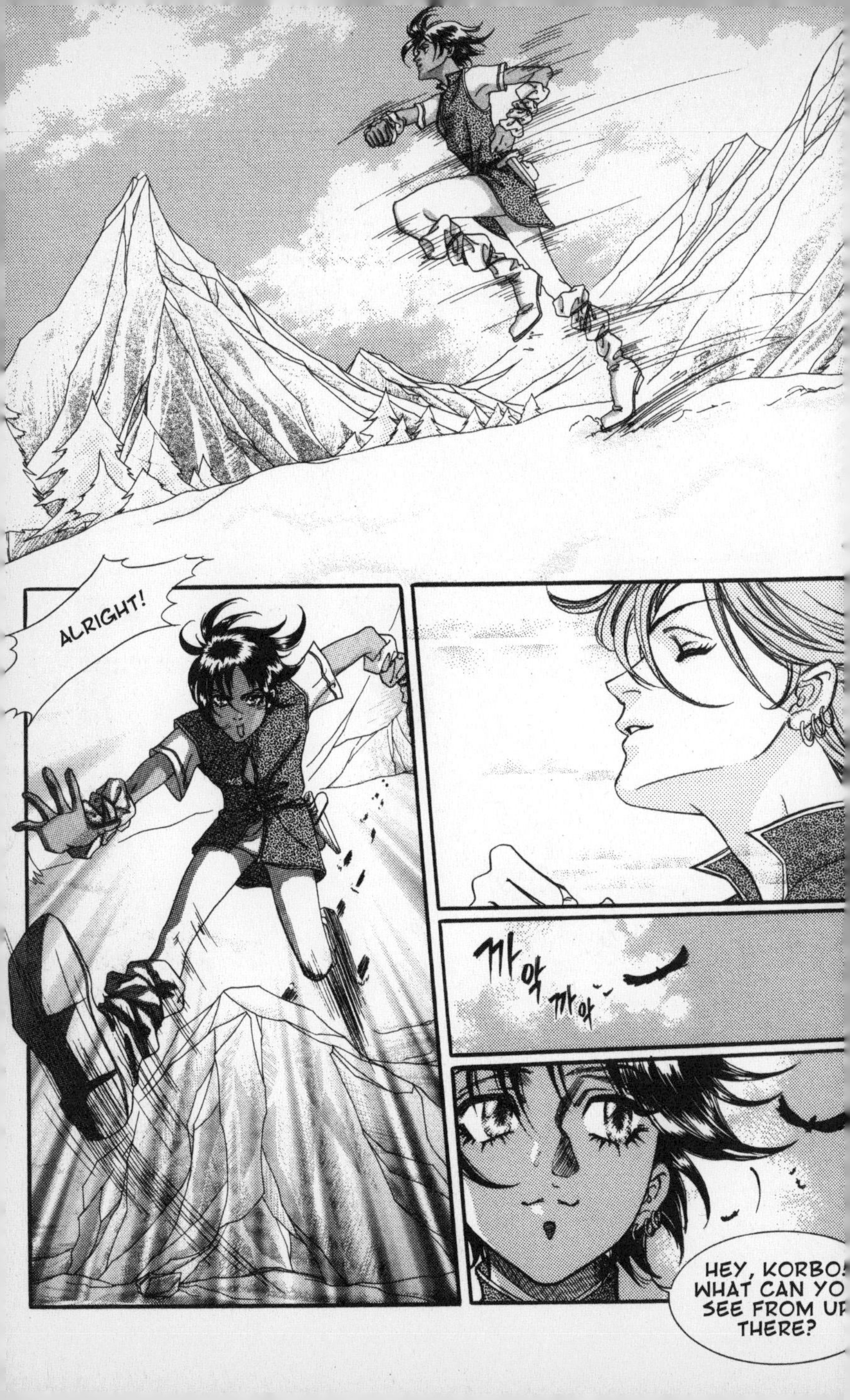
ALRIGHT!
까악 까악
HEY, KORBO!
WHAT CAN YO
SEE FROM UP
THERE?

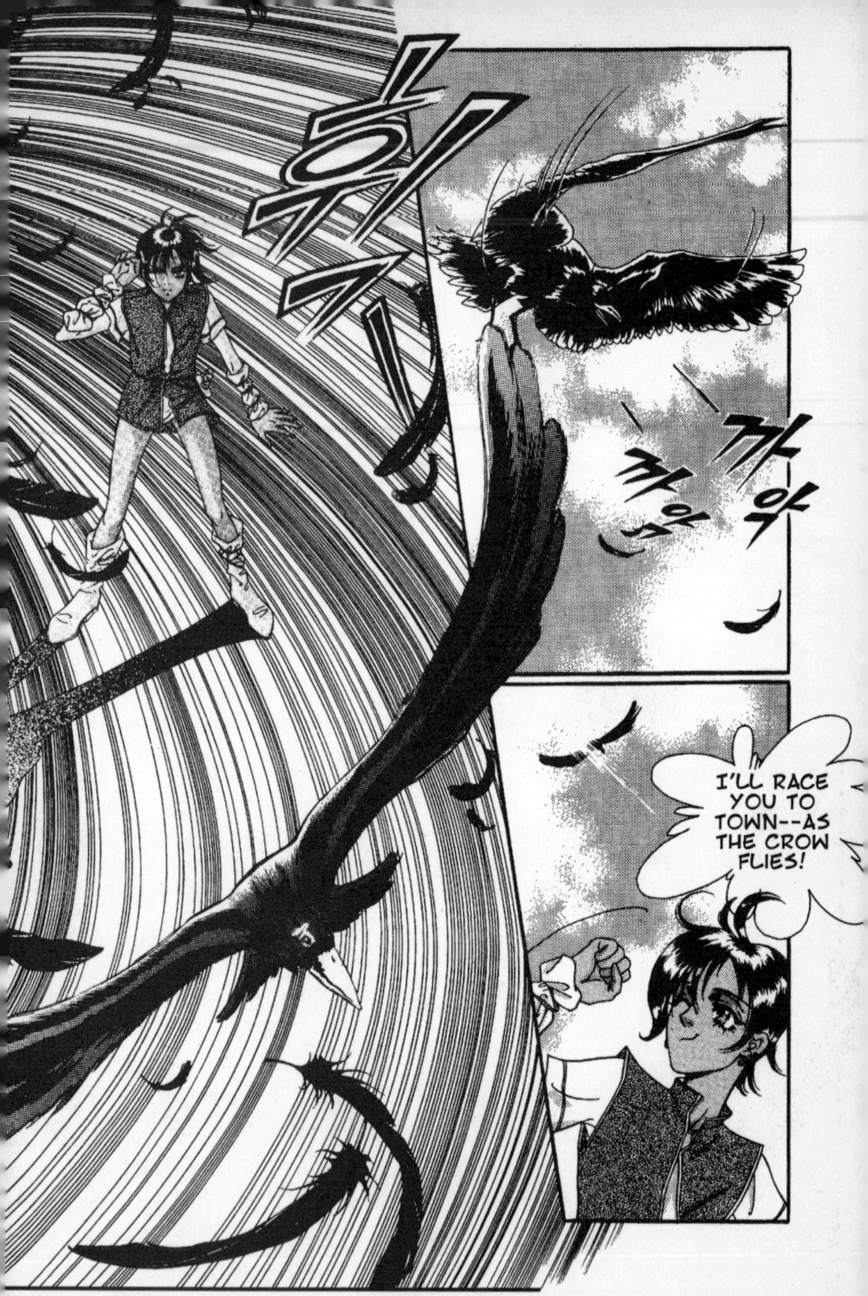
I'LL RACE YOU TO TOWN--AS THE CROW FLIES!

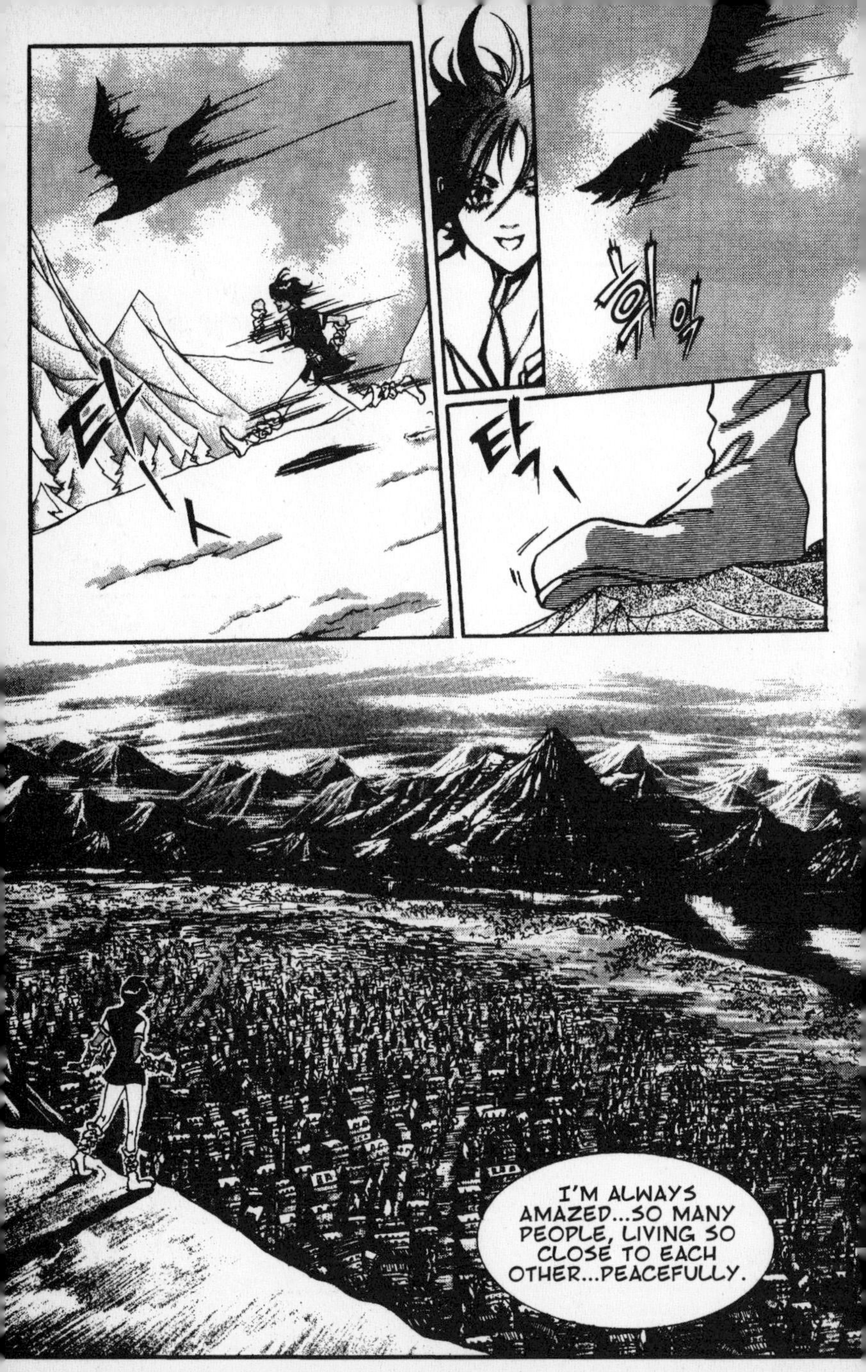
I'M ALWAYS AMAZED...SO MANY PEOPLE, LIVING SO CLOSE TO EACH OTHER...PEACEFULLY.

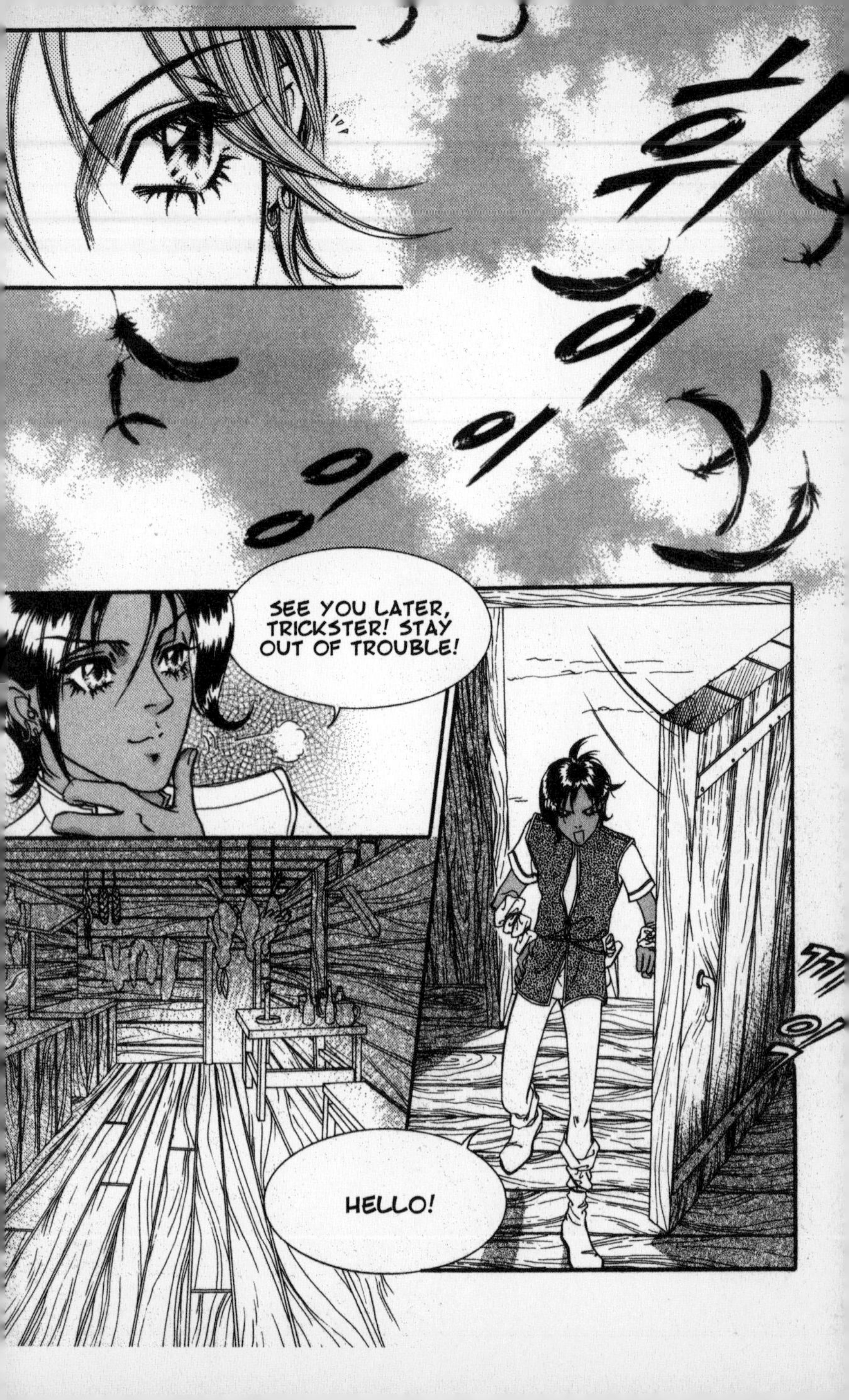
SEE YOU LATER, TRICKSTER! STAY OUT OF TROUBLE!
HELLO!

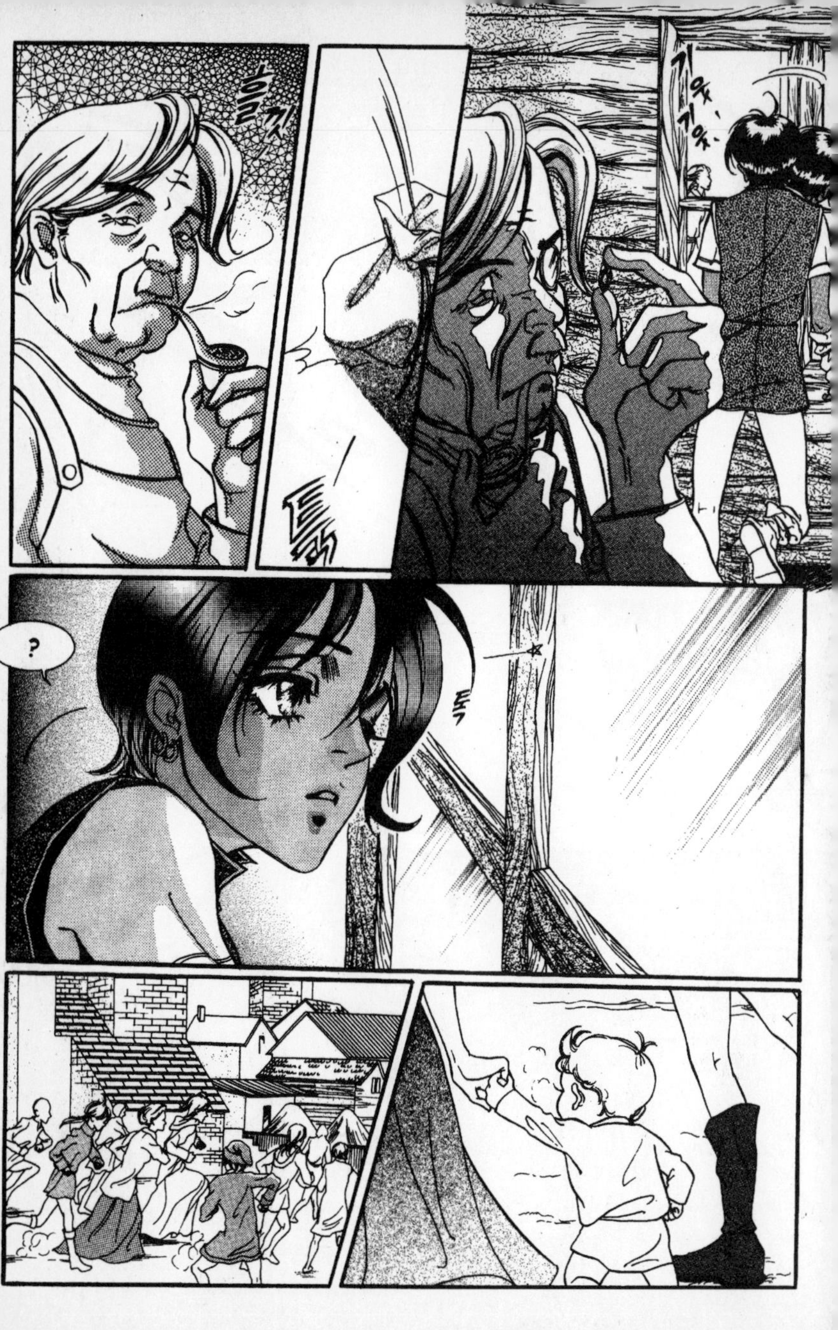
흘긋
기웃, 기웃.
?

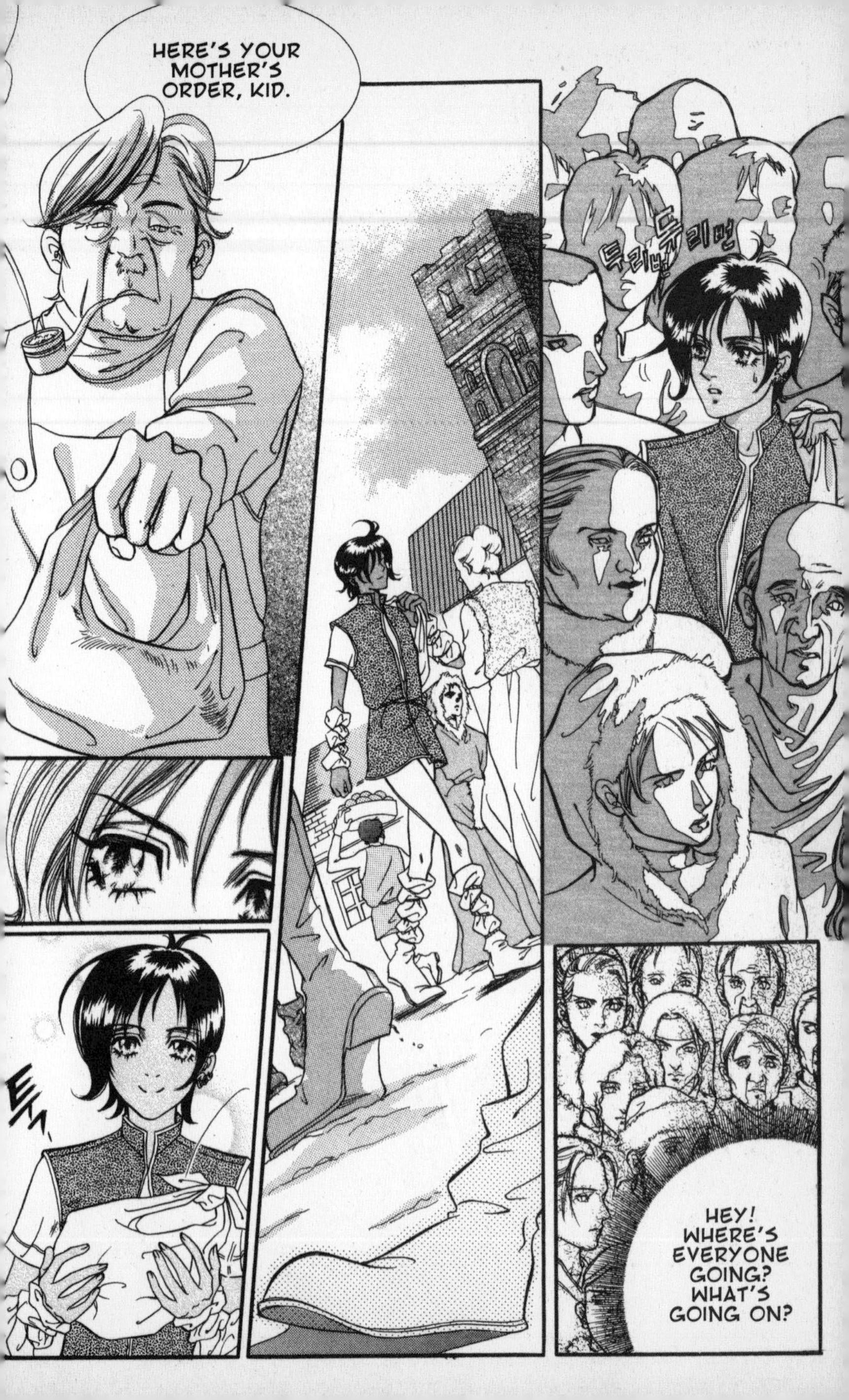
HERE'S YOUR MOTHER'S ORDER, KID.
두리번 두리번
HEY! WHERE'S EVERYONE GOING? WHAT'S GOING ON?

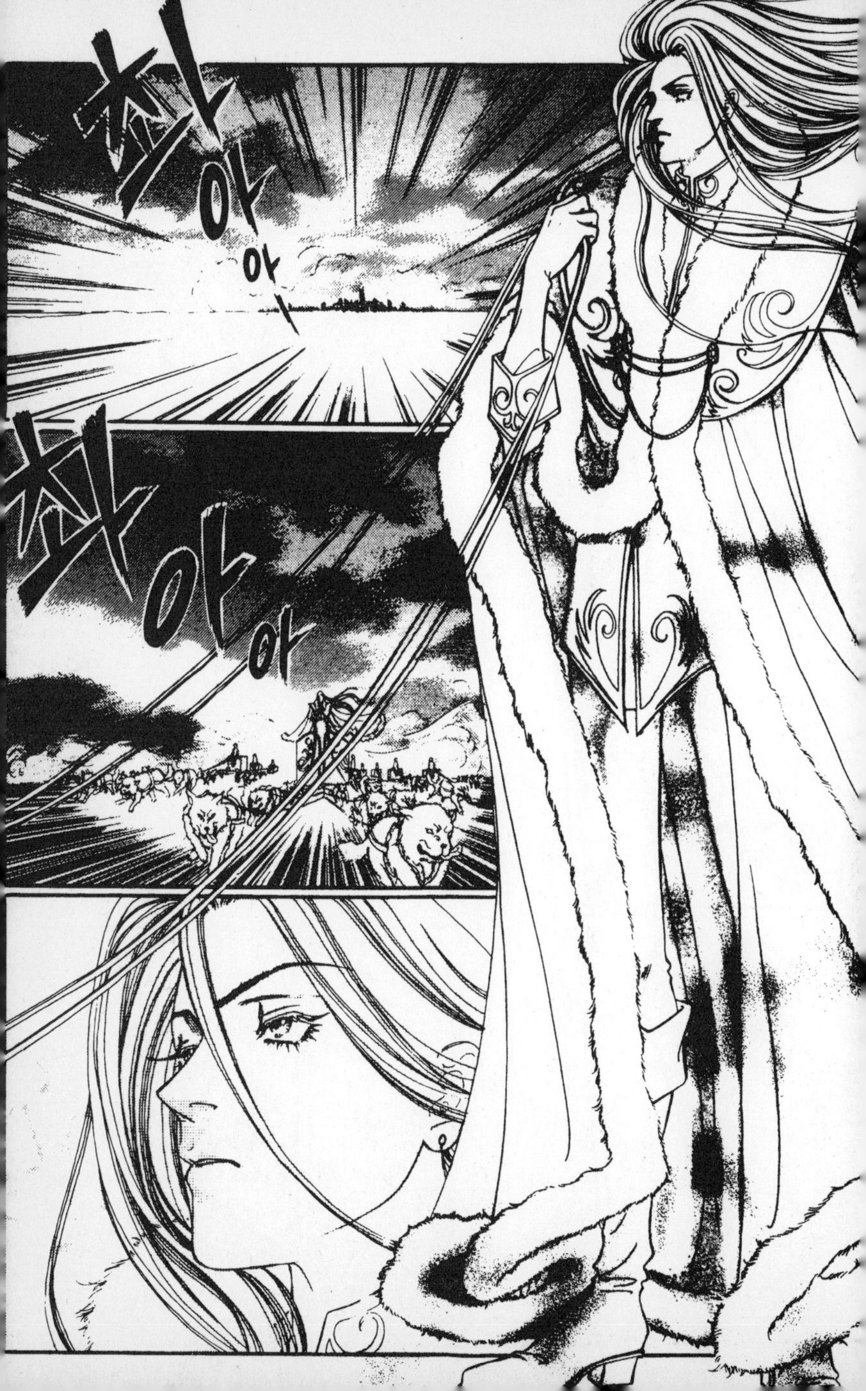

촤아아
촤아아

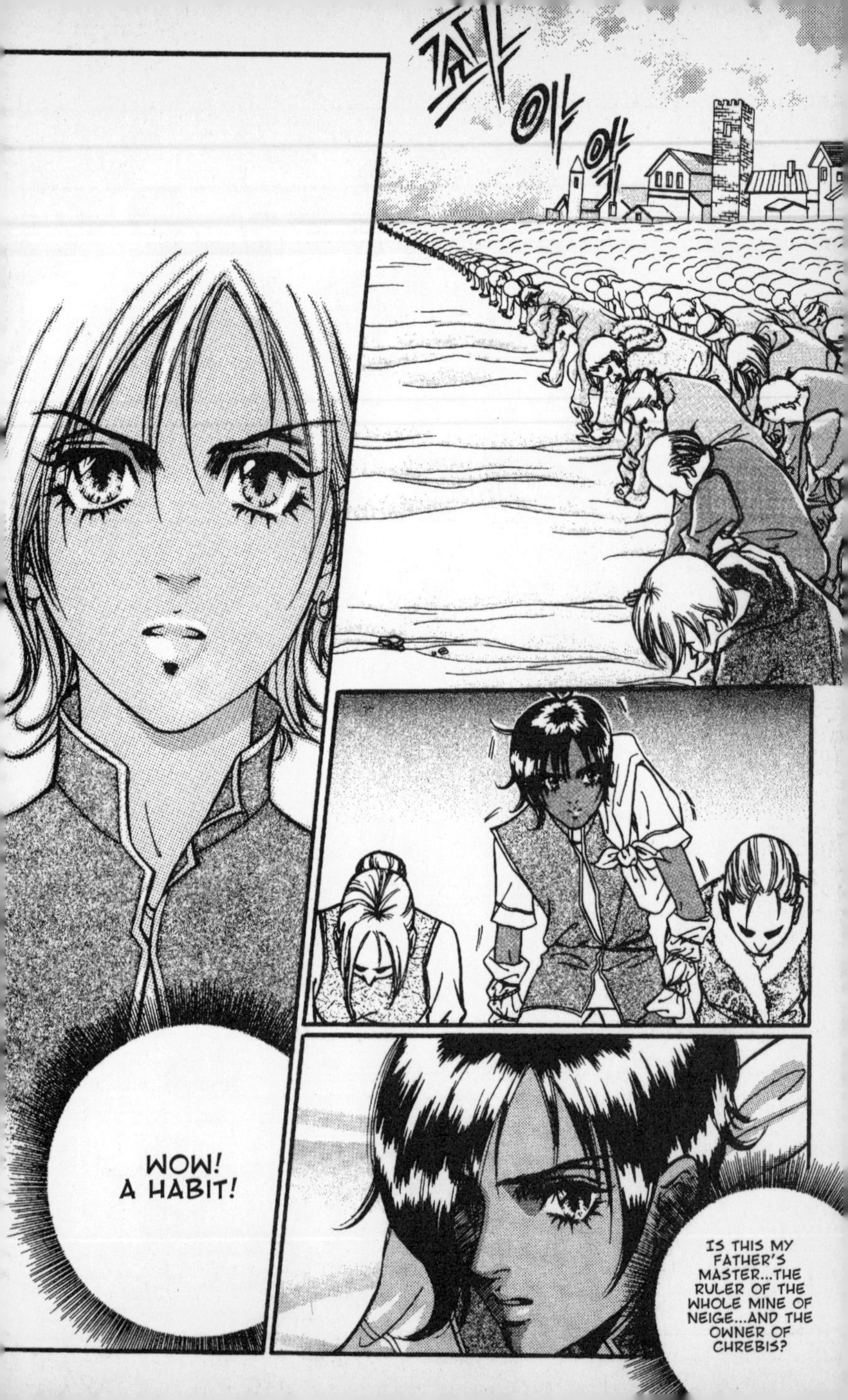

쫘아악
WOW!
A HABIT!
IS THIS MY FATHER'S MASTER...THE RULER OF THE WHOLE MINE OF NEIGE...AND THE OWNER OF CHREBIS?

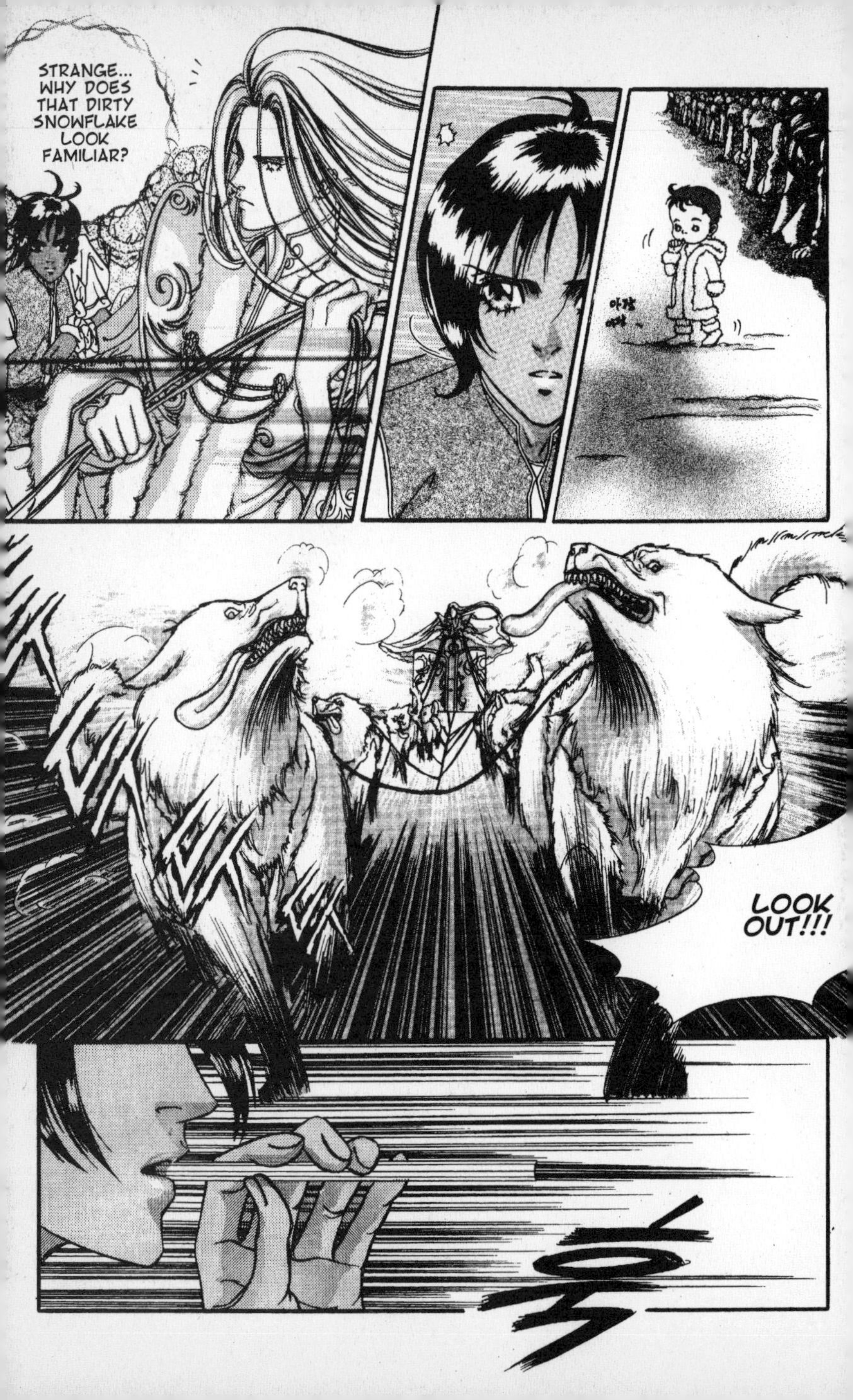
STRANGE... WHY DOES THAT DIRTY SNOWFLAKE LOOK FAMILIAR?
LOOK OUT!!!

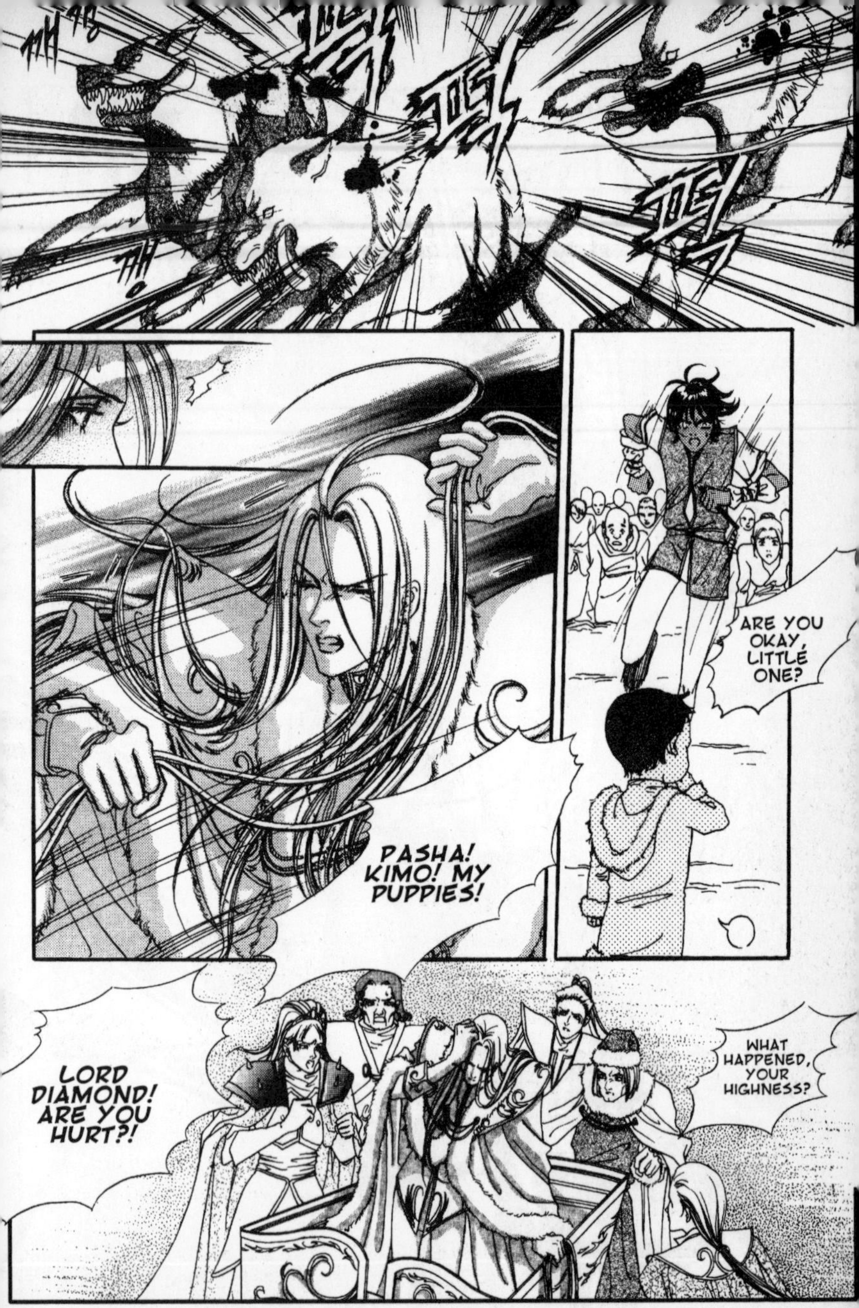
PASHA! KIMO! MY PUPPIES!
ARE YOU OKAY, LITTLE ONE?
LORD DIAMOND! ARE YOU HURT?!
WHAT HAPPENED, YOUR HIGHNESS?

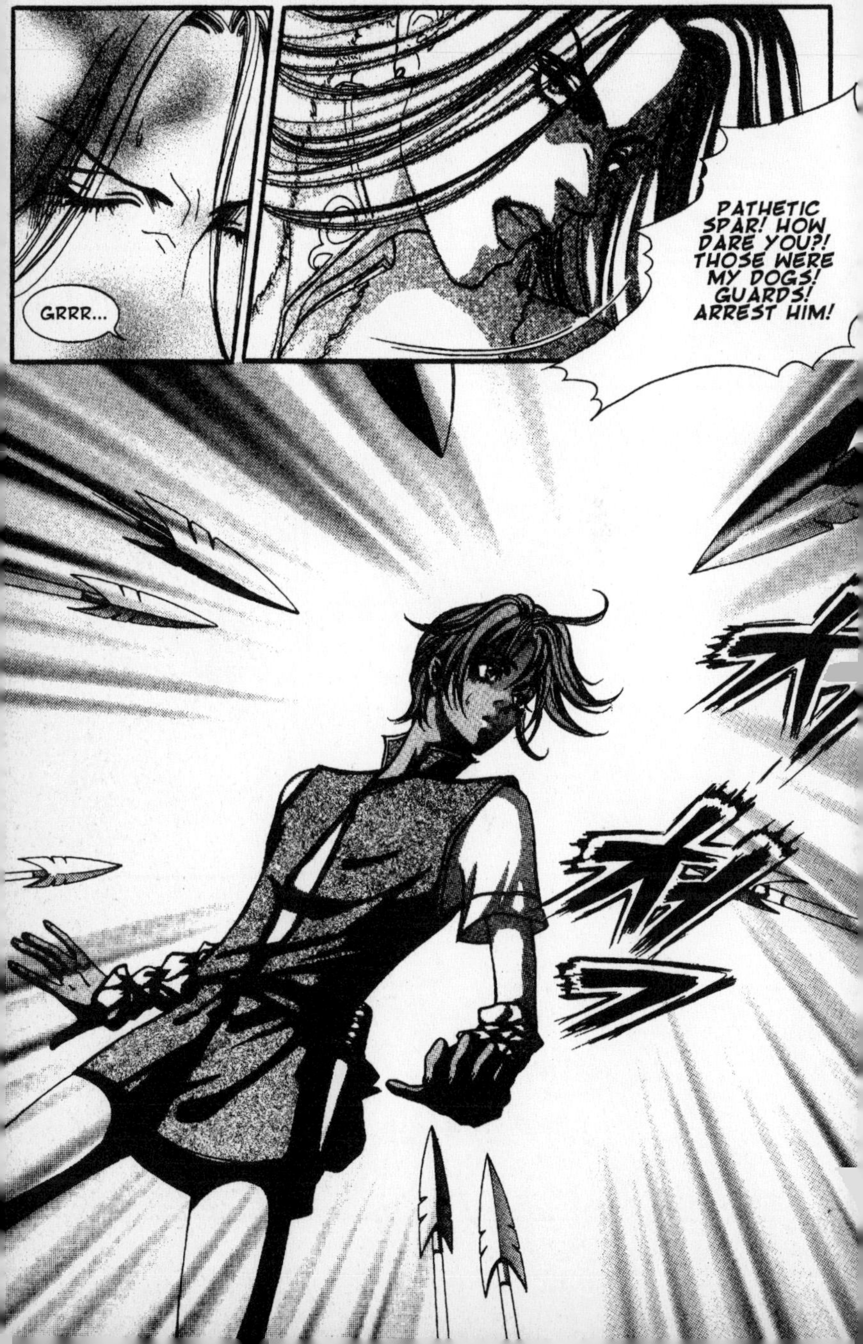
GRRR...
PATHETIC SPAR! HOW DARE YOU?! THOSE WERE MY DOGS! GUARDS! ARREST HIM!

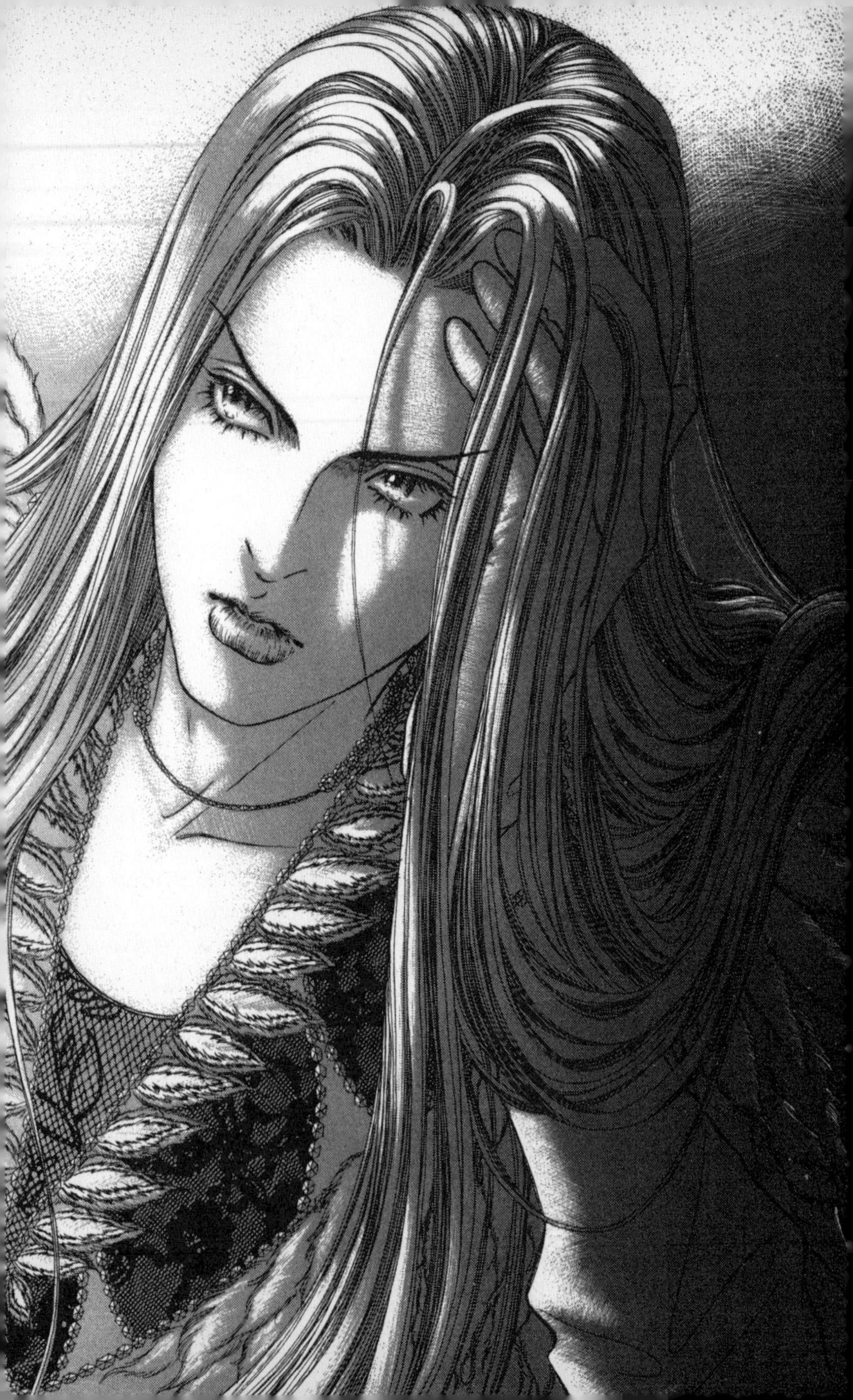

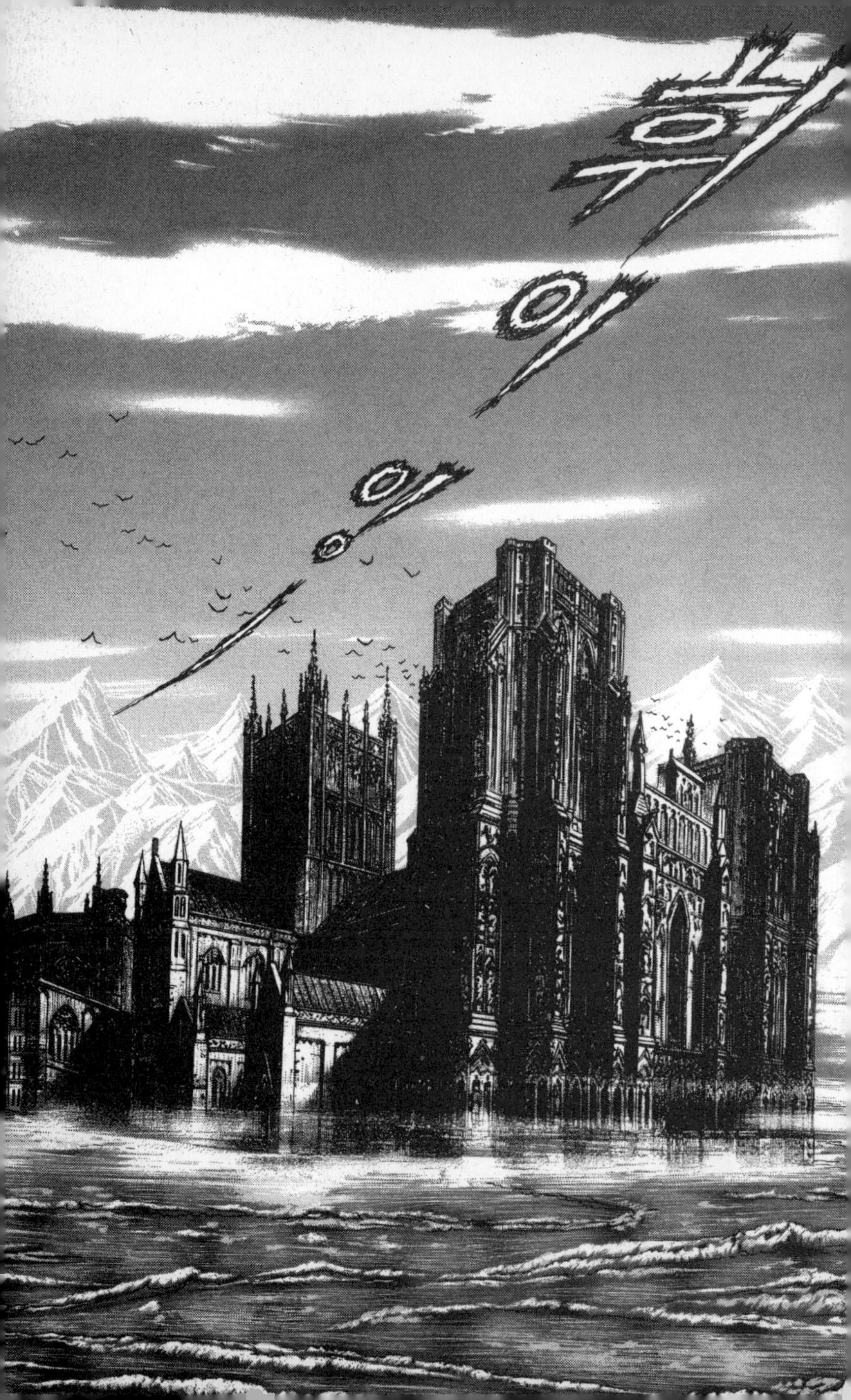
하아아아

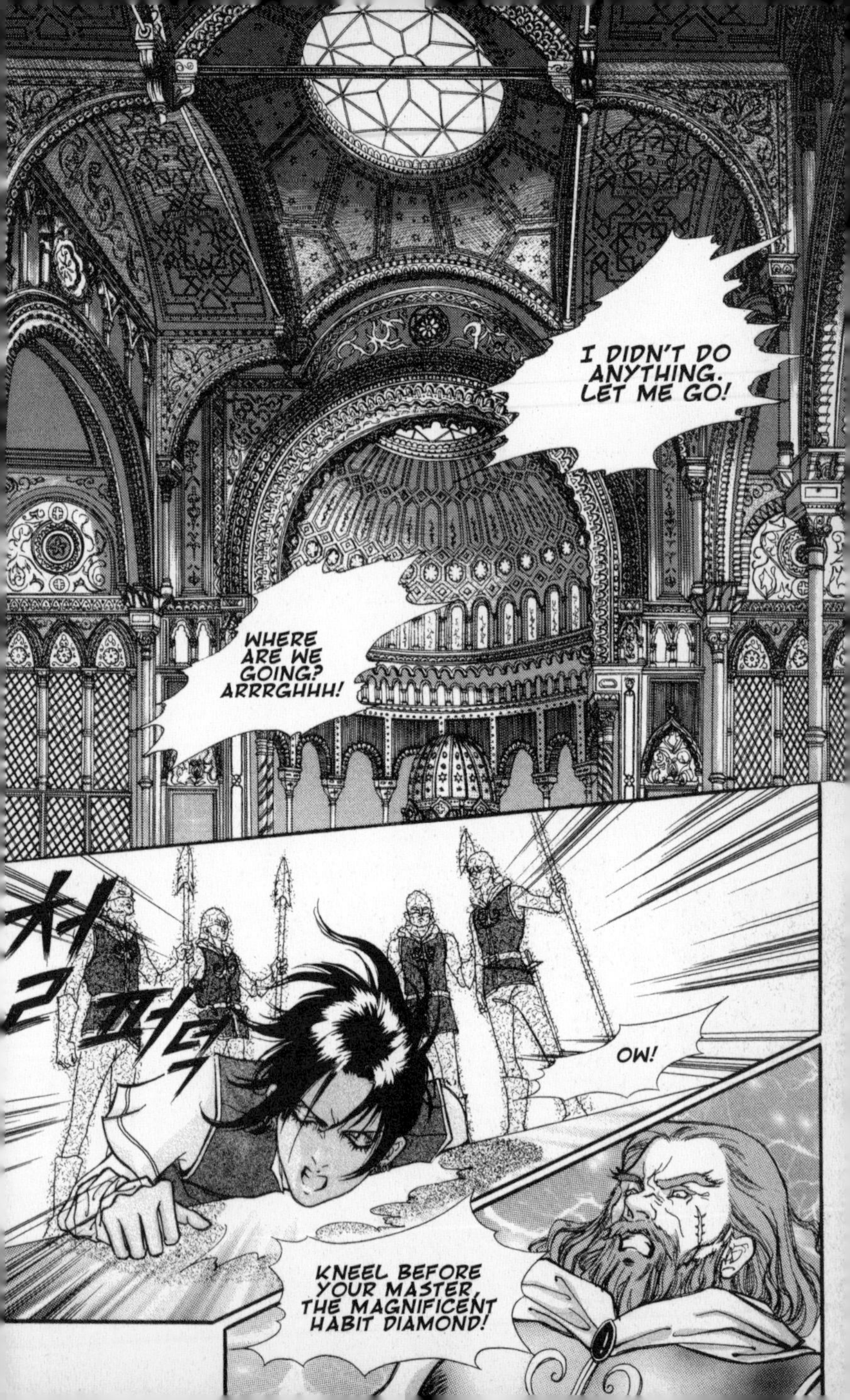

I DIDN'T DO ANYTHING. LET ME GO!
WHERE ARE WE GOING? ARRRGHHH!
OW!
KNEEL BEFORE YOUR MASTER, THE MAGNIFICENT HABIT DIAMOND!

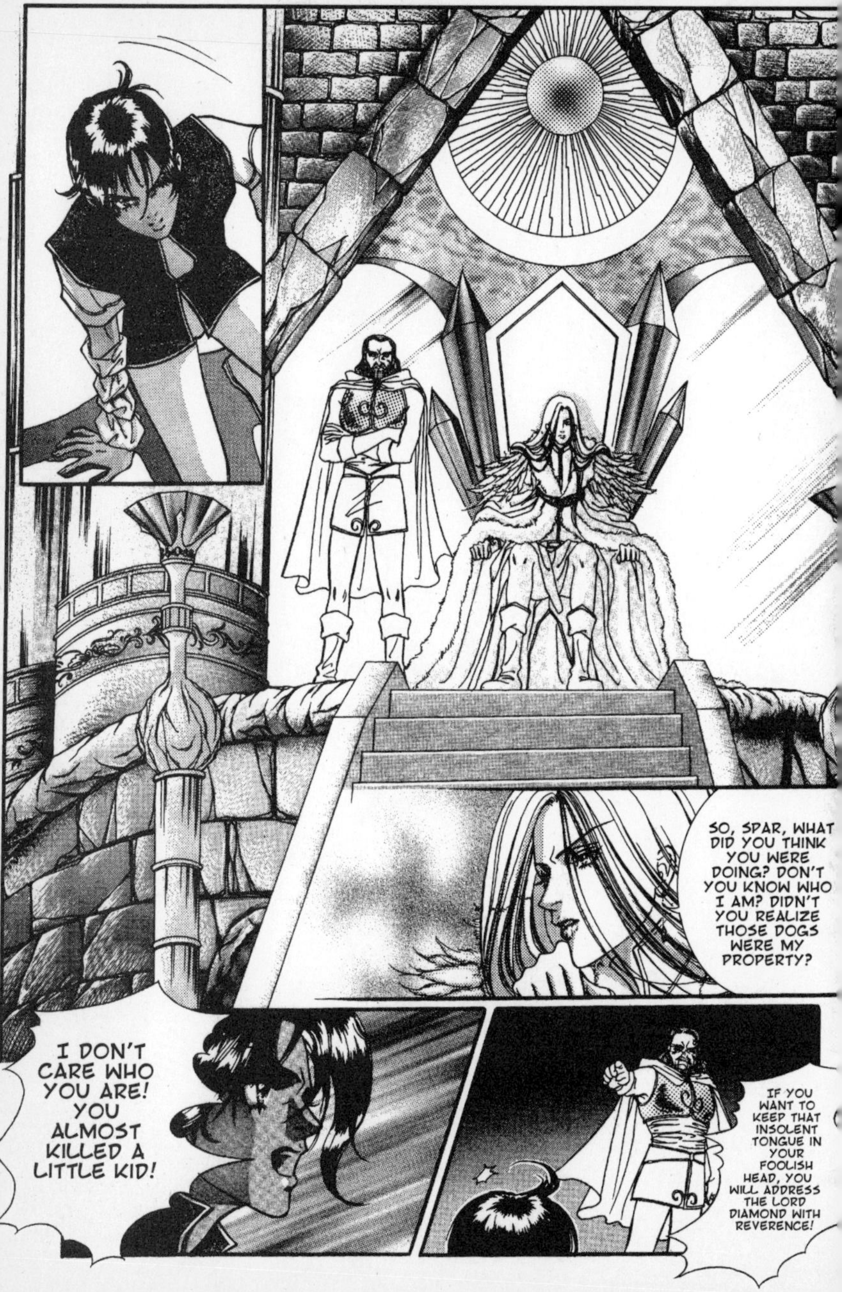
SO, SPAR, WHAT DID YOU THINK YOU WERE DOING? DON'T YOU KNOW WHO I AM? DIDN'T YOU REALIZE THOSE DOGS WERE MY PROPERTY?
I DON'T CARE WHO YOU ARE! YOU ALMOST KILLED A LITTLE KID!
IF YOU WANT TO KEEP THAT INSOLENT TONGUE IN YOUR FOOLISH HEAD, YOU WILL ADDRESS THE LORD DIAMOND WITH REVERENCE!

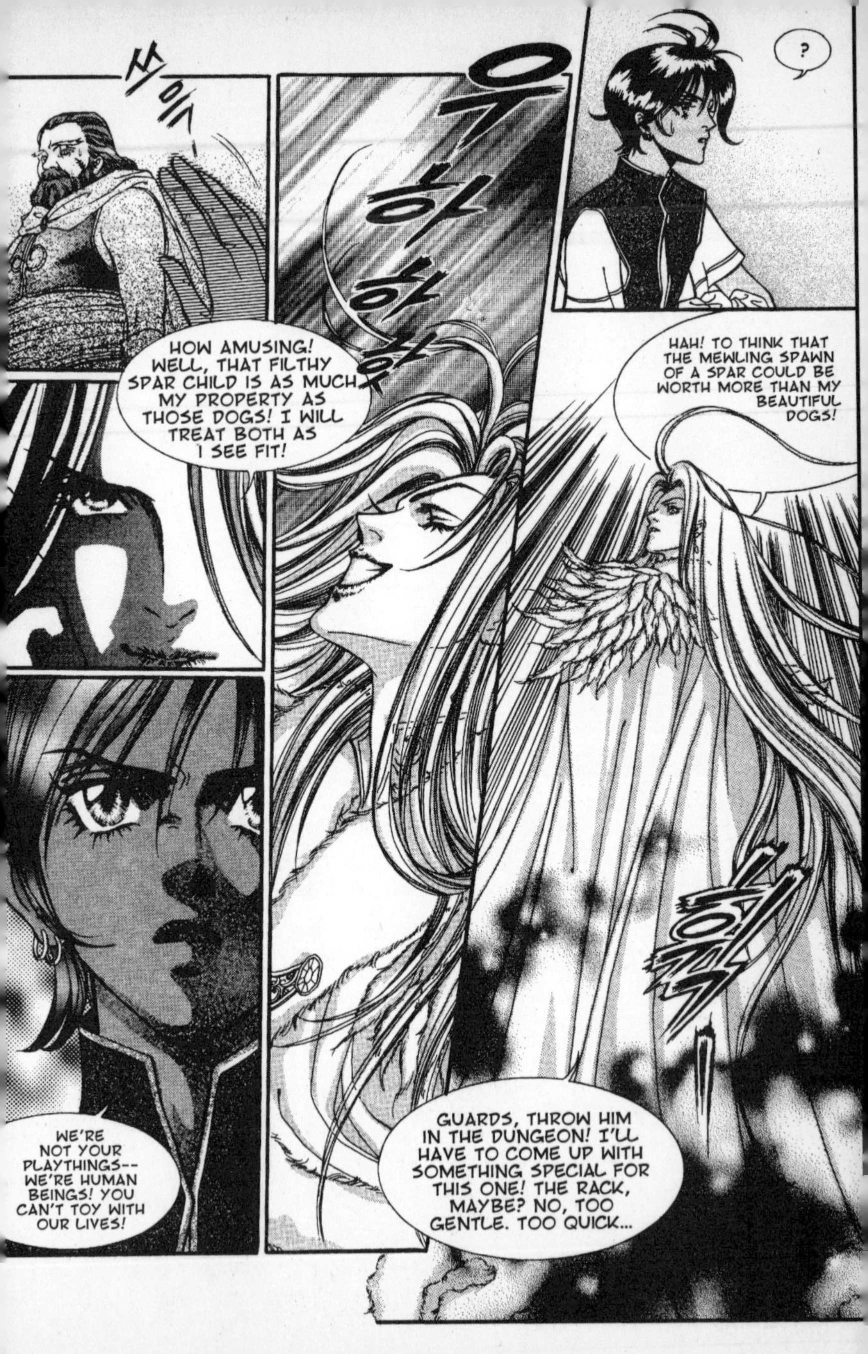
HOW AMUSING! WELL, THAT FILTHY SPAR CHILD IS AS MUCH MY PROPERTY AS THOSE DOGS! I WILL TREAT BOTH AS I SEE FIT!
?
HAH! TO THINK THAT THE MEWLING SPAWN OF A SPAR COULD BE WORTH MORE THAN MY BEAUTIFUL DOGS!
WE'RE NOT YOUR PLAYTHINGS-- WE'RE HUMAN BEINGS! YOU CAN'T TOY WITH OUR LIVES!
GUARDS, THROW HIM IN THE DUNGEON! I'LL HAVE TO COME UP WITH SOMETHING SPECIAL FOR THIS ONE! THE RACK, MAYBE? NO, TOO GENTLE. TOO QUICK...

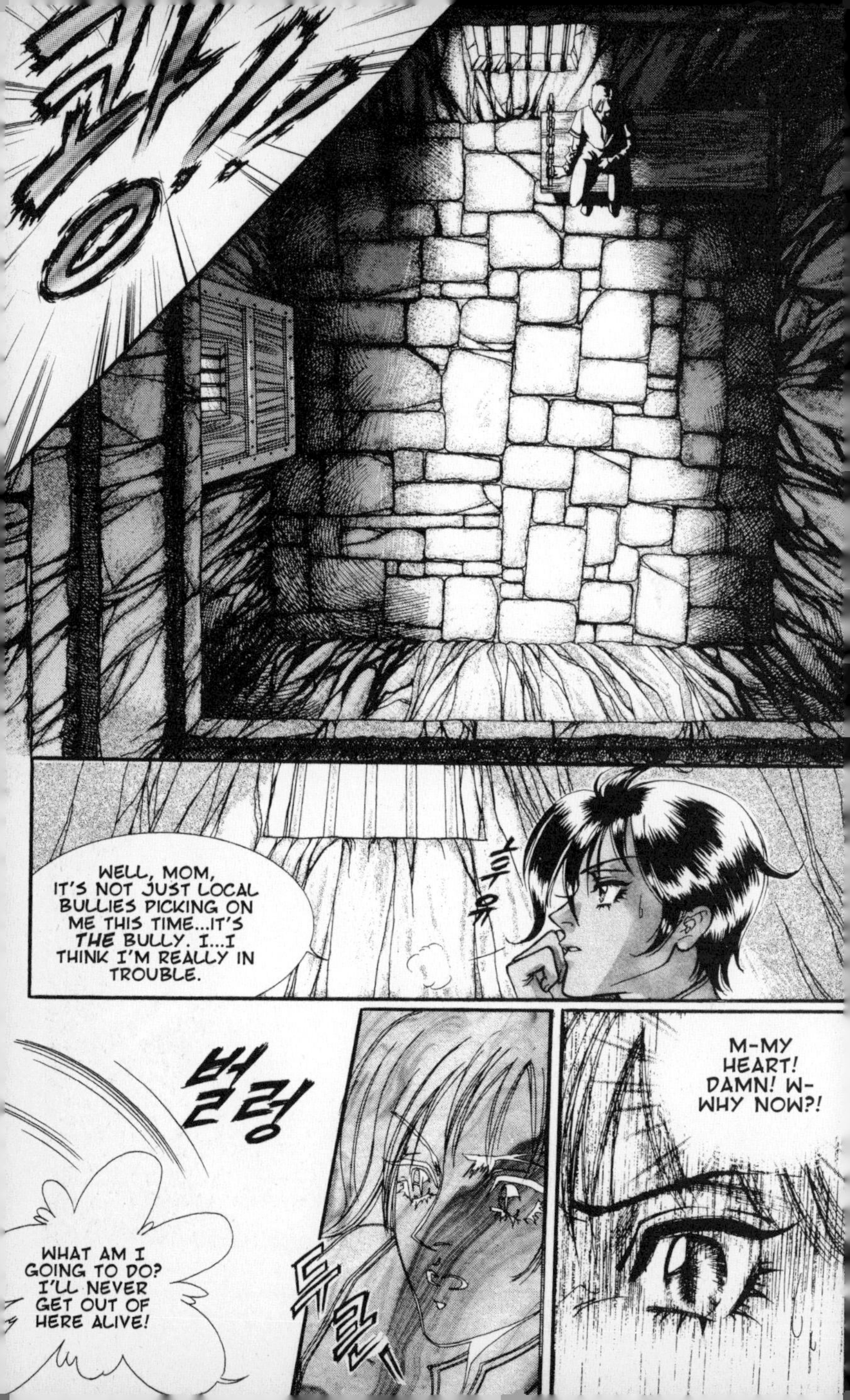
WELL, MOM, IT'S NOT JUST LOCAL BULLIES PICKING ON ME THIS TIME...IT'S *THE* BULLY. I...I THINK I'M REALLY IN TROUBLE.
벌렁
WHAT AM I GOING TO DO? I'LL NEVER GET OUT OF HERE ALIVE!
두근
M-MY HEART! DAMN! W-WHY NOW?!

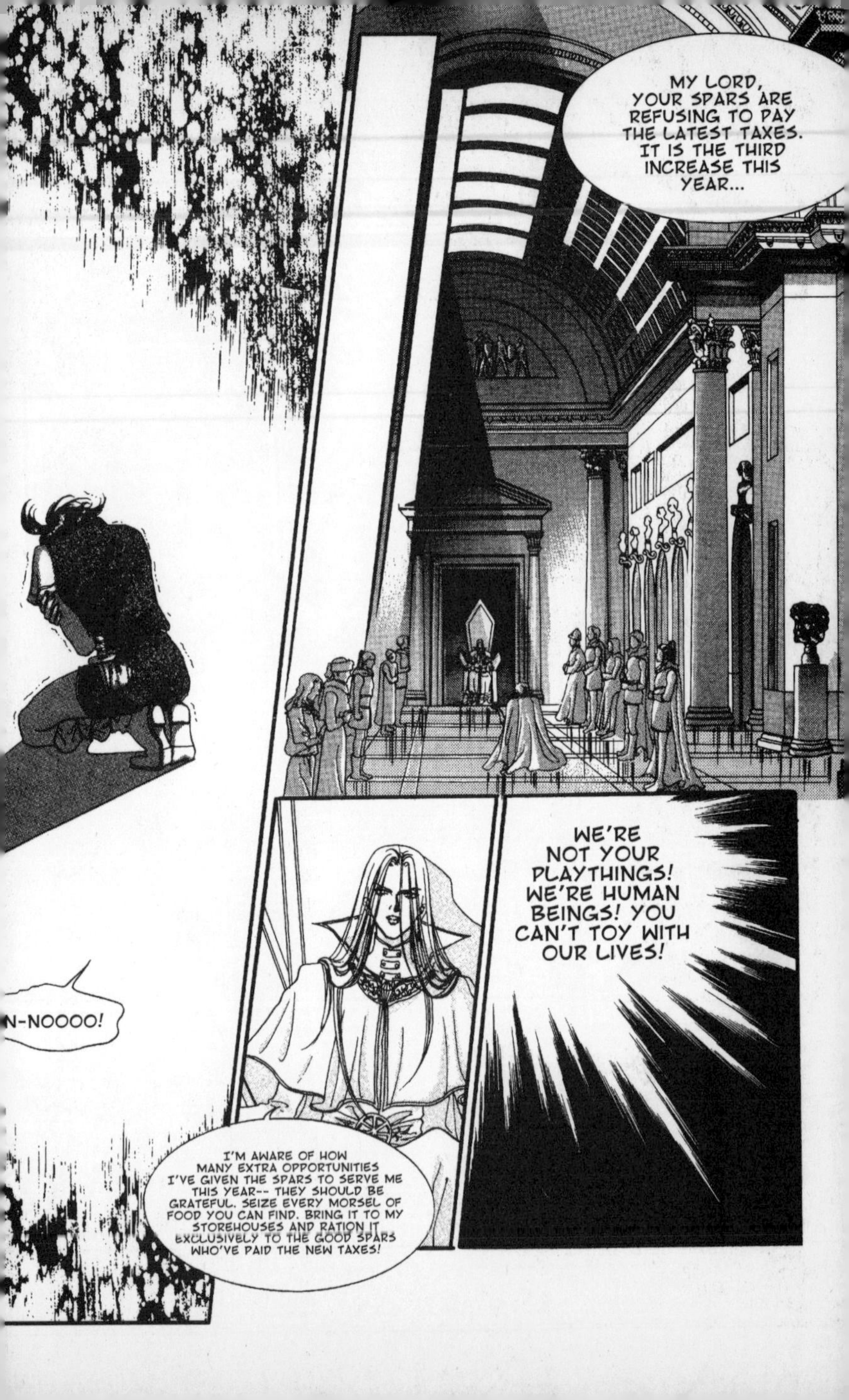
MY LORD, YOUR SPARS ARE REFUSING TO PAY THE LATEST TAXES. IT IS THE THIRD INCREASE THIS YEAR...
N-NOOOO!
WE'RE NOT YOUR PLAYTHINGS! WE'RE HUMAN BEINGS! YOU CAN'T TOY WITH OUR LIVES!
I'M AWARE OF HOW MANY EXTRA OPPORTUNITIES I'VE GIVEN THE SPARS TO SERVE ME THIS YEAR-- THEY SHOULD BE GRATEFUL. SEIZE EVERY MORSEL OF FOOD YOU CAN FIND. BRING IT TO MY STOREHOUSES AND RATION IT EXCLUSIVELY TO THE GOOD SPARS WHO'VE PAID THE NEW TAXES!

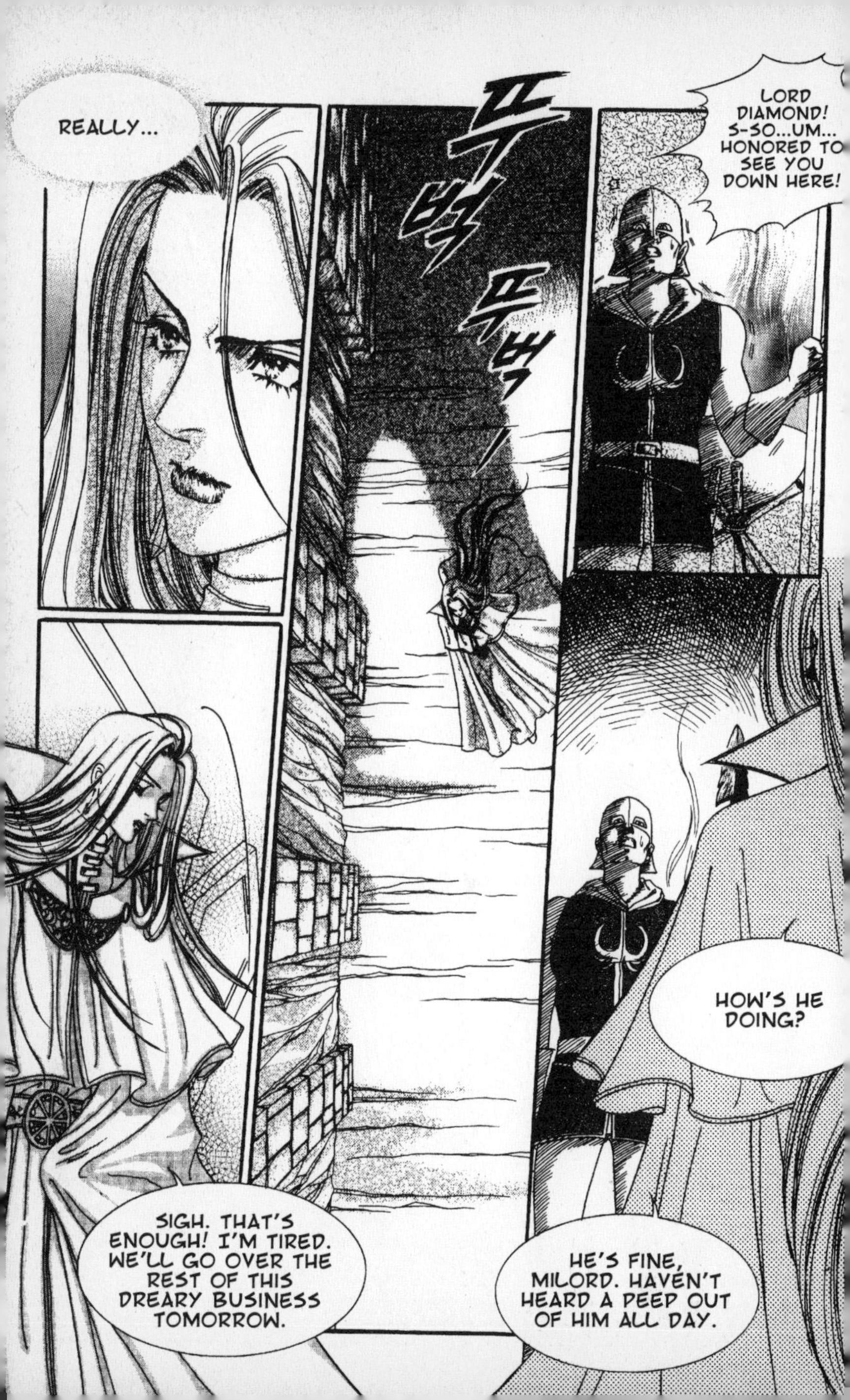
REALLY...
SIGH. THAT'S ENOUGH! I'M TIRED. WE'LL GO OVER THE REST OF THIS DREARY BUSINESS TOMORROW.
뚜벅 뚜벅
LORD DIAMOND! S-SO...UM... HONORED TO SEE YOU DOWN HERE!
HOW'S HE DOING?
HE'S FINE, MILORD. HAVEN'T HEARD A PEEP OUT OF HIM ALL DAY.

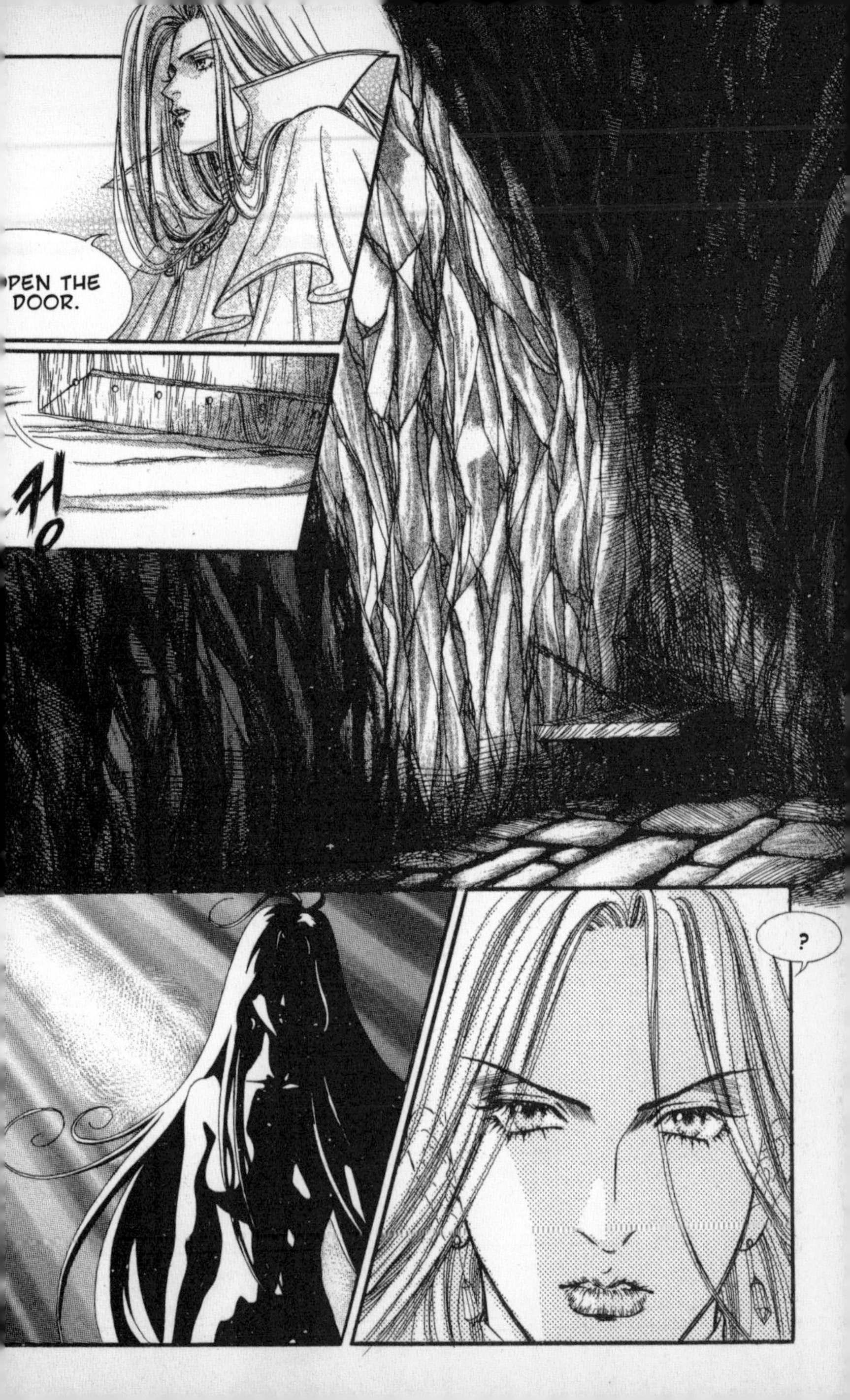
PEN THE
DOOR.
?

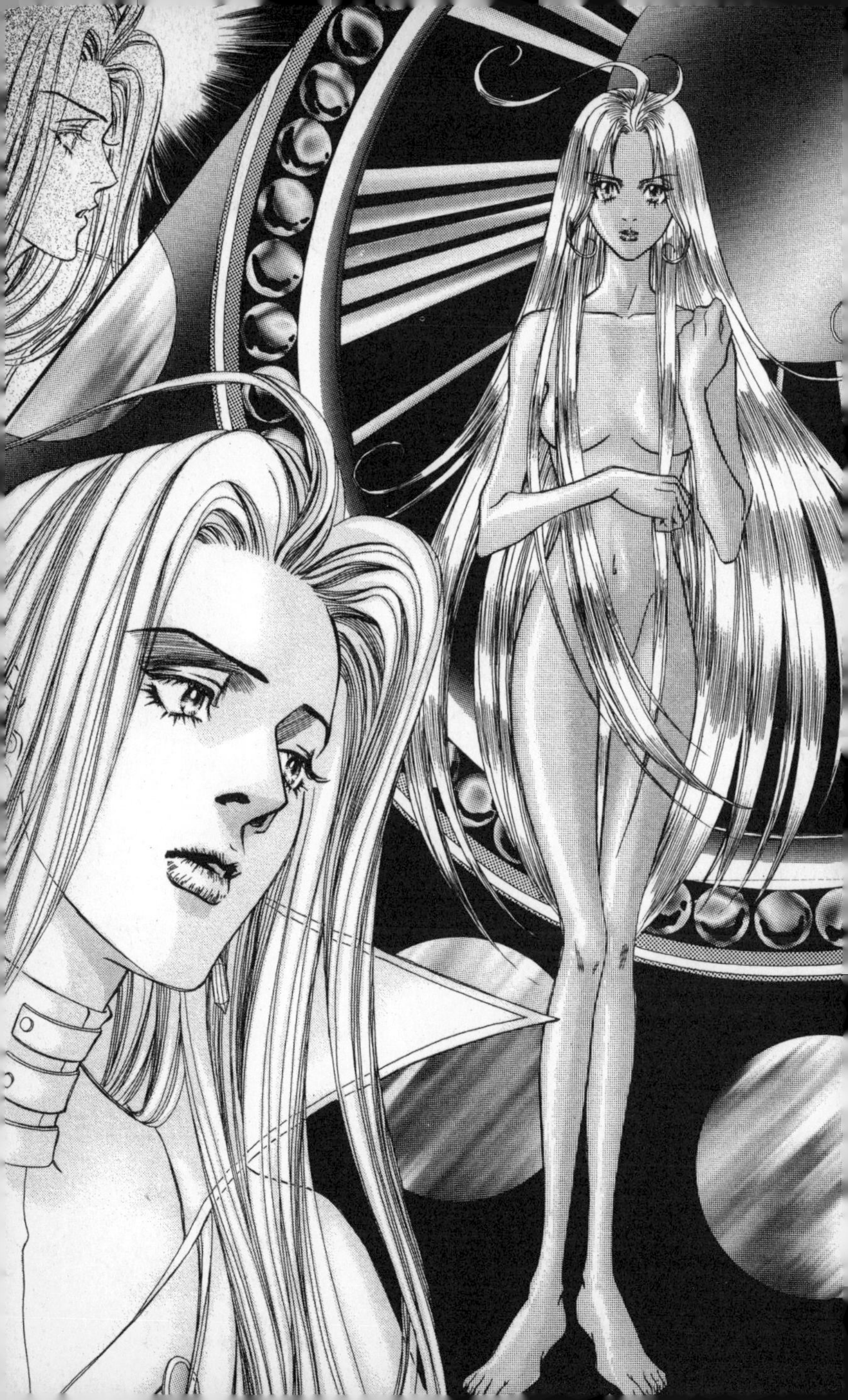

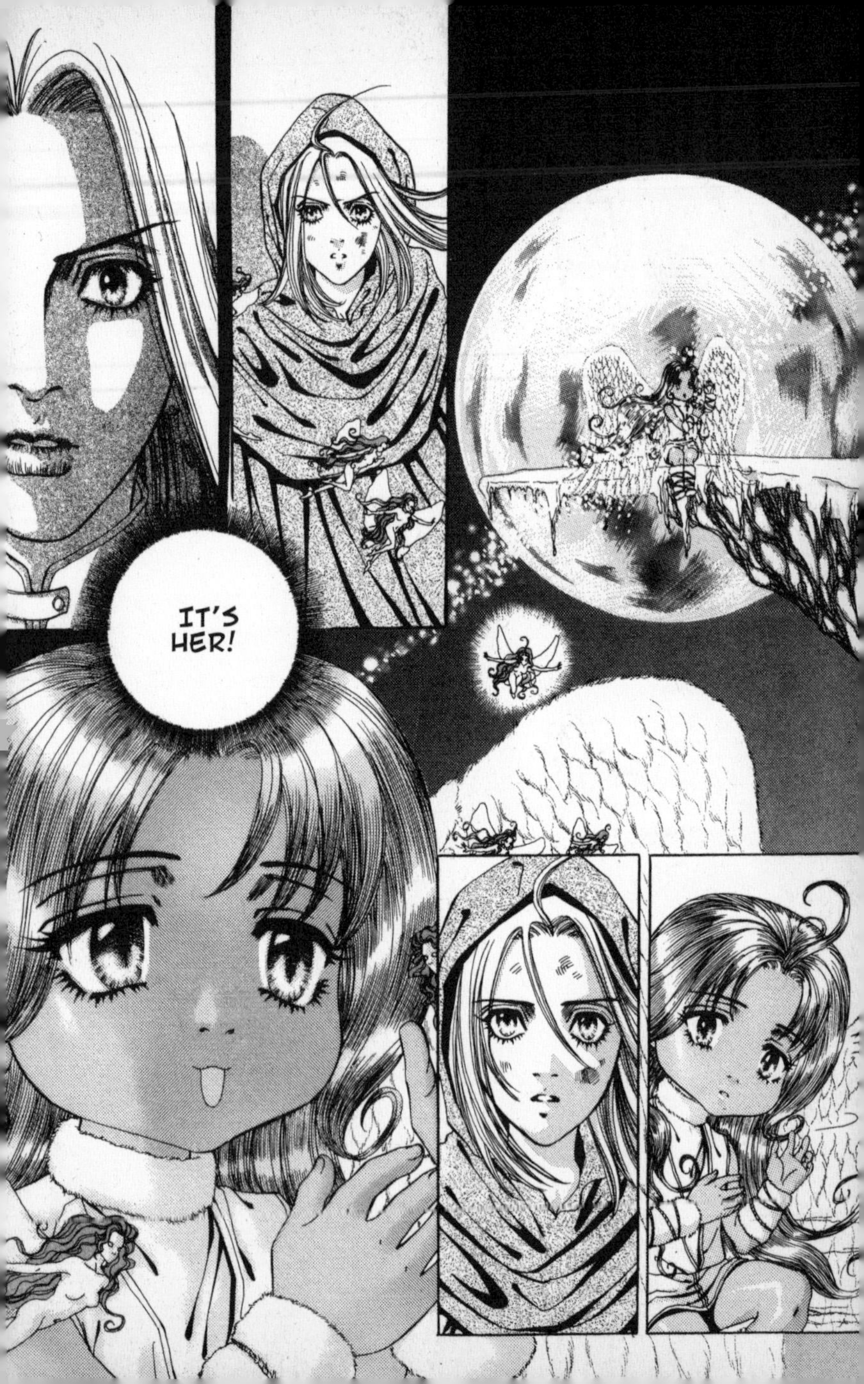
IT'S HER!

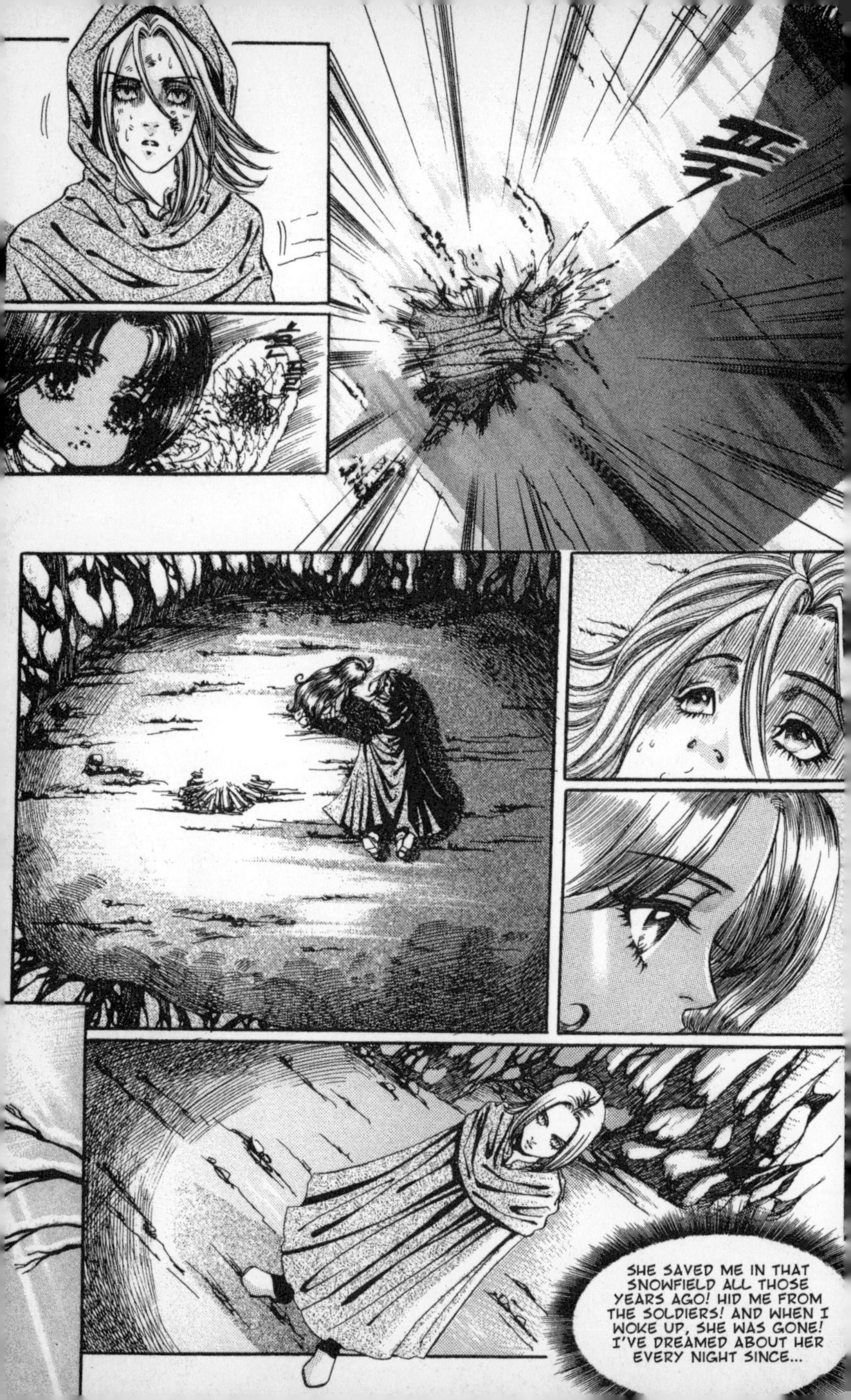
SHE SAVED ME IN THAT SNOWFIELD ALL THOSE YEARS AGO! HID ME FROM THE SOLDIERS! AND WHEN I WOKE UP, SHE WAS GONE! I'VE DREAMED ABOUT HER EVERY NIGHT SINCE...

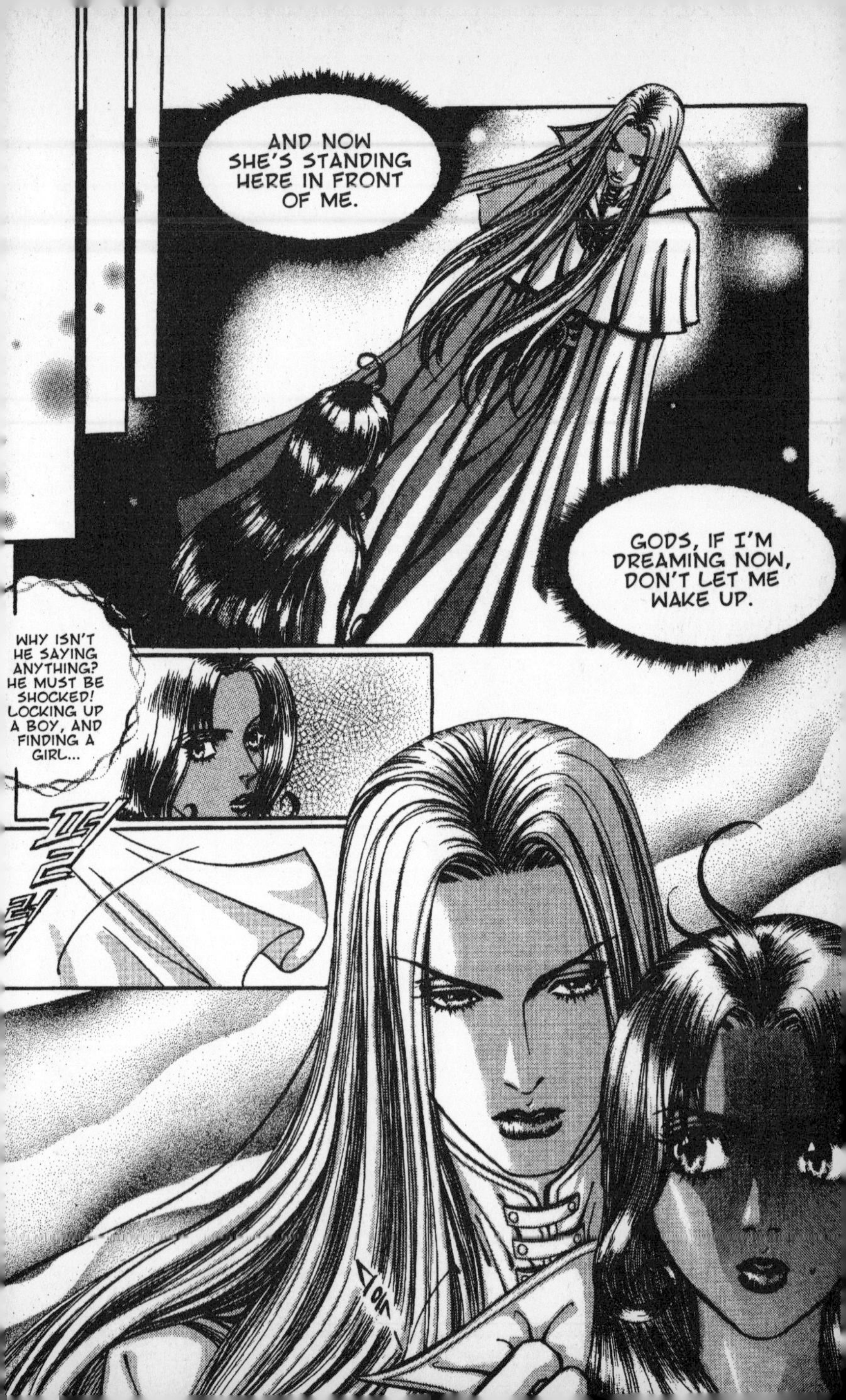
AND NOW SHE'S STANDING HERE IN FRONT OF ME.
GODS, IF I'M DREAMING NOW, DON'T LET ME WAKE UP.
WHY ISN'T HE SAYING ANYTHING? HE MUST BE SHOCKED! LOCKING UP A BOY, AND FINDING A GIRL...

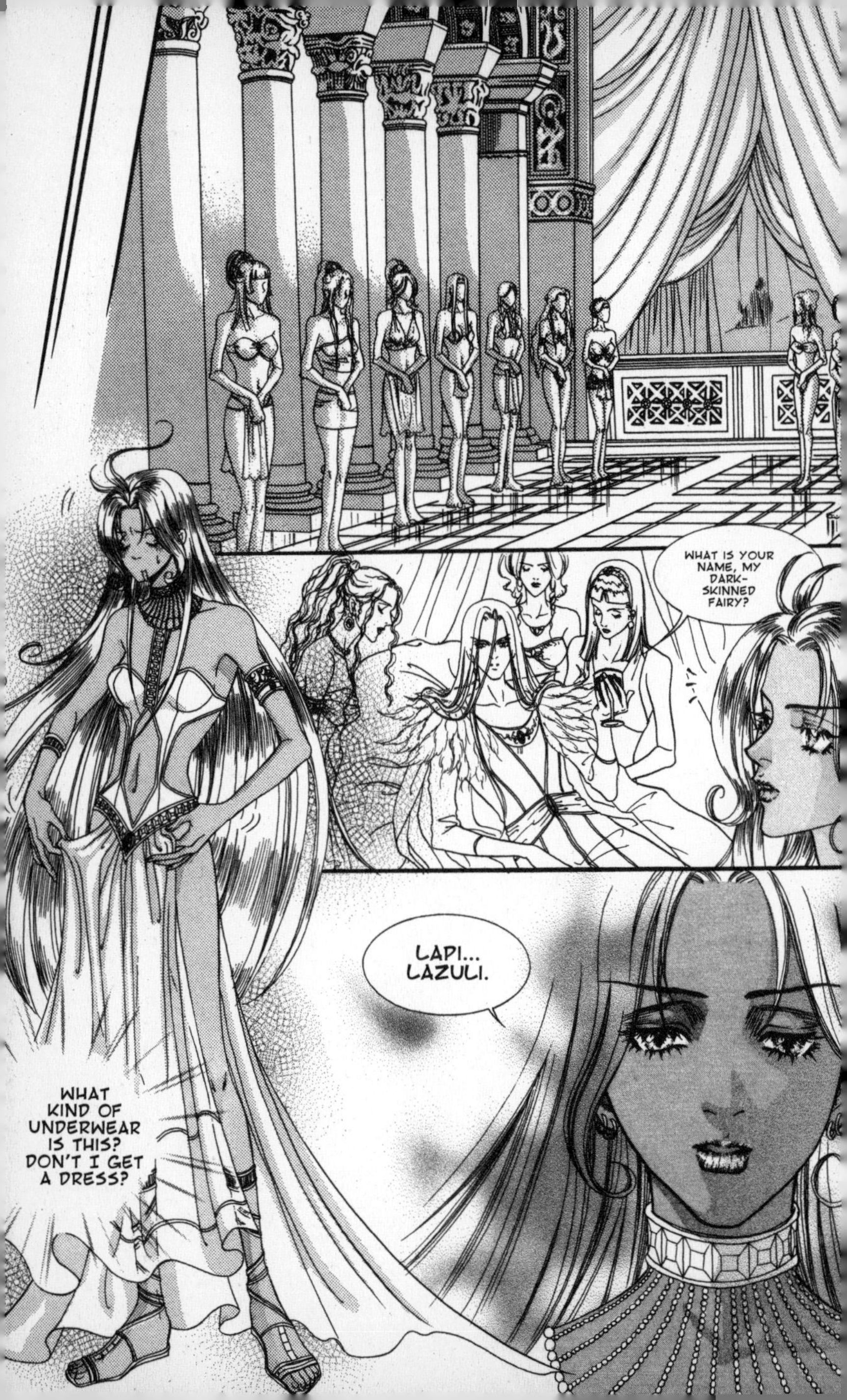
WHAT IS YOUR NAME, MY DARK-SKINNED FAIRY?
LAPI... LAZULI.
WHAT KIND OF UNDERWEAR IS THIS? DON'T I GET A DRESS?

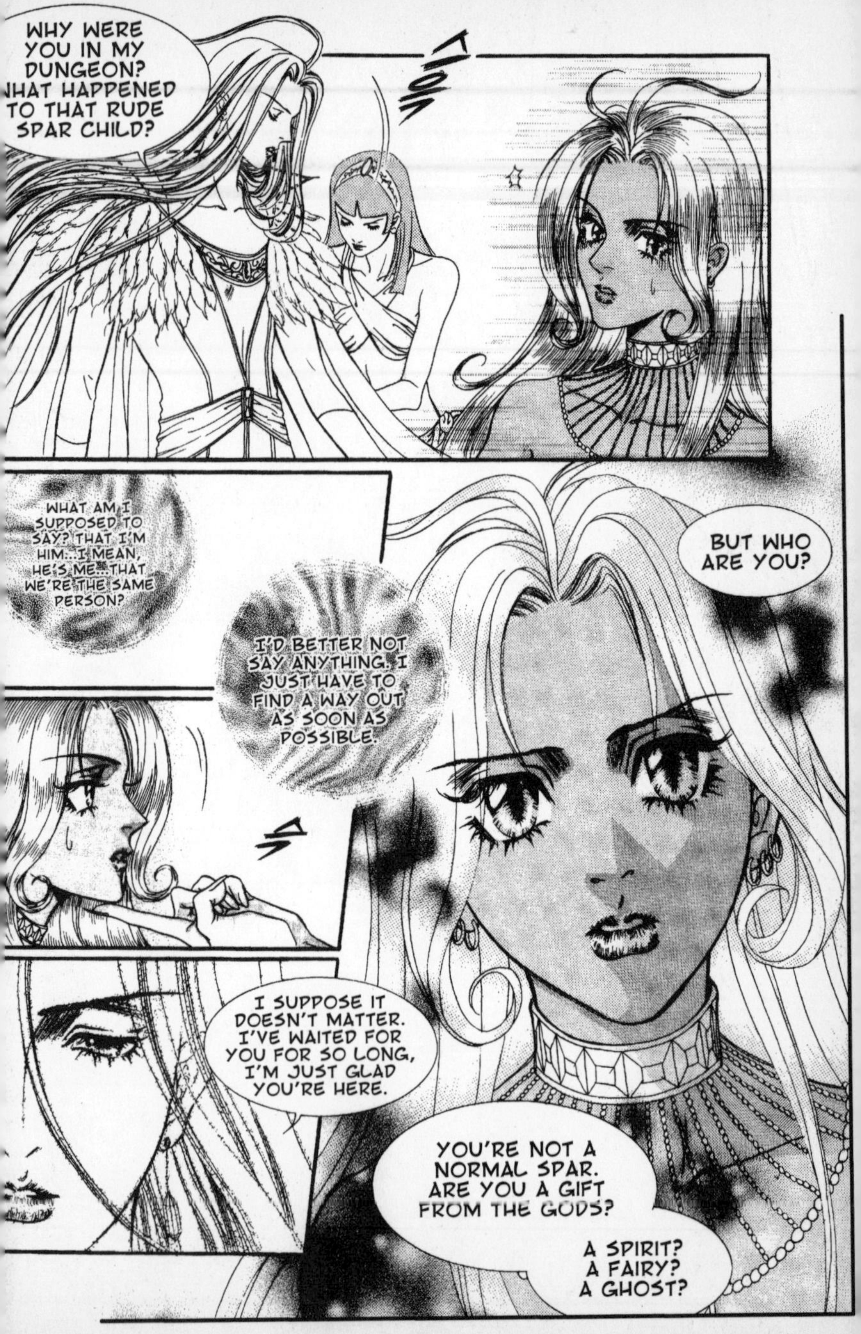
WHY WERE YOU IN MY DUNGEON? WHAT HAPPENED TO THAT RUDE SPAR CHILD?
BUT WHO ARE YOU?
WHAT AM I SUPPOSED TO SAY? THAT I'M HIM...I MEAN, HE'S ME...THAT WE'RE THE SAME PERSON?
I'D BETTER NOT SAY ANYTHING. I JUST HAVE TO FIND A WAY OUT AS SOON AS POSSIBLE.
I SUPPOSE IT DOESN'T MATTER. I'VE WAITED FOR YOU FOR SO LONG, I'M JUST GLAD YOU'RE HERE.
YOU'RE NOT A NORMAL SPAR. ARE YOU A GIFT FROM THE GODS?
A SPIRIT? A FAIRY? A GHOST?

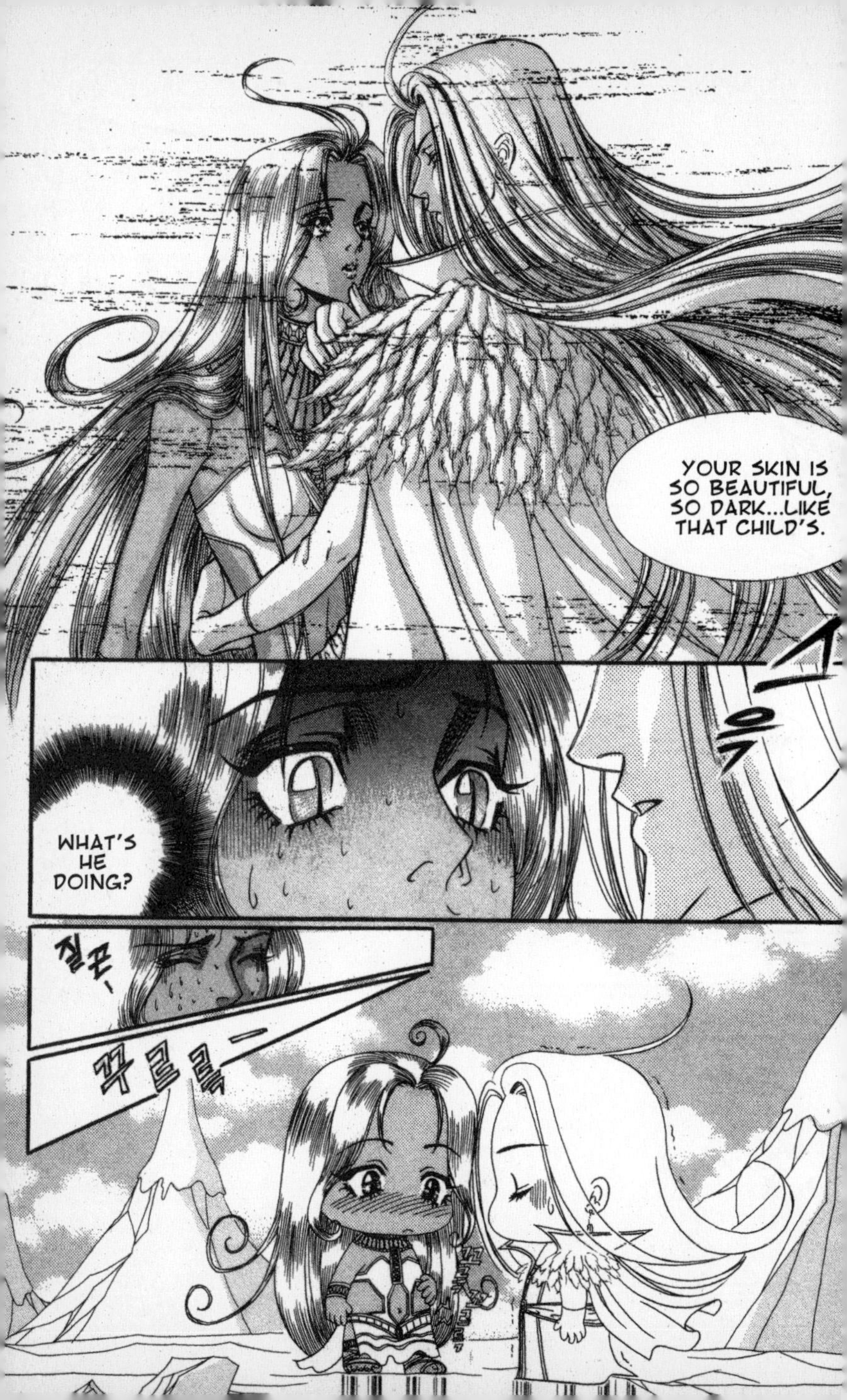
YOUR SKIN IS SO BEAUTIFUL, SO DARK...LIKE THAT CHILD'S.
WHAT'S HE DOING?
질끈
꾸르륵

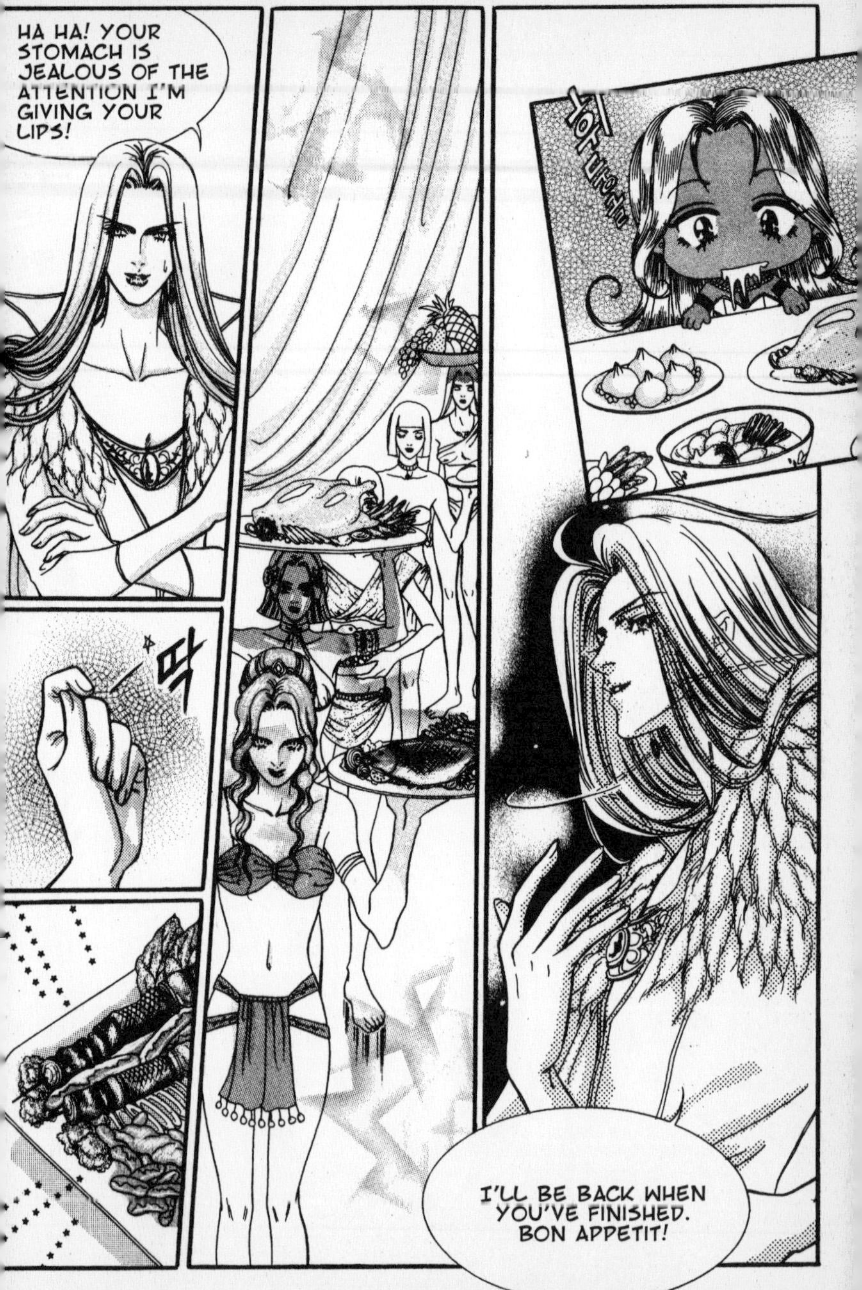
HA HA! YOUR STOMACH IS JEALOUS OF THE ATTENTION I'M GIVING YOUR LIPS!
딱
I'LL BE BACK WHEN YOU'VE FINISHED. BON APPETIT!

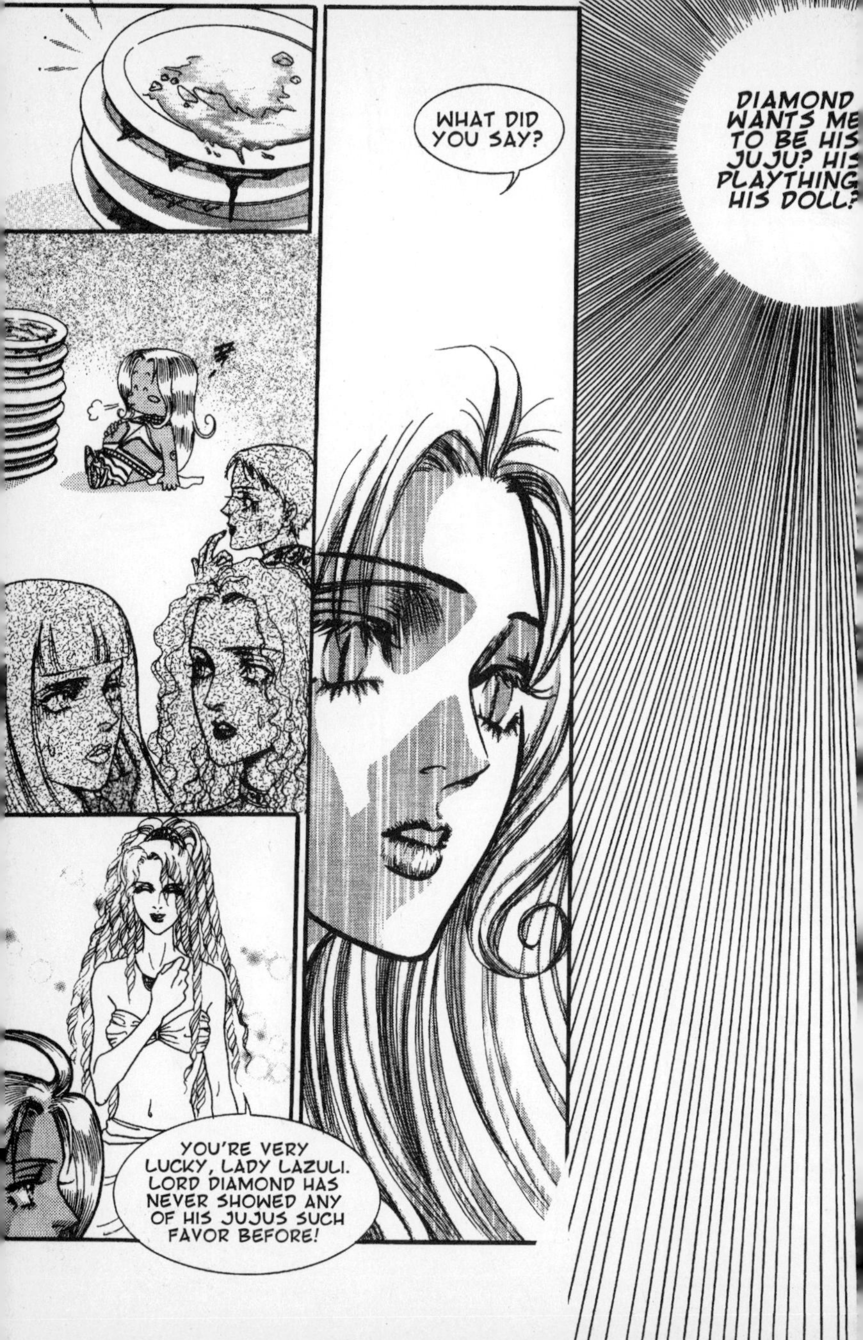
DIAMOND WANTS ME TO BE HIS JUJU? HIS PLAYTHING? HIS DOLL?
WHAT DID YOU SAY?
YOU'RE VERY LUCKY, LADY LAZULI. LORD DIAMOND HAS NEVER SHOWED ANY OF HIS JUJUS SUCH FAVOR BEFORE!

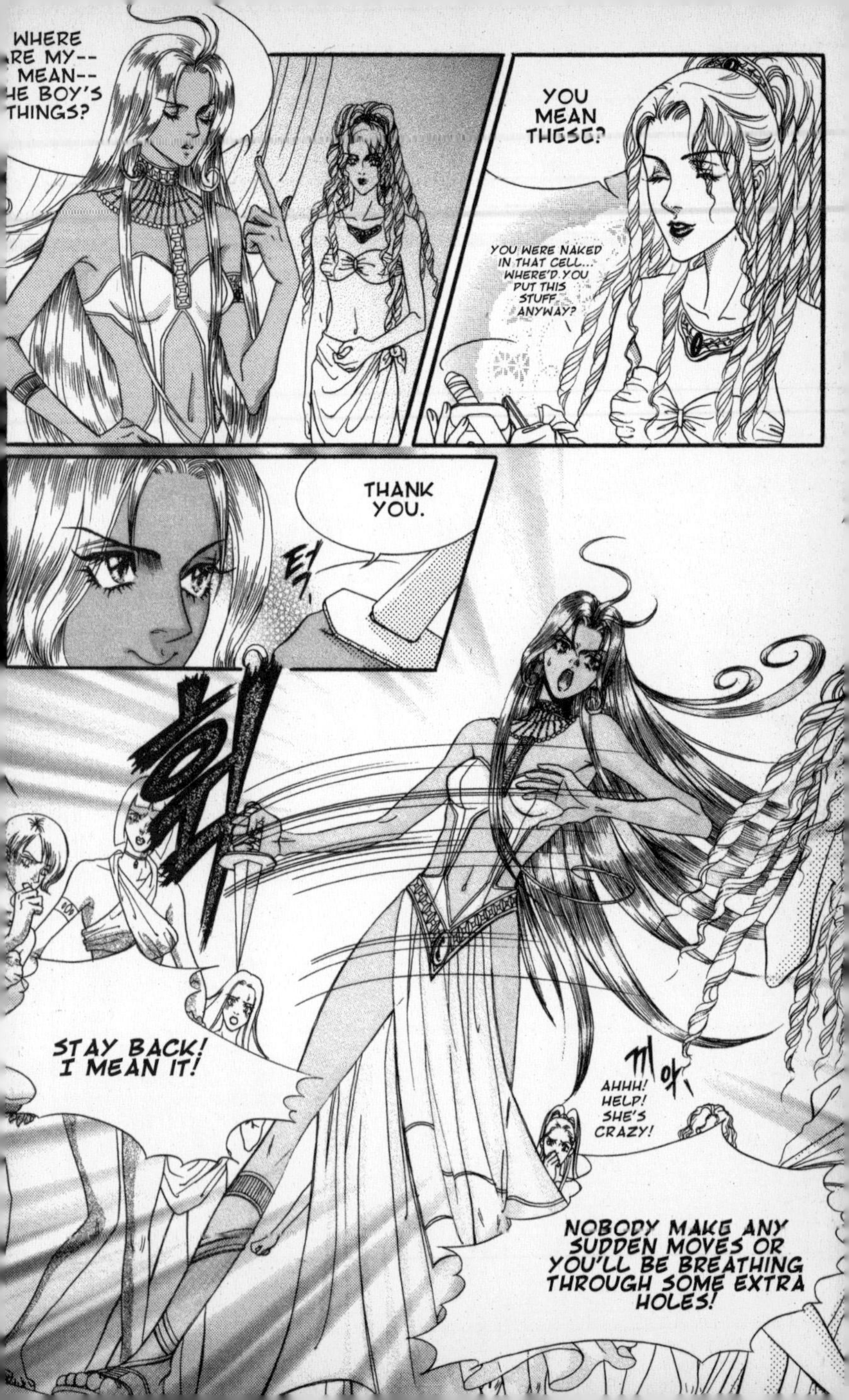
WHERE RE MY-- MEAN-- HE BOY'S THINGS?
YOU MEAN THESE?
YOU WERE NAKED IN THAT CELL... WHERE'D YOU PUT THIS STUFF ANYWAY?
THANK YOU.
턱
휙
STAY BACK! I MEAN IT!
꺄아
AHHH! HELP! SHE'S CRAZY!
NOBODY MAKE ANY SUDDEN MOVES OR YOU'LL BE BREATHING THROUGH SOME EXTRA HOLES!

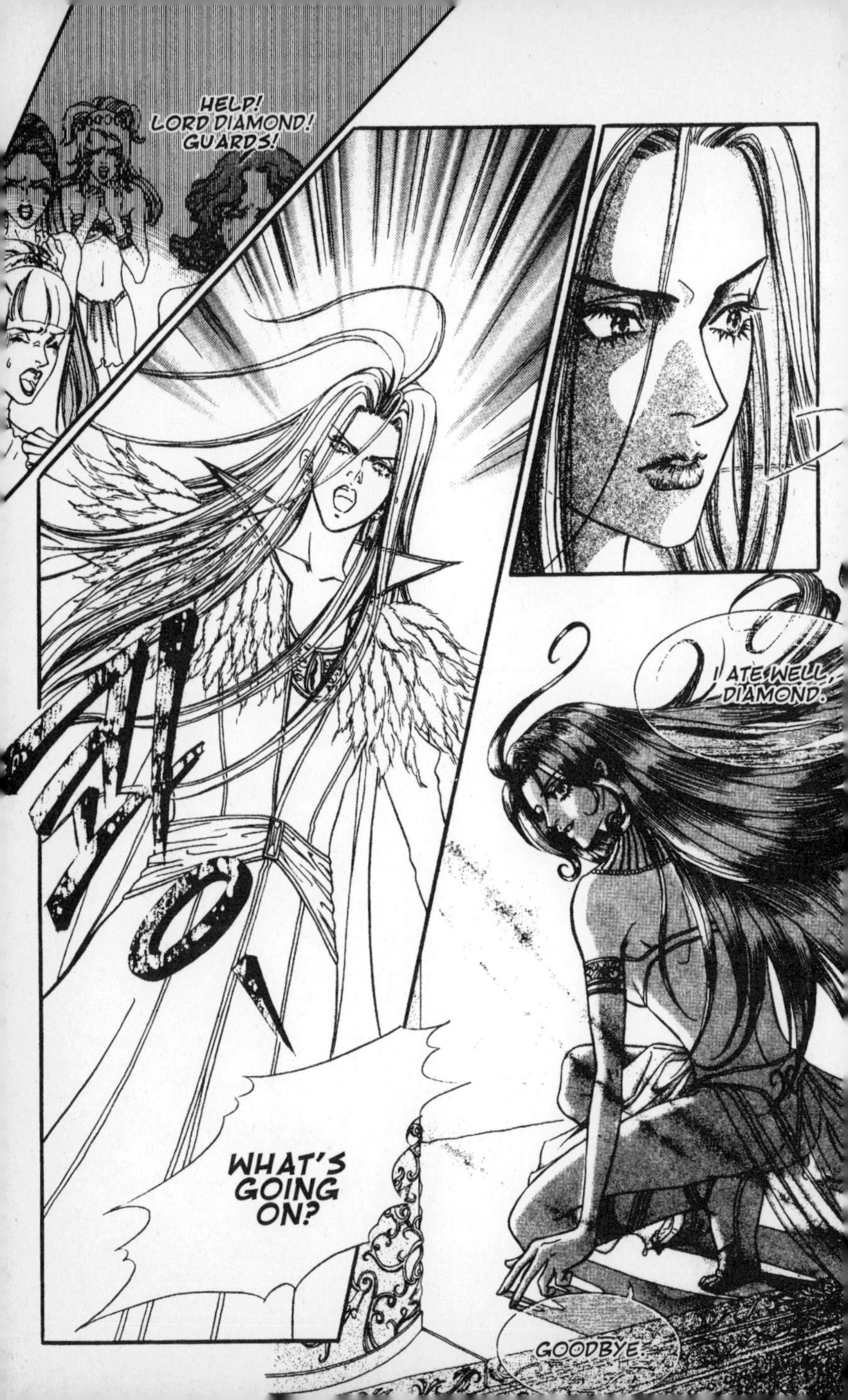
HELP! LORD DIAMOND! GUARDS!
WHAT'S GOING ON?
I ATE WELL, DIAMOND.
GOODBYE.

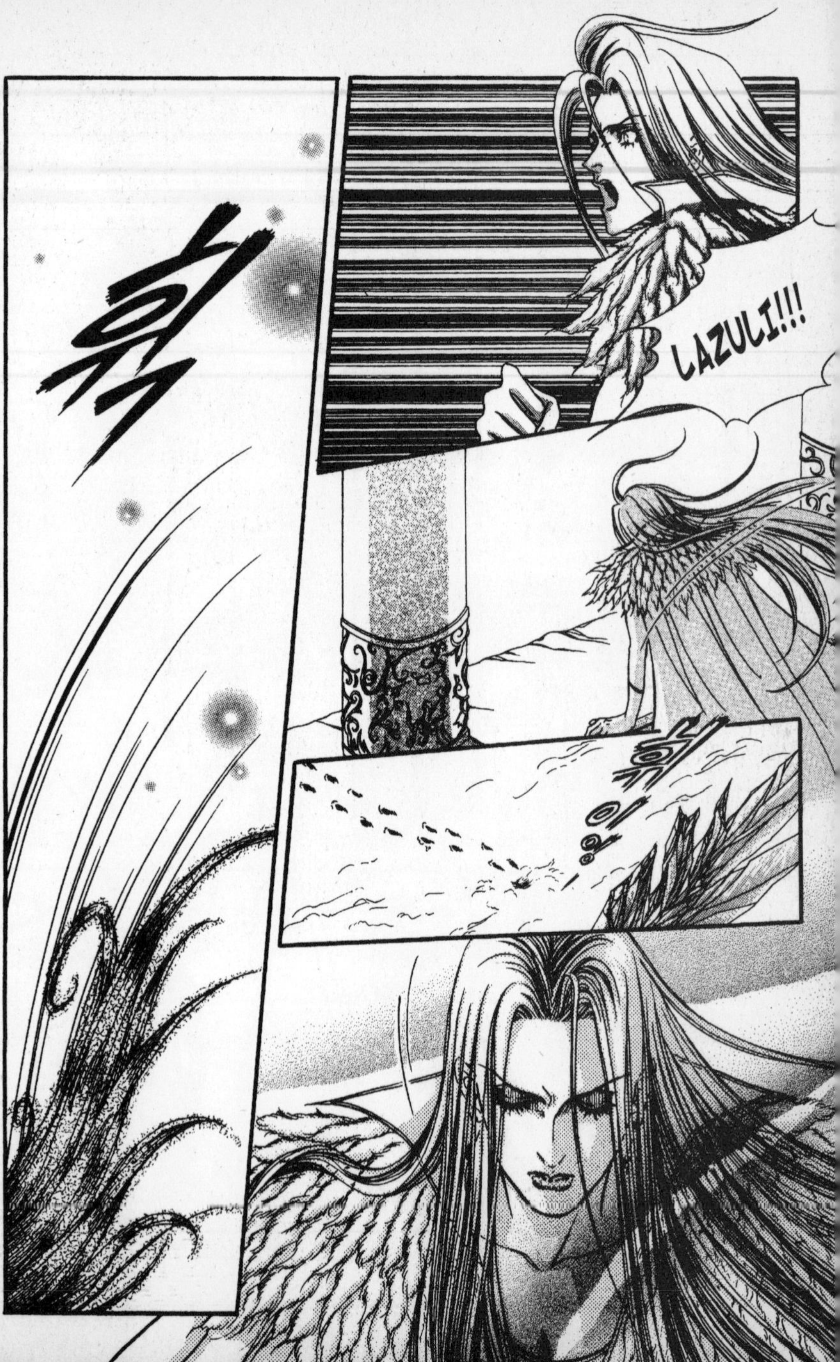
LAZULI!!!

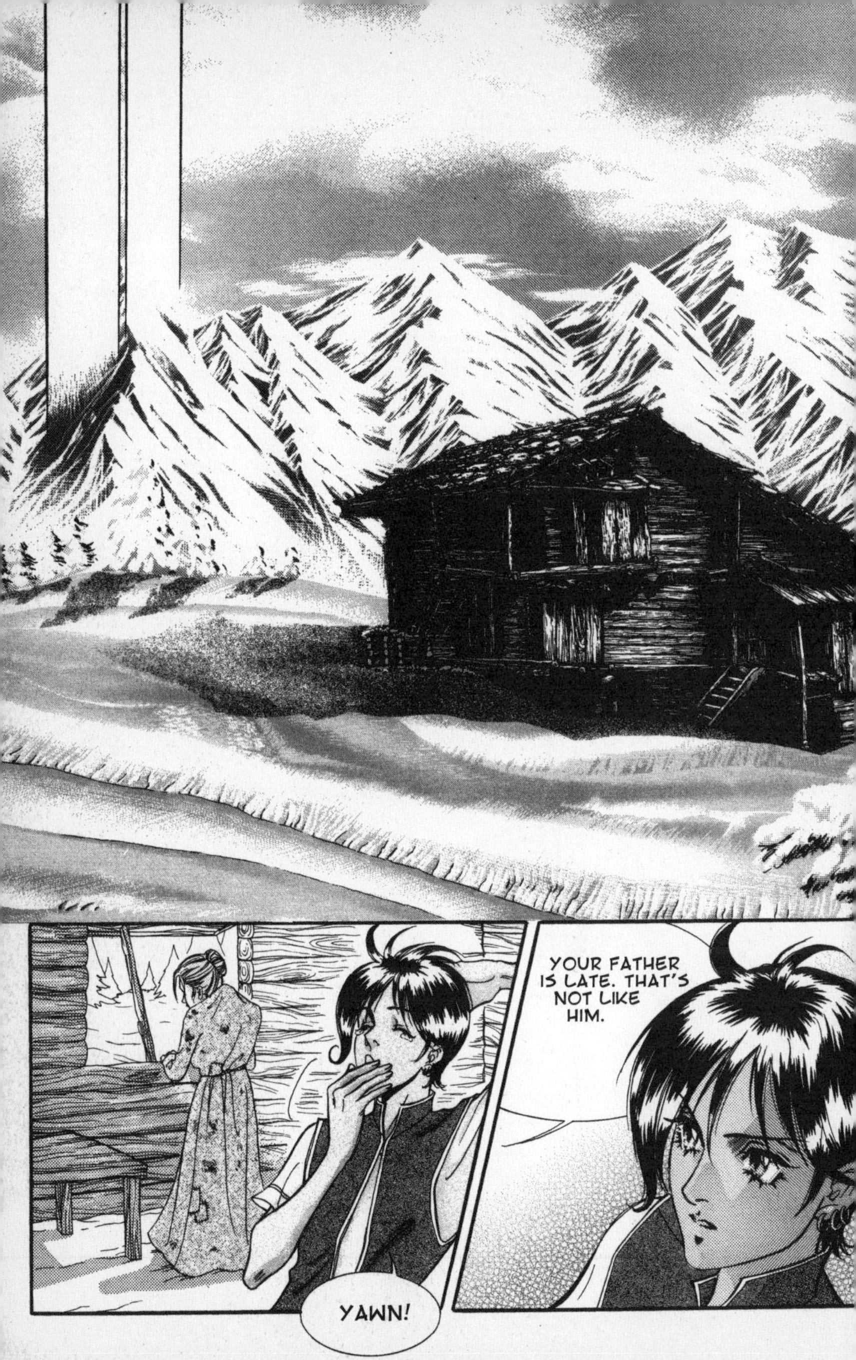
YOUR FATHER IS LATE. THAT'S NOT LIKE HIM.
YAWN!

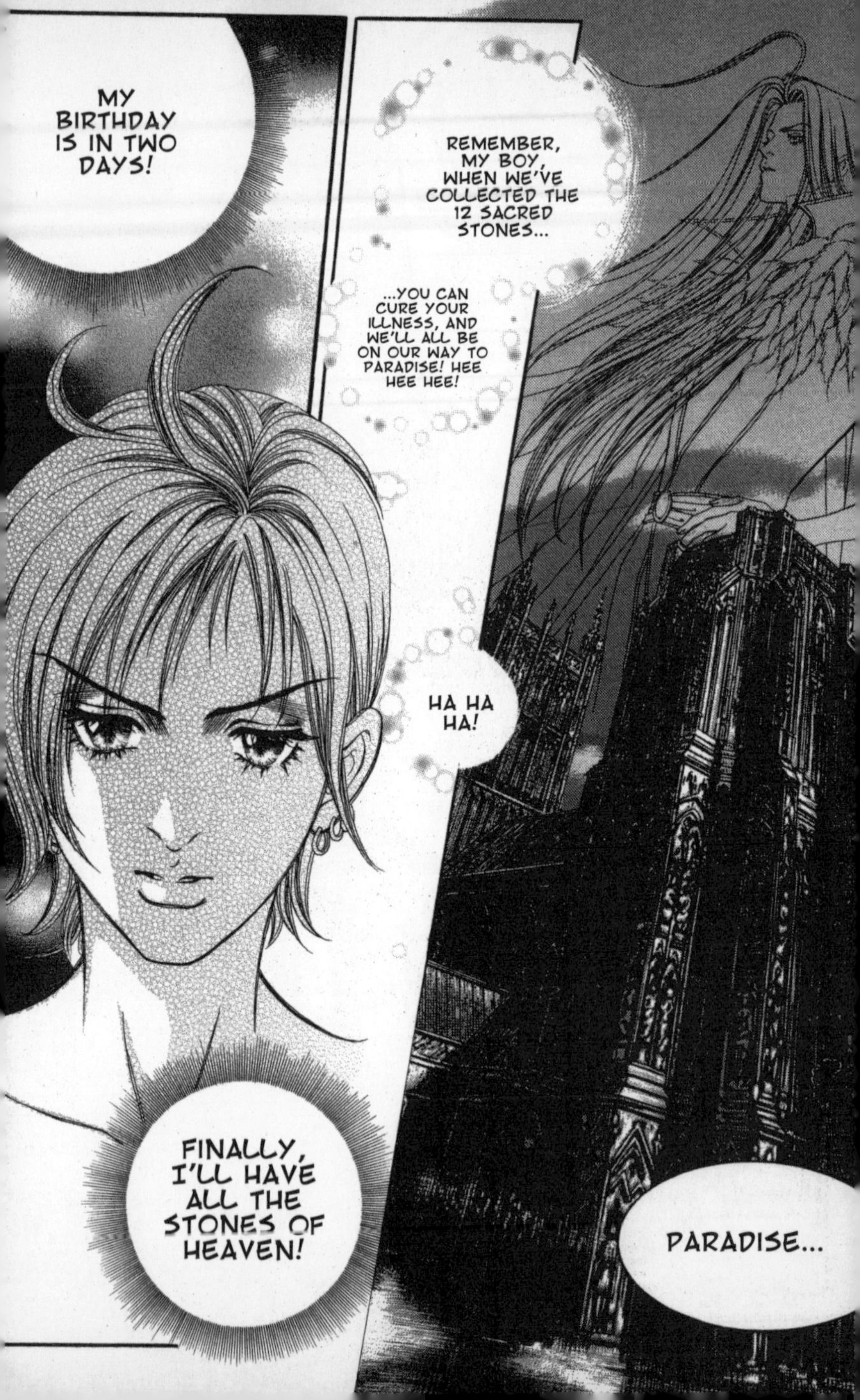
REMEMBER, MY BOY, WHEN WE'VE COLLECTED THE 12 SACRED STONES...
...YOU CAN CURE YOUR ILLNESS, AND WE'LL ALL BE ON OUR WAY TO PARADISE! HEE HEE HEE!
HA HA HA!
PARADISE...
MY BIRTHDAY IS IN TWO DAYS!
FINALLY, I'LL HAVE ALL THE STONES OF HEAVEN!

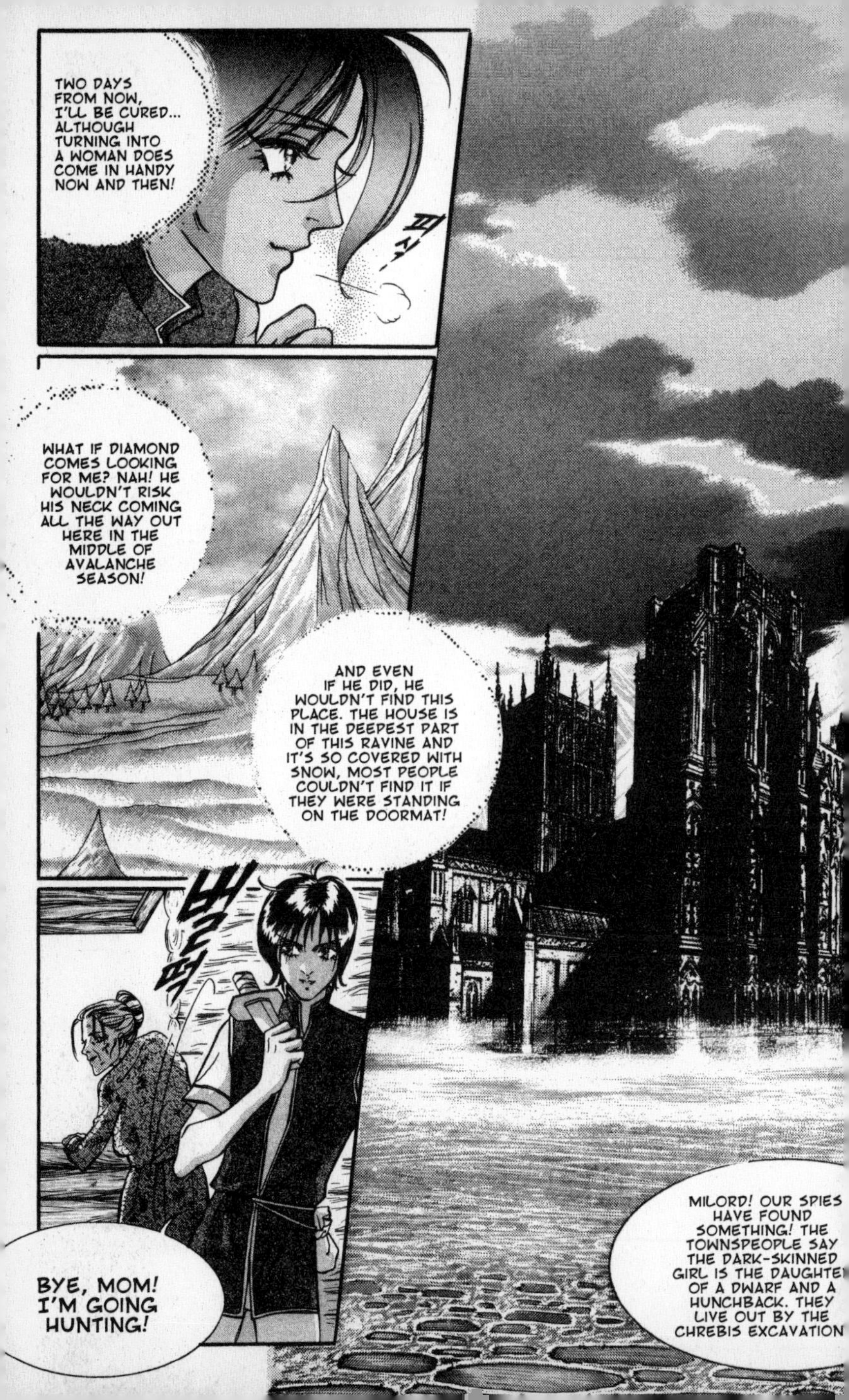
TWO DAYS FROM NOW, I'LL BE CURED... ALTHOUGH TURNING INTO A WOMAN DOES COME IN HANDY NOW AND THEN!
피식
WHAT IF DIAMOND COMES LOOKING FOR ME? NAH! HE WOULDN'T RISK HIS NECK COMING ALL THE WAY OUT HERE IN THE MIDDLE OF AVALANCHE SEASON!
AND EVEN IF HE DID, HE WOULDN'T FIND THIS PLACE. THE HOUSE IS IN THE DEEPEST PART OF THIS RAVINE AND IT'S SO COVERED WITH SNOW, MOST PEOPLE COULDN'T FIND IT IF THEY WERE STANDING ON THE DOORMAT!
벌떡
BYE, MOM! I'M GOING HUNTING!
MILORD! OUR SPIES HAVE FOUND SOMETHING! THE TOWNSPEOPLE SAY THE DARK-SKINNED GIRL IS THE DAUGHTE OF A DWARF AND A HUNCHBACK. THEY LIVE OUT BY THE CHREBIS EXCAVATION

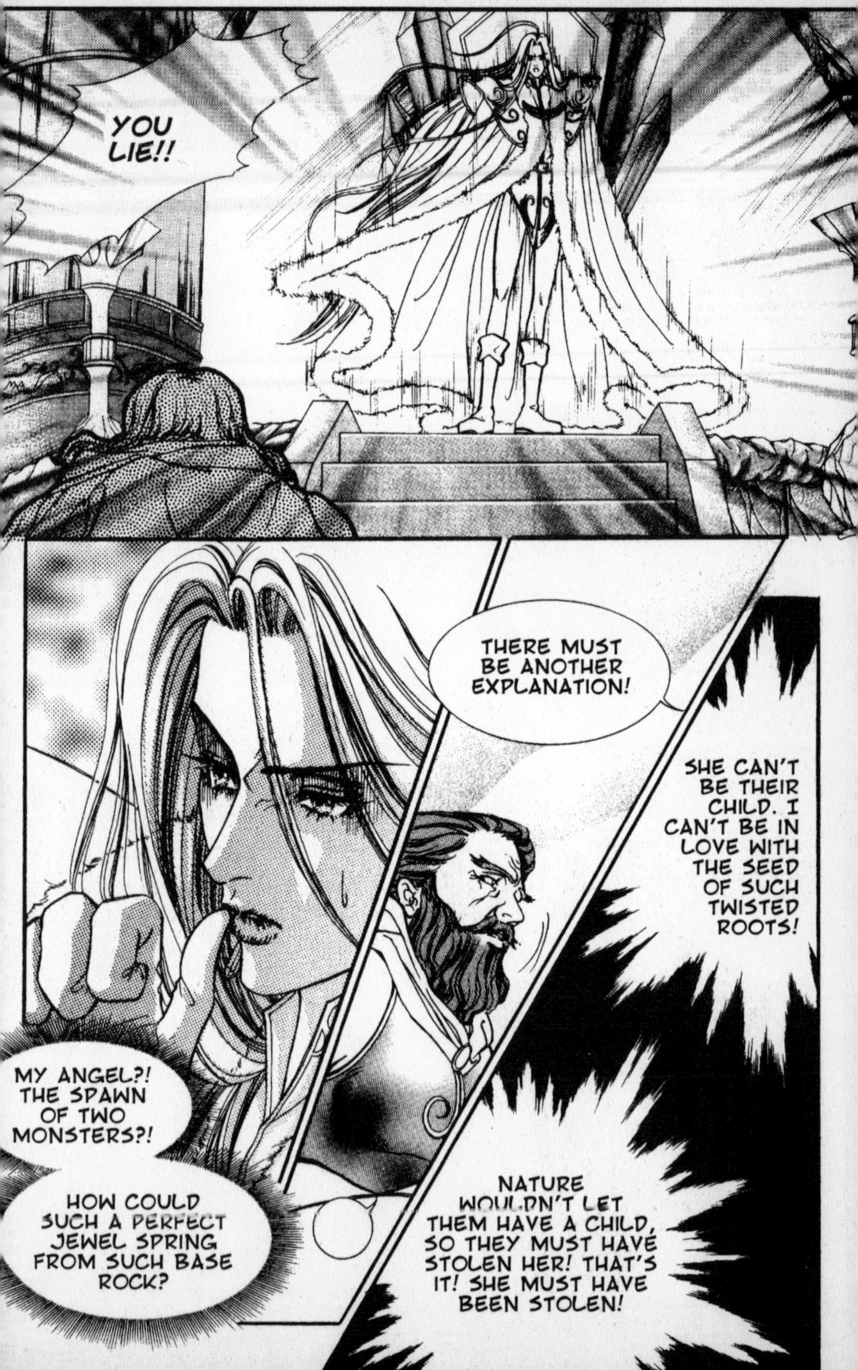
YOU LIE!!
THERE MUST BE ANOTHER EXPLANATION!
SHE CAN'T BE THEIR CHILD. I CAN'T BE IN LOVE WITH THE SEED OF SUCH TWISTED ROOTS!
MY ANGEL?! THE SPAWN OF TWO MONSTERS?!
HOW COULD SUCH A PERFECT JEWEL SPRING FROM SUCH BASE ROCK?
NATURE WOULDN'T LET THEM HAVE A CHILD, SO THEY MUST HAVE STOLEN HER! THAT'S IT! SHE MUST HAVE BEEN STOLEN!

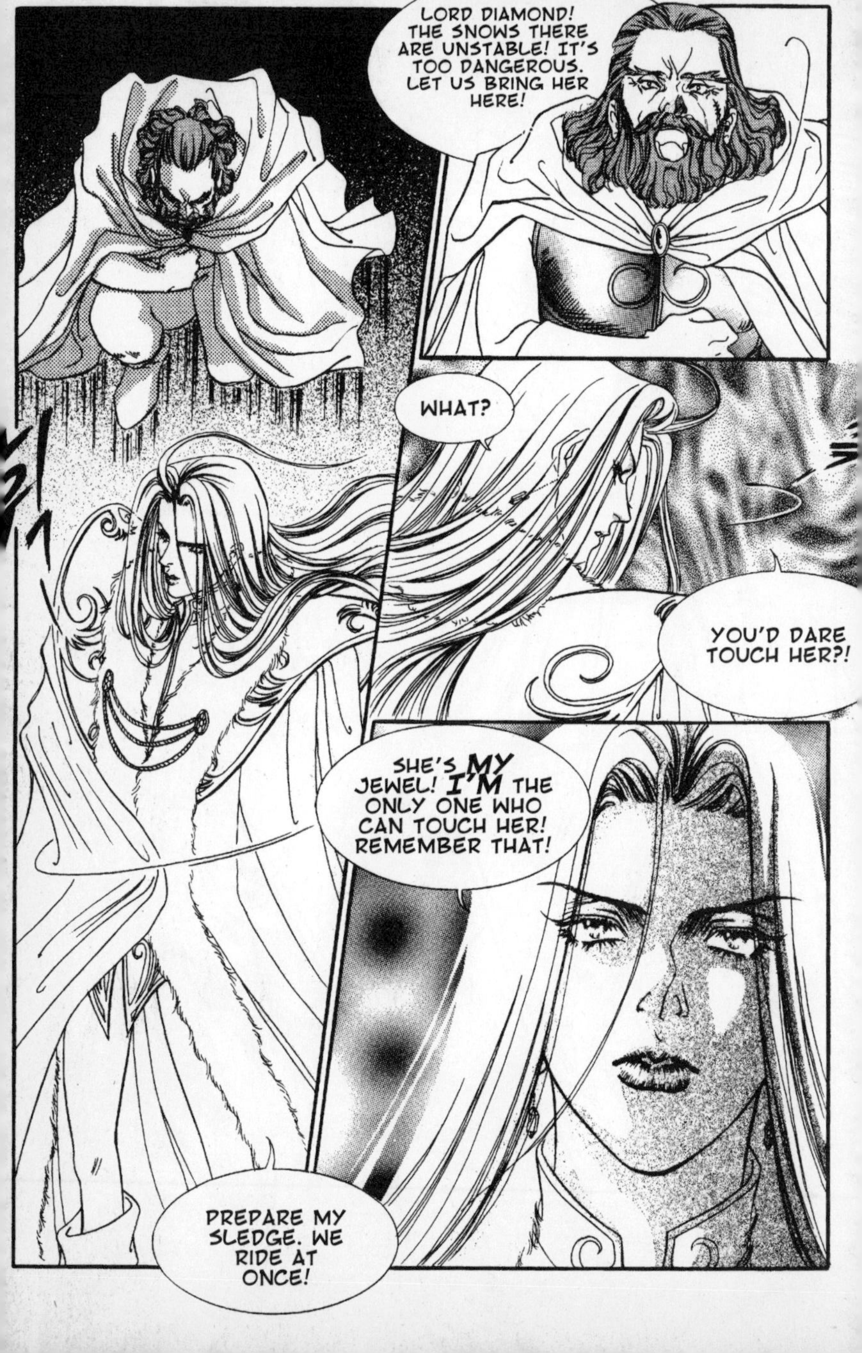
LORD DIAMOND! THE SNOWS THERE ARE UNSTABLE! IT'S TOO DANGEROUS. LET US BRING HER HERE!
WHAT?
YOU'D DARE TOUCH HER?!
SHE'S **MY** JEWEL! **I'M** THE ONLY ONE WHO CAN TOUCH HER! REMEMBER THAT!
PREPARE MY SLEDGE. WE RIDE AT ONCE!

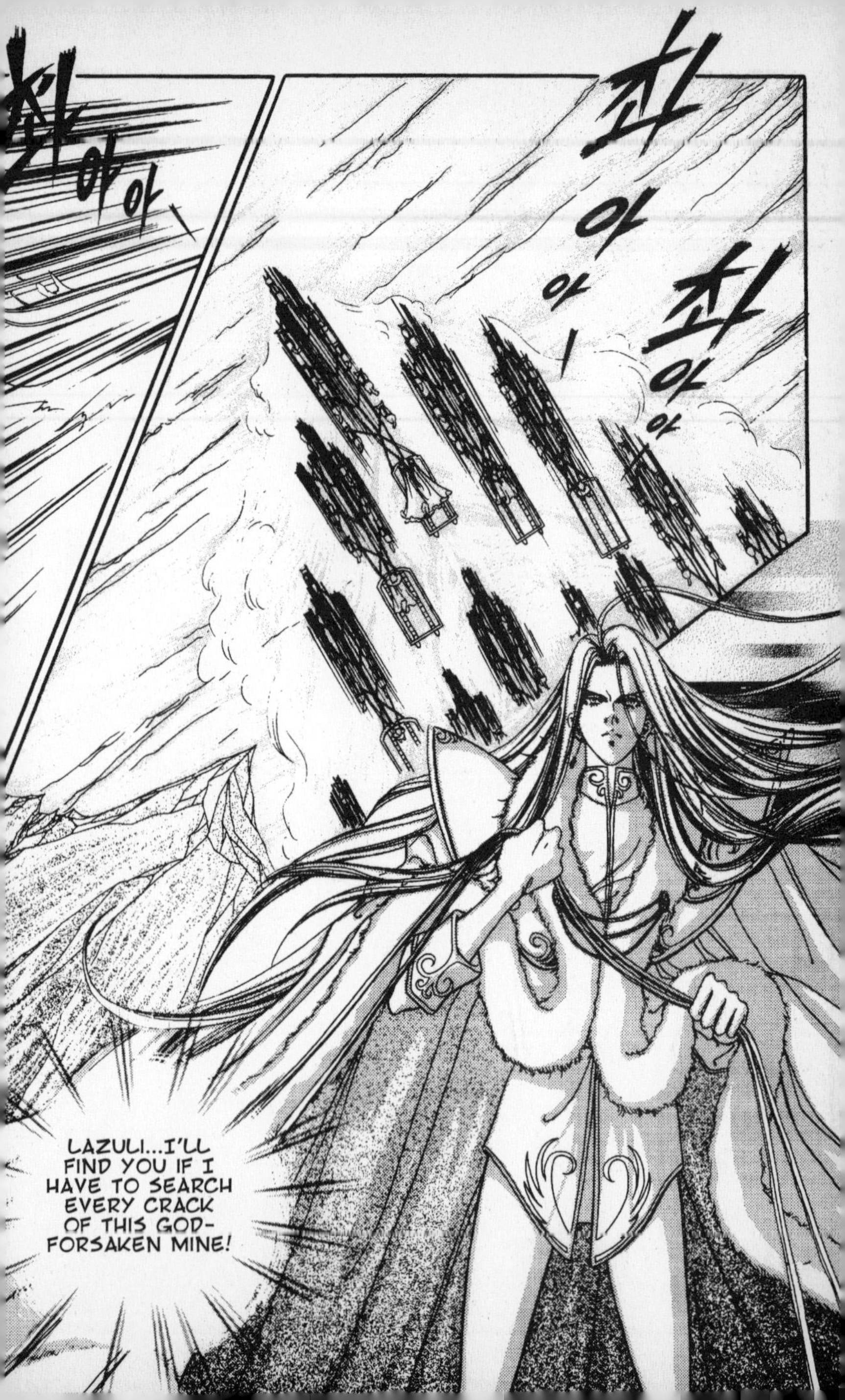
LAZULI...I'LL FIND YOU IF I HAVE TO SEARCH EVERY CRACK OF THIS GOD-FORSAKEN MINE!

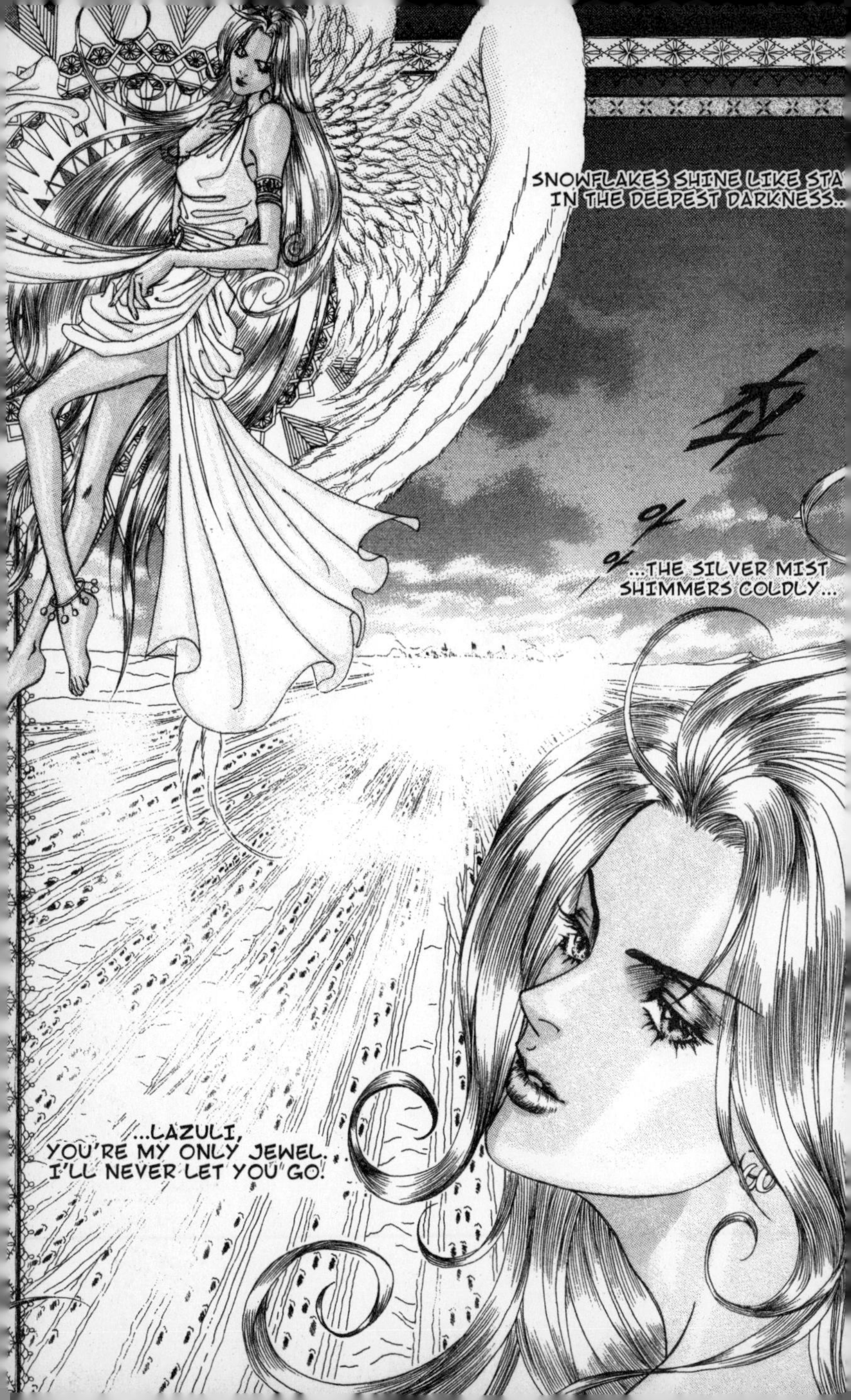
SNOWFLAKES SHINE LIKE STA
IN THE DEEPEST DARKNESS...
...THE SILVER MIST
SHIMMERS COLDLY...
...LAZULI,
YOU'RE MY ONLY JEWEL...
I'LL NEVER LET YOU GO.

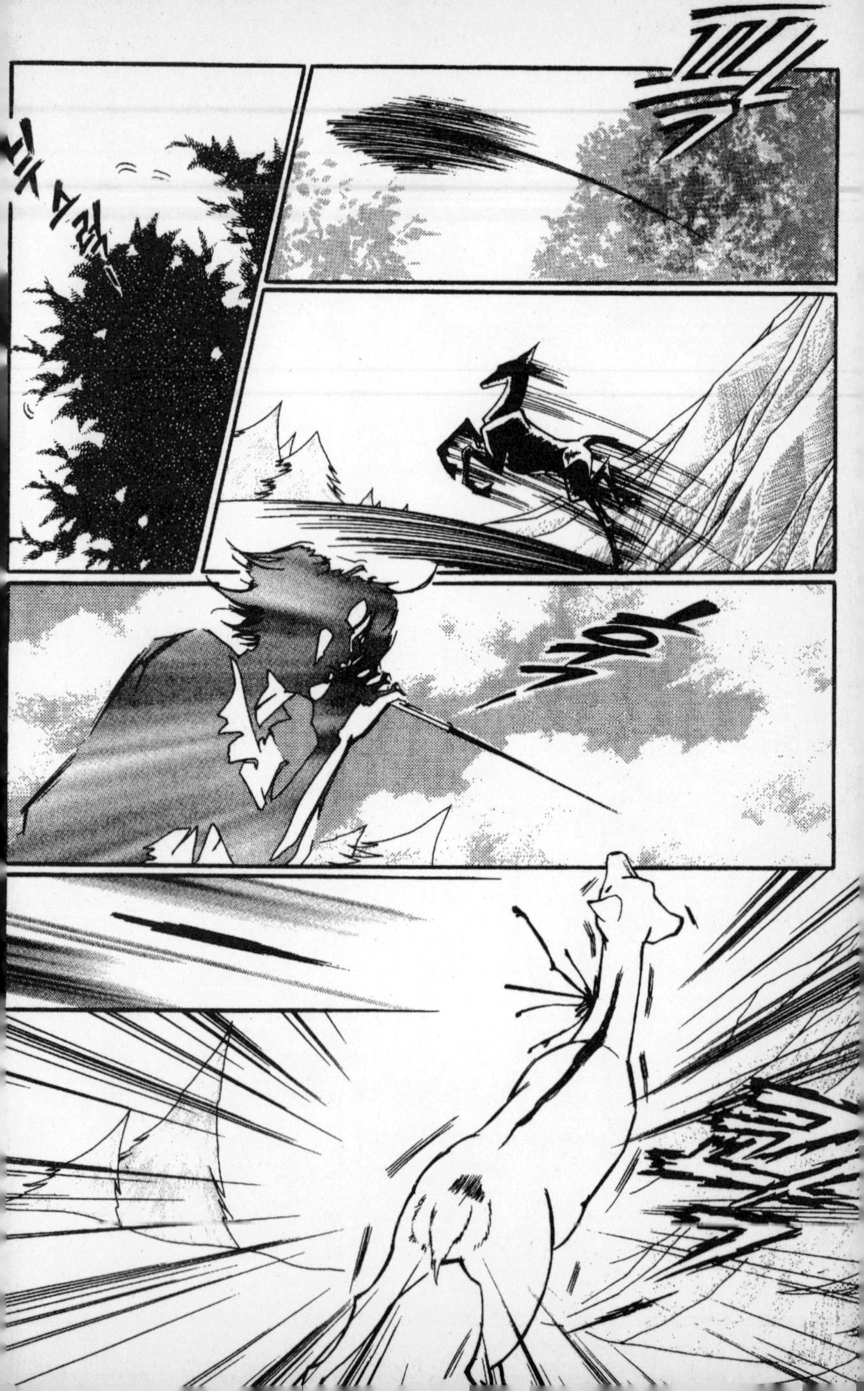
스럭

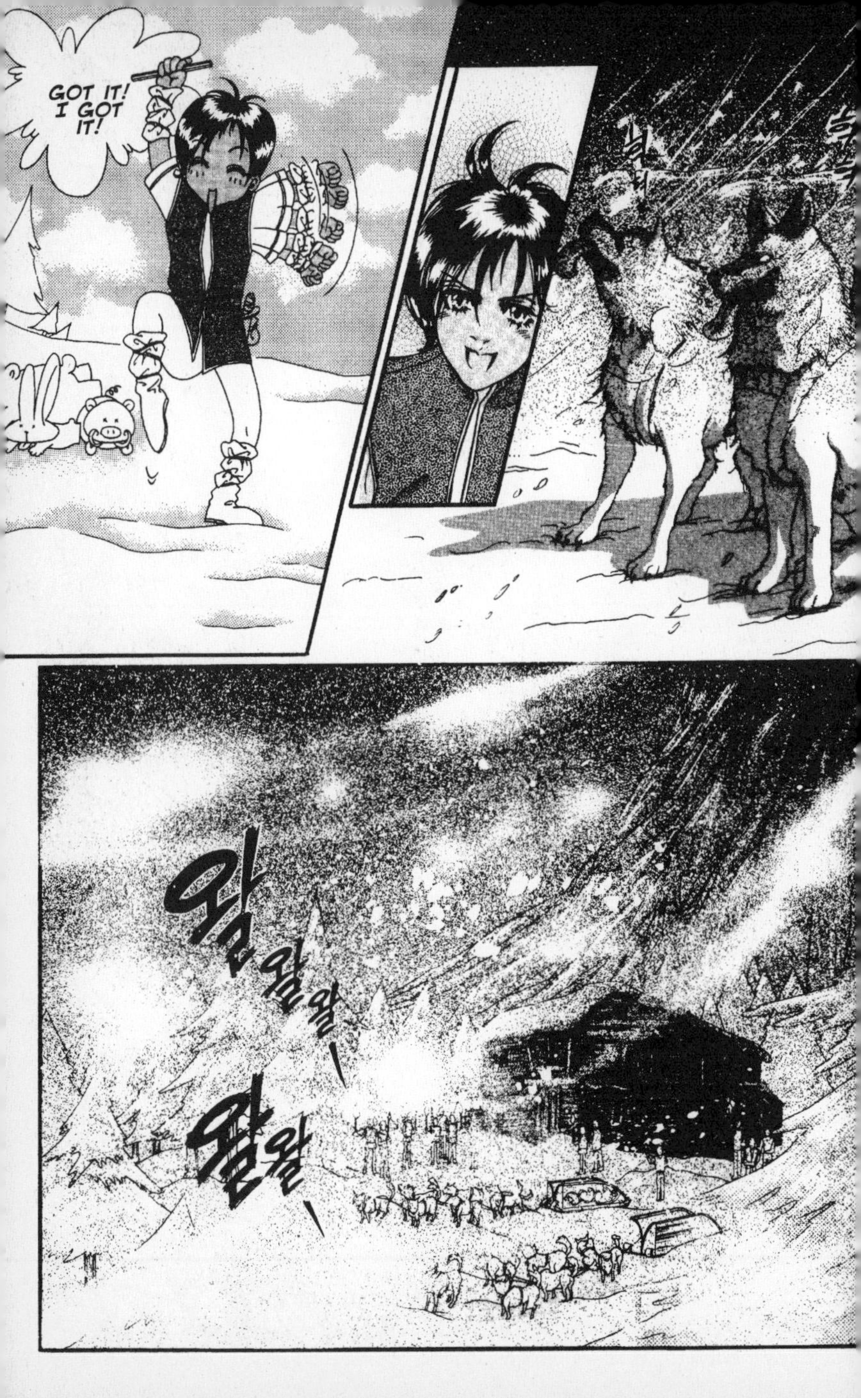
GOT IT! I GOT IT!
왈왈왈
왈왈

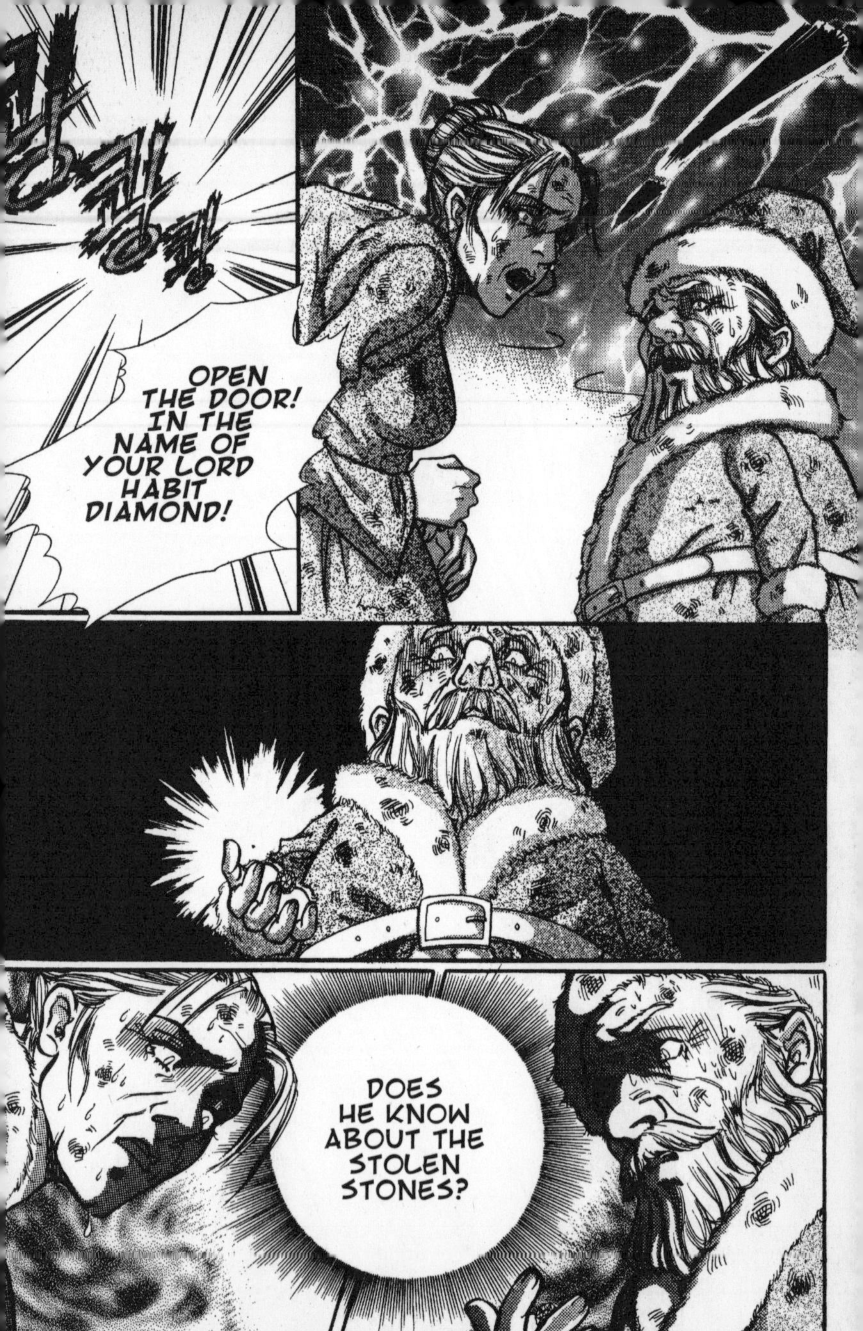
OPEN THE DOOR! IN THE NAME OF YOUR LORD HABIT DIAMOND!
DOES HE KNOW ABOUT THE STOLEN STONES?

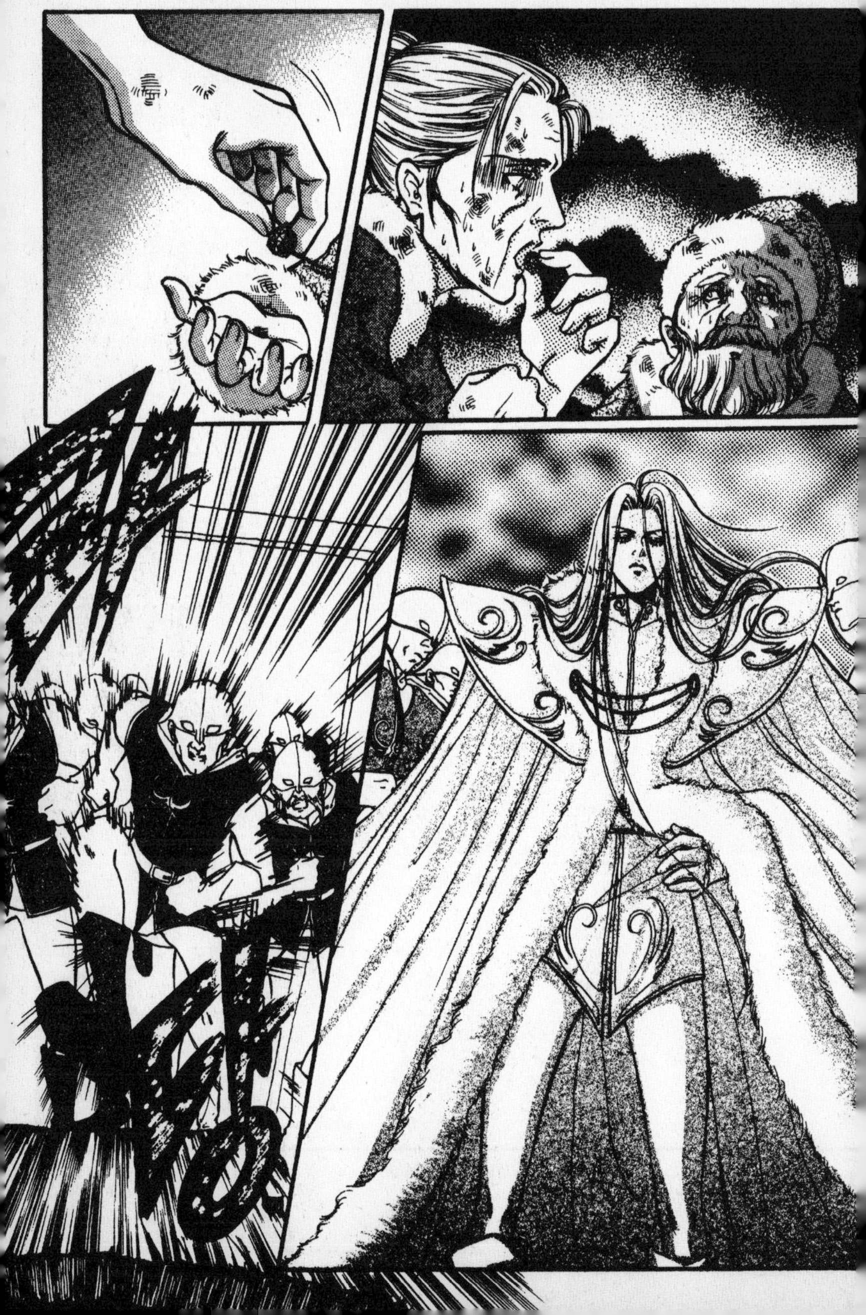

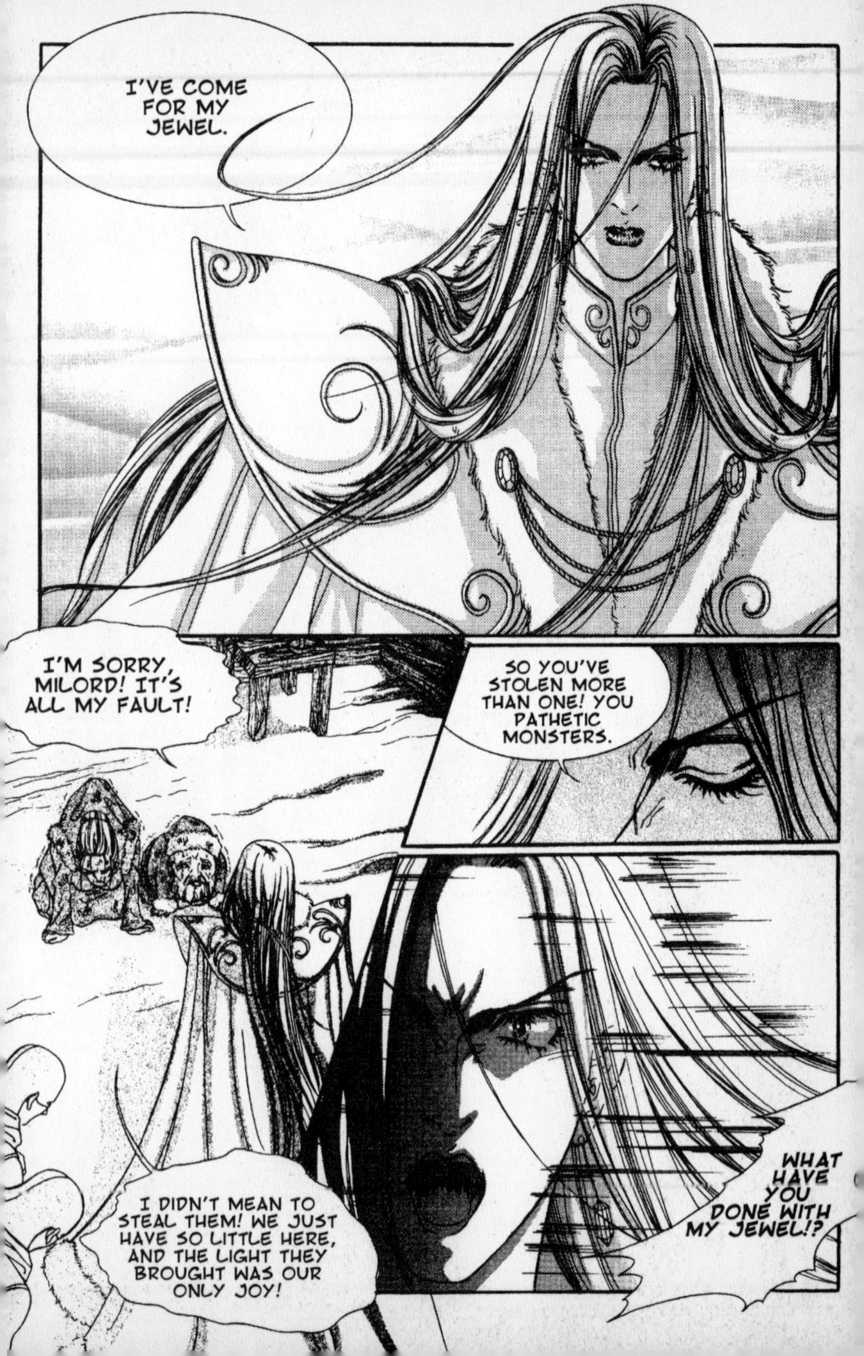
I'VE COME FOR MY JEWEL.
I'M SORRY, MILORD! IT'S ALL MY FAULT!
SO YOU'VE STOLEN MORE THAN ONE! YOU PATHETIC MONSTERS.
WHAT HAVE YOU DONE WITH MY JEWEL!?
I DIDN'T MEAN TO STEAL THEM! WE JUST HAVE SO LITTLE HERE, AND THE LIGHT THEY BROUGHT WAS OUR ONLY JOY!

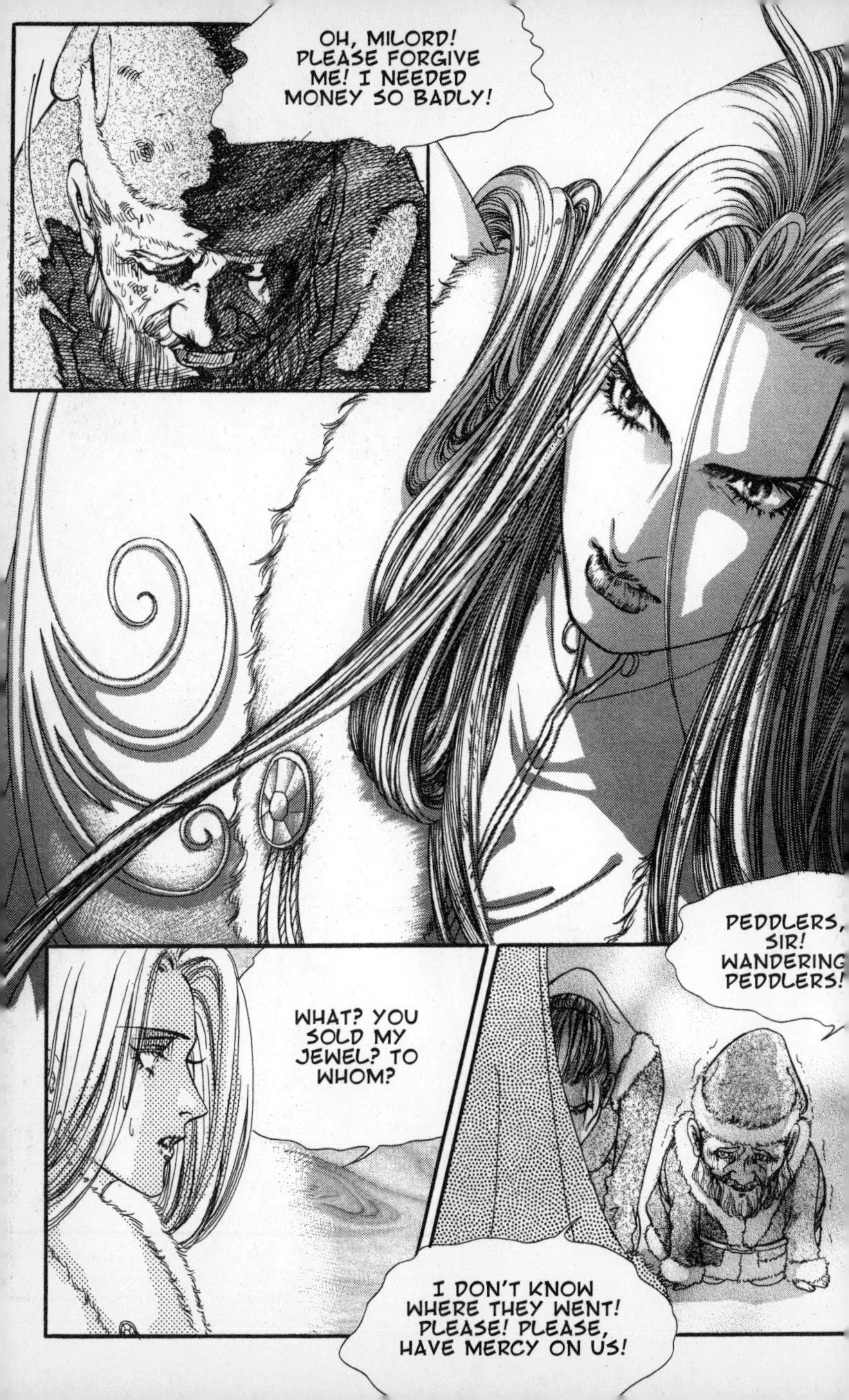
OH, MILORD! PLEASE FORGIVE ME! I NEEDED MONEY SO BADLY!
WHAT? YOU SOLD MY JEWEL? TO WHOM?
PEDDLERS, SIR! WANDERING PEDDLERS!
I DON'T KNOW WHERE THEY WENT! PLEASE! PLEASE, HAVE MERCY ON US!

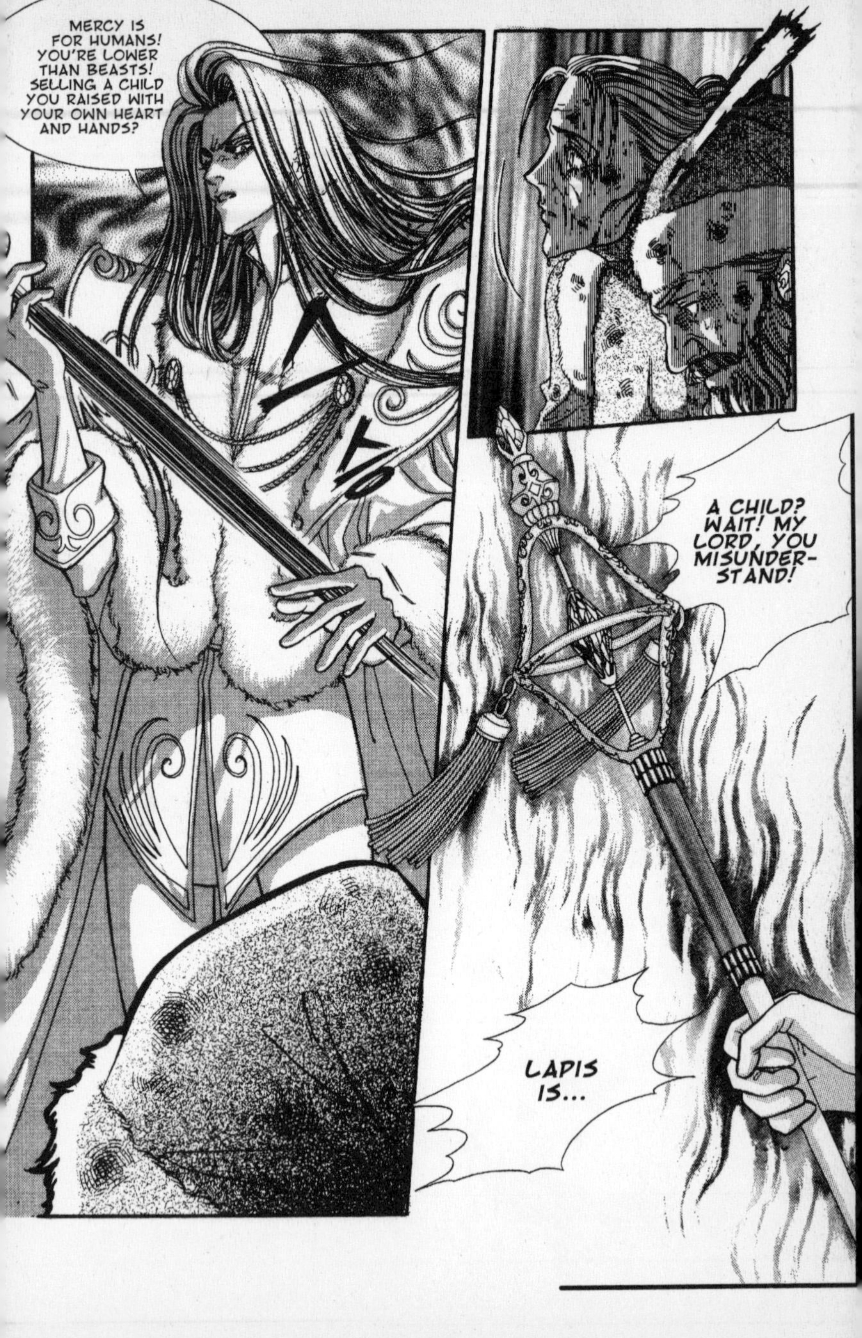
MERCY IS FOR HUMANS! YOU'RE LOWER THAN BEASTS! SELLING A CHILD YOU RAISED WITH YOUR OWN HEART AND HANDS?
A CHILD? WAIT! MY LORD, YOU MISUNDER-STAND!
LAPIS IS...

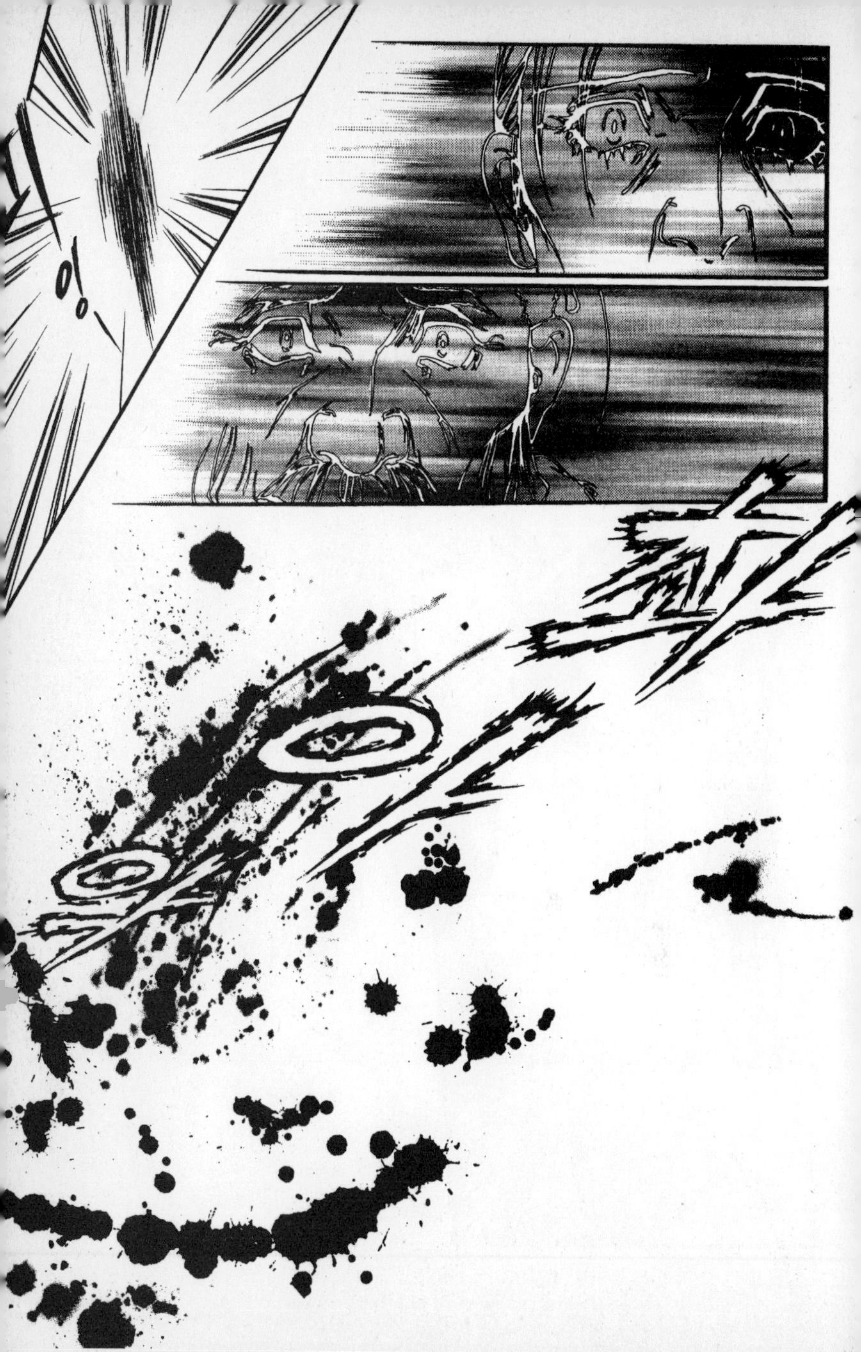

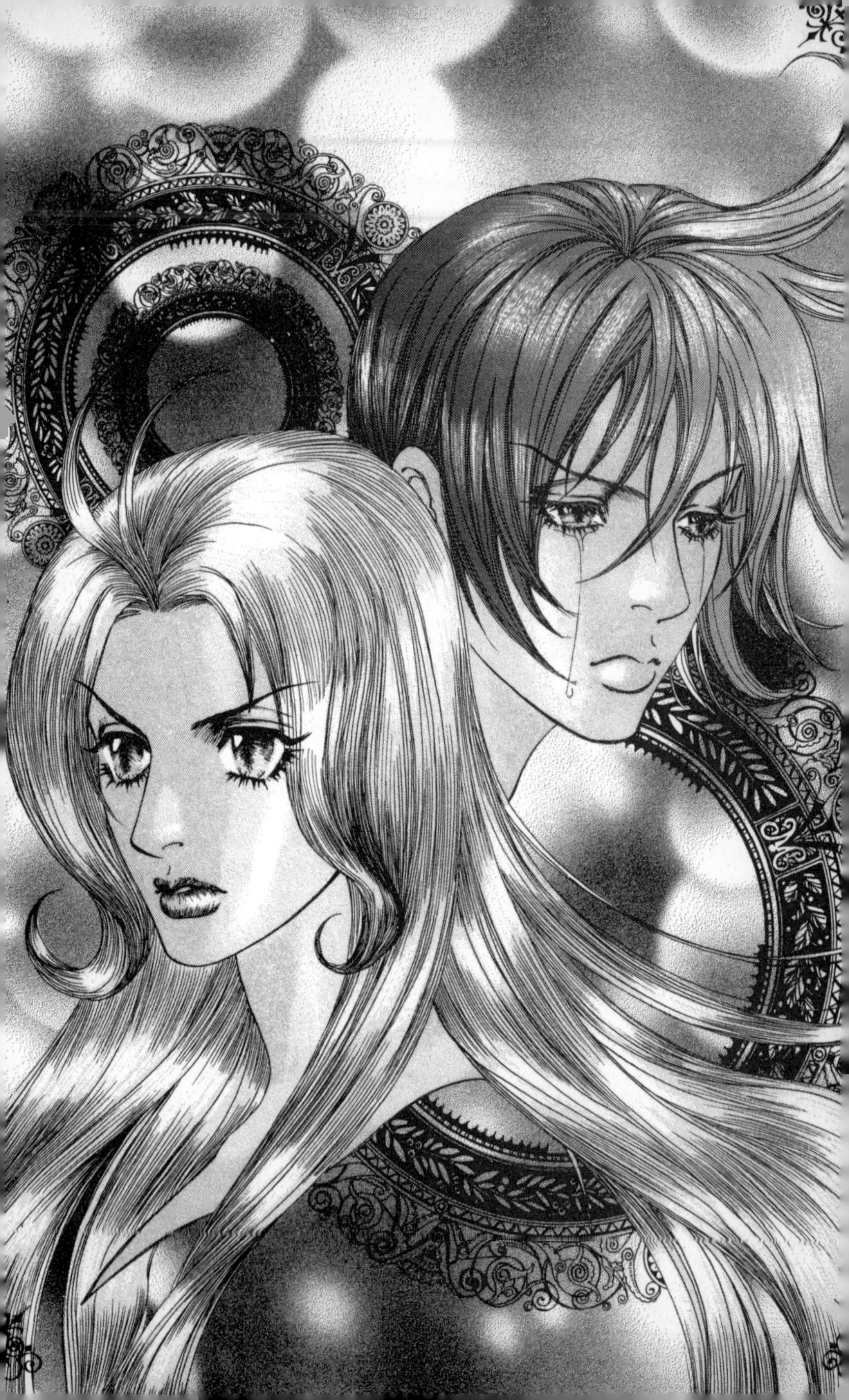

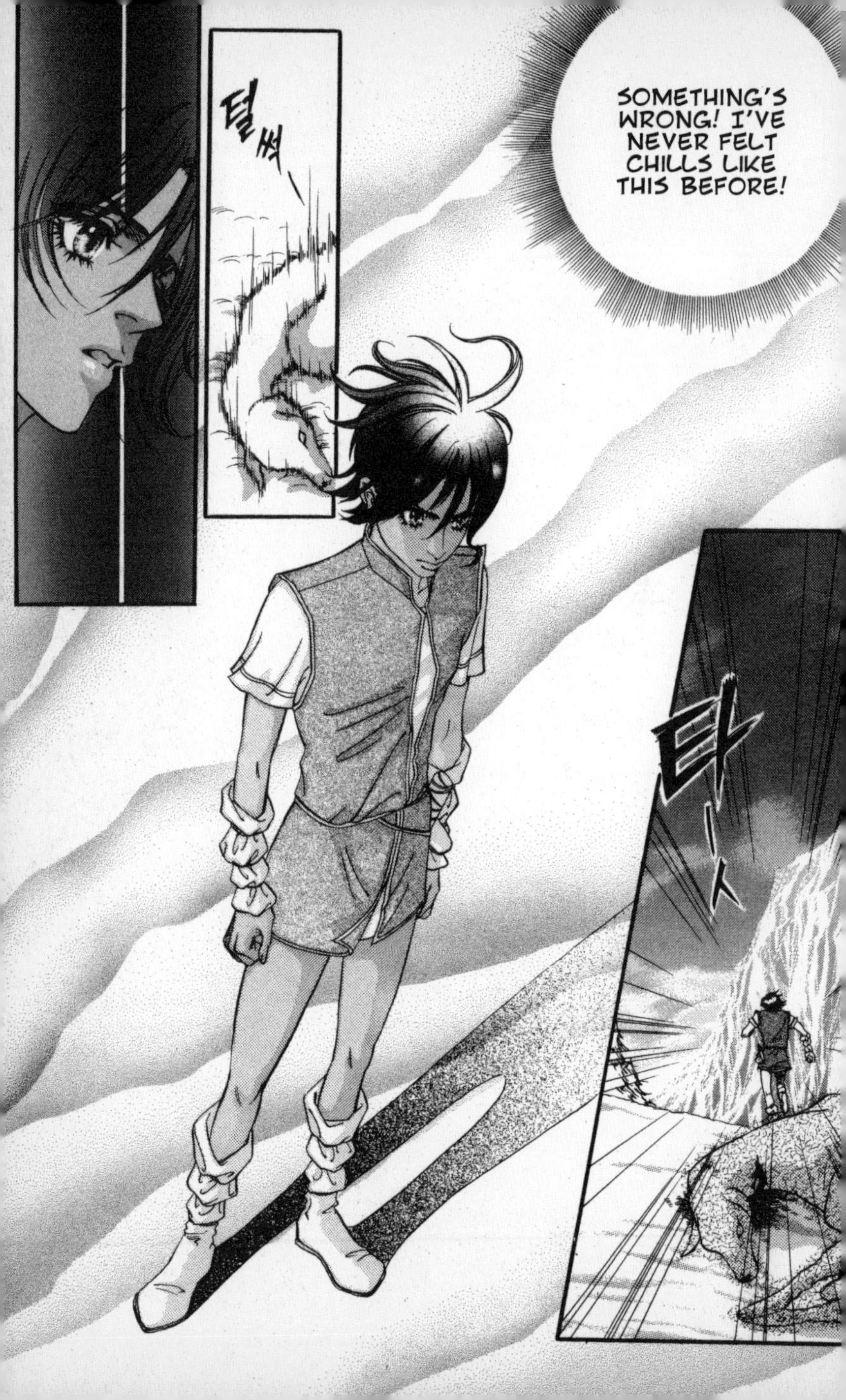
털썩
SOMETHING'S WRONG! I'VE NEVER FELT CHILLS LIKE THIS BEFORE!
탁

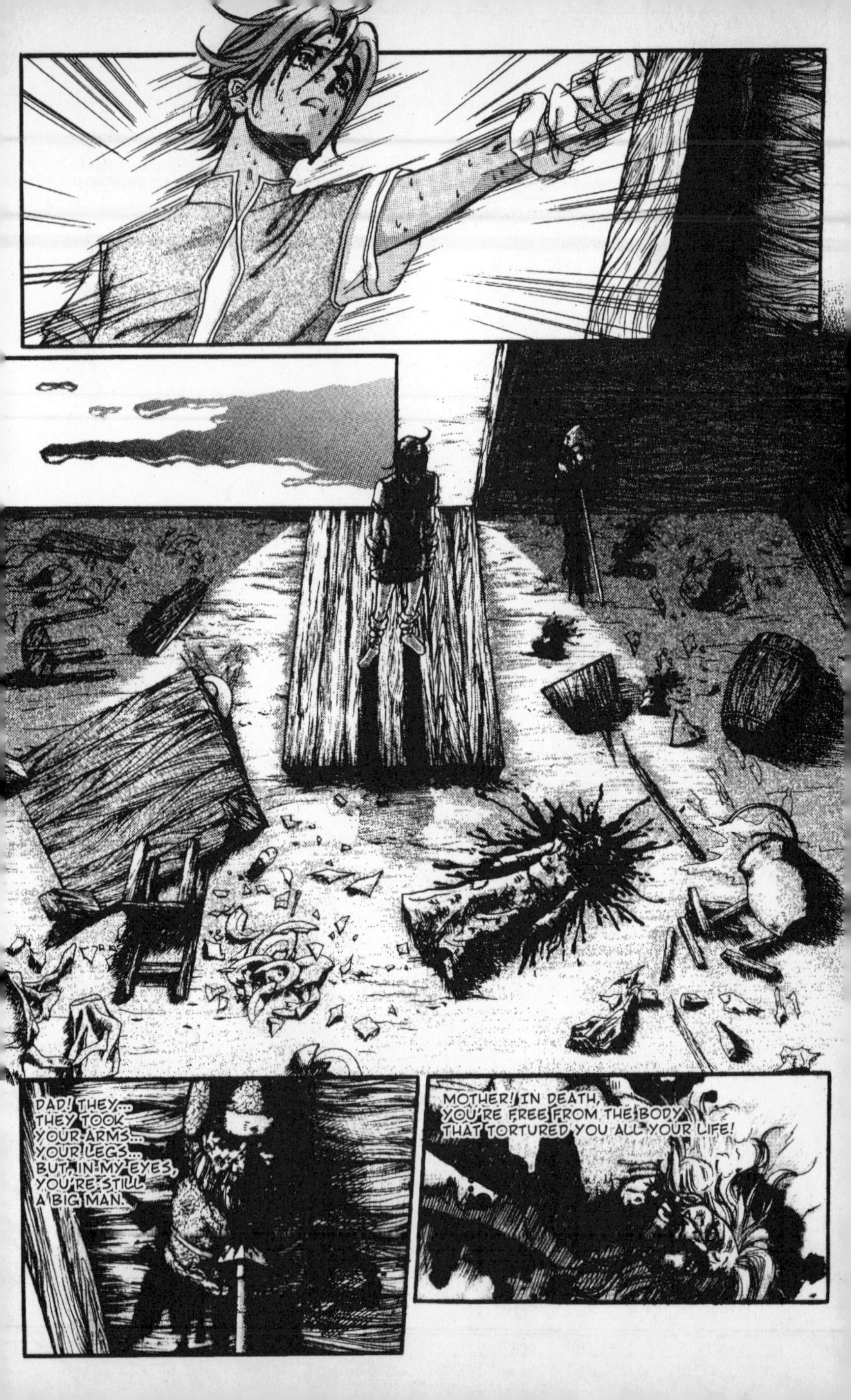
DAD! THEY... THEY TOOK YOUR ARMS... YOUR LEGS... BUT, IN MY EYES, YOU'RE STILL A BIG MAN.
MOTHER! IN DEATH, YOU'RE FREE FROM THE BODY THAT TORTURED YOU ALL YOUR LIFE!

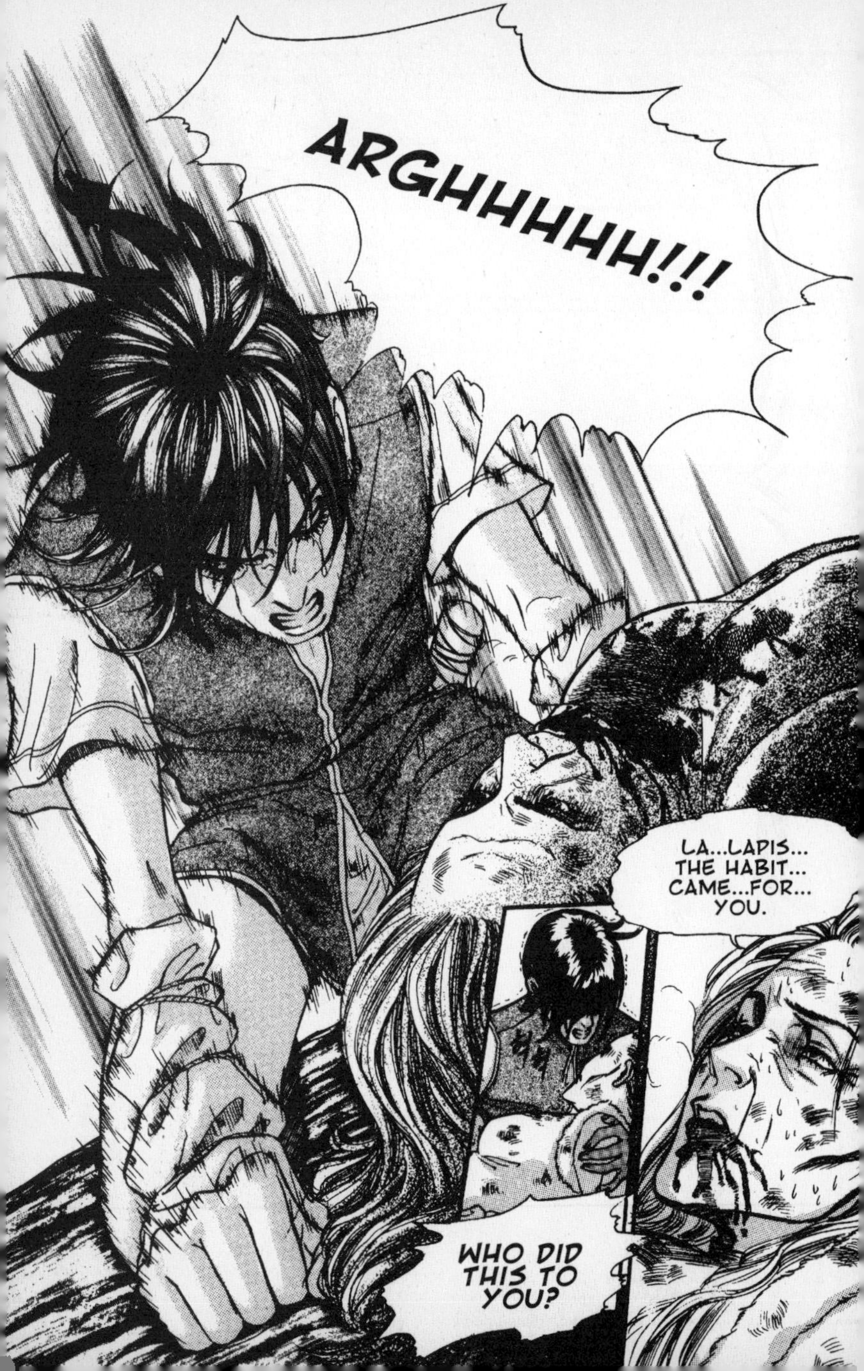
ARGHHHHH!!!
LA...LAPIS... THE HABIT... CAME...FOR... YOU.
WHO DID THIS TO YOU?

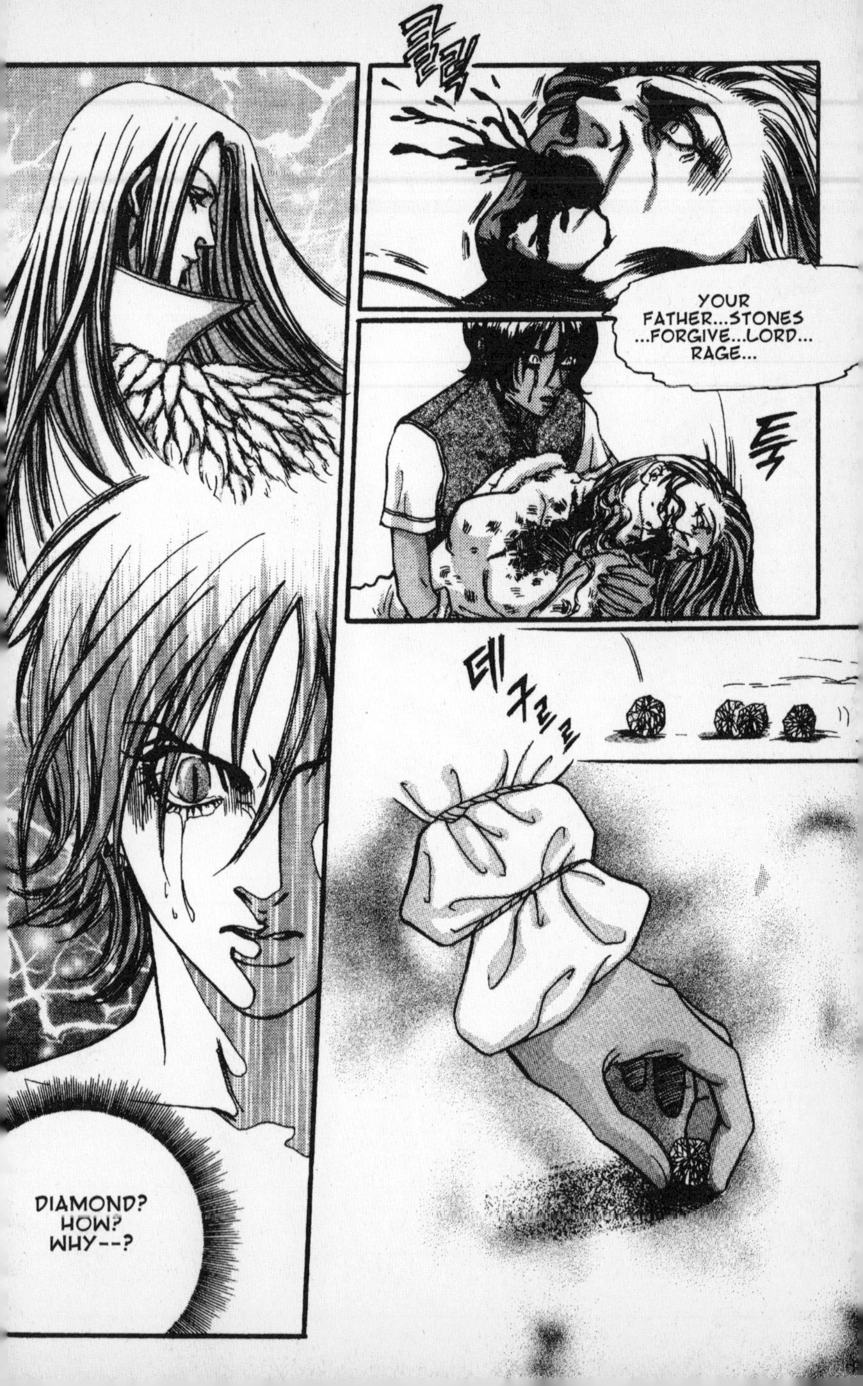
YOUR FATHER...STONES ...FORGIVE...LORD... RAGE...
DIAMOND? HOW? WHY--?

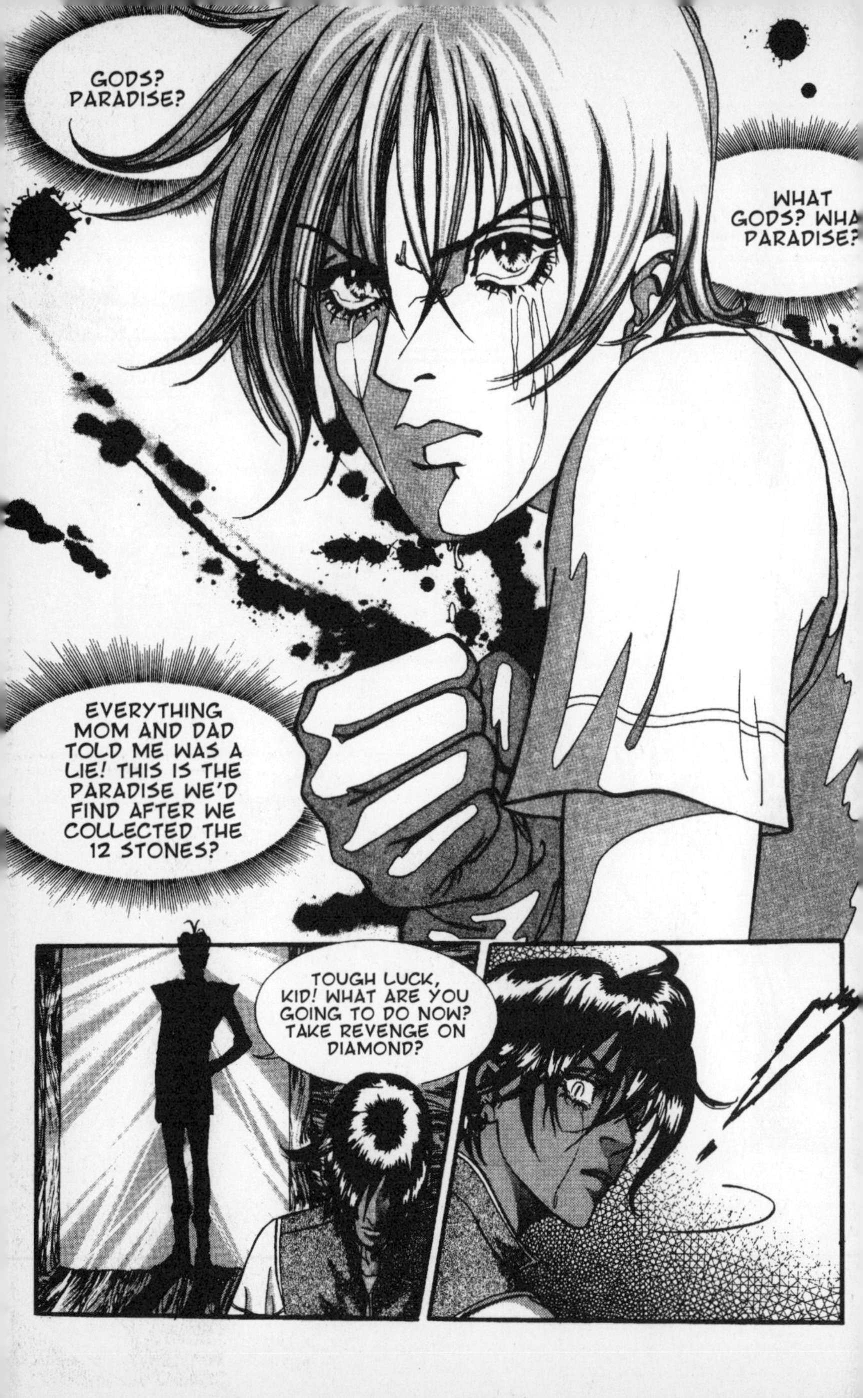
GODS? PARADISE?
WHAT GODS? WHA PARADISE?
EVERYTHING MOM AND DAD TOLD ME WAS A LIE! THIS IS THE PARADISE WE'D FIND AFTER WE COLLECTED THE 12 STONES?
TOUGH LUCK, KID! WHAT ARE YOU GOING TO DO NOW? TAKE REVENGE ON DIAMOND?

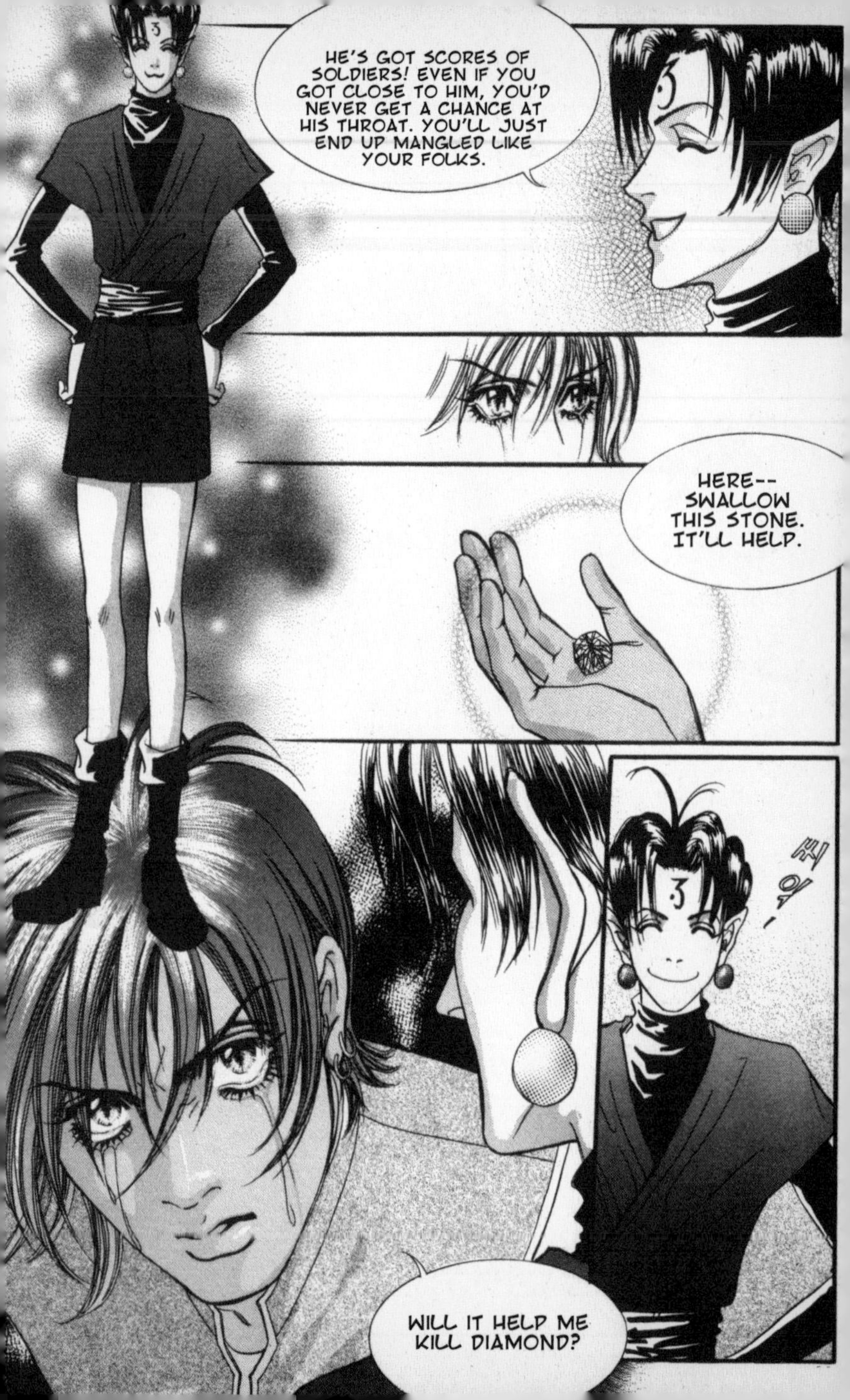
HE'S GOT SCORES OF SOLDIERS! EVEN IF YOU GOT CLOSE TO HIM, YOU'D NEVER GET A CHANCE AT HIS THROAT. YOU'LL JUST END UP MANGLED LIKE YOUR FOLKS.
HERE-- SWALLOW THIS STONE. IT'LL HELP.
WILL IT HELP ME KILL DIAMOND?

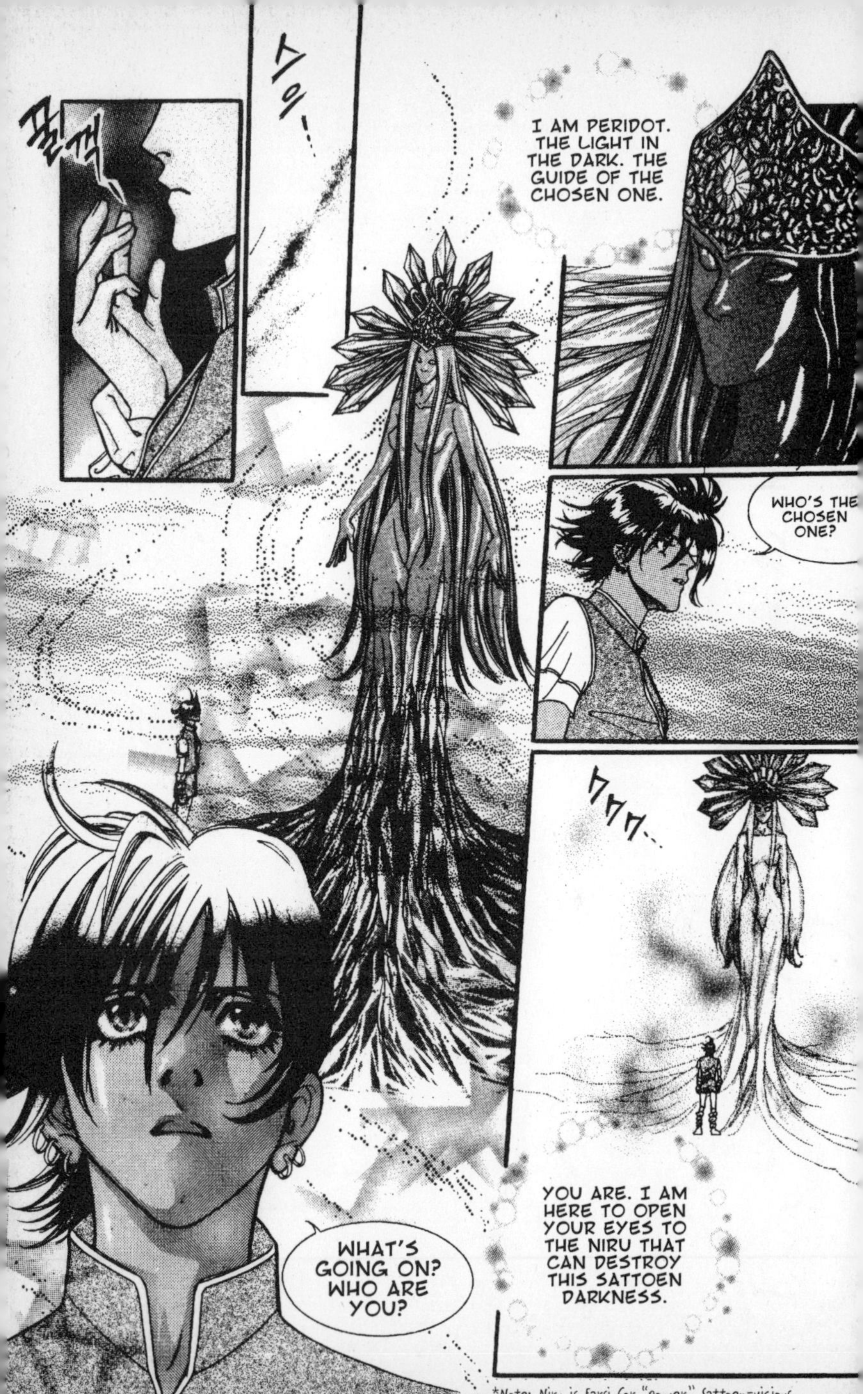
꿀꺽
스으...
WHAT'S GOING ON? WHO ARE YOU?
I AM PERIDOT. THE LIGHT IN THE DARK. THE GUIDE OF THE CHOSEN ONE.
WHO'S THE CHOSEN ONE?
YOU ARE. I AM HERE TO OPEN YOUR EYES TO THE NIRU THAT CAN DESTROY THIS SATTOEN DARKNESS.

*Note: Niru is Farsi for "power." Sattoen=vicious

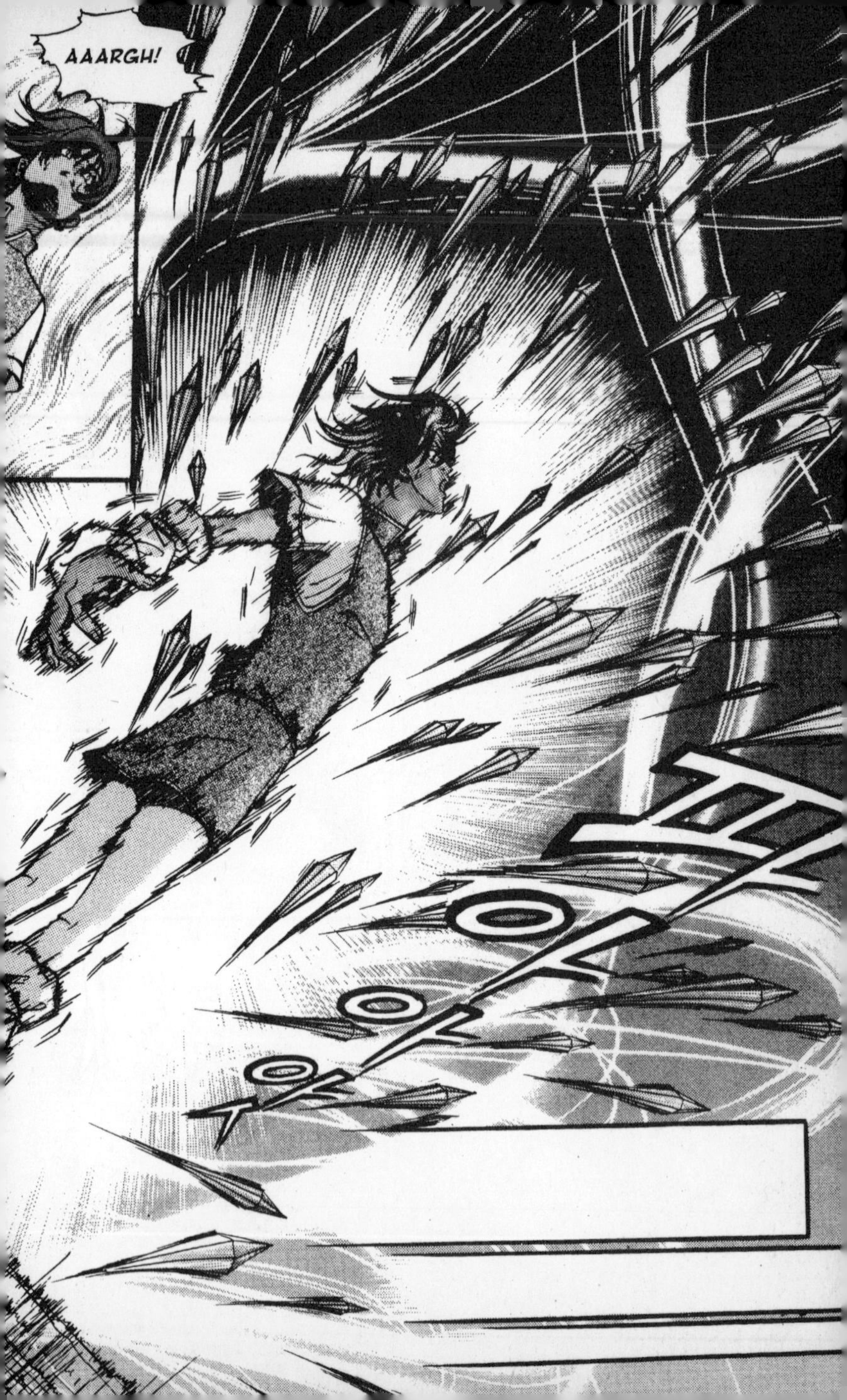
AAARGH!

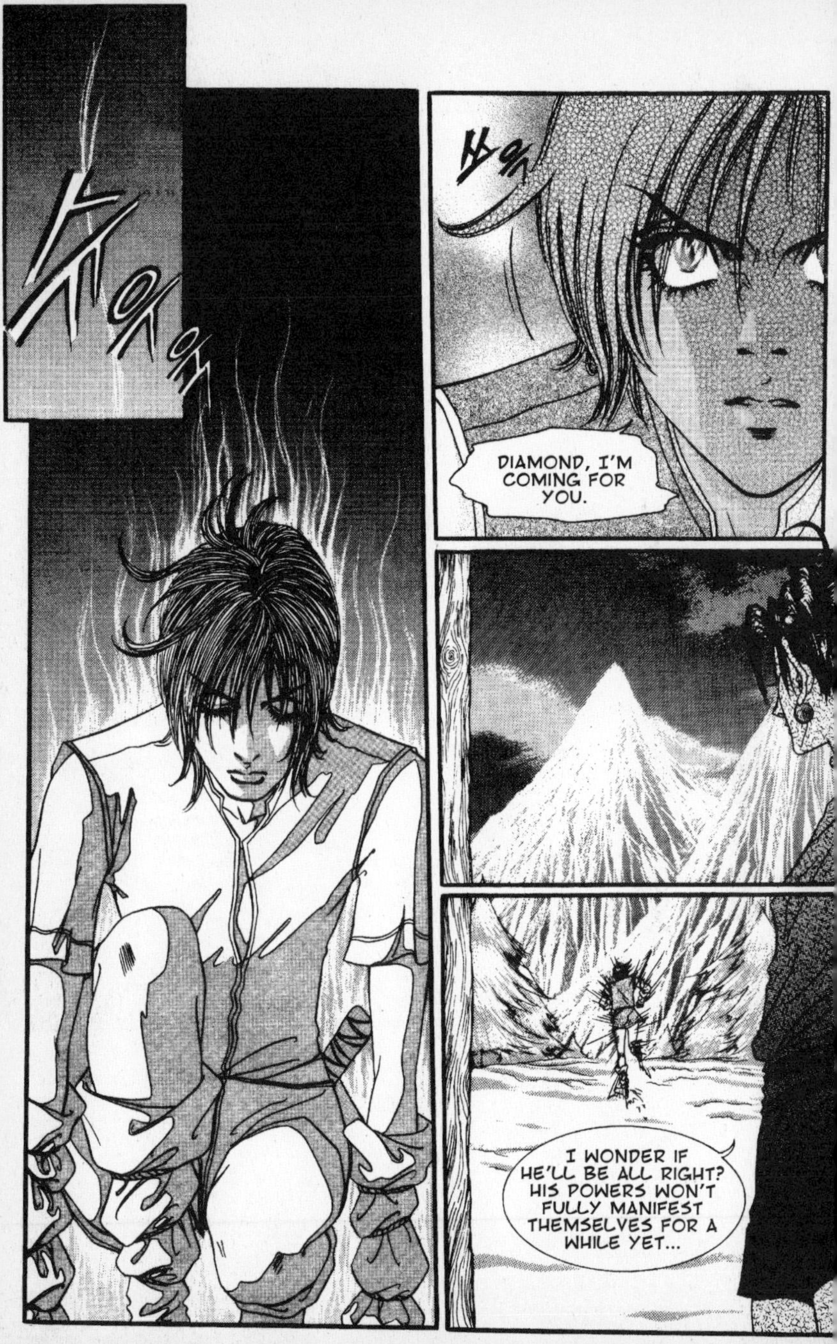
DIAMOND, I'M COMING FOR YOU.
I WONDER IF HE'LL BE ALL RIGHT? HIS POWERS WON'T FULLY MANIFEST THEMSELVES FOR A WHILE YET...

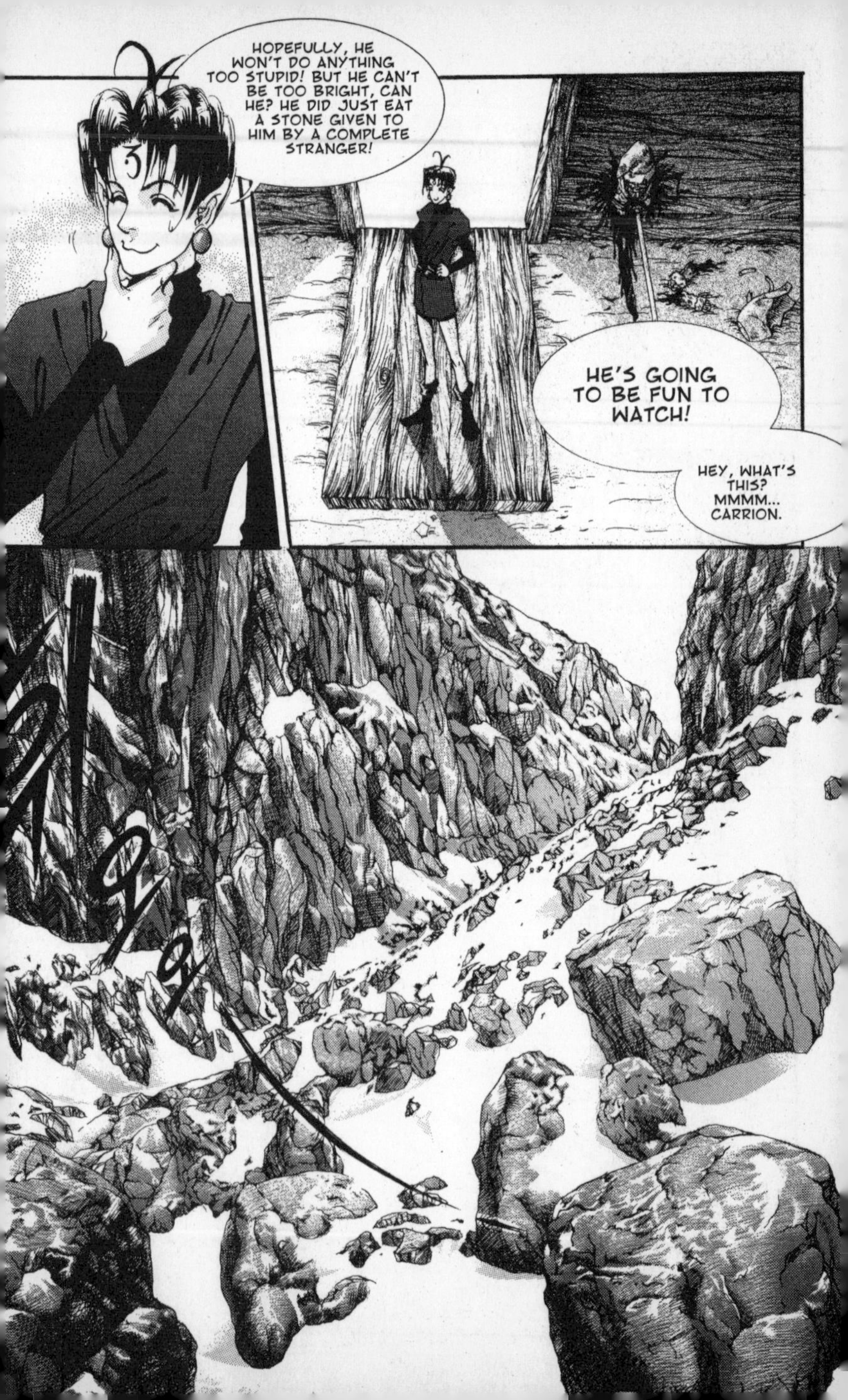
HOPEFULLY, HE WON'T DO ANYTHING TOO STUPID! BUT HE CAN'T BE TOO BRIGHT, CAN HE? HE DID JUST EAT A STONE GIVEN TO HIM BY A COMPLETE STRANGER!
HE'S GOING TO BE FUN TO WATCH!
HEY, WHAT'S THIS? MMMM... CARRION.

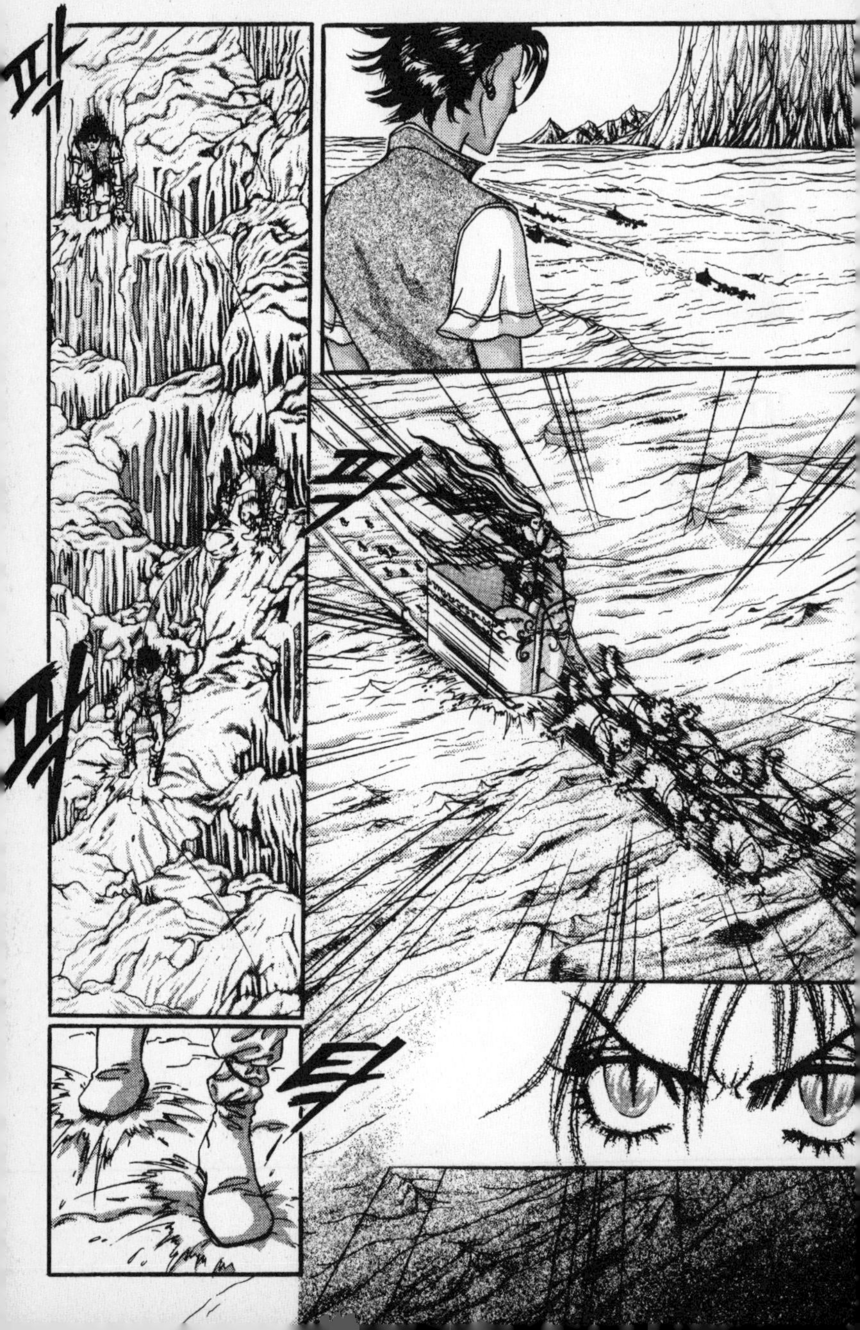
팍
팍
팍
탁

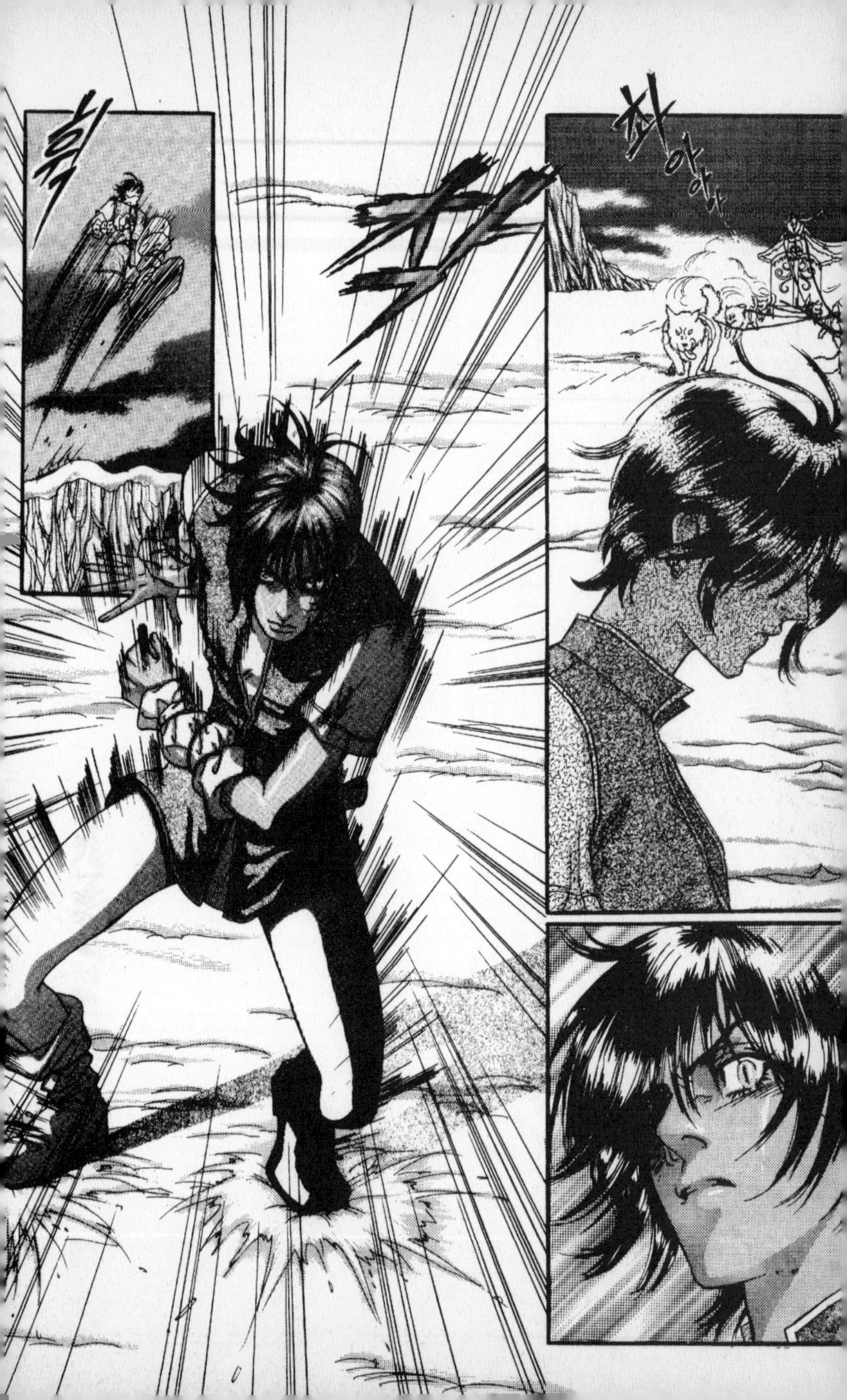
촤아아
휙

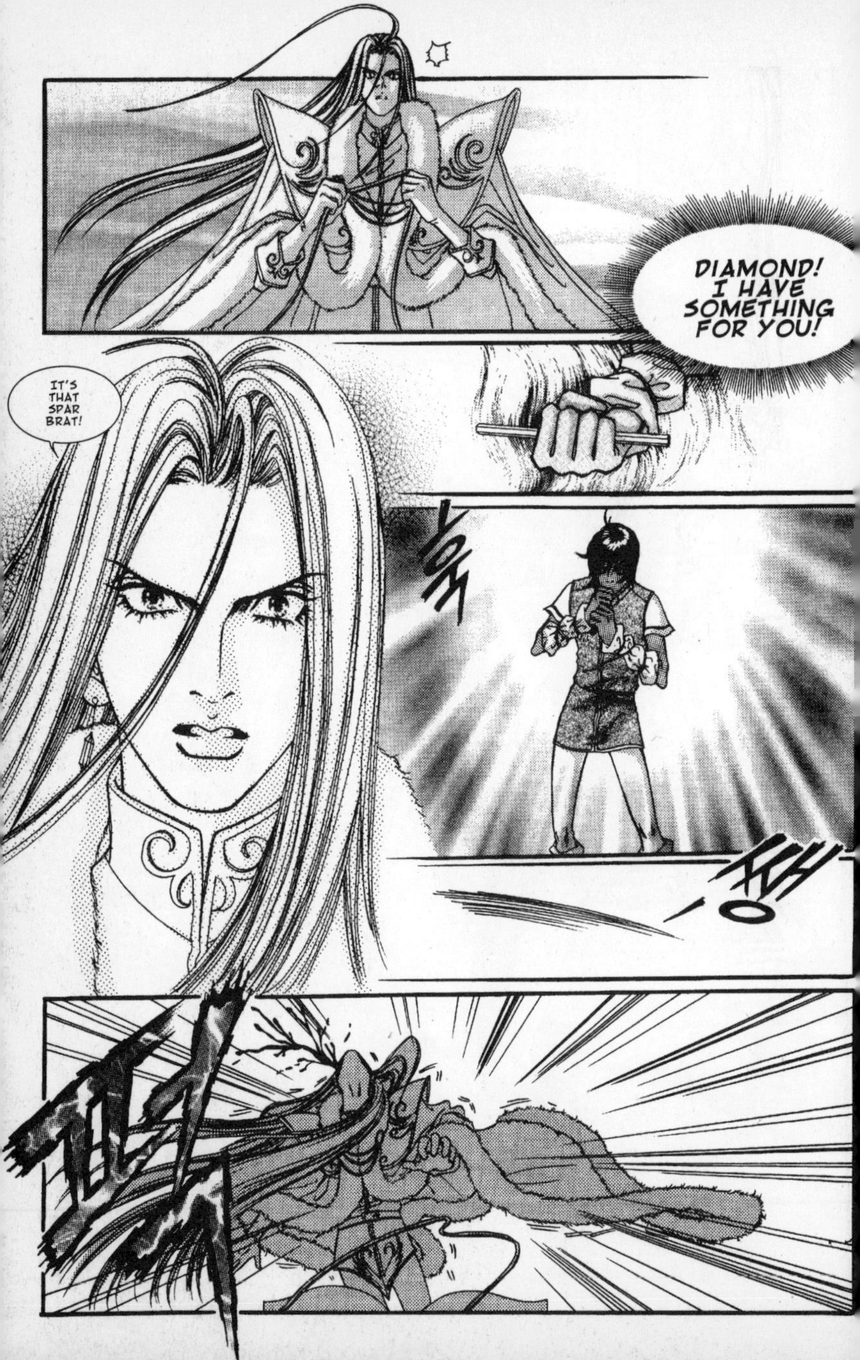
DIAMOND! I HAVE SOMETHING FOR YOU!
IT'S THAT SPAR BRAT!

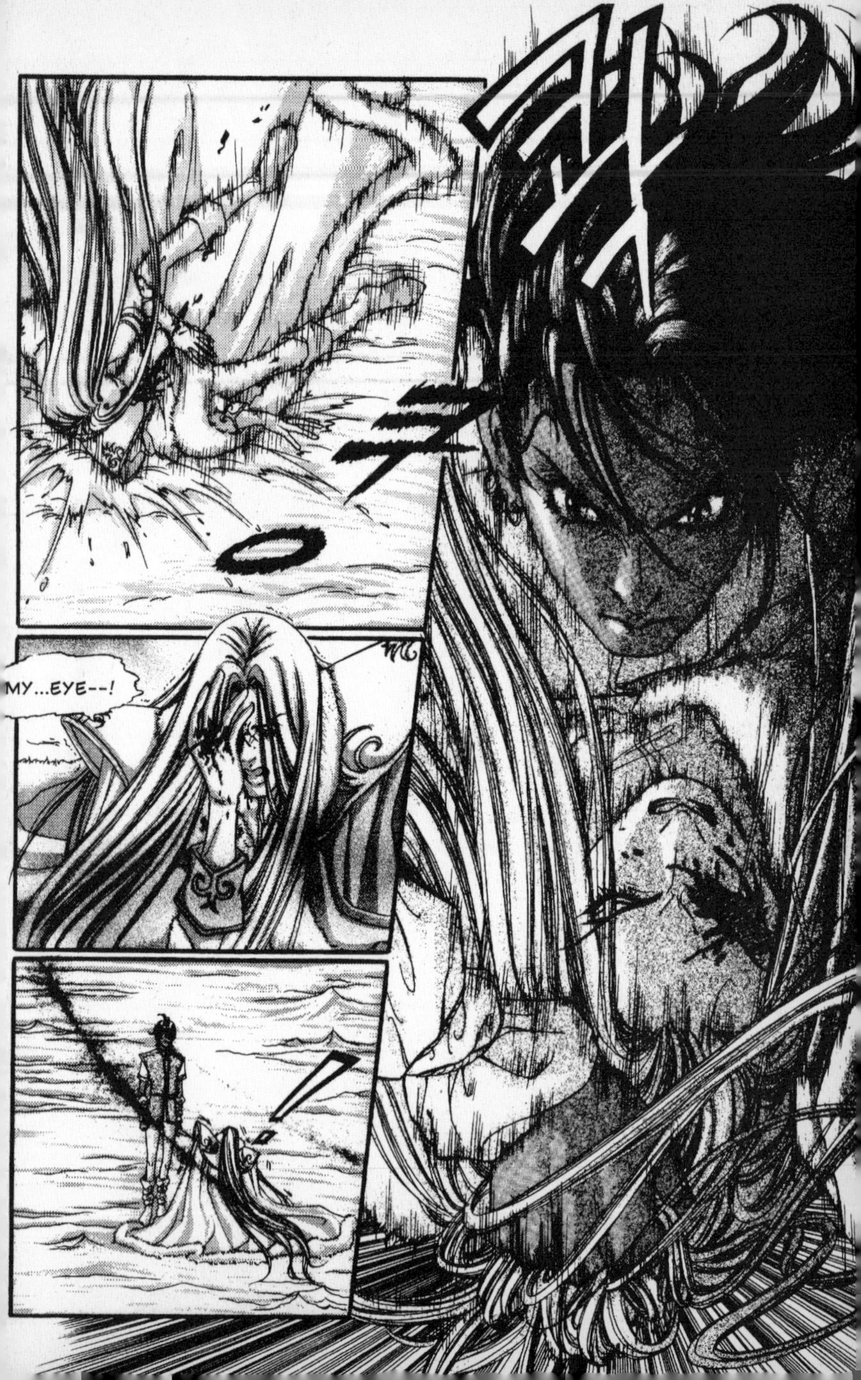
MY...EYE--!

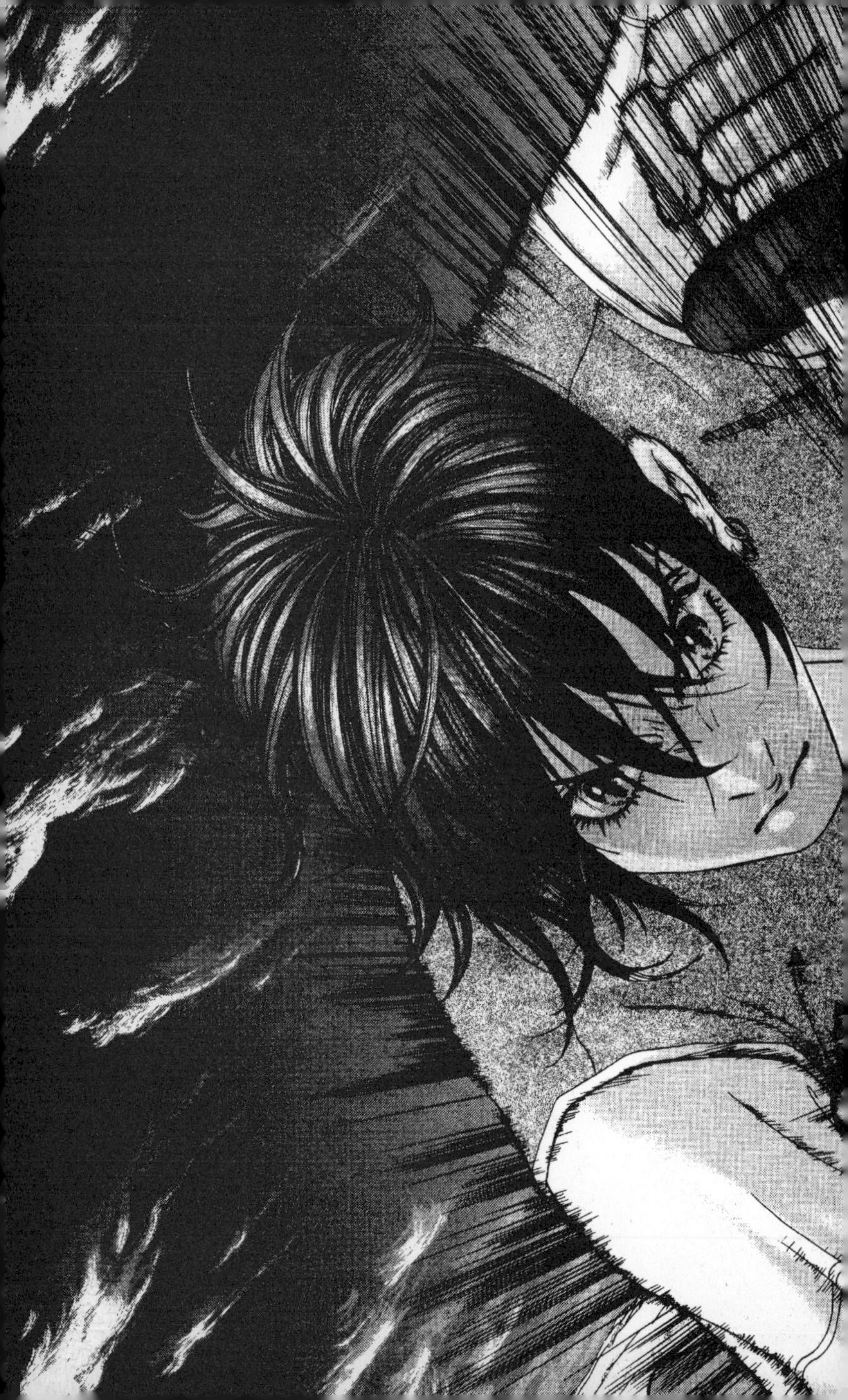

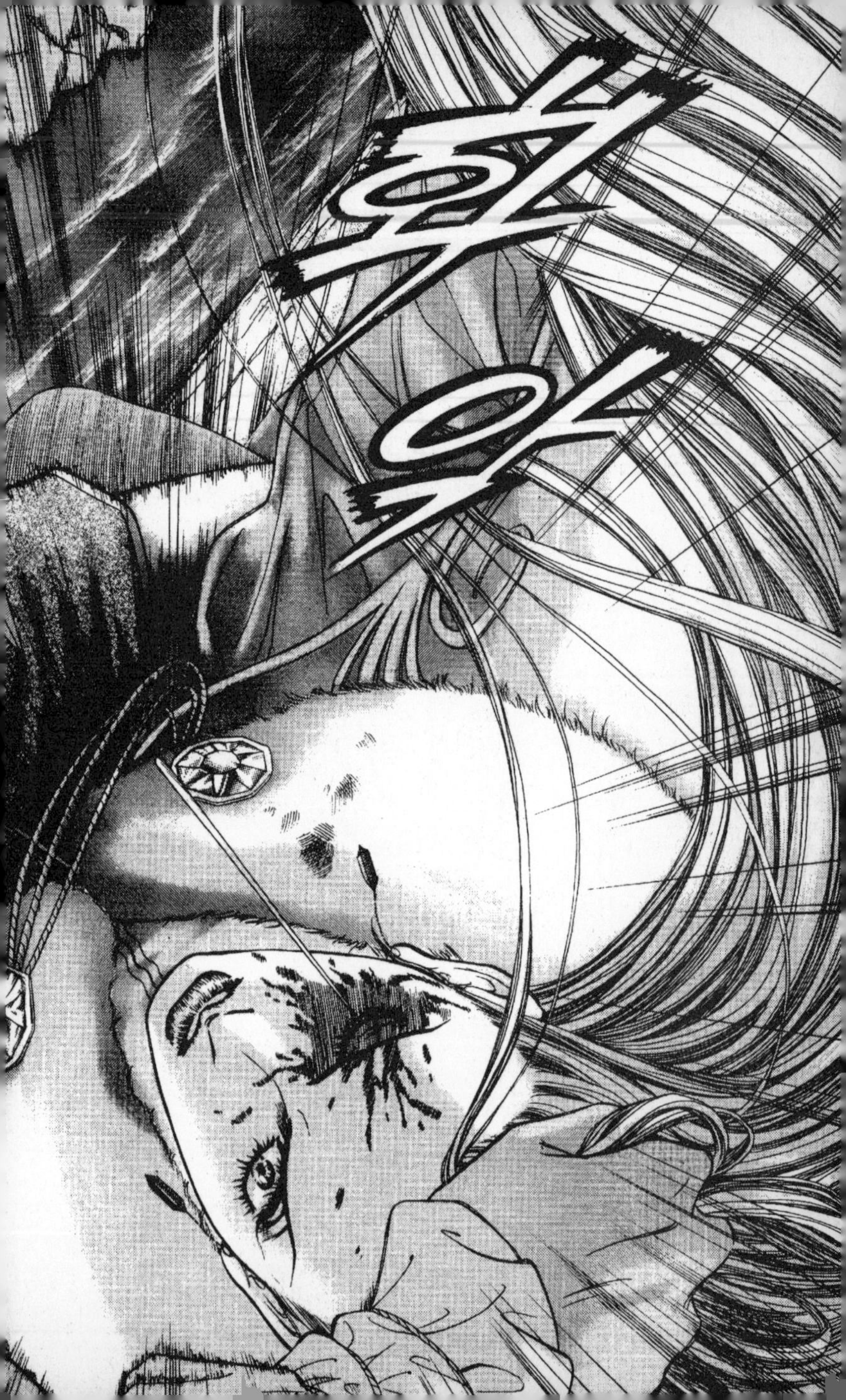

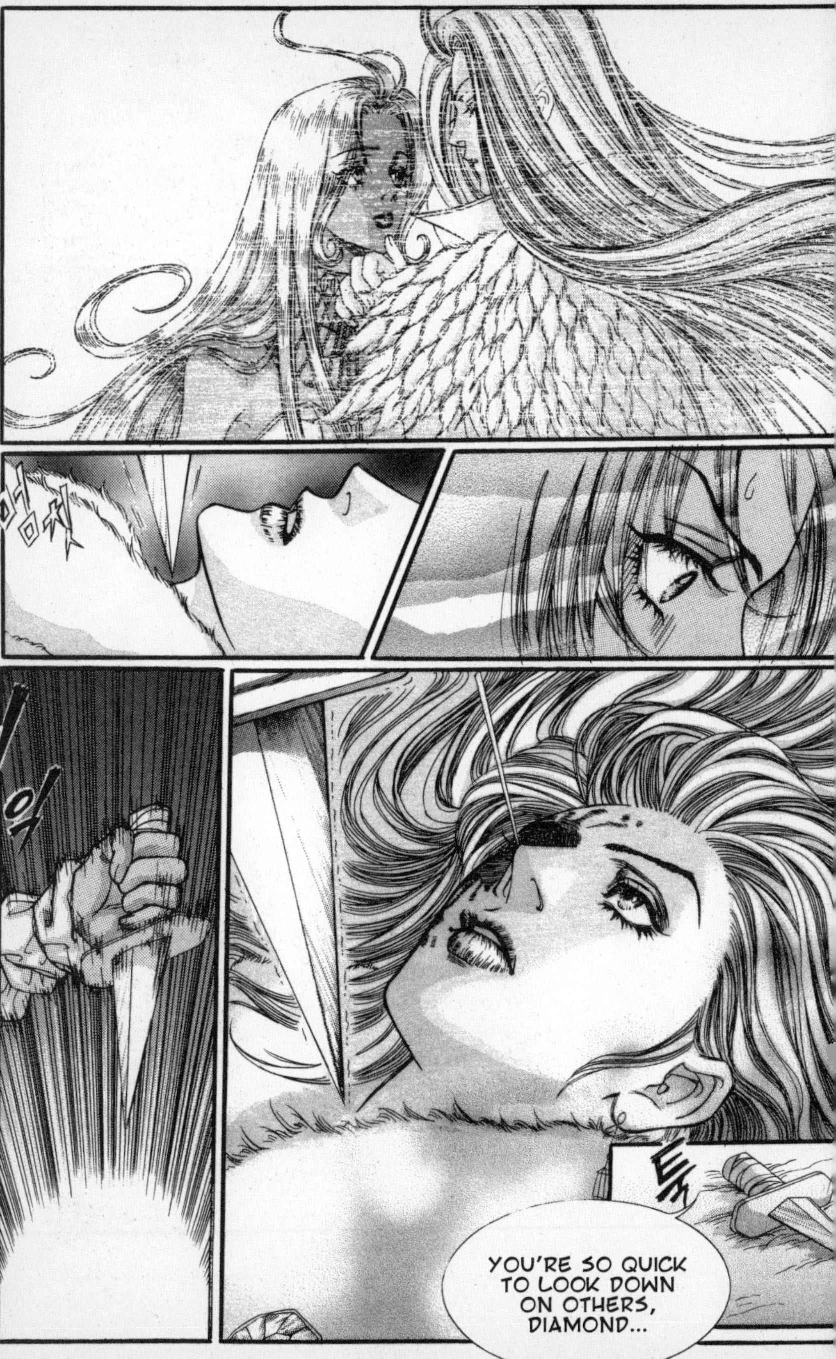
YOU'RE SO QUICK TO LOOK DOWN ON OTHERS, DIAMOND...

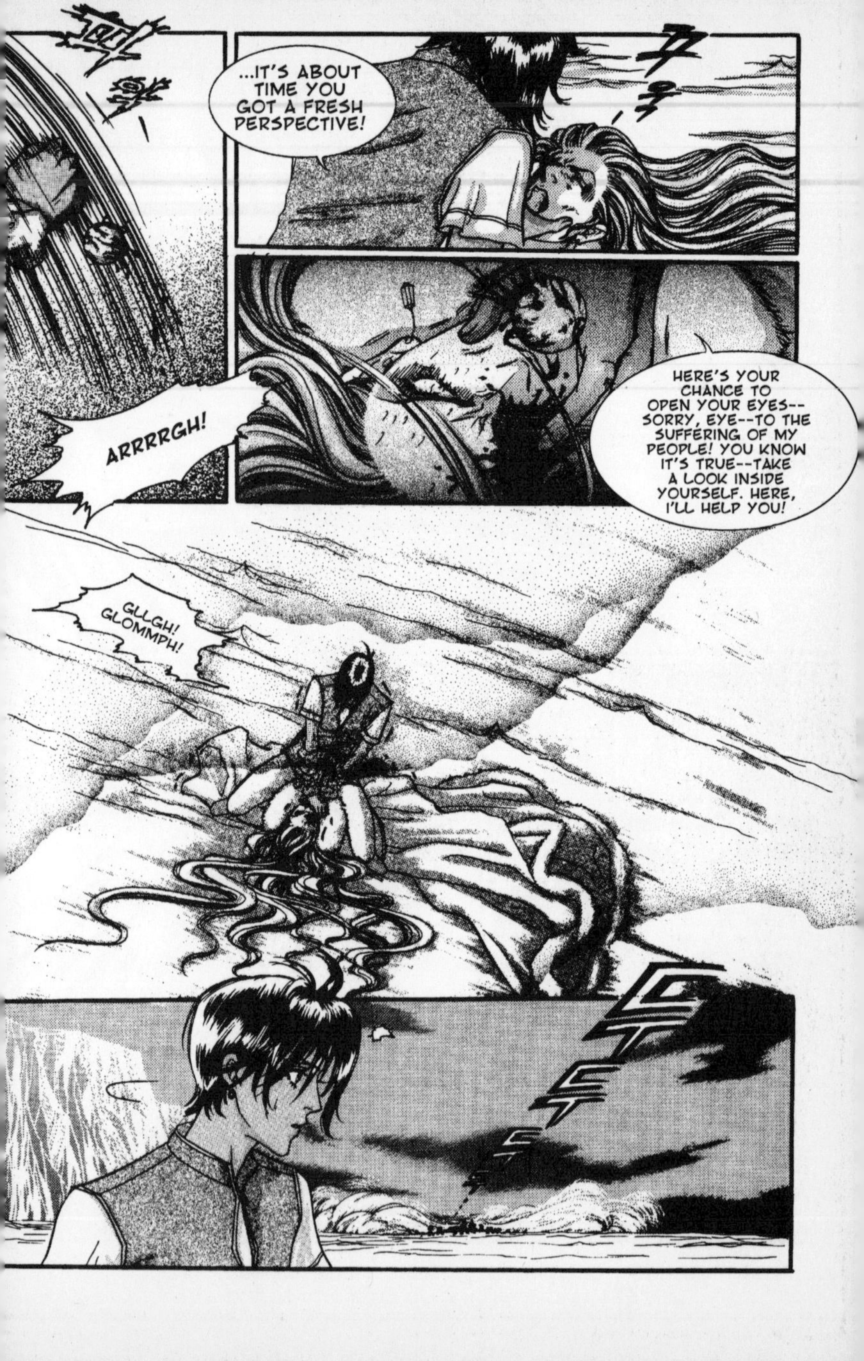
...IT'S ABOUT TIME YOU GOT A FRESH PERSPECTIVE!
ARRRRGH!
HERE'S YOUR CHANCE TO OPEN YOUR EYES--SORRY, EYE--TO THE SUFFERING OF MY PEOPLE! YOU KNOW IT'S TRUE--TAKE A LOOK INSIDE YOURSELF. HERE, I'LL HELP YOU!
GULGH! GLOMMPH!

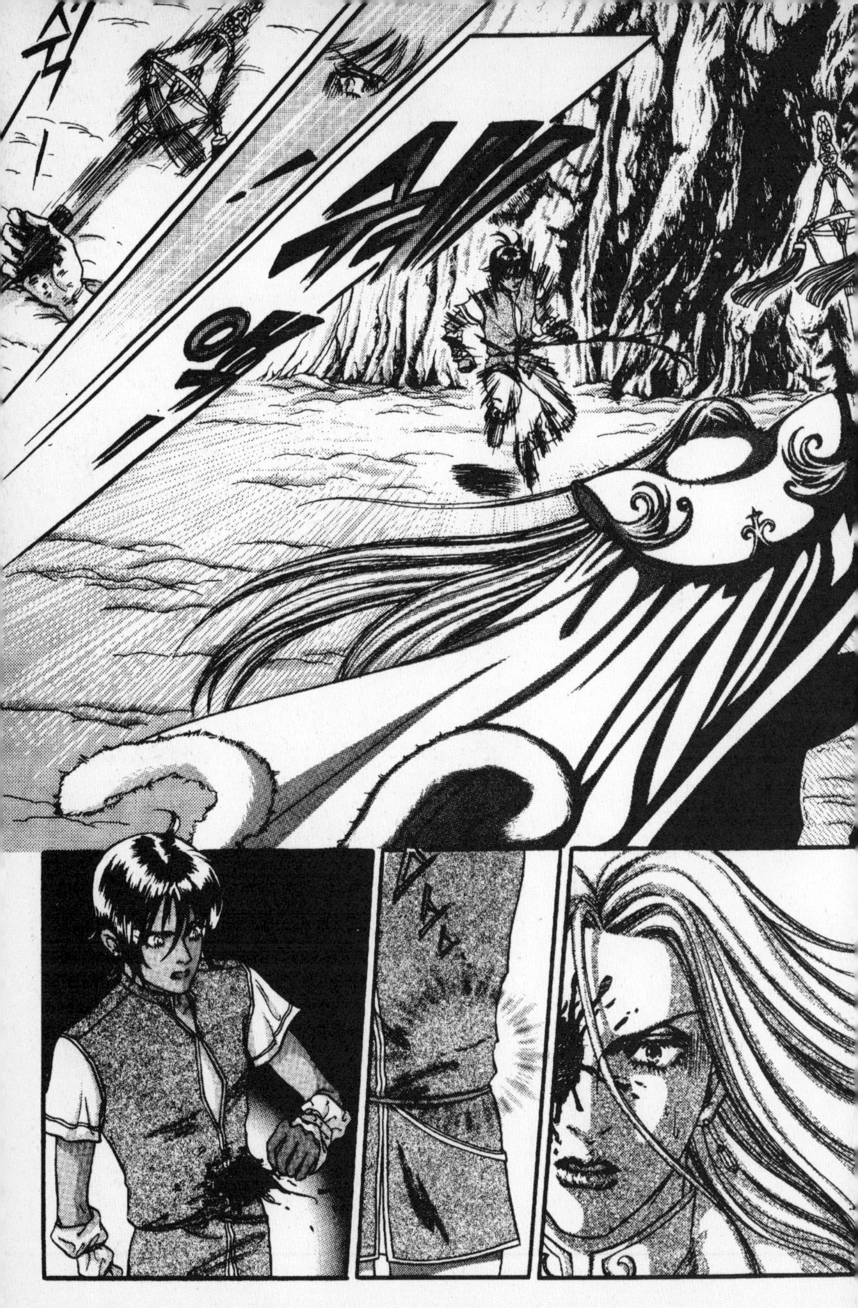
싸아—

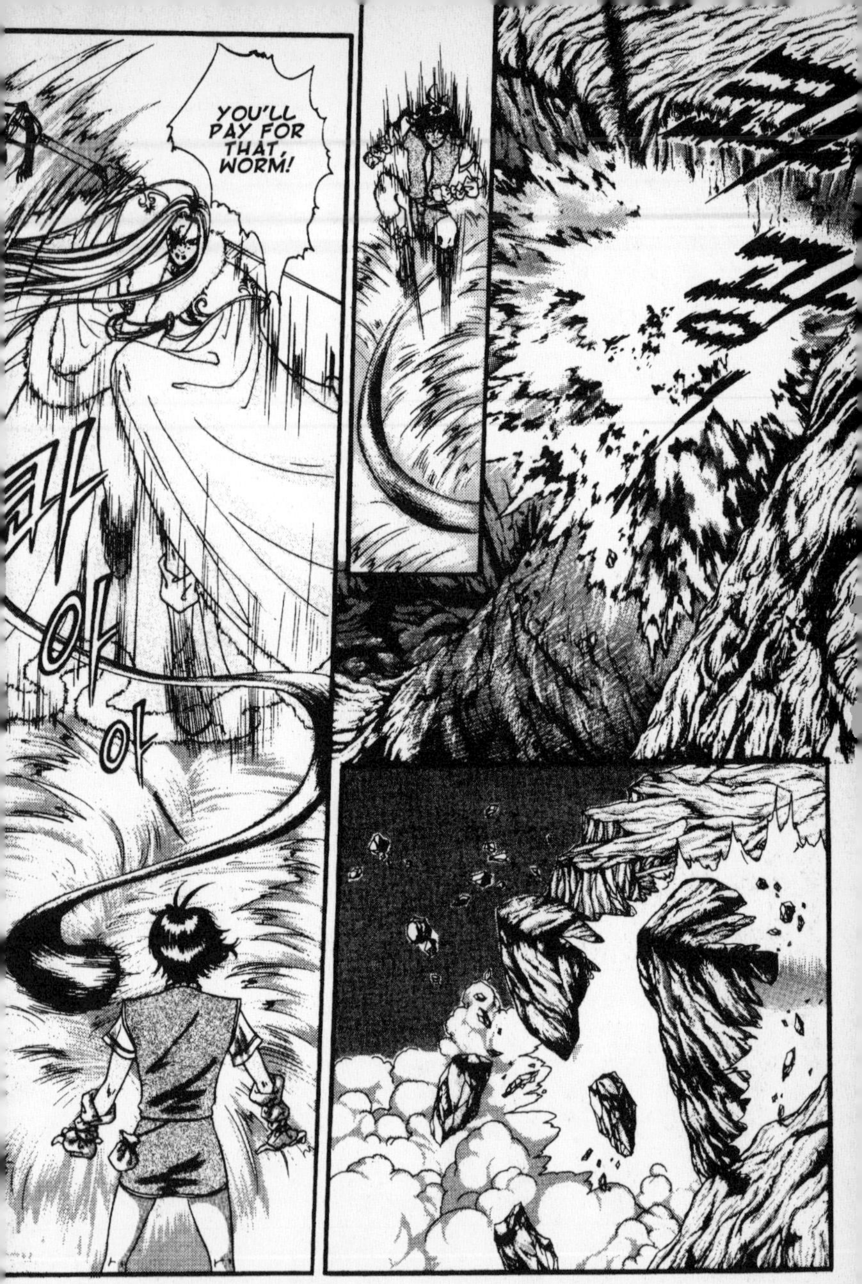
YOU'LL PAY FOR THAT, WORM!

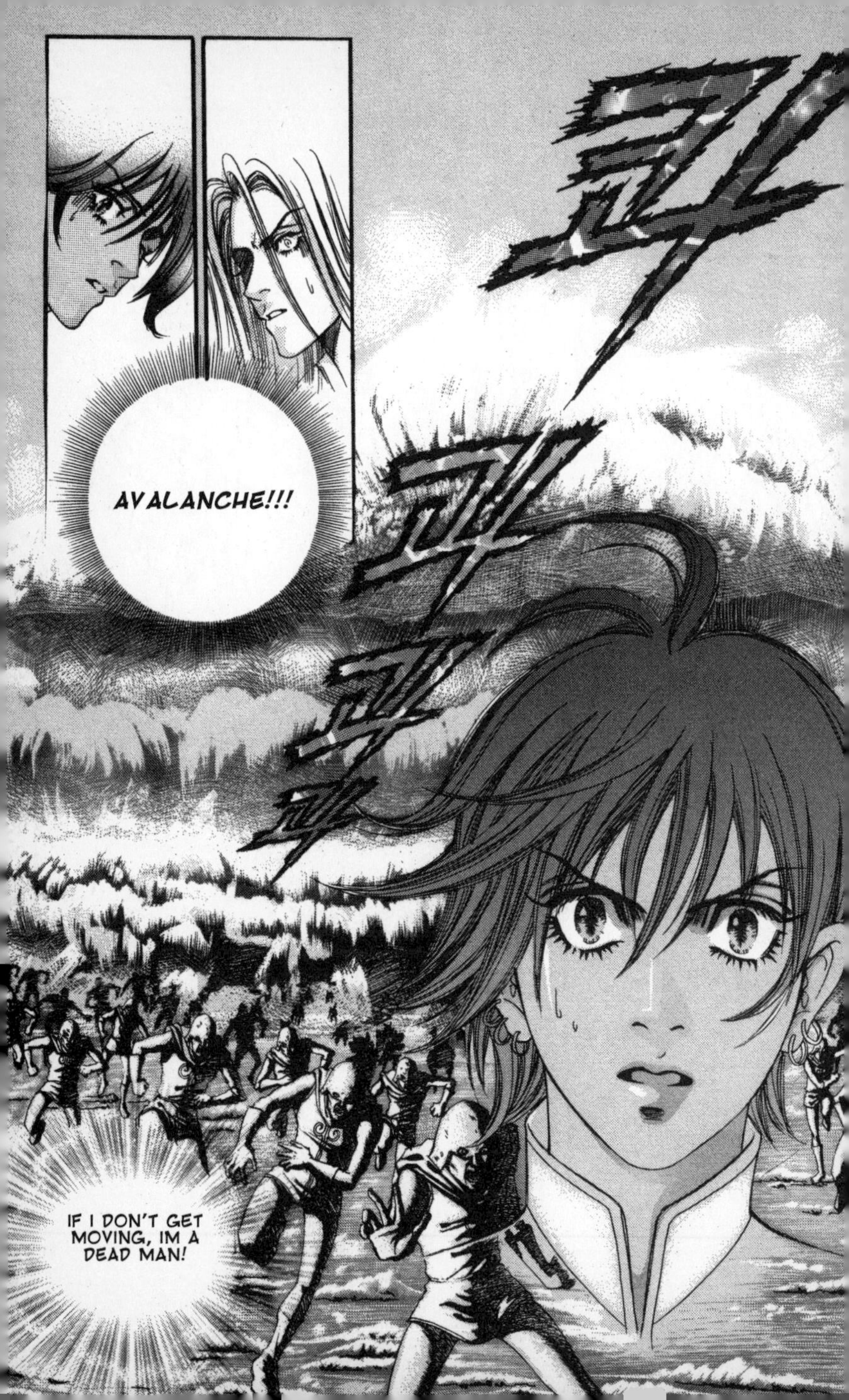
AVALANCHE!!!
IF I DON'T GET MOVING, IM A DEAD MAN!

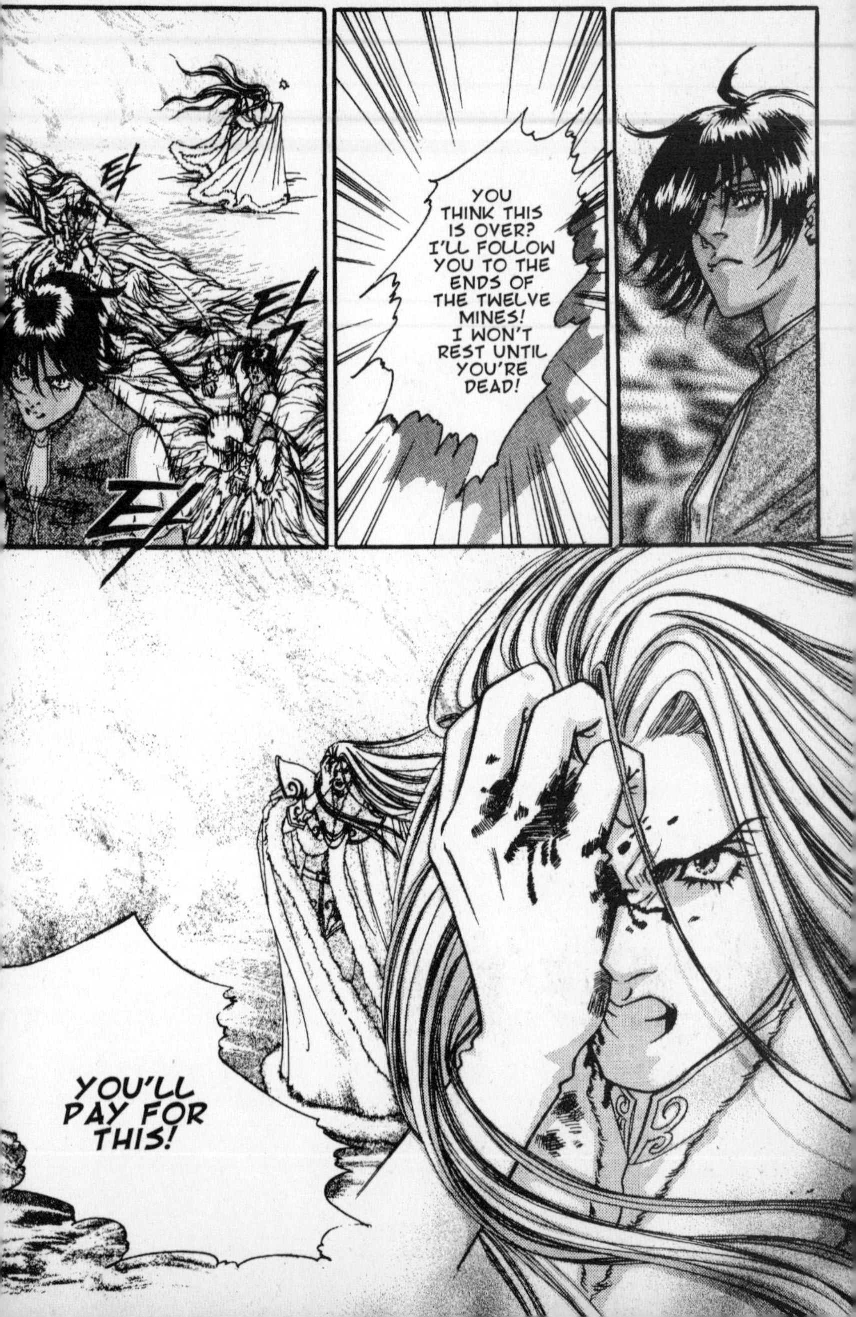
YOU THINK THIS IS OVER? I'LL FOLLOW YOU TO THE ENDS OF THE TWELVE MINES! I WON'T REST UNTIL YOU'RE DEAD!
YOU'LL PAY FOR THIS!

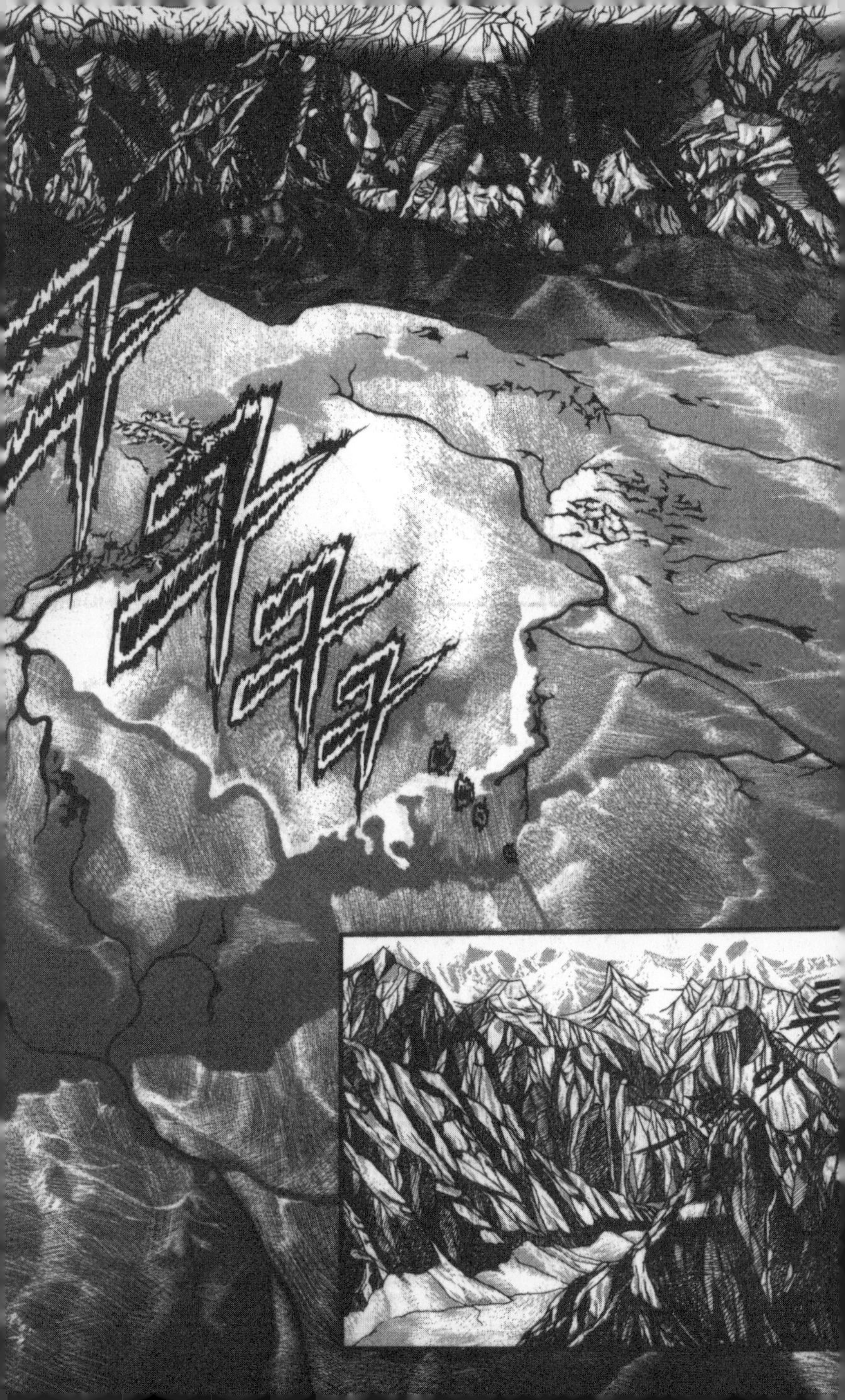

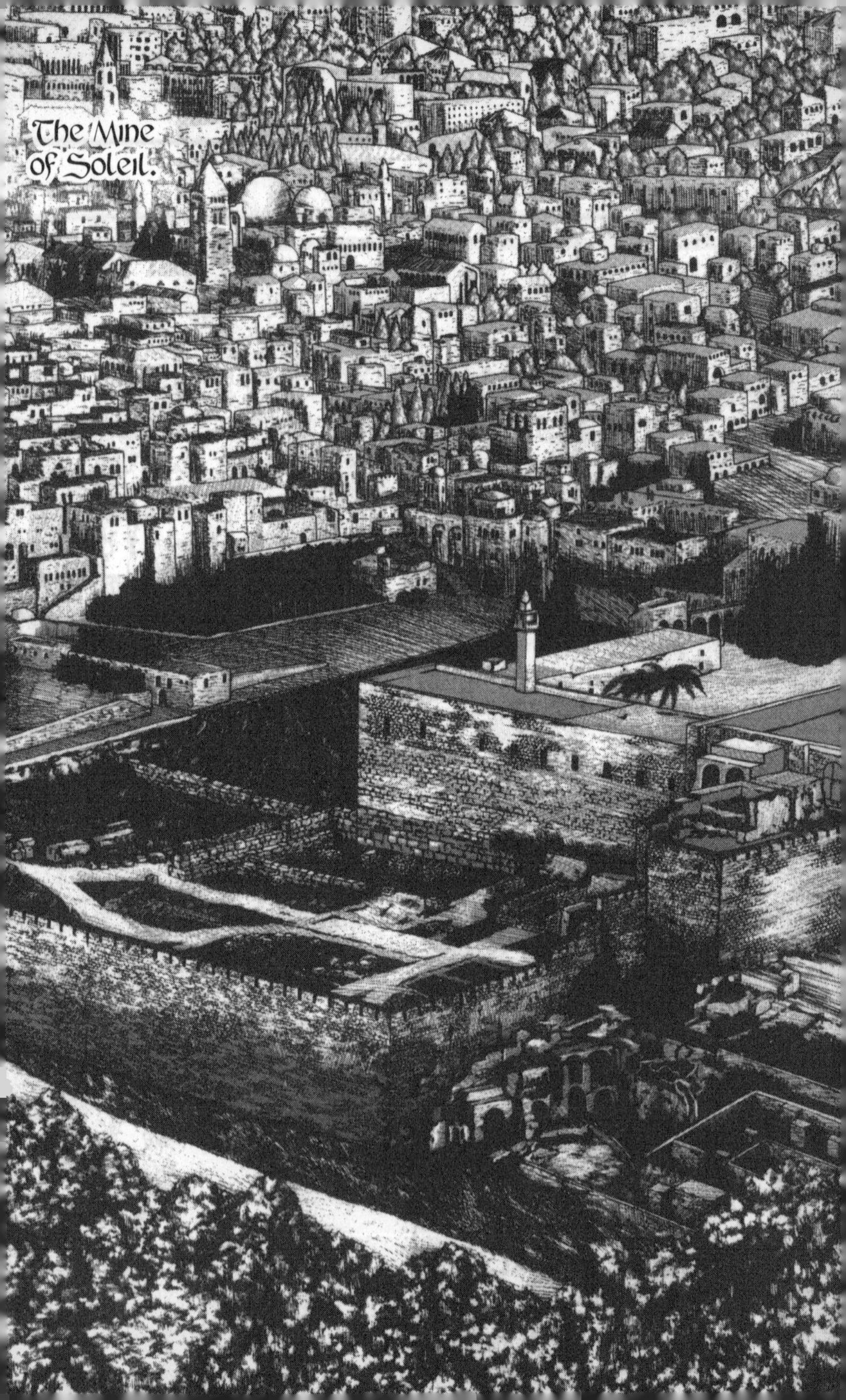
The Mine of Soleil.

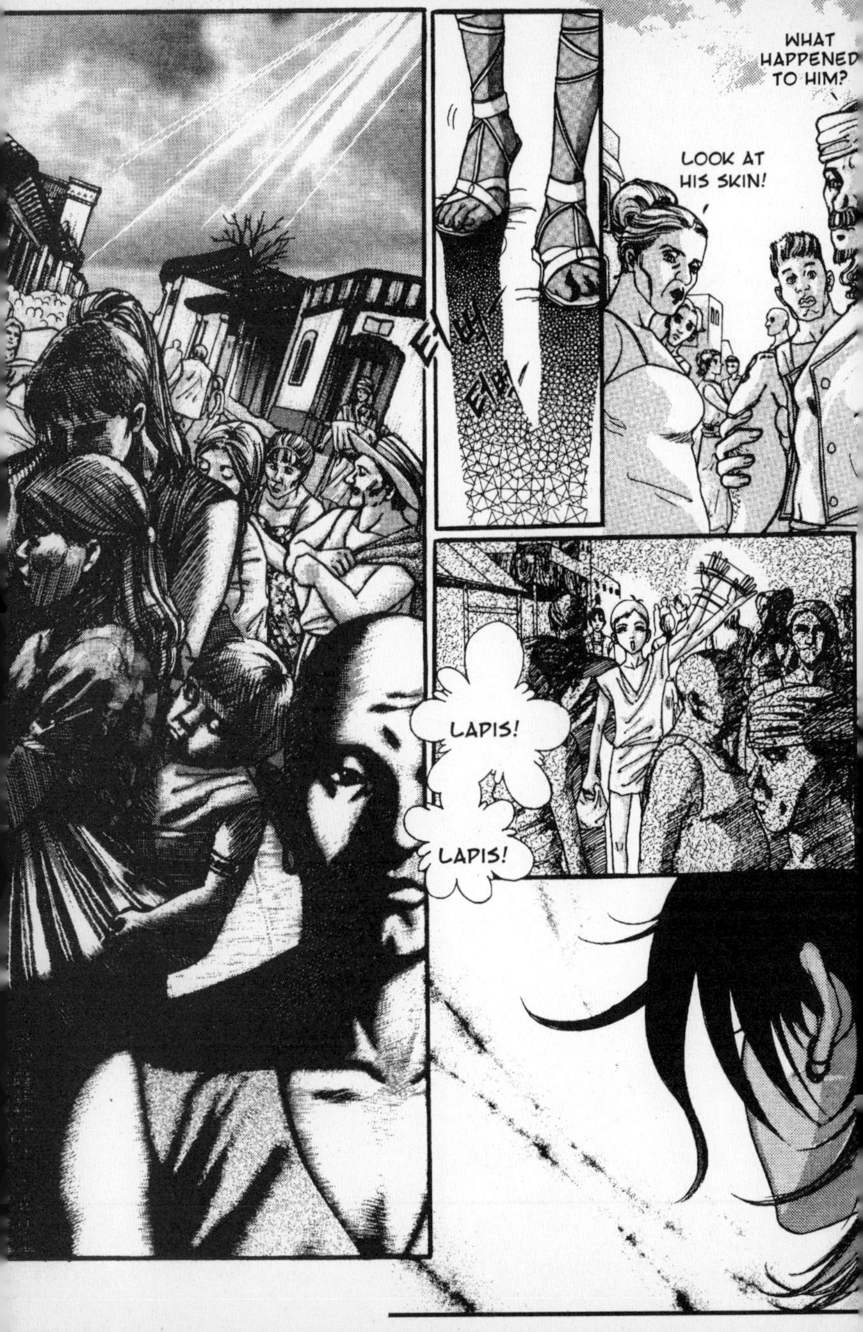

WHAT HAPPENED TO HIM?
LOOK AT HIS SKIN!
LAPIS!
LAPIS!

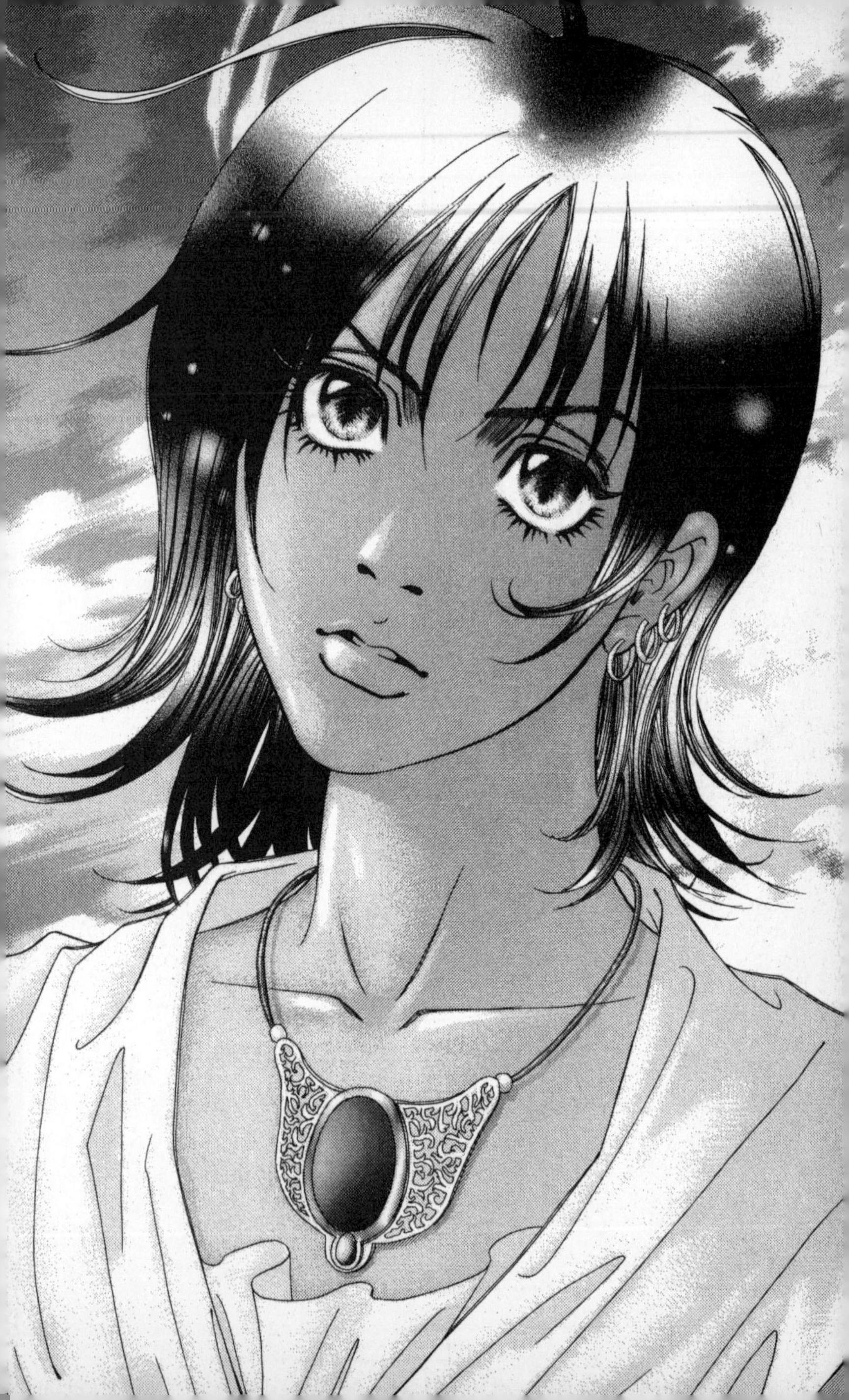

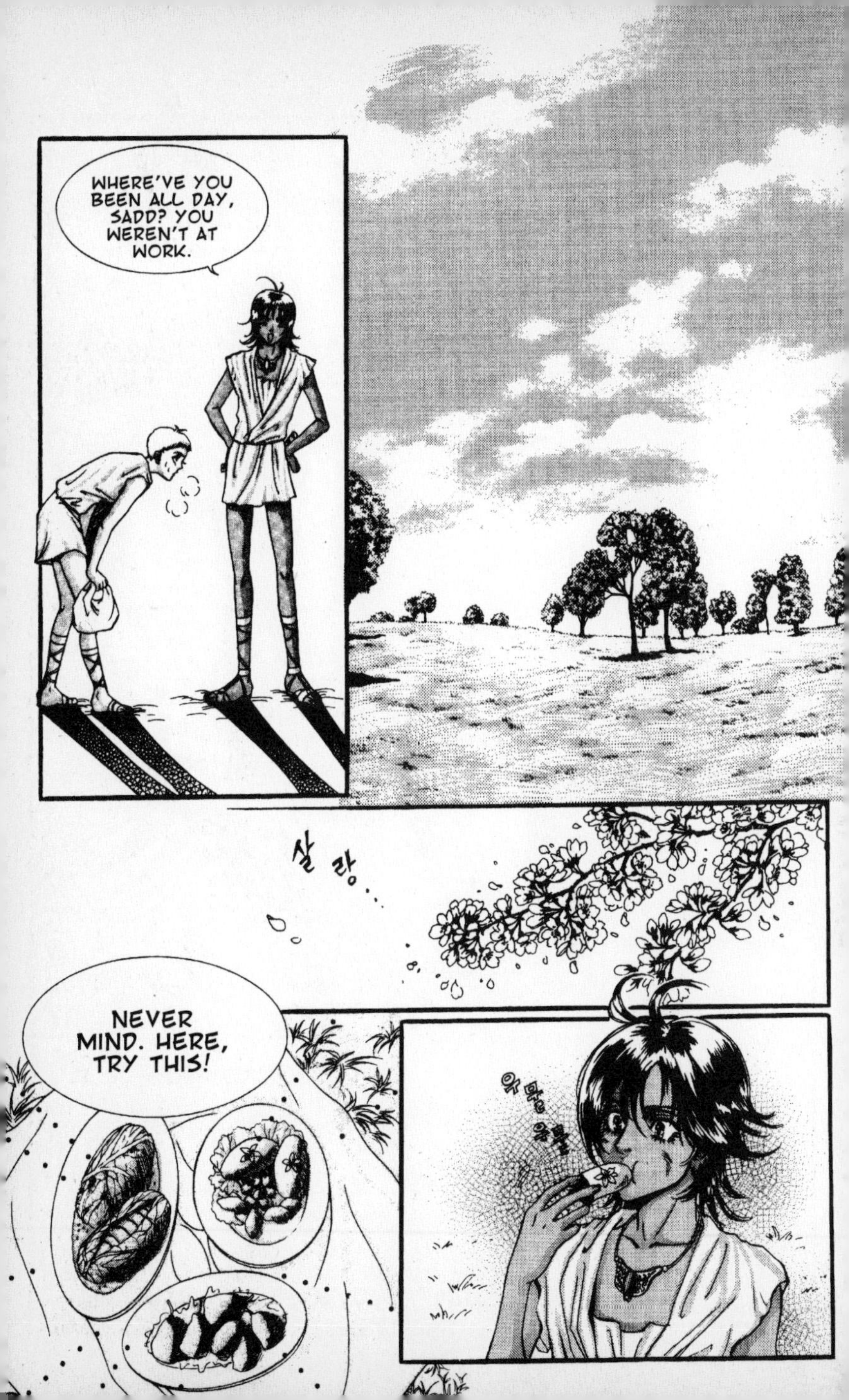
WHERE'VE YOU BEEN ALL DAY, SADD? YOU WEREN'T AT WORK.
살랑...
NEVER MIND. HERE, TRY THIS!
우물우물

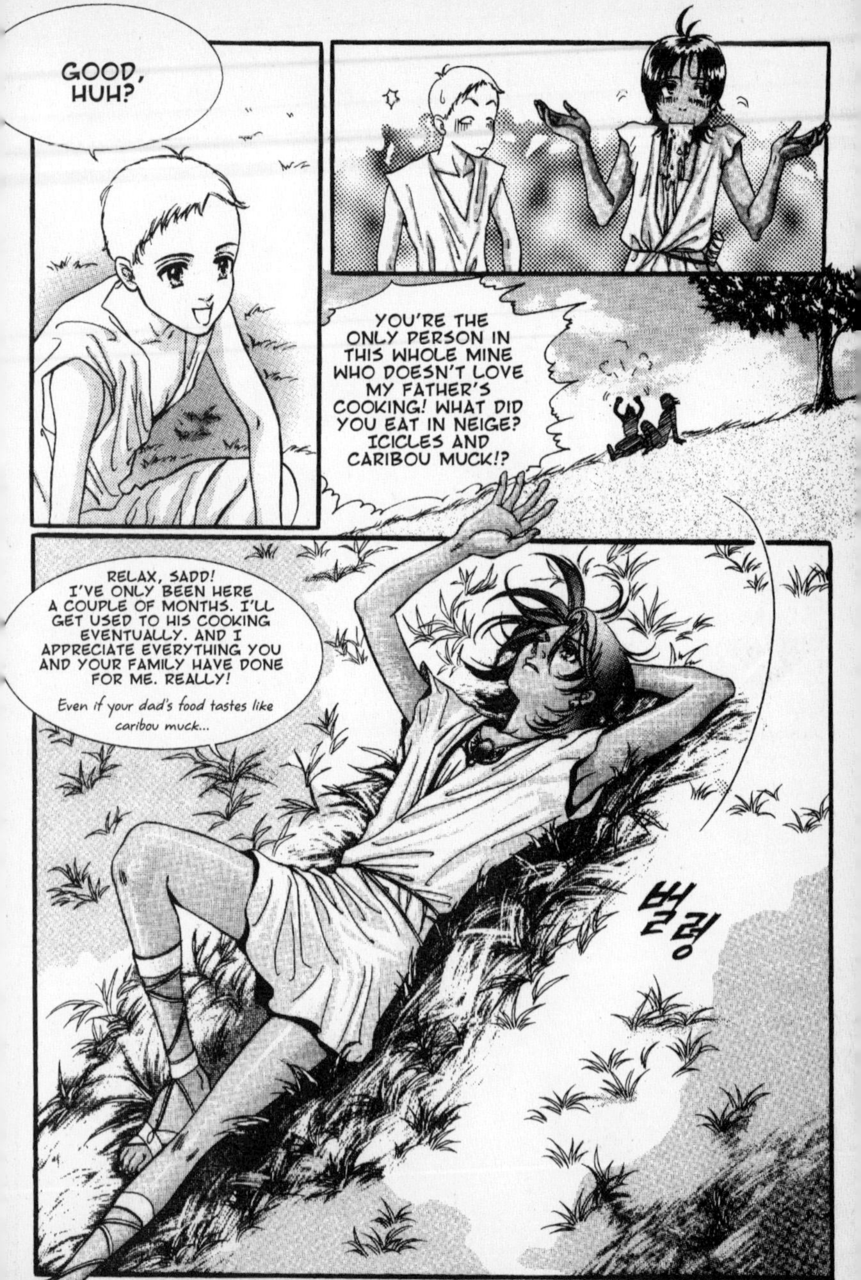
GOOD, HUH?
YOU'RE THE ONLY PERSON IN THIS WHOLE MINE WHO DOESN'T LOVE MY FATHER'S COOKING! WHAT DID YOU EAT IN NEIGE? ICICLES AND CARIBOU MUCK!?
RELAX, SADD! I'VE ONLY BEEN HERE A COUPLE OF MONTHS. I'LL GET USED TO HIS COOKING EVENTUALLY. AND I APPRECIATE EVERYTHING YOU AND YOUR FAMILY HAVE DONE FOR ME. REALLY!
Even if your dad's food tastes like caribou muck...
벌렁

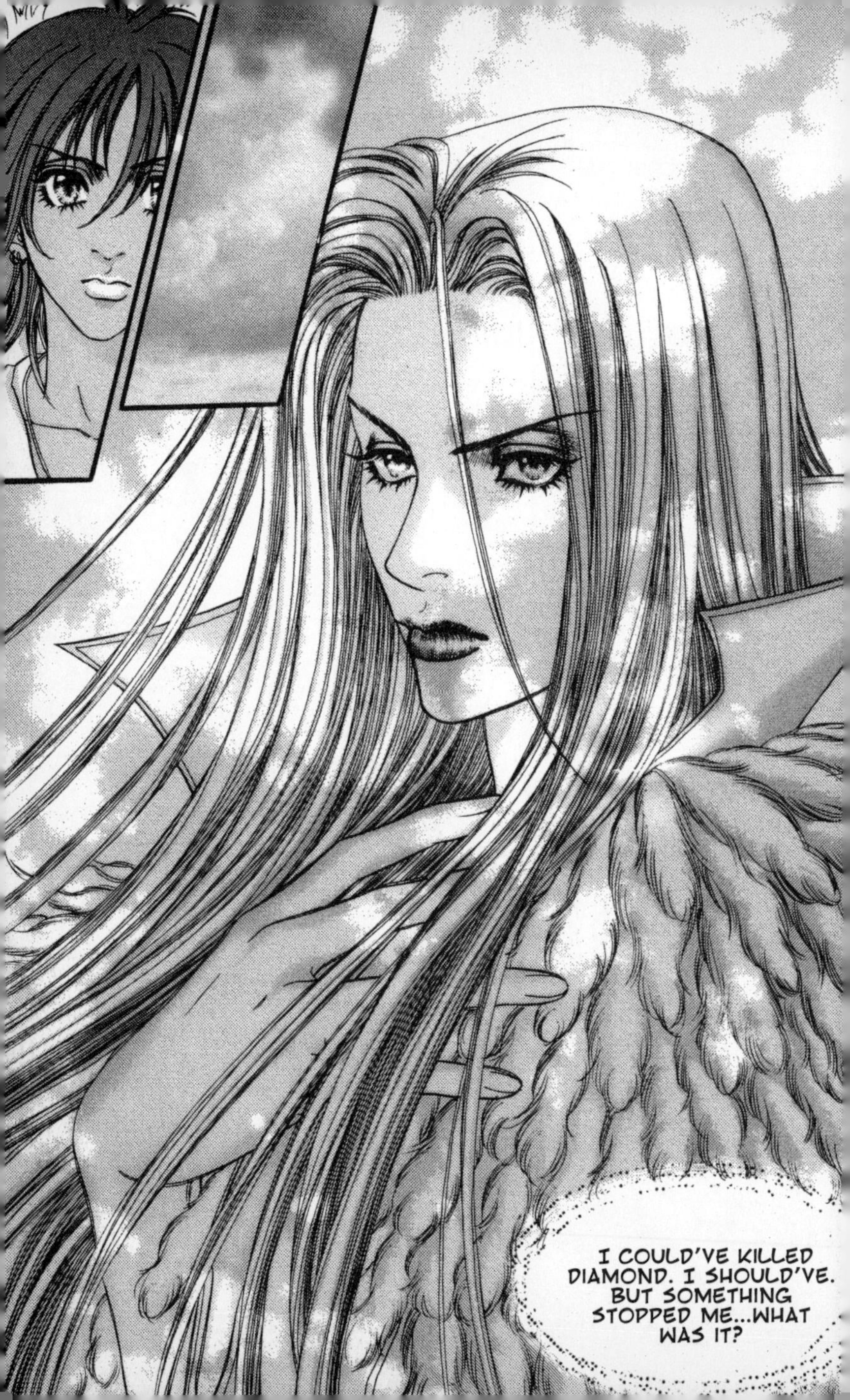
I COULD'VE KILLED DIAMOND. I SHOULD'VE. BUT SOMETHING STOPPED ME...WHAT WAS IT?

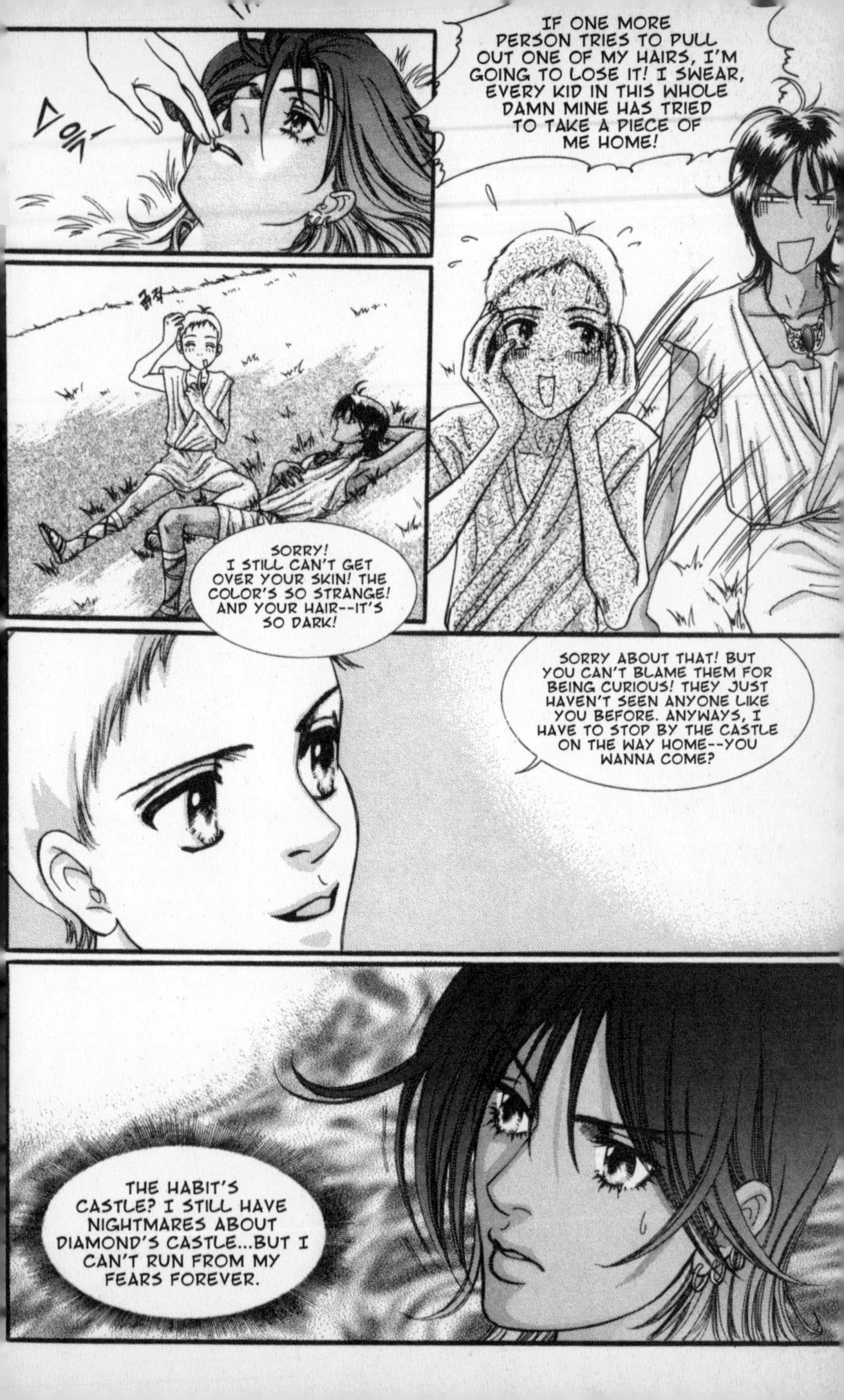
IF ONE MORE PERSON TRIES TO PULL OUT ONE OF MY HAIRS, I'M GOING TO LOSE IT! I SWEAR, EVERY KID IN THIS WHOLE DAMN MINE HAS TRIED TO TAKE A PIECE OF ME HOME!
SORRY! I STILL CAN'T GET OVER YOUR SKIN! THE COLOR'S SO STRANGE! AND YOUR HAIR--IT'S SO DARK!
SORRY ABOUT THAT! BUT YOU CAN'T BLAME THEM FOR BEING CURIOUS! THEY JUST HAVEN'T SEEN ANYONE LIKE YOU BEFORE. ANYWAYS, I HAVE TO STOP BY THE CASTLE ON THE WAY HOME--YOU WANNA COME?
THE HABIT'S CASTLE? I STILL HAVE NIGHTMARES ABOUT DIAMOND'S CASTLE...BUT I CAN'T RUN FROM MY FEARS FOREVER.

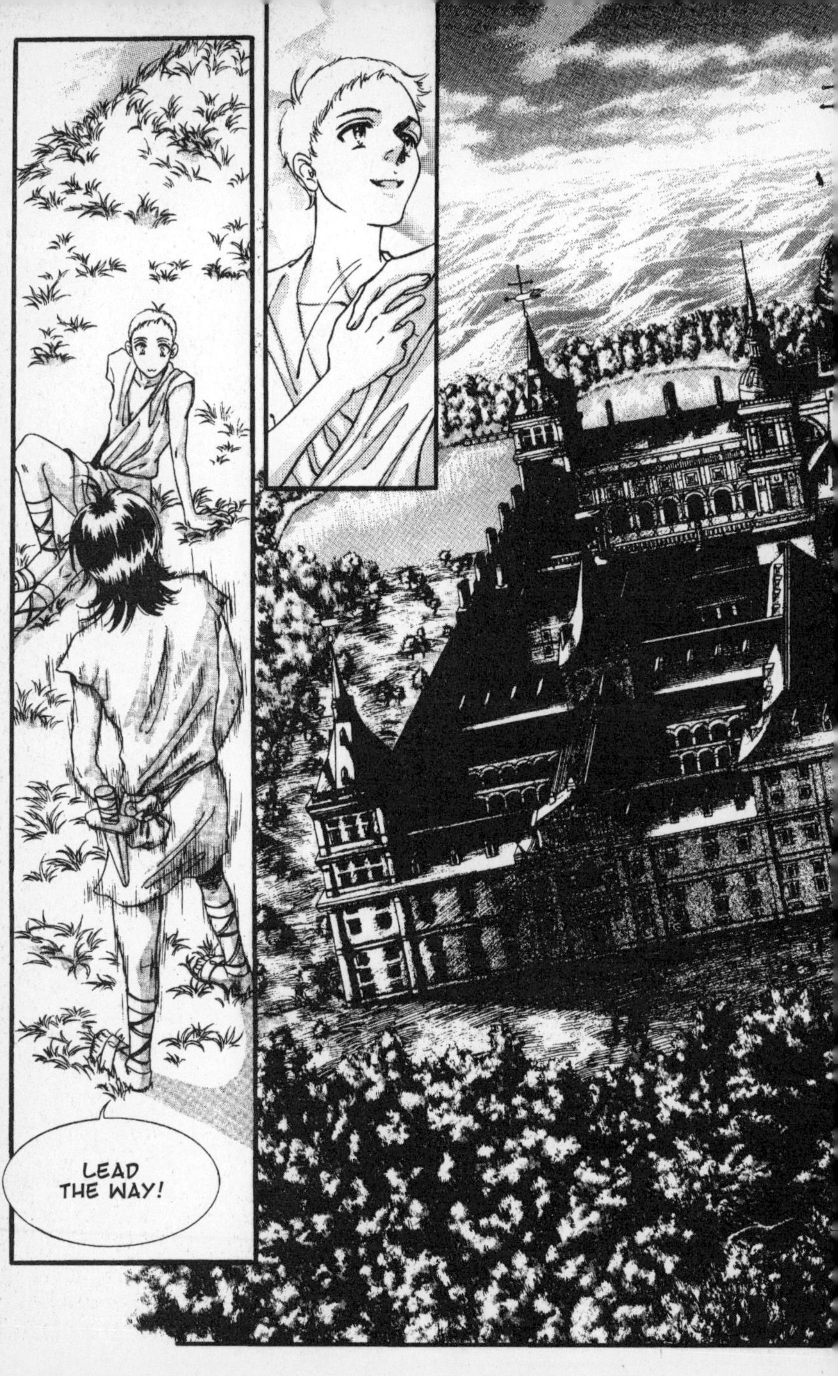
LEAD THE WAY!

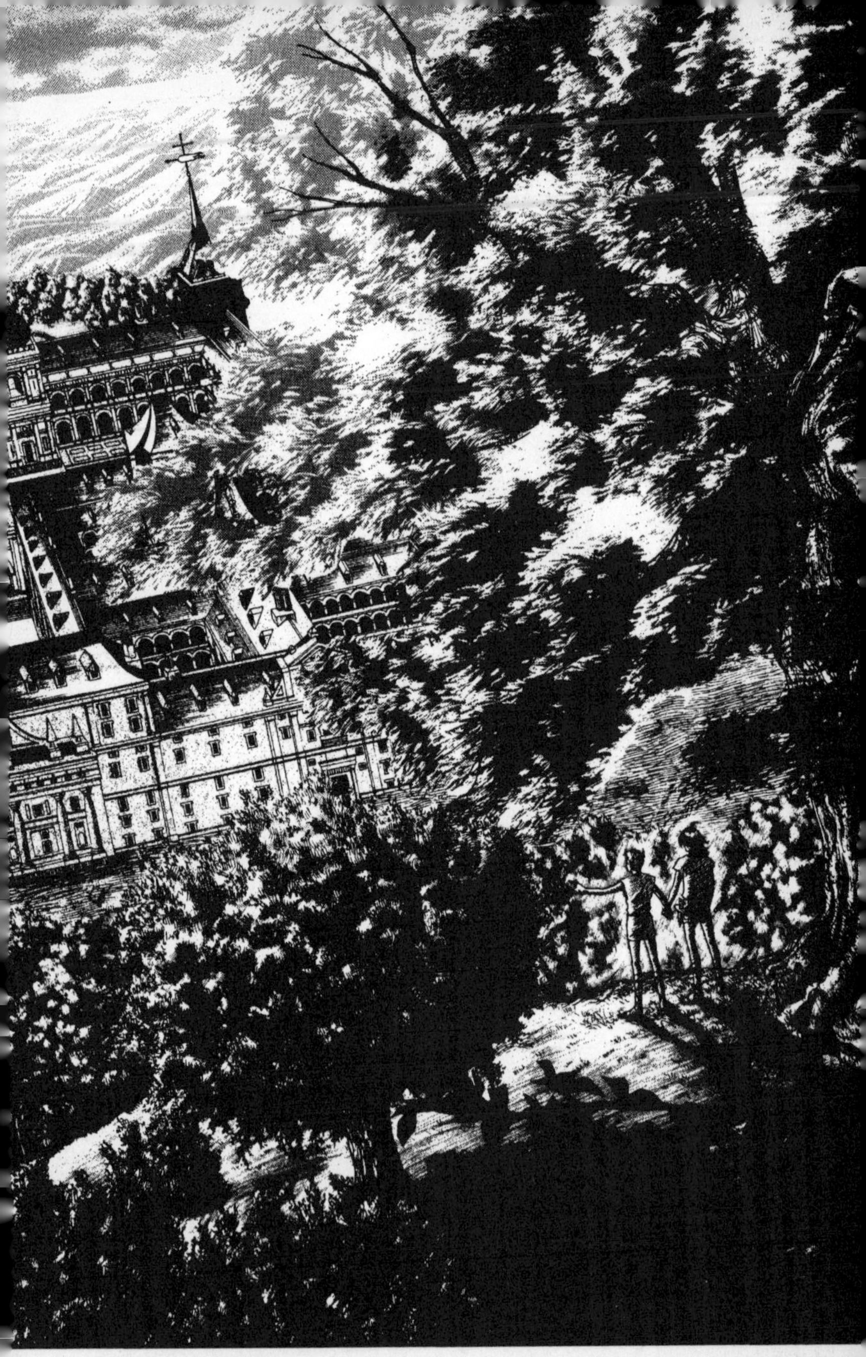

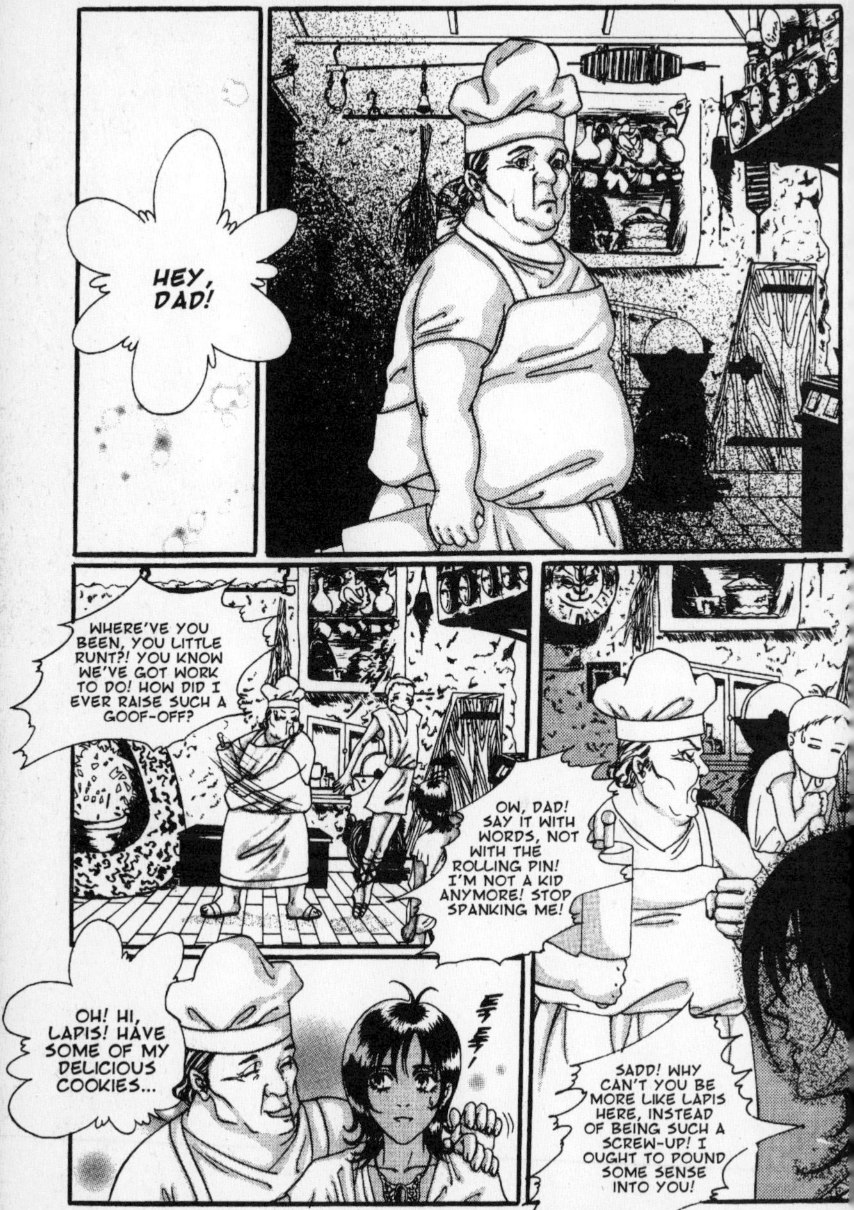
HEY, DAD!
WHERE'VE YOU BEEN, YOU LITTLE RUNT?! YOU KNOW WE'VE GOT WORK TO DO! HOW DID I EVER RAISE SUCH A GOOF-OFF?
OW, DAD! SAY IT WITH WORDS, NOT WITH THE ROLLING PIN! I'M NOT A KID ANYMORE! STOP SPANKING ME!
OH! HI, LAPIS! HAVE SOME OF MY DELICIOUS COOKIES...
SADD! WHY CAN'T YOU BE MORE LIKE LAPIS HERE, INSTEAD OF BEING SUCH A SCREW-UP! I OUGHT TO POUND SOME SENSE INTO YOU!

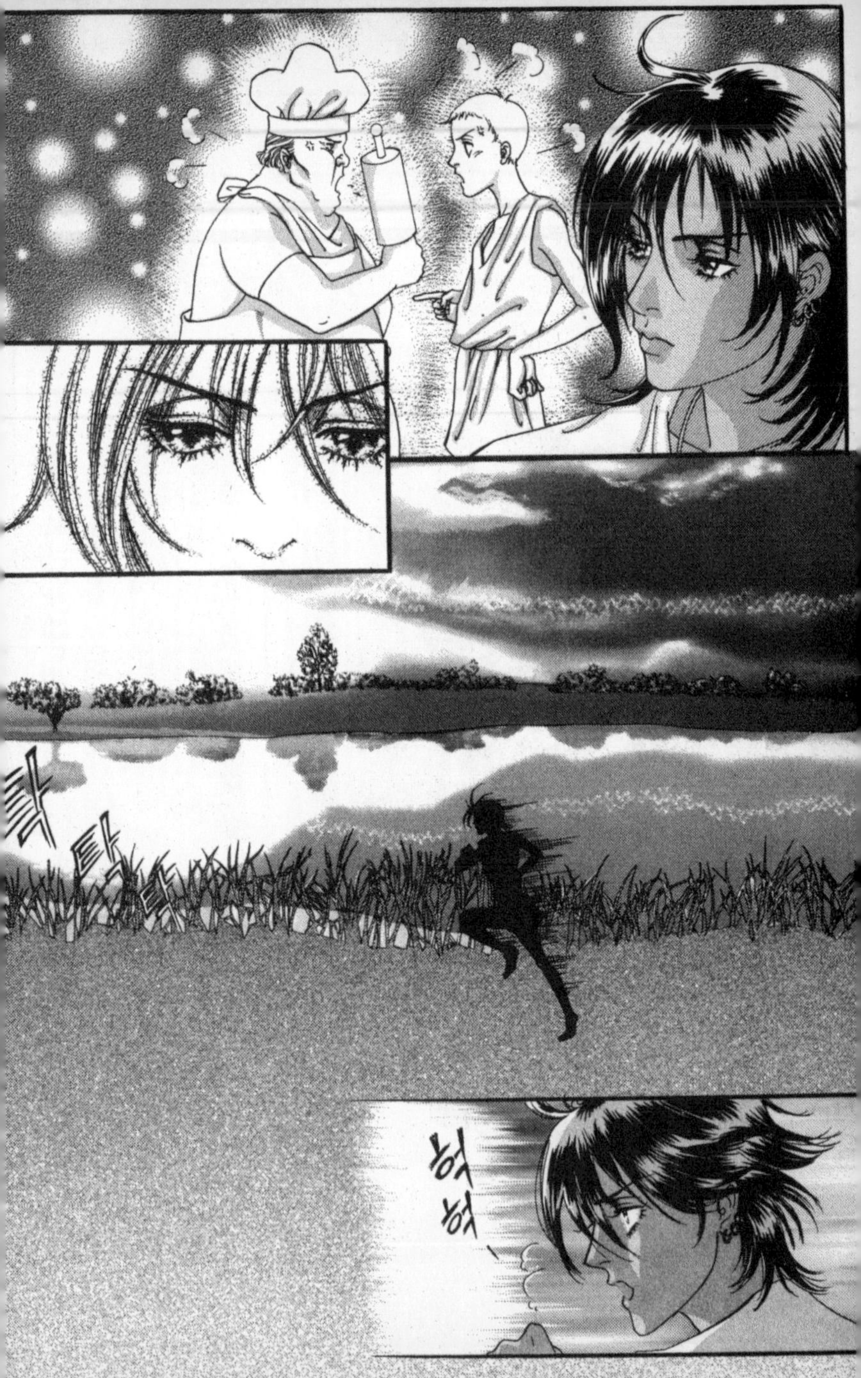
탁 탁 탁 탁
헉 헉

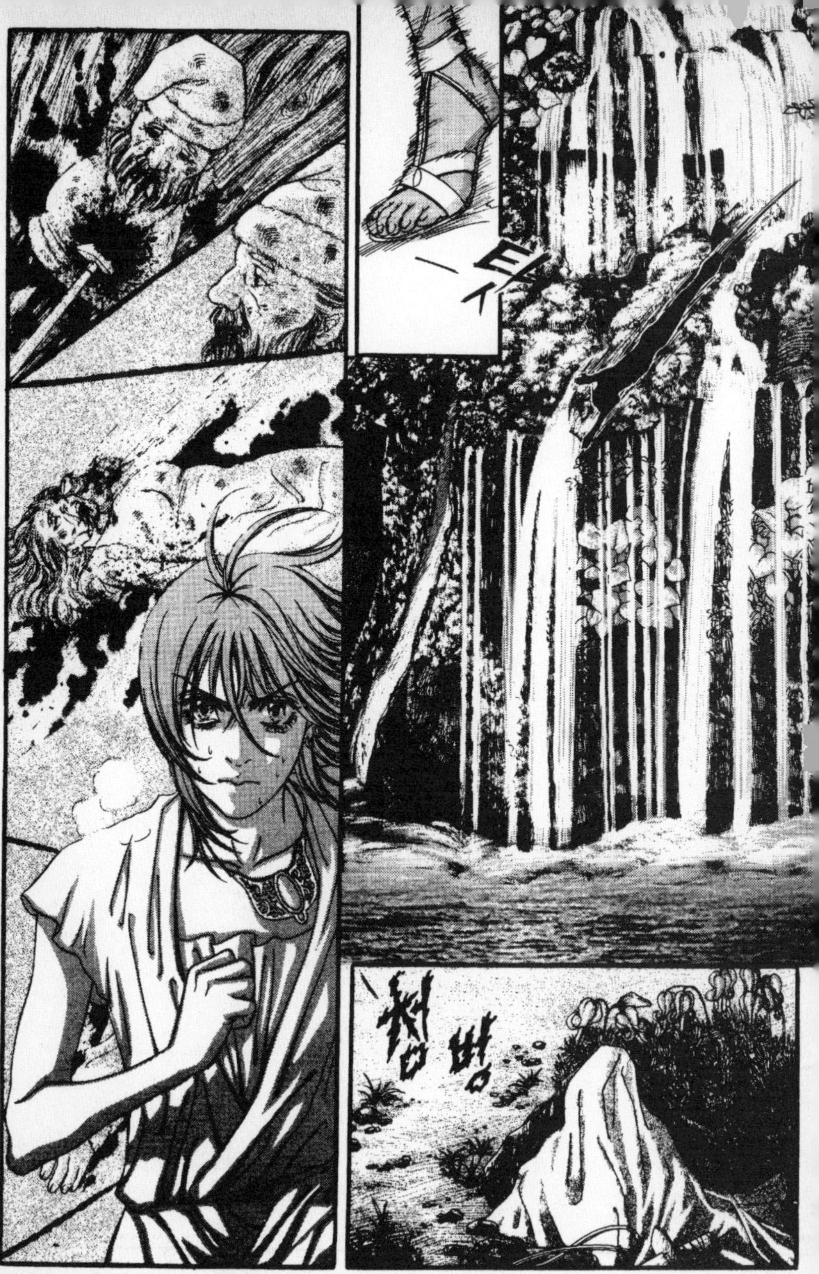
타이
첨벙

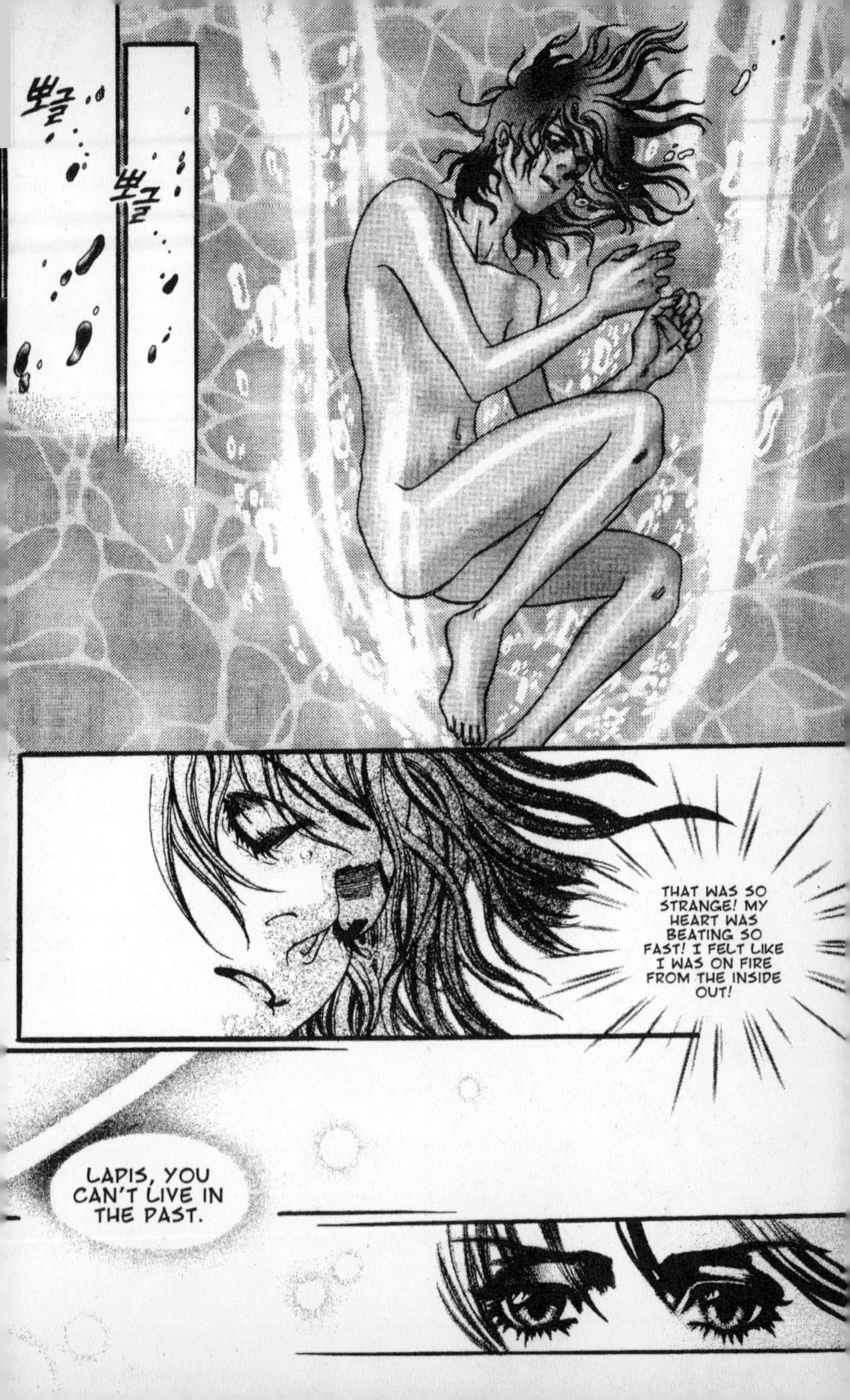
뽀글
뽀글
THAT WAS SO STRANGE! MY HEART WAS BEATING SO FAST! I FELT LIKE I WAS ON FIRE FROM THE INSIDE OUT!
LAPIS, YOU CAN'T LIVE IN THE PAST.

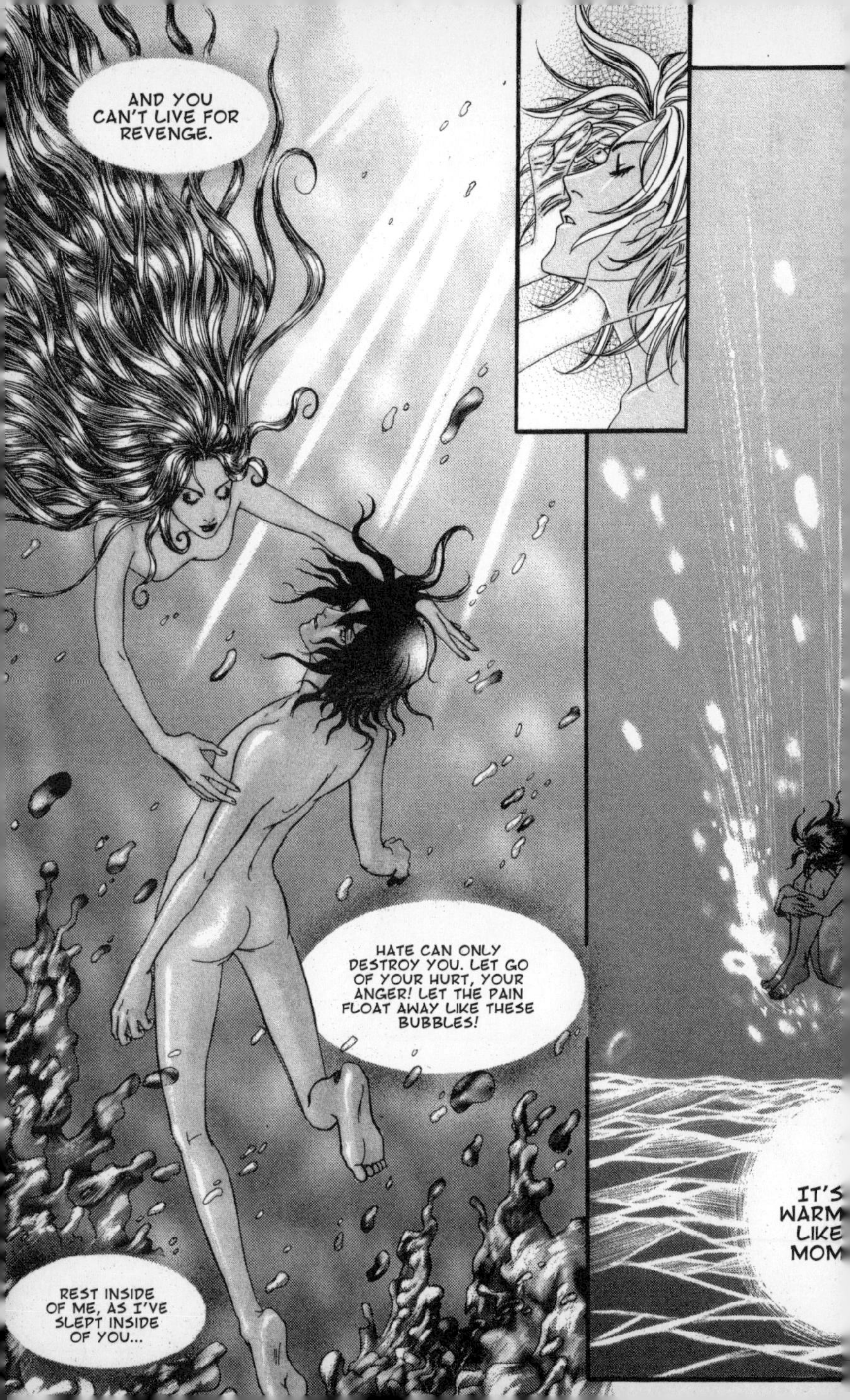
AND YOU CAN'T LIVE FOR REVENGE.
HATE CAN ONLY DESTROY YOU. LET GO OF YOUR HURT, YOUR ANGER! LET THE PAIN FLOAT AWAY LIKE THESE BUBBLES!
REST INSIDE OF ME, AS I'VE SLEPT INSIDE OF YOU...
IT'S WARM LIKE MOM

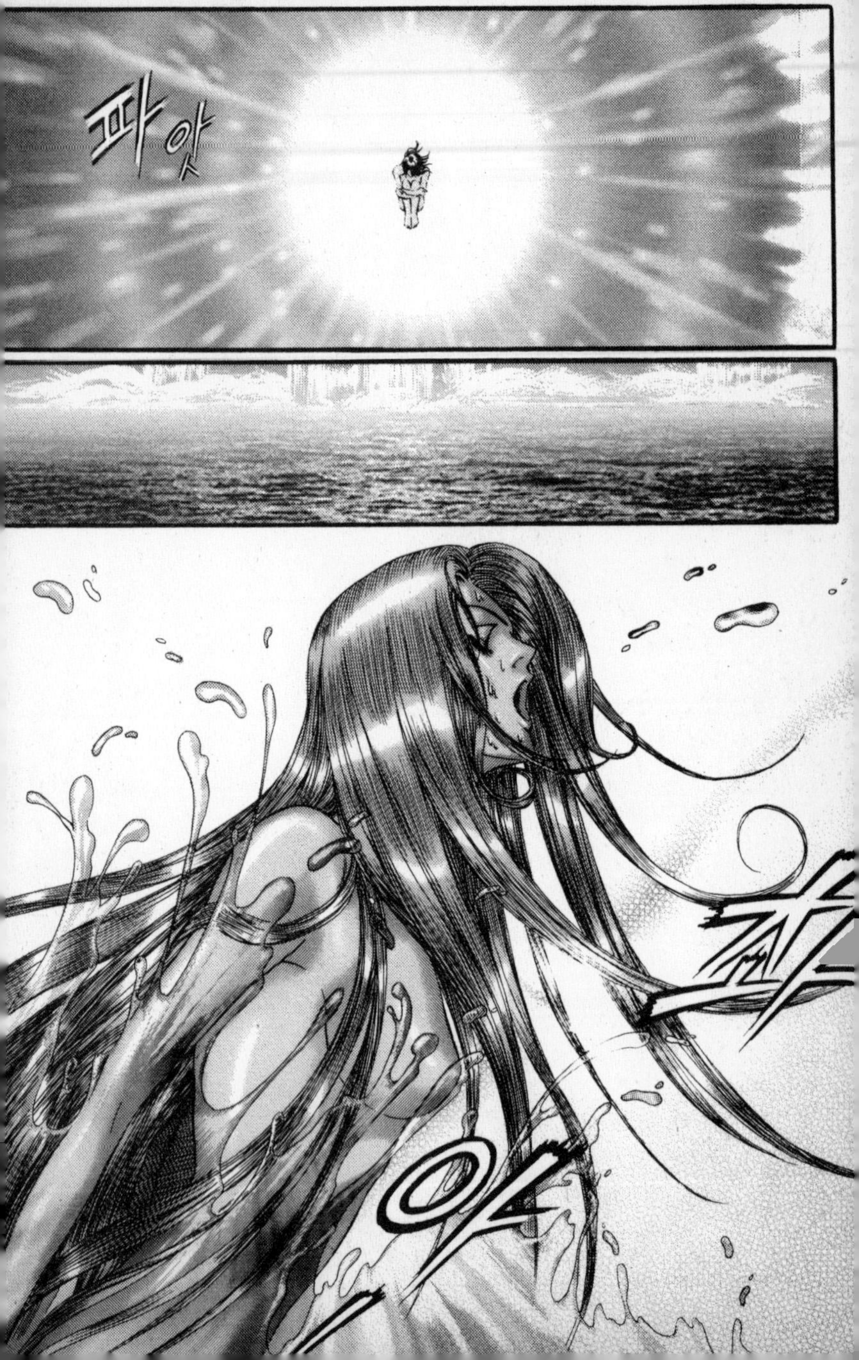
파앗

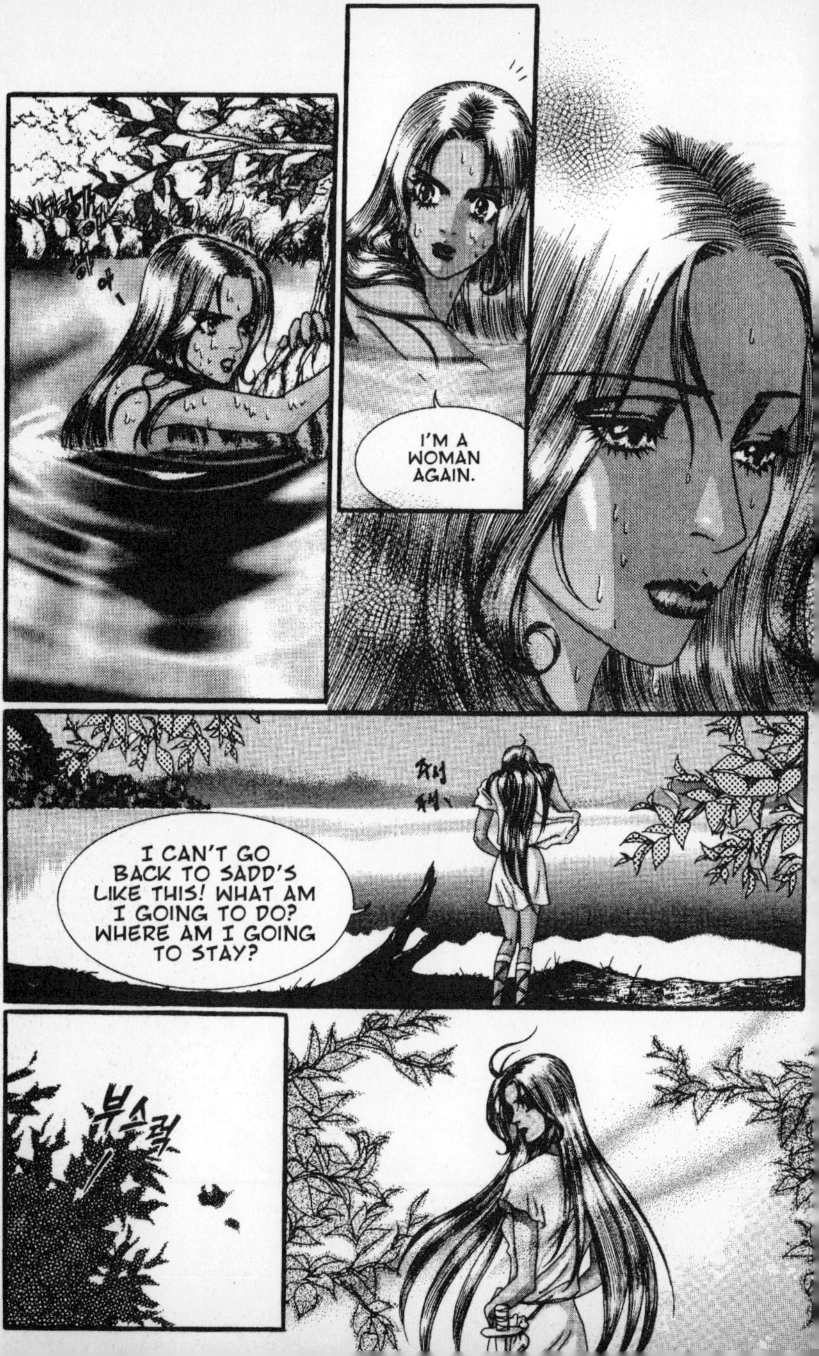
I'M A WOMAN AGAIN.
I CAN'T GO BACK TO SADD'S LIKE THIS! WHAT AM I GOING TO DO? WHERE AM I GOING TO STAY?

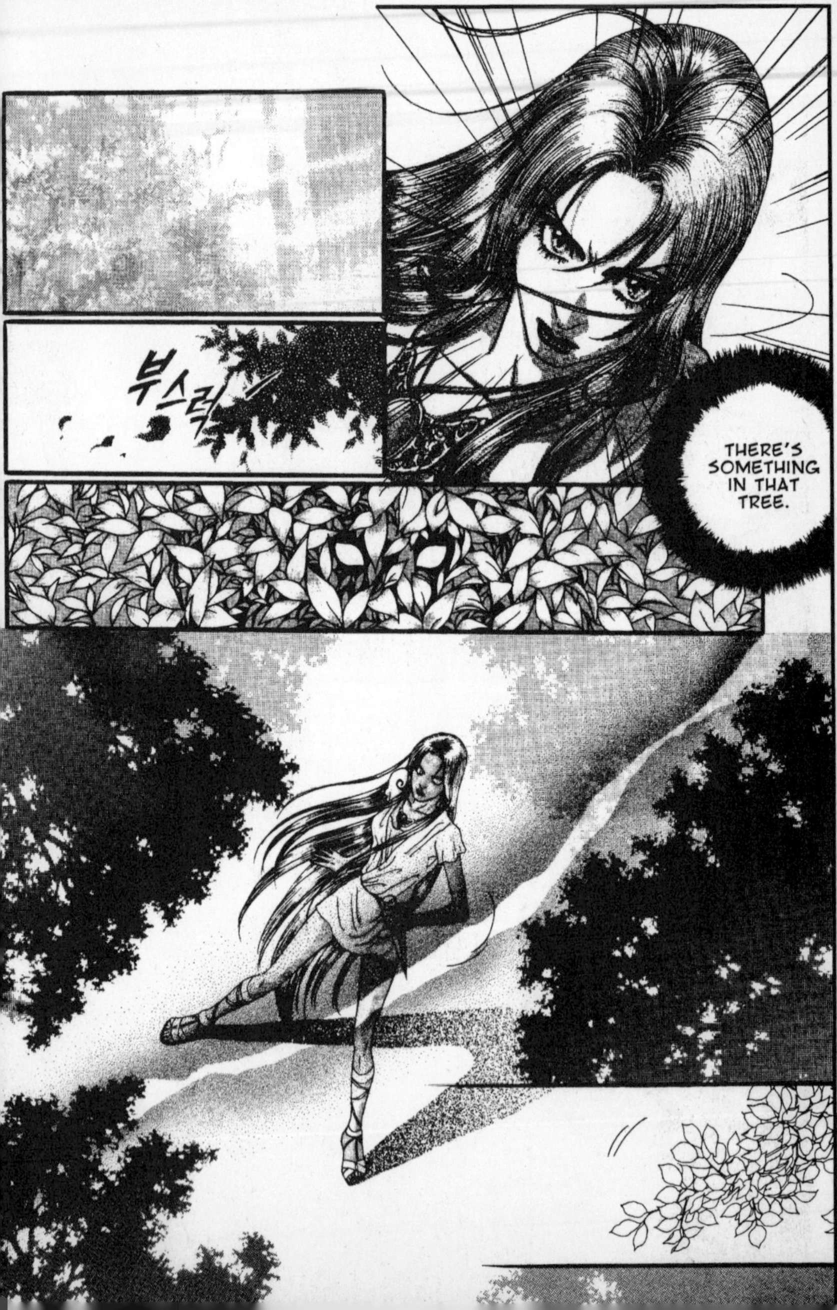

부스럭
THERE'S SOMETHING IN THAT TREE.

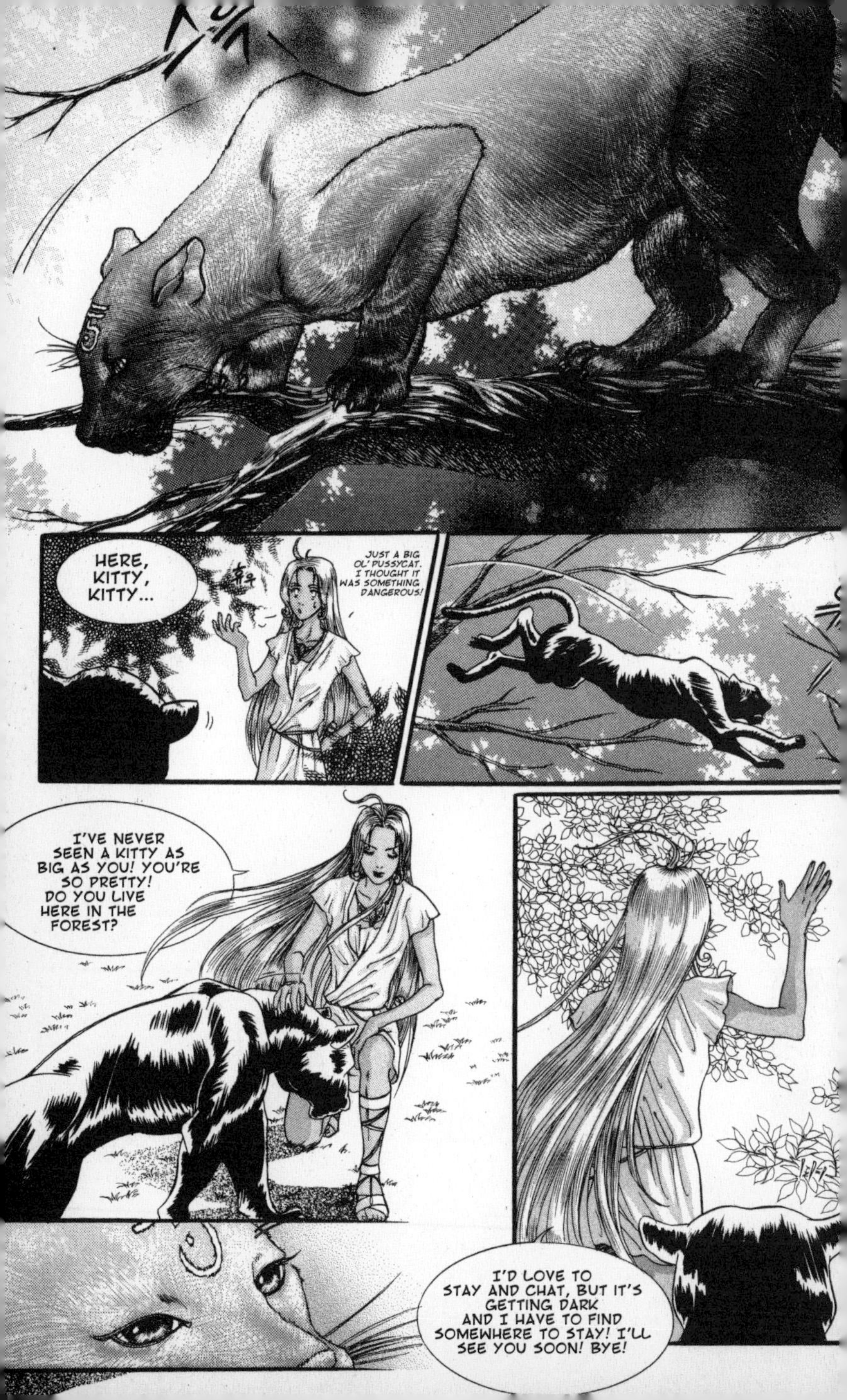
HERE, KITTY, KITTY...
JUST A BIG OL' PUSSYCAT. I THOUGHT IT WAS SOMETHING DANGEROUS!
I'VE NEVER SEEN A KITTY AS BIG AS YOU! YOU'RE SO PRETTY! DO YOU LIVE HERE IN THE FOREST?
I'D LOVE TO STAY AND CHAT, BUT IT'S GETTING DARK AND I HAVE TO FIND SOMEWHERE TO STAY! I'LL SEE YOU SOON! BYE!

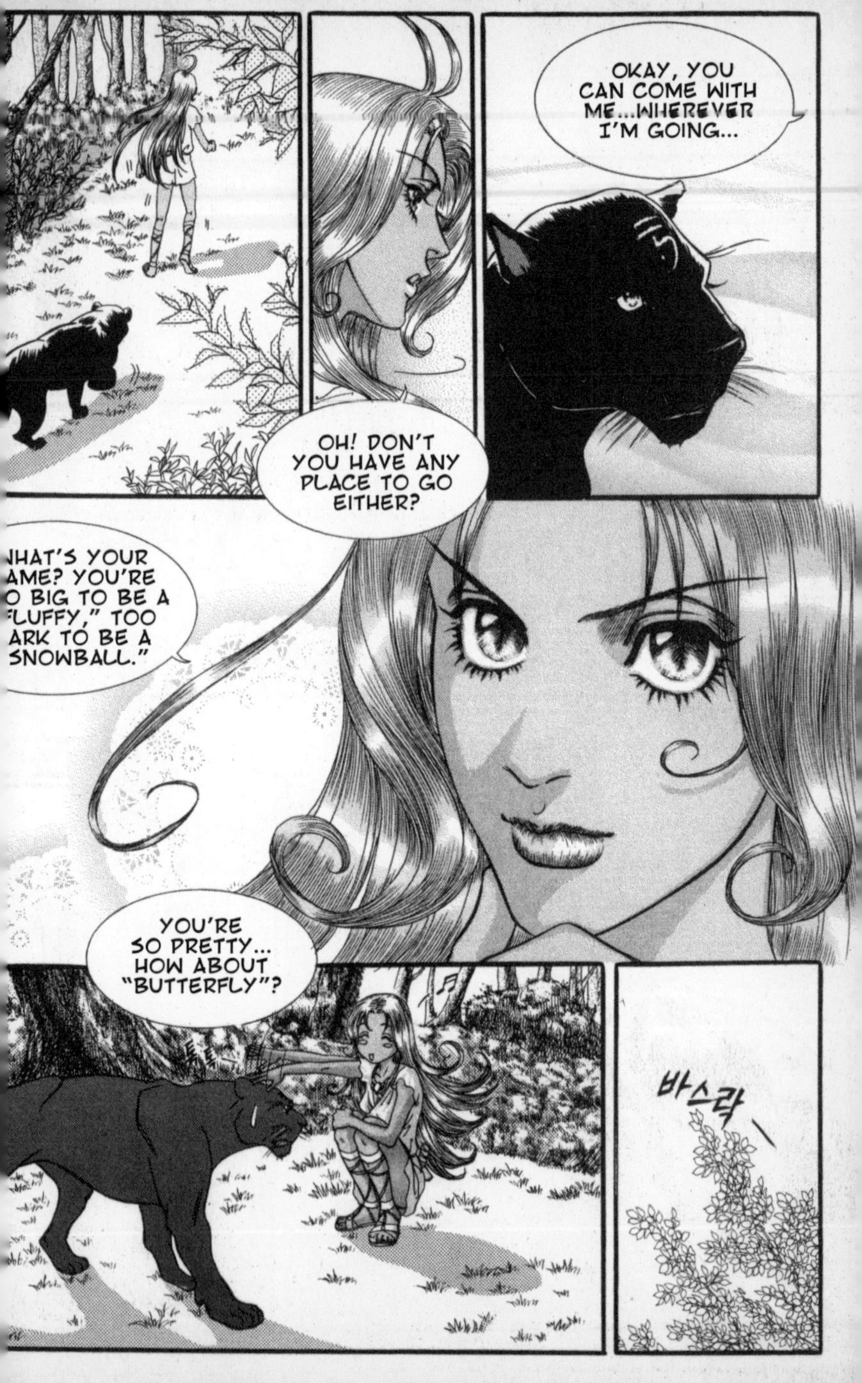
OKAY, YOU CAN COME WITH ME...WHEREVER I'M GOING...
OH! DON'T YOU HAVE ANY PLACE TO GO EITHER?
WHAT'S YOUR NAME? YOU'RE TOO BIG TO BE A "FLUFFY," TOO DARK TO BE A "SNOWBALL."
YOU'RE SO PRETTY... HOW ABOUT "BUTTERFLY"?
바스락

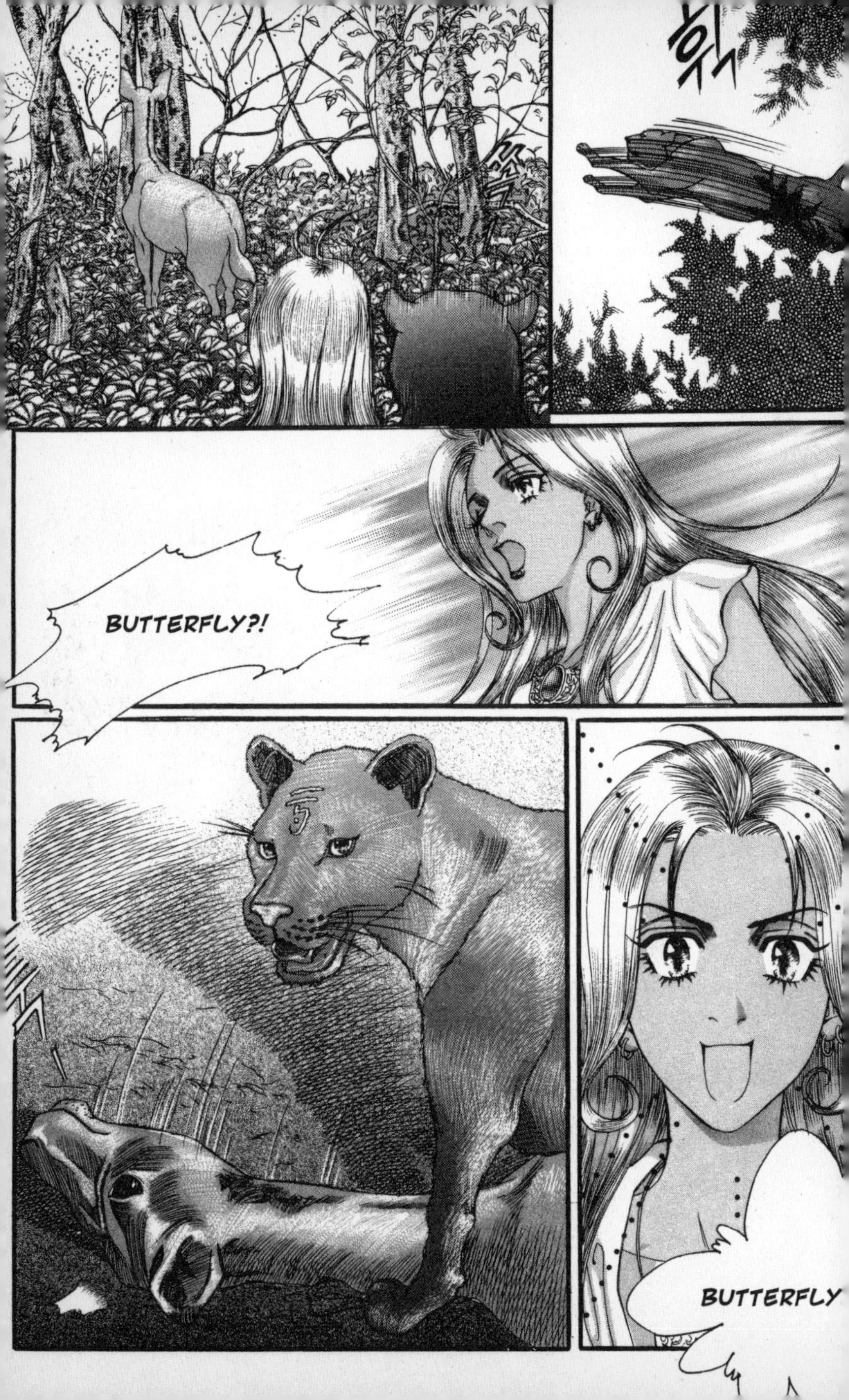
BUTTERFLY?!
BUTTERFLY

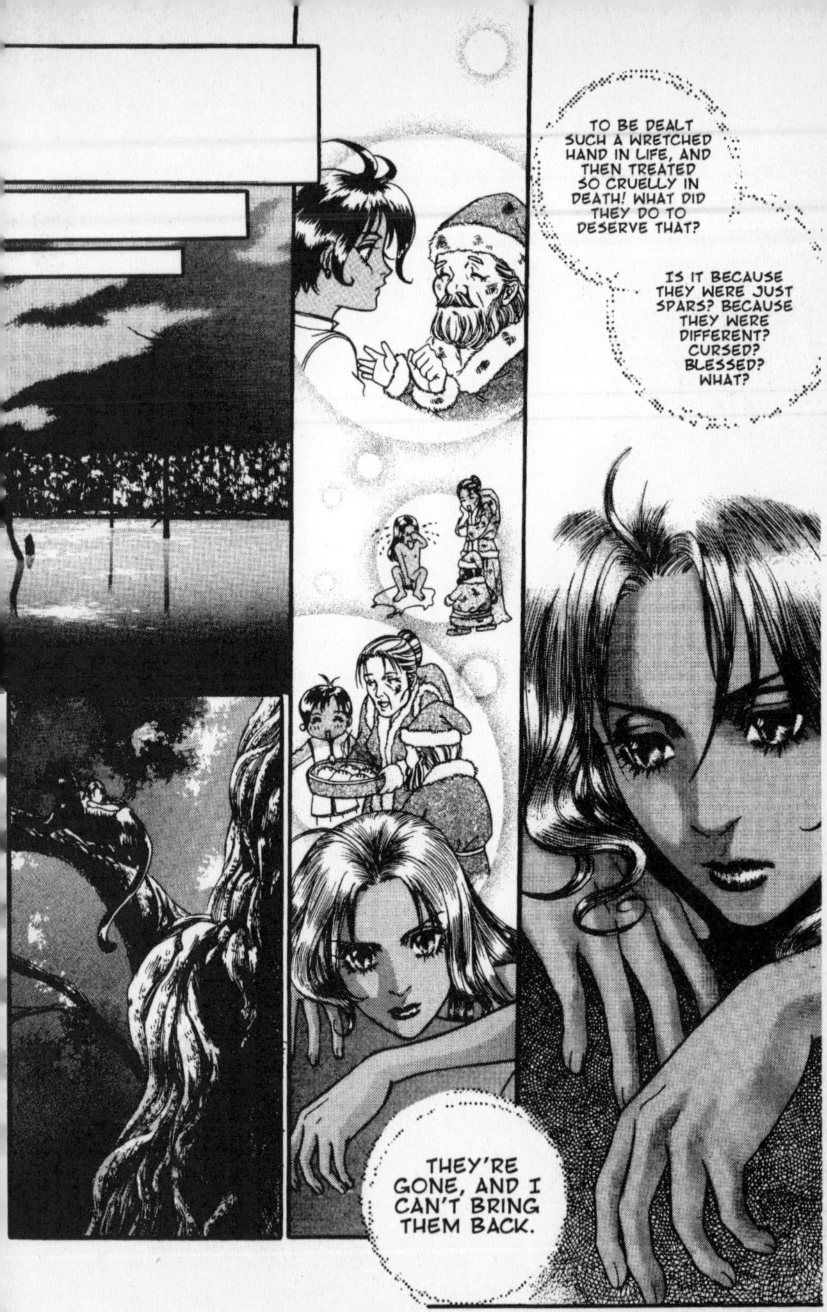
TO BE DEALT SUCH A WRETCHED HAND IN LIFE, AND THEN TREATED SO CRUELLY IN DEATH! WHAT DID THEY DO TO DESERVE THAT?
IS IT BECAUSE THEY WERE JUST SPARS? BECAUSE THEY WERE DIFFERENT? CURSED? BLESSED? WHAT?
THEY'RE GONE, AND I CAN'T BRING THEM BACK.

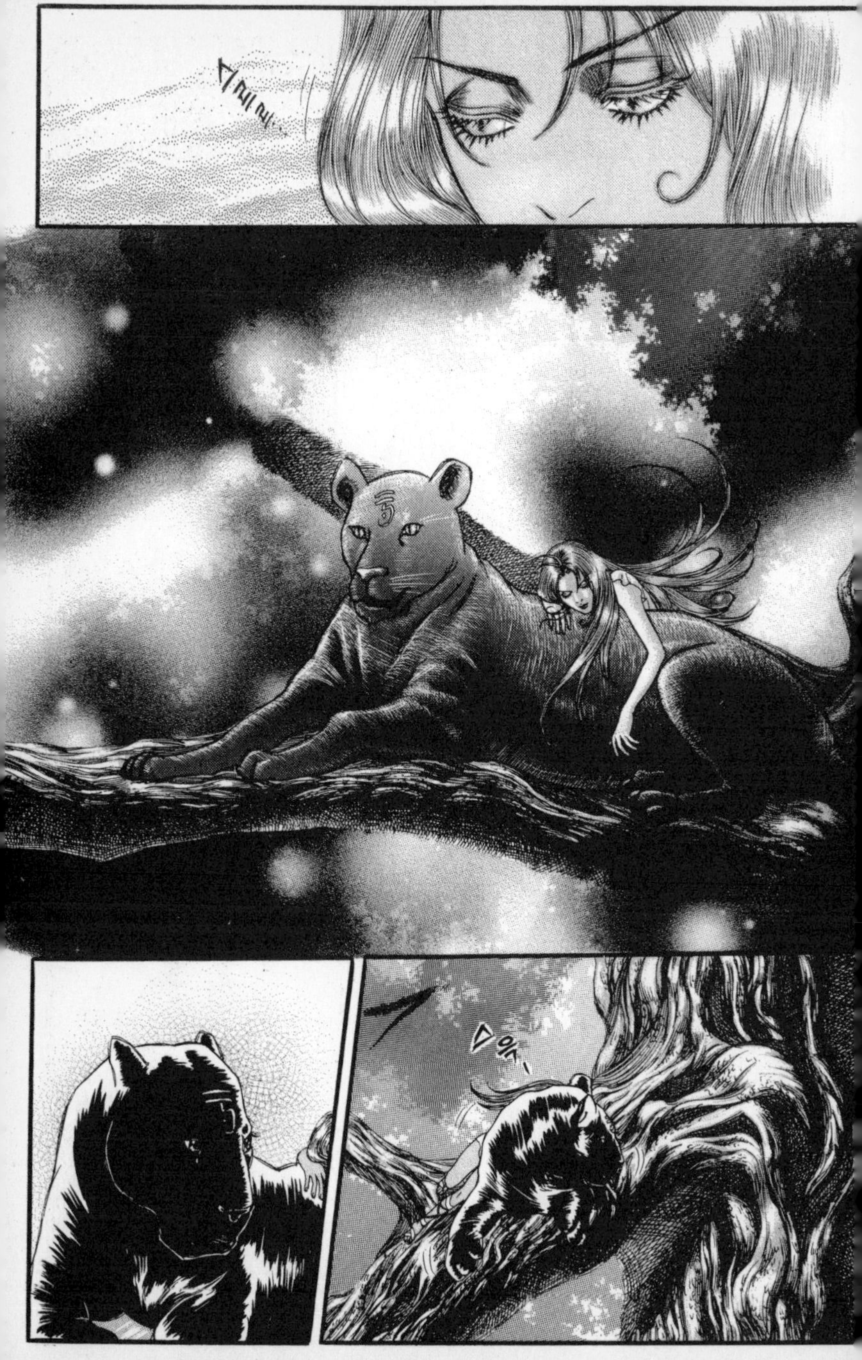

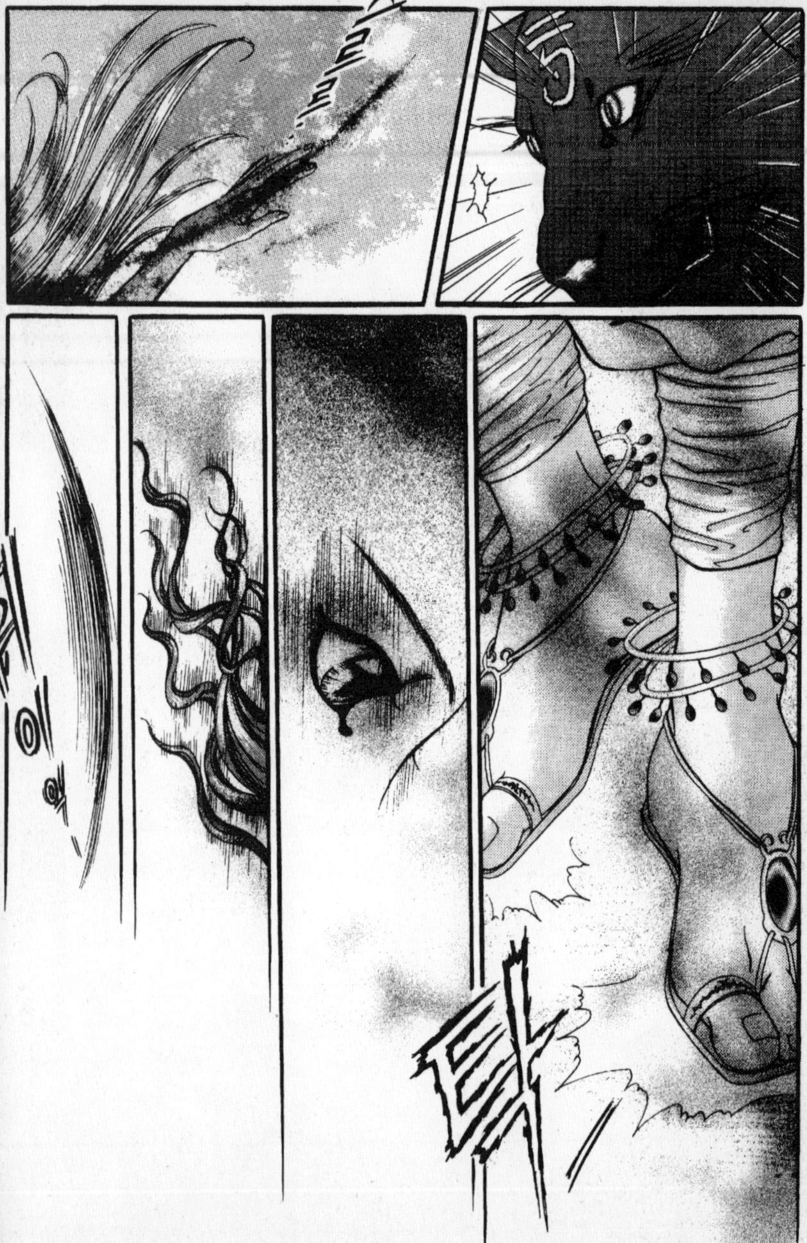
스르르...

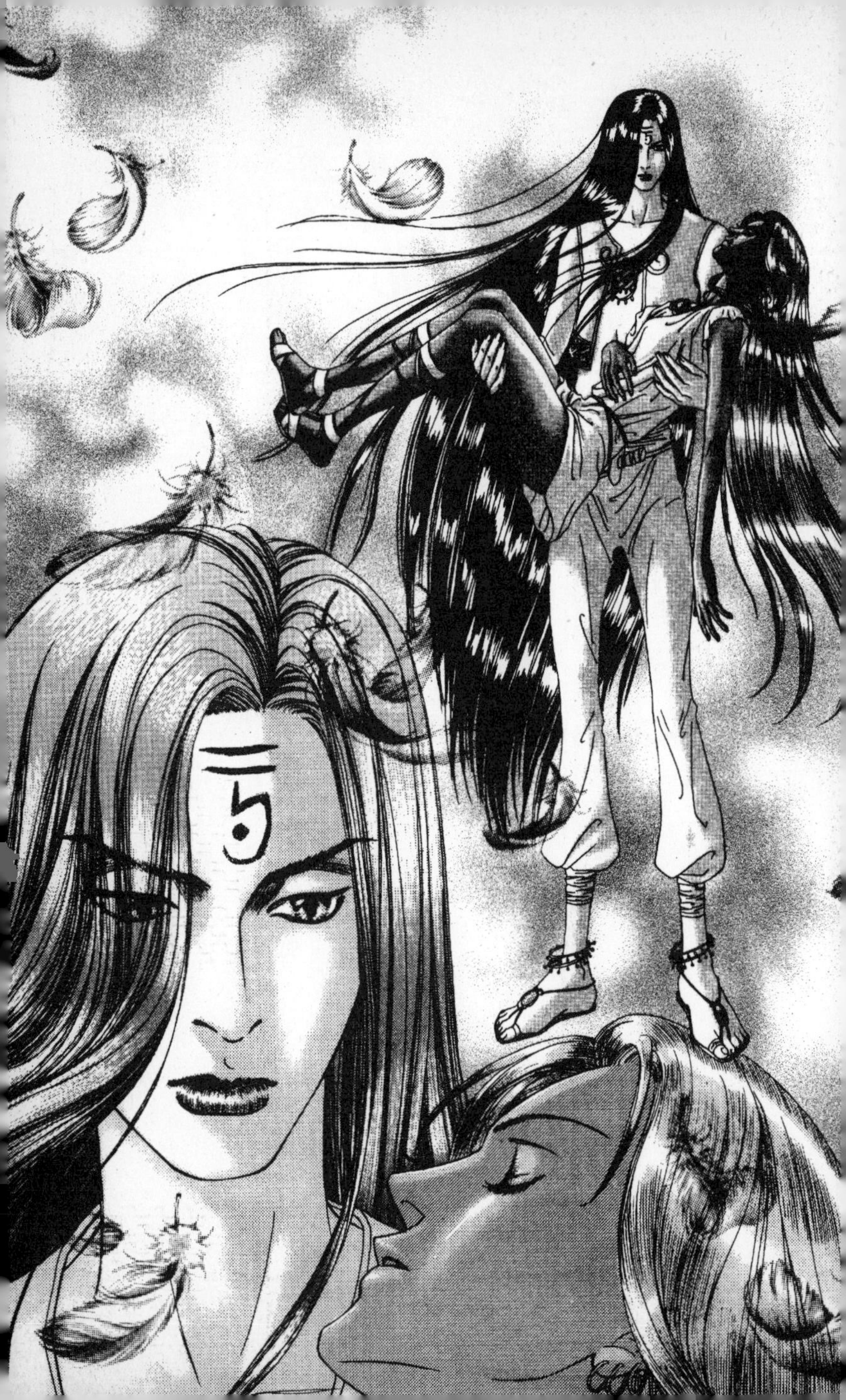

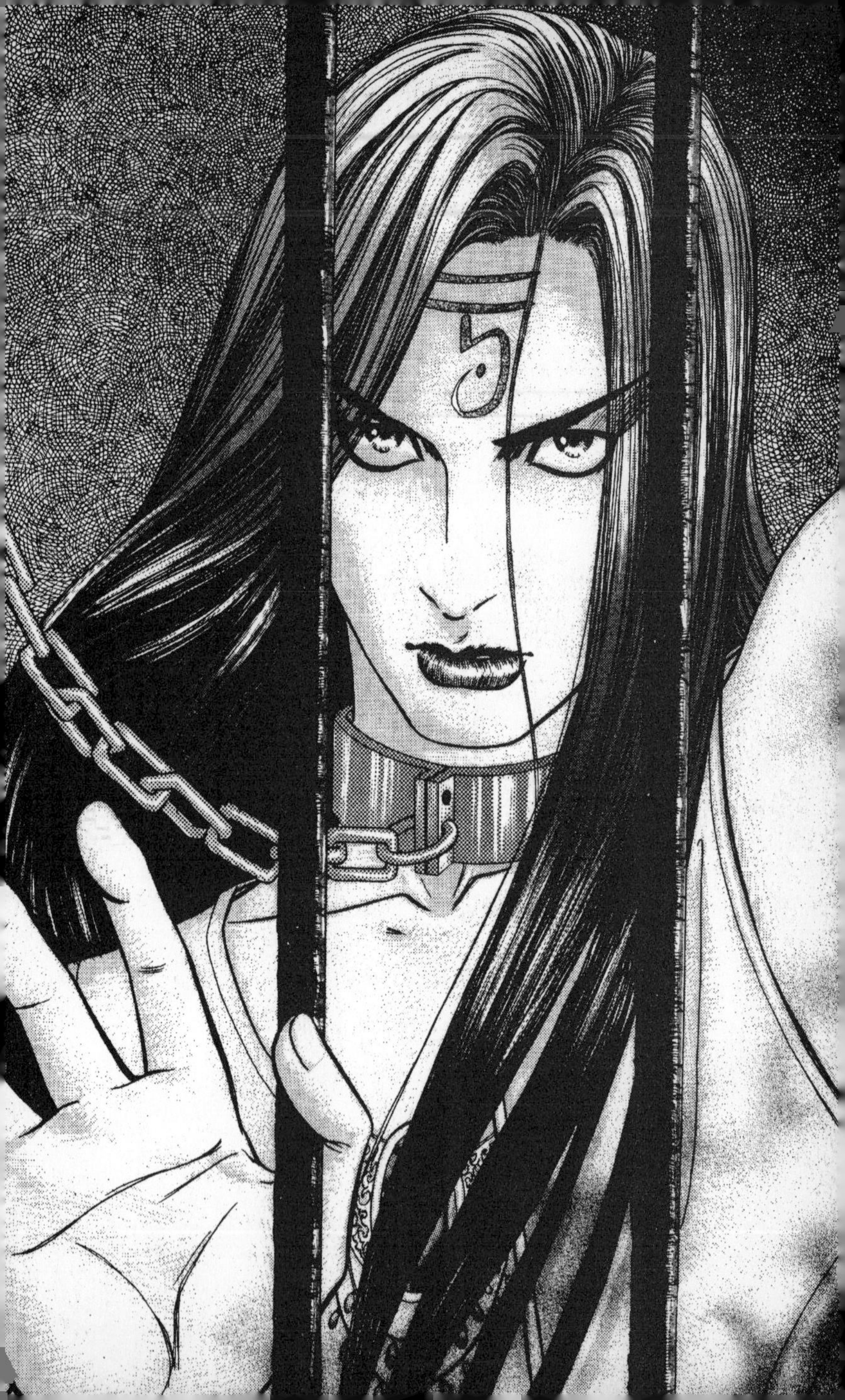

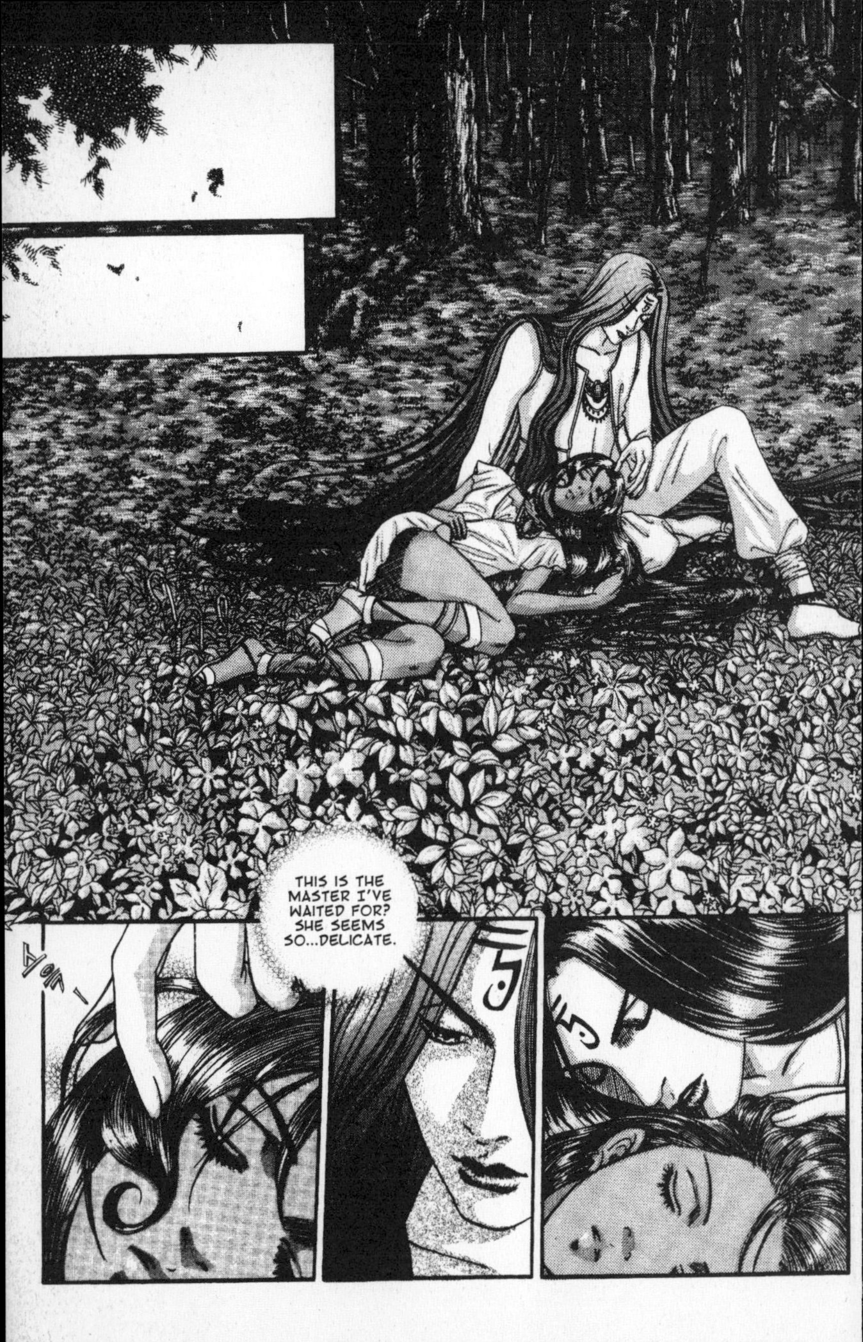
THIS IS THE MASTER I'VE WAITED FOR? SHE SEEMS SO...DELICATE.

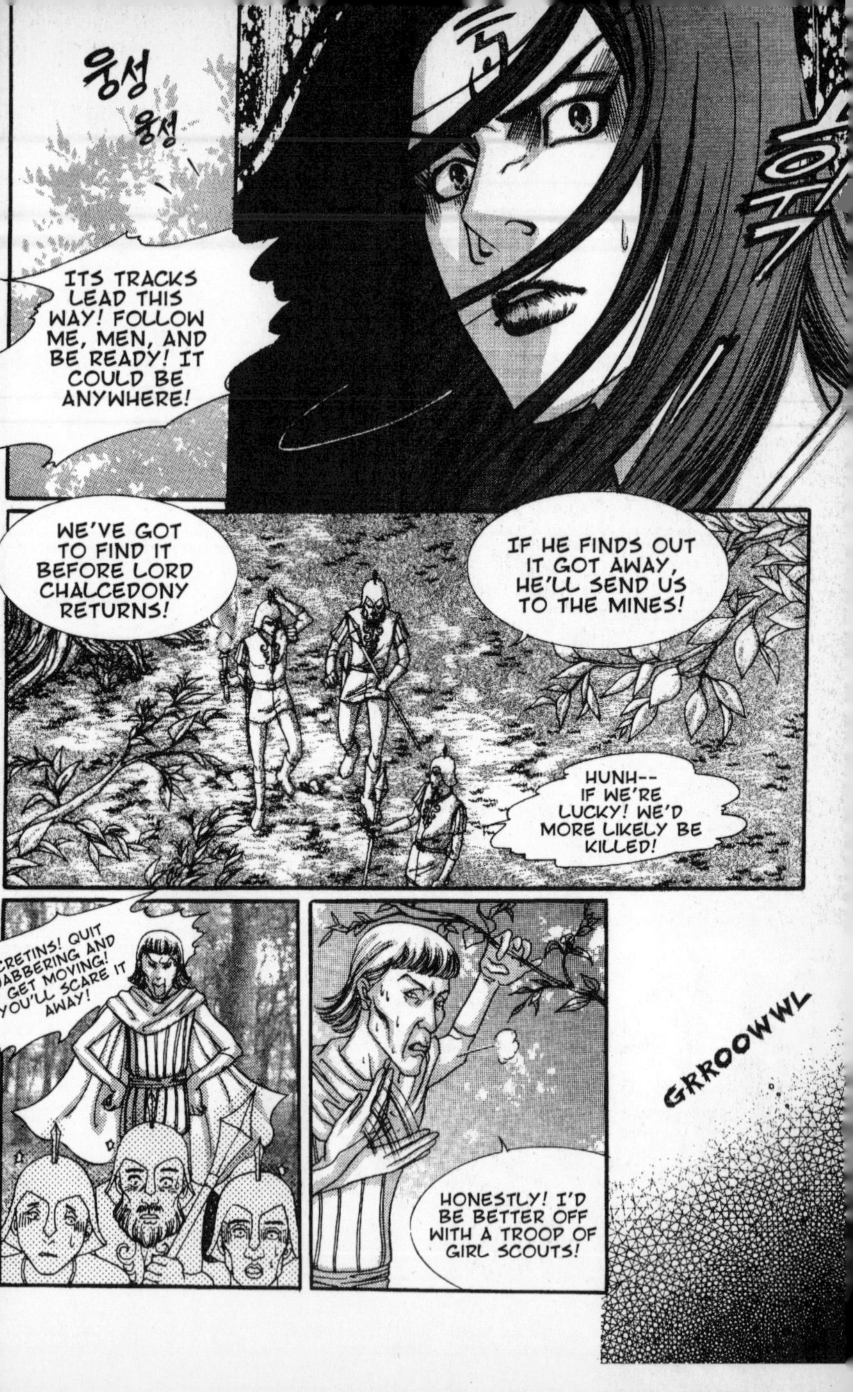
웅성
웅성
ITS TRACKS LEAD THIS WAY! FOLLOW ME, MEN, AND BE READY! IT COULD BE ANYWHERE!
WE'VE GOT TO FIND IT BEFORE LORD CHALCEDONY RETURNS!
IF HE FINDS OUT IT GOT AWAY, HE'LL SEND US TO THE MINES!
HUNH-- IF WE'RE LUCKY! WE'D MORE LIKELY BE KILLED!
CRETINS! QUIT JABBERING AND GET MOVING! YOU'LL SCARE IT AWAY!
HONESTLY! I'D BE BETTER OFF WITH A TROOP OF GIRL SCOUTS!
GRROOWWL

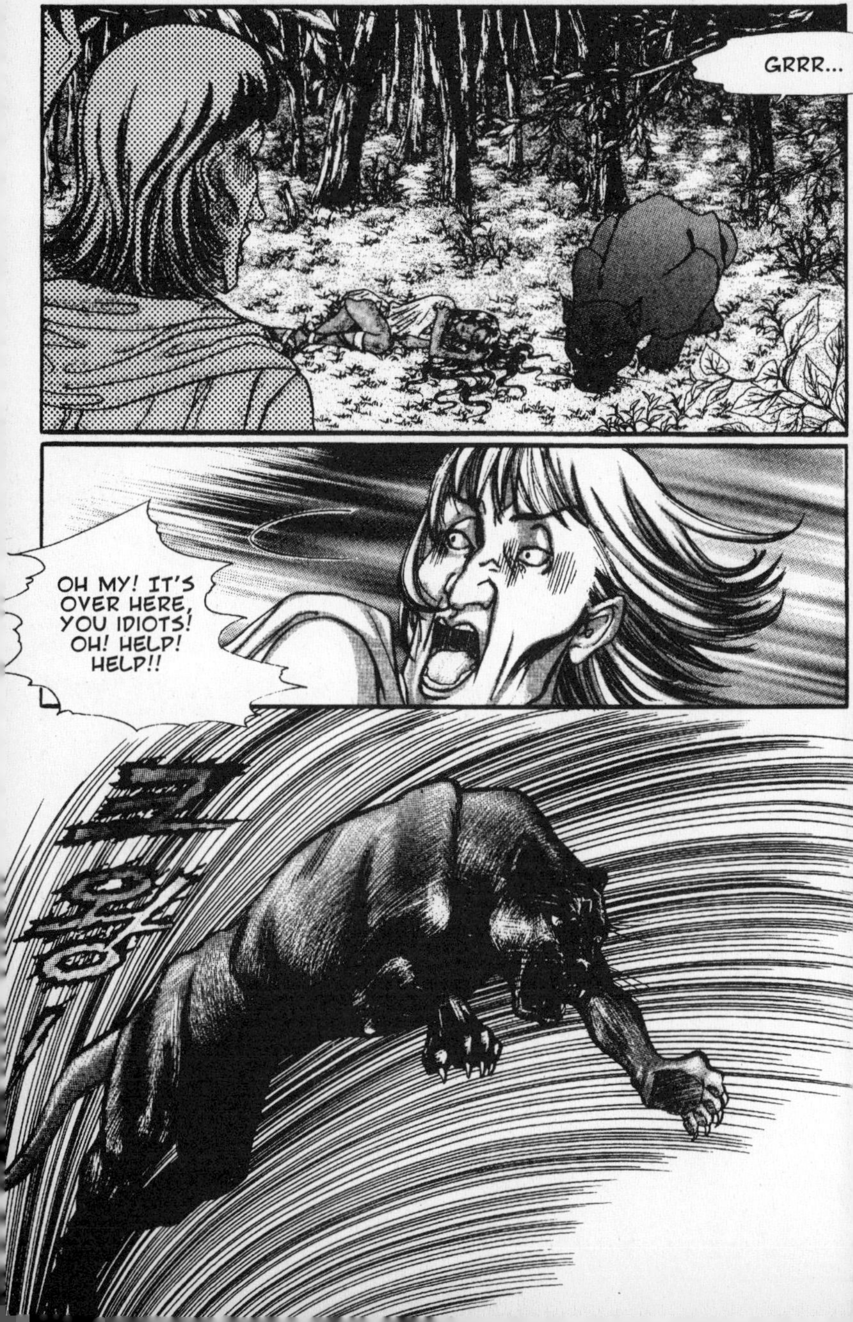
GRRR...
OH MY! IT'S OVER HERE, YOU IDIOTS! OH! HELP! HELP!!

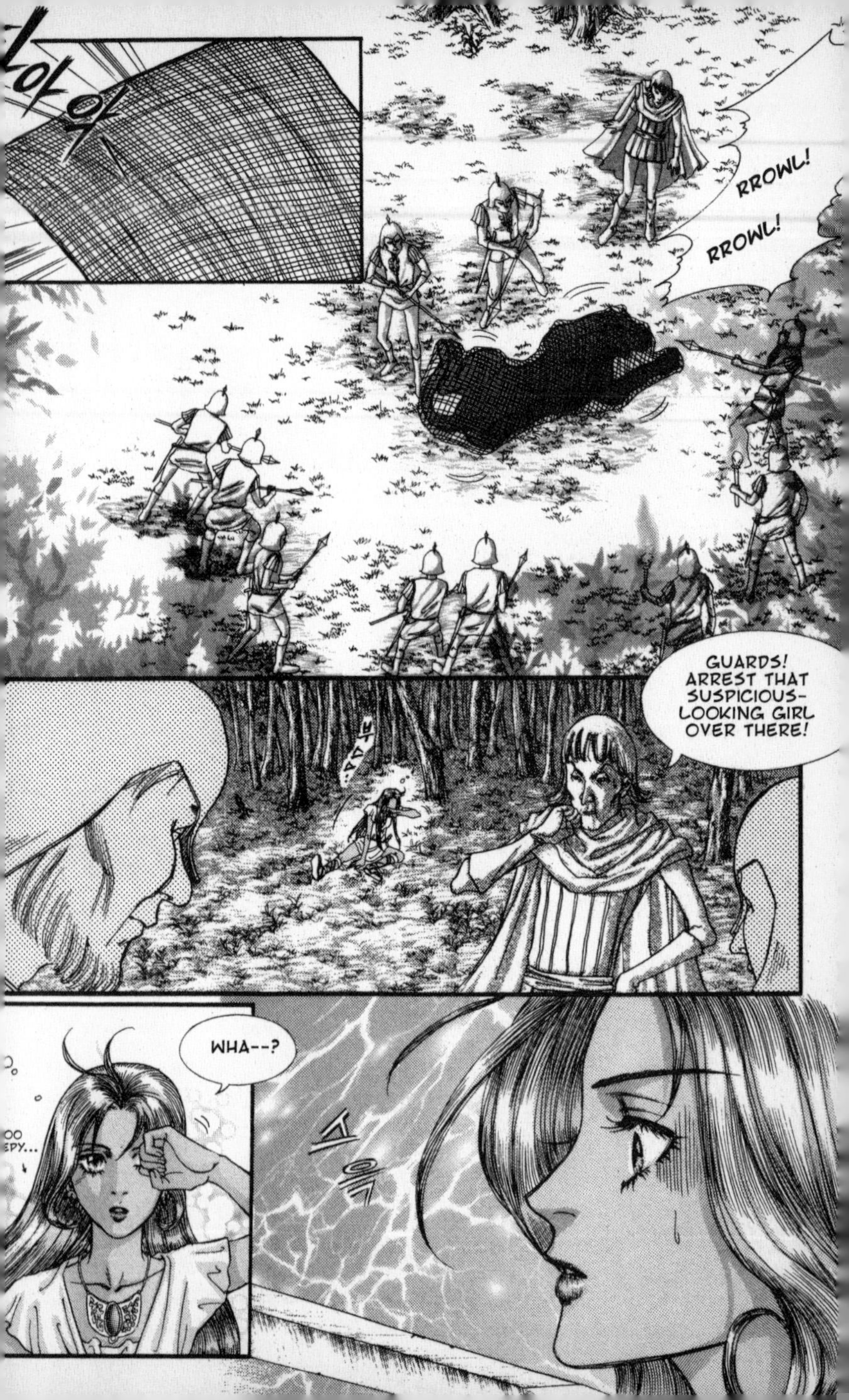
RROWL!
RROWL!
GUARDS! ARREST THAT SUSPICIOUS-LOOKING GIRL OVER THERE!
WHA--?

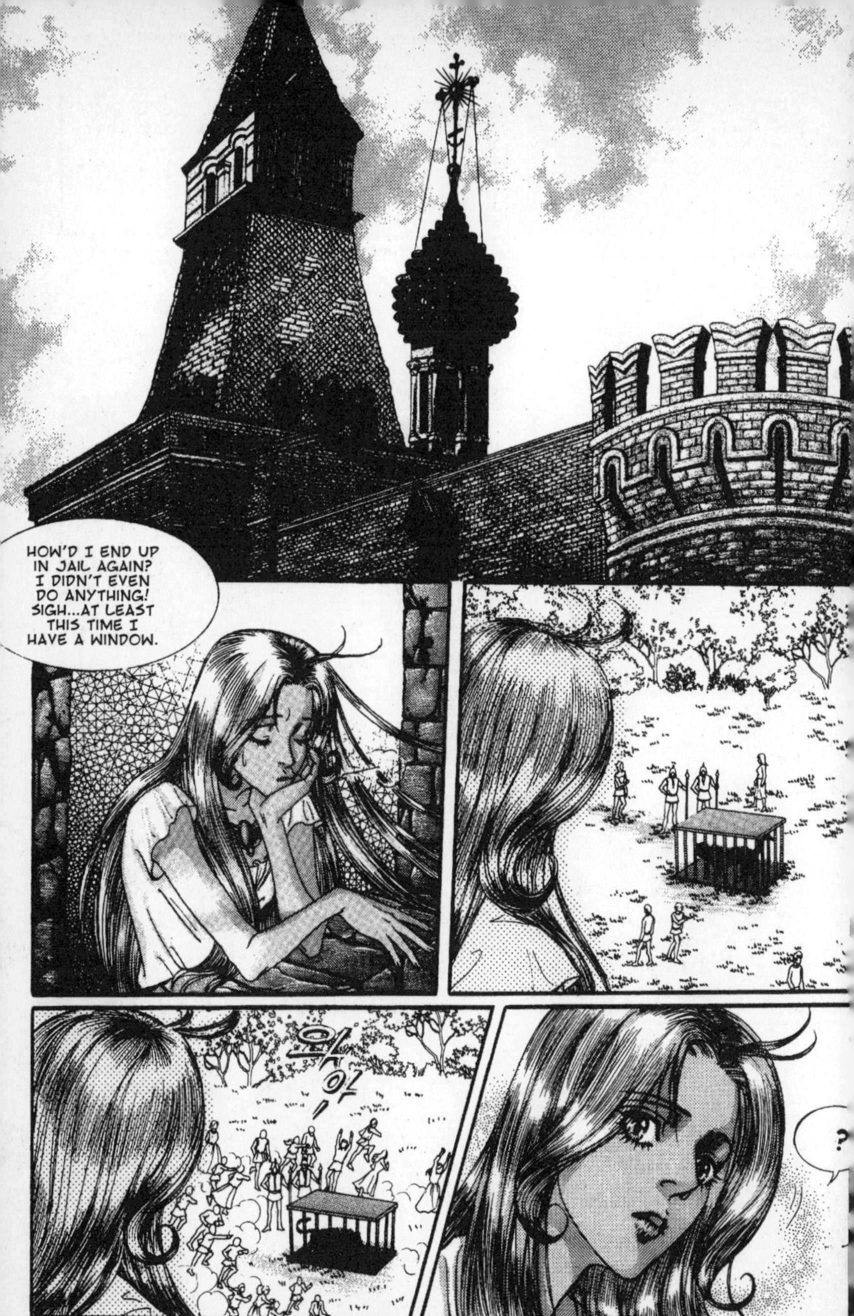
HOW'D I END UP IN JAIL AGAIN? I DIDN'T EVEN DO ANYTHING! SIGH...AT LEAST THIS TIME I HAVE A WINDOW.
와아!
?

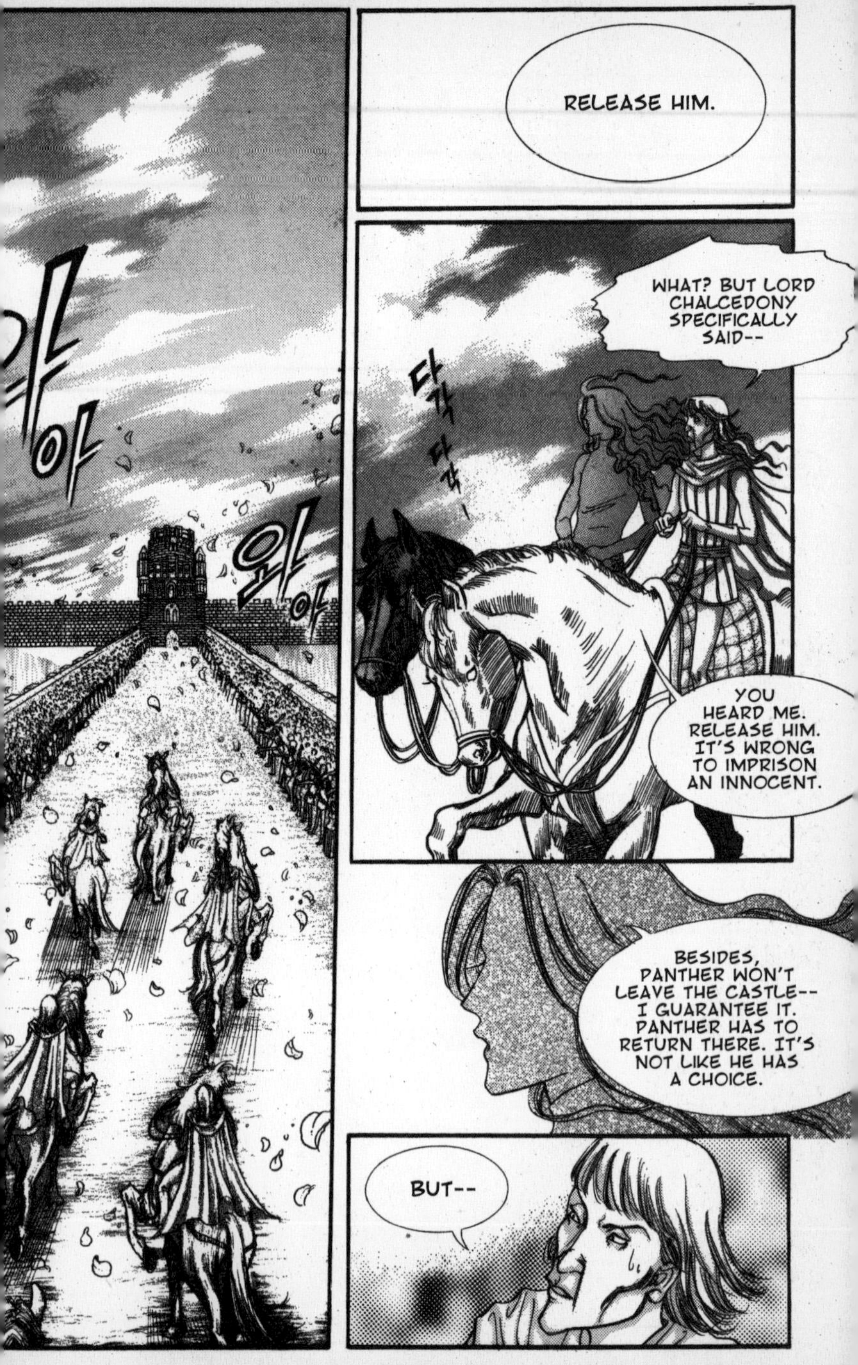
와아
RELEASE HIM.
다각 다각
WHAT? BUT LORD CHALCEDONY SPECIFICALLY SAID--
YOU HEARD ME. RELEASE HIM. IT'S WRONG TO IMPRISON AN INNOCENT.
BESIDES, PANTHER WON'T LEAVE THE CASTLE-- I GUARANTEE IT. PANTHER HAS TO RETURN THERE. IT'S NOT LIKE HE HAS A CHOICE.
BUT--

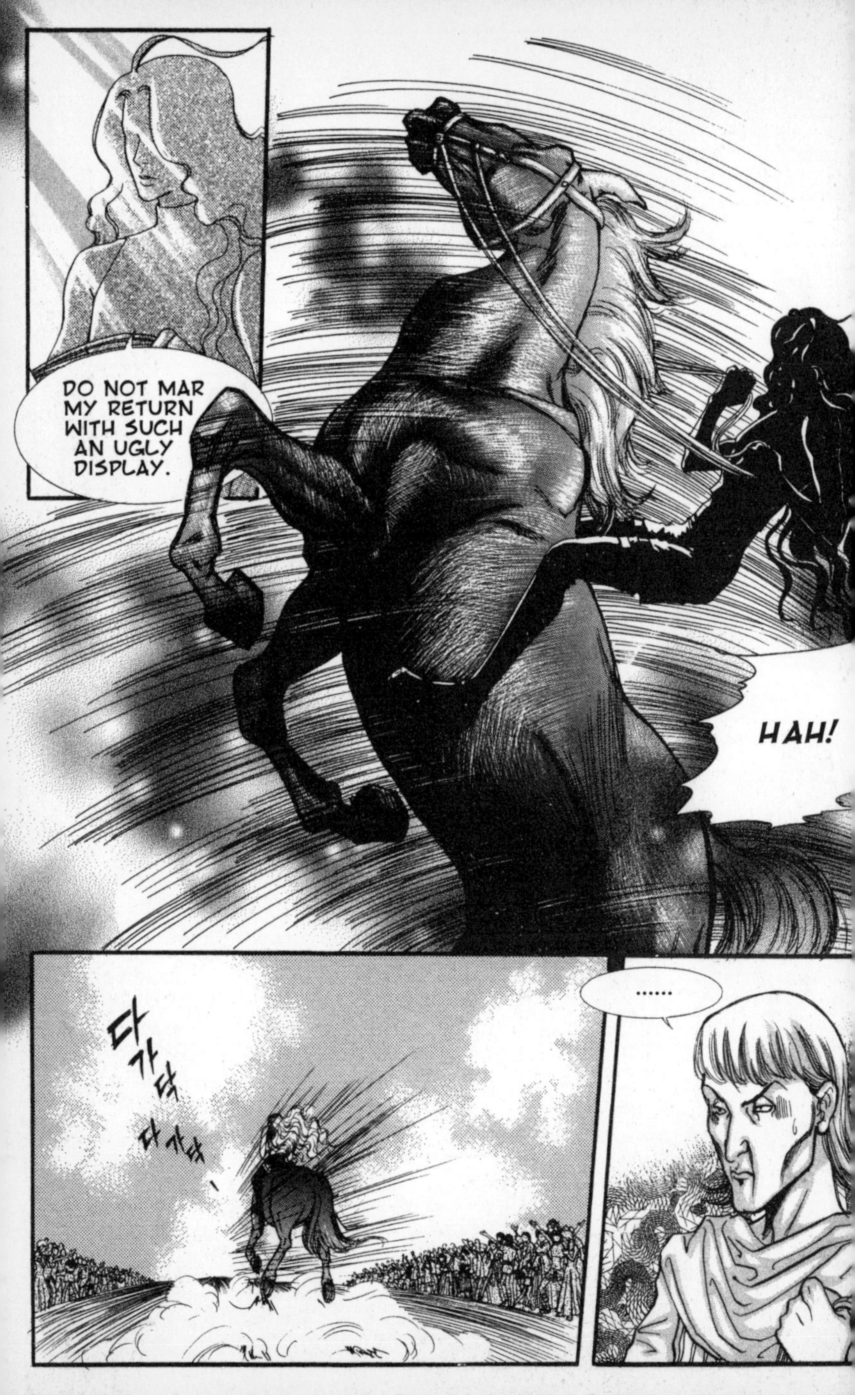
DO NOT MAR MY RETURN WITH SUCH AN UGLY DISPLAY.
HAH!
다가닥
다가닥
....

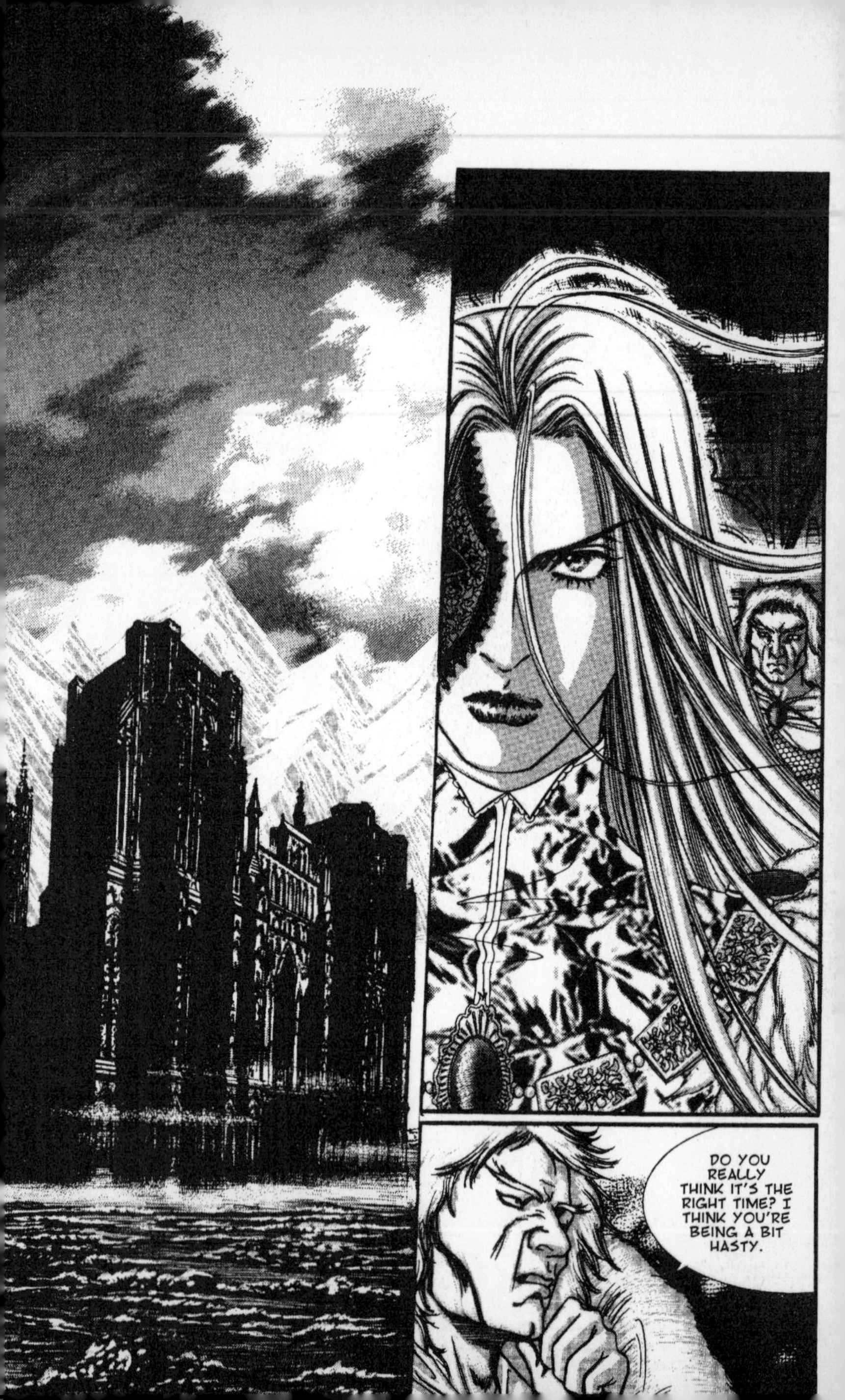
DO YOU REALLY THINK IT'S THE RIGHT TIME? I THINK YOU'RE BEING A BIT HASTY.

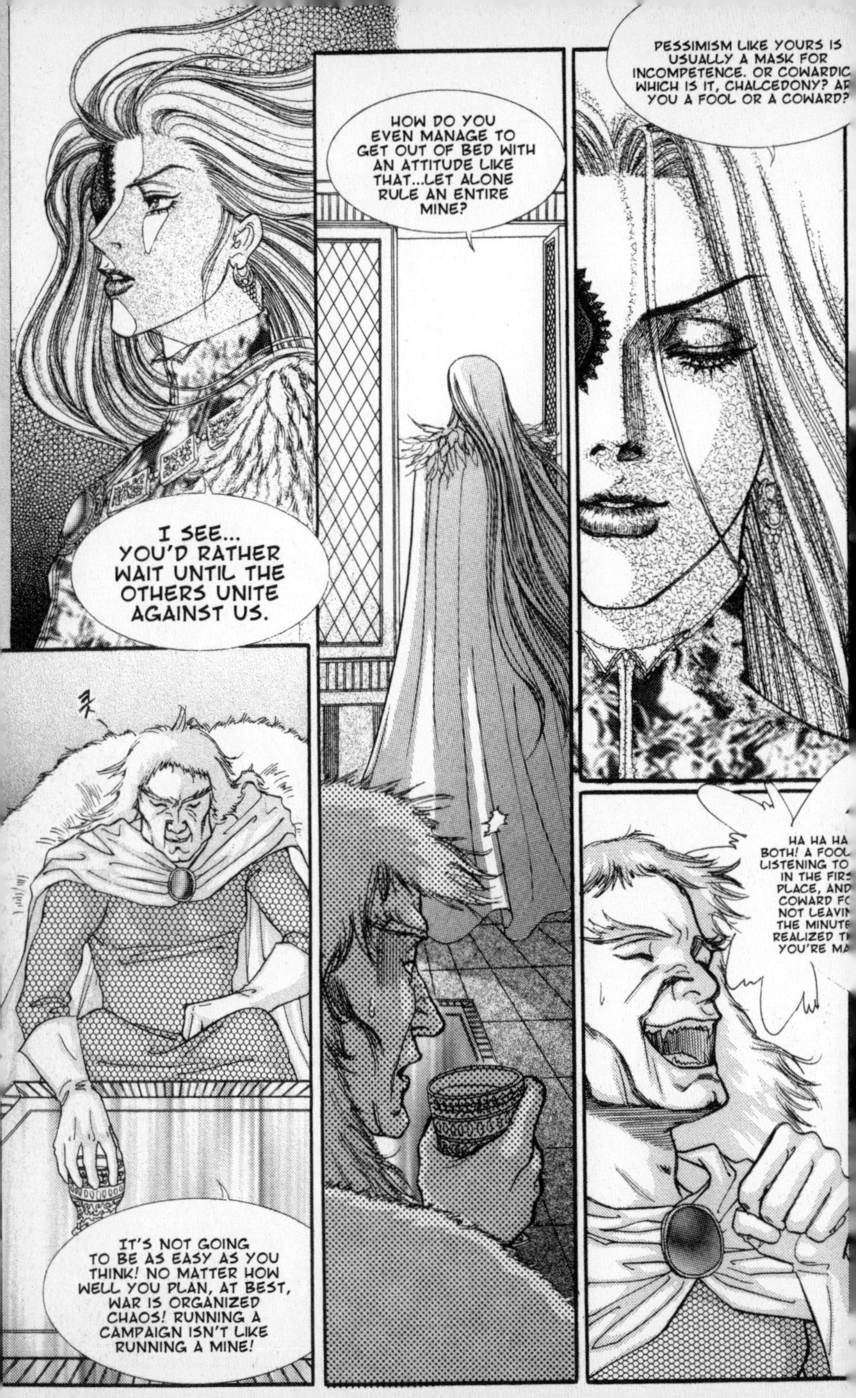
I SEE... YOU'D RATHER WAIT UNTIL THE OTHERS UNITE AGAINST US.
IT'S NOT GOING TO BE AS EASY AS YOU THINK! NO MATTER HOW WELL YOU PLAN, AT BEST, WAR IS ORGANIZED CHAOS! RUNNING A CAMPAIGN ISN'T LIKE RUNNING A MINE!
HOW DO YOU EVEN MANAGE TO GET OUT OF BED WITH AN ATTITUDE LIKE THAT...LET ALONE RULE AN ENTIRE MINE?
PESSIMISM LIKE YOURS IS USUALLY A MASK FOR INCOMPETENCE. OR COWARDIC WHICH IS IT, CHALCEDONY? AR YOU A FOOL OR A COWARD?
HA HA HA BOTH! A FOOL LISTENING TO IN THE FIRS PLACE, AND COWARD FO NOT LEAVIN THE MINUTE REALIZED T YOU'RE MA

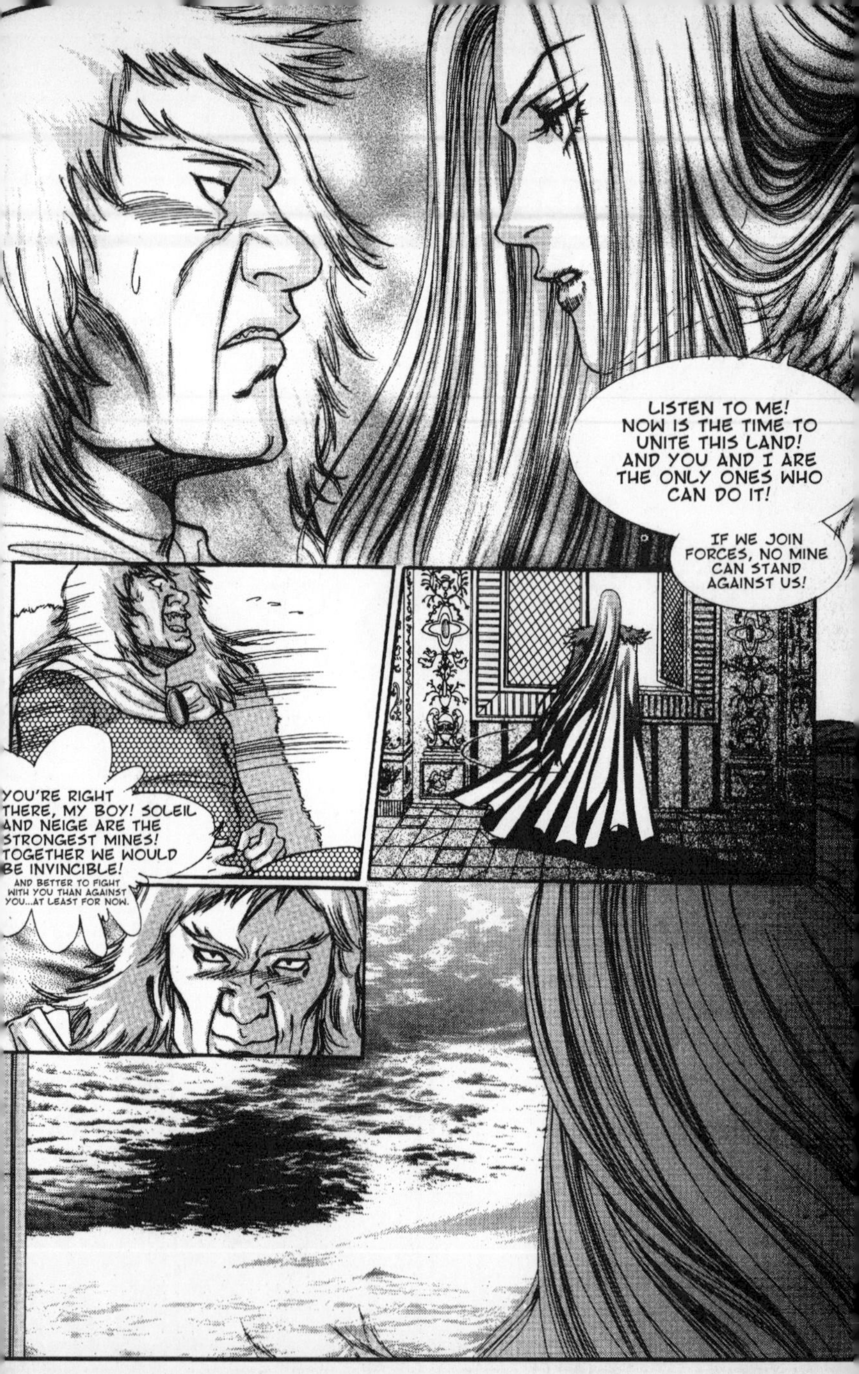
LISTEN TO ME! NOW IS THE TIME TO UNITE THIS LAND! AND YOU AND I ARE THE ONLY ONES WHO CAN DO IT!
IF WE JOIN FORCES, NO MINE CAN STAND AGAINST US!
YOU'RE RIGHT THERE, MY BOY! SOLEIL AND NEIGE ARE THE STRONGEST MINES! TOGETHER WE WOULD BE INVINCIBLE!
AND BETTER TO FIGHT WITH YOU THAN AGAINST YOU...AT LEAST FOR NOW.

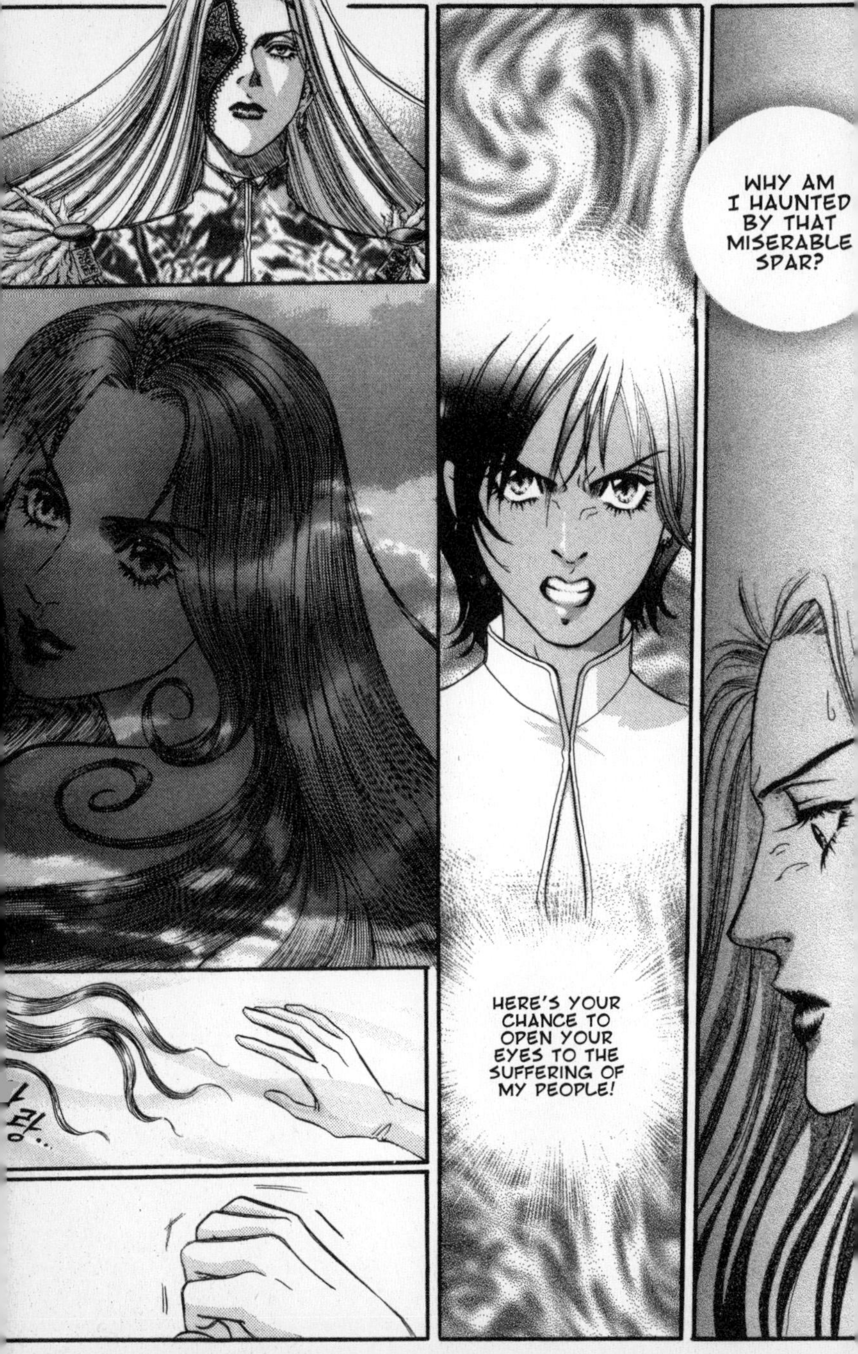
HERE'S YOUR CHANCE TO OPEN YOUR EYES TO THE SUFFERING OF MY PEOPLE!
WHY AM I HAUNTED BY THAT MISERABLE SPAR?

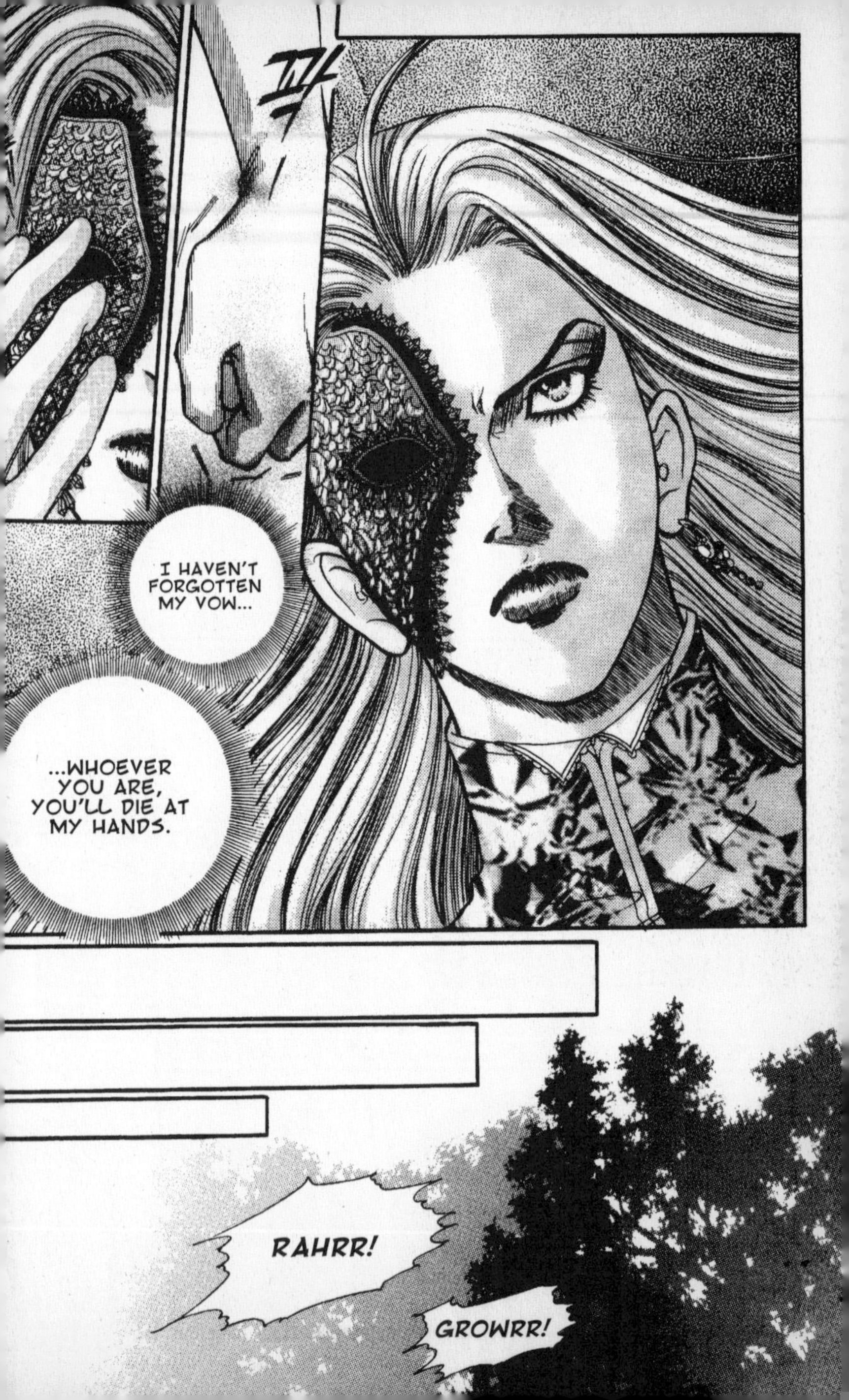
I HAVEN'T FORGOTTEN MY VOW...
...WHOEVER YOU ARE, YOU'LL DIE AT MY HANDS.
RAHRR!
GROWRR!

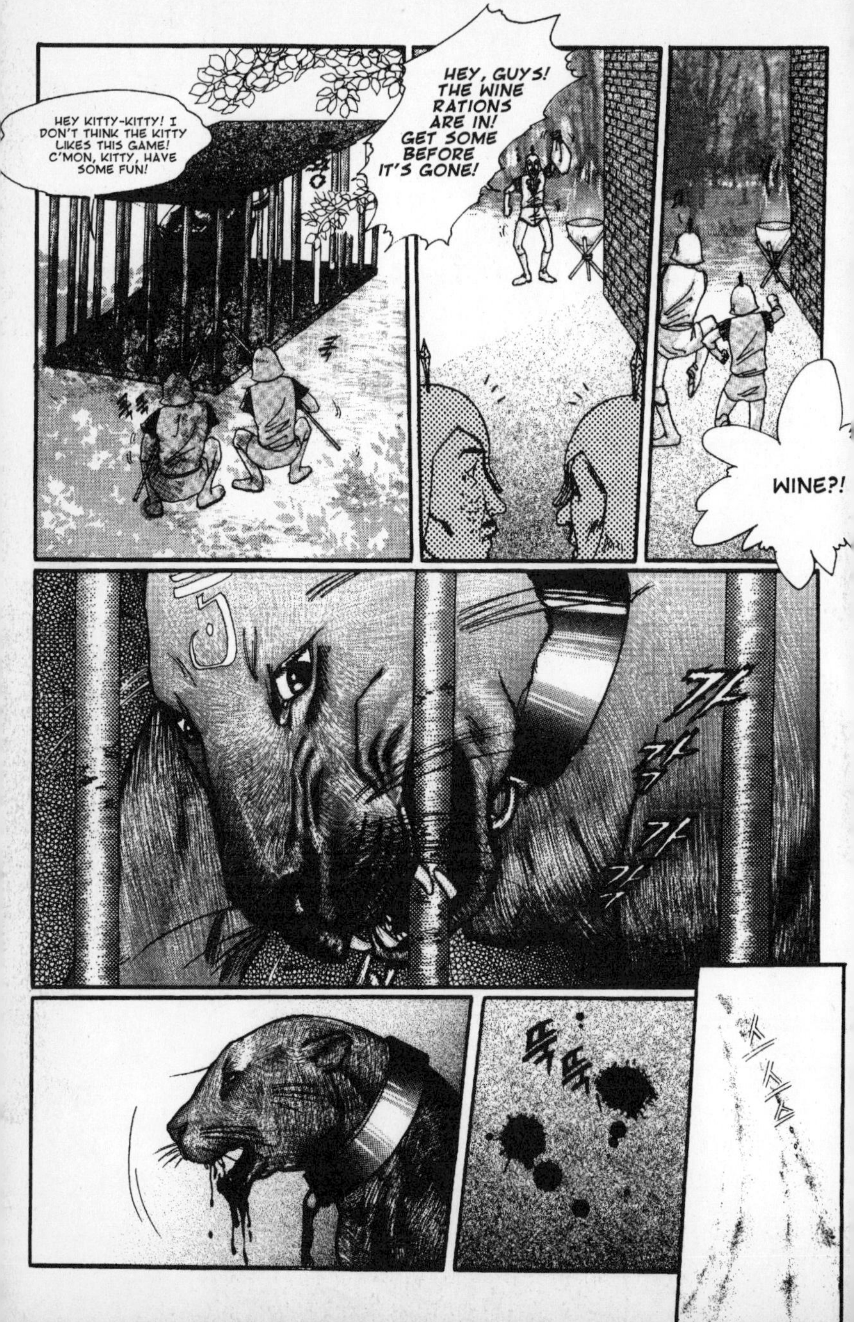
HEY KITTY-KITTY! I DON'T THINK THE KITTY LIKES THIS GAME! C'MON, KITTY, HAVE SOME FUN!
HEY, GUYS! THE WINE RATIONS ARE IN! GET SOME BEFORE IT'S GONE!
WINE?!

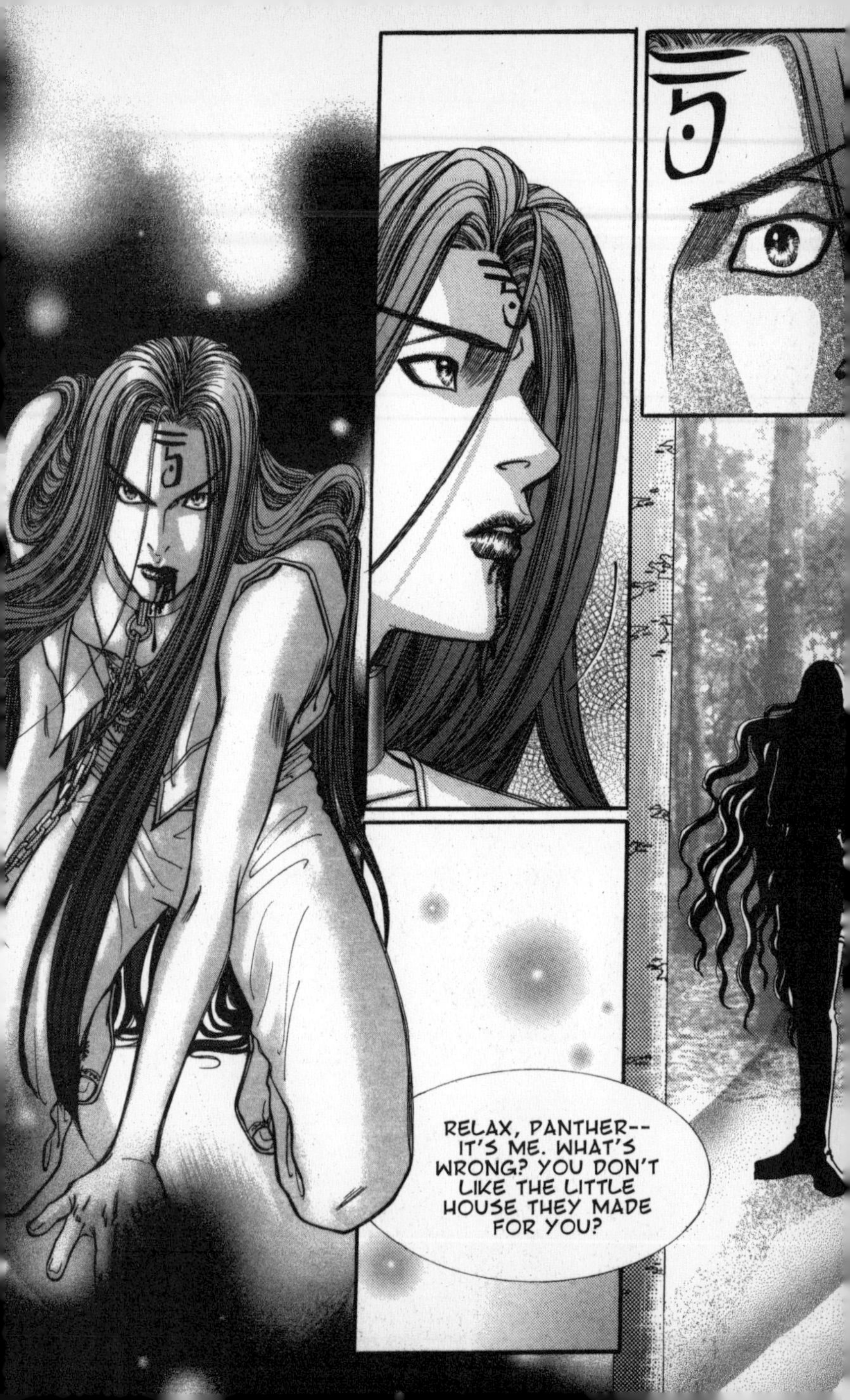
RELAX, PANTHER-- IT'S ME. WHAT'S WRONG? YOU DON'T LIKE THE LITTLE HOUSE THEY MADE FOR YOU?

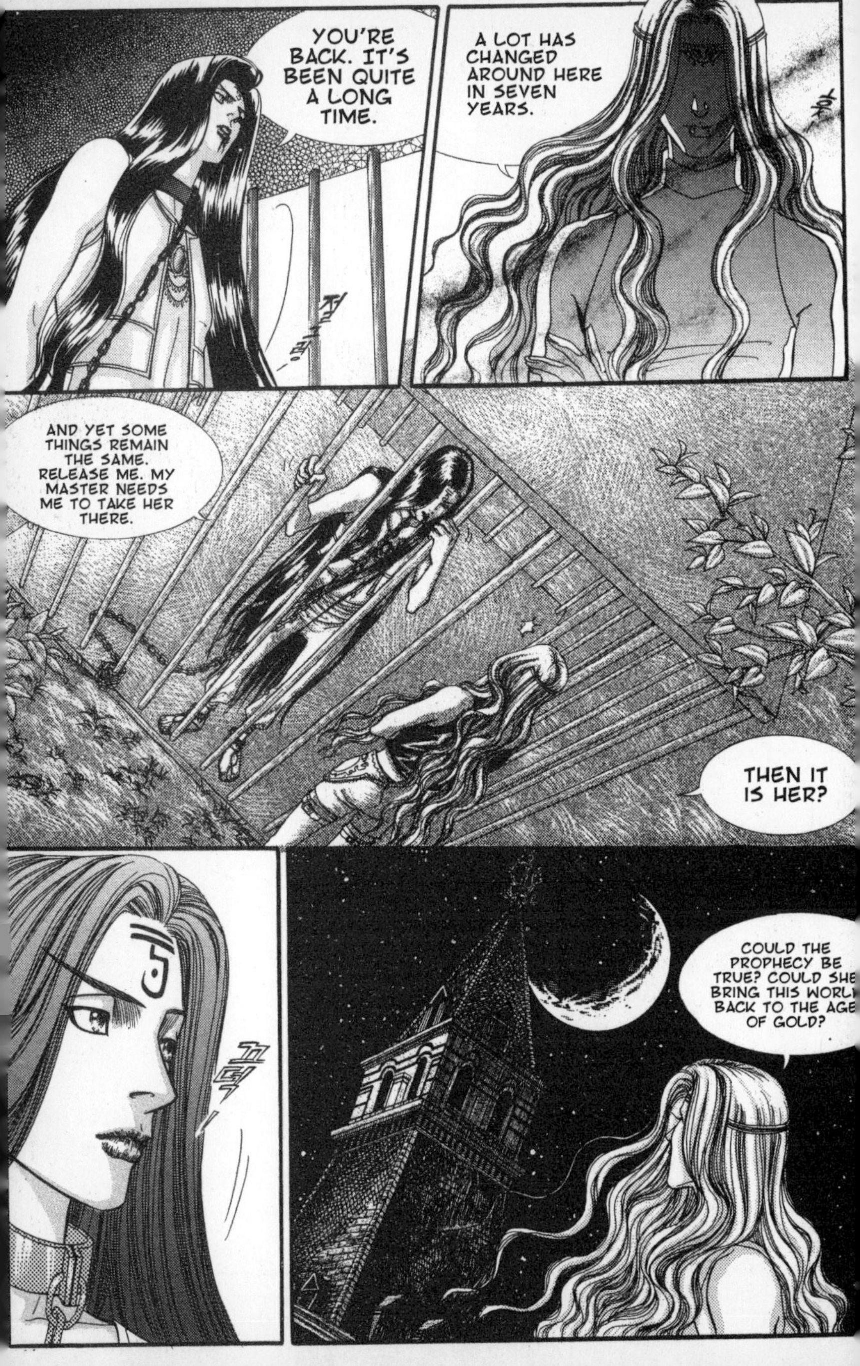
YOU'RE BACK. IT'S BEEN QUITE A LONG TIME.
A LOT HAS CHANGED AROUND HERE IN SEVEN YEARS.
AND YET SOME THINGS REMAIN THE SAME. RELEASE ME. MY MASTER NEEDS ME TO TAKE HER THERE.
THEN IT IS HER?
COULD THE PROPHECY BE TRUE? COULD SHE BRING THIS WORLD BACK TO THE AGE OF GOLD?

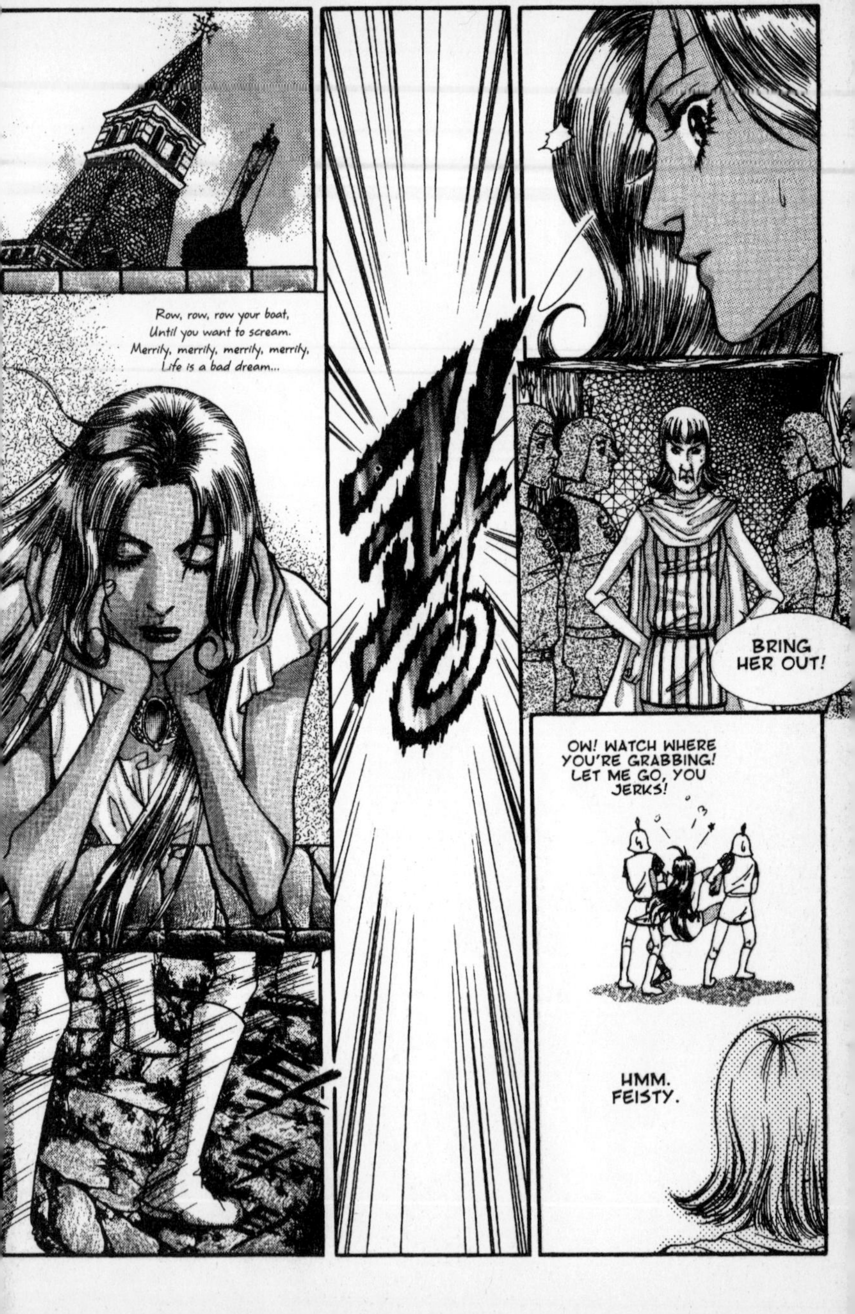
Row, row, row your boat,
Until you want to scream.
Merrily, merrily, merrily, merrily,
Life is a bad dream...
BRING HER OUT!
OW! WATCH WHERE YOU'RE GRABBING! LET ME GO, YOU JERKS!
HMM. FEISTY.

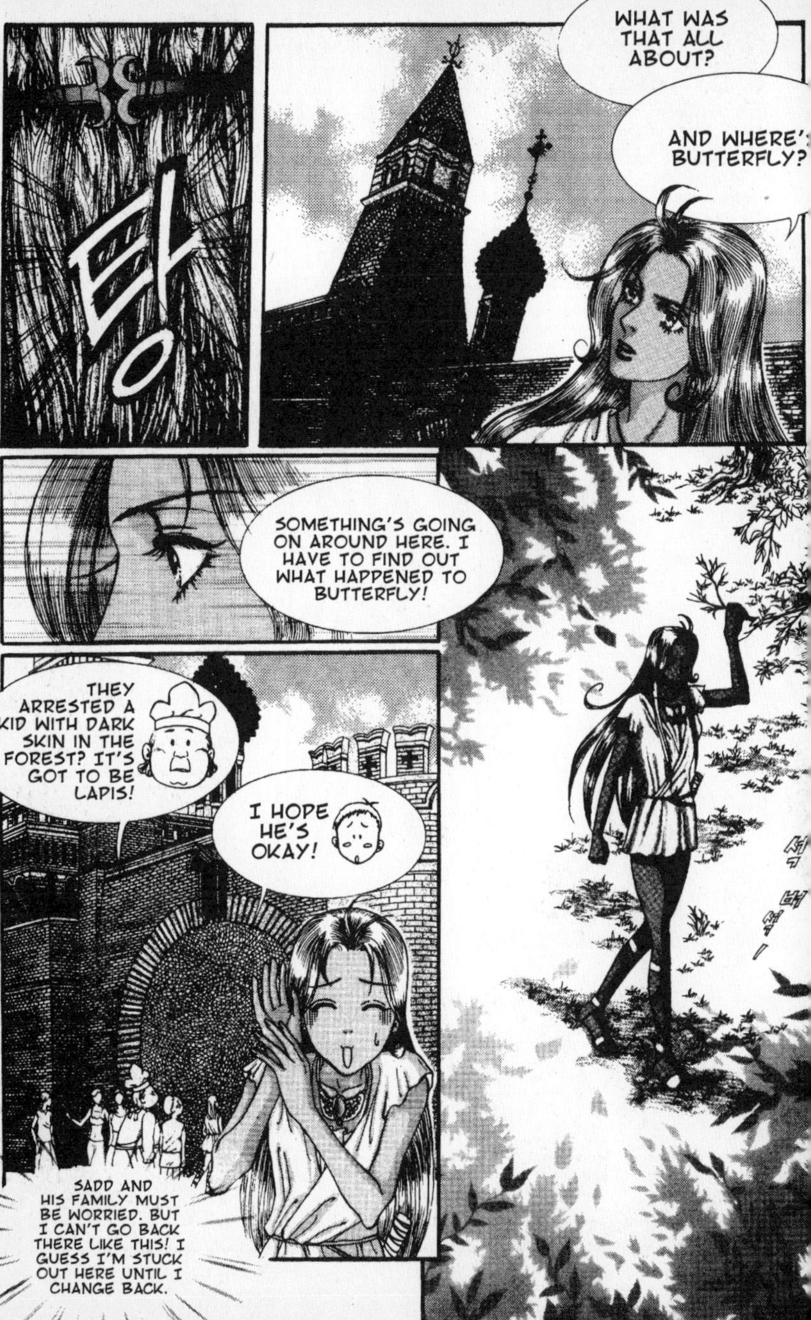
WHAT WAS THAT ALL ABOUT?
AND WHERE'S BUTTERFLY?
SOMETHING'S GOING ON AROUND HERE. I HAVE TO FIND OUT WHAT HAPPENED TO BUTTERFLY!
THEY ARRESTED A KID WITH DARK SKIN IN THE FOREST? IT'S GOT TO BE LAPIS!
I HOPE HE'S OKAY!
SADD AND HIS FAMILY MUST BE WORRIED. BUT I CAN'T GO BACK THERE LIKE THIS! I GUESS I'M STUCK OUT HERE UNTIL I CHANGE BACK.

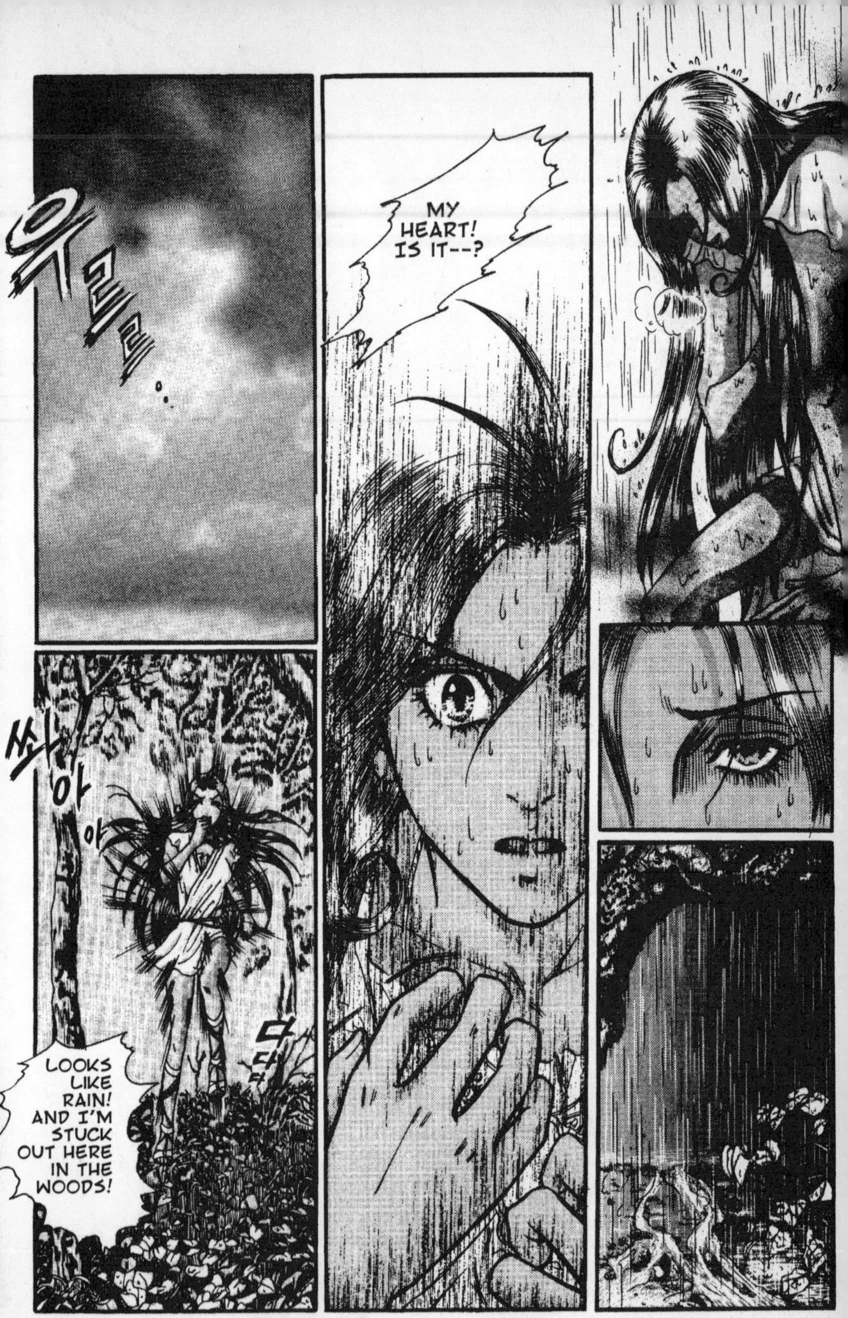
우르릉
쏴아아
LOOKS LIKE RAIN! AND I'M STUCK OUT HERE IN THE WOODS!
MY HEART! IS IT--?

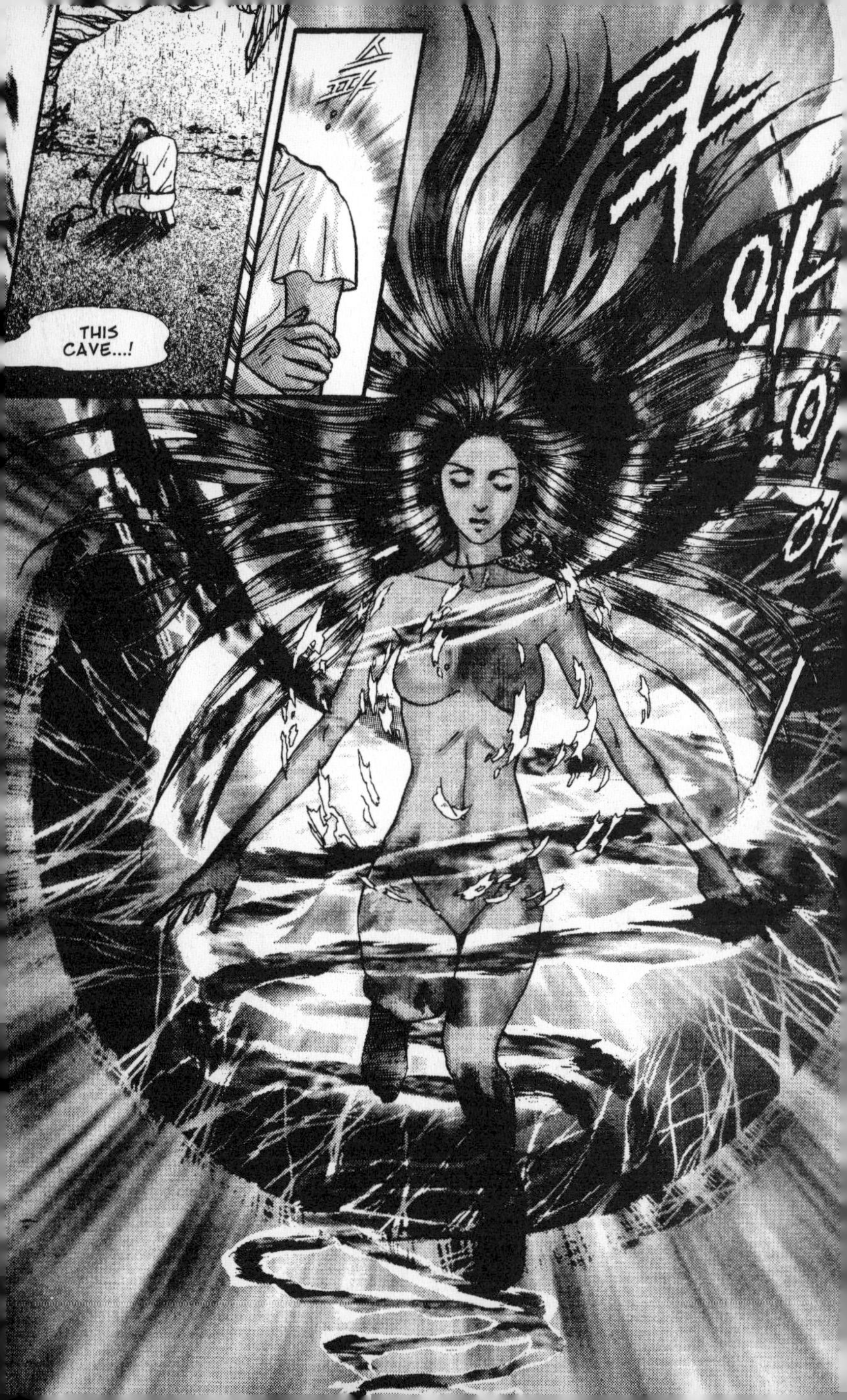
THIS CAVE...!

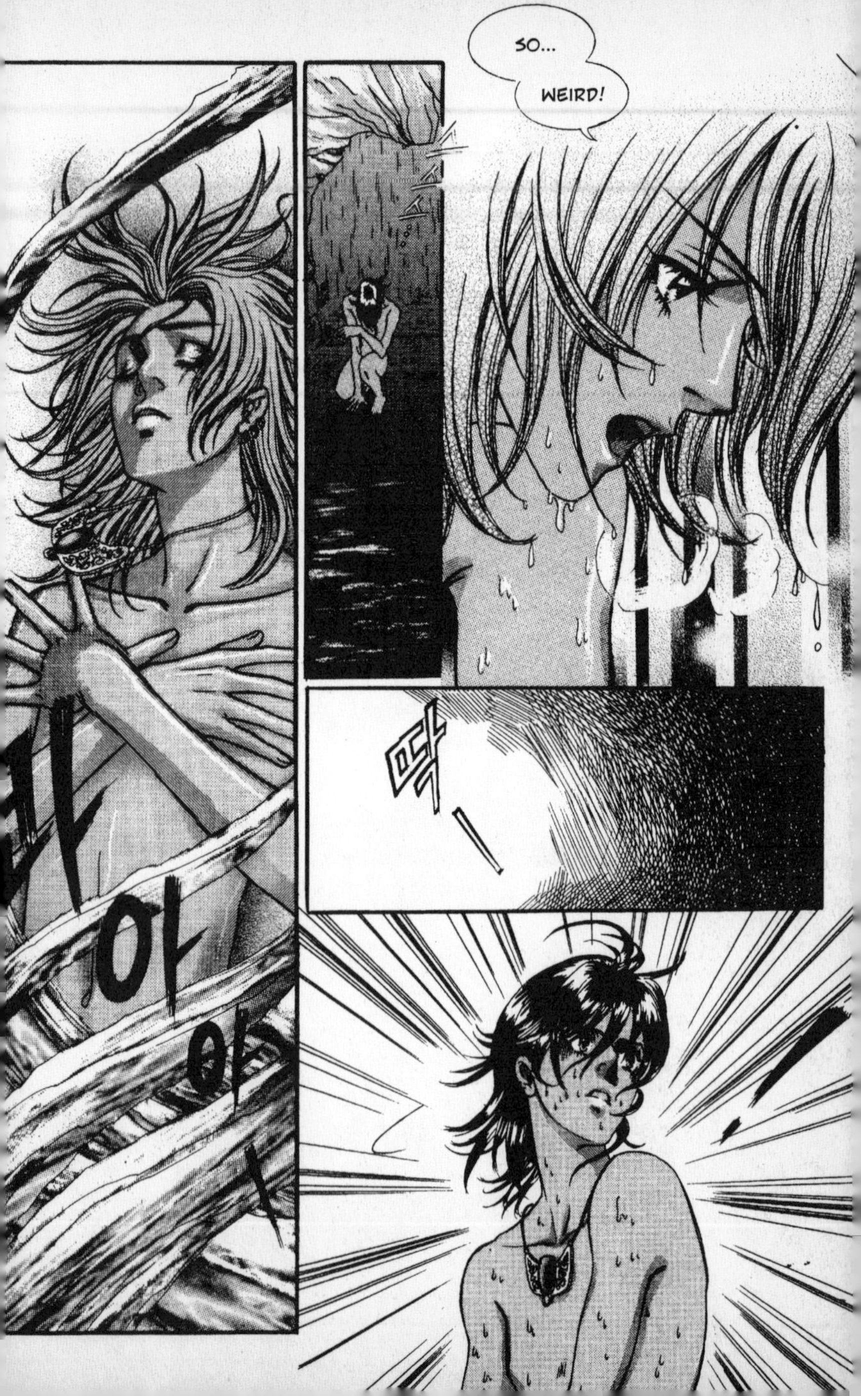
SO... WEIRD!

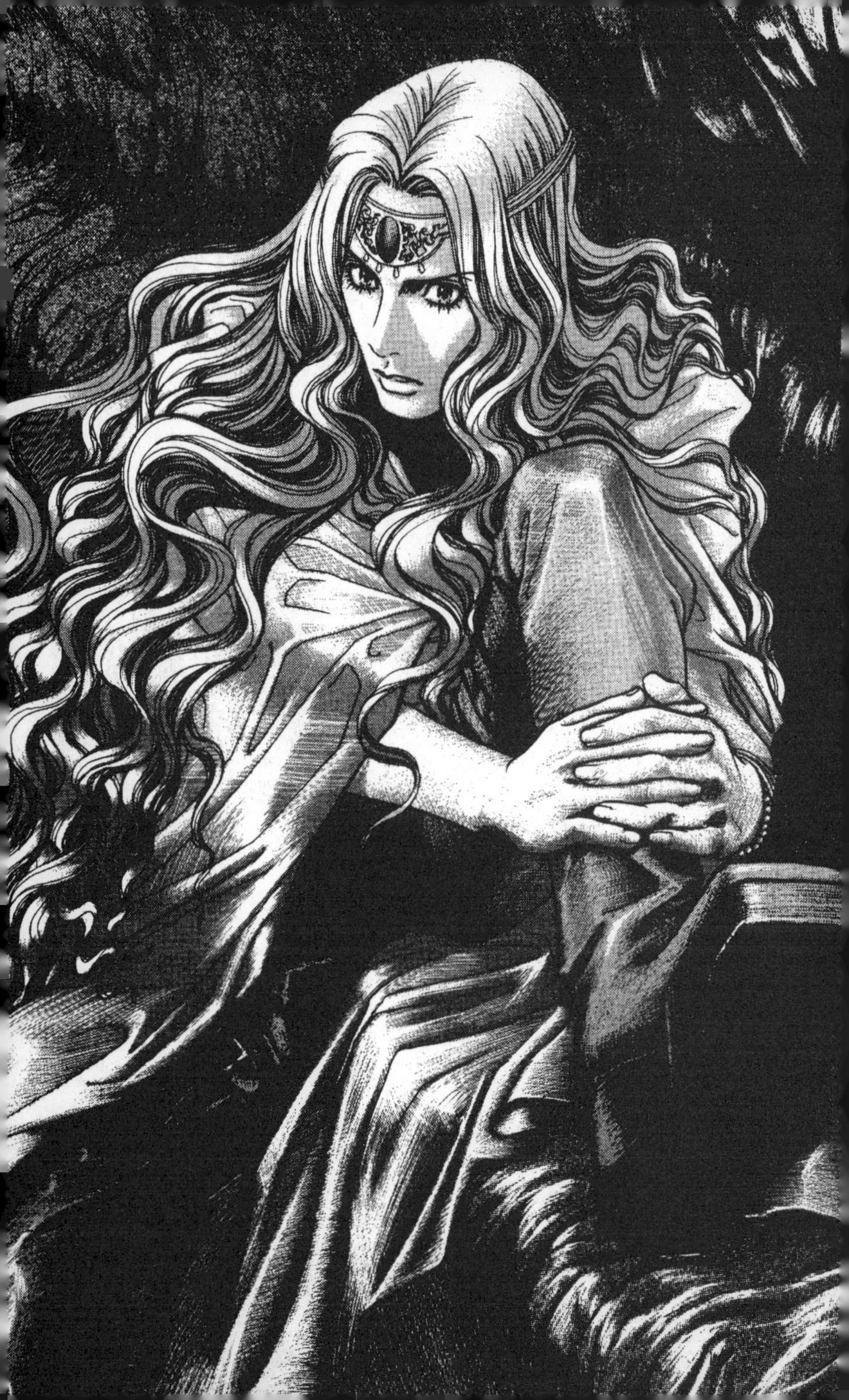

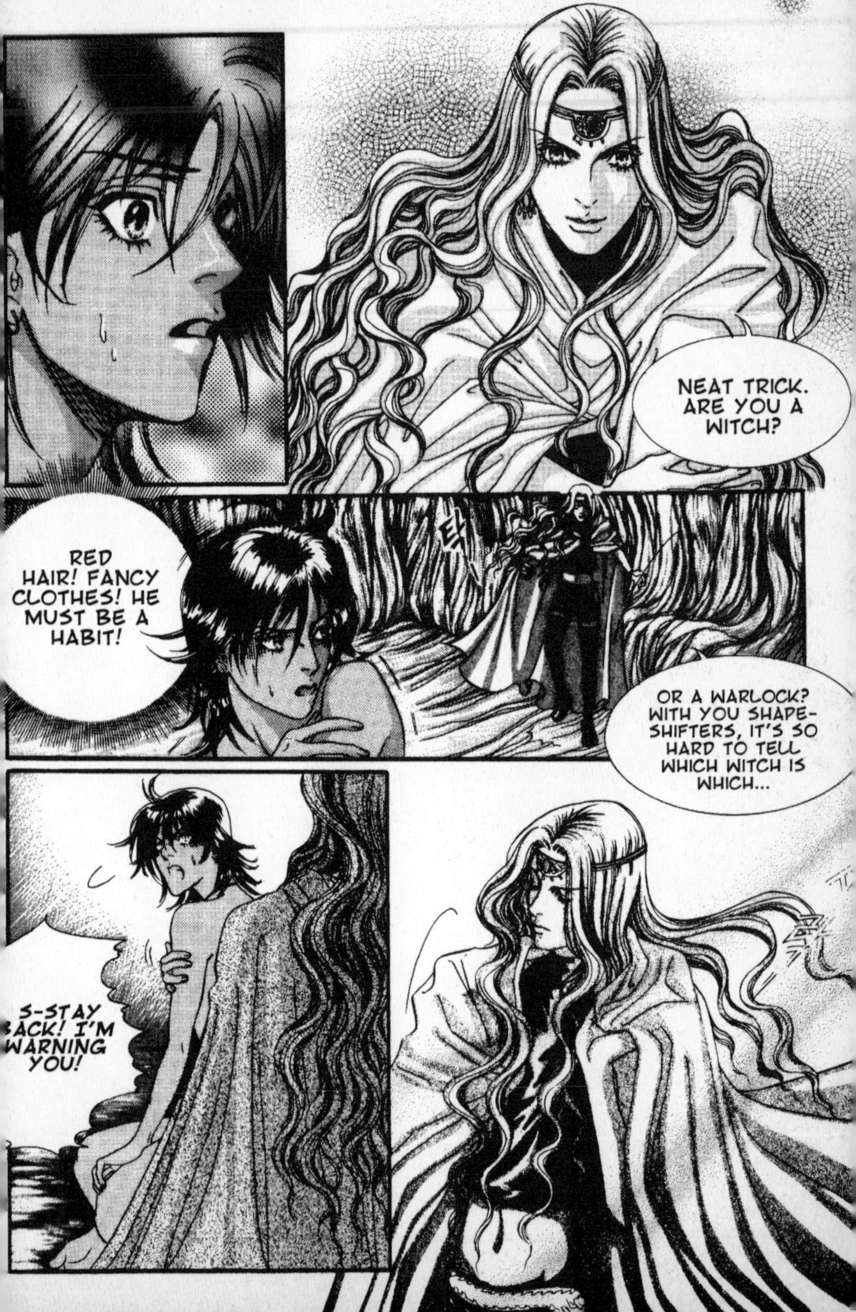

NEAT TRICK. ARE YOU A WITCH?
RED HAIR! FANCY CLOTHES! HE MUST BE A HABIT!
OR A WARLOCK? WITH YOU SHAPE-SHIFTERS, IT'S SO HARD TO TELL WHICH WITCH IS WHICH...
S-STAY BACK! I'M WARNING YOU!

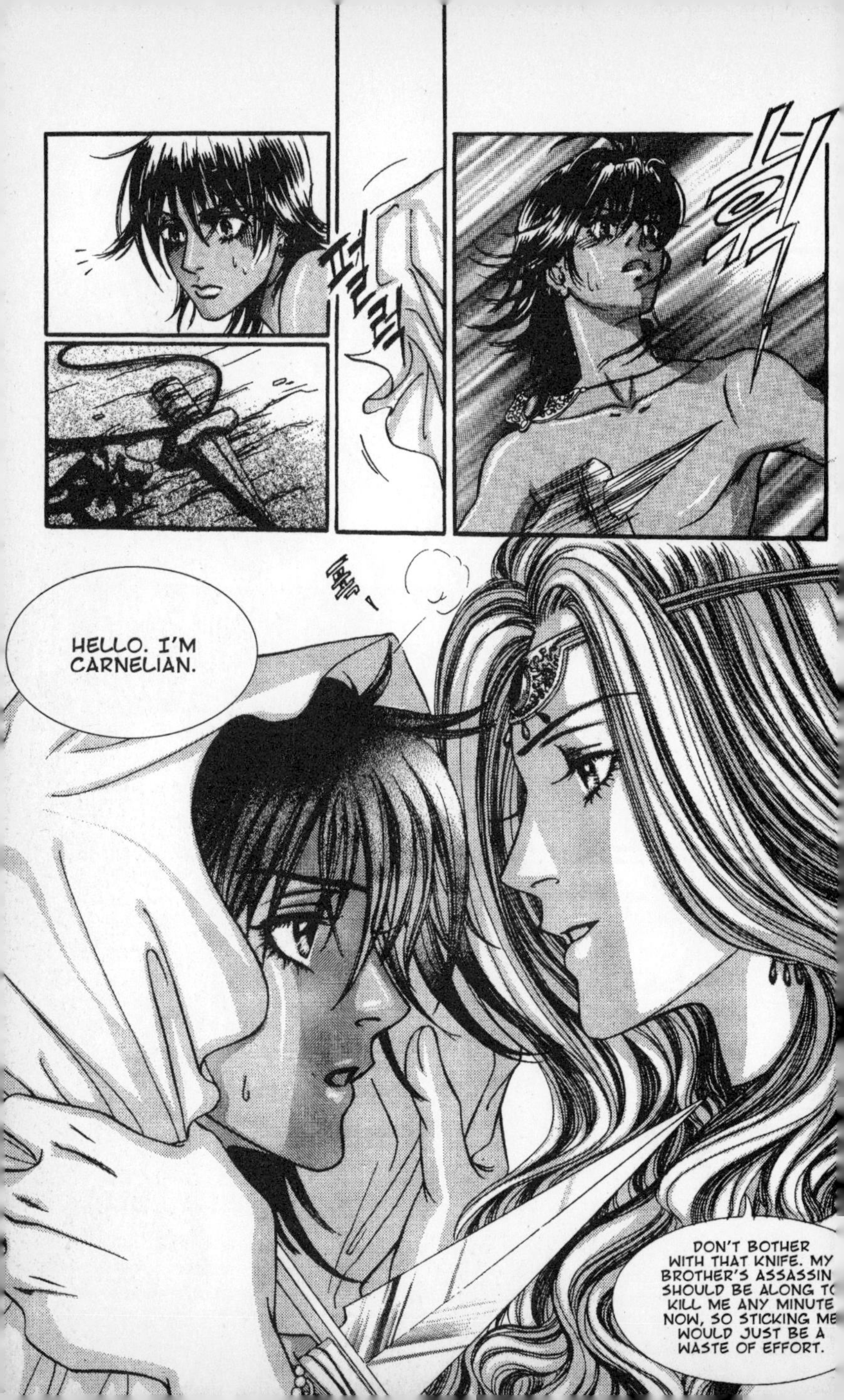
HELLO. I'M CARNELIAN.
DON'T BOTHER WITH THAT KNIFE. MY BROTHER'S ASSASSIN SHOULD BE ALONG TO KILL ME ANY MINUTE NOW, SO STICKING ME WOULD JUST BE A WASTE OF EFFORT.

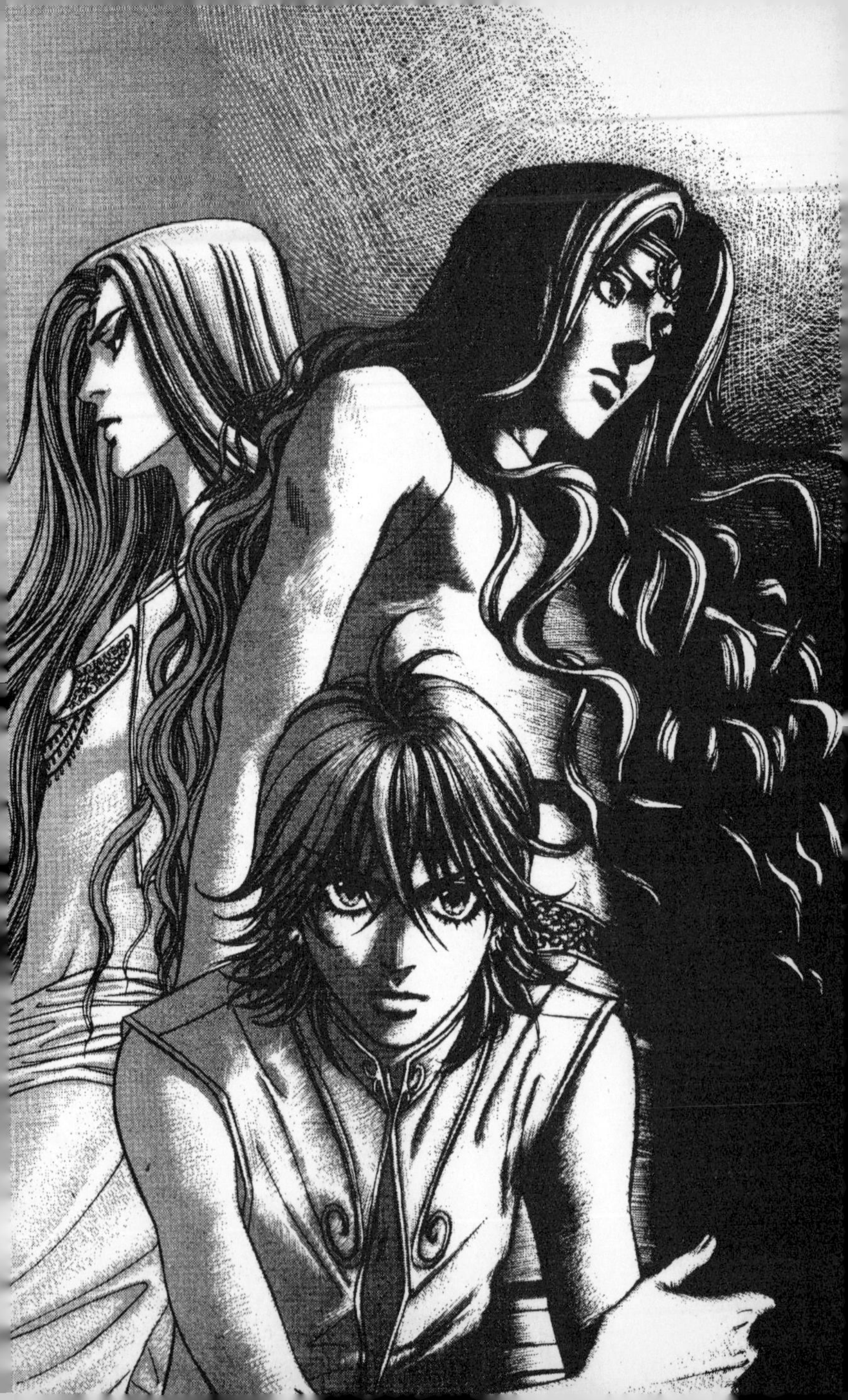

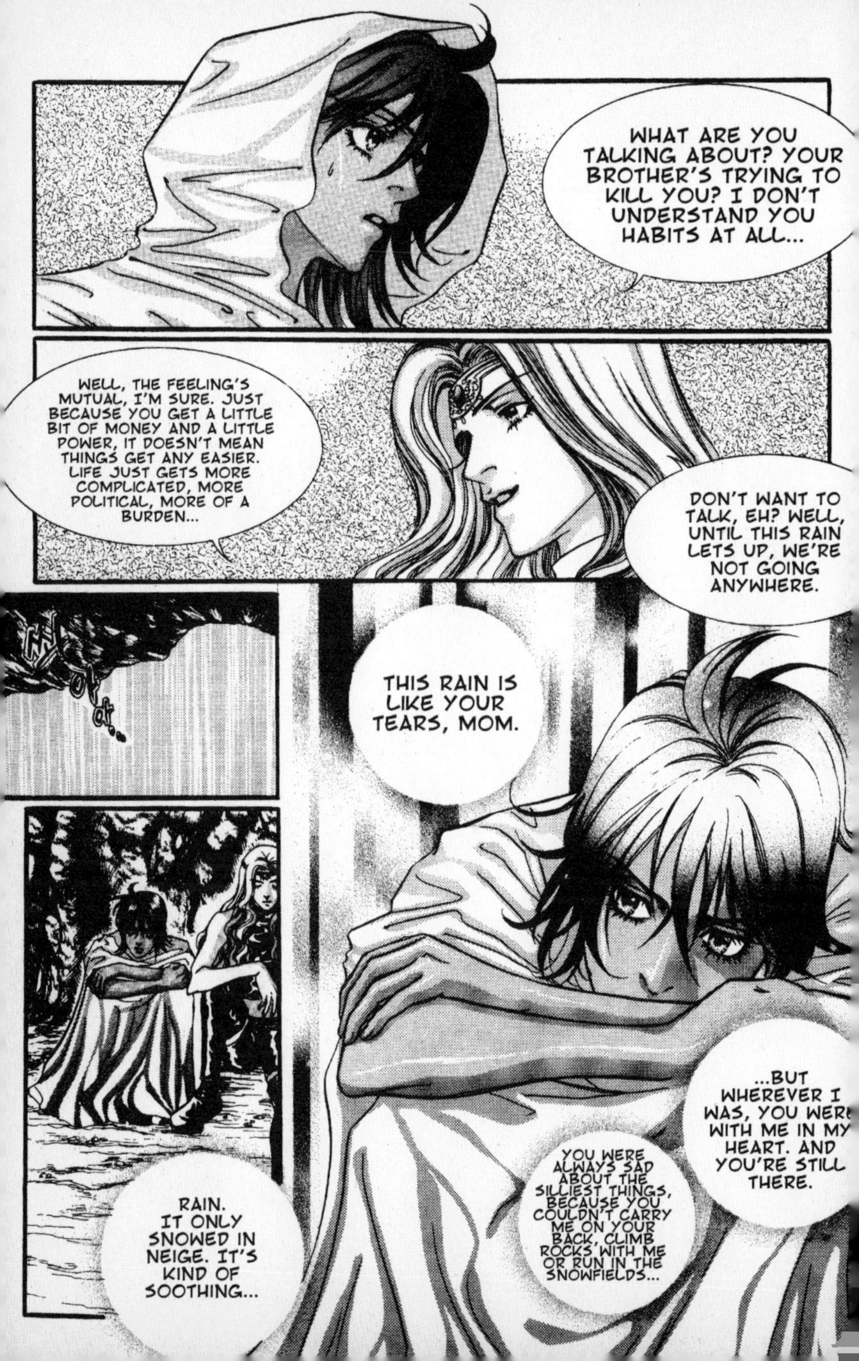
WHAT ARE YOU TALKING ABOUT? YOUR BROTHER'S TRYING TO KILL YOU? I DON'T UNDERSTAND YOU HABITS AT ALL...
WELL, THE FEELING'S MUTUAL, I'M SURE. JUST BECAUSE YOU GET A LITTLE BIT OF MONEY AND A LITTLE POWER, IT DOESN'T MEAN THINGS GET ANY EASIER. LIFE JUST GETS MORE COMPLICATED, MORE POLITICAL, MORE OF A BURDEN...
DON'T WANT TO TALK, EH? WELL, UNTIL THIS RAIN LETS UP, WE'RE NOT GOING ANYWHERE.
THIS RAIN IS LIKE YOUR TEARS, MOM.
RAIN. IT ONLY SNOWED IN NEIGE. IT'S KIND OF SOOTHING...
YOU WERE ALWAYS SAD ABOUT THE SILLIEST THINGS, BECAUSE YOU COULDN'T CARRY ME ON YOUR BACK, CLIMB ROCKS WITH ME OR RUN IN THE SNOWFIELDS...
...BUT WHEREVER I WAS, YOU WERE WITH ME IN MY HEART. AND YOU'RE STILL THERE.

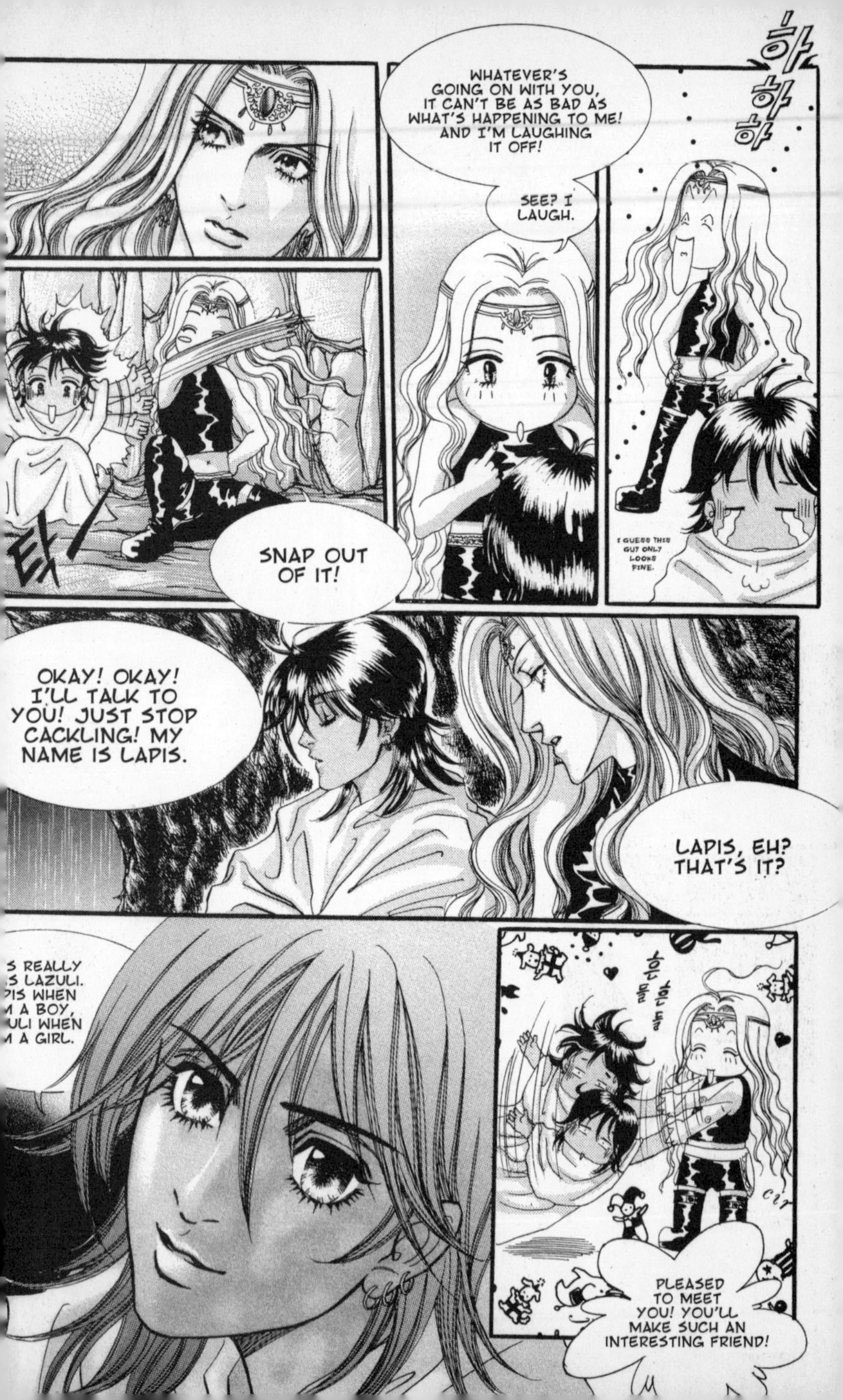
WHATEVER'S GOING ON WITH YOU, IT CAN'T BE AS BAD AS WHAT'S HAPPENING TO ME! AND I'M LAUGHING IT OFF!
SEE? I LAUGH.
하하하
I GUESS THIS GUY ONLY LOOKS FINE.
탁
SNAP OUT OF IT!
OKAY! OKAY! I'LL TALK TO YOU! JUST STOP CACKLING! MY NAME IS LAPIS.
LAPIS, EH? THAT'S IT?
S REALLY S LAZULI. PIS WHEN M A BOY, ULI WHEN M A GIRL.
PLEASED TO MEET YOU! YOU'LL MAKE SUCH AN INTERESTING FRIEND!

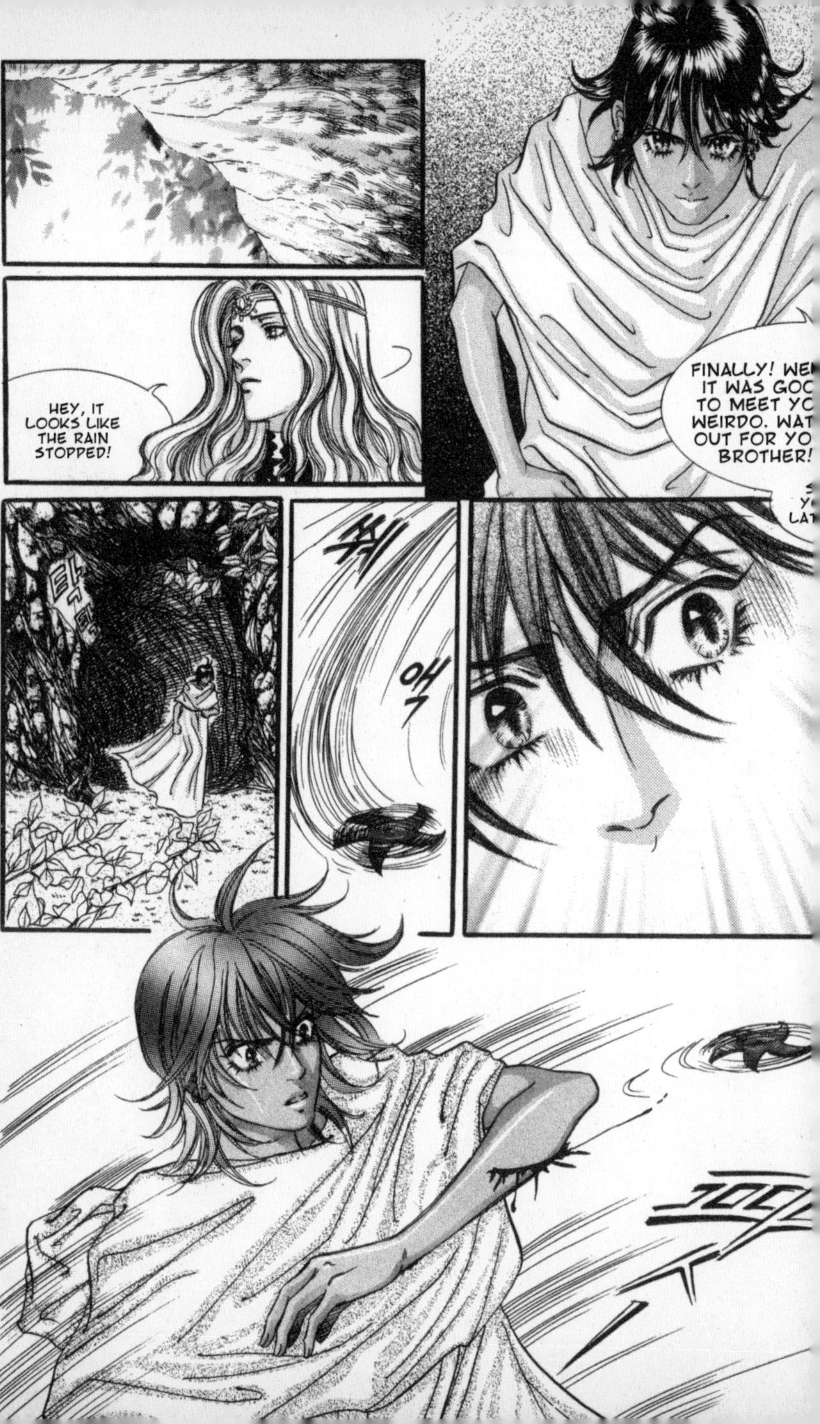
HEY, IT LOOKS LIKE THE RAIN STOPPED!
FINALLY! WE
IT WAS GOO
TO MEET YO
WEIRDO. WAT
OUT FOR YO
BROTHER!

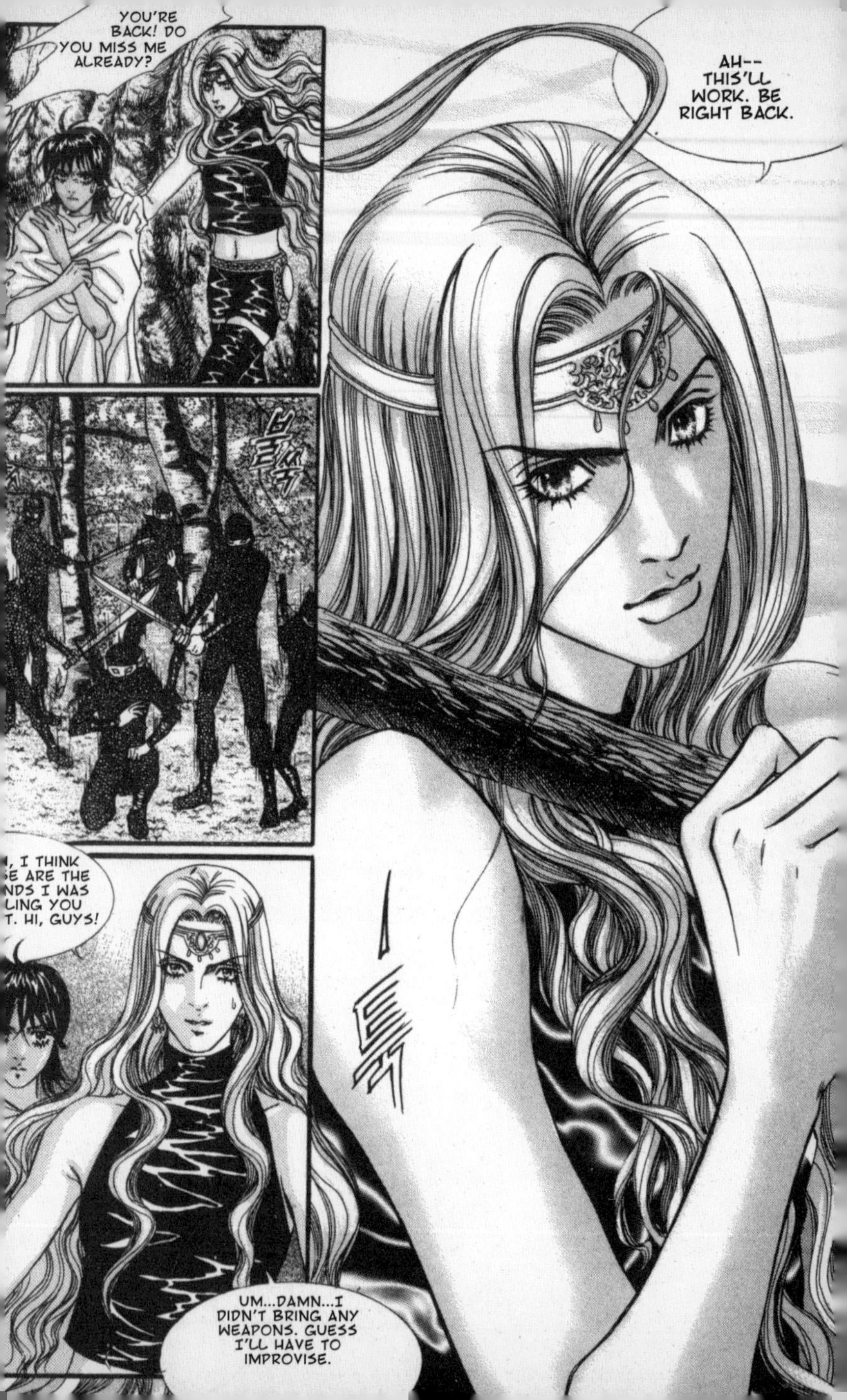
YOU'RE BACK! DO YOU MISS ME ALREADY?
, I THINK SE ARE THE NDS I WAS LING YOU T. HI, GUYS!
UM...DAMN...I DIDN'T BRING ANY WEAPONS. GUESS I'LL HAVE TO IMPROVISE.
AH-- THIS'LL WORK. BE RIGHT BACK.

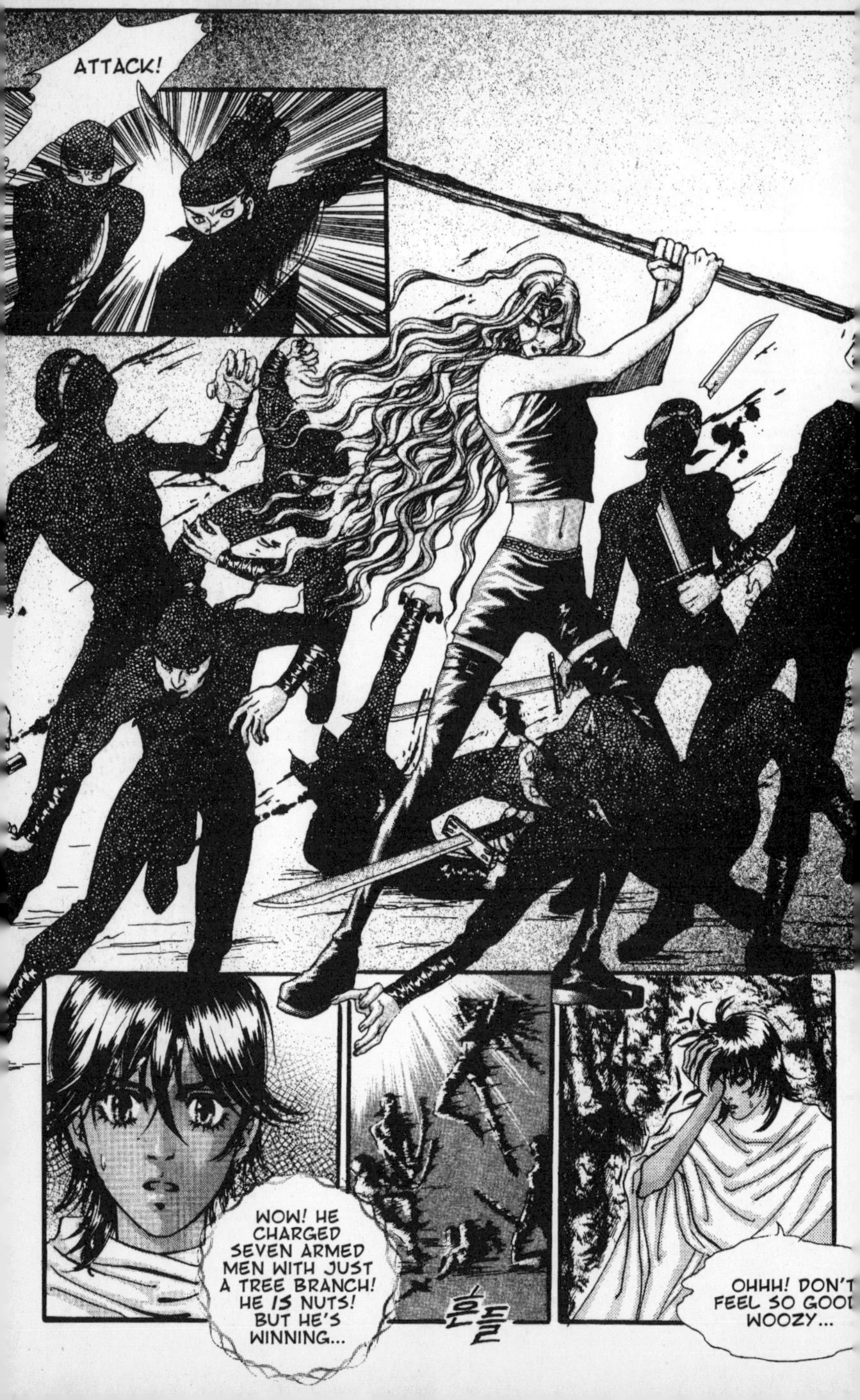
ATTACK!
WOW! HE CHARGED SEVEN ARMED MEN WITH JUST A TREE BRANCH! HE IS NUTS! BUT HE'S WINNING...
OHHH! DON'T FEEL SO GOOD WOOZY...

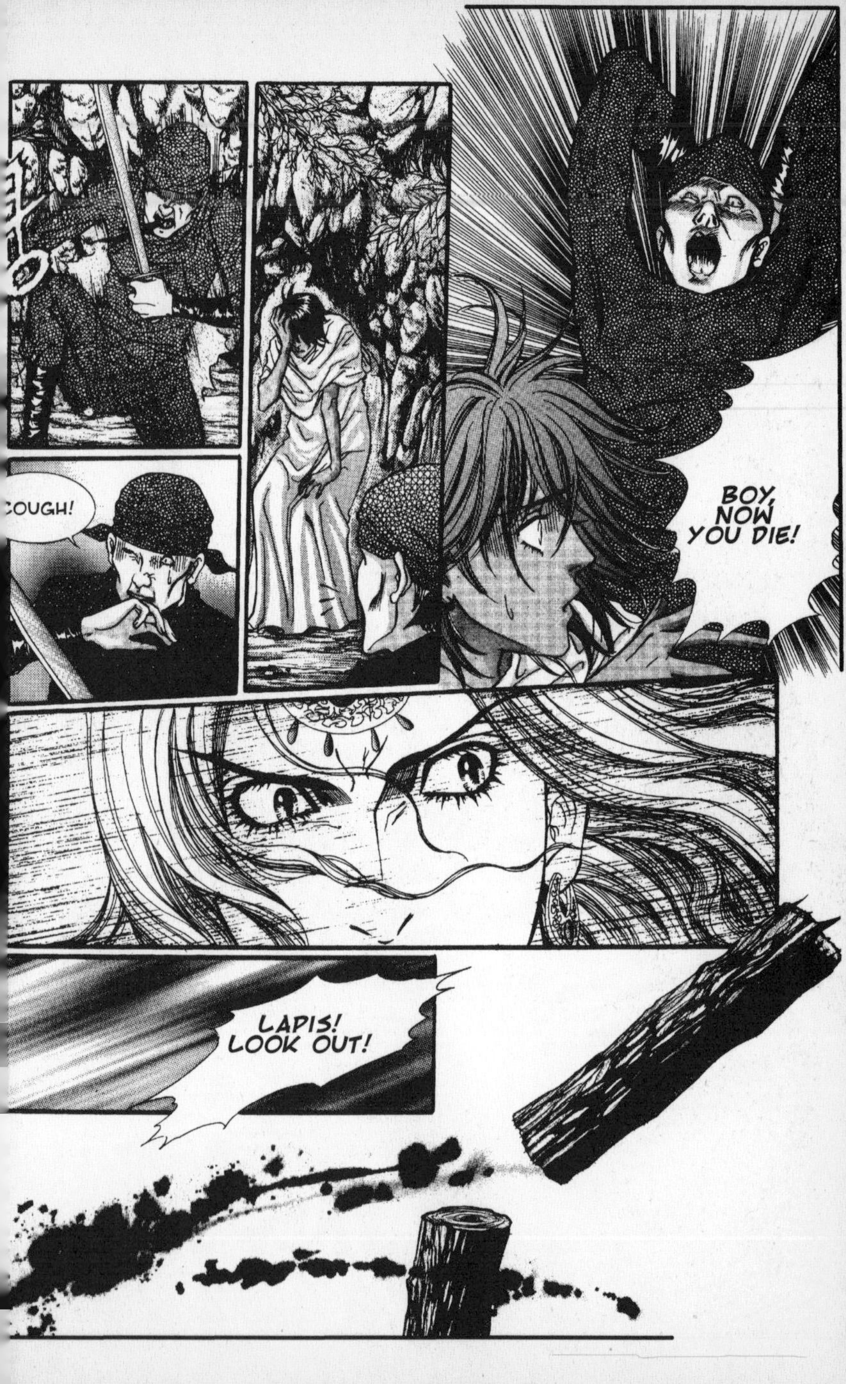
BOY, NOW YOU DIE!
COUGH!
LAPIS! LOOK OUT!

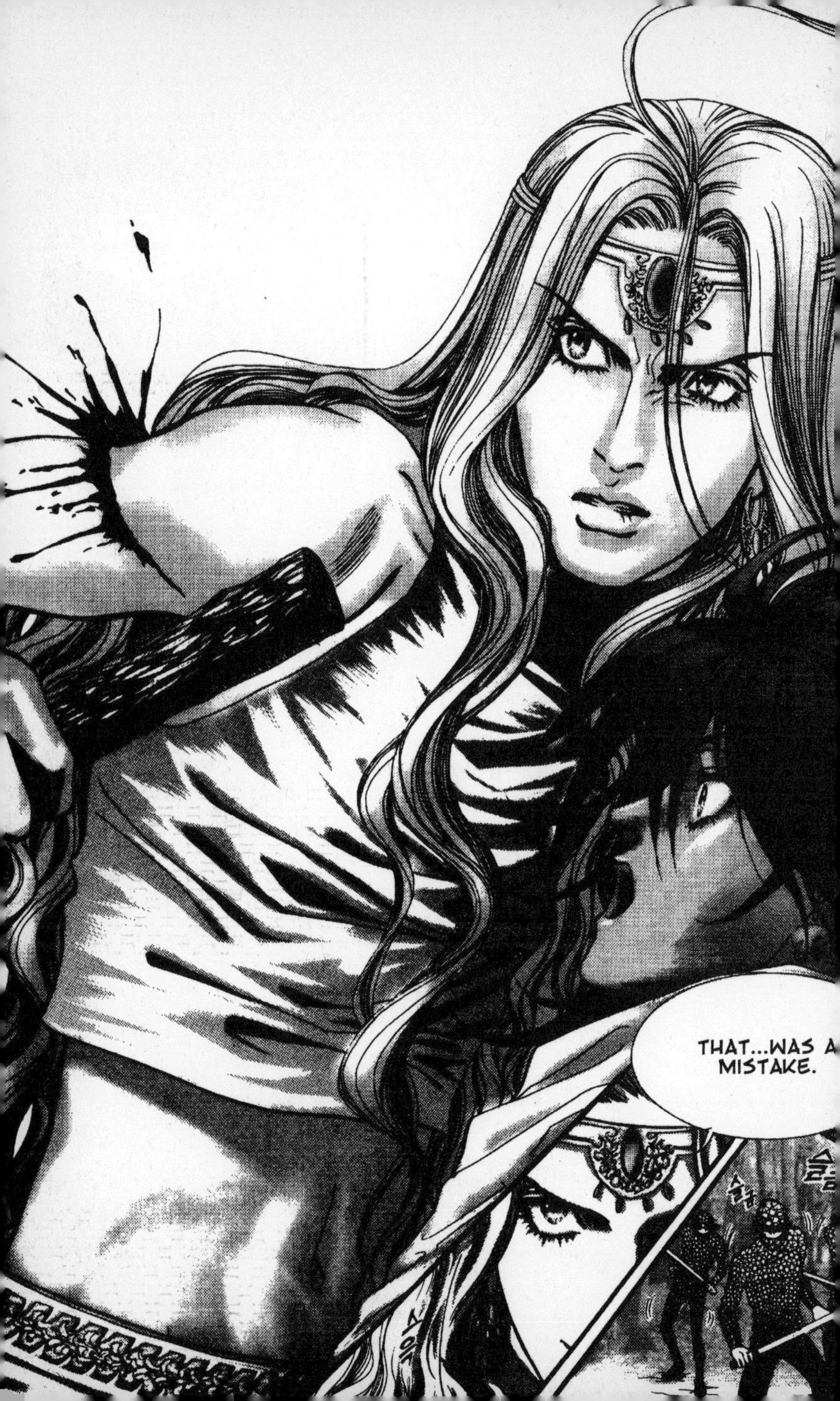
THAT...WAS A MISTAKE.

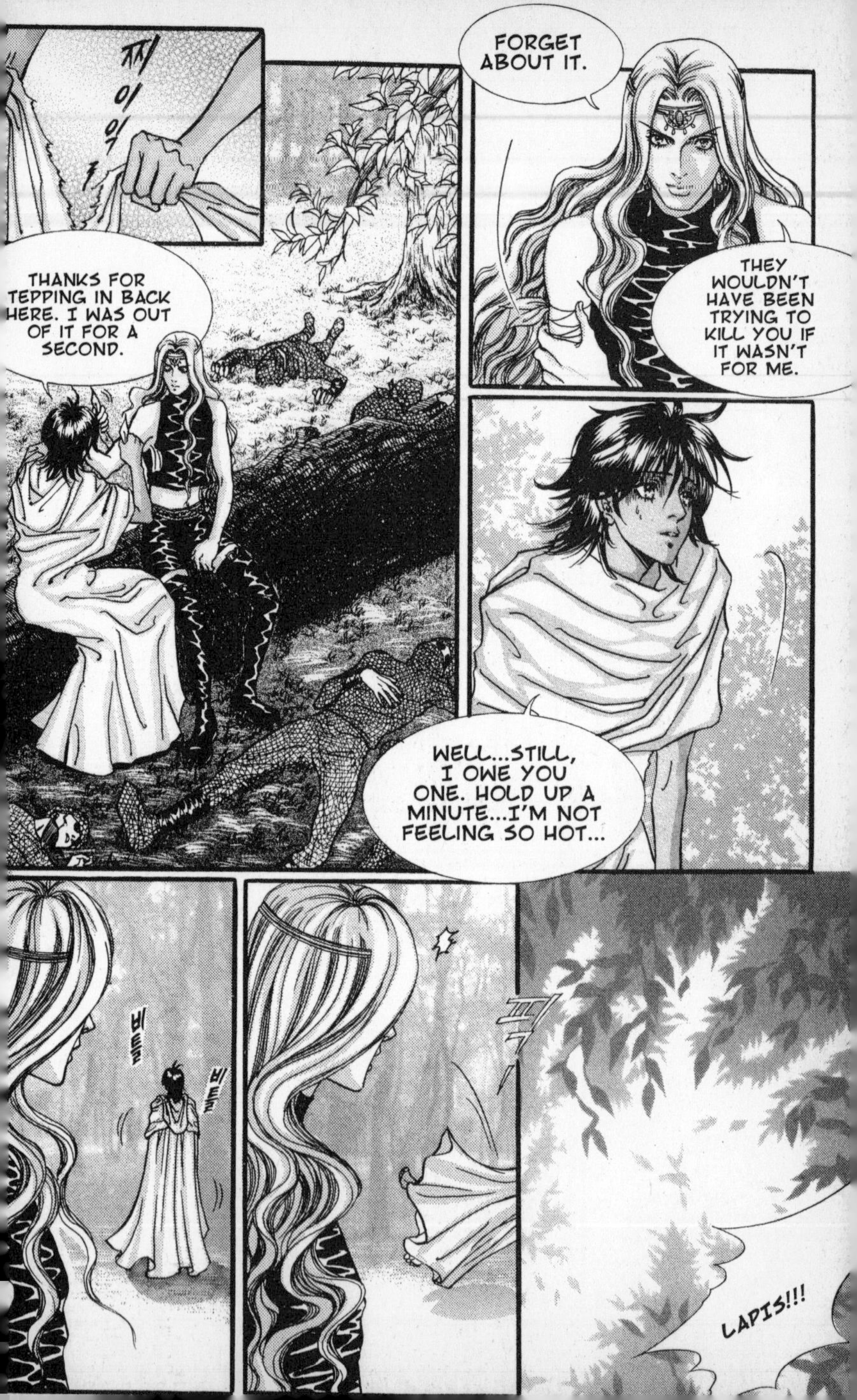
찌이익
THANKS FOR
TEPPING IN BACK
HERE. I WAS OUT
OF IT FOR A
SECOND.
FORGET
ABOUT IT.
THEY
WOULDN'T
HAVE BEEN
TRYING TO
KILL YOU IF
IT WASN'T
FOR ME.
WELL...STILL,
I OWE YOU
ONE. HOLD UP A
MINUTE...I'M NOT
FEELING SO HOT...
비틀
비틀
LAPIS!!!

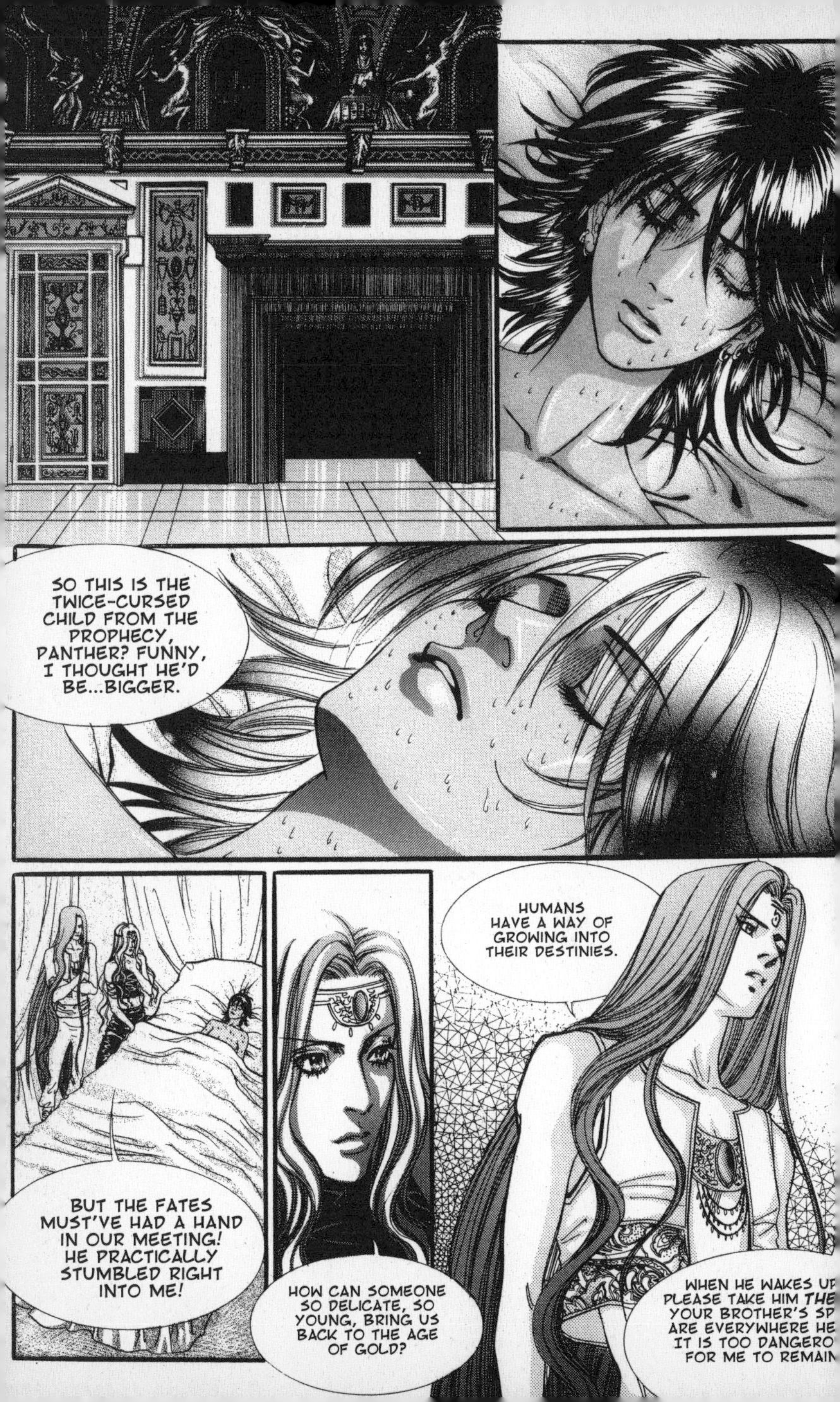

SO THIS IS THE TWICE-CURSED CHILD FROM THE PROPHECY, PANTHER? FUNNY, I THOUGHT HE'D BE...BIGGER.
BUT THE FATES MUST'VE HAD A HAND IN OUR MEETING! HE PRACTICALLY STUMBLED RIGHT INTO ME!
HOW CAN SOMEONE SO DELICATE, SO YOUNG, BRING US BACK TO THE AGE OF GOLD?
HUMANS HAVE A WAY OF GROWING INTO THEIR DESTINIES.

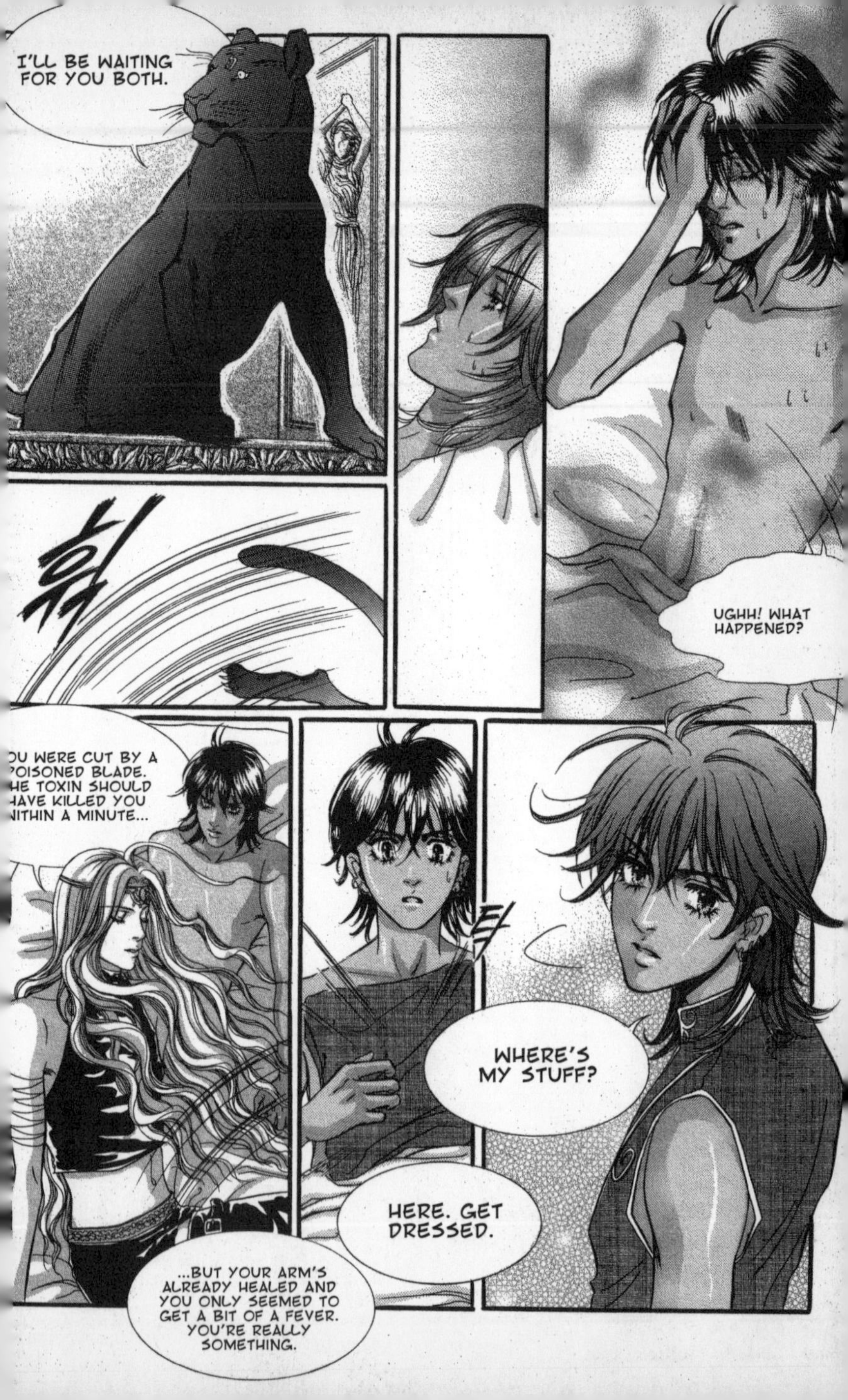

I'LL BE WAITING FOR YOU BOTH.
UGHH! WHAT HAPPENED?
OU WERE CUT BY A POISONED BLADE. HE TOXIN SHOULD HAVE KILLED YOU WITHIN A MINUTE...
...BUT YOUR ARM'S ALREADY HEALED AND YOU ONLY SEEMED TO GET A BIT OF A FEVER. YOU'RE REALLY SOMETHING.
WHERE'S MY STUFF?
HERE. GET DRESSED.

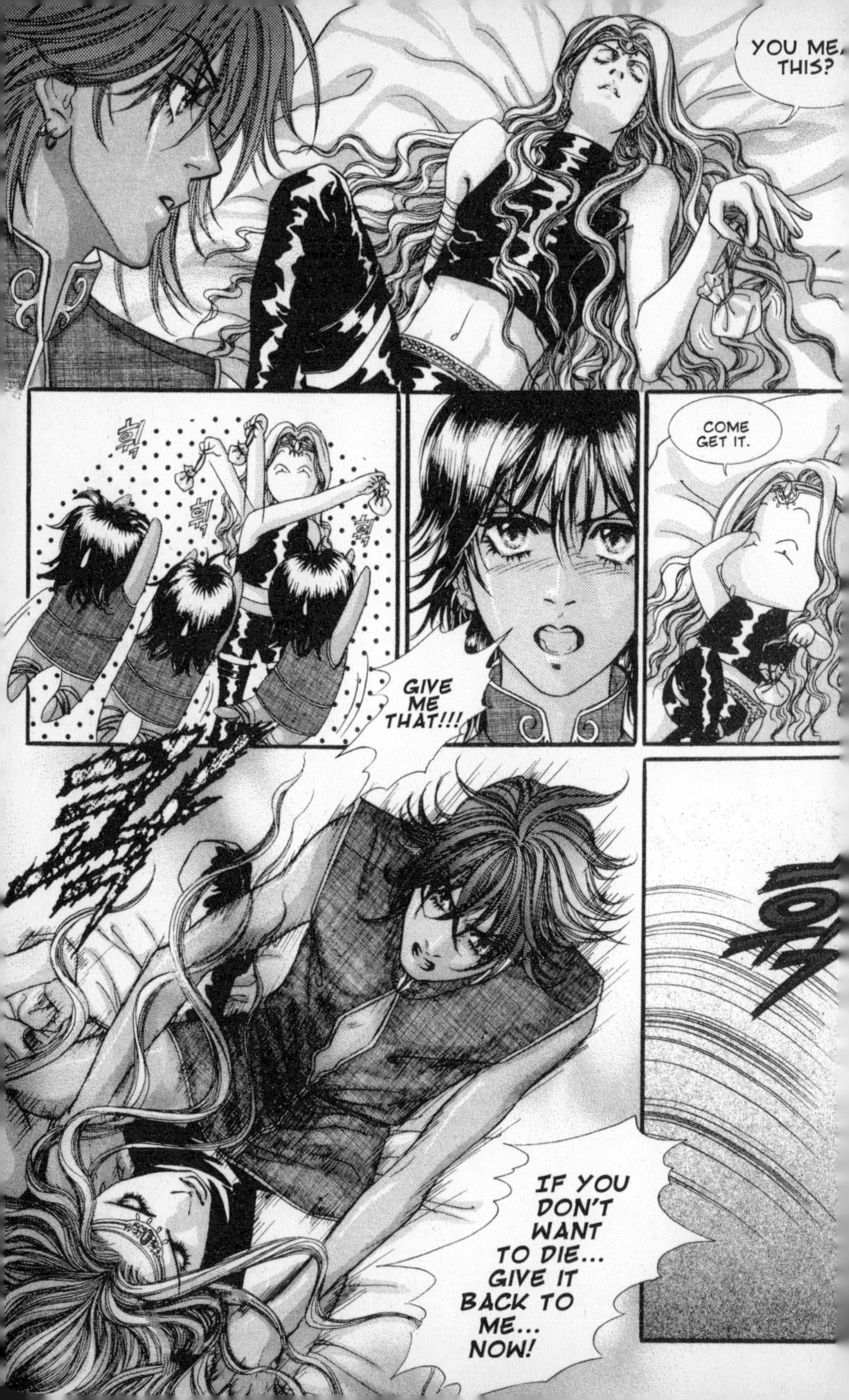
YOU ME THIS?
COME GET IT.
GIVE ME THAT!!!
IF YOU DON'T WANT TO DIE... GIVE IT BACK TO ME... NOW!

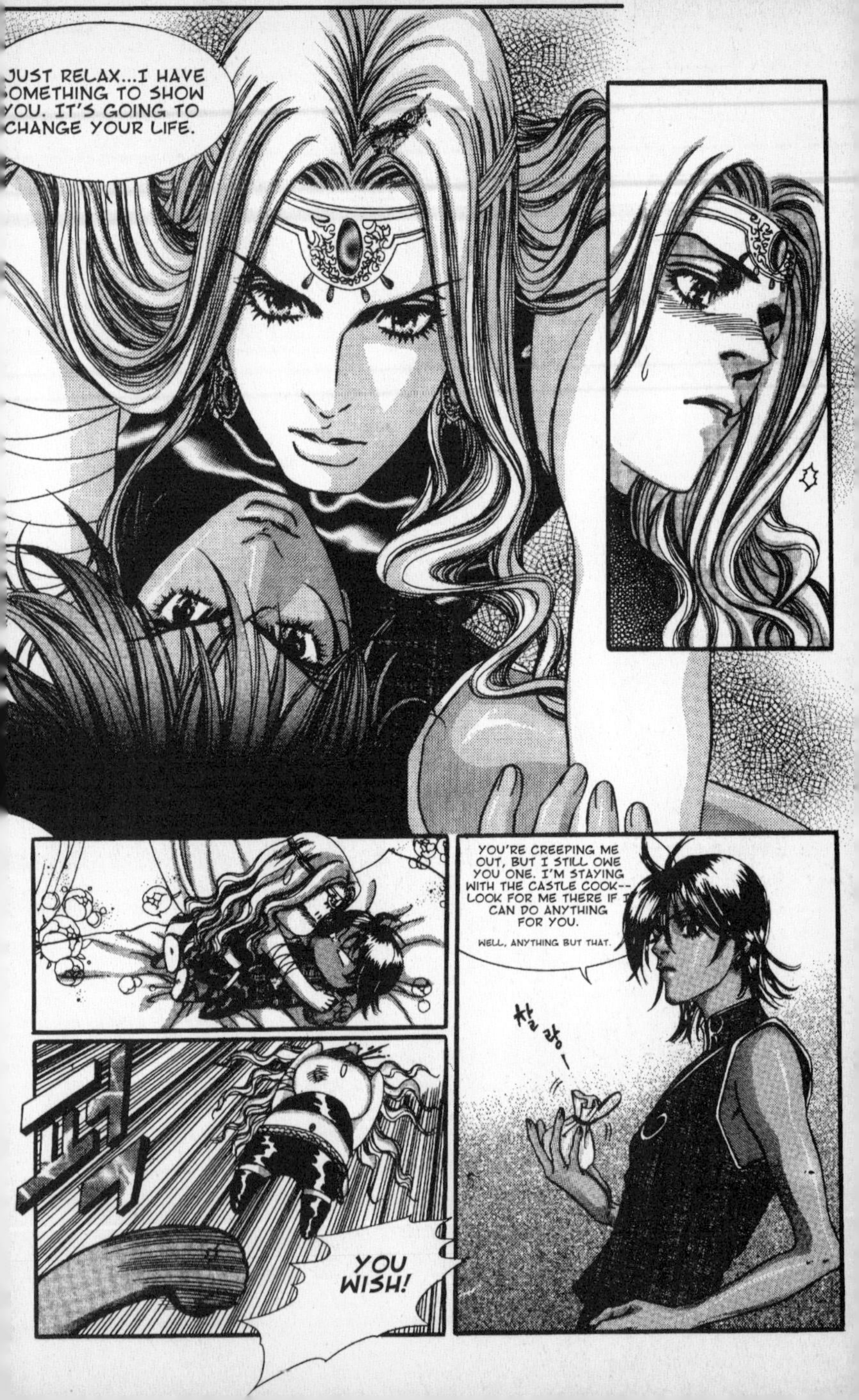

JUST RELAX...I HAVE SOMETHING TO SHOW YOU. IT'S GOING TO CHANGE YOUR LIFE.
YOU WISH!
YOU'RE CREEPING ME OUT, BUT I STILL OWE YOU ONE. I'M STAYING WITH THE CASTLE COOK--LOOK FOR ME THERE IF I CAN DO ANYTHING FOR YOU.
WELL, ANYTHING BUT THAT.
찰랑-

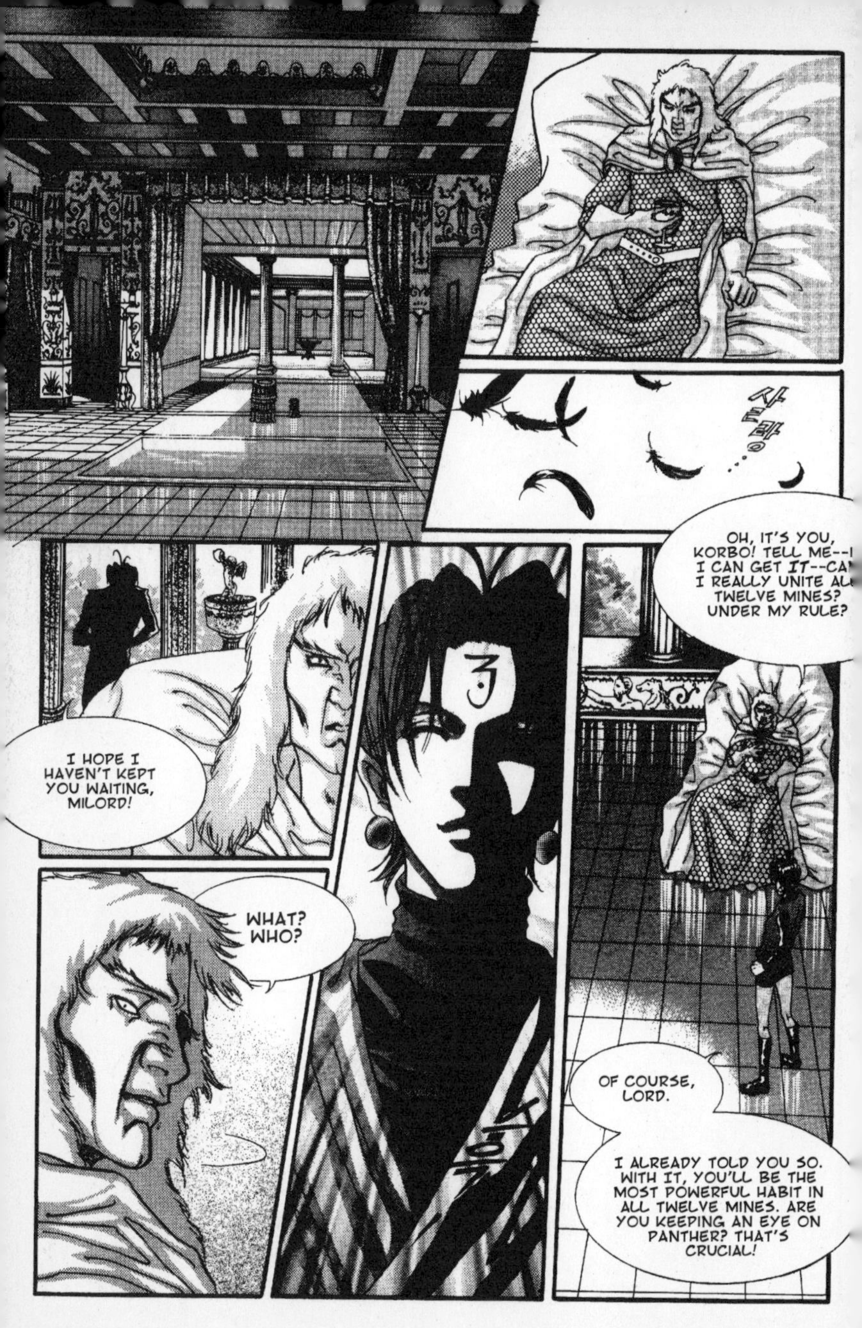
OH, IT'S YOU, KORBO! TELL ME--I CAN GET IT--CAN I REALLY UNITE ALL TWELVE MINES? UNDER MY RULE?
I HOPE I HAVEN'T KEPT YOU WAITING, MILORD!
WHAT? WHO?
OF COURSE, LORD.
I ALREADY TOLD YOU SO. WITH IT, YOU'LL BE THE MOST POWERFUL HABIT IN ALL TWELVE MINES. ARE YOU KEEPING AN EYE ON PANTHER? THAT'S CRUCIAL!

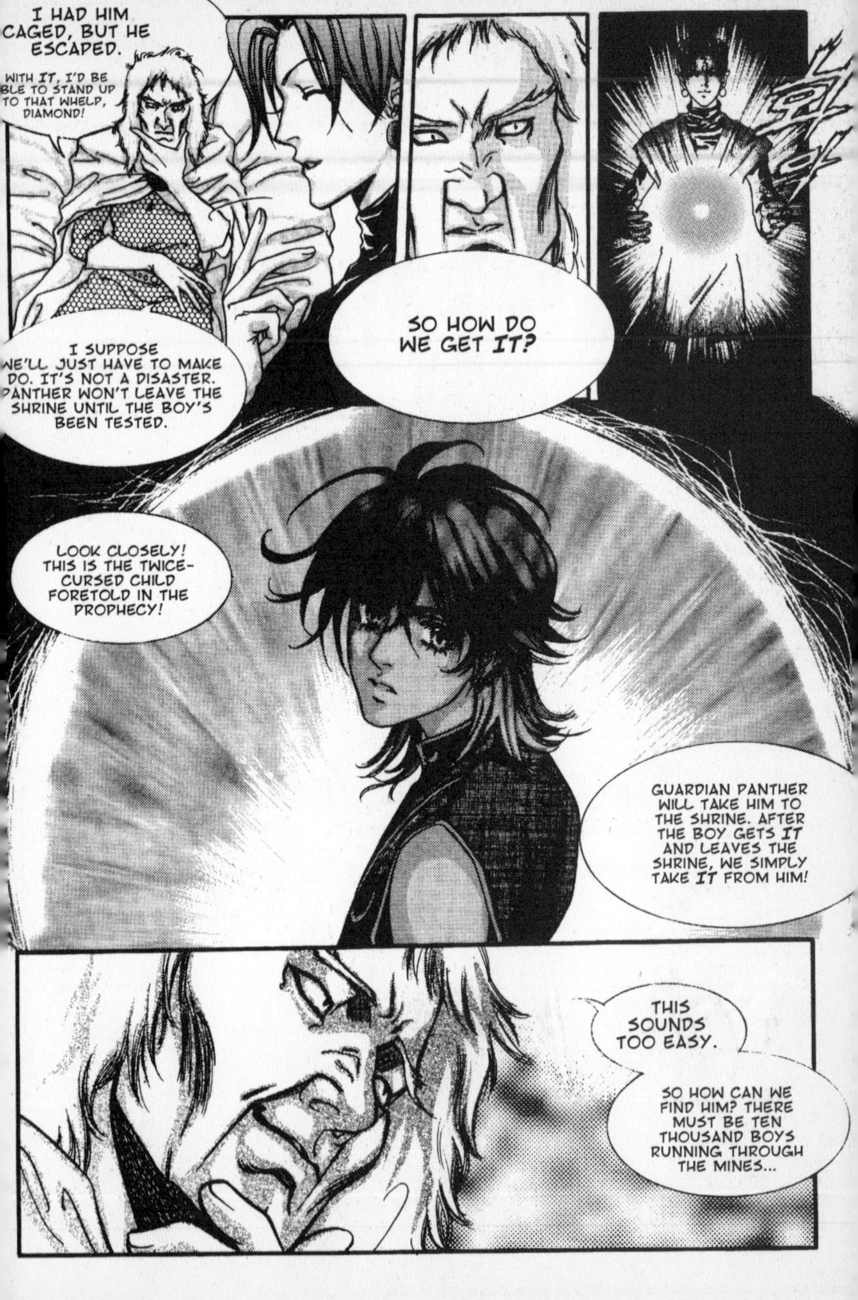

I HAD HIM CAGED, BUT HE ESCAPED.
WITH IT, I'D BE ABLE TO STAND UP TO THAT WHELP, DIAMOND!
I SUPPOSE WE'LL JUST HAVE TO MAKE DO. IT'S NOT A DISASTER. PANTHER WON'T LEAVE THE SHRINE UNTIL THE BOY'S BEEN TESTED.
SO HOW DO WE GET IT?
LOOK CLOSELY! THIS IS THE TWICE-CURSED CHILD FORETOLD IN THE PROPHECY!
GUARDIAN PANTHER WILL TAKE HIM TO THE SHRINE. AFTER THE BOY GETS IT AND LEAVES THE SHRINE, WE SIMPLY TAKE IT FROM HIM!
THIS SOUNDS TOO EASY.
SO HOW CAN WE FIND HIM? THERE MUST BE TEN THOUSAND BOYS RUNNING THROUGH THE MINES...

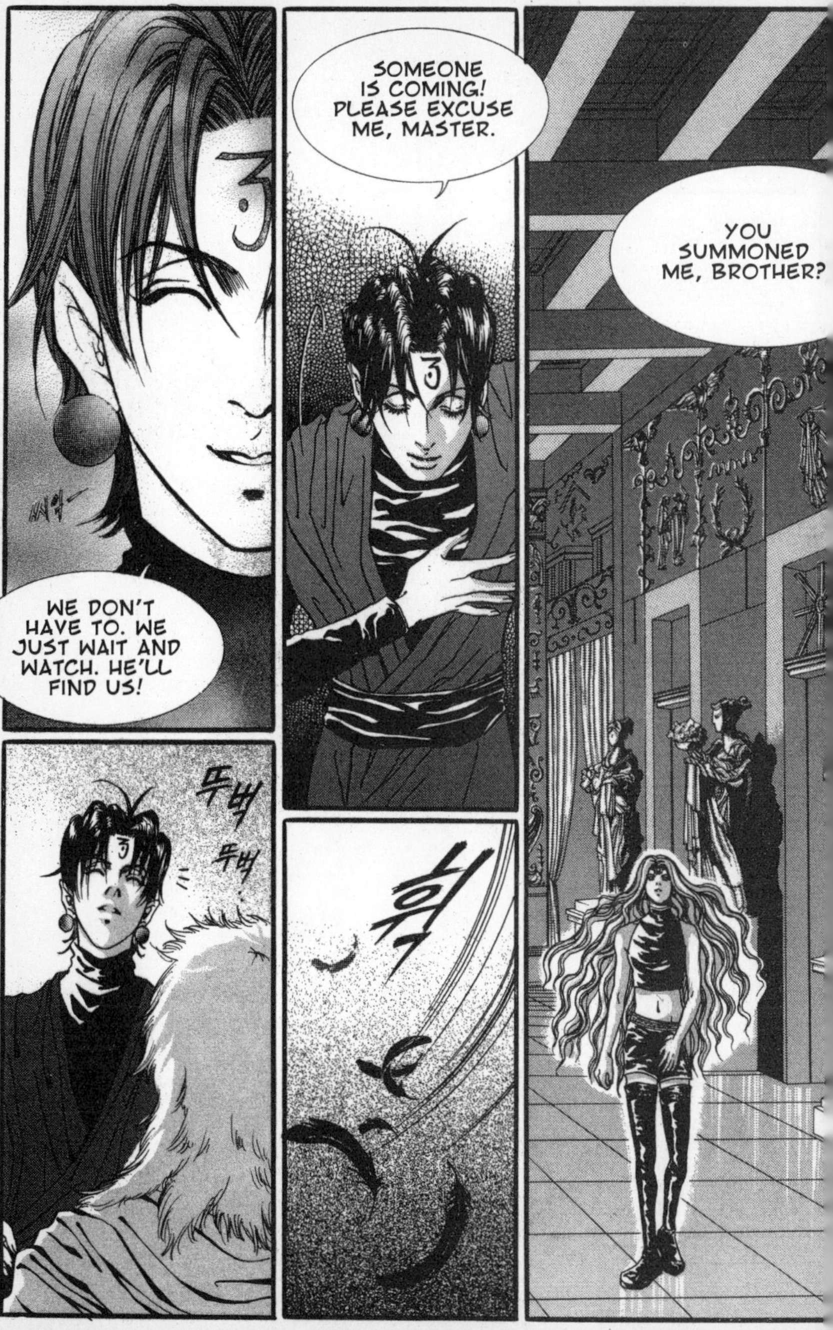
WE DON'T HAVE TO. WE JUST WAIT AND WATCH. HE'LL FIND US!
SOMEONE IS COMING! PLEASE EXCUSE ME, MASTER.
뚜벅 뚜벅
YOU SUMMONED ME, BROTHER?

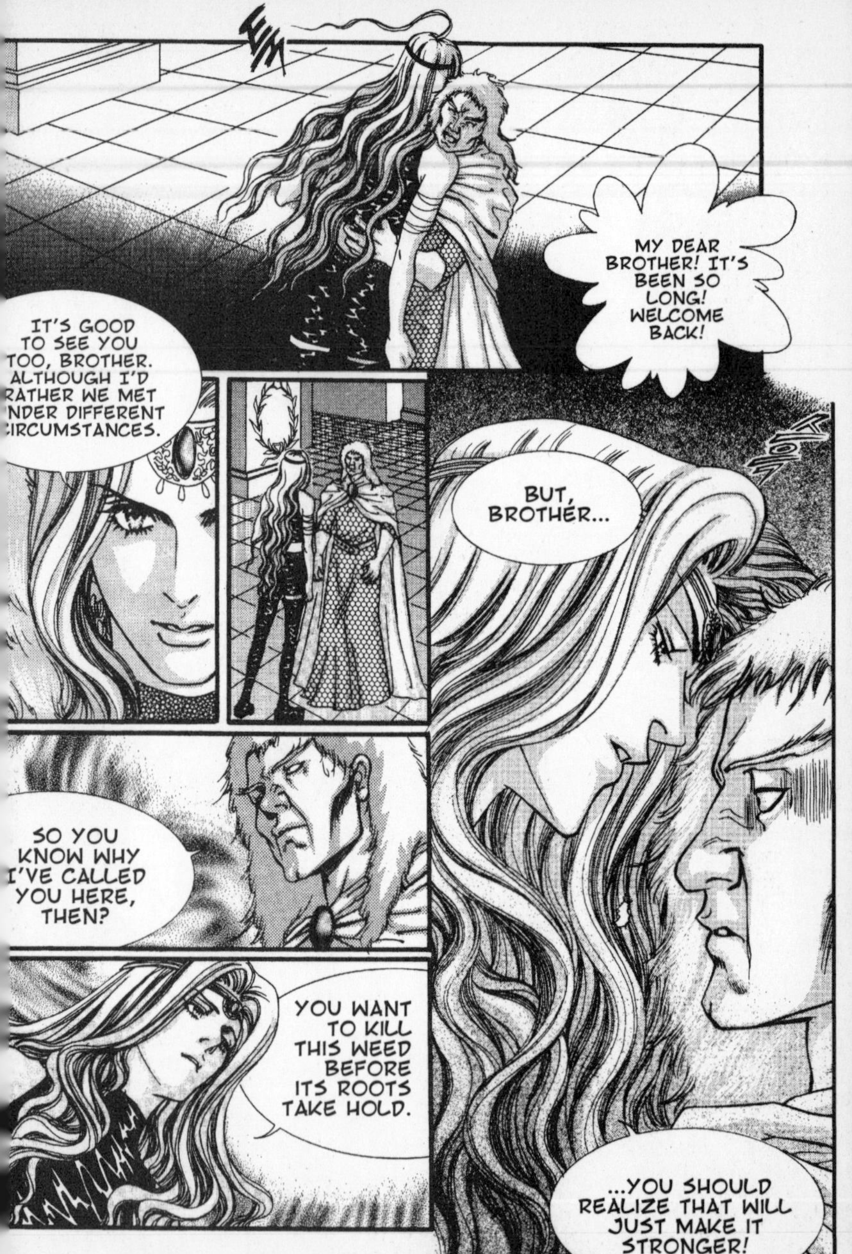
MY DEAR BROTHER! IT'S BEEN SO LONG! WELCOME BACK!
IT'S GOOD TO SEE YOU TOO, BROTHER. ALTHOUGH I'D RATHER WE MET UNDER DIFFERENT CIRCUMSTANCES.
SO YOU KNOW WHY I'VE CALLED YOU HERE, THEN?
YOU WANT TO KILL THIS WEED BEFORE ITS ROOTS TAKE HOLD.
BUT, BROTHER...
...YOU SHOULD REALIZE THAT WILL JUST MAKE IT STRONGER!

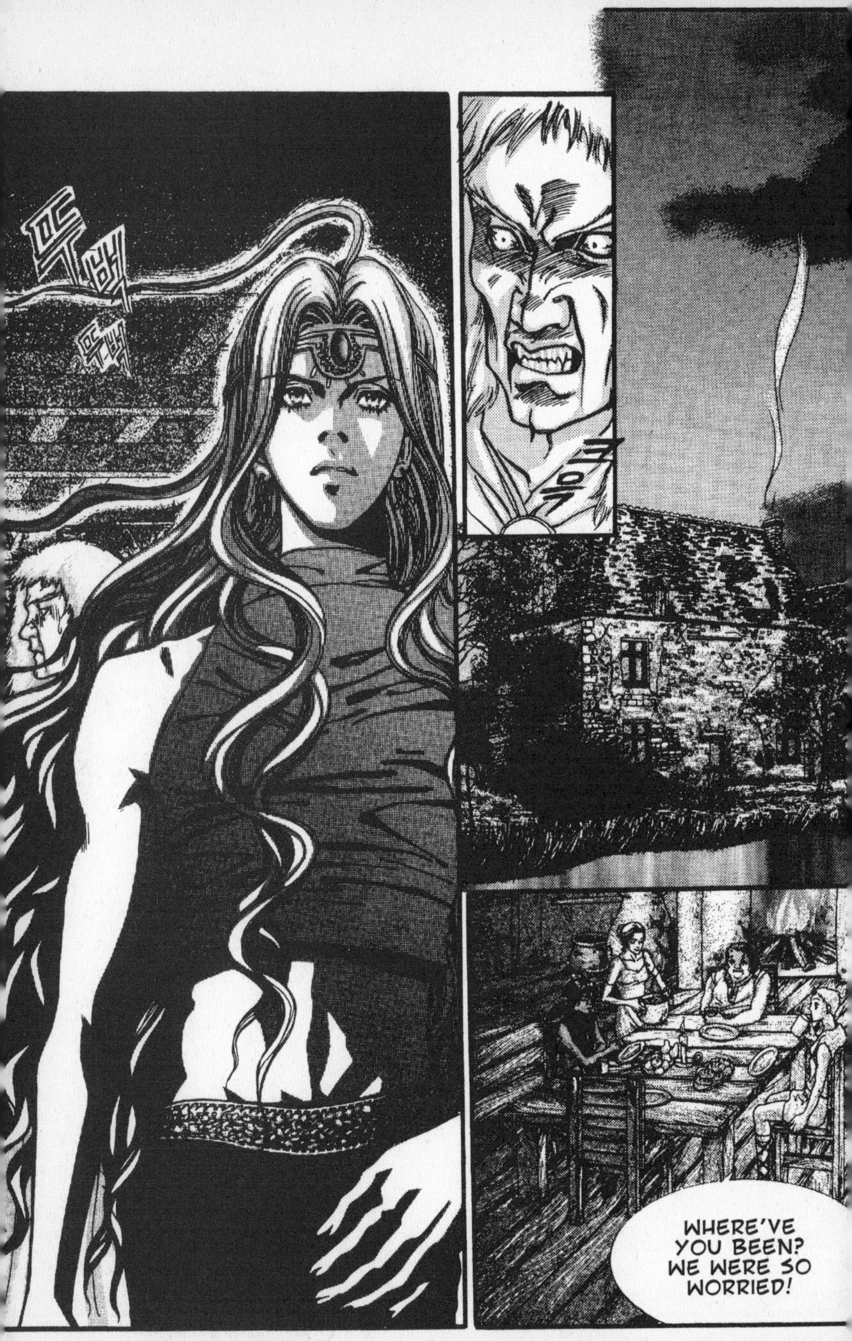
WHERE'VE YOU BEEN? WE WERE SO WORRIED!

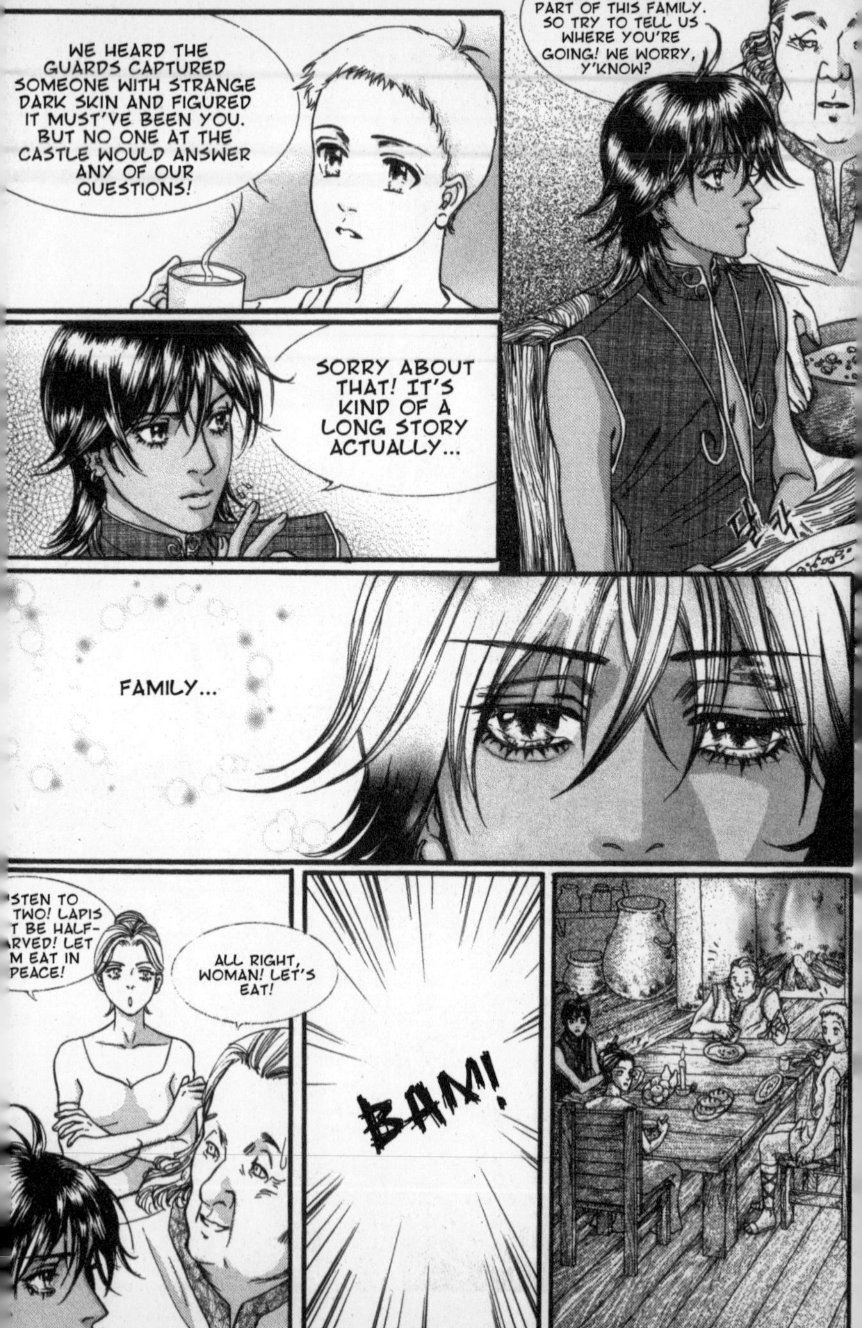
WE HEARD THE GUARDS CAPTURED SOMEONE WITH STRANGE DARK SKIN AND FIGURED IT MUST'VE BEEN YOU. BUT NO ONE AT THE CASTLE WOULD ANSWER ANY OF OUR QUESTIONS!
SORRY ABOUT THAT! IT'S KIND OF A LONG STORY ACTUALLY...
LAPIS, WE THINK OF YOU AS PART OF THIS FAMILY. SO TRY TO TELL US WHERE YOU'RE GOING! WE WORRY, Y'KNOW?
FAMILY...
'STEN TO TWO! LAPIS T BE HALF-ARVED! LET M EAT IN PEACE!
ALL RIGHT, WOMAN! LET'S EAT!
BAM!

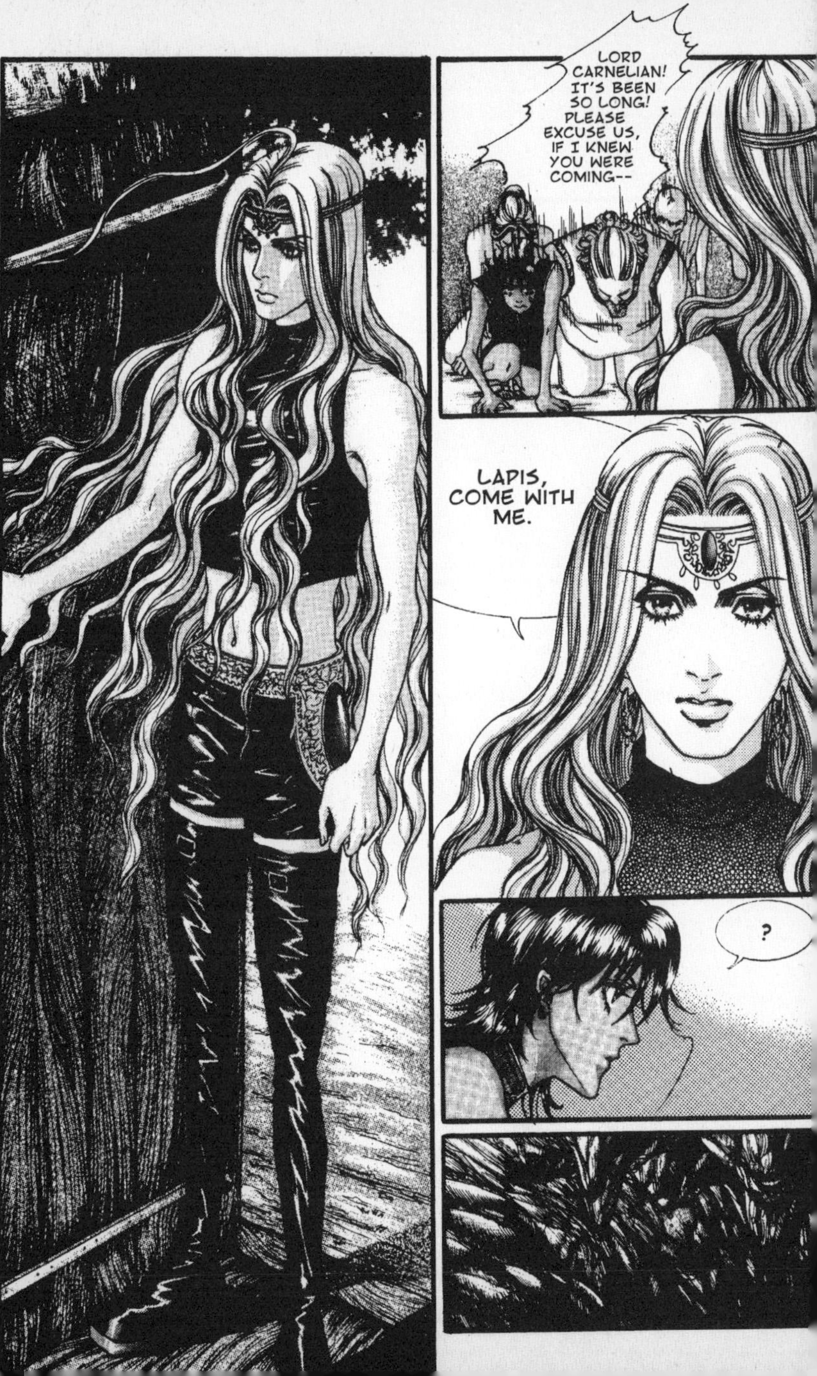
LORD CARNELIAN! IT'S BEEN SO LONG! PLEASE EXCUSE US, IF I KNEW YOU WERE COMING--
LAPIS, COME WITH ME.
?

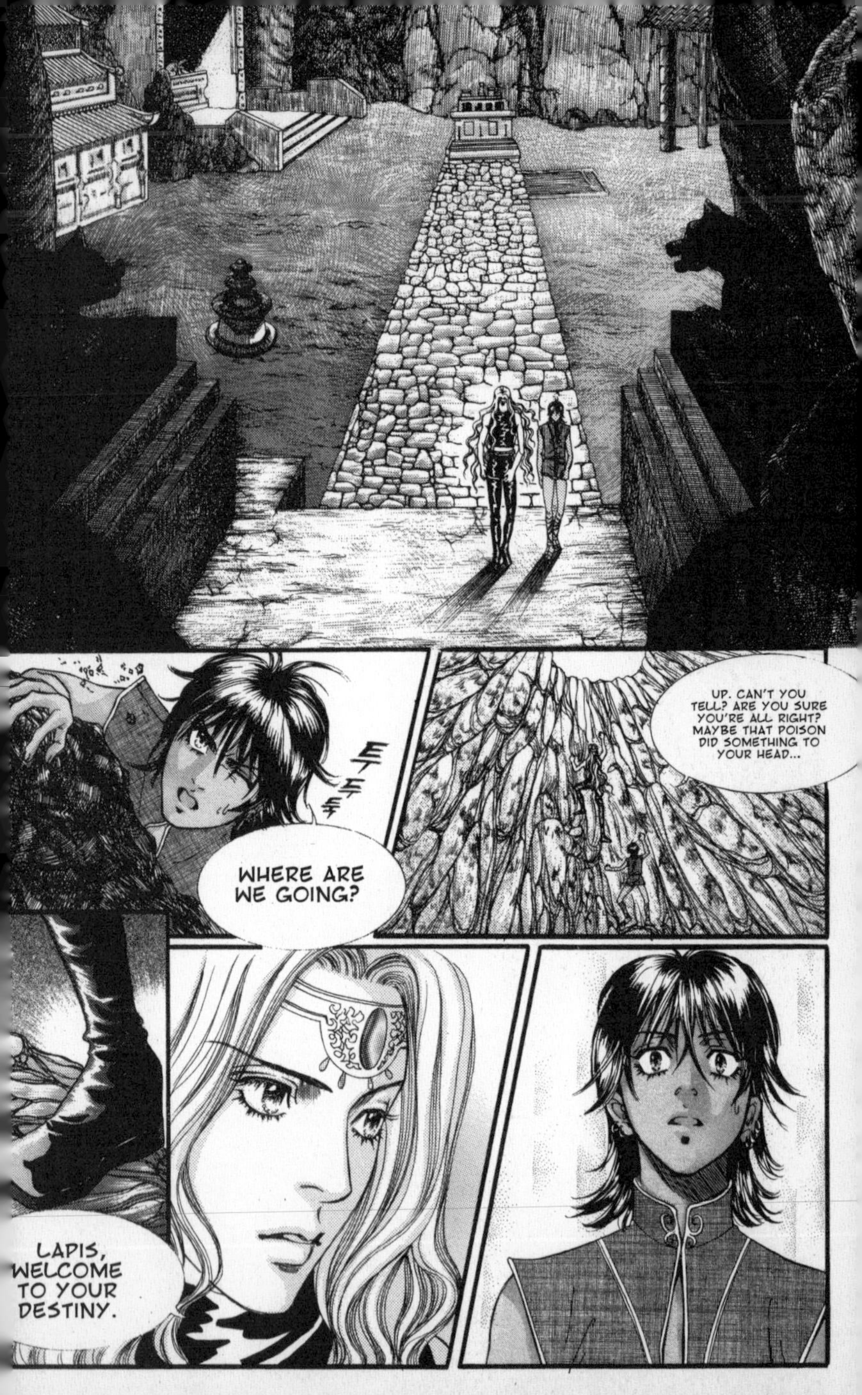
WHERE ARE WE GOING?
UP. CAN'T YOU TELL? ARE YOU SURE YOU'RE ALL RIGHT? MAYBE THAT POISON DID SOMETHING TO YOUR HEAD...
LAPIS, WELCOME TO YOUR DESTINY.

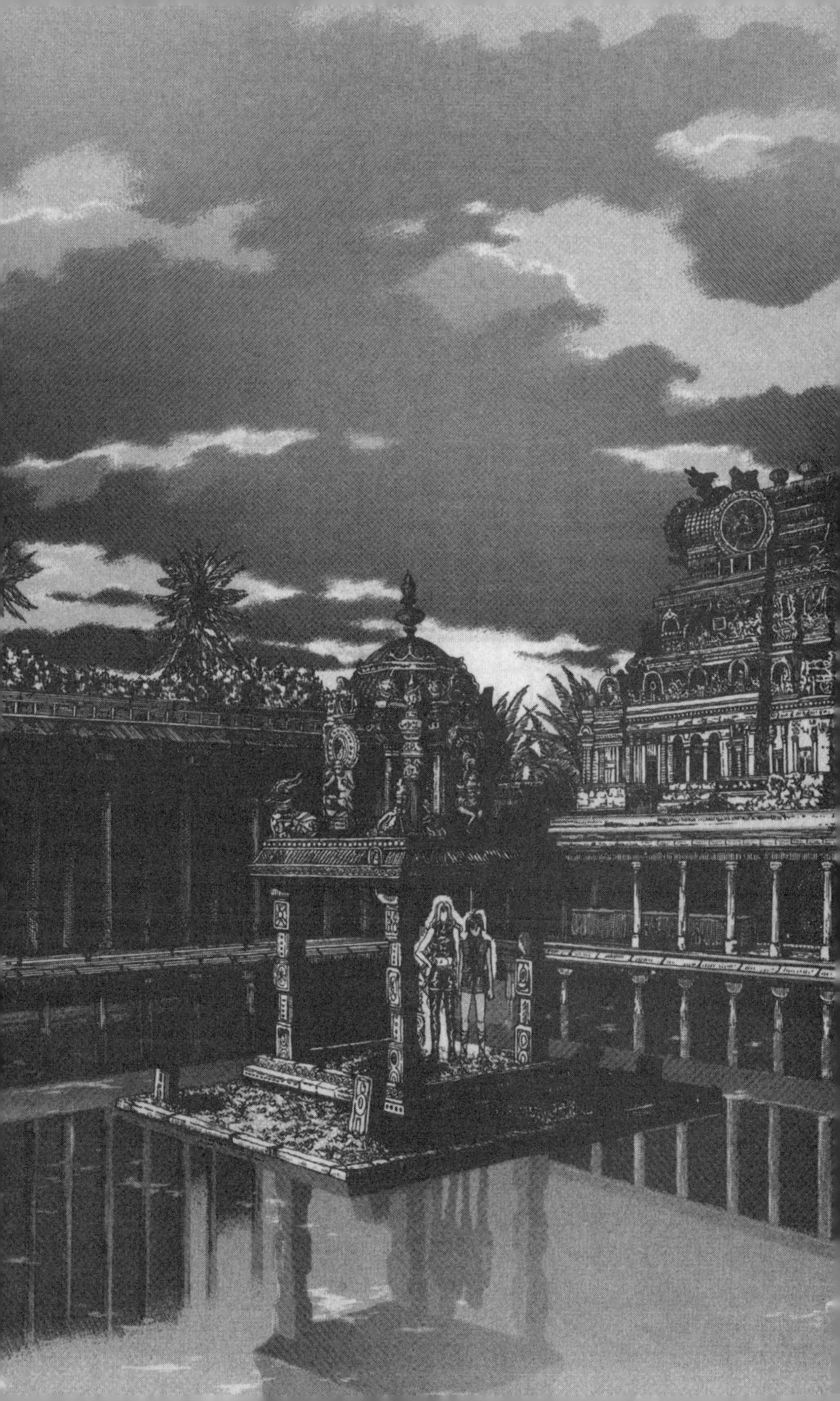

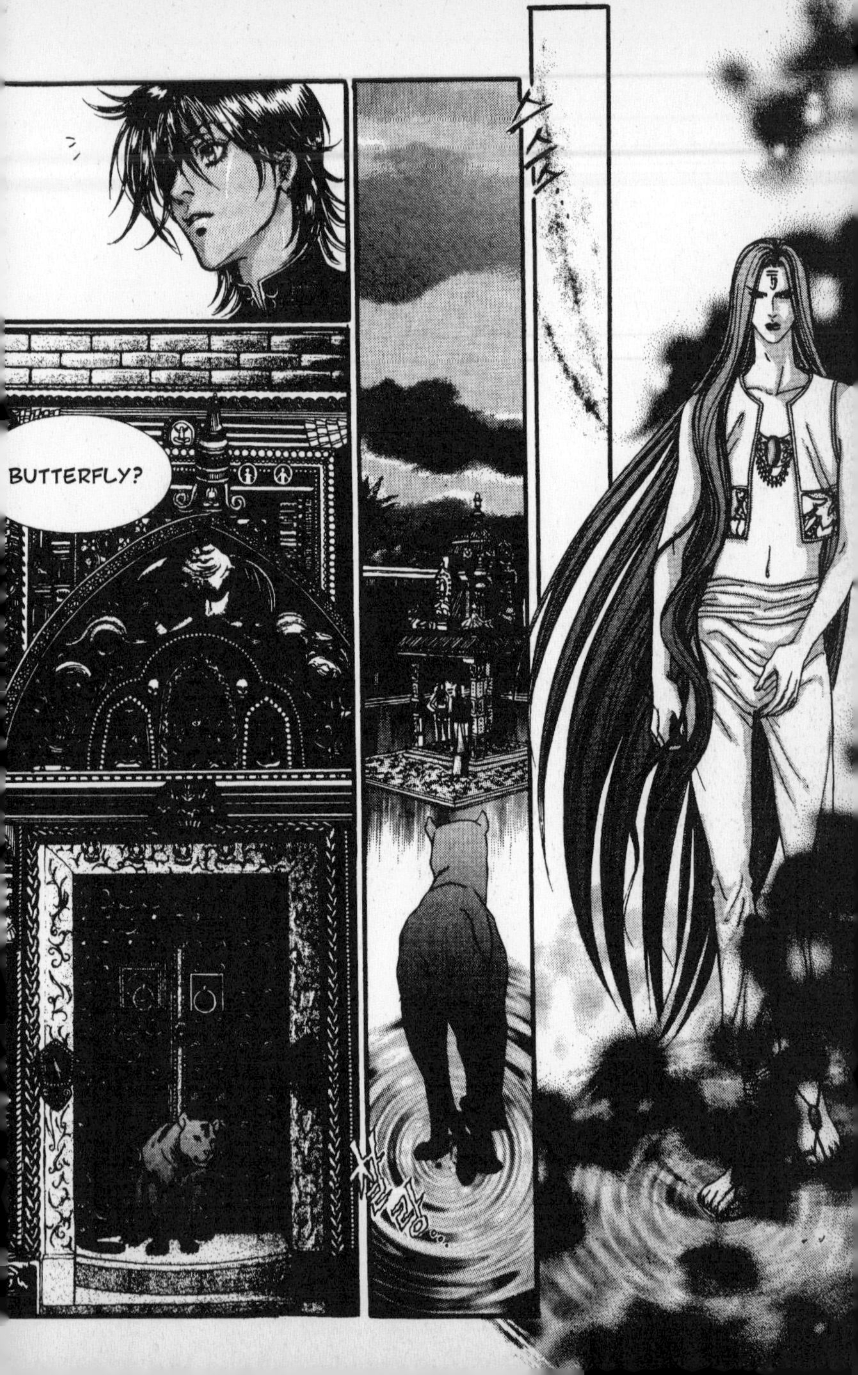
BUTTERFLY?

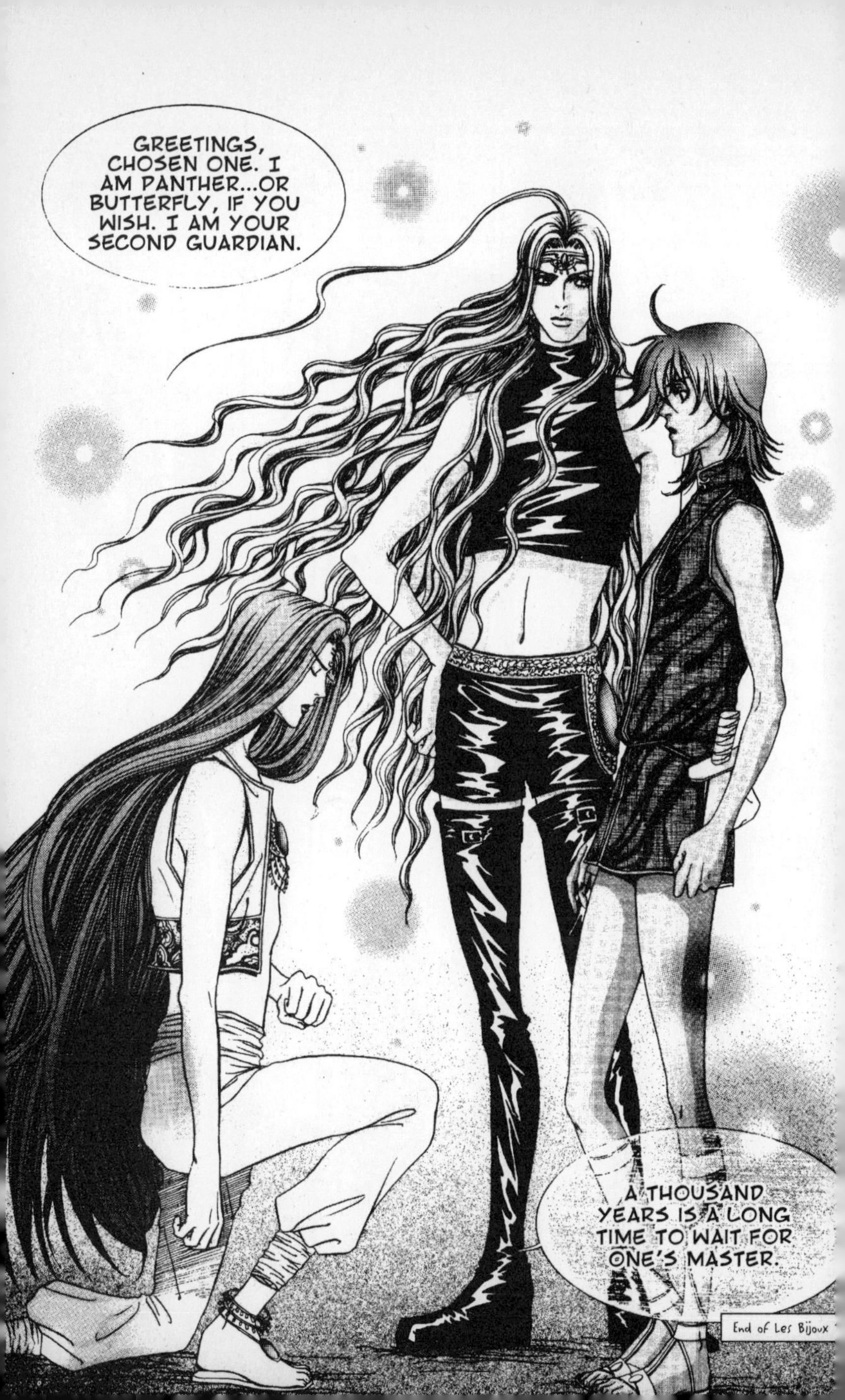
GREETINGS, CHOSEN ONE. I AM PANTHER...OR BUTTERFLY, IF YOU WISH. I AM YOUR SECOND GUARDIAN.
A THOUSAND YEARS IS A LONG TIME TO WAIT FOR ONE'S MASTER.
End of Les Bijoux

WELCOME TO THE WORLD OF STONES

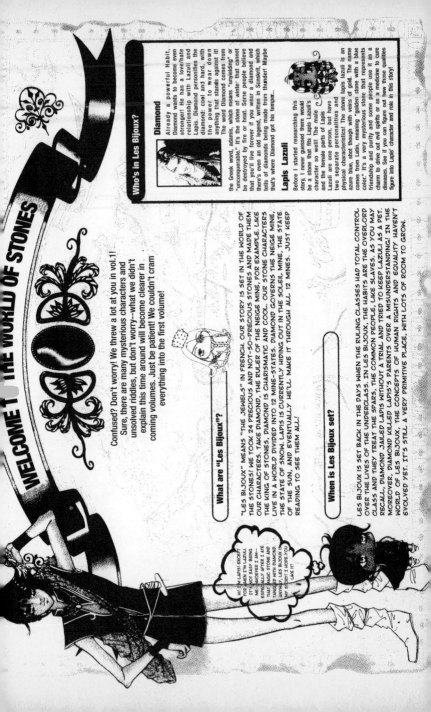

Confused? Don't worry! We threw a lot at you in vol.1! Sure, there are many mysterious characters and unsolved riddles, but don't worry--what we didn't explain this time around will become clearer in coming volumes. Just be patient! We couldn't cram everything into the first volume!

What are "Les Bijoux"?

"LES BIJOUX" MEANS "THE JEWELS" IN FRENCH. OUR STORY IS SET IN THE WORLD OF THE STONES! WE TOOK 24 PRECIOUS AND NOT-SO-PRECIOUS STONES AND MADE THEM OUR CHARACTERS. TAKE DIAMOND, THE RULER OF THE NEIGE MINE, FOR EXAMPLE. LIKE THE KING OF STONES, DIAMOND IS CHARISMATIC AND COOL. OUR STONE CHARACTERS LIVE IN A WORLD DIVIDED INTO 12 MINE-STATES. DIAMOND GOVERNS THE NEIGE MINE, THE STATE OF SNOW. LAPIS IS CURRENTLY HIDING OUT IN THE SOLEIL MINE, THE STATE OF THE SUN, AND EVENTUALLY HE'LL MAKE IT THROUGH ALL 12 MINES. JUST KEEP READING TO SEE THEM ALL!

When is Les Bijoux set?

LES BIJOUX IS SET BACK IN THE DAYS WHEN THE RULING CLASSES HAD TOTAL CONTROL OVER THE LIVES OF THE UNDERCLASS. IN LES BIJOUX, THE HABITS ARE THE OVERLORD CLASS AND THEY TREAT THE SPARS, THE COMMON PEOPLE, LIKE SLAVES. AS YOU MAY RECALL, DIAMOND JAILED LAPIS WITHOUT A TRIAL AND TRIED TO KEEP LAZULI AS A PET. MOREOVER, DIAMOND KILLED LAPIS'S PARENTS OVER A MISUNDERSTANDING! IN THE WORLD OF LES BIJOUX, THE CONCEPTS OF HUMAN RIGHTS AND EQUALITY HAVEN'T EVOLVED YET. IT'S STILL A VERY PRIMITIVE PLACE, WITH LOTS OF ROOM TO GROW.

Who's in Les Bijoux?

Diamond

Already a powerful Habit, Diamond wants to become even stronger! He has a love/hate relationship with Lazuli and Lapis. Diamond personifies the diamond: cool and hard, with the power to wear down anything that stands against it! The word Diamond comes from the Greek word, adamis, which means "unyielding" or "unconquerable." It's the stone of winter that cannot be destroyed by fire or heat. Some people believe that you'll live forever if you wear a diamond and there's even an old legend, written in Sanskrit, which tells of diamonds being made from thunder! Maybe that's where Diamond got his temper...

Lapis Lazuli

Before I started researching this story, I never guessed there would be a stone that fits Lapis Lazuli's character so well! The male Lapis and the female parts of Lapis Lazuli are one person, but have two separate personalities! The stone lapis lazuli is an physical characteristics! The name lazuli comes from a stain, meaning "golden stone with a blue azure blue, skies with veins of gold. The name lapis comes from a Latin, mysterious stone that represents friendship and purity and some people use it as a charm to drive out evil spirits or as a medicine to cure diseases. See if you can figure out how these qualities figure into Lapis' character and role in this story!

ME! I'M LAPIS EXCEPT WHEN I'M LAZULI! IT'S NOT EASY BEING ME... ESPECIALLY AFTER I ATE THAT MAGIC STONE AND CHANGED INTO DIAMOND! ANYWAY, LIKE OUR BOOK. I HOPE YOU LIKE IT!

THE WORD "HABIT" REFERS TO THE TENDENCY OF A STONE'S CRYSTAL TO TAKE A CERTAIN SHAPE. THE HABITS ARE WHITE MEN AND WOMEN WITH COLORED EYES AND CURLY HAIR. "SPAR" IS A KIND OF NEARLY VALUELESS GYPSUM ROCK. IN LES BIJOUX, LAPIS AND HIS PARENTS BELONG TO THE SPAR UNDERCLASS. BONUE SPARS LIVE OUTSIDE THE CASTLE AND WORK FOR THE BENEFIT OF THE HABITS, WHILE THE JUJU SPARS SERVE AS THE HABITS' TOYS. SADD'S FATHER IN THE MINE OF SOLEIL IS A BONUE SPAR WHO COOKS AS THE SOLEIL CASTLE. LAPIS IS ONLY A SPAR, BUT HE'S ALREADY BUCKING THE SYSTEM BY STANDING UP TO DIAMOND FOR SOMETHING HE BELIEVES IN! SOMETIMES ALL IT TAKES IS ONE PERSON WITH VISION TO CHANGE THE WHOLE WORLD. AND THE WORLD OF LES BIJOUX NEEDS CHANGE BADLY...

Question: Okay so what's going on with Lapis Lazuli anyway?

WHAT A COMPLICATED CHARACTER! TWO IN ONE, MALE AND FEMALE! AN EXTRAORDINARY PERSON WITH AN EXTRAORDINARY DESTINY! LAPIS WAS BORN TO DESTROY THE MASTER-SLAVE RELATIONSHIP BETWEEN THE HABITS AND THE SPARS, WHILE LAZULI FINDS HERSELF SMITTEN BY DIAMOND, THE MAN WHO KILLED HER PARENTS! CAN YOU SEE THE CONFLICT BREWING? IT'S GOING TO BE A HARD ROAD AHEAD FOR LAPIS LAZULI...

Question: How far did we get in vol. 1?

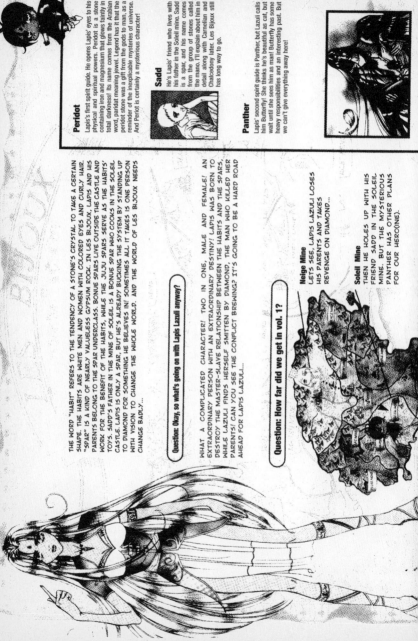

Neige Mine
LET'S SEE, LAPIS LAZULI LOSES HIS PARENTS AND TAKES REVENGE ON DIAMOND...

Soleil Mine
THEN HE HOLES UP WITH HIS FRIEND SADD IN THE SOLEIL MINE. BUT THE MYSTERIOUS PANTHER HAS OTHER PLANS FOR OUR HERO(INE).

Peridot

Lapis's first spirit guide. He opens Lapis' eyes to his physical and spiritual powers. Peridot is a stone containing iron and magnesium that glows faintly in total darkness! Its name comes from the Arabian word, paridat meaning jewel. Legend has it that the peridot stone was a gift from the gods to man, as a reminder of the inexplicable mysteries of universe. And Periot is certainly a mysterious character!

Sadd

He's Lapis' friend who lives with his father in the Soleil mine. Sadd is a spar, and his name comes from the group of stones called the mano. I'll explain about him in detail along with Carnelian and Chalcedony later. Les Bijoux still has long way to go.

Panther

Lapis' second spirit guide. But Lazuli calls him Panther! She thinks he's beautiful as cat, but wait until she sees him as man! Butterfly has some heavy responsibilities and an interesting past. But we can't give everything away here!

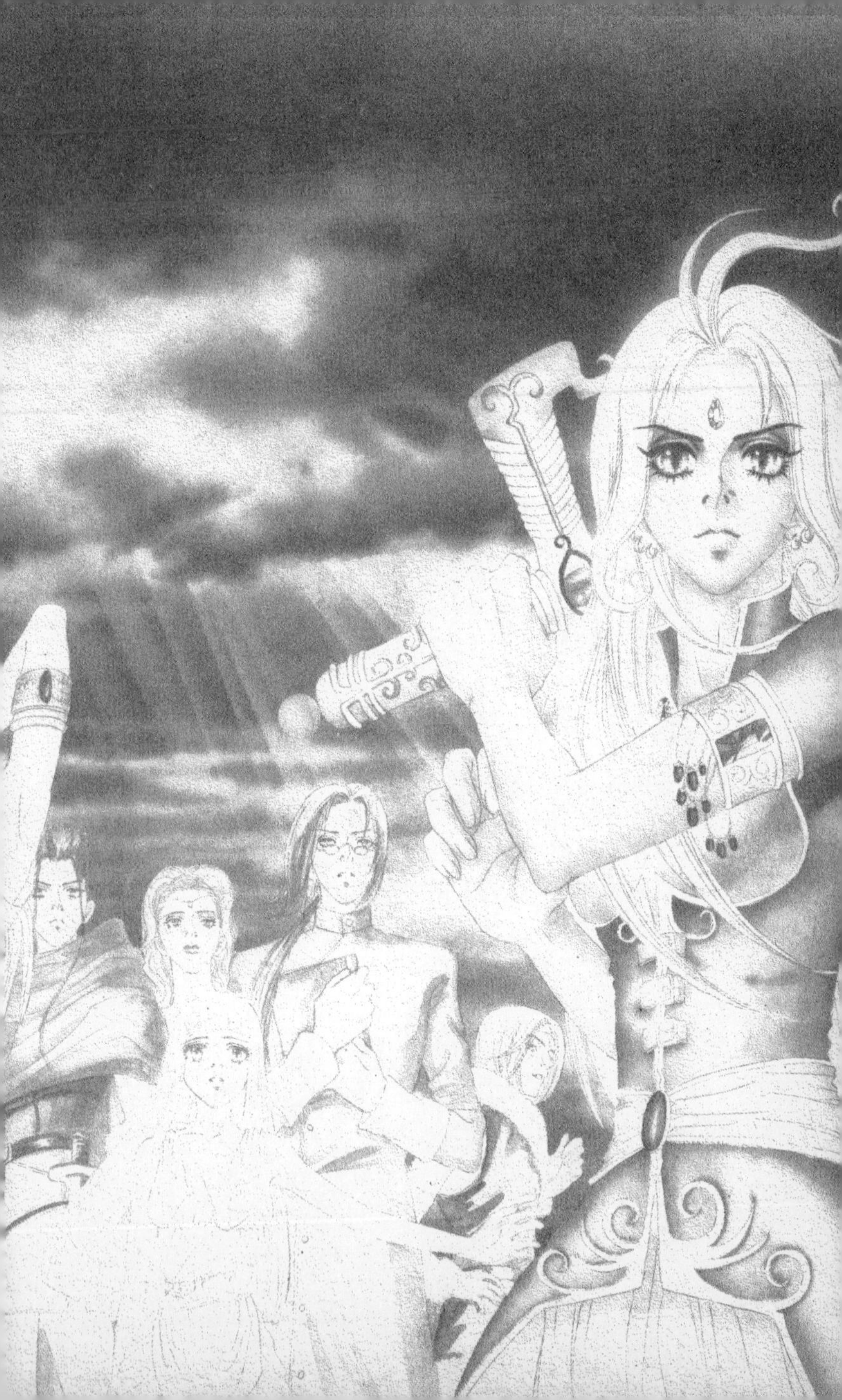

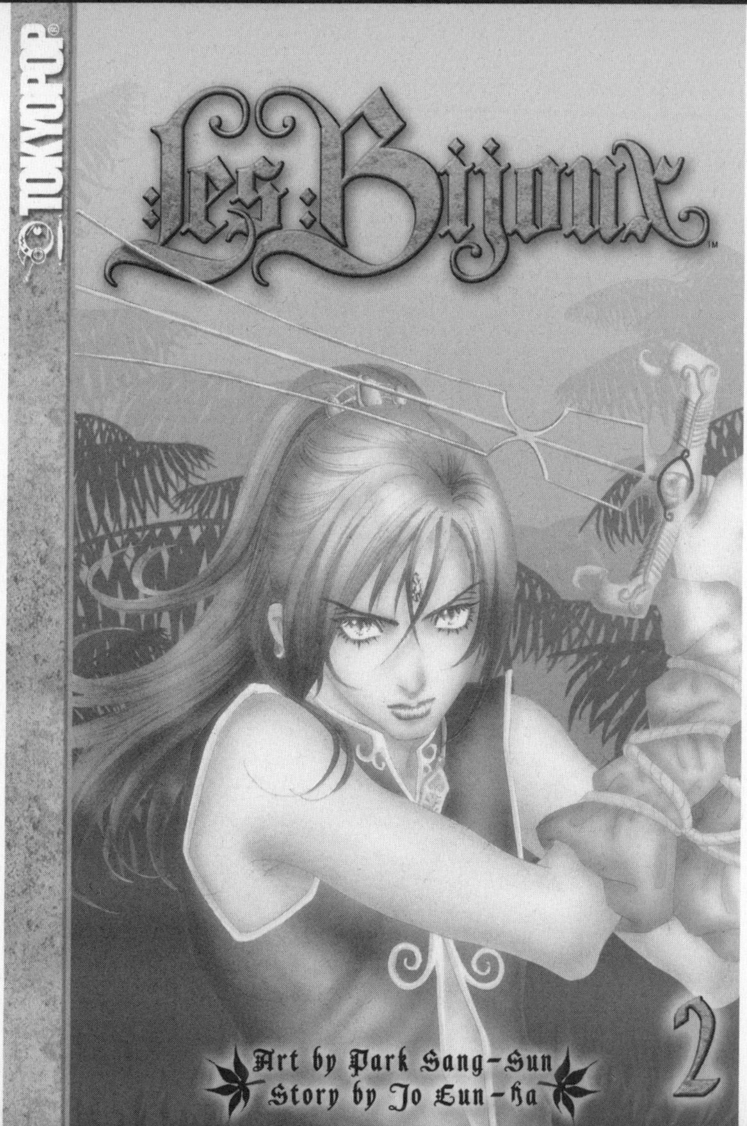
TOKYOPOP
Les Bijoux
2
Art by Park Sang-Sun
Story by Jo Eun-Ha

IN THE NEXT VOLUME OF

Les Bijoux

Destiny and Death

Lapis gains new allies and new enemies as
he faces his role as the one who will
overthrow the tyrannical Habits.

Though Lapis' path is preordained, it is also
perilous--for him and those he loves. Lapis'
parents were slaughtered by the vicious ruler
of his former homeland...could Lapis' new
quest for a divine artifact cost him the lives
of his new friends and family?

Jo Eun-Ha
- Writer -

Dear readers, I'd like to introduce you to Les Bijoux, a world of fantasy, told through a rainbow of gems! It's a beautiful land beset by terrible evils, and its creation took a long time and a lot of hard work. But the book you're holding is proof that with sufficient determination you CAN get blood from a stone. If you try hard enough, you can squeeze out a whole world! It's been a long time since anyone's tried to tell a story on this scale in shojo manga, and the process took more mental and physical strength than I knew I had. However, due of the painful reality of deadlines, the series isn't as good as it could've been. But, if you look closely enough, even the most perfect diamond has its flaws! So, since I can't change history, I just hope you enjoy Les Bijoux, flaws and all! And I'd be grateful for any encouragement you can send my way!

Date of Birth: 9/20/1973

Jo Eun-Ha debuted as writer in 1996, with *Xtra Syndrome*, which placed in Daewon's New Fiction Writers Contest.

Major Works
I am a Deer, *A Monday Man* and *Pasa*

Note: The episodes of Les Bijoux contained in this volume were serialized from 10/15/1999 to 1/1/2000 in the bi-weekly shojo manga magazine, *Issue*.

Park Sang-Sun

- Artist -

Illustrating Les Bijoux was one of the most difficult things I've ever done. This wasn't my story, so I had a tough time conveying the emotion and passion of Eun-Ha's characters. And creating the worlds of Les Bijoux, with all the detail they required, was much more demanding than I was used to. I had to work so fast! Unfortunately, being locked away with Les Bijoux created a whole lot of conflicts with my good friends...and some of my relationships even ended because of it! So for a while there, I was blaming Les Bijoux for all the bad things that were happening in my life. I was so stressed, I even started losing my hair! On one deadline, I ended up in emergency room and had to have surgery! But now I consider working on Les Bijoux as a test from above, and I believe I'll finish this series a stronger person than when I began it.

Because Les Bijoux caused me so much pain, I love it that much more. I'm putting everything I have into it, with the focus of a gem cutter faceting a jewel from raw crystal. I hope you love Les Bijoux as much as I do! And I hope you have fun trying to figure out what's going to happen to Diamond, Lapis and his friends. Finally, I would like Eun-Ha and Ink-Yong to know how much their concessions meant to me!

Date of Birth: 8/9/1974

Park Sang-Sun made her debut in 1997 with *Broken Toy* published in *Issue* magazine and the same year placed in the *White* magazine Super Manga Contest.

Major Works
Requiem of the Soul, Lost Wings

ALSO AVAILABLE FROM ☁ TOKYOPOP®

MANGA

.HACK//LEGEND OF THE TWILIGHT
@LARGE
A.I. LOVE YOU
AI YORI AOSHI
ANGELIC LAYER
ARM OF KANNON May 2004
BABY BIRTH
BATTLE ROYALE
BATTLE VIXENS April 2004
BRAIN POWERED
BRIGADOON
B'TX
CANDIDATE FOR GODDESS, THE April 2004
CARDCAPTOR SAKURA
CARDCAPTOR SAKURA - MASTER OF THE CLOW
CARDCAPTOR SAKURA AUTHENTIC May 2004
CHOBITS
CHRONICLES OF THE CURSED SWORD
CLAMP SCHOOL DETECTIVES
CLOVER
COMIC PARTY June 2004
CONFIDENTIAL CONFESSIONS
CORRECTOR YUI
COWBOY BEBOP
COWBOY BEBOP: SHOOTING STAR
CRESCENT MOON May 2004
CYBORG 009
DEMON DIARY
DEMON ORORON, THE April 2004
DEUS VITAE June 2004
DIGIMON
DIGIMON ZERO TWO
DIGIMON SERIES 3 April 2004
DNANGEL April 2004
DOLL - HARDCOVER May 2004
DRAGON HUNTER
DRAGON KNIGHTS
DUKLYON: CLAMP SCHOOL DEFENDERS
ERICA SAKURAZAWA WORKS
FAERIES' LANDING
FAKE
FLCL
FORBIDDEN DANCE
FRUITS BASKET
G GUNDAM
GATE KEEPERS
GETBACKERS
GHOST! March 2004
GIRL GOT GAME
GRAVITATION
GTO
GUNDAM WING

GUNDAM WING: BATTLEFIELD OF PACIFISTS
GUNDAM WING: ENDLESS WALTZ
GUNDAM WING: THE LAST OUTPOST (G-UNIT)
HAPPY MANIA
HARLEM BEAT
I.N.V.U.
IMMORTAL RAIN June 2004
INITIAL D
ISLAND
JING: KING OF BANDITS
JULINE
JUROR 13 Coming Soon
KARE KANO
KILL ME, KISS ME
KINDAICHI CASE FILES, THE
KING OF HELL
KODOCHA: SANA'S STAGE
LAMENT OF THE LAMB May 2004
LES BIJOUX
LOVE HINA
LUPIN III
MAGIC KNIGHT RAYEARTH I
MAGIC KNIGHT RAYEARTH II
MAHOROMATIC: AUTOMATIC MAIDEN May 2004
MAN OF MANY FACES
MARMALADE BOY
MARS
MINK April 2004
MIRACLE GIRLS
MIYUKI-CHAN IN WONDERLAND
MODEL May 2004
ONE April 2004
PARADISE KISS
PARASYTE
PEACH GIRL
PEACH GIRL: CHANGE OF HEART
PEACH GIRL: AUTHENTIC COLLECTORS BOX SET May 2004
PET SHOP OF HORRORS
PITA-TEN
PLANET LADDER
PLANETES
PRIEST
PSYCHIC ACADEMY March 2004
RAGNAROK
RAVE MASTER
REALITY CHECK
REBIRTH
REBOUND
REMOTE June 2004
RISING STARS OF MANGA
SABER MARIONETTE J
SAILOR MOON
SAINT TAIL

11.20.03 T

ALSO AVAILABLE FROM TOKYOPOP.

SAIYUKI March 2004
SAMURAI DEEPER KYO
SAMURAI GIRL REAL BOUT HIGH SCHOOL
SCRYED
SEIKAI TRILOGY, THE CREST OF THE STARS June 2004
SGT. FROG March 2004
SHAOLIN SISTERS
SHIRAHIME-SYO: SNOW GODDESS TALES HARDCOVER
SHIRAHIME-SYO: SNOW GODDESS TALES SOFTCOVER
June 2004
SHUTTERBOX
SKULL MAN, THE
SNOW DROP
SOKORA REFUGEES Coming Soon
SORCERER HUNTERS
SUIKODEN III May 2004
SUKI
TOKYO BABYLON May 2004
TOKYO MEW MEW
UNDER THE GLASS MOON
VAMPIRE GAME
VISION OF ESCAFLOWNE, THE
WILD ACT
WISH
WORLD OF HARTZ Coming Soon
X-DAY
ZODIAC P.I.

NOVELS

KARMA CLUB Coming Soon
SAILOR MOON

ART BOOKS

CARDCAPTOR SAKURA
MAGIC KNIGHT RAYEARTH
PEACH GIRL ART BOOK April 2004

ANIME GUIDES

COWBOY BEBOP ANIME GUIDES
GUNDAM TECHNICAL MANUALS
SAILOR MOON SCOUT GUIDES

TOKYOPOP KIDS

STRAY SHEEP

CINE-MANGA™

CARDCAPTORS
FAIRLY ODDPARENTS March 2004
FINDING NEMO
G.I. JOE SPY TROOPS
JACKIE CHAN ADVENTURES
JIMMY NEUTRON BOY GENIUS, THE ADVENTURES OF
KIM POSSIBLE
LIZZIE MCGUIRE
POWER RANGERS: NINJA STORM
SHREK Coming Soon
SPONGEBOB SQUAREPANTS
SPY KIDS 2
SPY KIDS 3-D Game Over March 2004
TRANSFORMERS: ARMADA
TRANSFORMERS: ENERGON May 2004

**For more
information visit
www.TOKYOPOP.com**

11.20.03 T

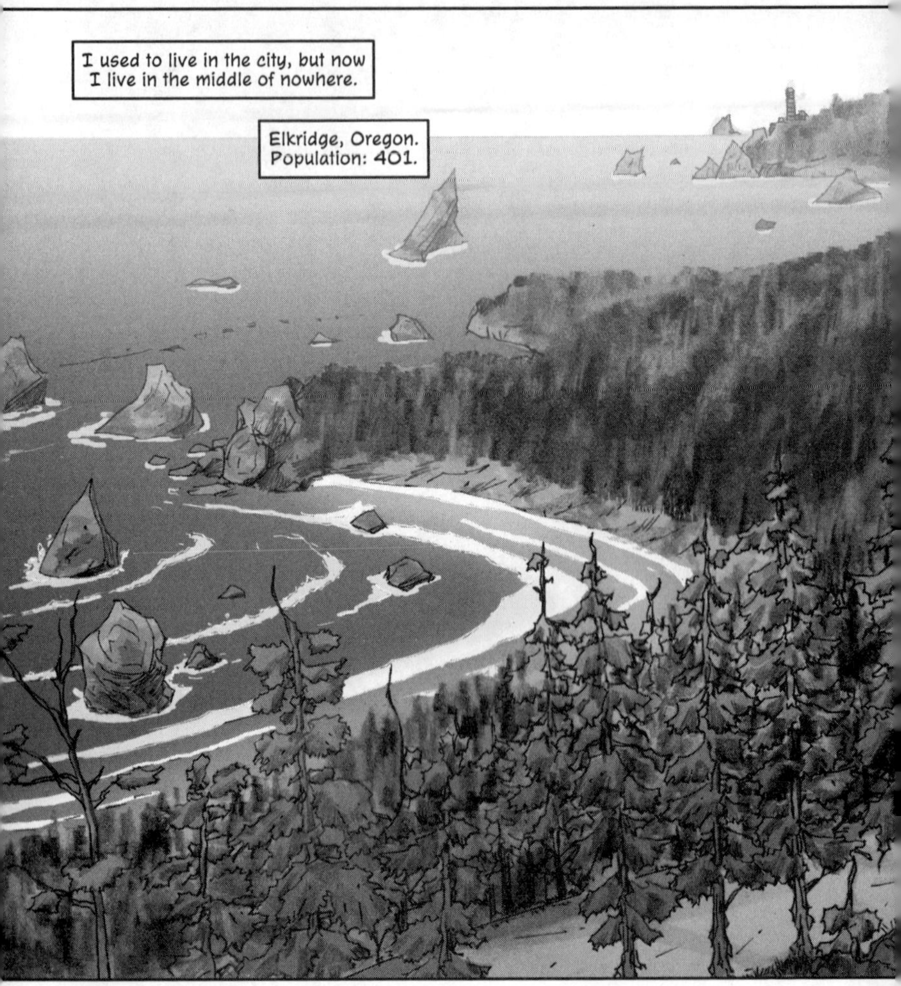
I used to live in the city, but now I live in the middle of nowhere.
Elkridge, Oregon. Population: 401.

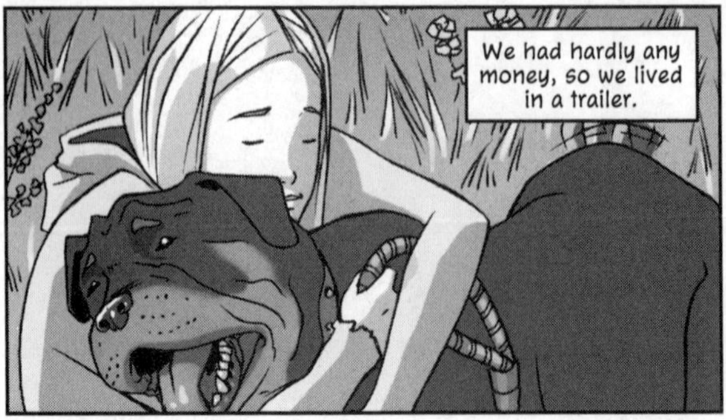
We had hardly any money, so we lived in a trailer.

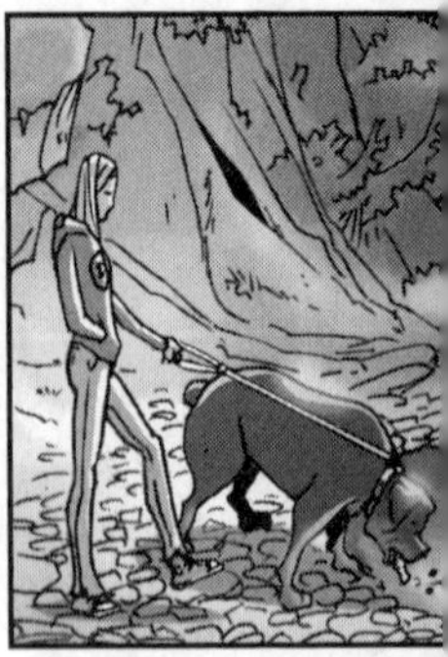

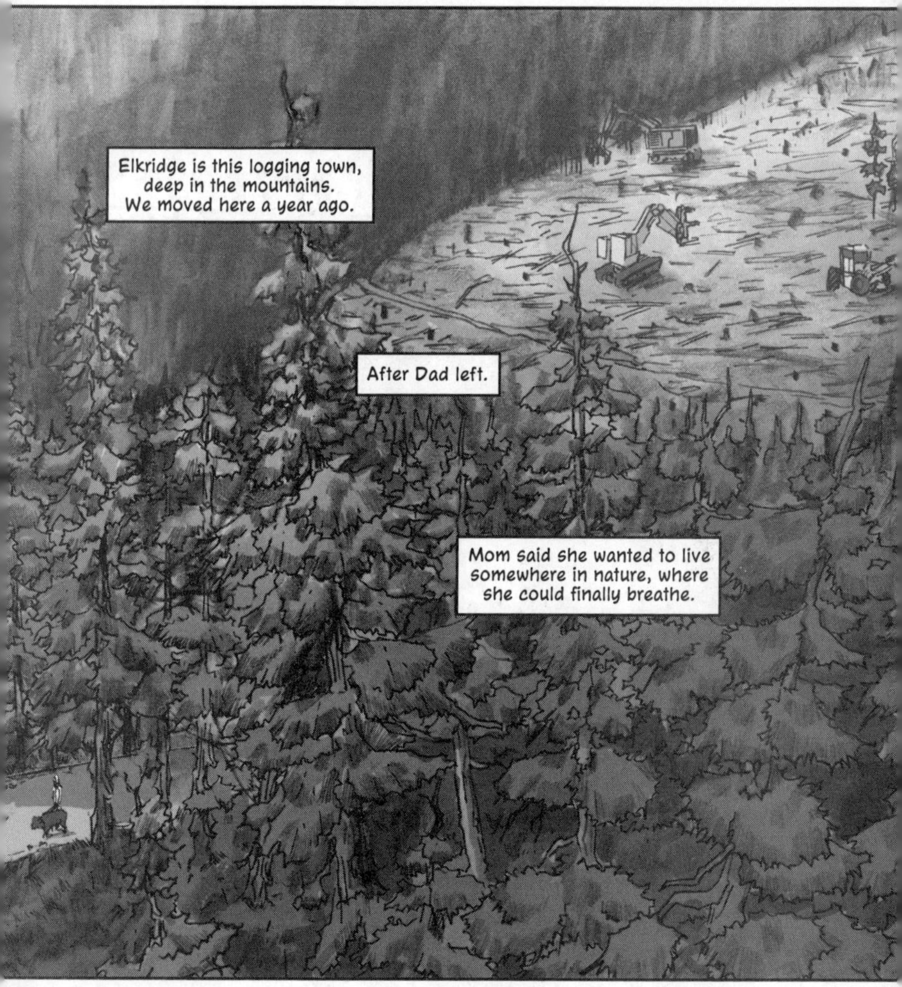
Elkridge is this logging town, deep in the mountains. We moved here a year ago.
After Dad left.
Mom said she wanted to live somewhere in nature, where she could finally breathe.

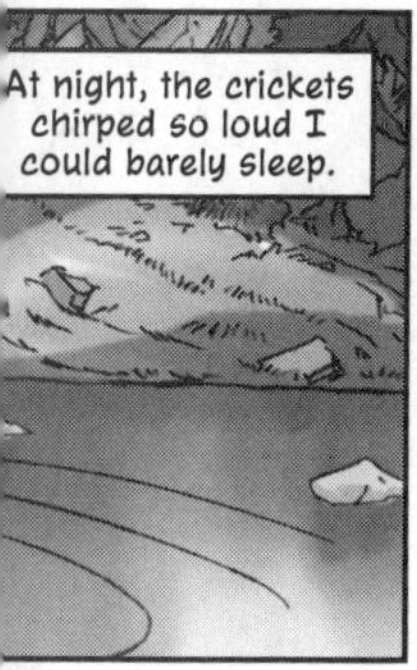
At night, the crickets chirped so loud I could barely sleep.

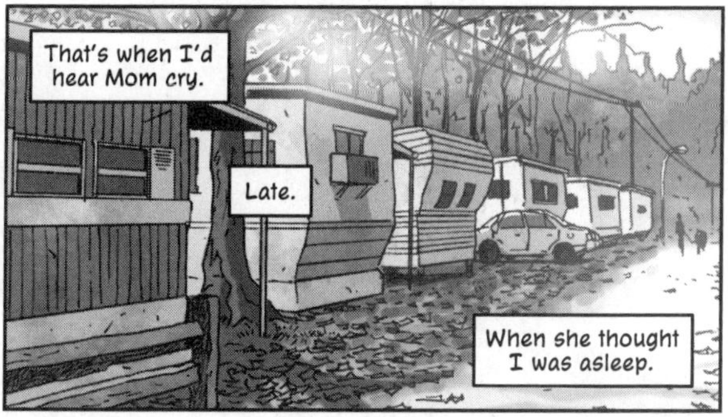
That's when I'd hear Mom cry.
Late.
When she thought I was asleep.

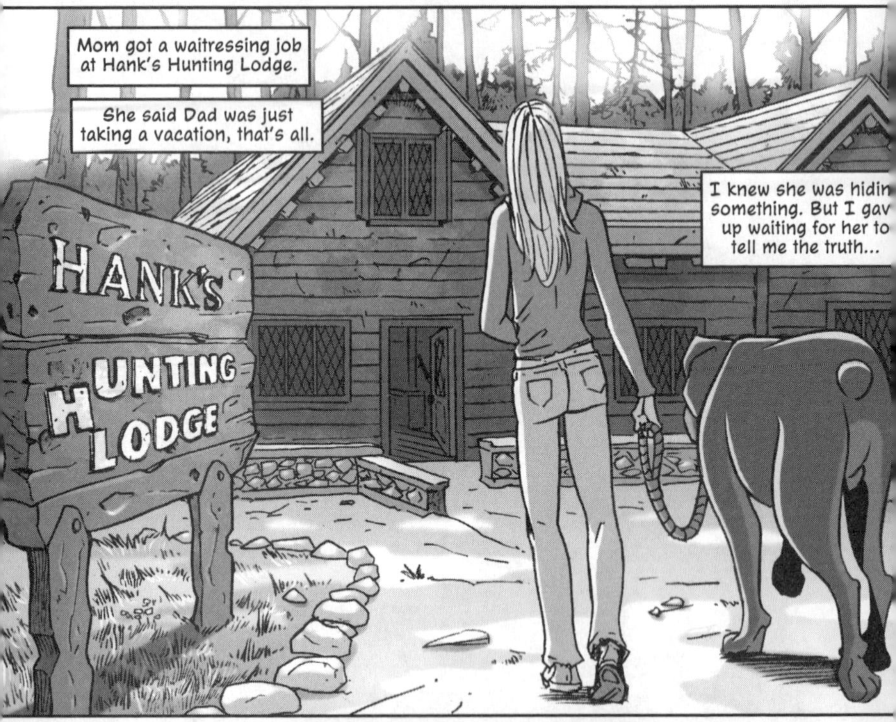
Mom got a waitressing job at Hank's Hunting Lodge.
She said Dad was just taking a vacation, that's all.
HANK'S HUNTING LODGE
I knew she was hidin something. But I gav up waiting for her to tell me the truth...

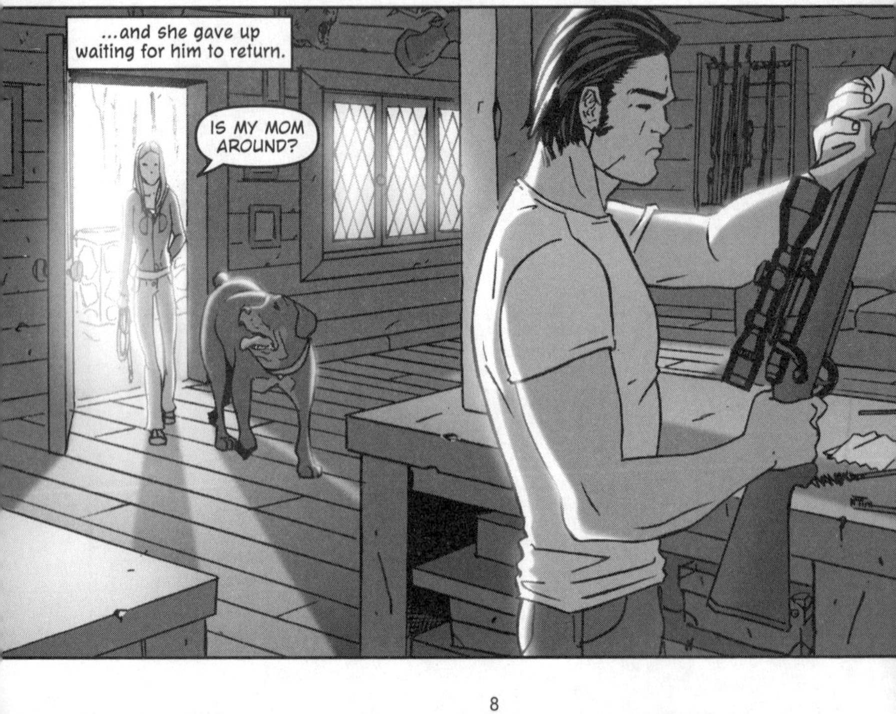
...and she gave up waiting for him to return.
IS MY MOM AROUND?

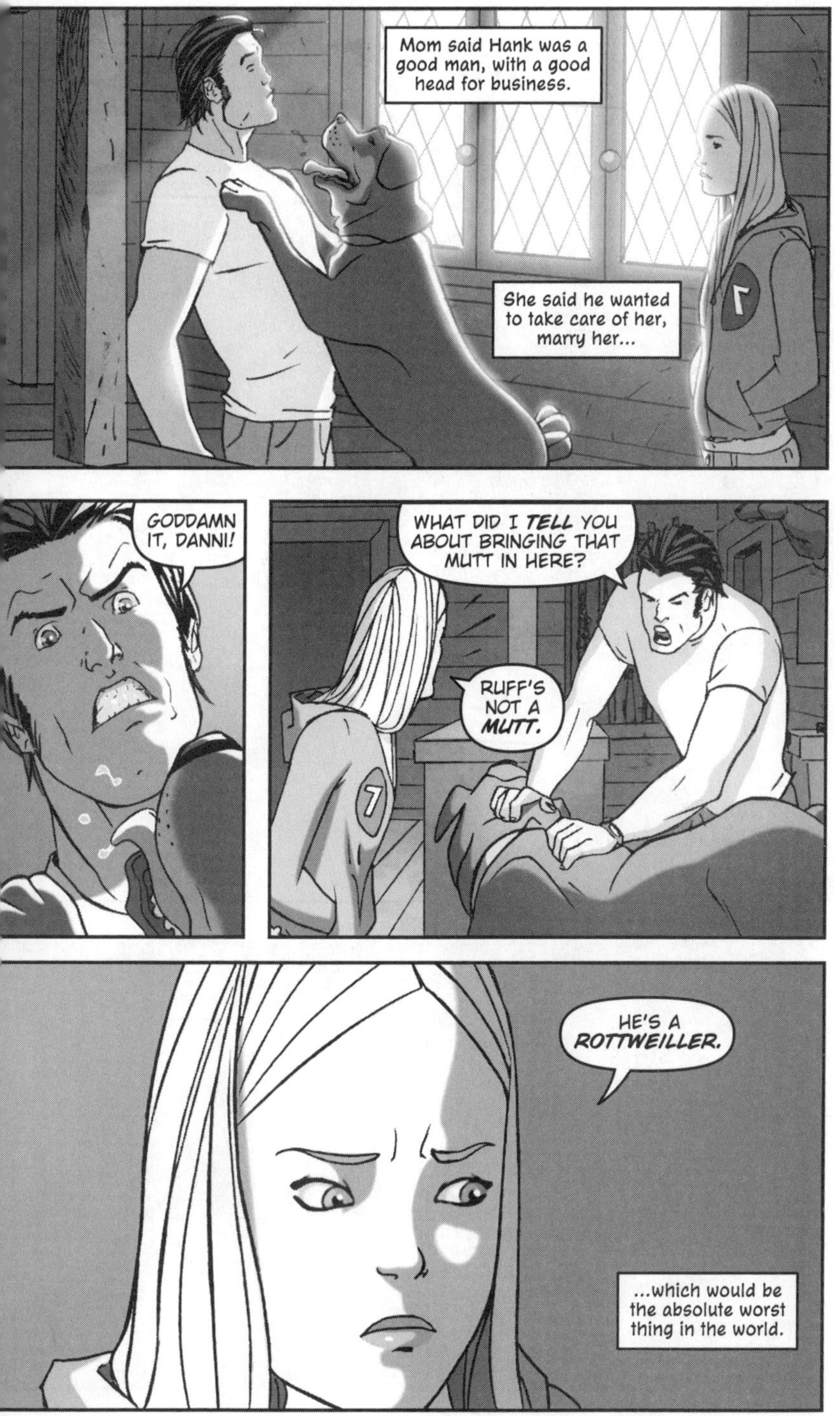
Mom said Hank was a good man, with a good head for business.
She said he wanted to take care of her, marry her...
GODDAMN IT, DANNI!
WHAT DID I *TELL* YOU ABOUT BRINGING THAT MUTT IN HERE?
RUFF'S NOT A *MUTT.*
HE'S A *ROTTWEILLER.*
...which would be the absolute worst thing in the world.

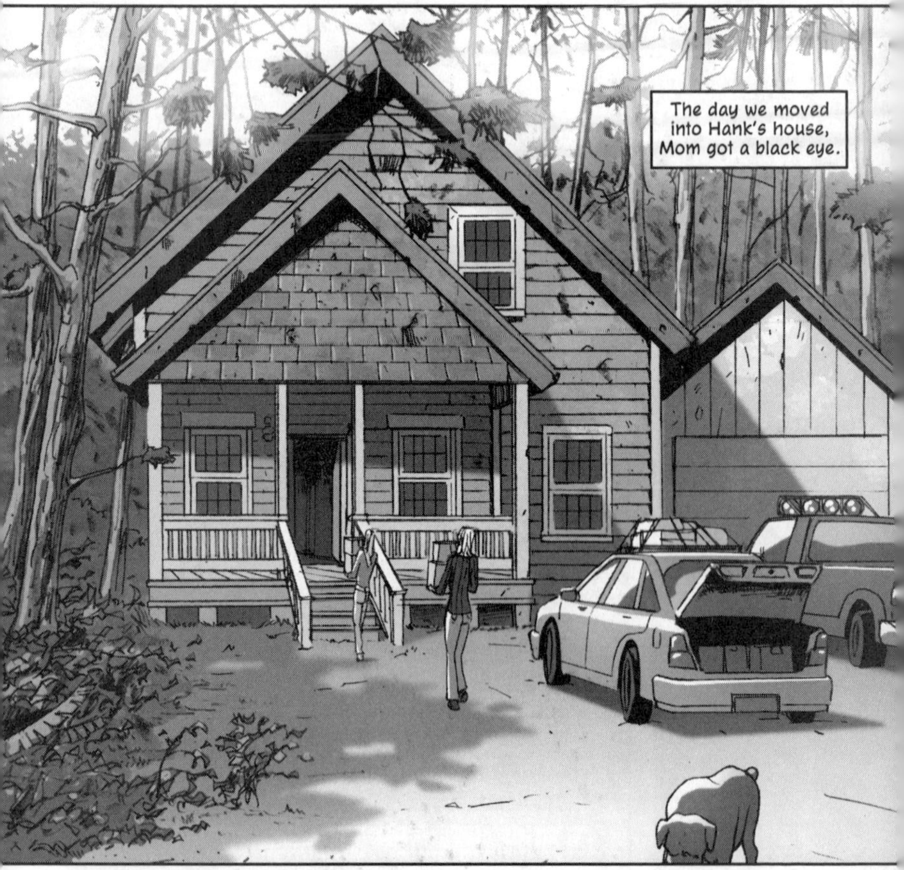
The day we moved into Hank's house, Mom got a black eye.

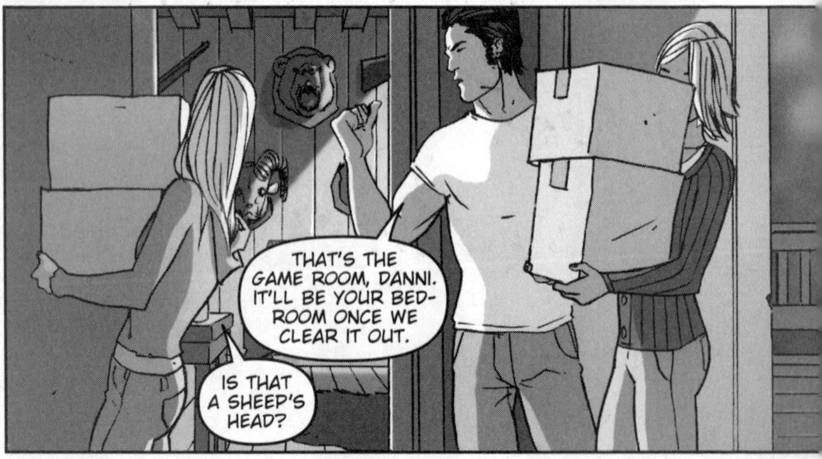
THAT'S THE GAME ROOM, DANNI. IT'LL BE YOUR BED-ROOM ONCE WE CLEAR IT OUT.
IS THAT A SHEEP'S HEAD?

'TIL THEN YOU'RE GONNA HAVE TO SHARE A ROOM WITH HASKELL.

IT'S THE ONE ON THE RIGHT.

I'LL GET THE SUITCASES-- THEY LOOK PRETTY DARN HEAVY.

WHAT ABOUT THE BOXES?

WE CAN HANDLE IT, HANK. YOU GO BACK TO THE LODGE.

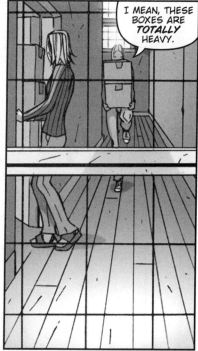

I MEAN, THESE BOXES ARE *TOTALLY* HEAVY.

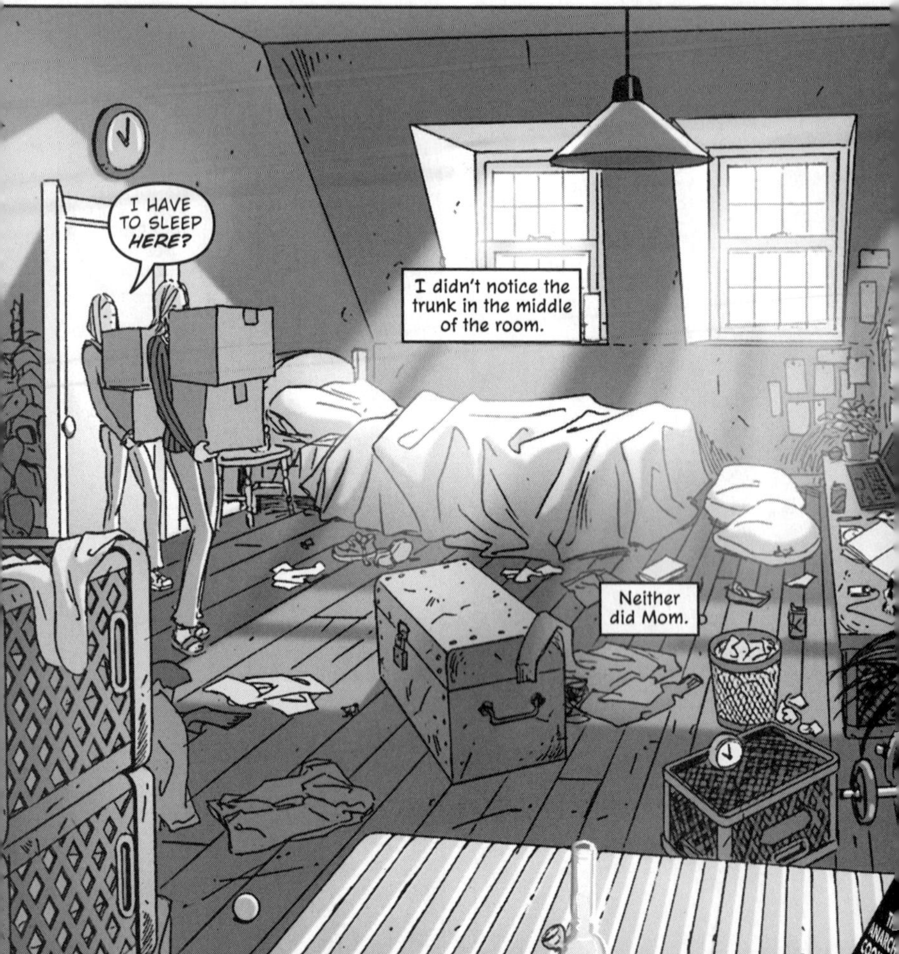
I HAVE TO SLEEP *HERE?*
I didn't notice the trunk in the middle of the room.
Neither did Mom.
ON THE ROAD
JACK KEROUAC
SIDDHARTHA
HERMANN HESSE

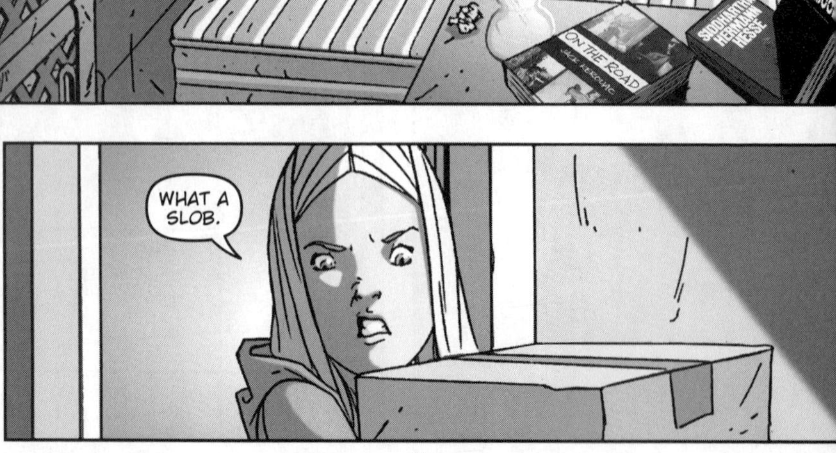
WHAT A SLOB.

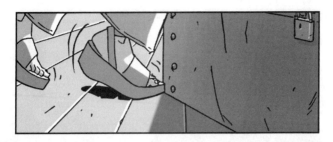

MOM!

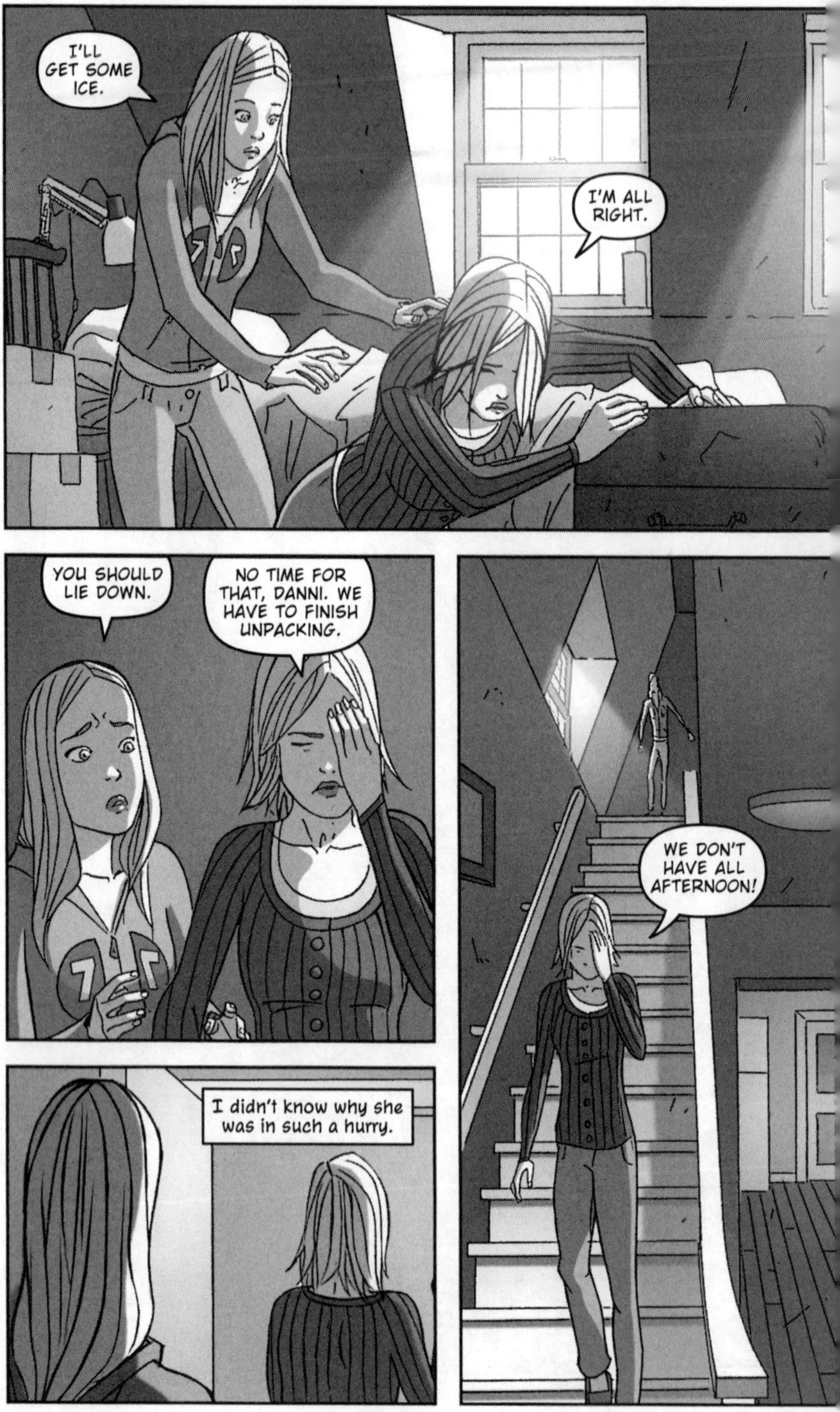
I'LL GET SOME ICE.
I'M ALL RIGHT.
YOU SHOULD LIE DOWN.
NO TIME FOR THAT, DANNI. WE HAVE TO FINISH UNPACKING.
WE DON'T HAVE ALL AFTERNOON!
I didn't know why she was in such a hurry.

What was she talking about?

We *did* have all afternoon.

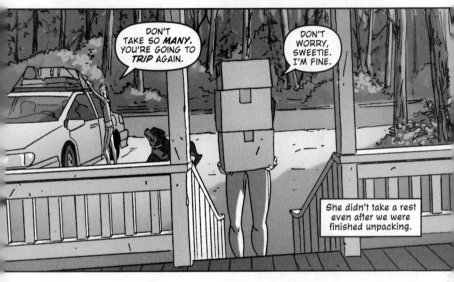

DON'T TAKE SO *MANY*. YOU'RE GOING TO *TRIP* AGAIN.

DON'T WORRY, SWEETIE. I'M FINE.

She didn't take a rest even after we were finished unpacking.

SSSS
SSS
CRACKLE

She said she had to get dinner on the table before Hank came back.

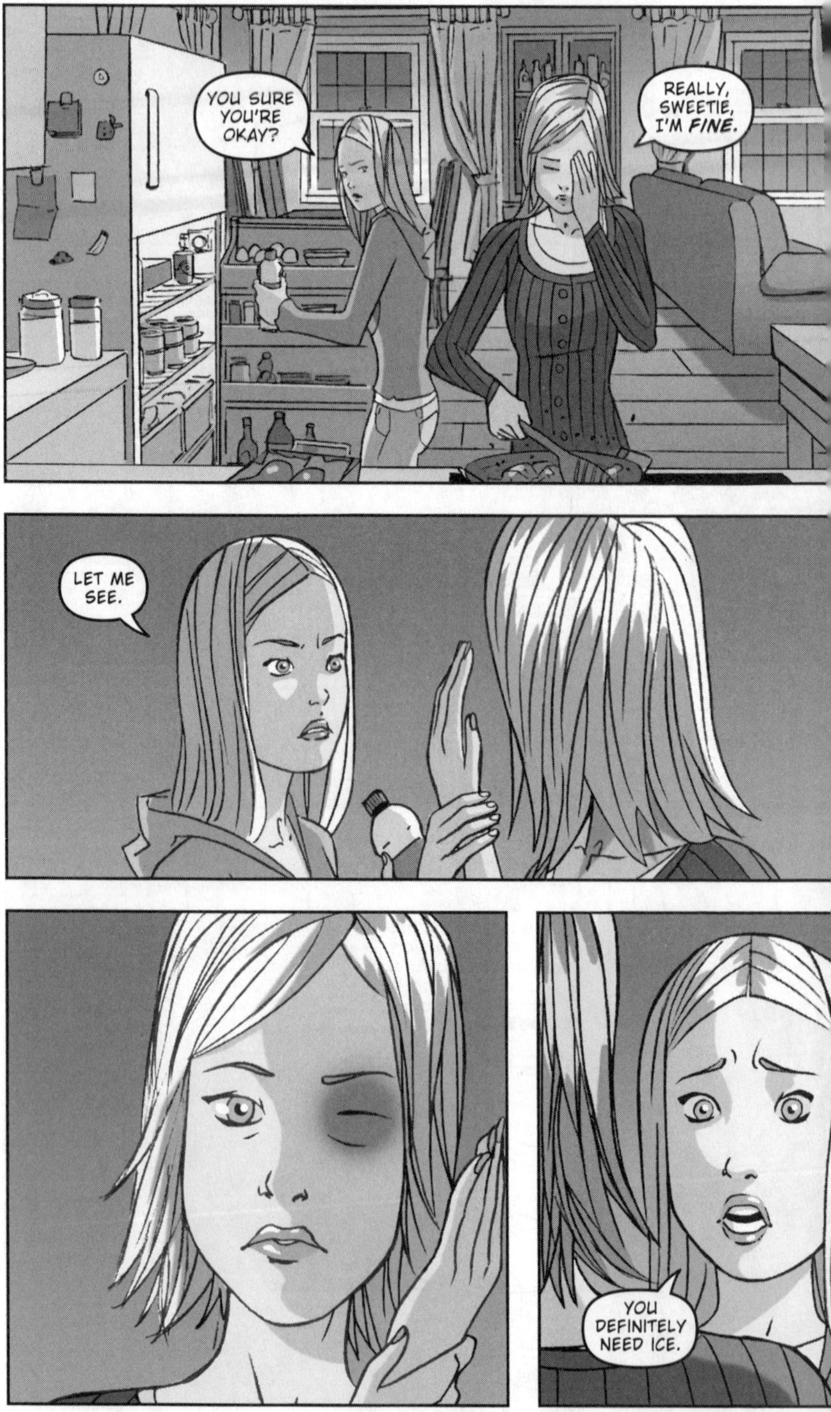
YOU SURE YOU'RE OKAY?
REALLY, SWEETIE, I'M *FINE*.
LET ME SEE.
YOU DEFINITELY NEED ICE.

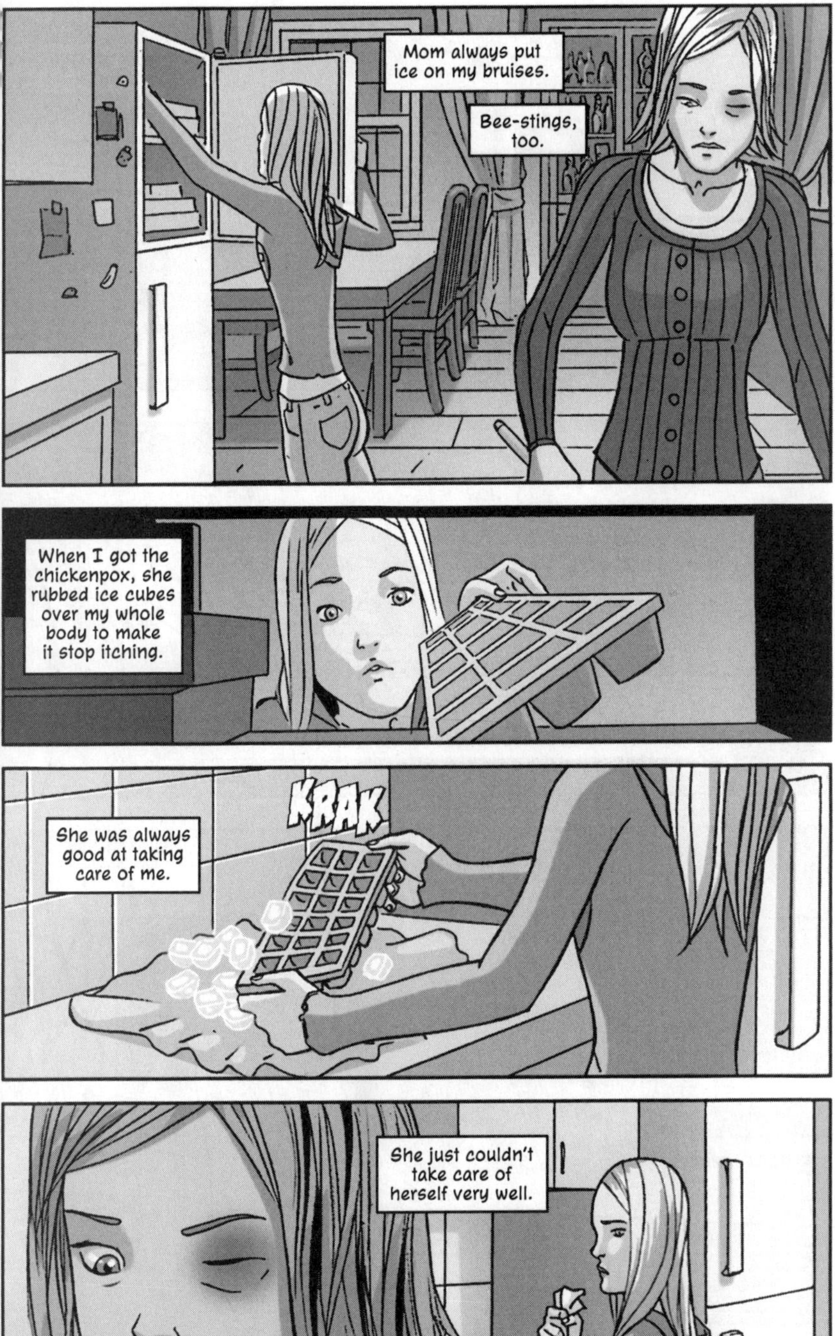
Mom always put ice on my bruises.
Bee-stings, too.
When I got the chickenpox, she rubbed ice cubes over my whole body to make it stop itching.
KRAK
She was always good at taking care of me.
She just couldn't take care of herself very well.

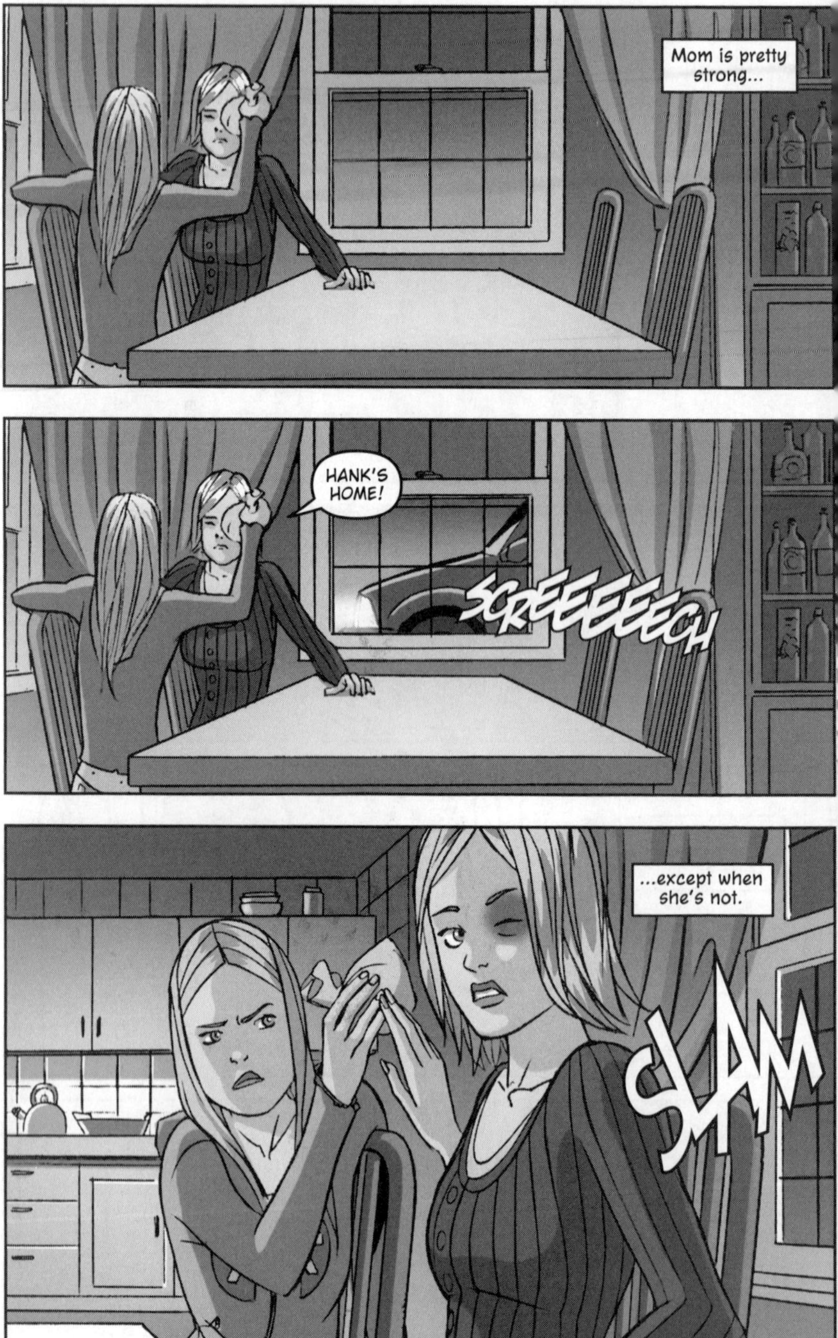
Mom is pretty strong...
HANK'S HOME!
SCREEEEEECH
...except when she's not.
SLAM

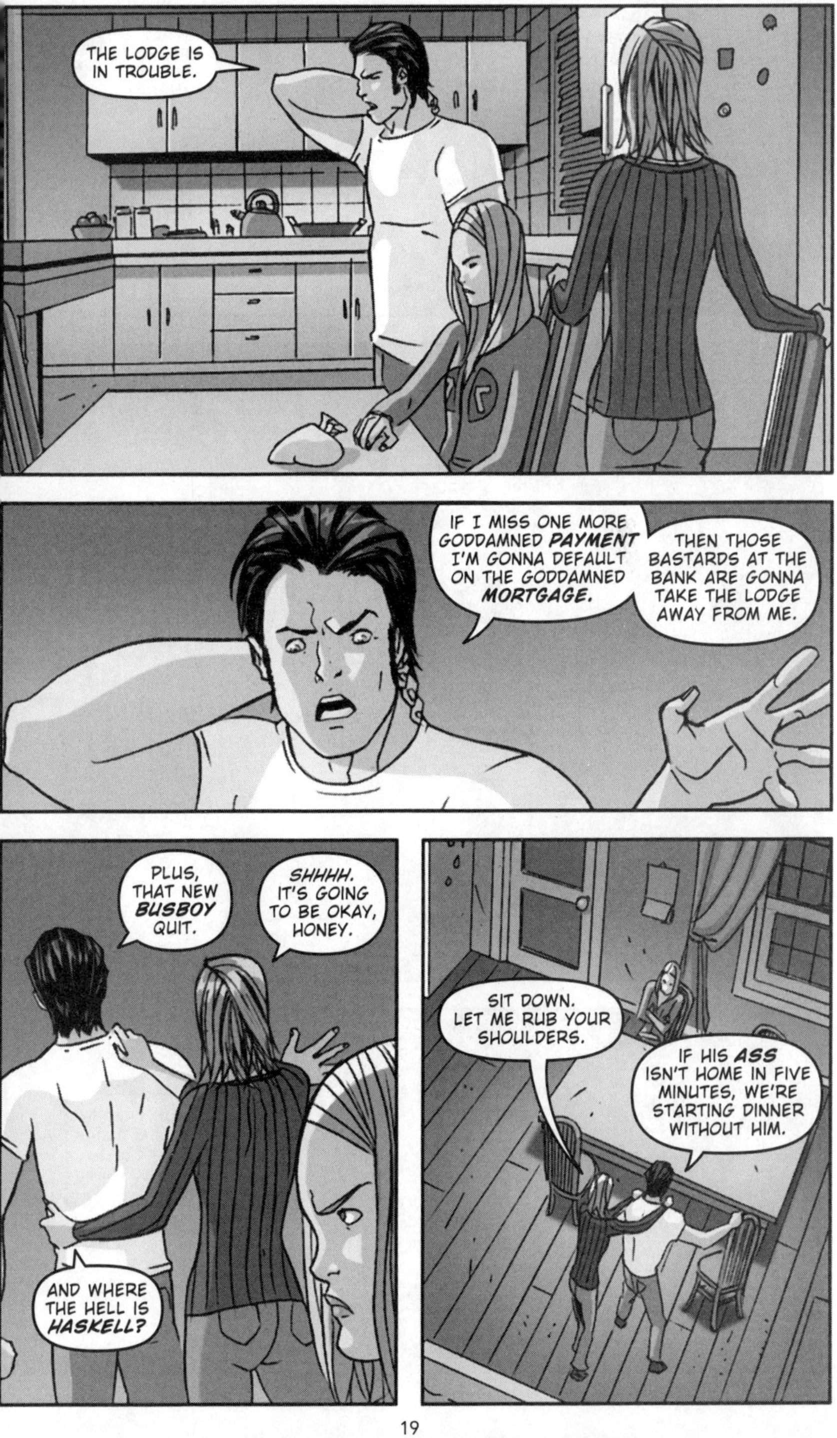
THE LODGE IS IN TROUBLE.
IF I MISS ONE MORE GODDAMNED PAYMENT I'M GONNA DEFAULT ON THE GODDAMNED MORTGAGE.
THEN THOSE BASTARDS AT THE BANK ARE GONNA TAKE THE LODGE AWAY FROM ME.
PLUS, THAT NEW BUSBOY QUIT.
SHHHH. IT'S GOING TO BE OKAY, HONEY.
AND WHERE THE HELL IS HASKELL?
SIT DOWN. LET ME RUB YOUR SHOULDERS.
IF HIS ASS ISN'T HOME IN FIVE MINUTES, WE'RE STARTING DINNER WITHOUT HIM.

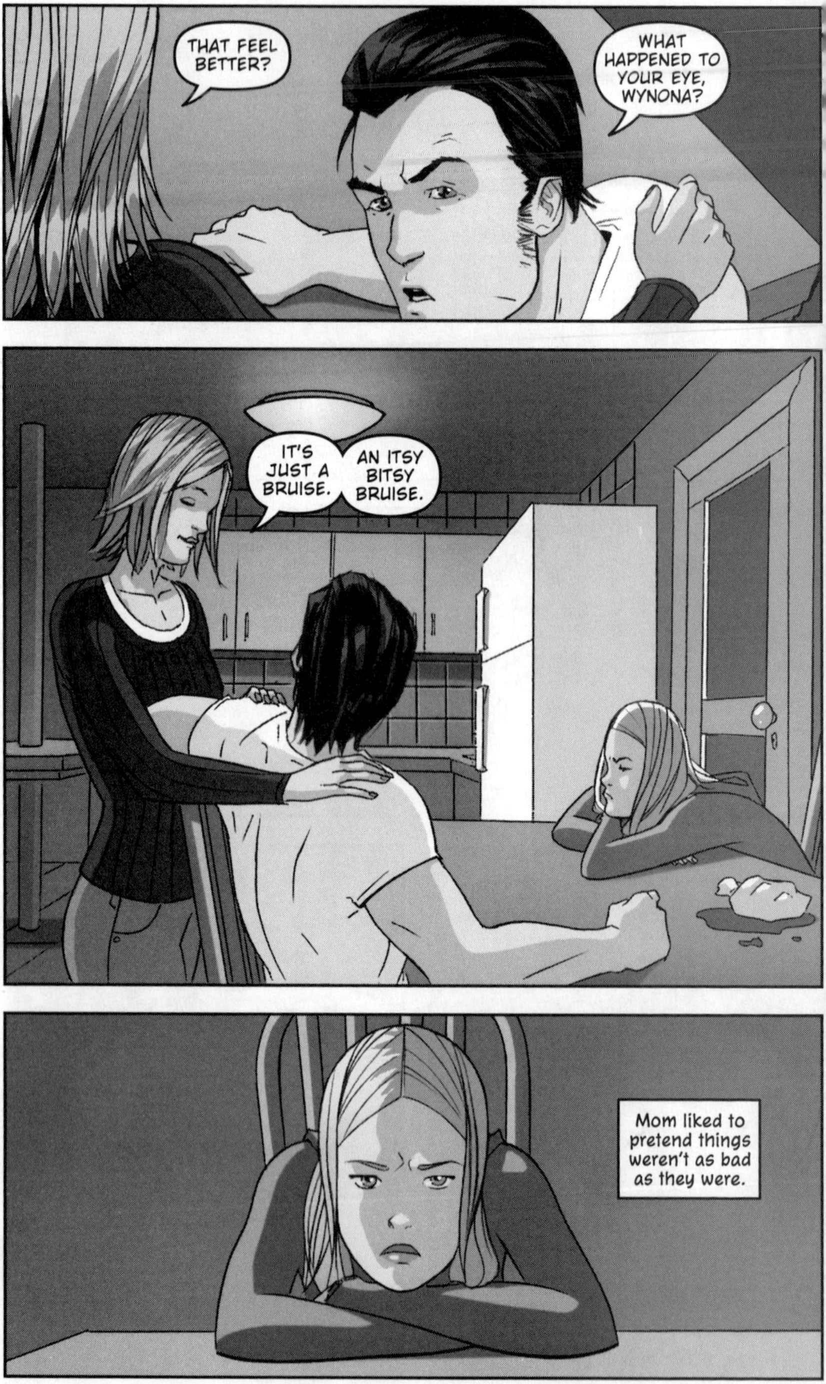
THAT FEEL BETTER?
WHAT HAPPENED TO YOUR EYE, WYNONA?
IT'S JUST A BRUISE.
AN ITSY BITSY BRUISE.
Mom liked to pretend things weren't as bad as they were.

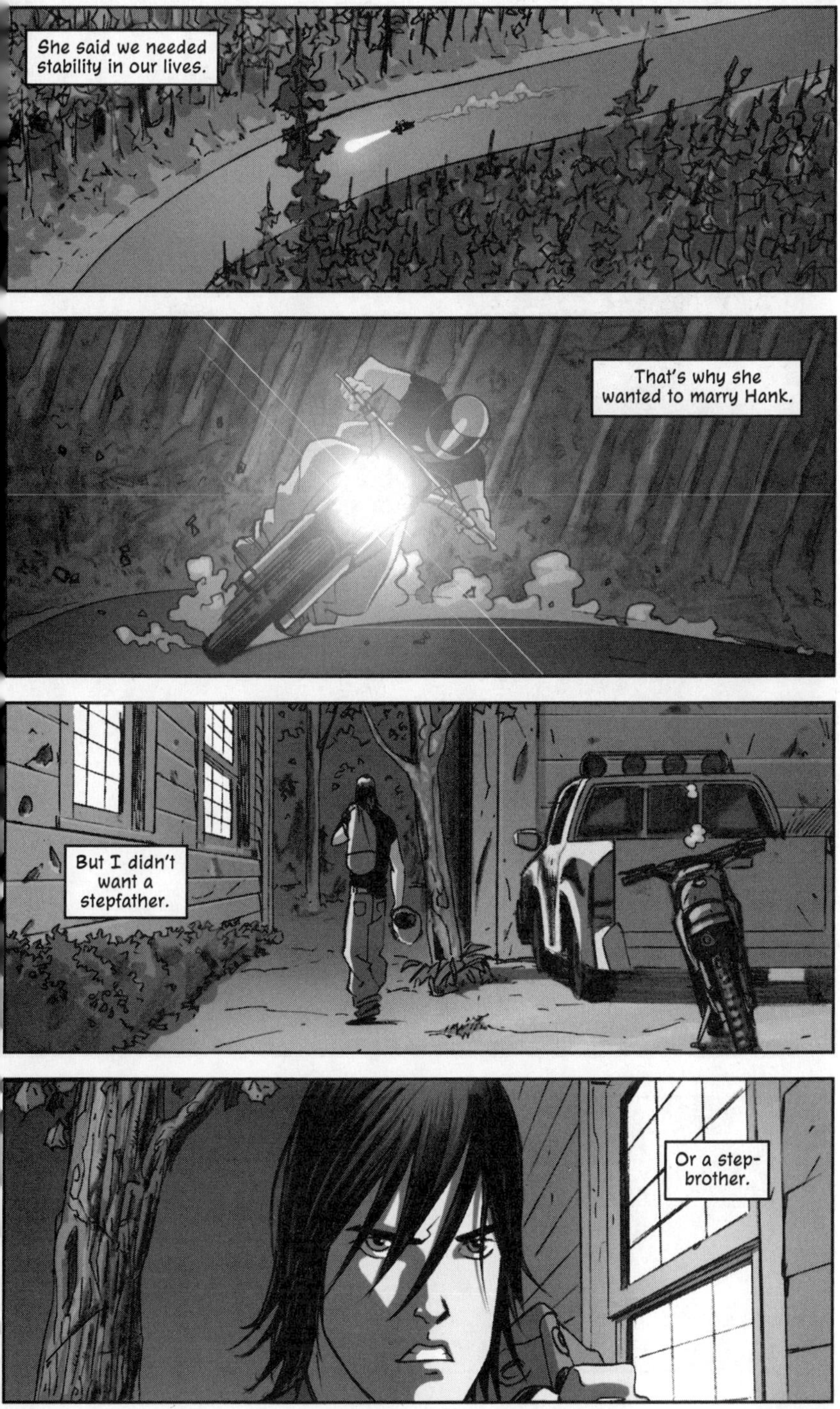
She said we needed stability in our lives.
That's why she wanted to marry Hank.
But I didn't want a stepfather.
Or a step-brother.

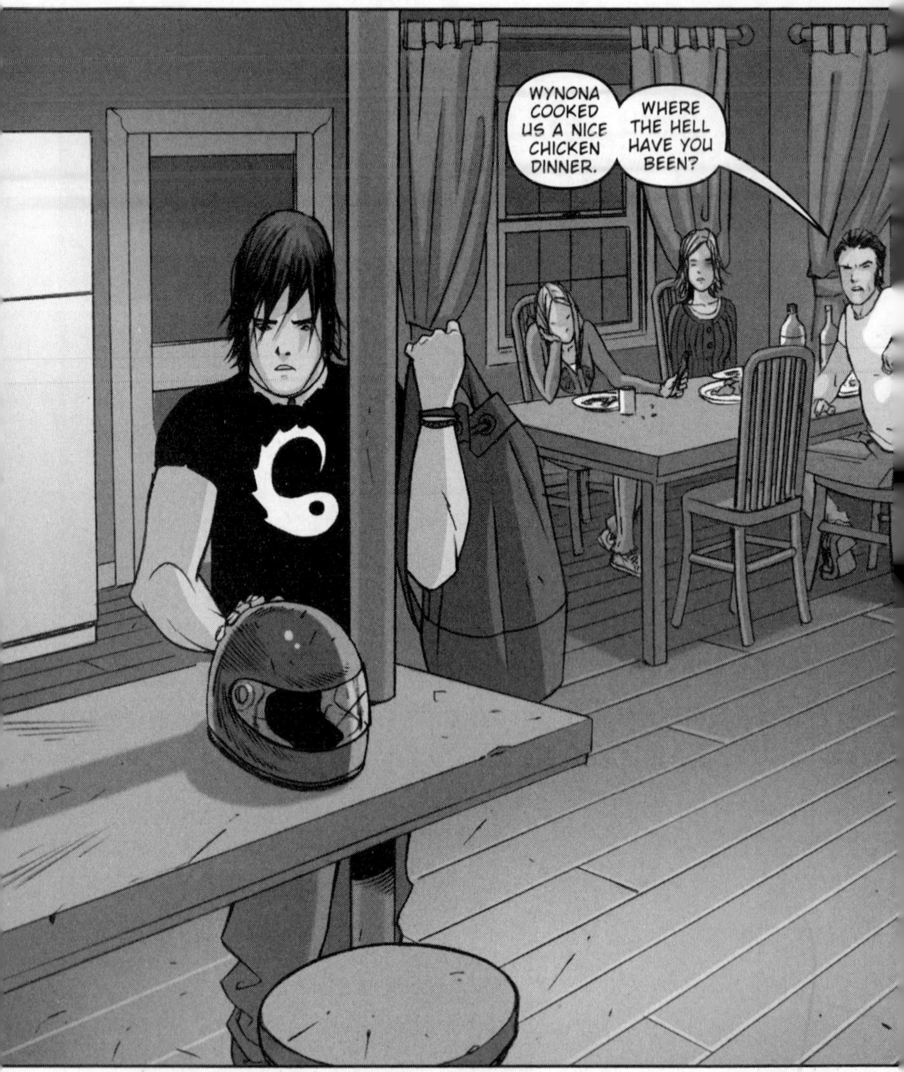
WHERE THE HELL HAVE YOU BEEN?
WYNONA COOKED US A NICE CHICKEN DINNER.

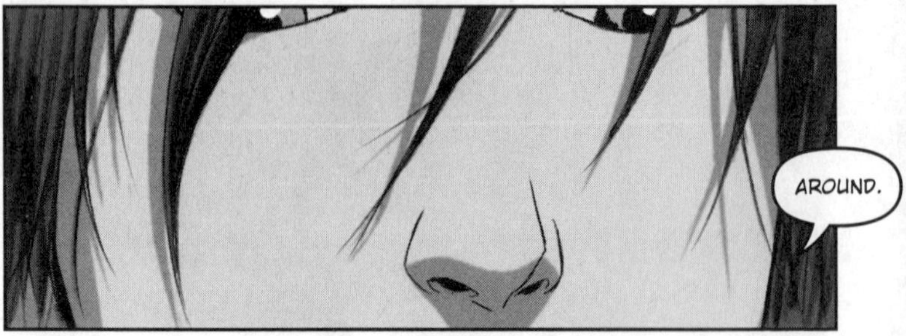
AROUND.

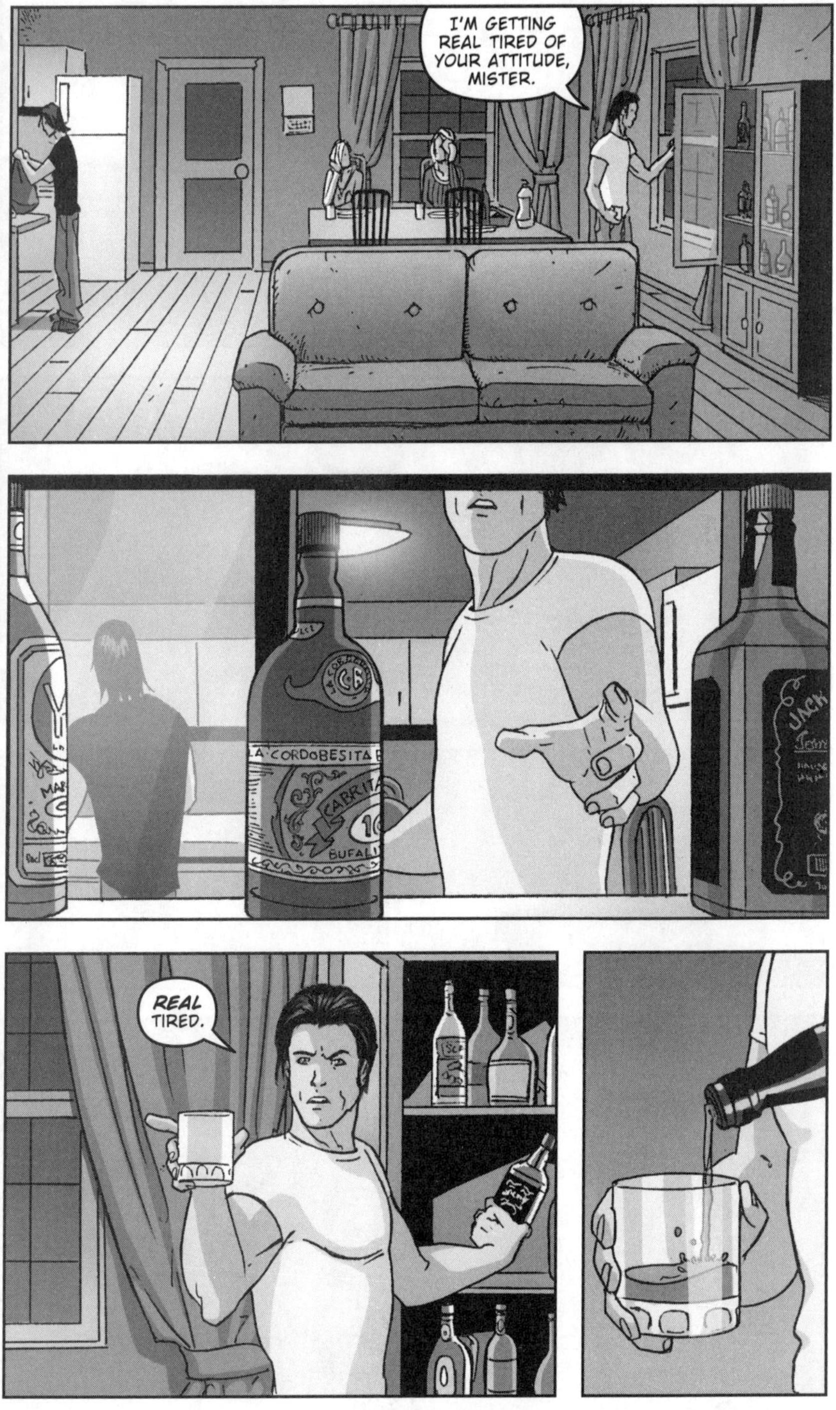
I'M GETTING REAL TIRED OF YOUR ATTITUDE, MISTER.
LA CORDOBESITA
CABRITA
BUFALI
REAL TIRED.

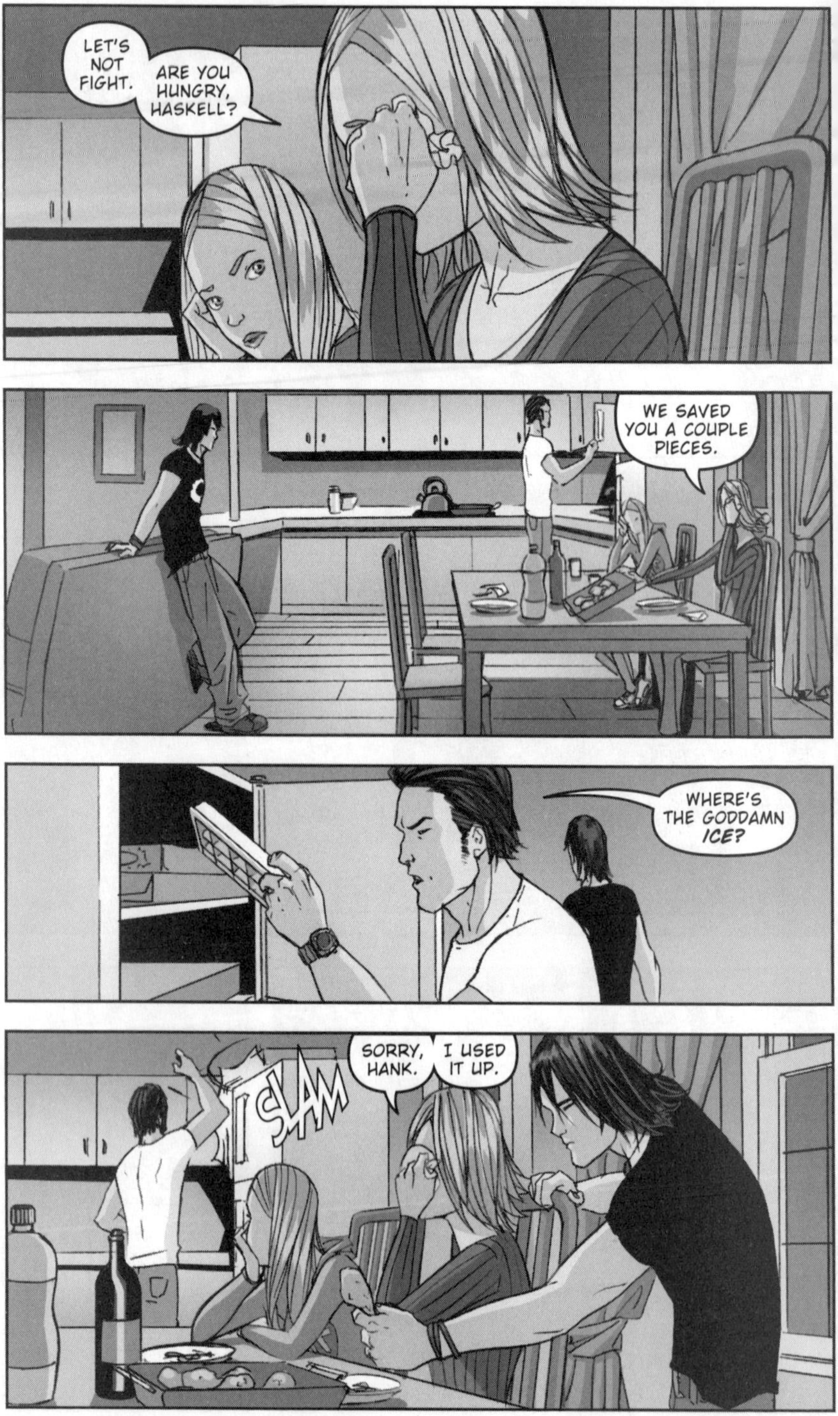
LET'S NOT FIGHT.
ARE YOU HUNGRY, HASKELL?
WE SAVED YOU A COUPLE PIECES.
WHERE'S THE GODDAMN *ICE?*
SLAM
SORRY, HANK.
I USED IT UP.

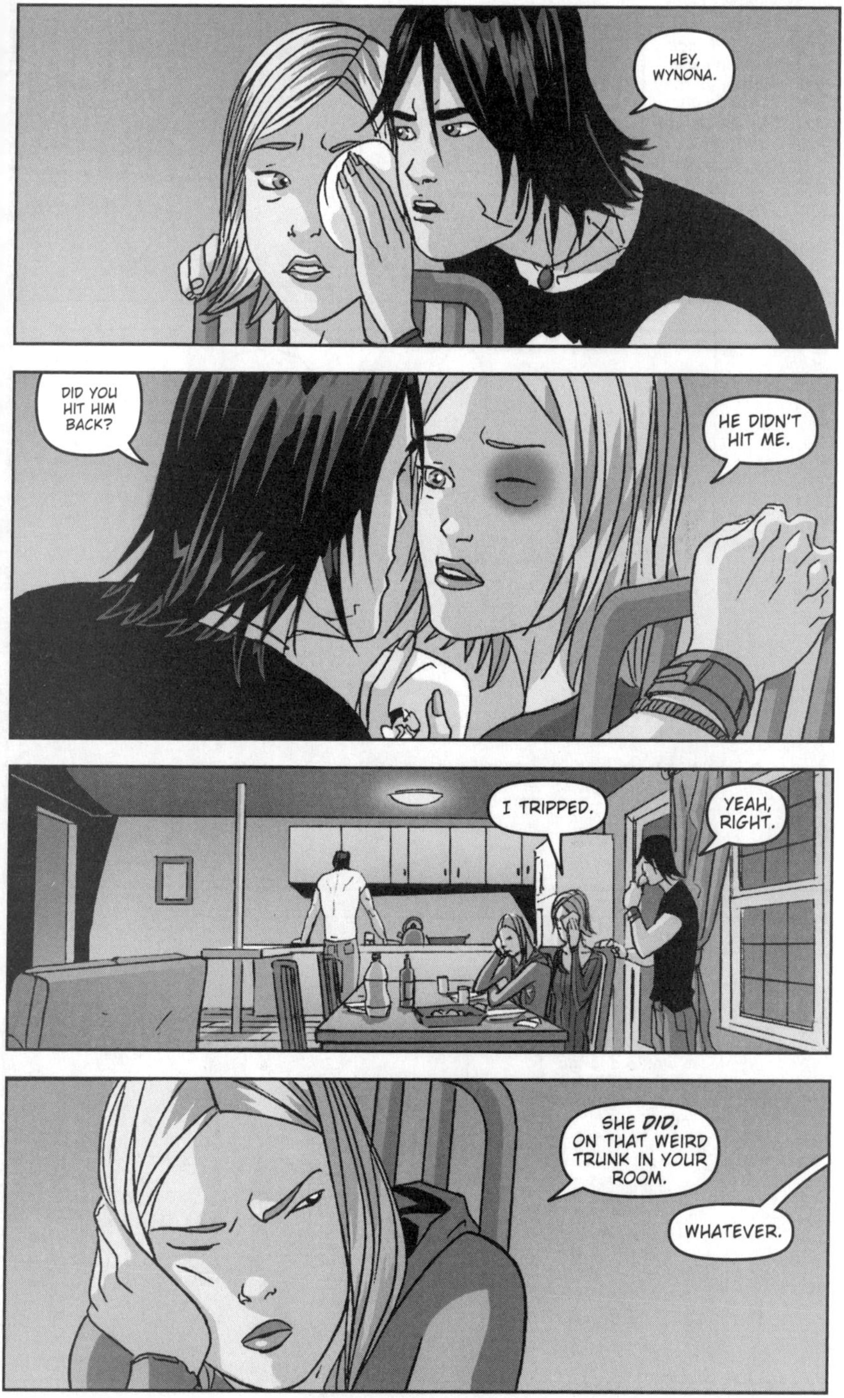
HEY, WYNONA.
DID YOU HIT HIM BACK?
HE DIDN'T HIT ME.
I TRIPPED.
YEAH, RIGHT.
SHE DID. ON THAT WEIRD TRUNK IN YOUR ROOM.
WHATEVER.

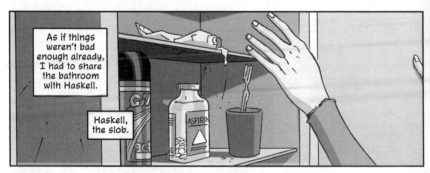

As if things weren't bad enough already, I had to share the bathroom with Haskell.

Haskell, the slob.

GROSS.

I kept telling myself that it was just temporary.

Mom would change her mind about Hank, and then we'd move out of here.

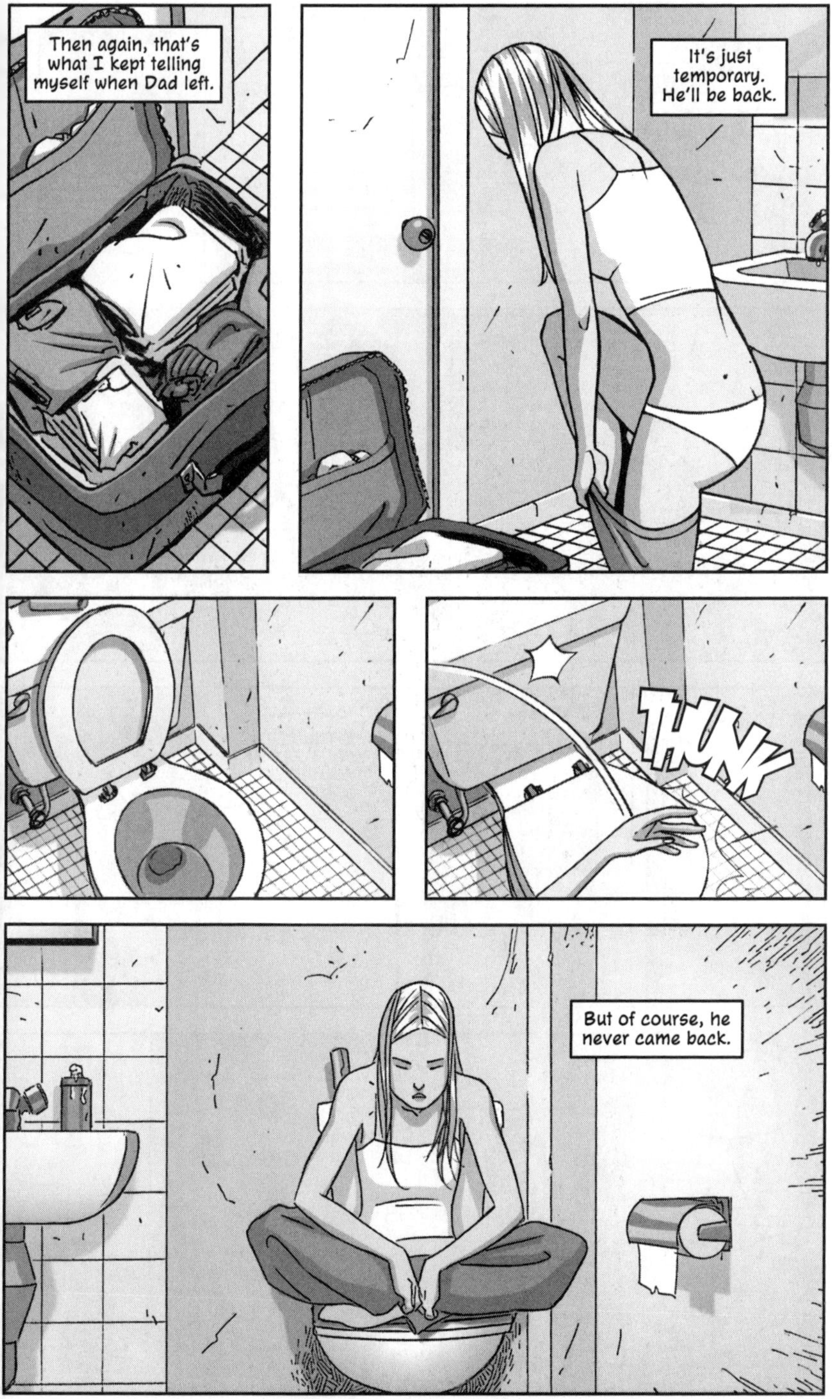

Then again, that's what I kept telling myself when Dad left.
It's just temporary. He'll be back.
THUNK
But of course, he never came back.

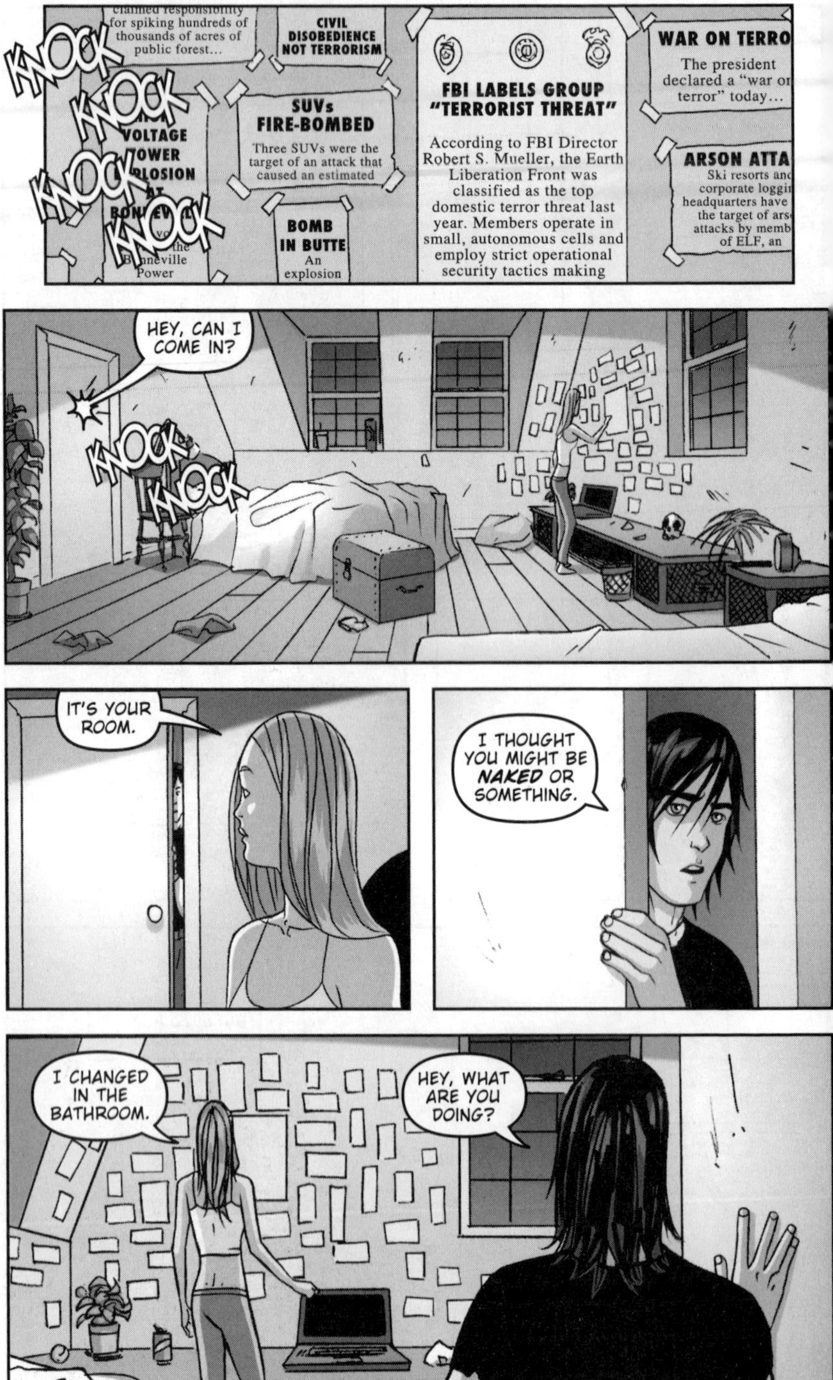
claimed responsibility for spiking hundreds of thousands of acres of public forest...
CIVIL DISOBEDIENCE NOT TERRORISM
KNOCK KNOCK KNOCK KNOCK
SUVs FIRE-BOMBED
Three SUVs were the target of an attack that caused an estimated
VOLTAGE POWER PLOSION AT
BOMB IN BUTTE
An explosion
FBI LABELS GROUP "TERRORIST THREAT"
According to FBI Director Robert S. Mueller, the Earth Liberation Front was classified as the top domestic terror threat last year. Members operate in small, autonomous cells and employ strict operational security tactics making
WAR ON TERRO
The president declared a "war on terror" today...
ARSON ATTA
Ski resorts and corporate loggi headquarters have the target of ars attacks by memb of ELF, an
HEY, CAN I COME IN?
KNOCK KNOCK
IT'S YOUR ROOM.
I THOUGHT YOU MIGHT BE *NAKED* OR SOMETHING.
I CHANGED IN THE BATHROOM.
HEY, WHAT ARE YOU DOING?

29

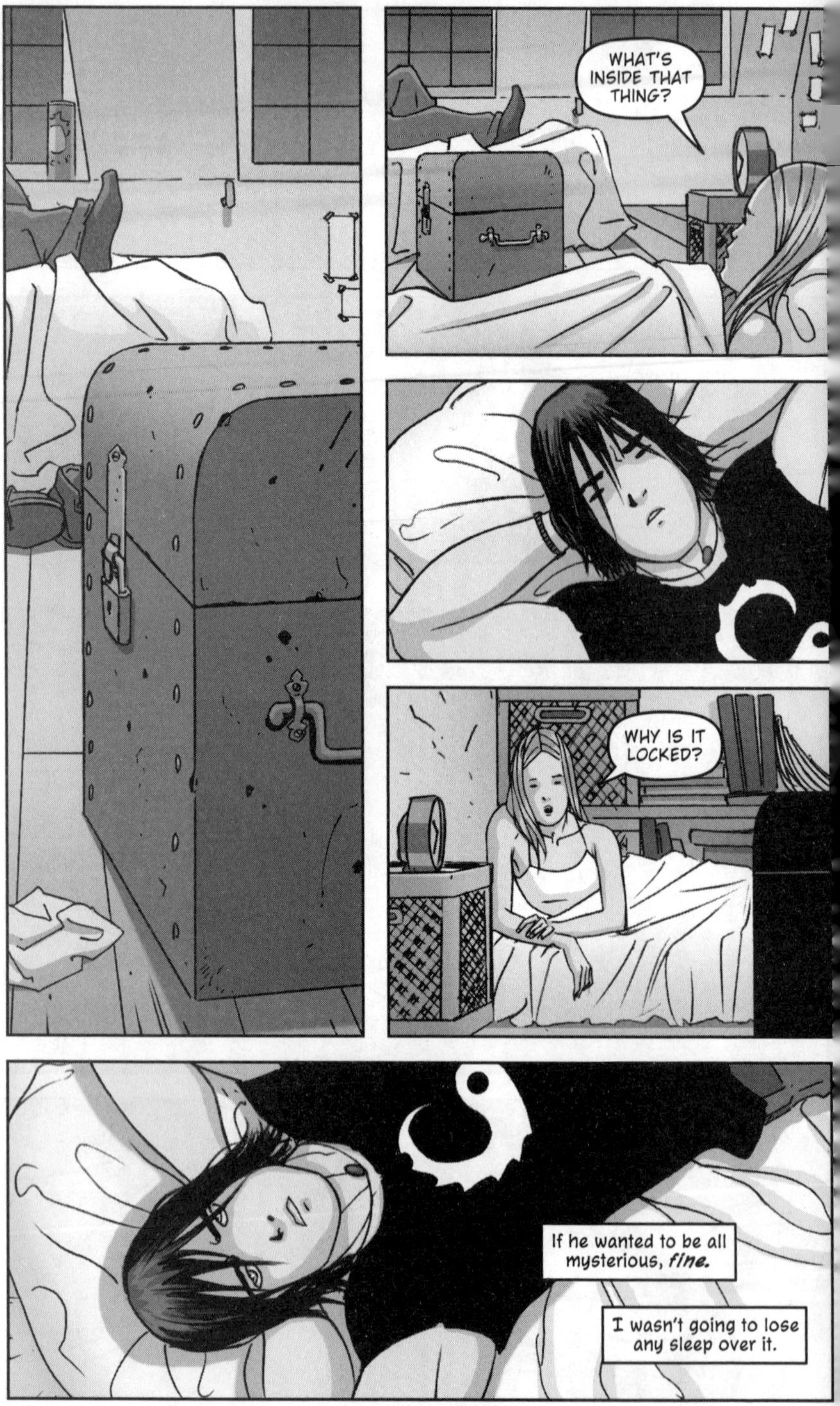
WHAT'S INSIDE THAT THING?
WHY IS IT LOCKED?
If he wanted to be all mysterious, *fine.*
I wasn't going to lose any sleep over it.

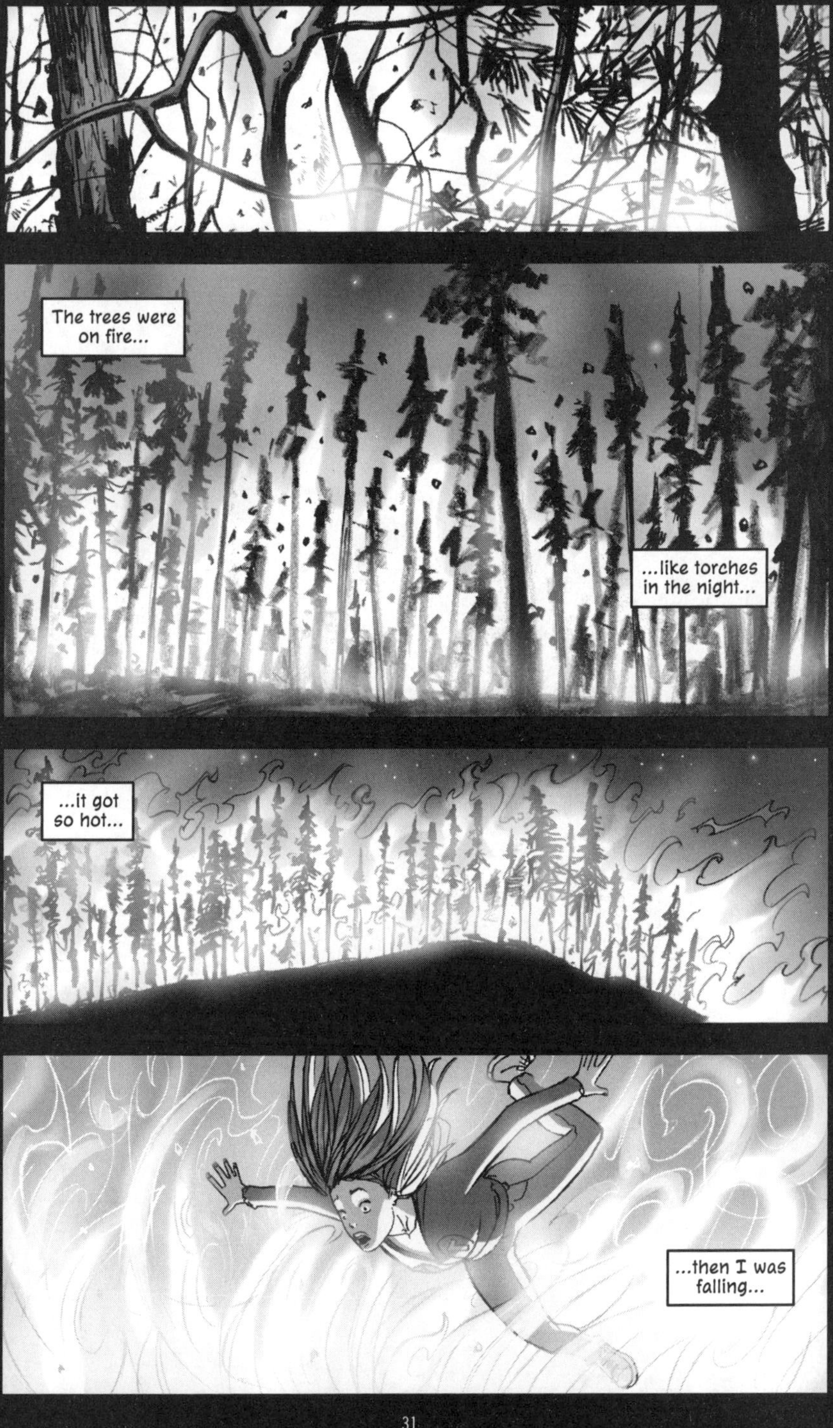
The trees were on fire...
...like torches in the night...
...it got so hot...
...then I was falling...

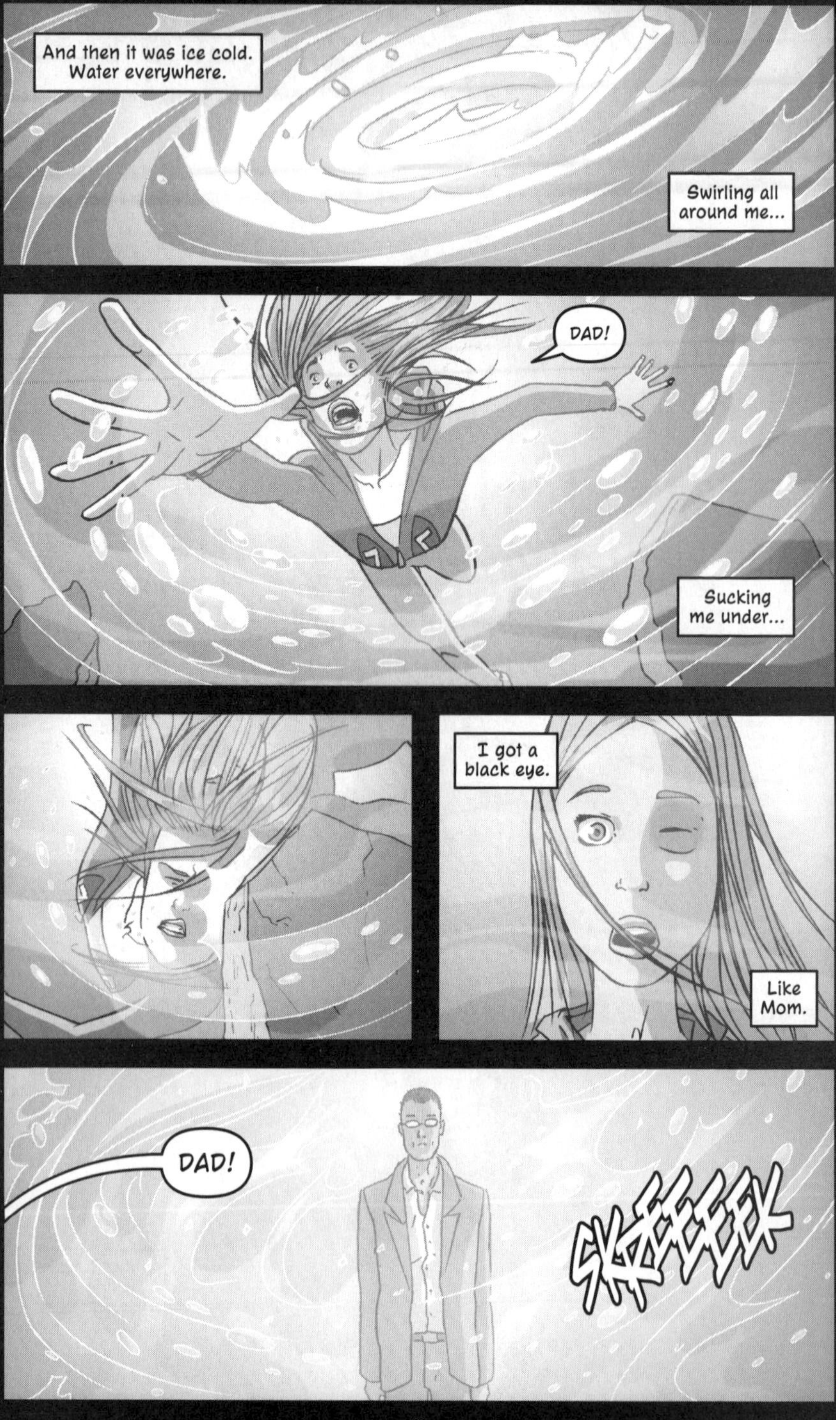
And then it was ice cold. Water everywhere.
Swirling all around me...
DAD!
Sucking me under...
I got a black eye.
Like Mom.
DAD!
SKREEEEK

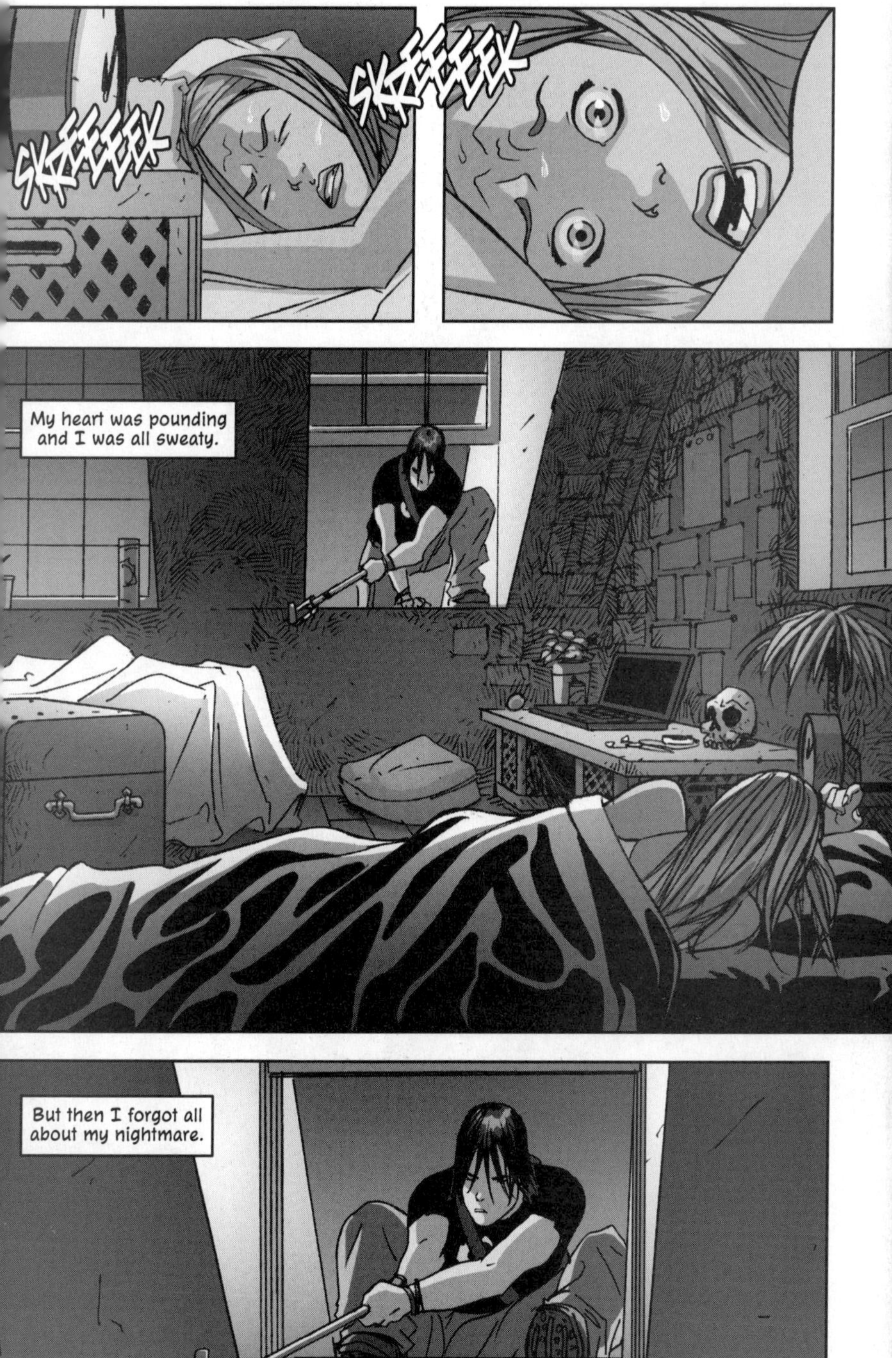
SKREEEEK
SKREEEEK
My heart was pounding and I was all sweaty.
But then I forgot all about my nightmare.

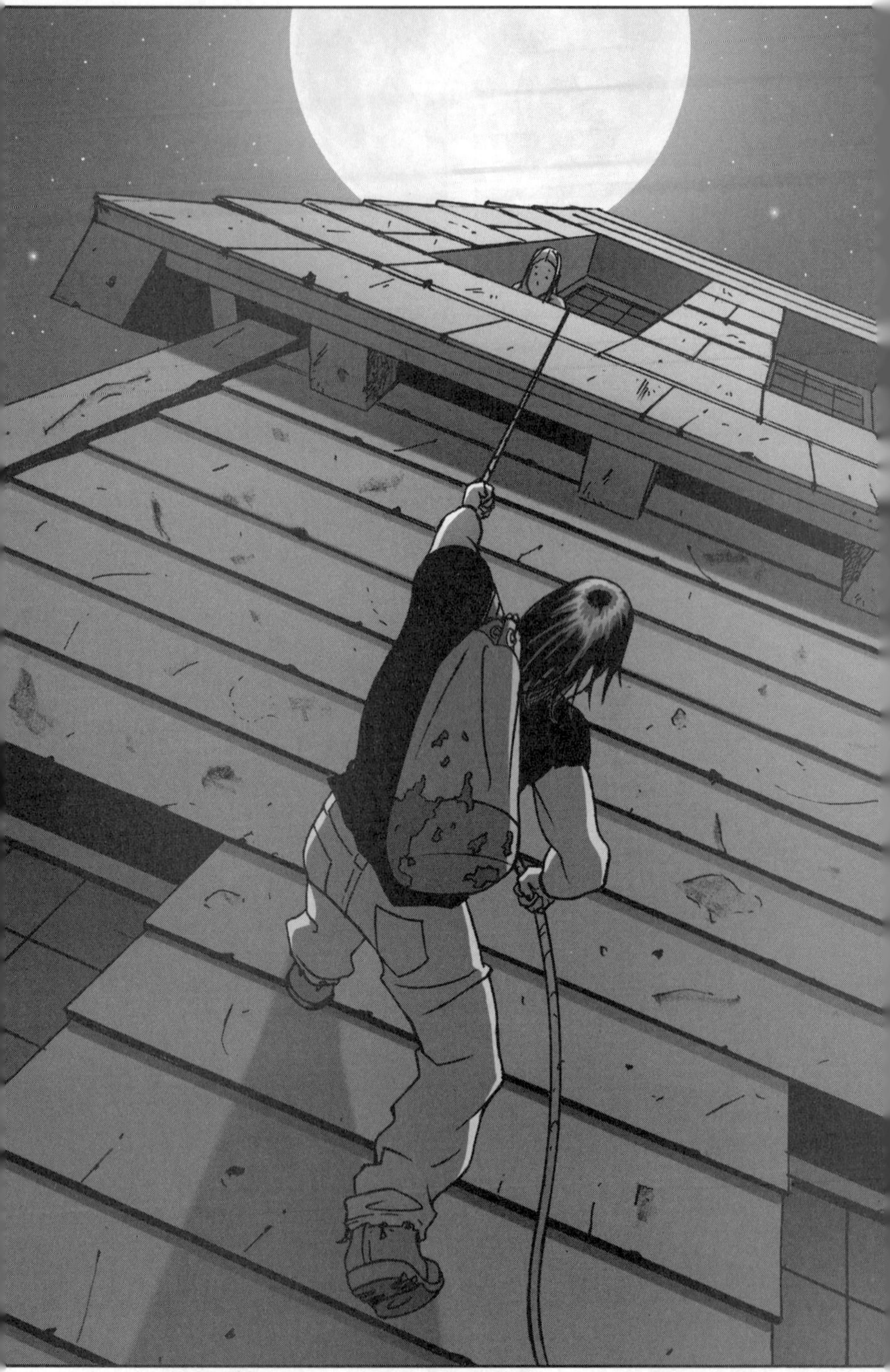

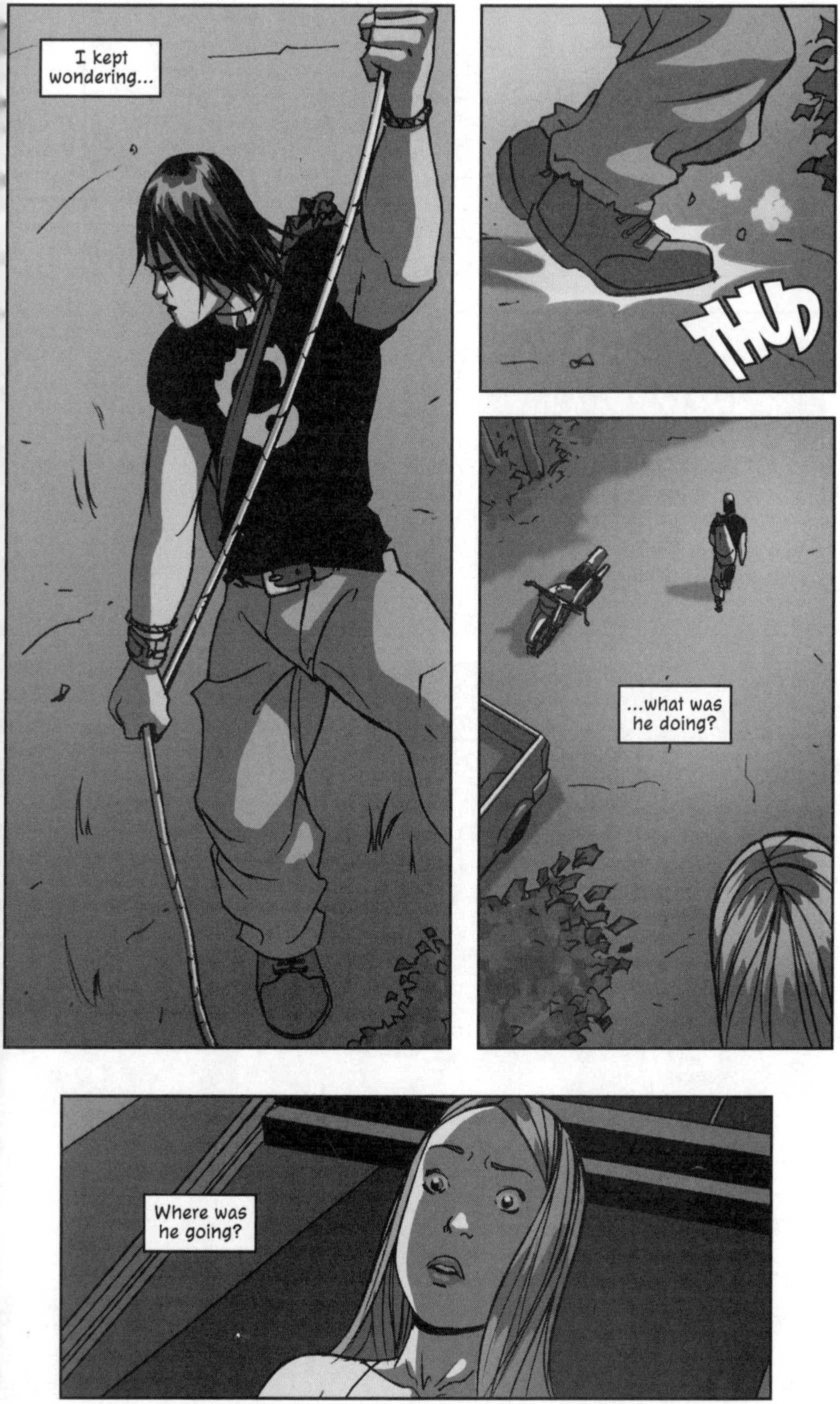
I kept wondering...
THUD
...what was he doing?
Where was he going?

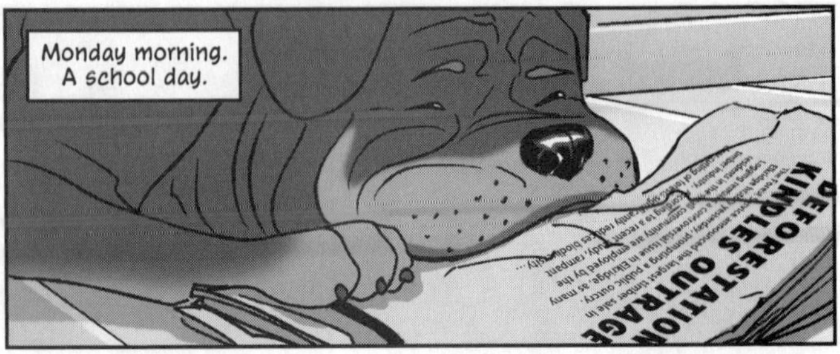
Monday morning.
A school day.
DEFORESTATION
KINDLES OUTRAGE

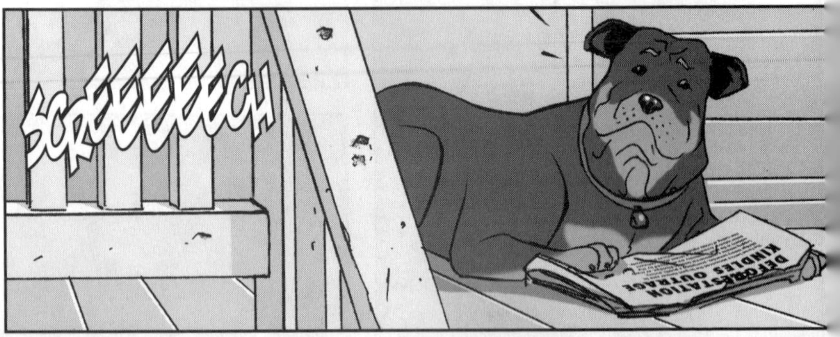
SCREEEEEECH
DEFORESTATION
KINDLES OUTRAGE

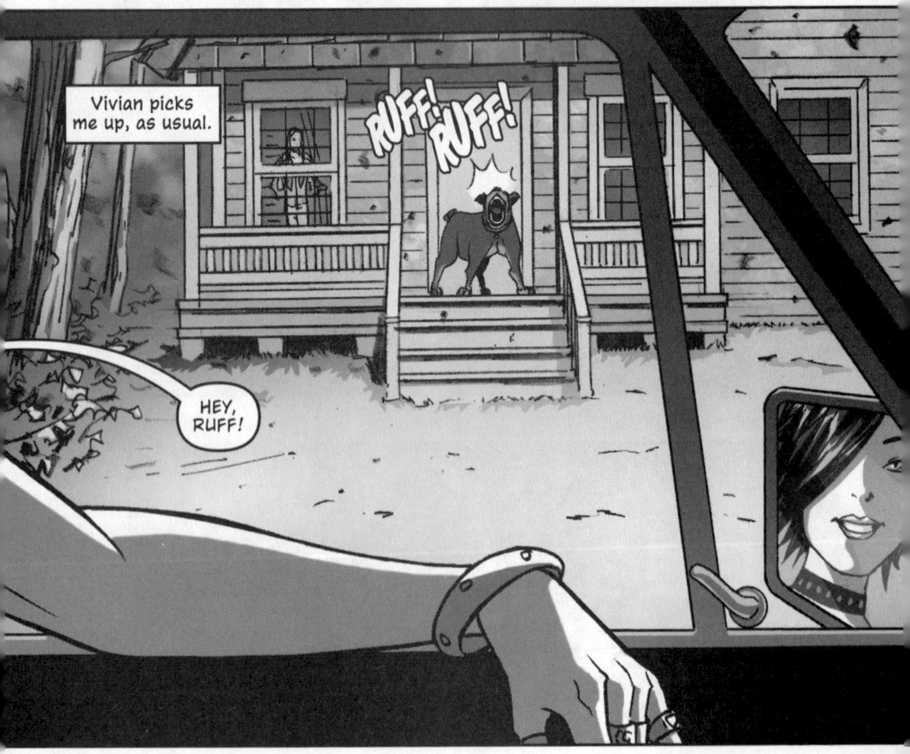
Vivian picks
me up, as usual.
RUFF! RUFF!
HEY,
RUFF!

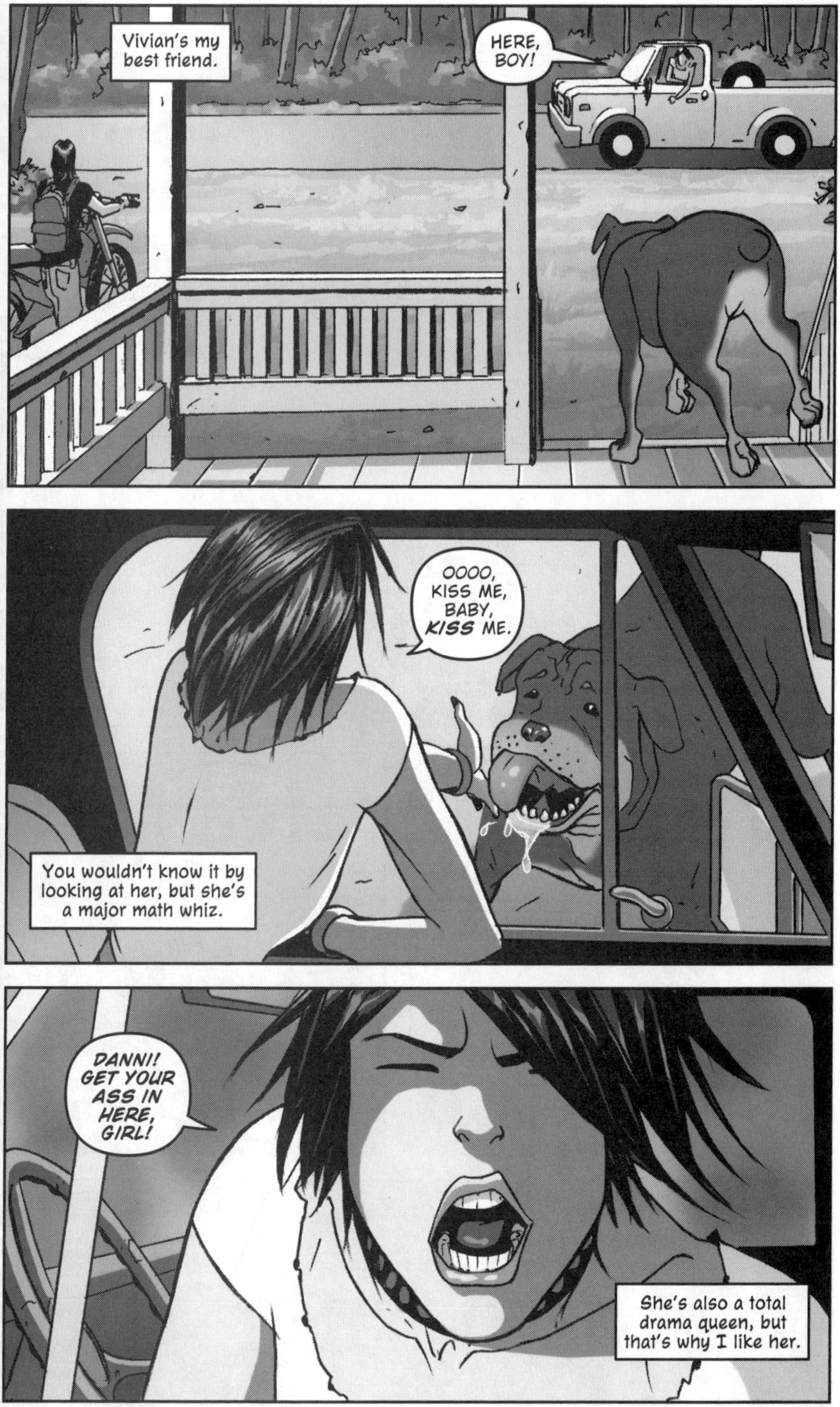
Vivian's my best friend.
HERE, BOY!
OOOO, KISS ME, BABY, KISS ME.
You wouldn't know it by looking at her, but she's a major math whiz.
DANNI! GET YOUR ASS IN HERE, GIRL!
She's also a total drama queen, but that's why I like her.

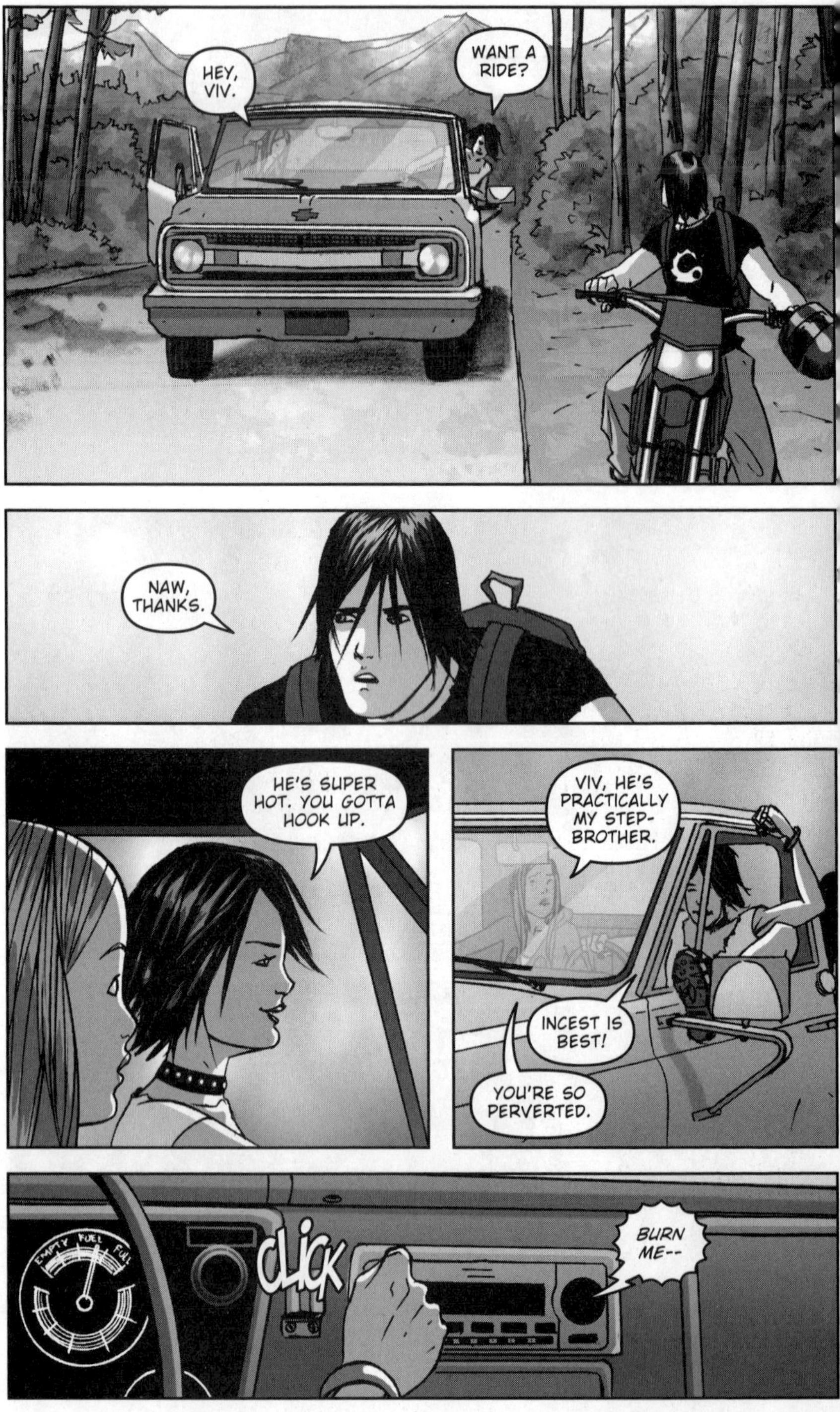
HEY, VIV.
WANT A RIDE?
NAW, THANKS.
HE'S SUPER HOT. YOU GOTTA HOOK UP.
VIV, HE'S PRACTICALLY MY STEP-BROTHER.
INCEST IS BEST!
YOU'RE SO PERVERTED.
EMPTY FUEL FULL
CLICK
BURN ME--

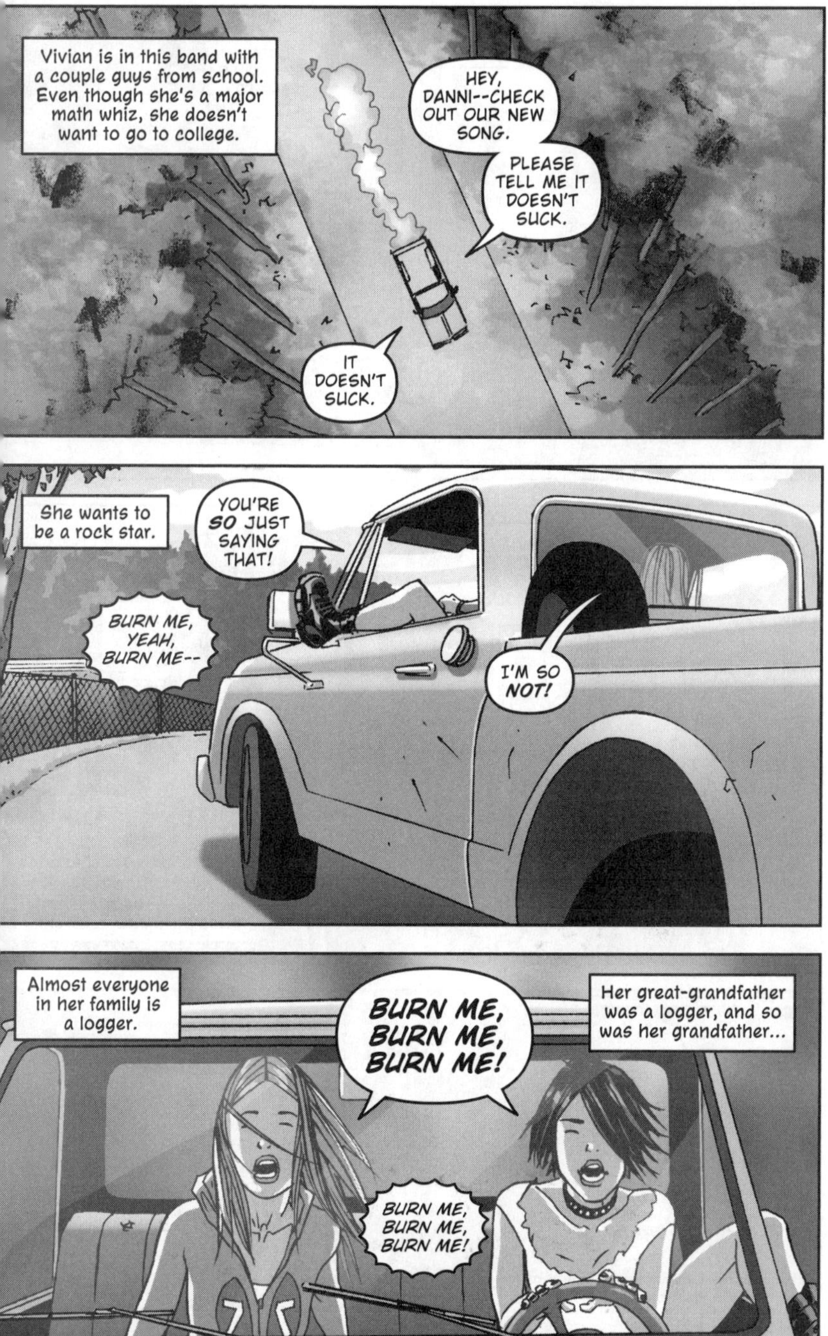
Vivian is in this band with a couple guys from school. Even though she's a major math whiz, she doesn't want to go to college.
HEY, DANNI--CHECK OUT OUR NEW SONG.
PLEASE TELL ME IT DOESN'T SUCK.
IT DOESN'T SUCK.
She wants to be a rock star.
YOU'RE SO JUST SAYING THAT!
BURN ME, YEAH, BURN ME--
I'M SO NOT!
Almost everyone in her family is a logger.
BURN ME, BURN ME, BURN ME!
Her great-grandfather was a logger, and so was her grandfather...
BURN ME, BURN ME, BURN ME!

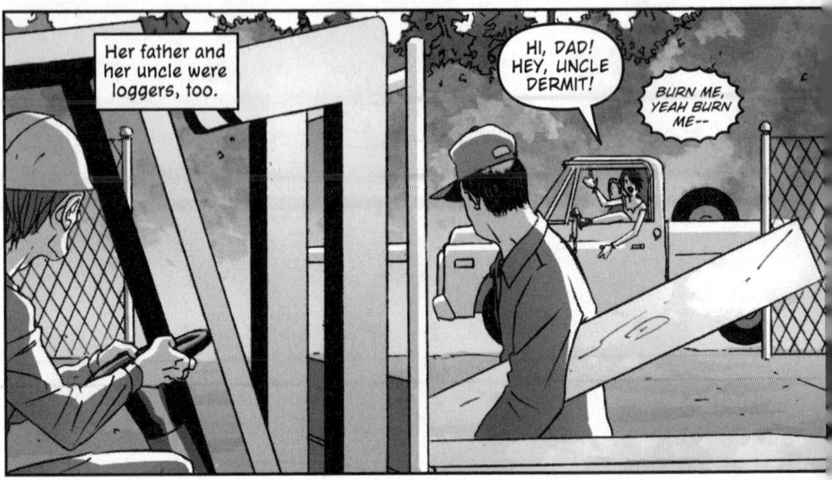
Her father and her uncle were loggers, too.
HI, DAD! HEY, UNCLE DERMIT!
BURN ME, YEAH BURN ME--

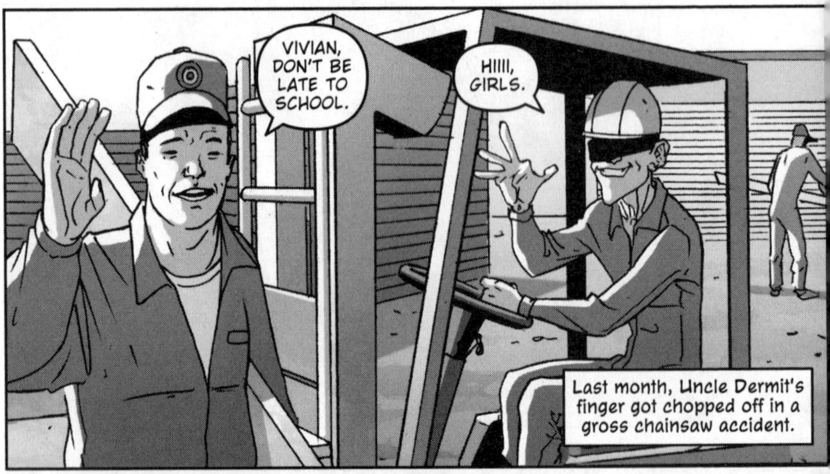
VIVIAN, DON'T BE LATE TO SCHOOL.
HIIII, GIRLS.
Last month, Uncle Dermit's finger got chopped off in a gross chainsaw accident.

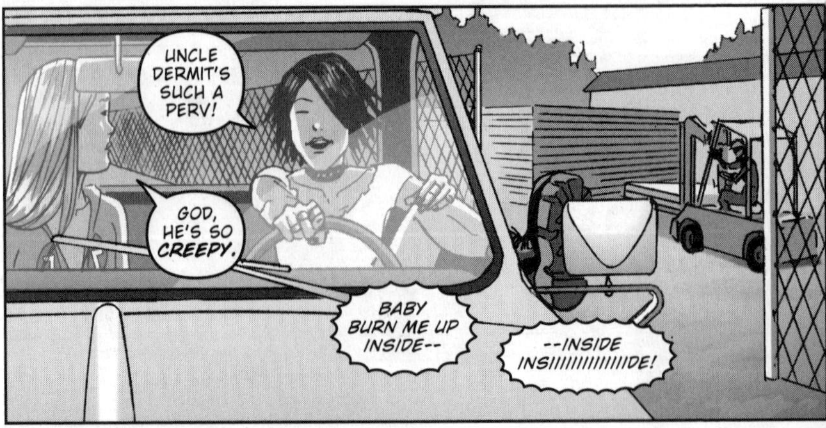
UNCLE DERMIT'S SUCH A PERV!
GOD, HE'S SO CREEPY.
BABY BURN ME UP INSIDE--
--INSIDE INSIIIIIIIIIIIIIDE!

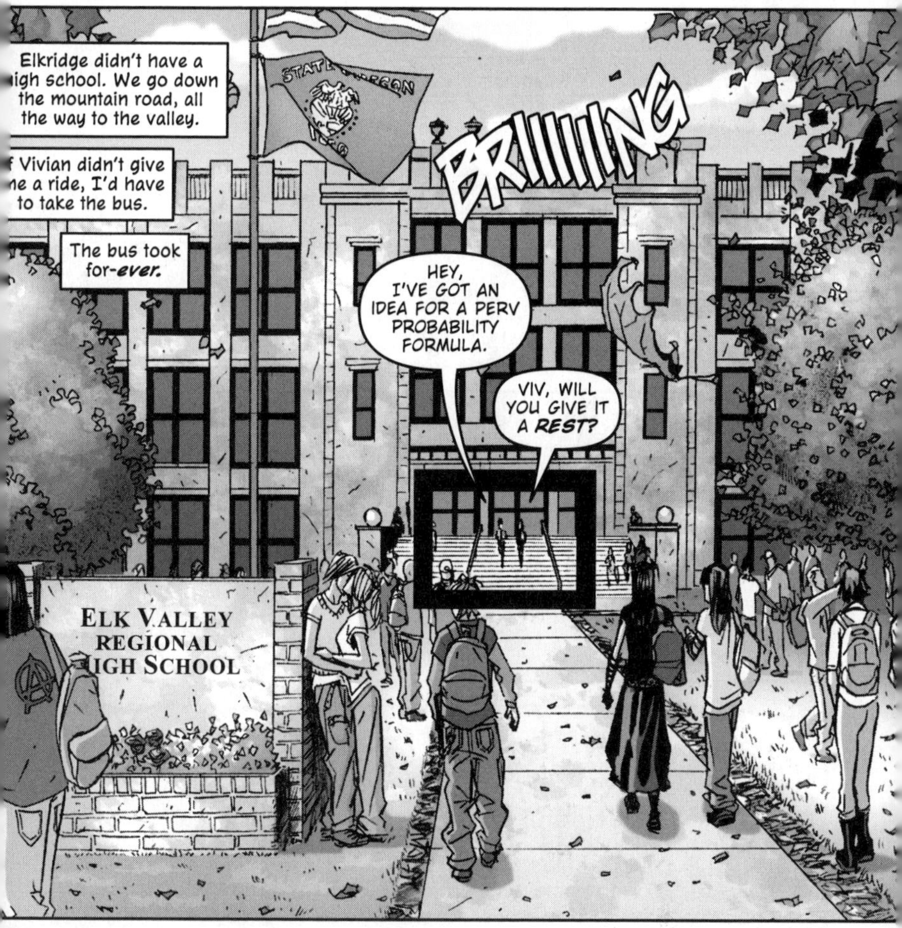

Elkridge didn't have a
igh school. We go down
the mountain road, all
the way to the valley.
f Vivian didn't give
ne a ride, I'd have
to take the bus.
The bus took
for-*ever.*
BRIIIIING
HEY, I'VE GOT AN IDEA FOR A PERV PROBABILITY FORMULA.
VIV, WILL YOU GIVE IT A *REST?*
ELK VALLEY
REGIONAL
IGH SCHOOL

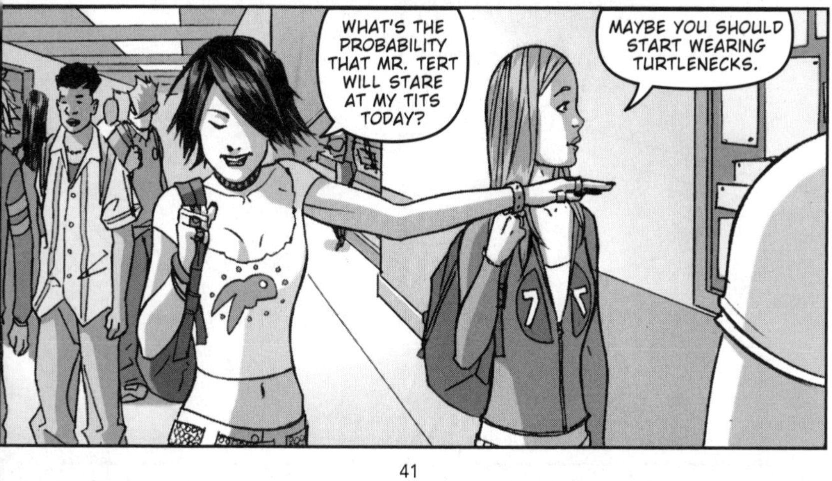

WHAT'S THE PROBABILITY THAT MR. TERT WILL STARE AT MY TITS TODAY?
MAYBE YOU SHOULD START WEARING TURTLENECKS.

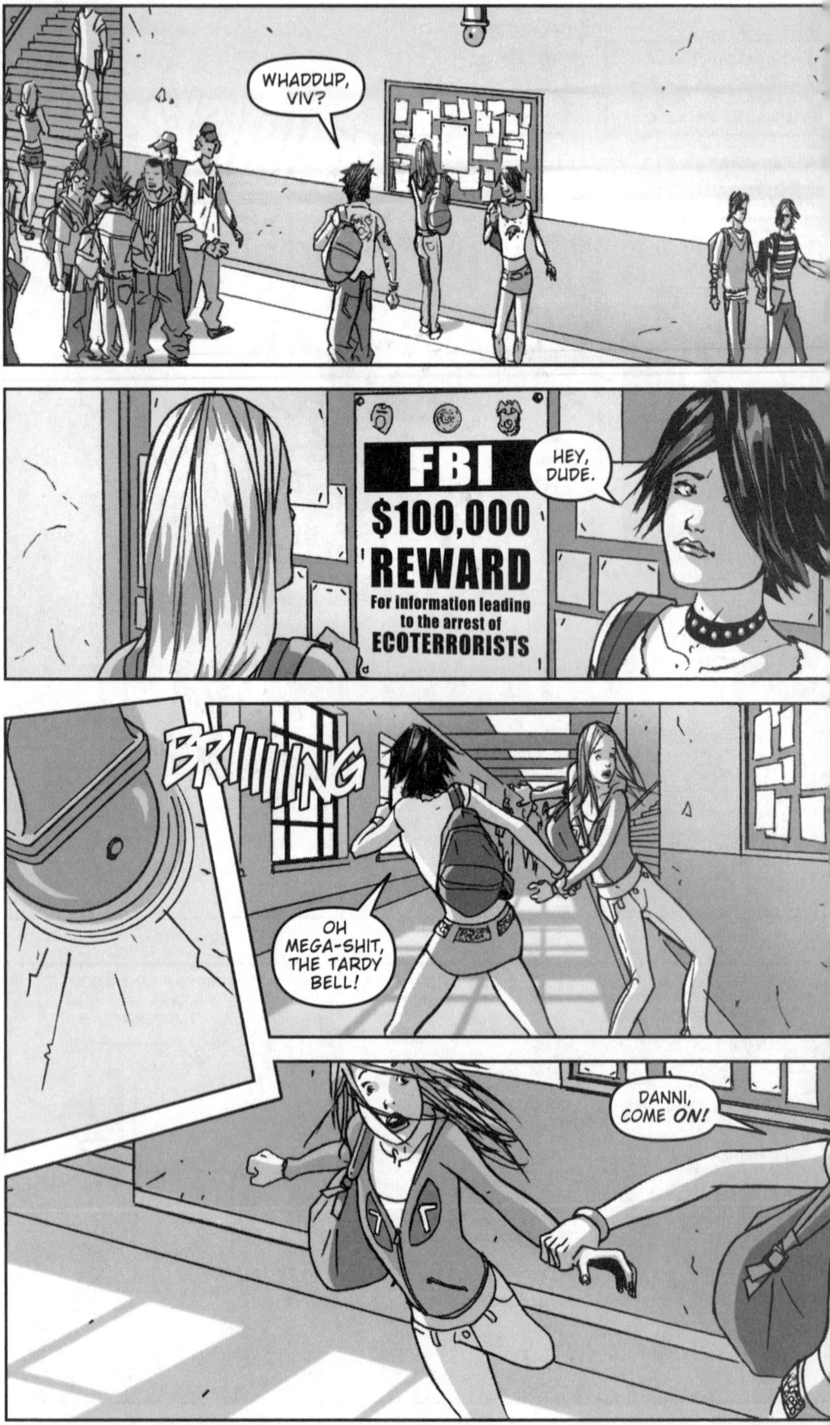
WHADDUP, VIV?
FBI
$100,000
REWARD
For information leading to the arrest of
ECOTERRORISTS
HEY, DUDE.
BRIIIIING
OH MEGA-SHIT, THE TARDY BELL!
DANNI, COME ON!

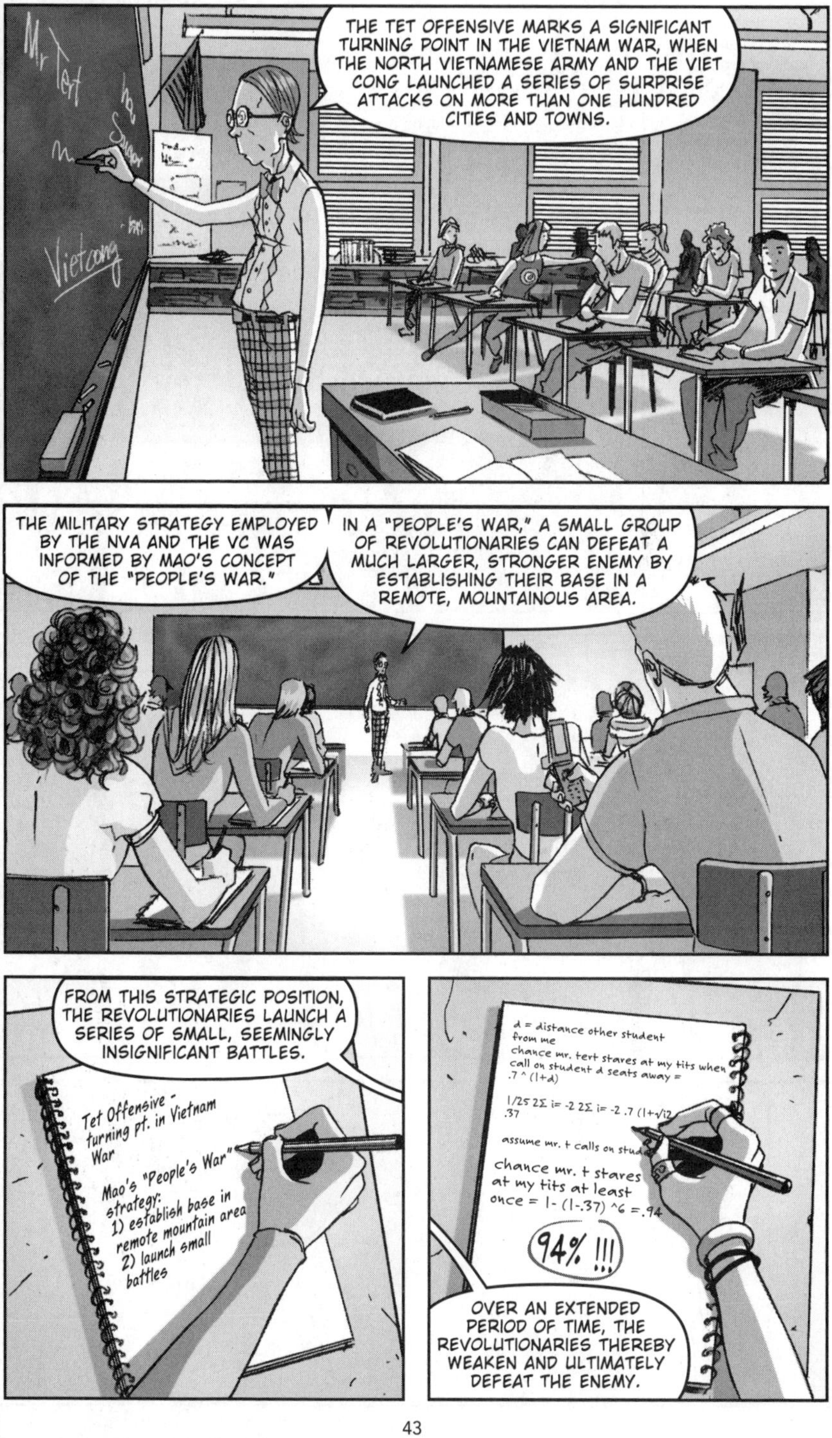
Mr Tert
Vietcong
THE TET OFFENSIVE MARKS A SIGNIFICANT TURNING POINT IN THE VIETNAM WAR, WHEN THE NORTH VIETNAMESE ARMY AND THE VIET CONG LAUNCHED A SERIES OF SURPRISE ATTACKS ON MORE THAN ONE HUNDRED CITIES AND TOWNS.
THE MILITARY STRATEGY EMPLOYED BY THE NVA AND THE VC WAS INFORMED BY MAO'S CONCEPT OF THE "PEOPLE'S WAR."
IN A "PEOPLE'S WAR," A SMALL GROUP OF REVOLUTIONARIES CAN DEFEAT A MUCH LARGER, STRONGER ENEMY BY ESTABLISHING THEIR BASE IN A REMOTE, MOUNTAINOUS AREA.
FROM THIS STRATEGIC POSITION, THE REVOLUTIONARIES LAUNCH A SERIES OF SMALL, SEEMINGLY INSIGNIFICANT BATTLES.
Tet Offensive - turning pt. in Vietnam War
Mao's "People's War" strategy:
1) establish base in remote mountain area
2) launch small battles
d = distance other student from me
chance mr. tert stares at my tits when call on student d seats away = .7 ^ (1+d)
1/25 2Σ i= -2 2Σ i= -2 .7 (1+√i2
.37
assume mr. t calls on stud
chance mr. t stares at my tits at least once = 1- (1-.37) ^6 =.94
94% !!!
OVER AN EXTENDED PERIOD OF TIME, THE REVOLUTIONARIES THEREBY WEAKEN AND ULTIMATELY DEFEAT THE ENEMY.

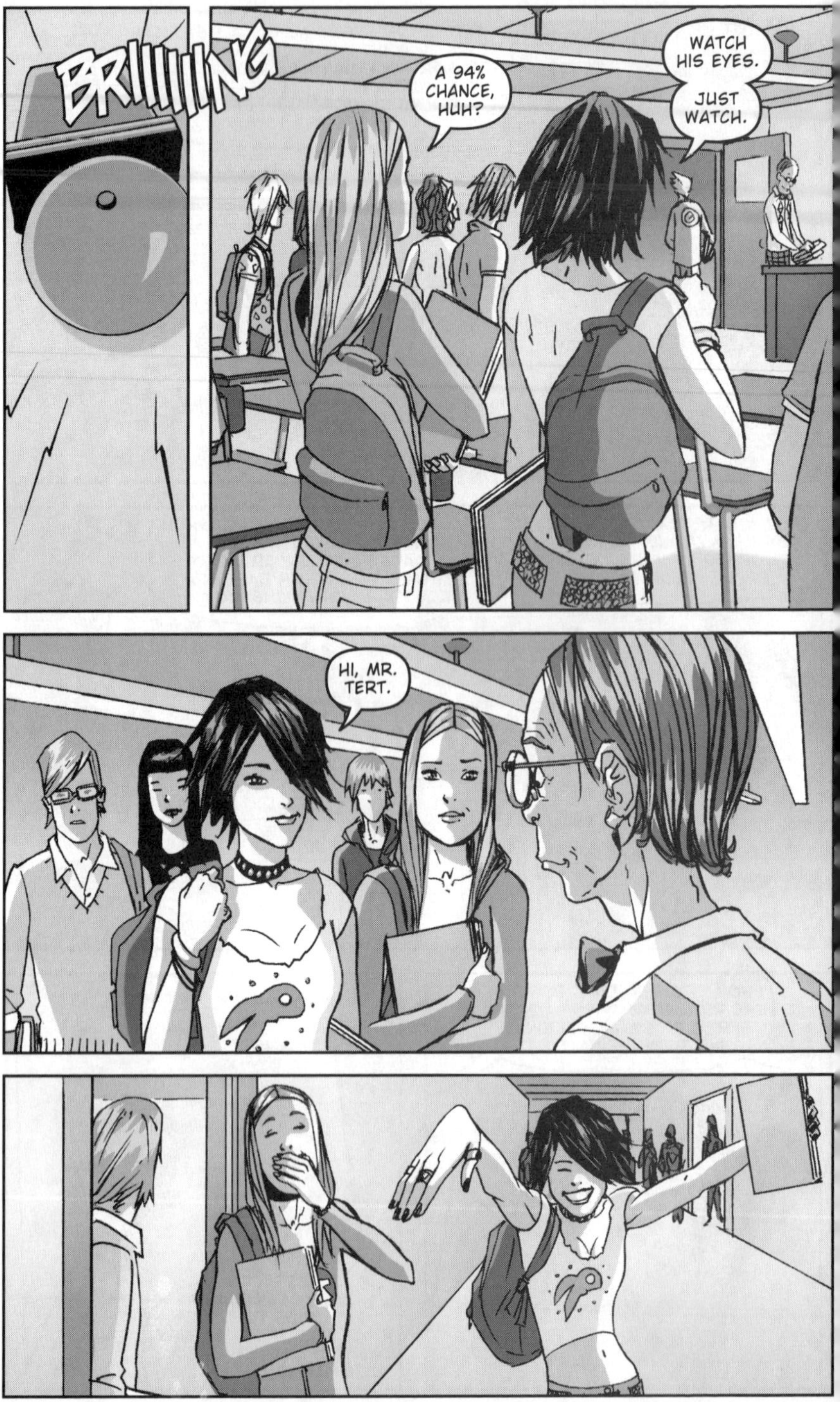
BRIIIIIING
A 94% CHANCE, HUH?
WATCH HIS EYES.
JUST WATCH.
HI, MR. TERT.

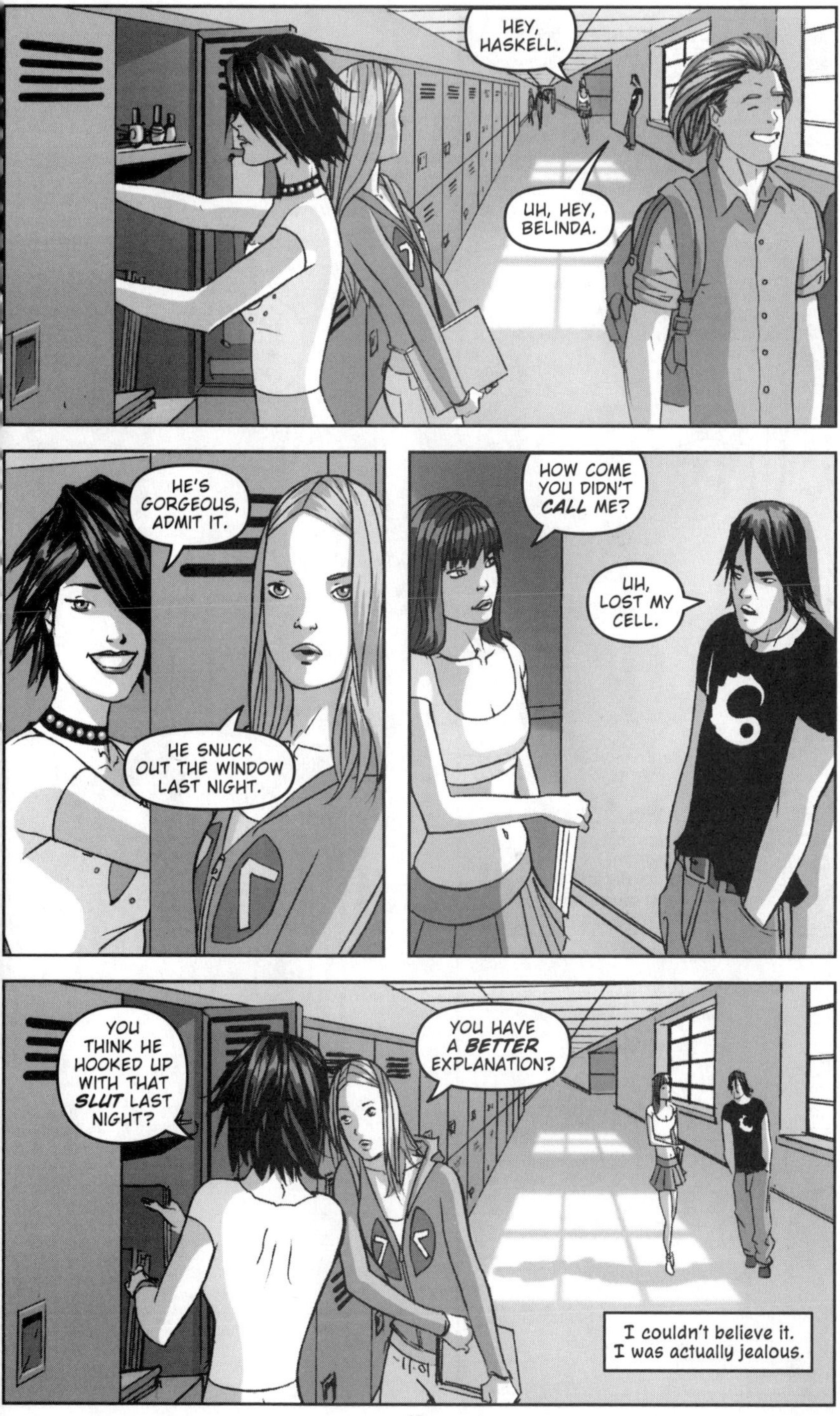
HEY, HASKELL.
UH, HEY, BELINDA.
HE'S GORGEOUS, ADMIT IT.
HE SNUCK OUT THE WINDOW LAST NIGHT.
HOW COME YOU DIDN'T *CALL* ME?
UH, LOST MY CELL.
YOU THINK HE HOOKED UP WITH THAT *SLUT* LAST NIGHT?
YOU HAVE A *BETTER* EXPLANATION?
I couldn't believe it. I was actually jealous.

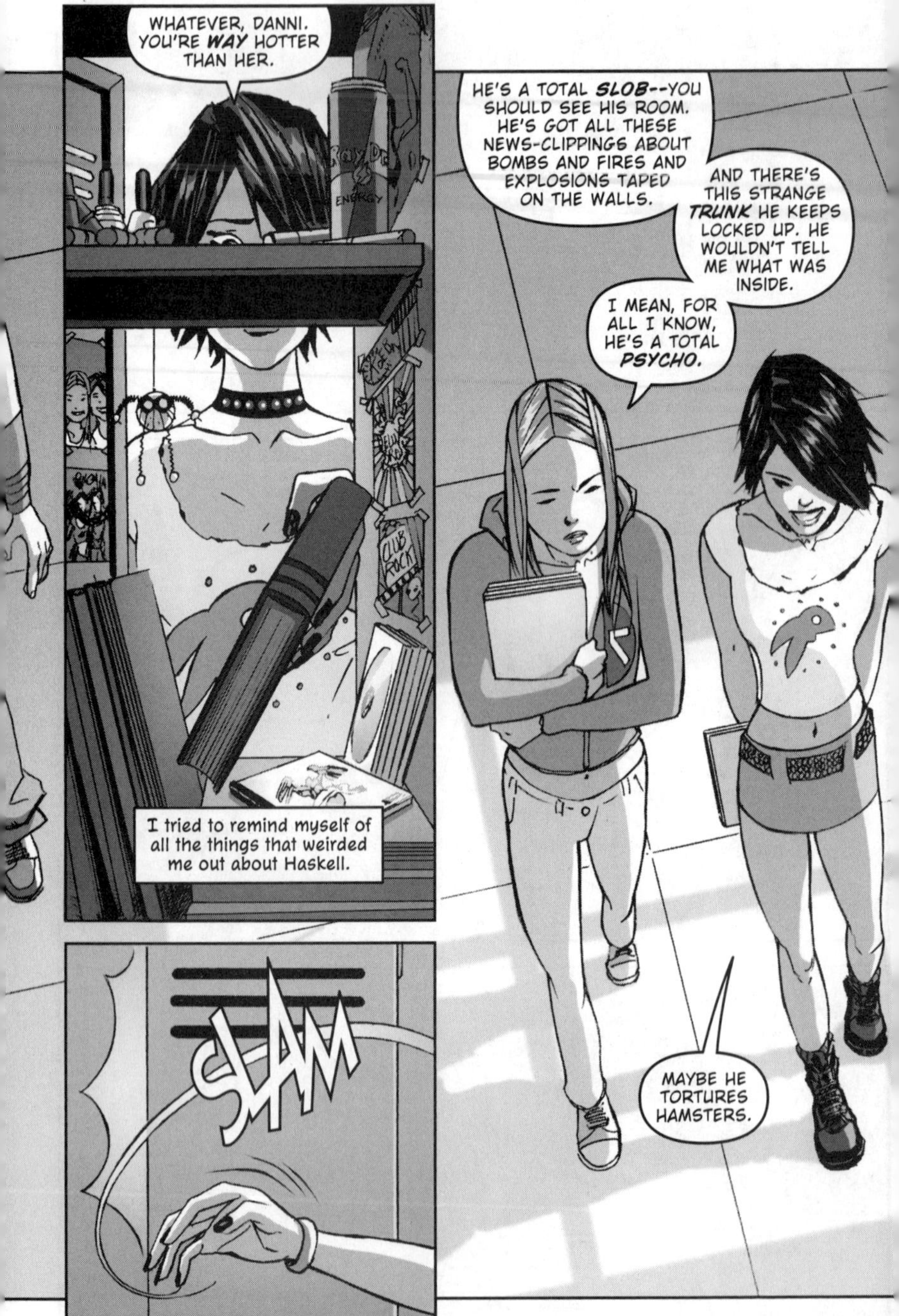
WHATEVER, DANNI. YOU'RE WAY HOTTER THAN HER.
HE'S A TOTAL SLOB--YOU SHOULD SEE HIS ROOM. HE'S GOT ALL THESE NEWS-CLIPPINGS ABOUT BOMBS AND FIRES AND EXPLOSIONS TAPED ON THE WALLS.
AND THERE'S THIS STRANGE TRUNK HE KEEPS LOCKED UP. HE WOULDN'T TELL ME WHAT WAS INSIDE.
I MEAN, FOR ALL I KNOW, HE'S A TOTAL PSYCHO.
I tried to remind myself of all the things that weirded me out about Haskell.
SLAM
MAYBE HE TORTURES HAMSTERS.

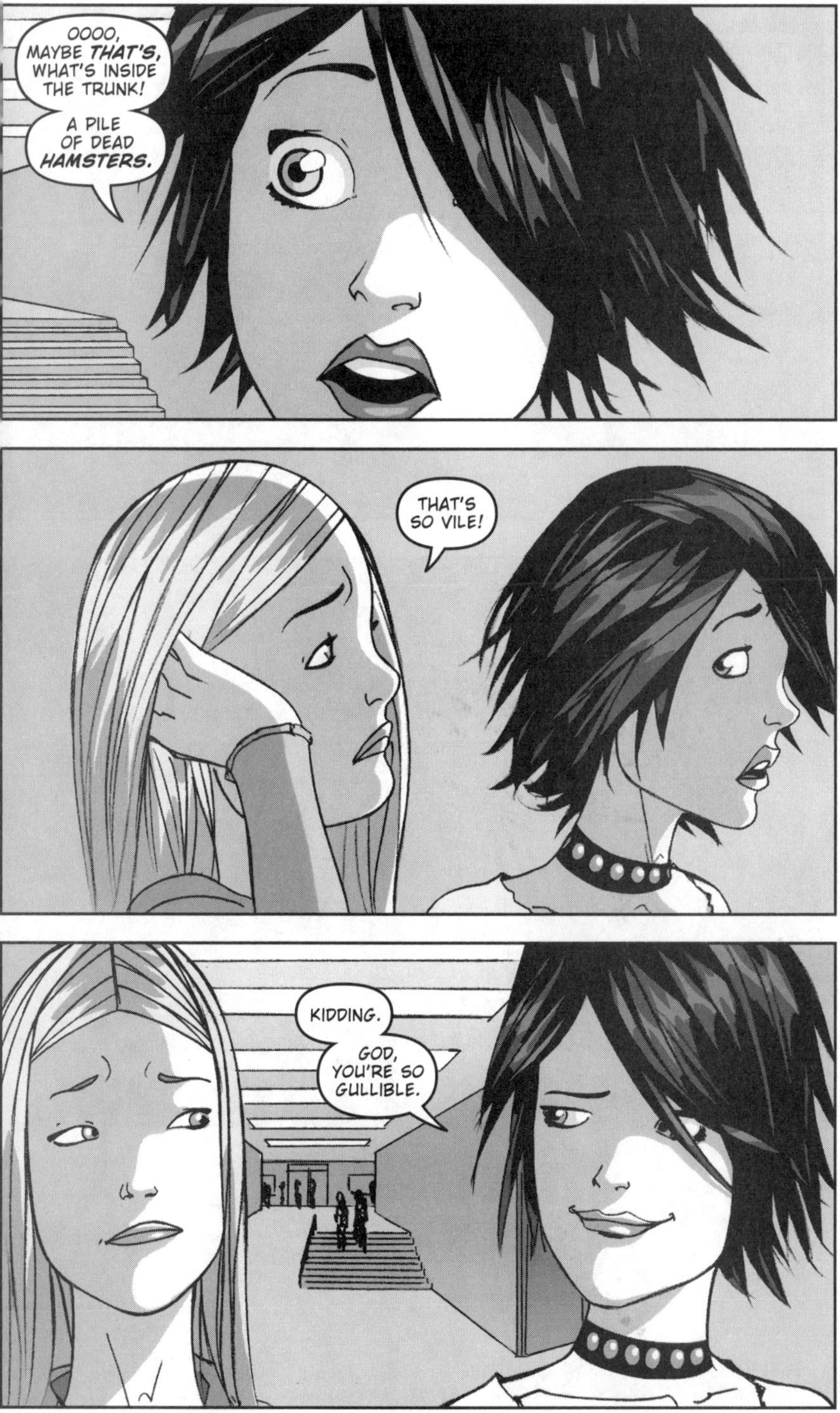
OOOO, MAYBE ***THAT'S,*** WHAT'S INSIDE THE TRUNK!
A PILE OF DEAD ***HAMSTERS.***
THAT'S SO VILE!
KIDDING.
GOD, YOU'RE SO GULLIBLE.

That night, when I came back from taking Ruff out for a walk, Hank was yelling at Haskell.

And for the first time, I felt bad for him...

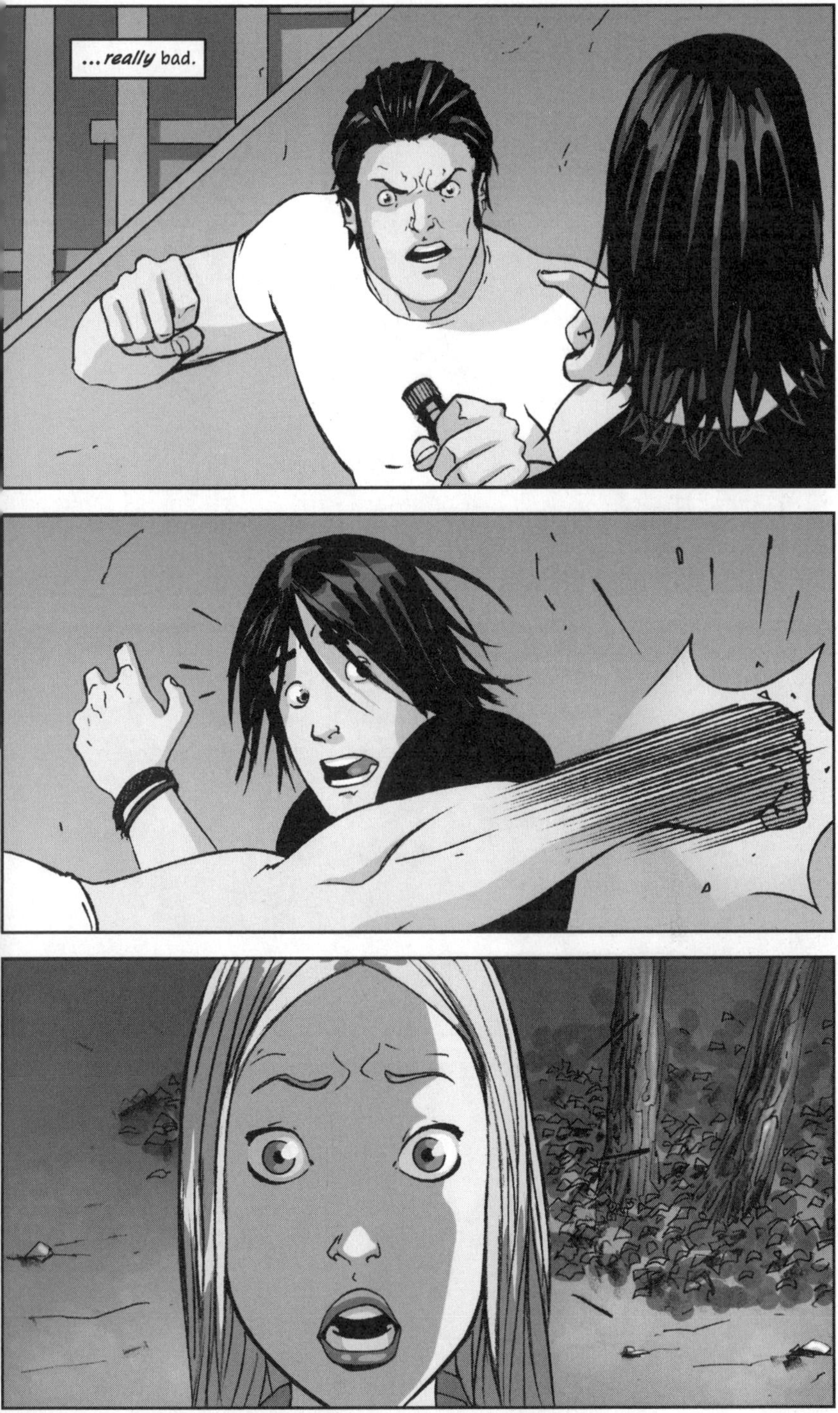
...*really* bad.

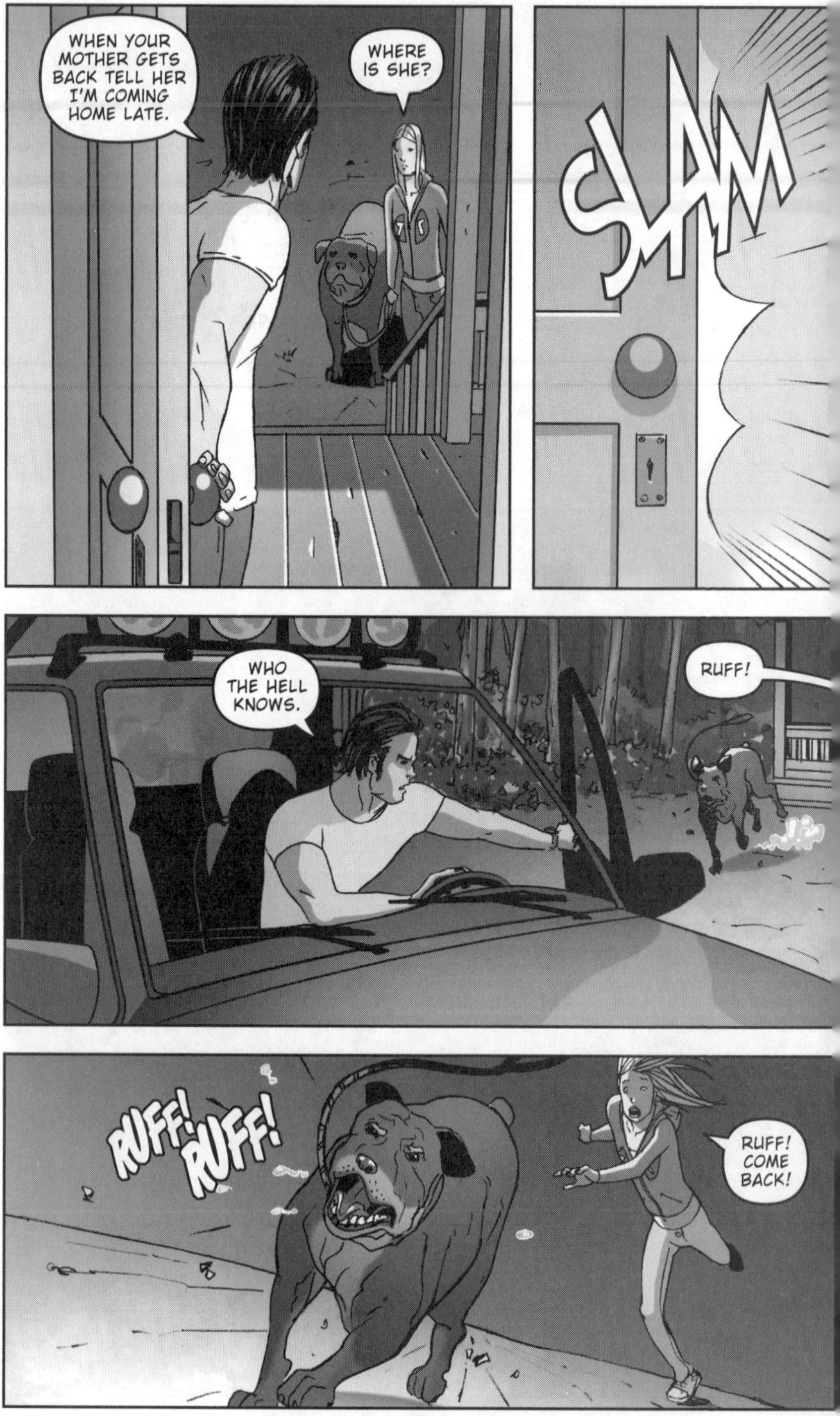
WHEN YOUR MOTHER GETS BACK TELL HER I'M COMING HOME LATE.
WHERE IS SHE?
SLAM
WHO THE HELL KNOWS.
RUFF!
RUFF! RUFF!
RUFF! COME BACK!

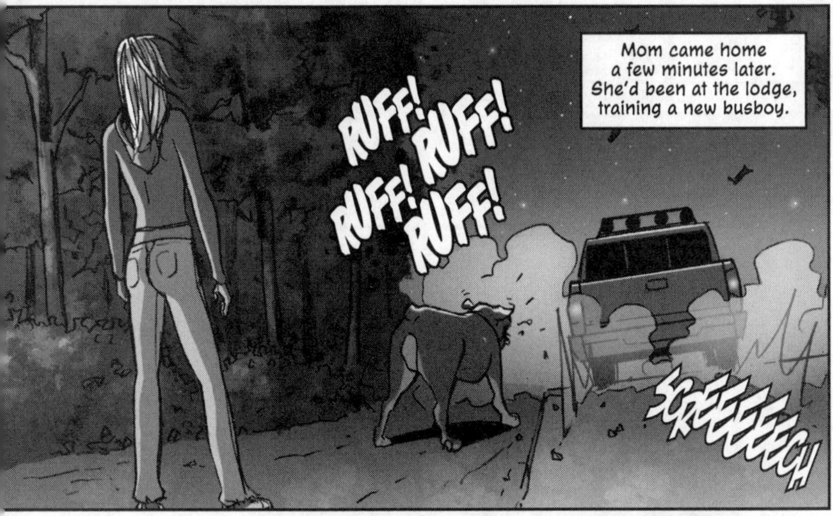
Mom came home a few minutes later. She'd been at the lodge, training a new busboy.
RUFF! RUFF! RUFF! RUFF!
SCREEEEEECH

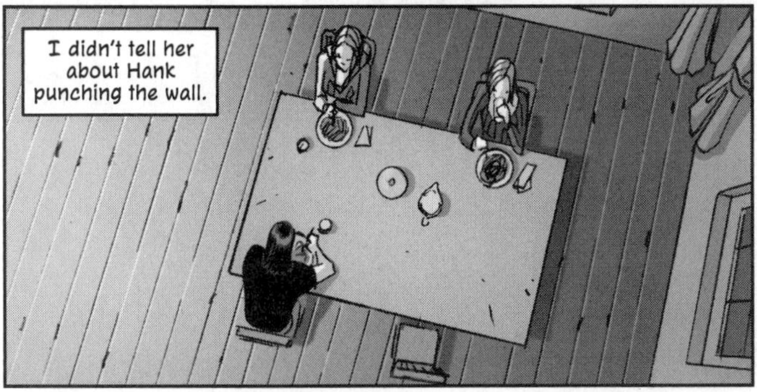
I didn't tell her about Hank punching the wall.

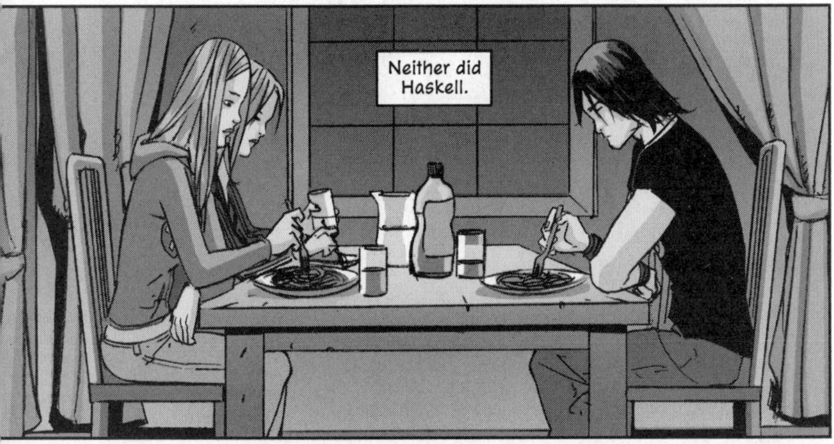
Neither did Haskell.

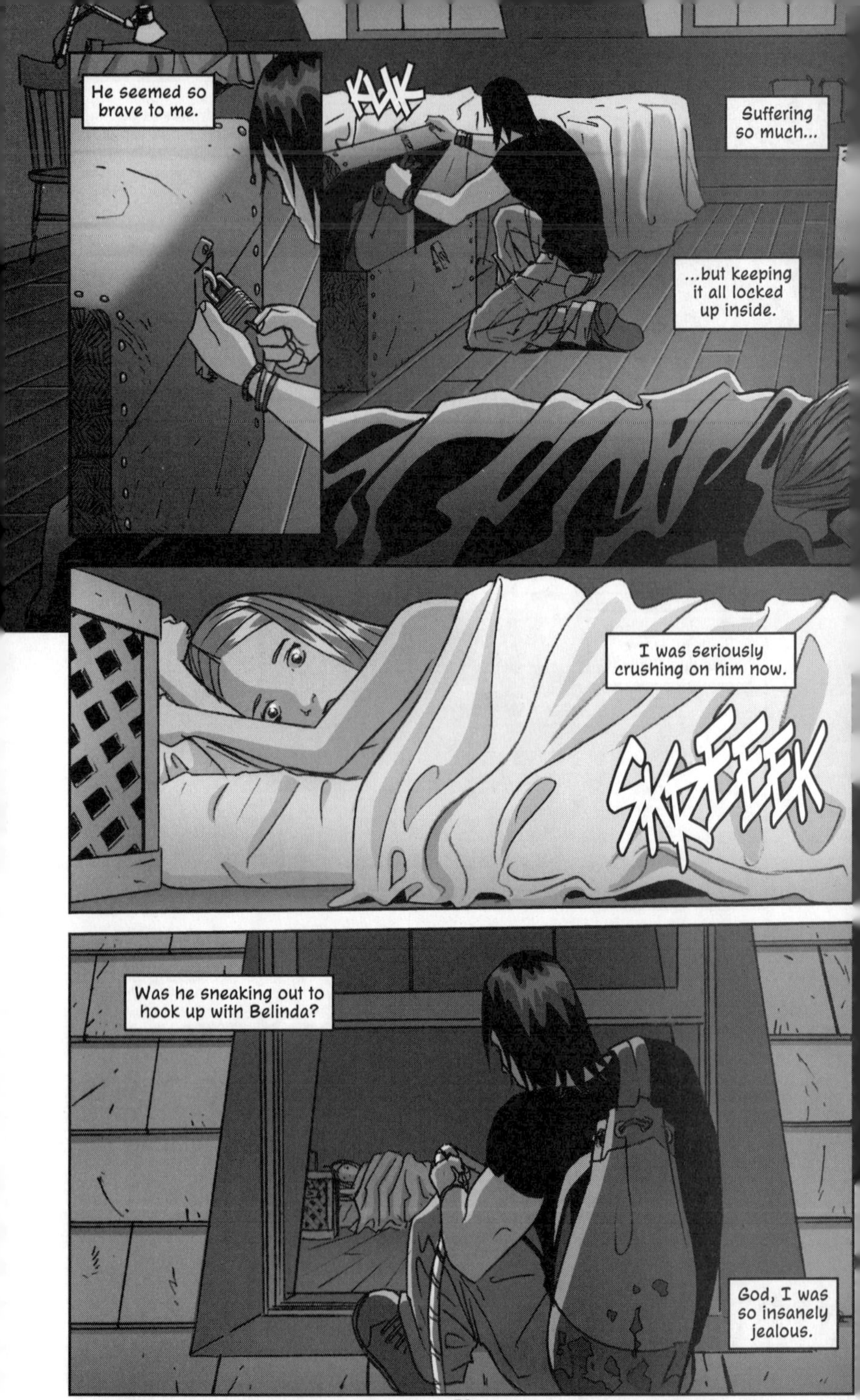

He seemed so brave to me.
KLIK
Suffering so much...
...but keeping it all locked up inside.
I was seriously crushing on him now.
SKREEEK
Was he sneaking out to hook up with Belinda?
God, I was so insanely jealous.

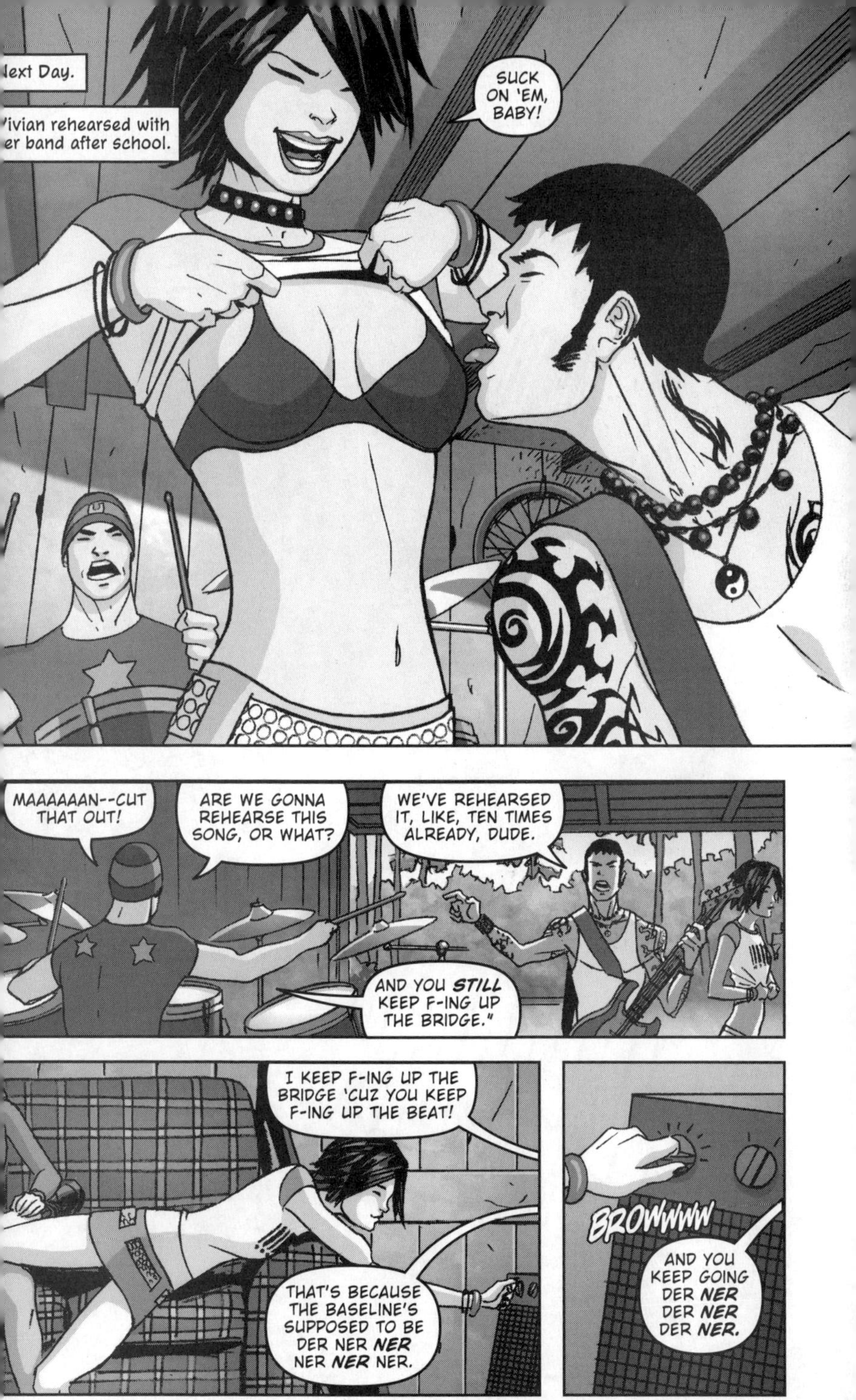
ext Day.
ivian rehearsed with
er band after school.
SUCK ON 'EM, BABY!
MAAAAAAN--CUT THAT OUT!
ARE WE GONNA REHEARSE THIS SONG, OR WHAT?
WE'VE REHEARSED IT, LIKE, TEN TIMES ALREADY, DUDE.
AND YOU ***STILL*** KEEP F-ING UP THE BRIDGE."
I KEEP F-ING UP THE BRIDGE 'CUZ YOU KEEP F-ING UP THE BEAT!
THAT'S BECAUSE THE BASELINE'S SUPPOSED TO BE DER NER ***NER*** NER ***NER*** NER.
BROWWWW
AND YOU KEEP GOING DER ***NER*** DER ***NER*** DER ***NER.***

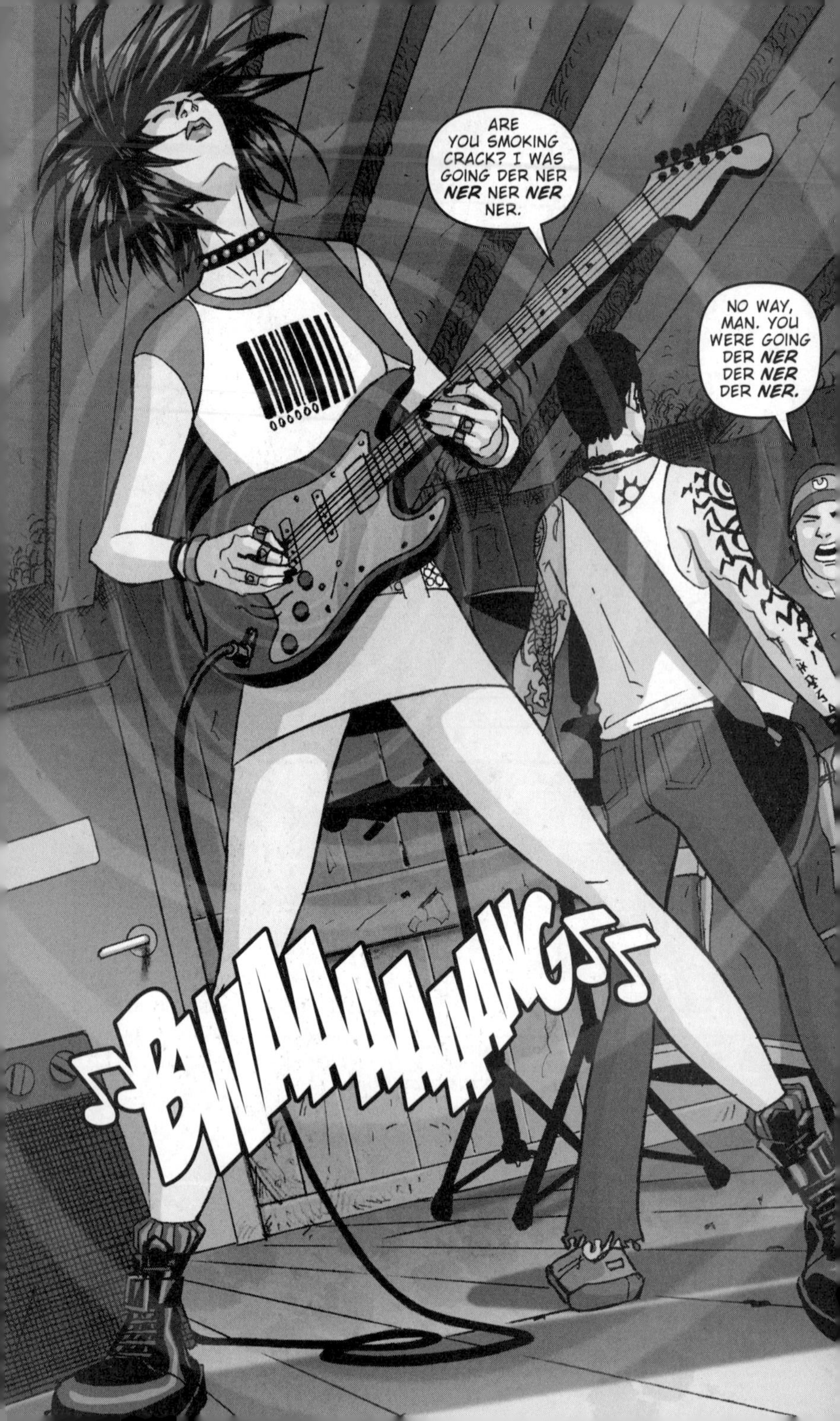
ARE YOU SMOKING CRACK? I WAS GOING DER NER **NER** NER **NER** NER.
NO WAY, MAN. YOU WERE GOING DER **NER** DER **NER** DER **NER.**
BWAAAAAANG

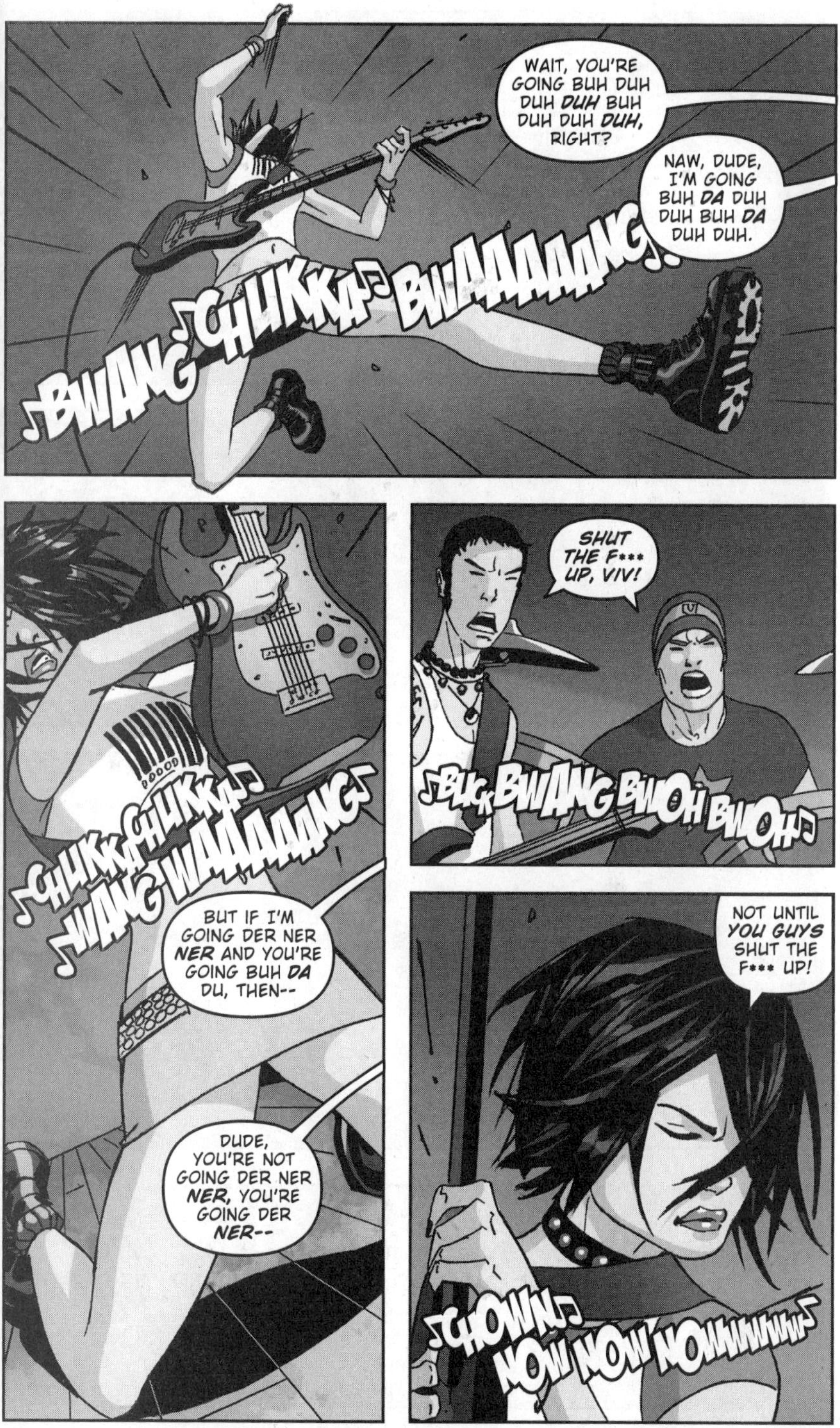
WAIT, YOU'RE GOING BUH DUH DUH *DUH* BUH DUH DUH *DUH*, RIGHT?
NAW, DUDE, I'M GOING BUH *DA* DUH DUH BUH *DA* DUH DUH.
BWANG CHUKKA BWAAAAAANG
CHUKKA CHUKKA WANG WAAAAAANG
BUT IF I'M GOING DER NER *NER* AND YOU'RE GOING BUH *DA* DU, THEN--
DUDE, YOU'RE NOT GOING DER NER *NER*, YOU'RE GOING DER *NER*--
*SHUT THE F*** UP, VIV!*
BUCK BWANG BWOH BWOH
NOT UNTIL *YOU GUYS* SHUT THE F*** UP!
CHOWN NOW NOW NOWWWWW

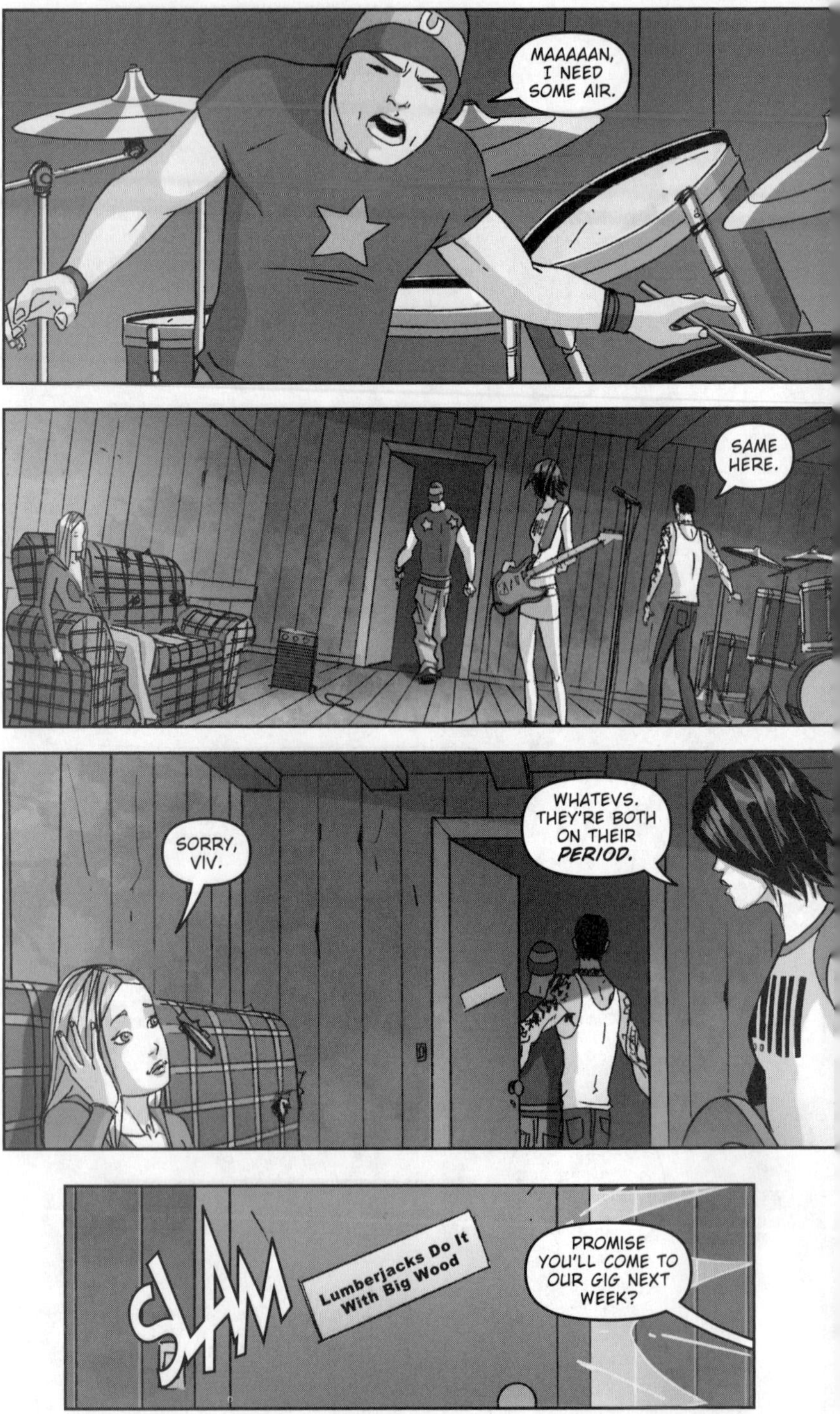

MAAAAAN, I NEED SOME AIR.
SAME HERE.
SORRY, VIV.
WHATEVS. THEY'RE BOTH ON THEIR *PERIOD.*
SLAM
Lumberjacks Do It With Big Wood
PROMISE YOU'LL COME TO OUR GIG NEXT WEEK?

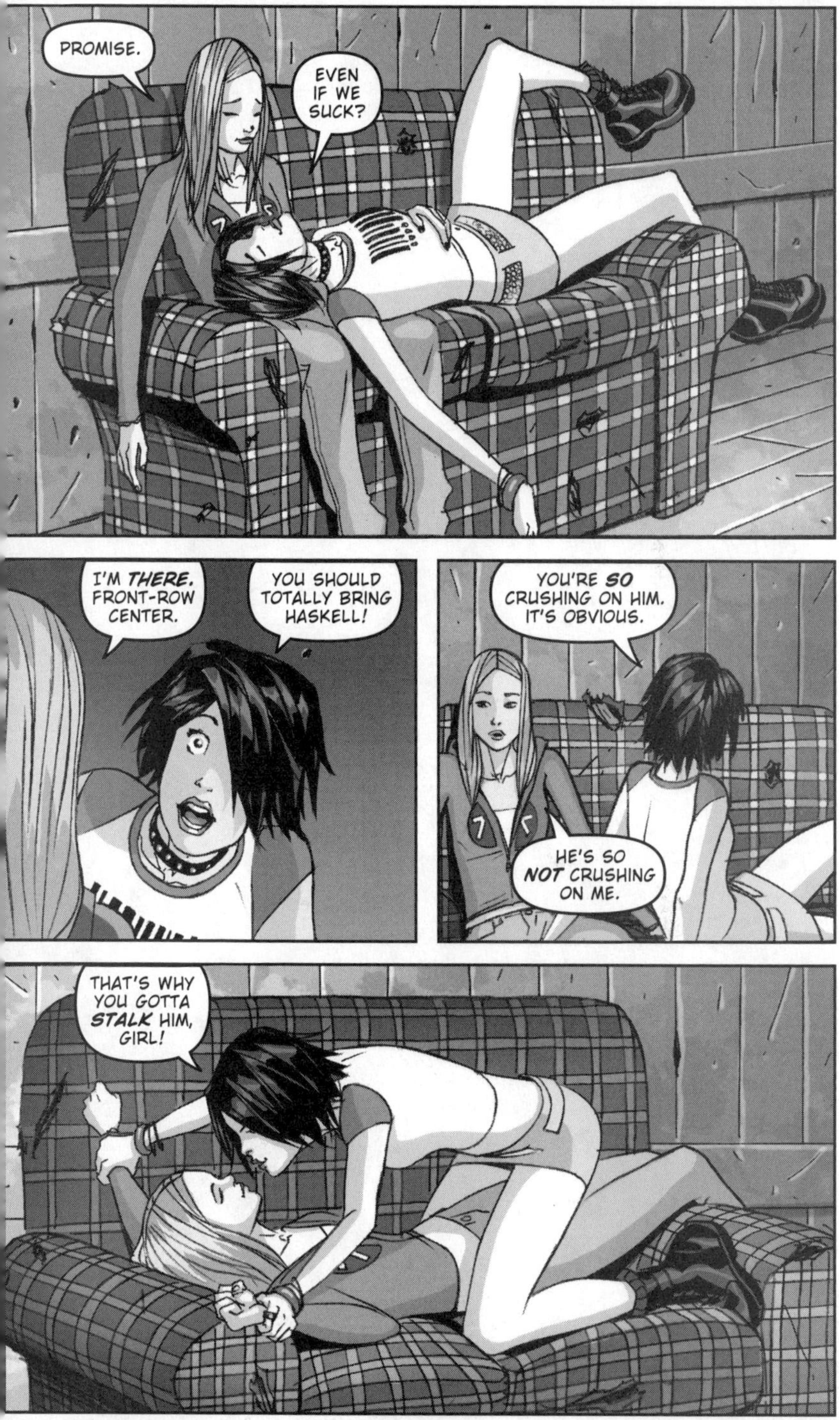
PROMISE.
EVEN IF WE SUCK?
I'M **THERE.** FRONT-ROW CENTER.
YOU SHOULD TOTALLY BRING HASKELL!
YOU'RE **SO** CRUSHING ON HIM. IT'S OBVIOUS.
HE'S SO **NOT** CRUSHING ON ME.
THAT'S WHY YOU GOTTA **STALK** HIM, GIRL!

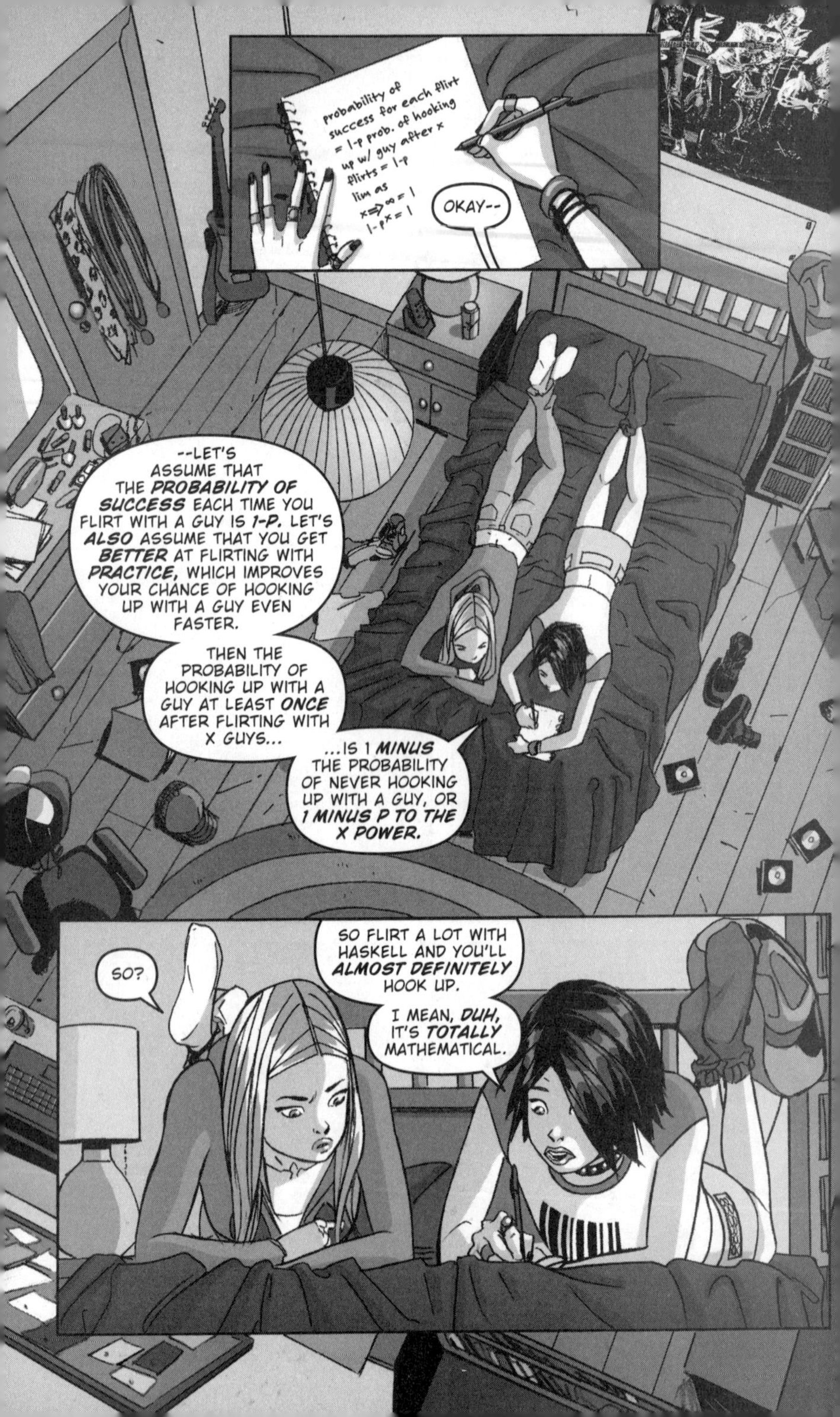
probability of success for each flirt = 1-p prob. of hooking up w/ guy after x flirts = 1-p
lim as x⟹∞ = 1
1-p^x = 1
OKAY--
--LET'S ASSUME THAT THE PROBABILITY OF SUCCESS EACH TIME YOU FLIRT WITH A GUY IS 1-P. LET'S ALSO ASSUME THAT YOU GET BETTER AT FLIRTING WITH PRACTICE, WHICH IMPROVES YOUR CHANCE OF HOOKING UP WITH A GUY EVEN FASTER.
THEN THE PROBABILITY OF HOOKING UP WITH A GUY AT LEAST ONCE AFTER FLIRTING WITH X GUYS...
...IS 1 MINUS THE PROBABILITY OF NEVER HOOKING UP WITH A GUY, OR 1 MINUS P TO THE X POWER.
SO?
SO FLIRT A LOT WITH HASKELL AND YOU'LL ALMOST DEFINITELY HOOK UP.
I MEAN, DUH, IT'S TOTALLY MATHEMATICAL.

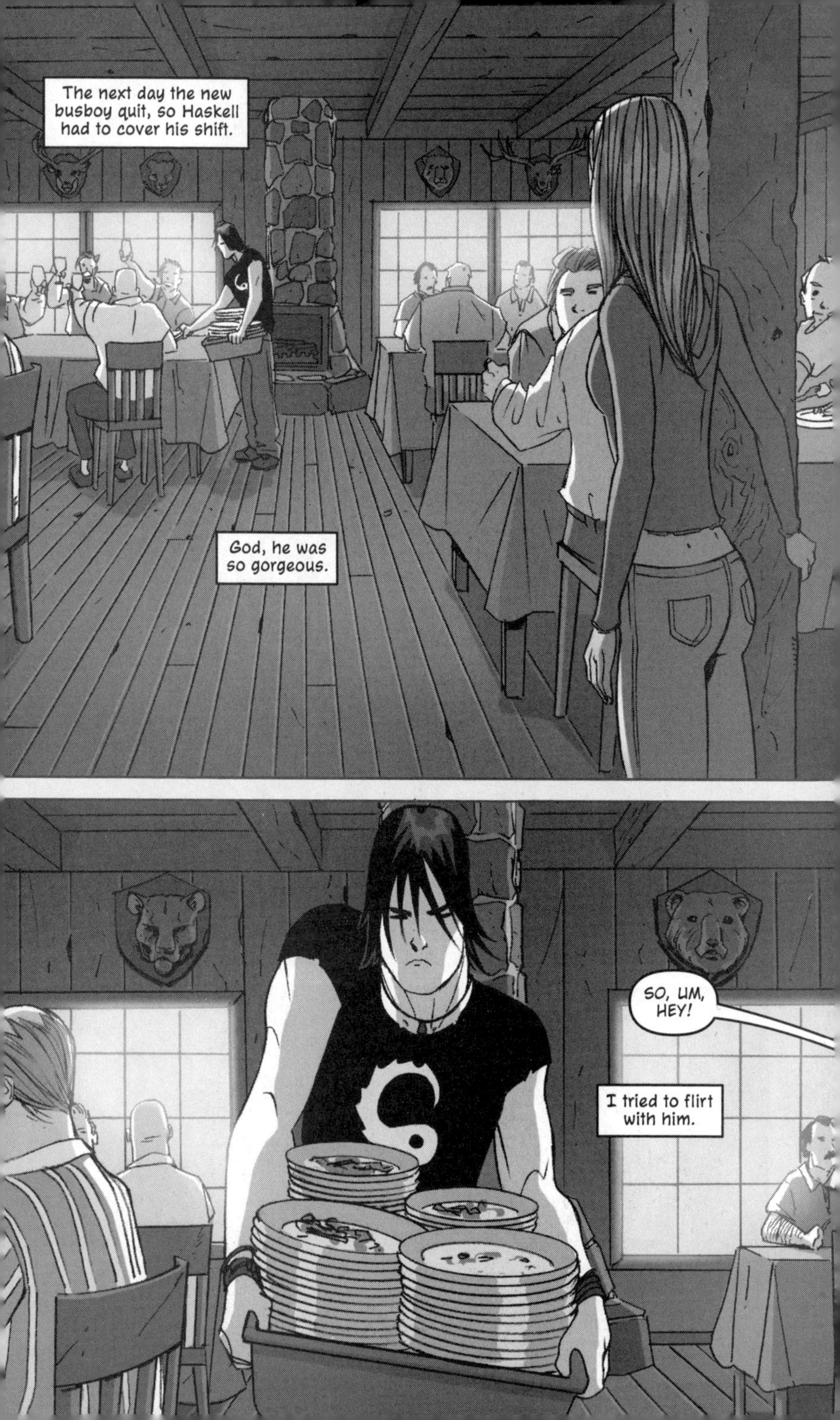
The next day the new busboy quit, so Haskell had to cover his shift.
God, he was so gorgeous.
SO, UM, HEY!
I tried to flirt with him.

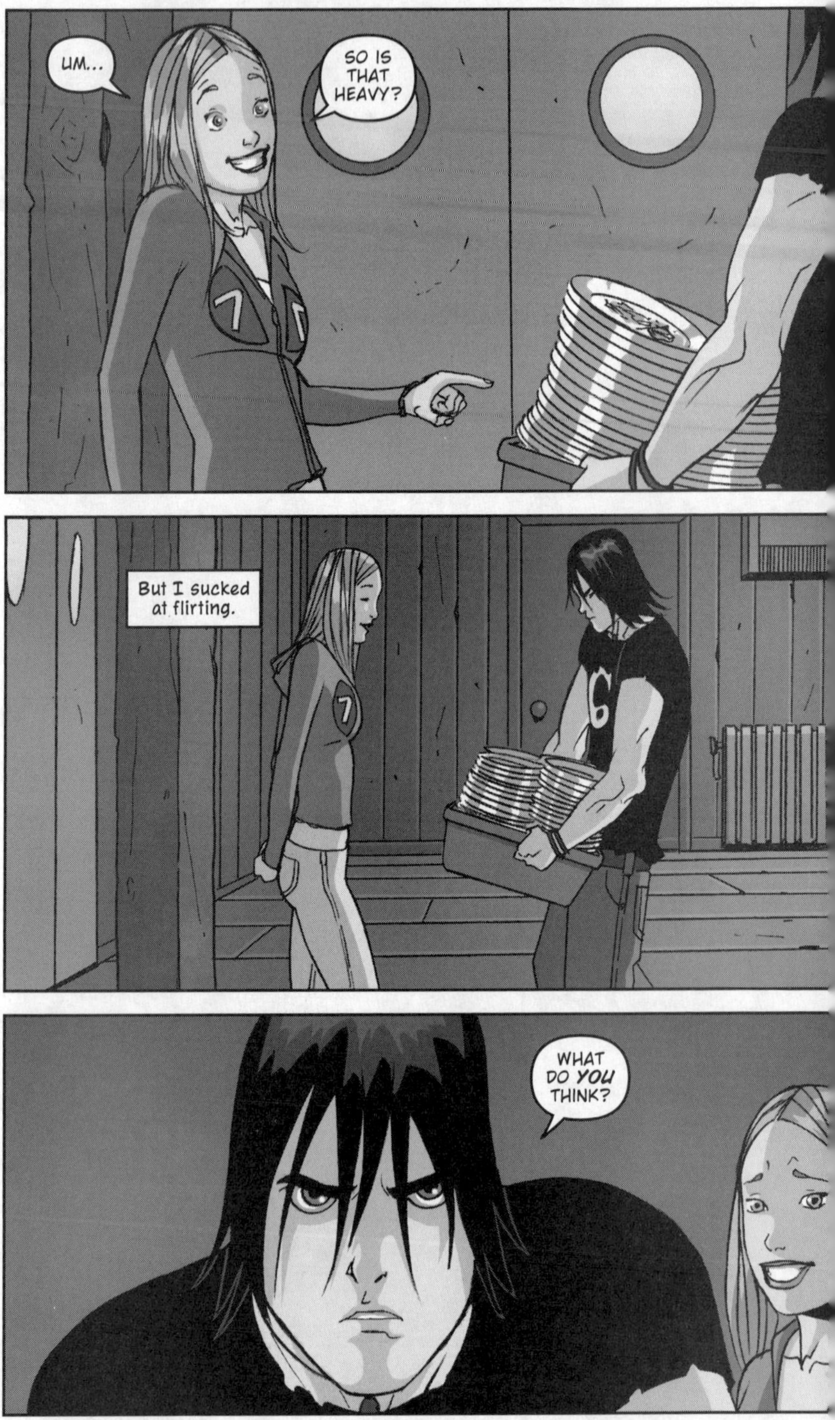
UM...
SO IS THAT HEAVY?
But I sucked at flirting.
WHAT DO YOU THINK?

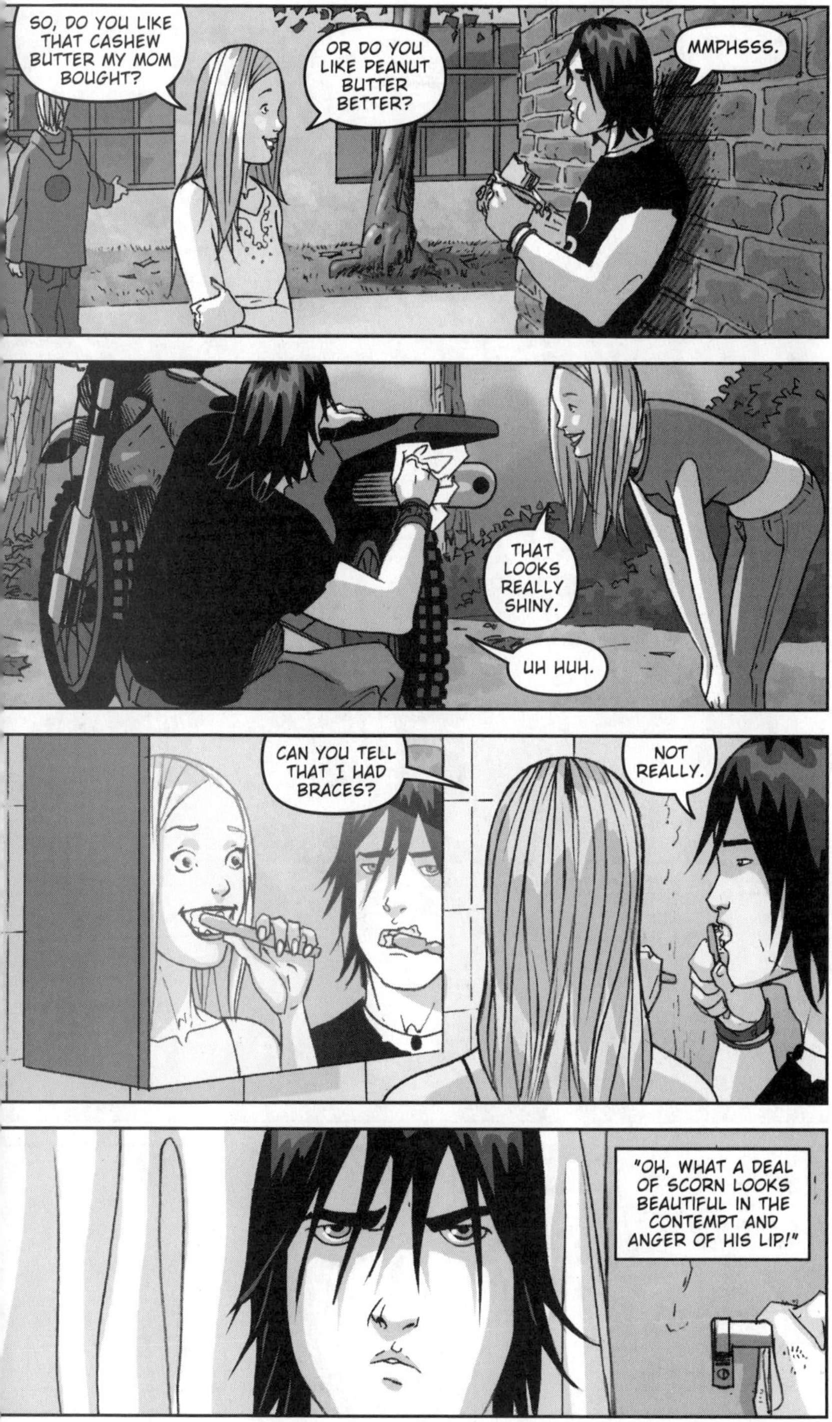
SO, DO YOU LIKE THAT CASHEW BUTTER MY MOM BOUGHT?
OR DO YOU LIKE PEANUT BUTTER BETTER?
MMPHSSS.
THAT LOOKS REALLY SHINY.
UH HUH.
CAN YOU TELL THAT I HAD BRACES?
NOT REALLY.
"OH, WHAT A DEAL OF SCORN LOOKS BEAUTIFUL IN THE CONTEMPT AND ANGER OF HIS LIP!"

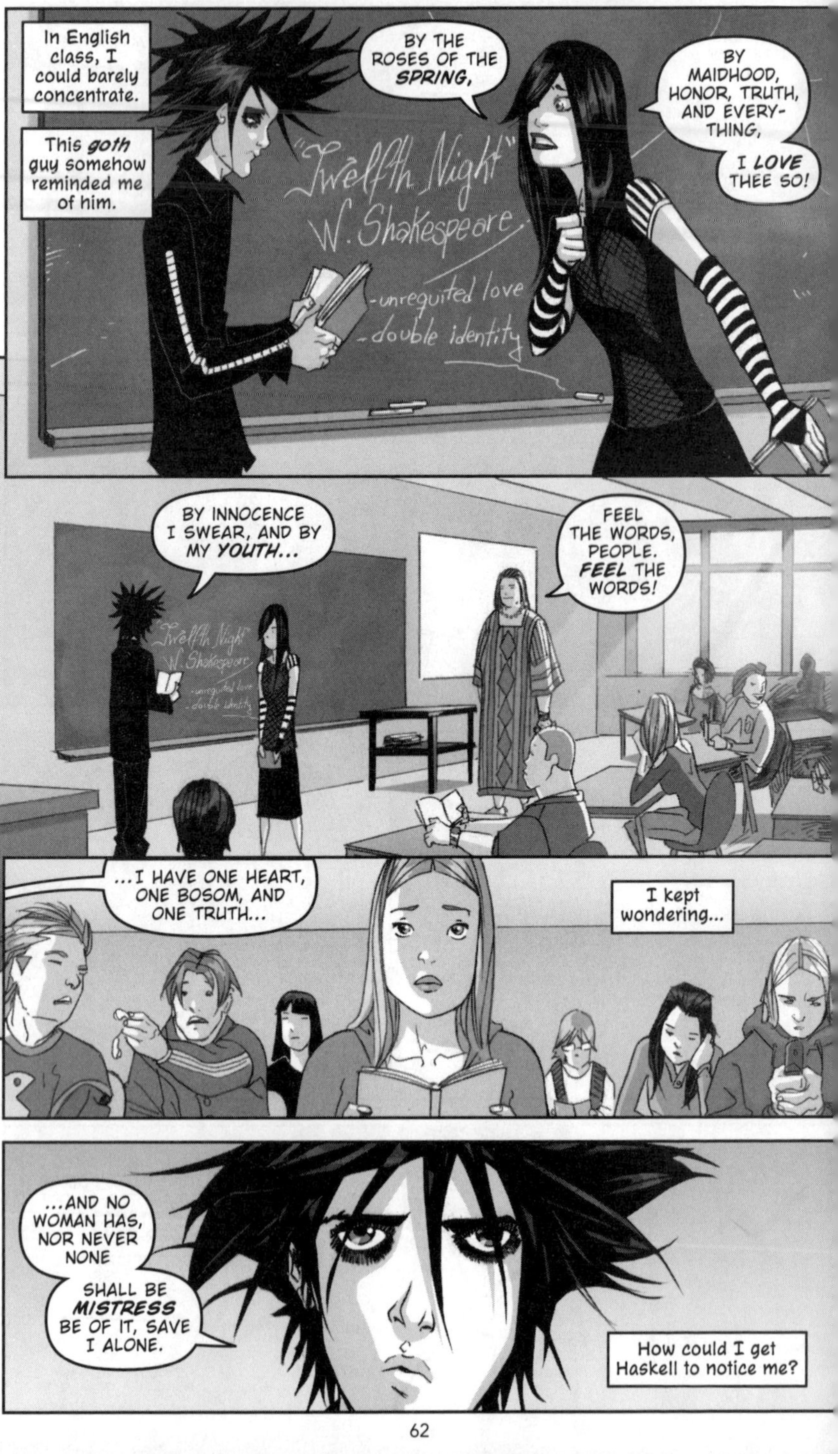
In English class, I could barely concentrate.
This goth guy somehow reminded me of him.
BY THE ROSES OF THE SPRING,
BY MAIDHOOD, HONOR, TRUTH, AND EVERY-THING,
I LOVE THEE SO!
"Twelfth Night" W. Shakespeare
-unrequited love
-double identity
BY INNOCENCE I SWEAR, AND BY MY YOUTH...
FEEL THE WORDS, PEOPLE. FEEL THE WORDS!
...I HAVE ONE HEART, ONE BOSOM, AND ONE TRUTH...
I kept wondering...
...AND NO WOMAN HAS, NOR NEVER NONE
SHALL BE MISTRESS BE OF IT, SAVE I ALONE.
How could I get Haskell to notice me?

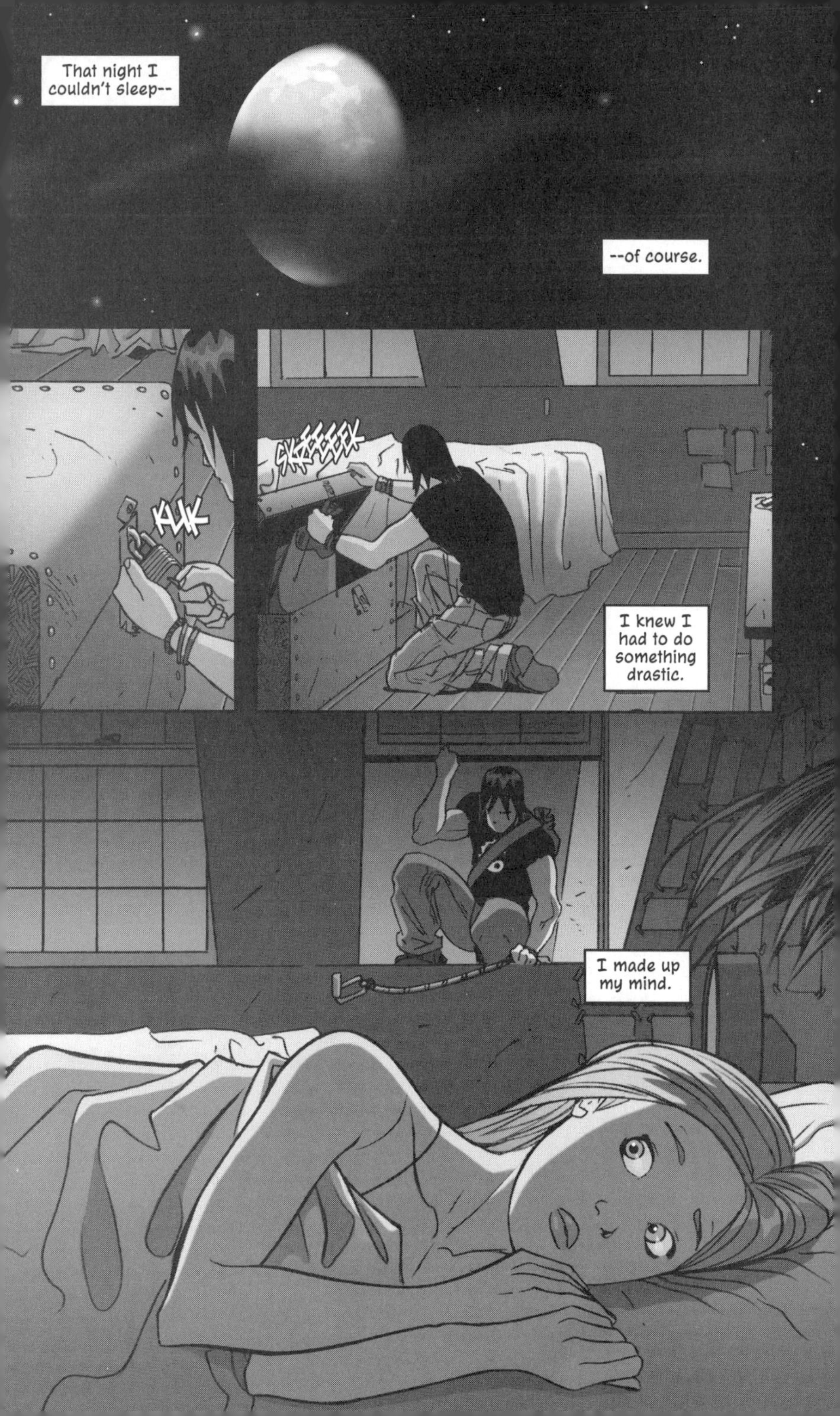
That night I couldn't sleep--
--of course.
KLIK
SKREEEEEK
I knew I had to do something drastic.
I made up my mind.

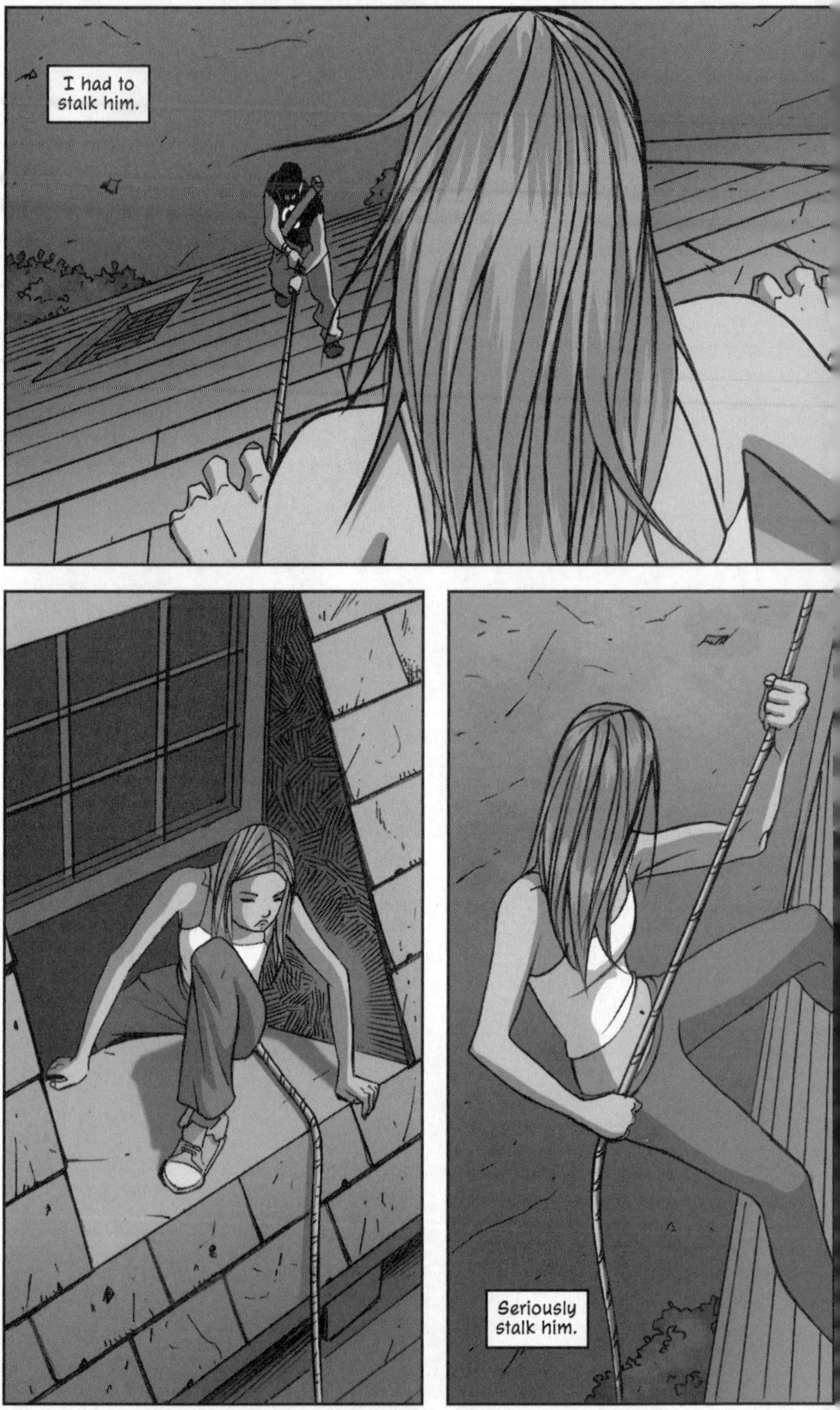
I had to stalk him.
Seriously stalk him.

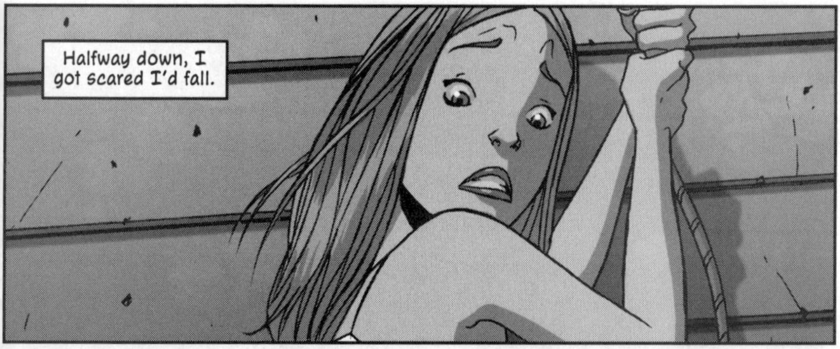
Halfway down, I got scared I'd fall.

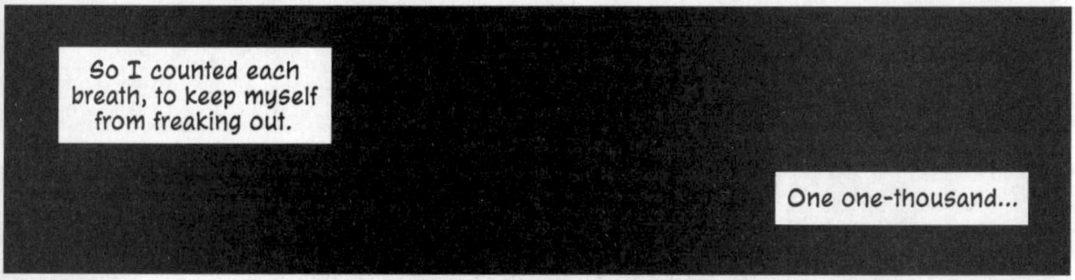
So I counted each breath, to keep myself from freaking out.
One one-thousand...

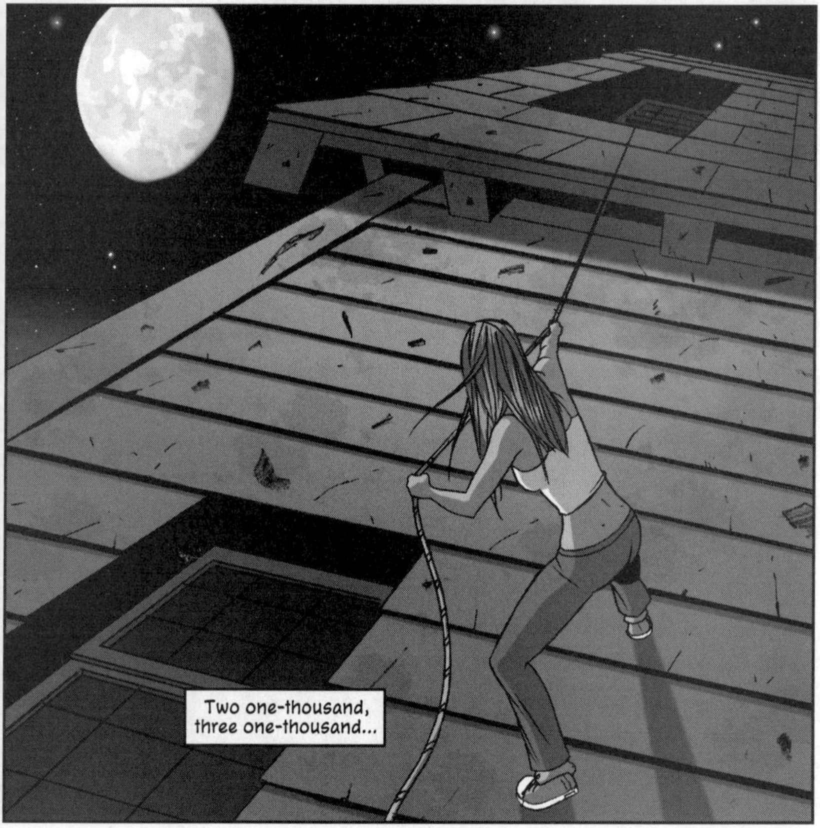
Two one-thousand, three one-thousand...

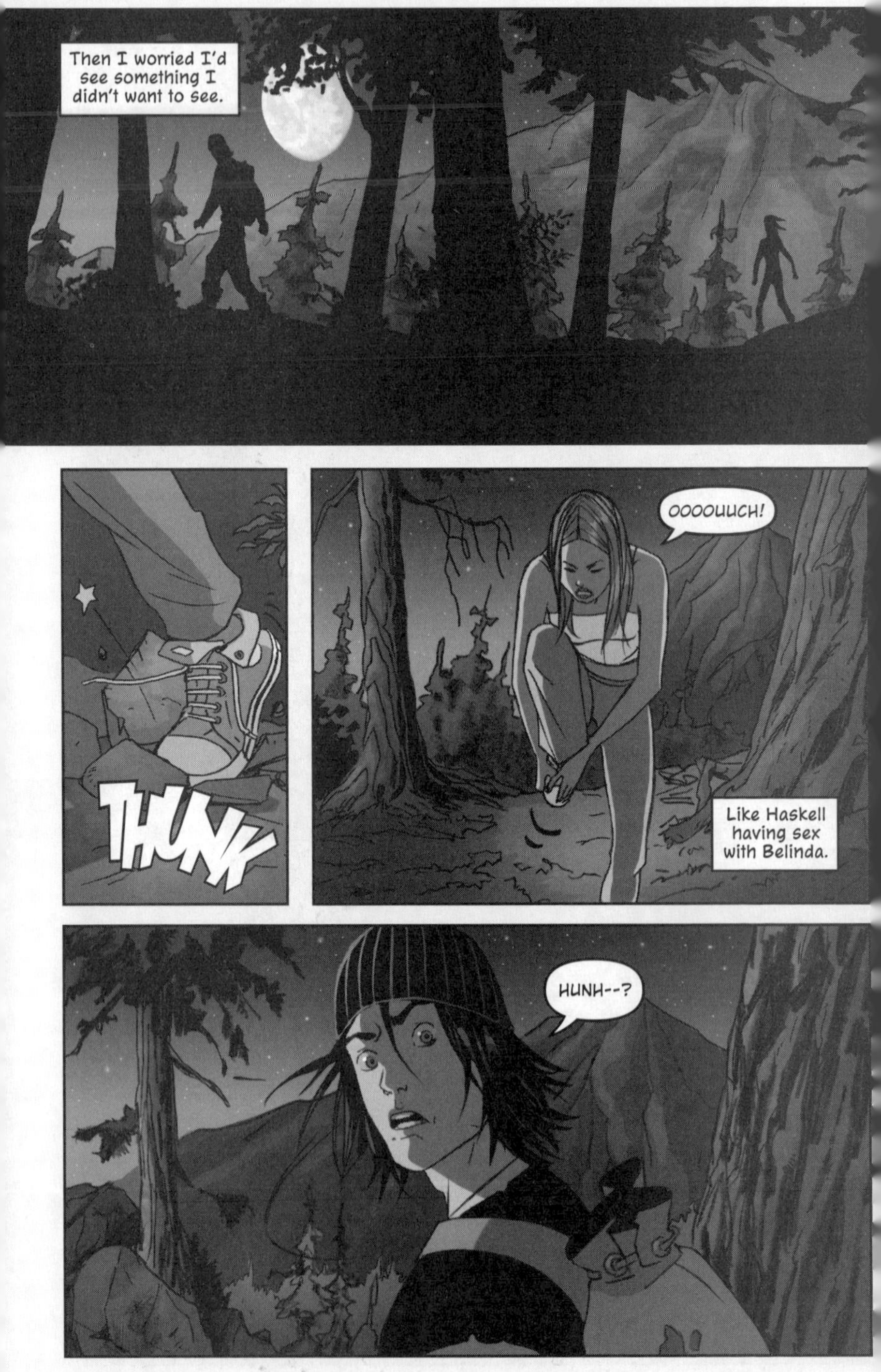
Then I worried I'd see something I didn't want to see.
THUNK
OOOOUUCH!
Like Haskell having sex with Belinda.
HUNH--?

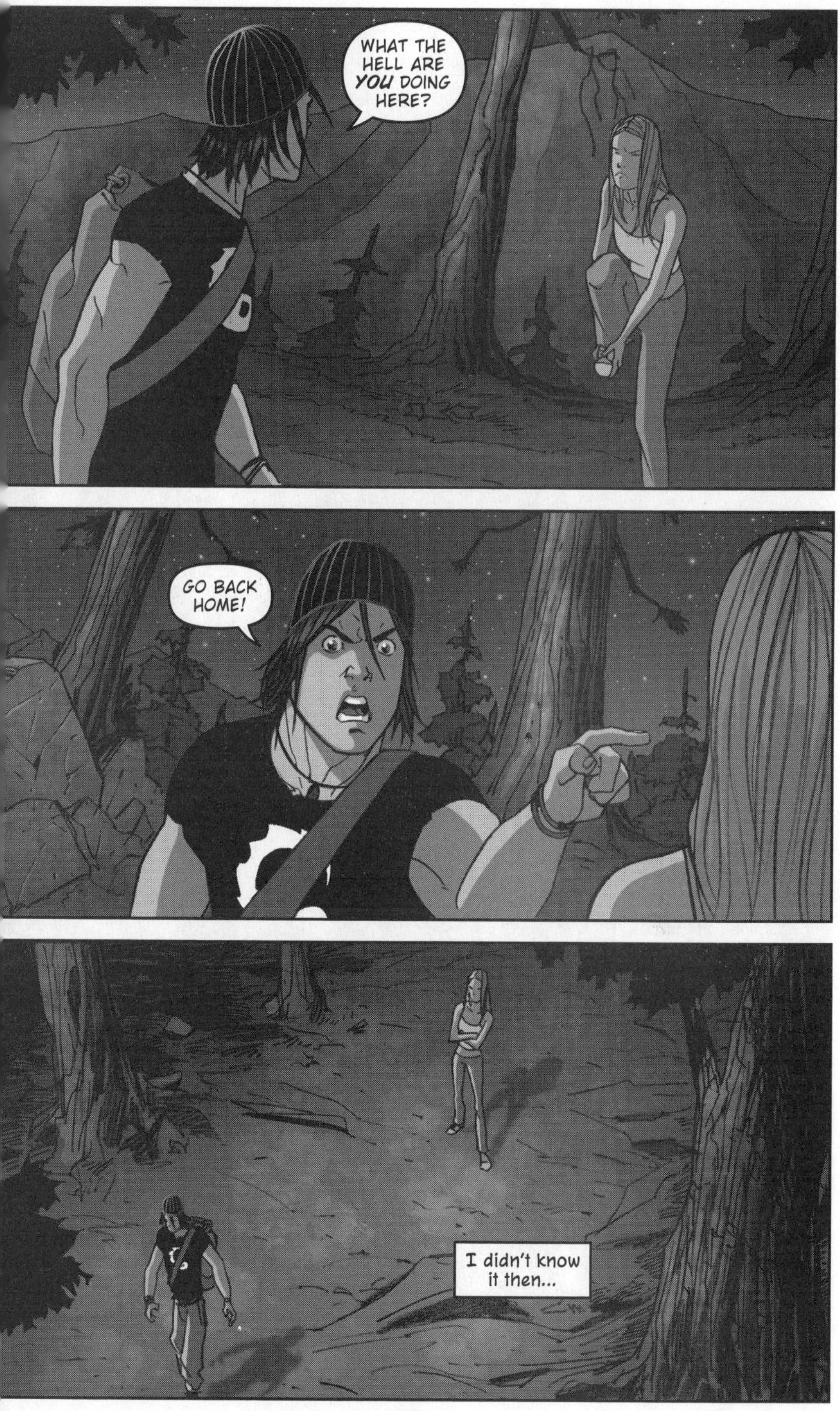
WHAT THE HELL ARE YOU DOING HERE?
GO BACK HOME!
I didn't know it then...

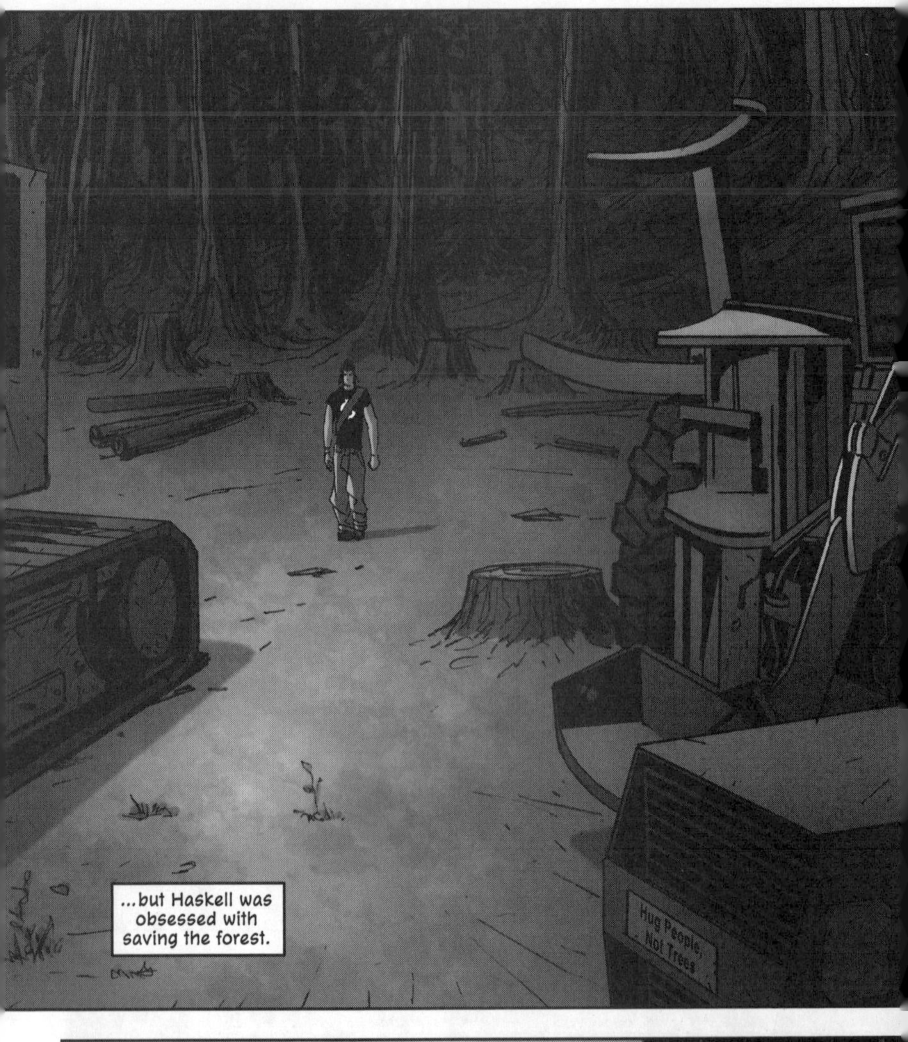
...but Haskell was obsessed with saving the forest.
Hug People, Not Trees

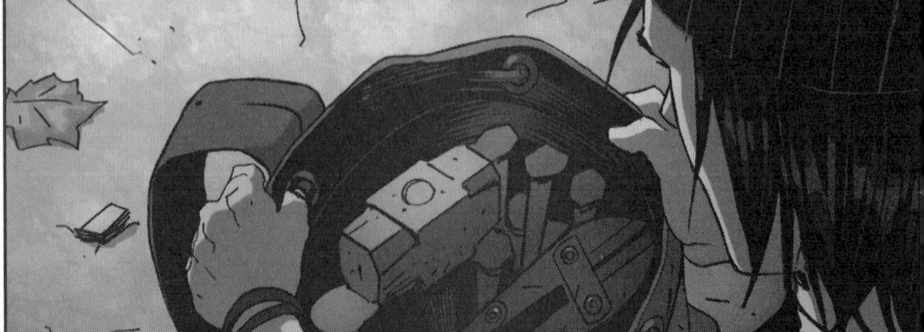

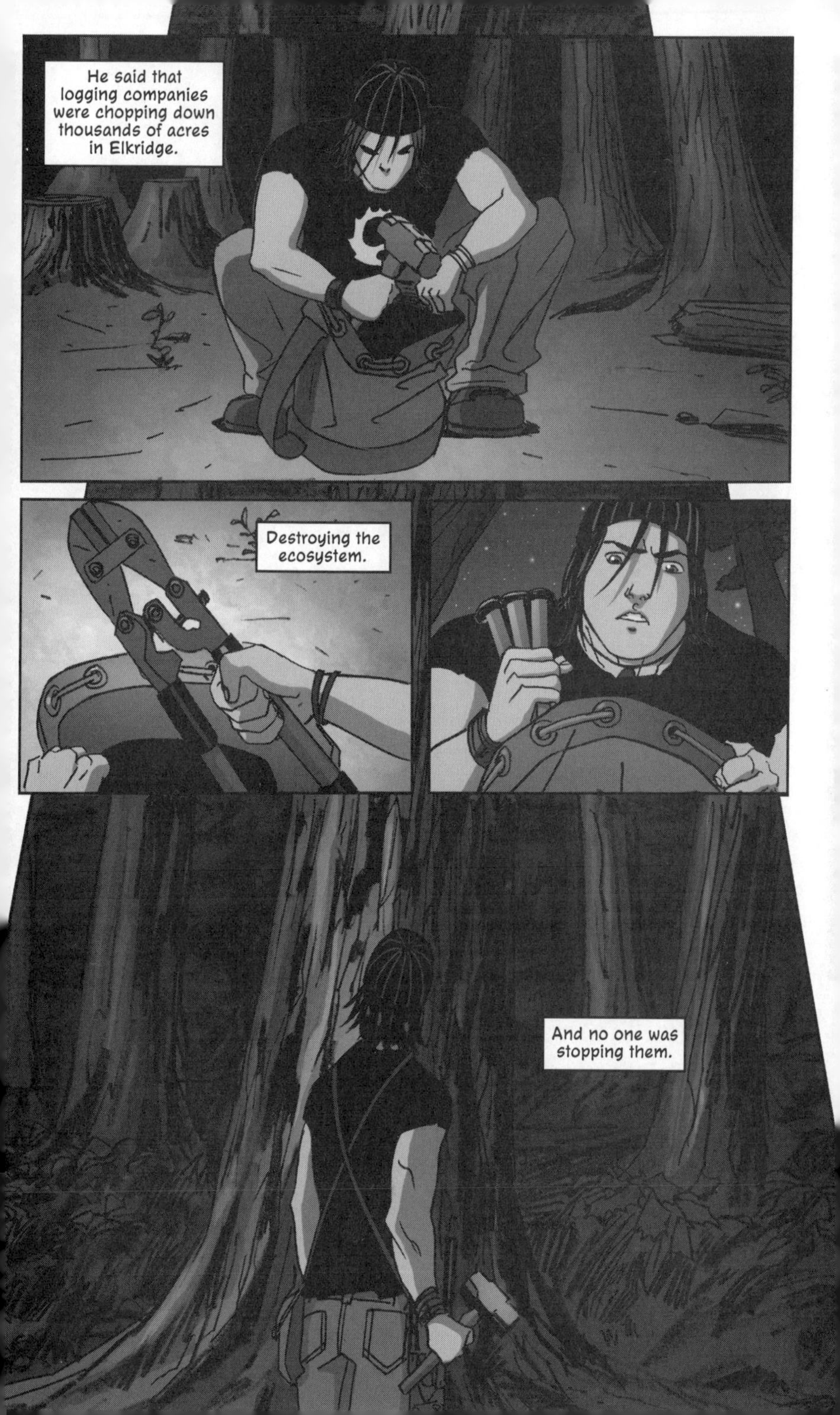
He said that logging companies were chopping down thousands of acres in Elkridge.
Destroying the ecosystem.
And no one was stopping them.

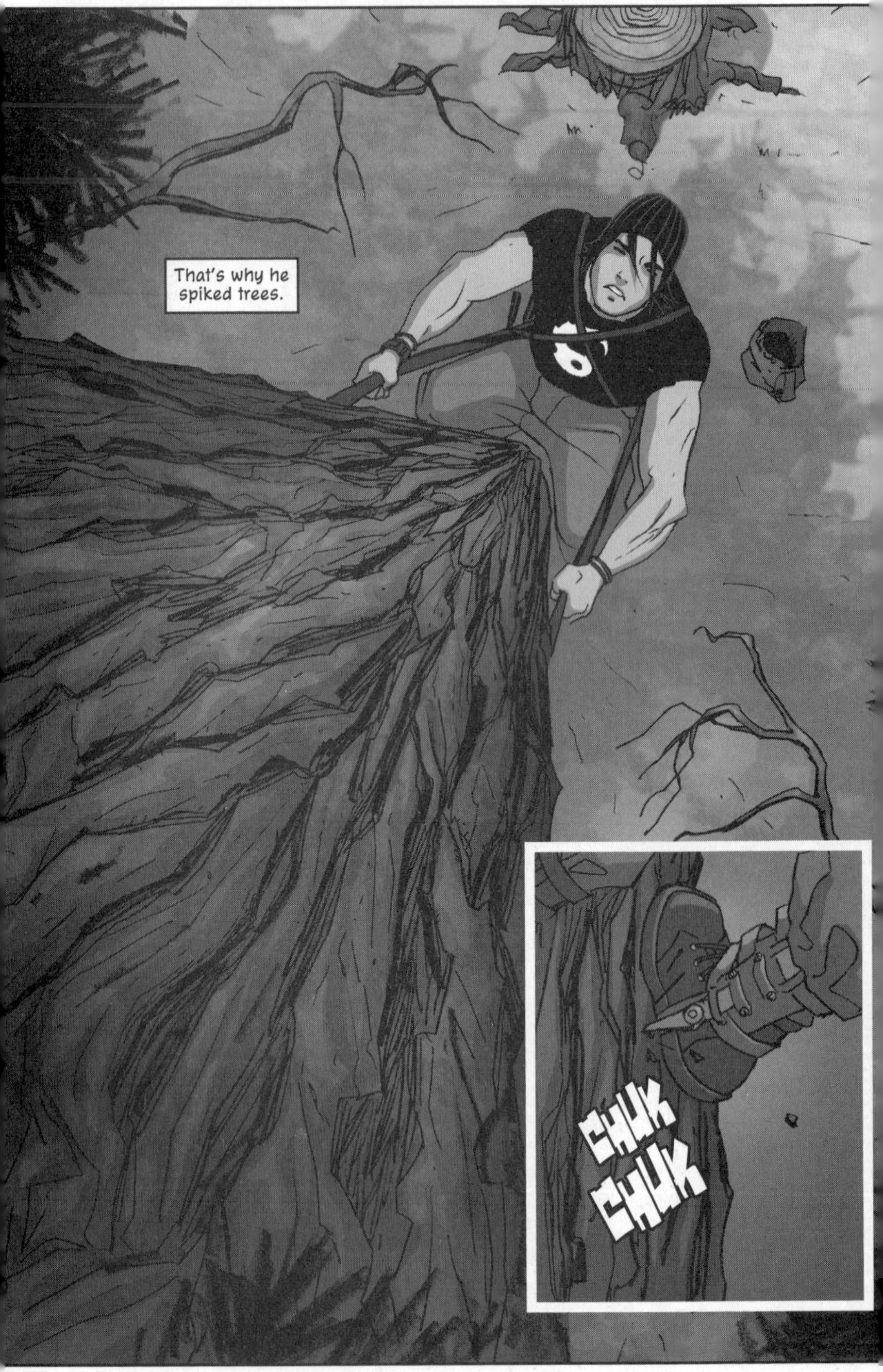
That's why he spiked trees.
CHUK
CHUK

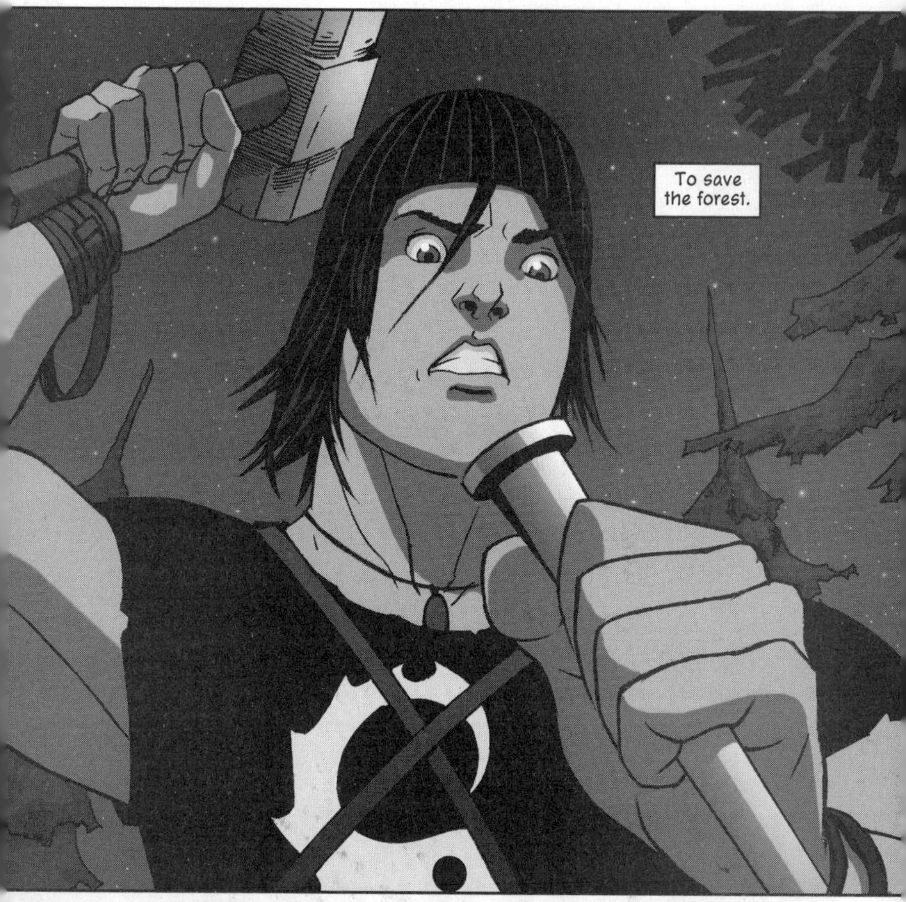
To save the forest.

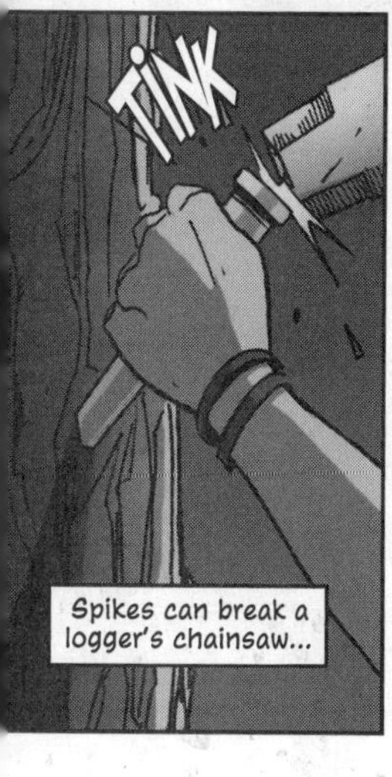
TINK
Spikes can break a logger's chainsaw...

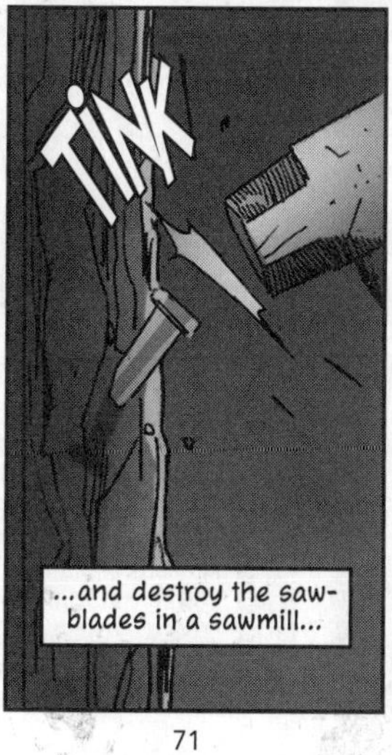
TINK
...and destroy the saw-blades in a sawmill...

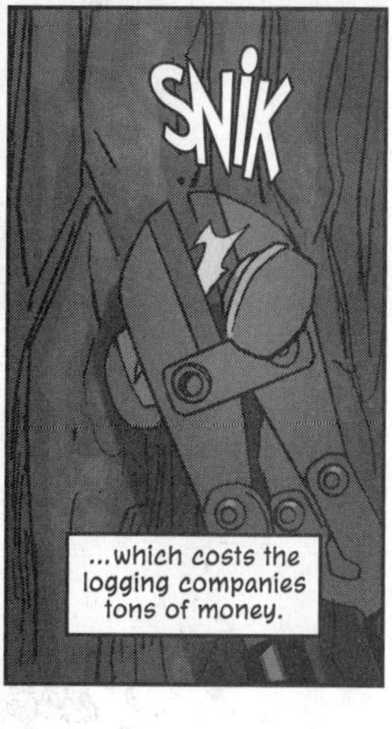
SNIK
...which costs the logging companies tons of money.

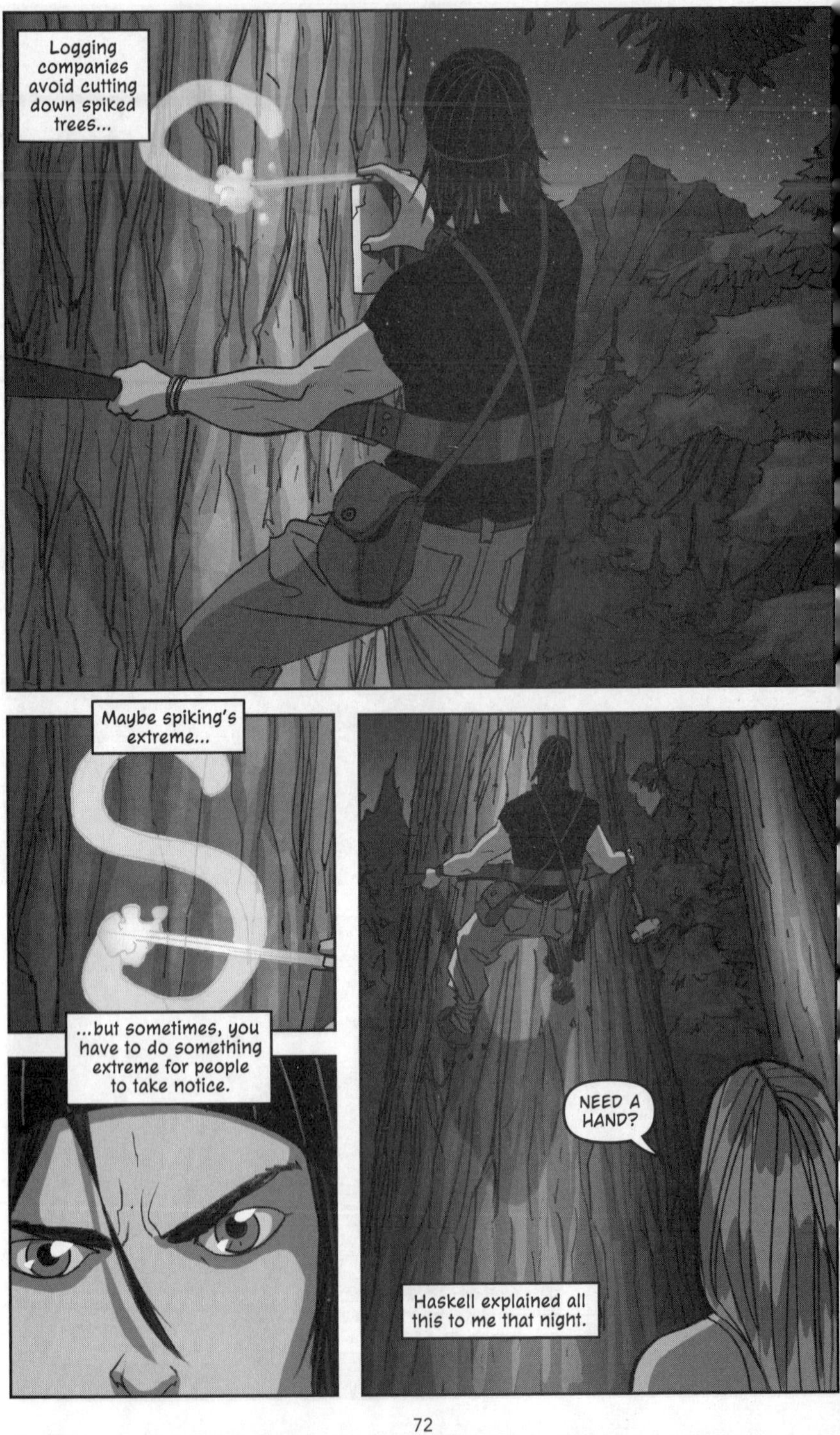
Logging companies avoid cutting down spiked trees...
Maybe spiking's extreme...
...but sometimes, you have to do something extreme for people to take notice.
NEED A HAND?
Haskell explained all this to me that night.

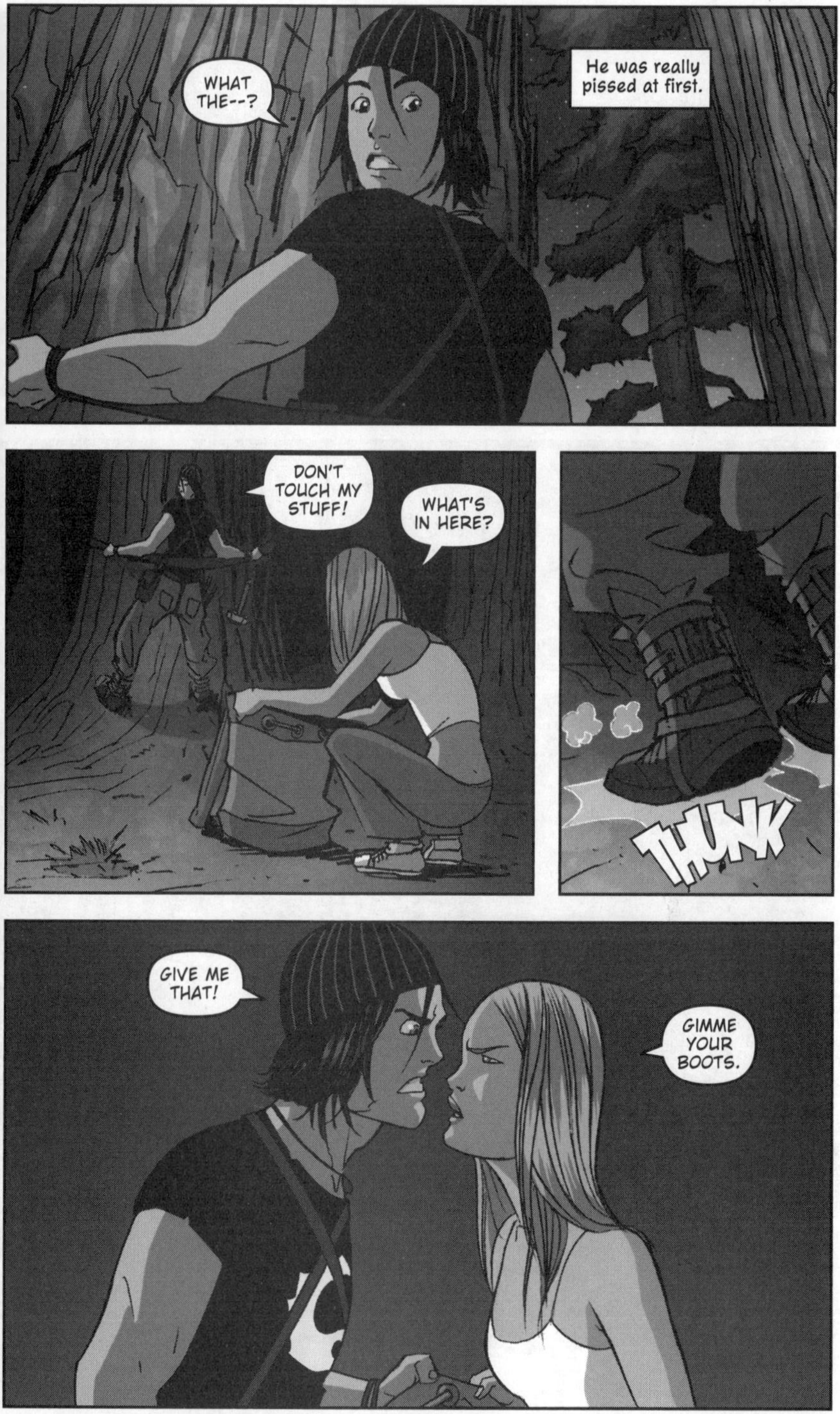
WHAT THE--?
He was really pissed at first.
DON'T TOUCH MY STUFF!
WHAT'S IN HERE?
THUNK
GIVE ME THAT!
GIMME YOUR BOOTS.

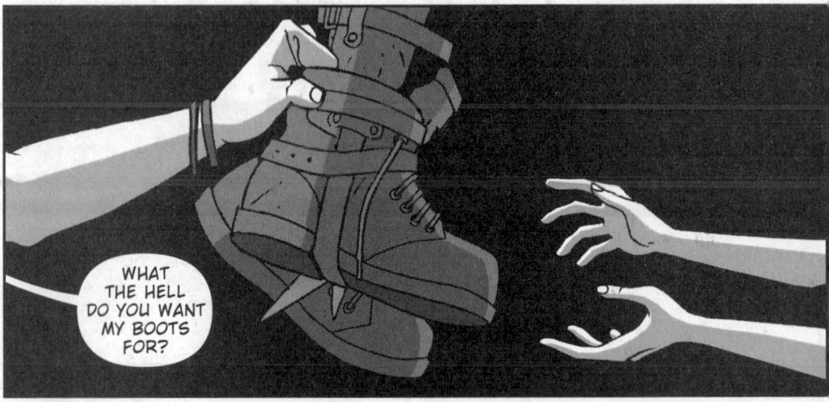
WHAT THE HELL DO YOU WANT MY BOOTS FOR?

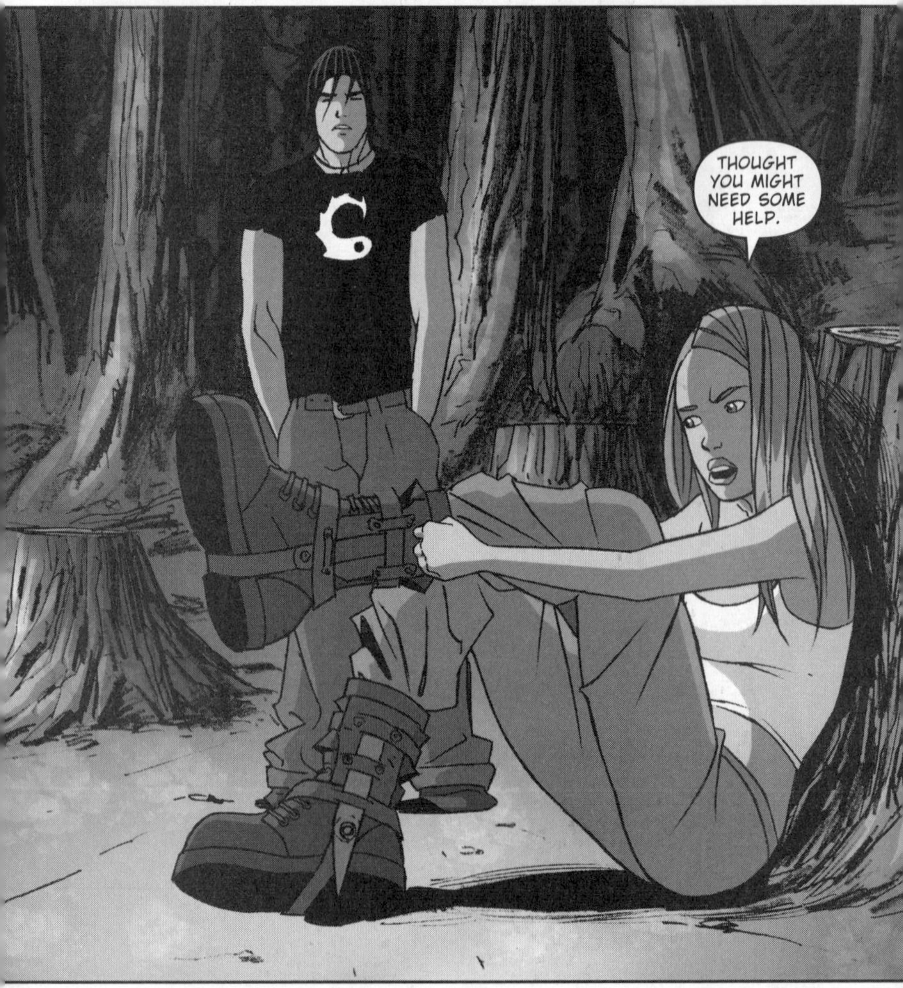
THOUGHT YOU MIGHT NEED SOME HELP.

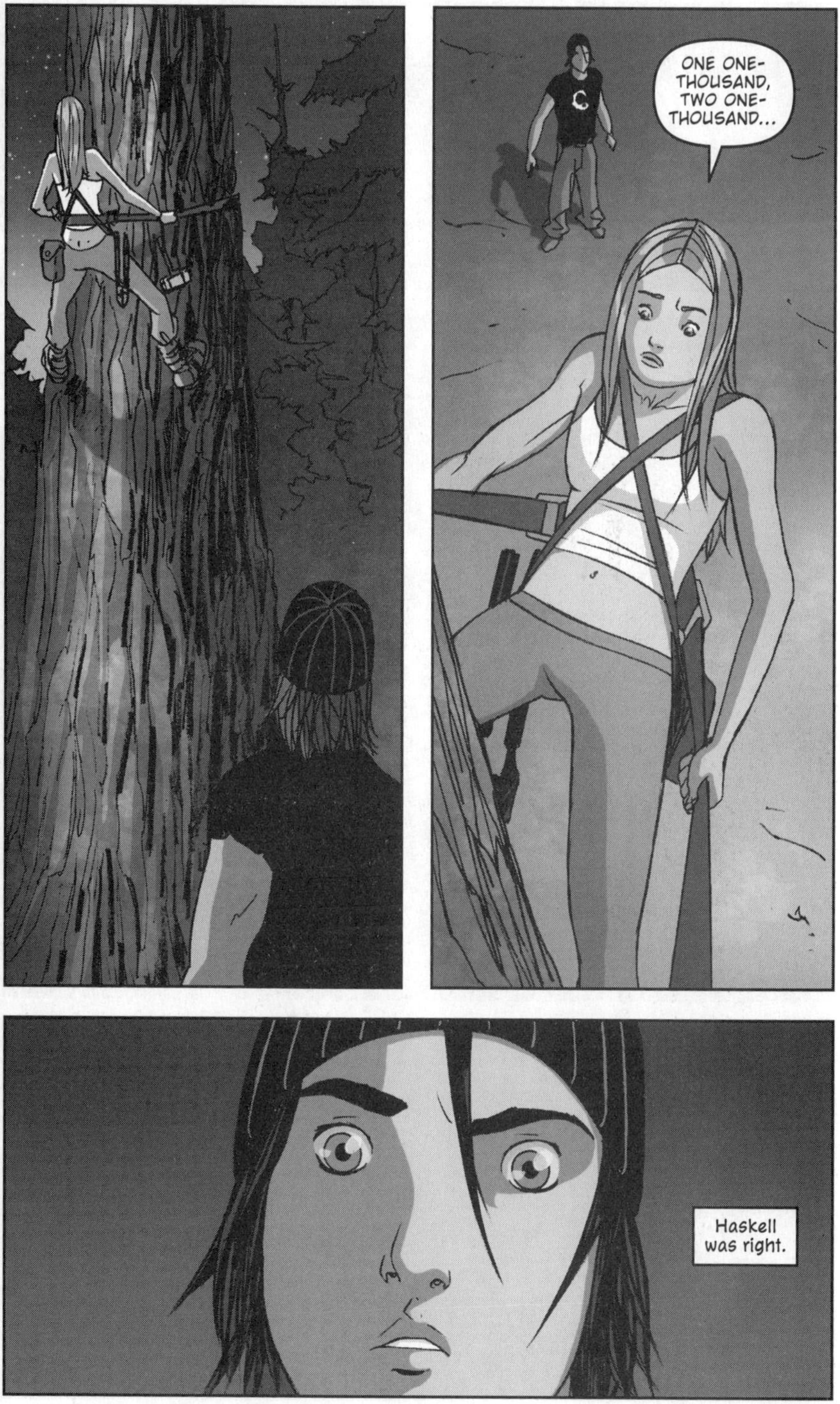
ONE ONE-THOUSAND, TWO ONE-THOUSAND...
Haskell was right.

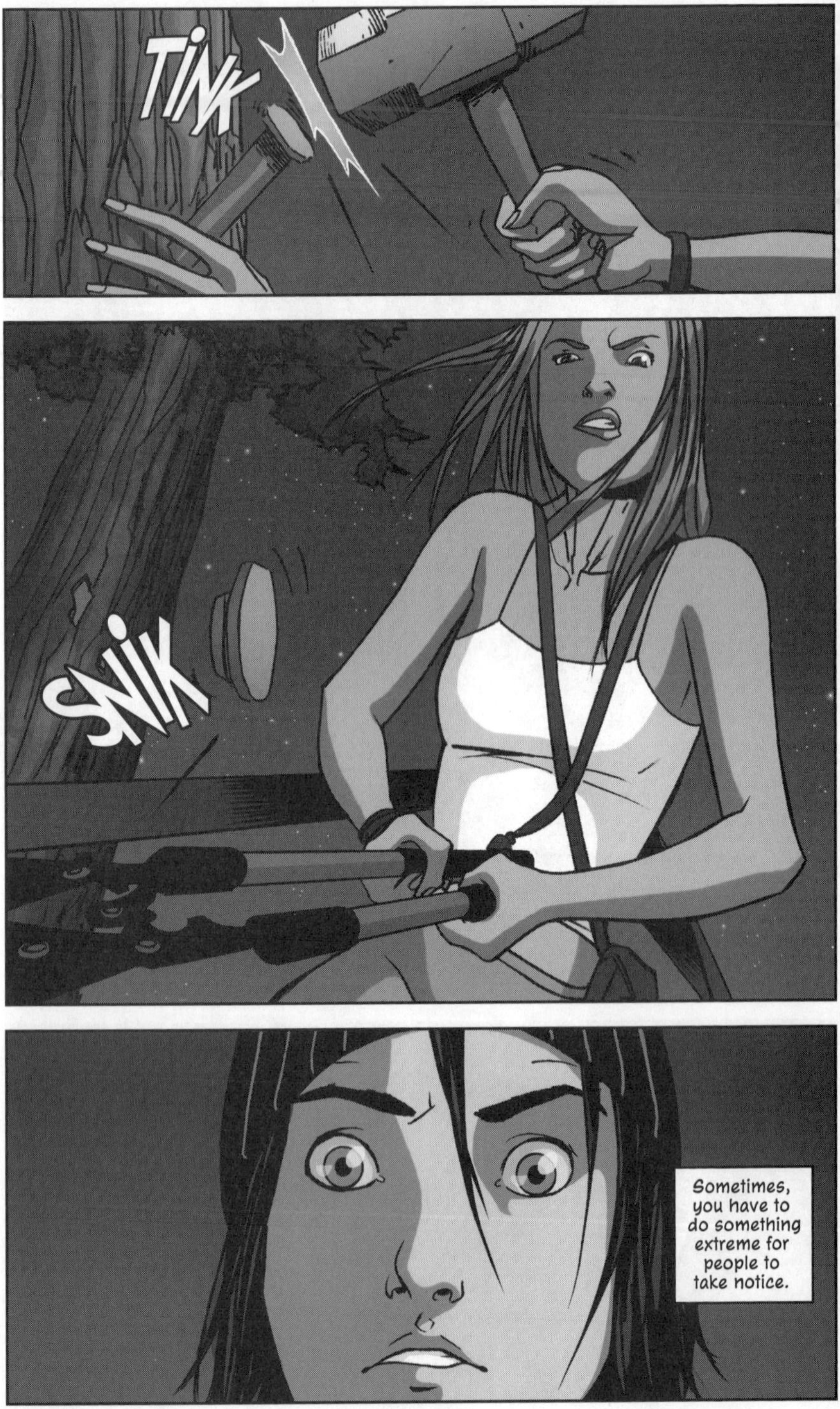
TINK
SNIK
Sometimes, you have to do something extreme for people to take notice.

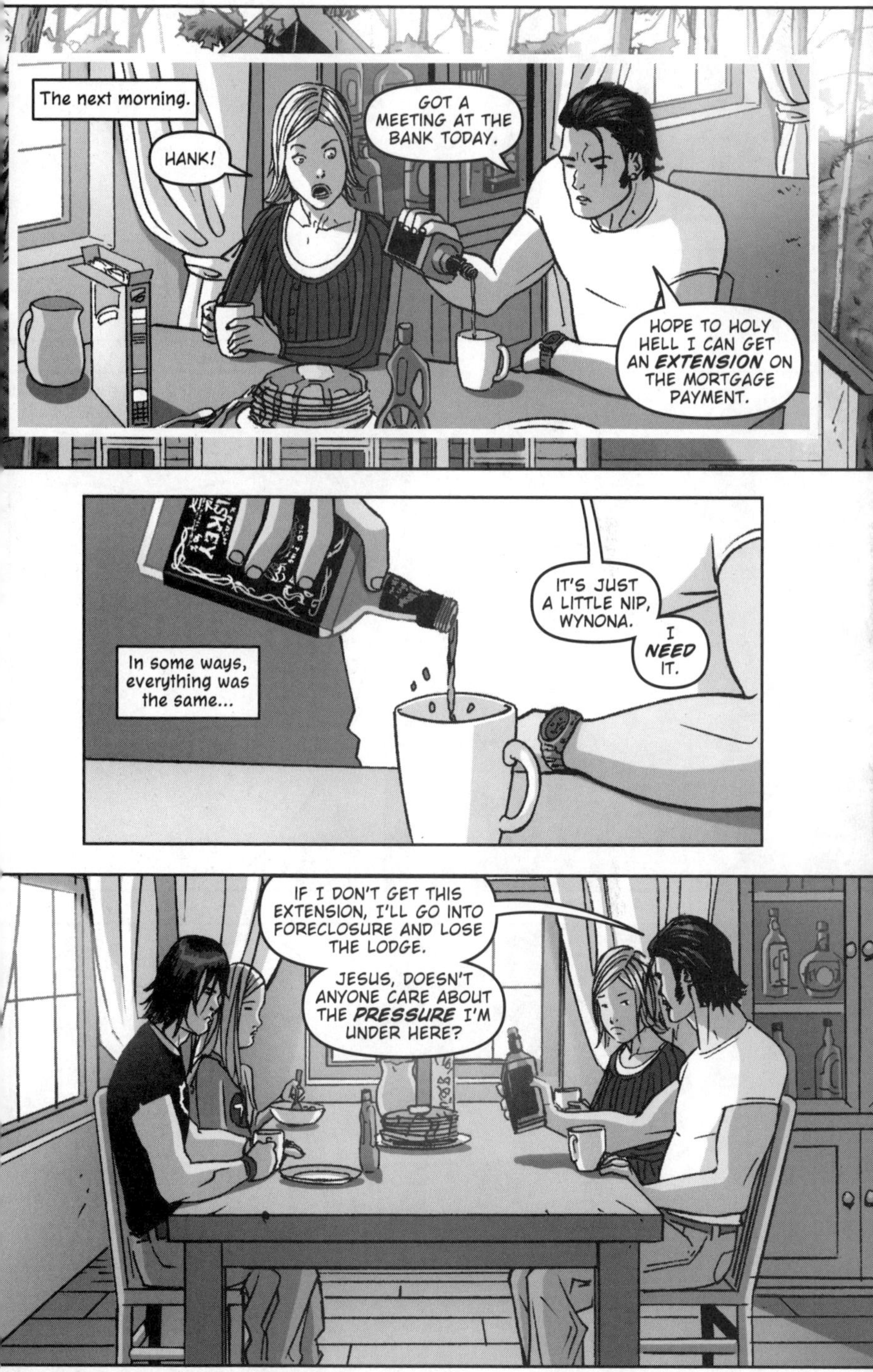

The next morning.
HANK!
GOT A MEETING AT THE BANK TODAY.
HOPE TO HOLY HELL I CAN GET AN **EXTENSION** ON THE MORTGAGE PAYMENT.
In some ways, everything was the same...
IT'S JUST A LITTLE NIP, WYNONA.
I **NEED** IT.
IF I DON'T GET THIS EXTENSION, I'LL GO INTO FORECLOSURE AND LOSE THE LODGE.
JESUS, DOESN'T ANYONE CARE ABOUT THE **PRESSURE** I'M UNDER HERE?

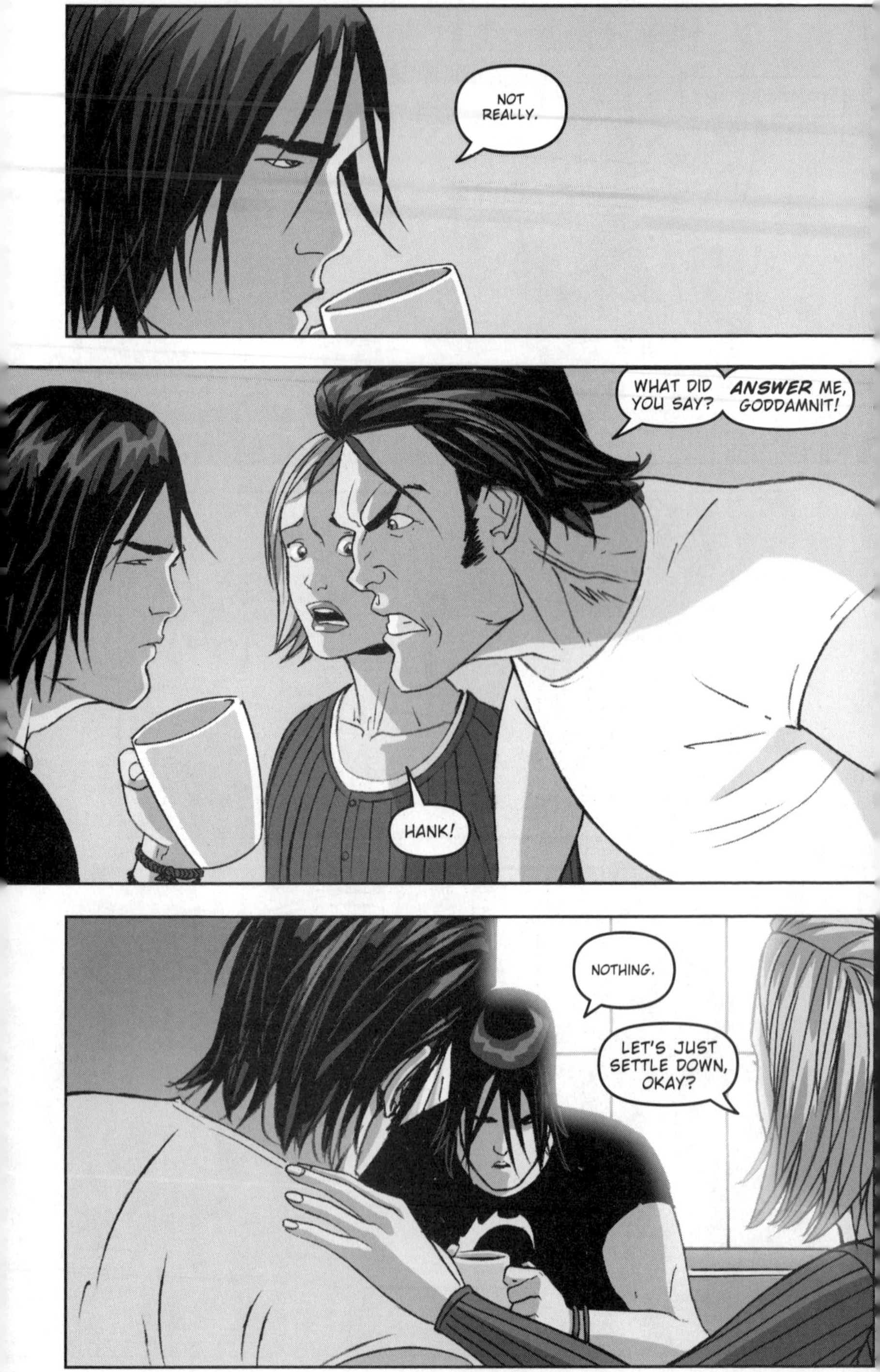
NOT REALLY.
WHAT DID YOU SAY?
ANSWER ME, GODDAMNIT!
HANK!
NOTHING.
LET'S JUST SETTLE DOWN, OKAY?

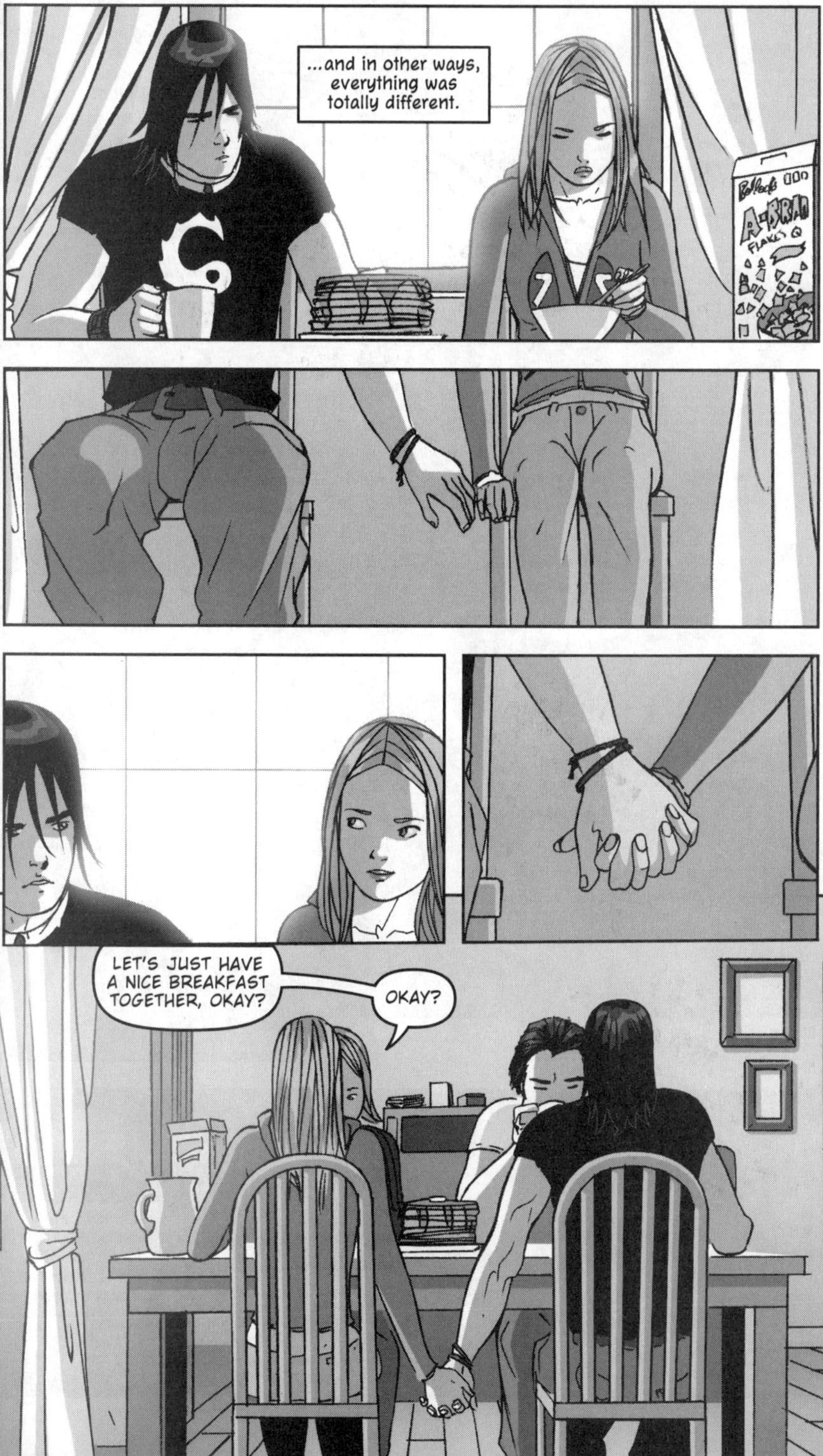
...and in other ways, everything was totally different.
LET'S JUST HAVE A NICE BREAKFAST TOGETHER, OKAY?
OKAY?

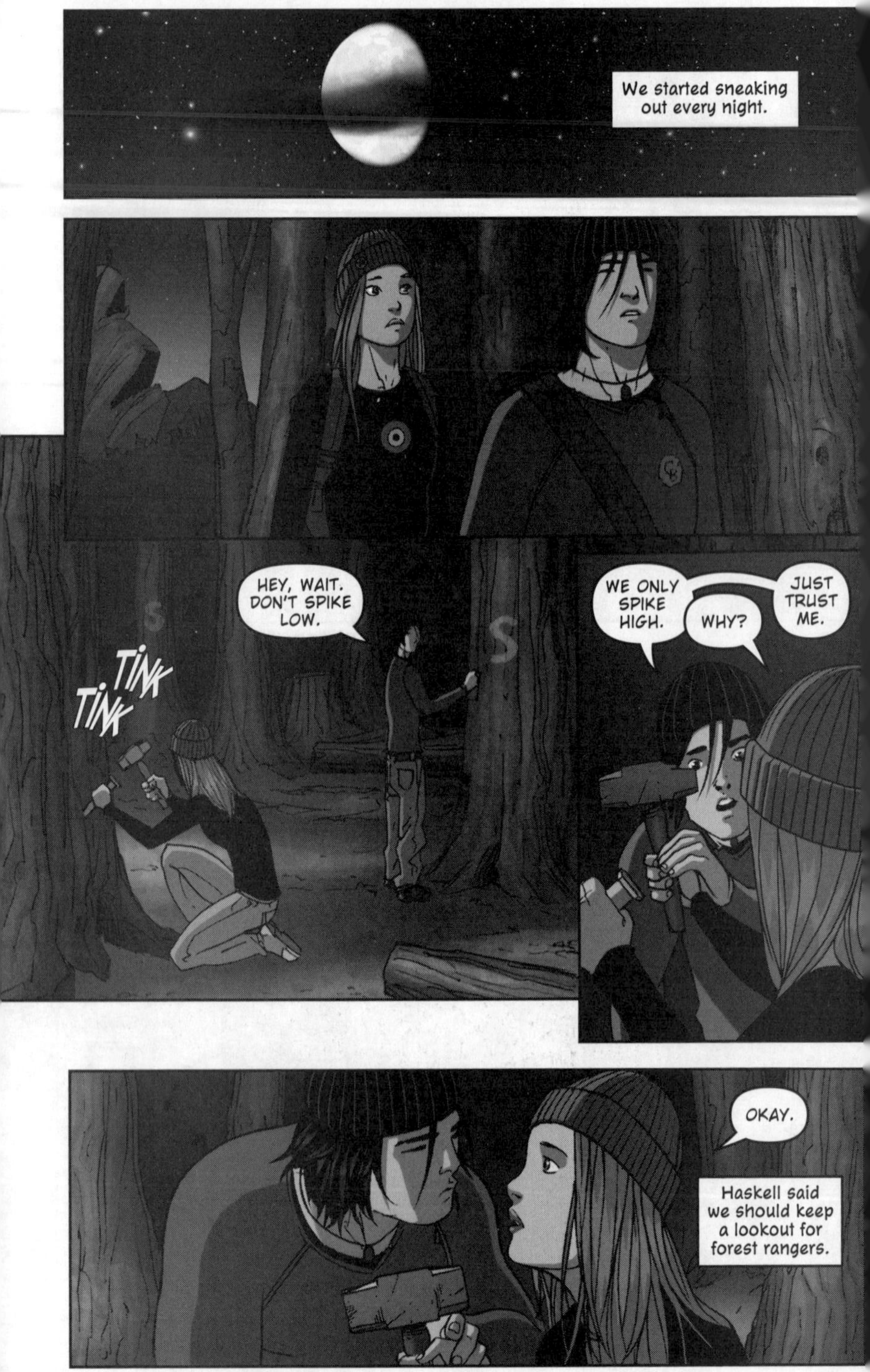

We started sneaking out every night.
TINK
TINK
HEY, WAIT. DON'T SPIKE LOW.
WE ONLY SPIKE HIGH.
WHY?
JUST TRUST ME.
OKAY.
Haskell said we should keep a lookout for forest rangers.

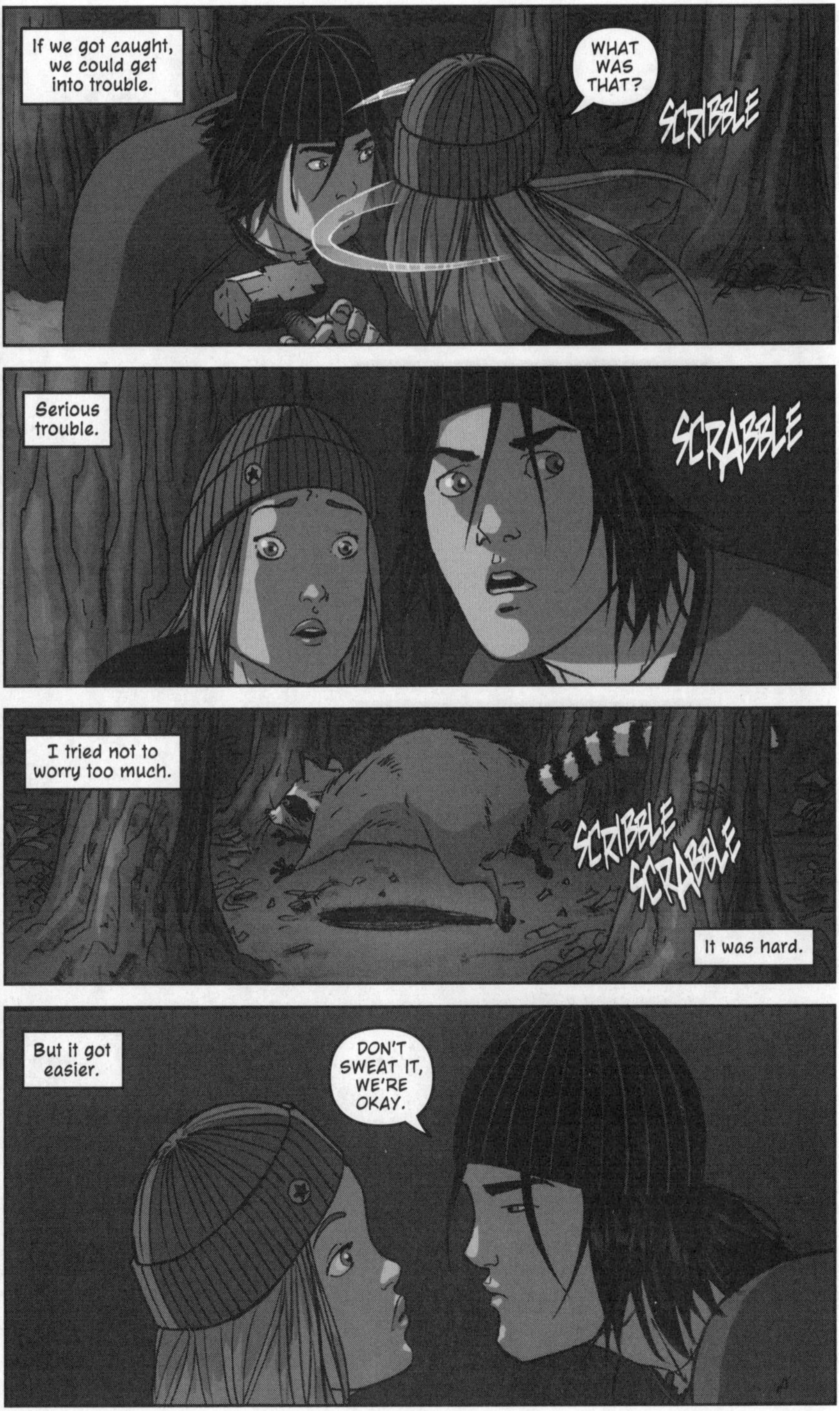
If we got caught, we could get into trouble.
WHAT WAS THAT?
SCRIBBLE
Serious trouble.
SCRABBLE
I tried not to worry too much.
SCRIBBLE
SCRABBLE
It was hard.
But it got easier.
DON'T SWEAT IT, WE'RE OKAY.

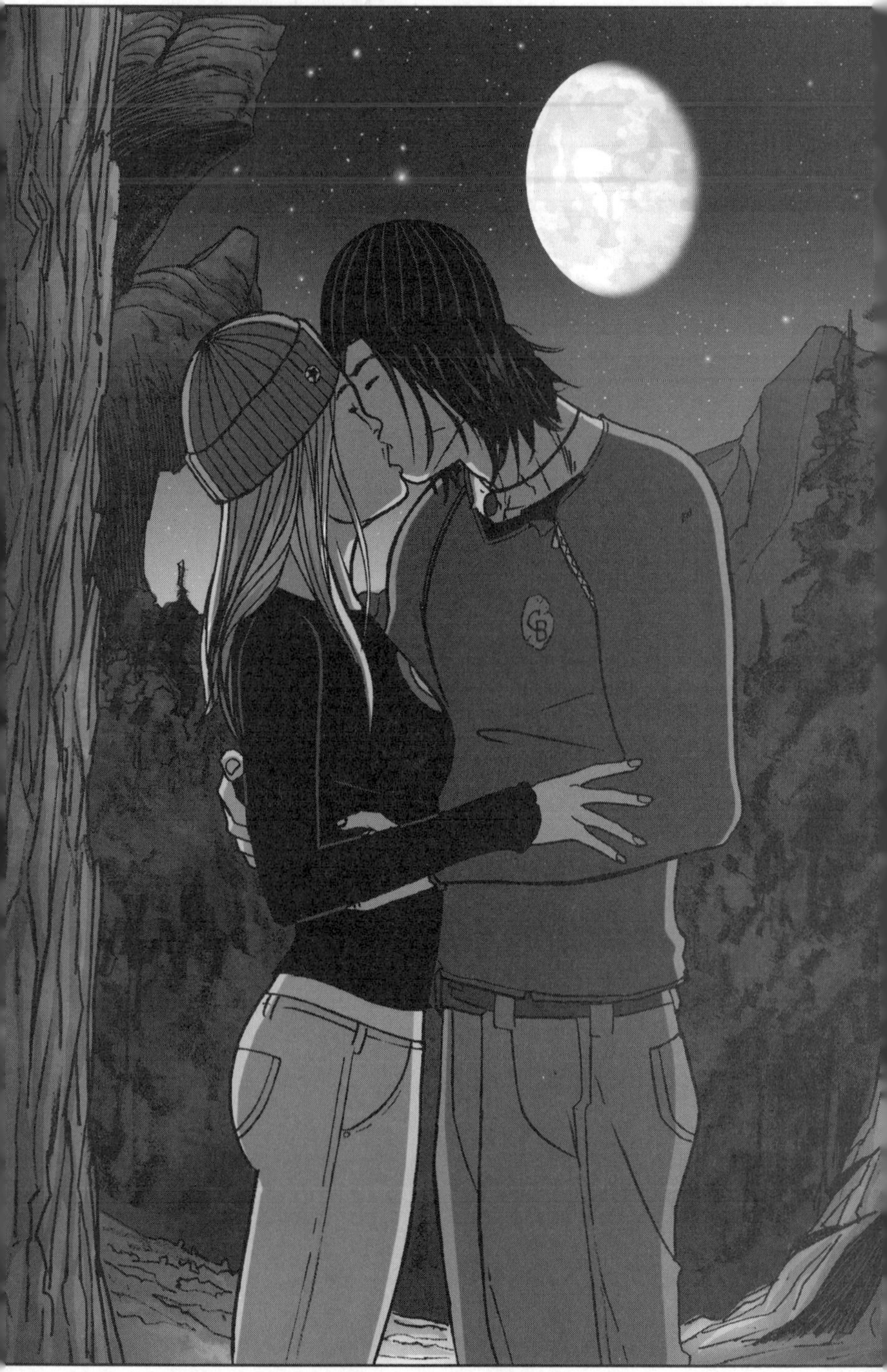

Danni–
Where
r u?
Back Send
New Message
Danni–
Where
r u?
Back Send
Hel–LO?
Back Send
New Message
Hel–LO?
Back Send
U r
such a
bitch!
Back Send
New Message
U r
such a
bitch!
Back Send

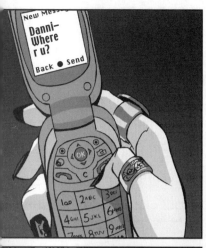

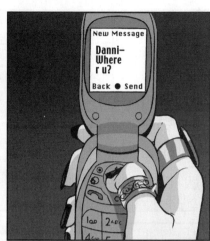

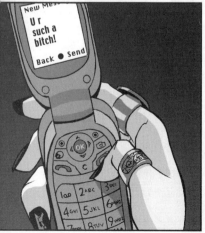

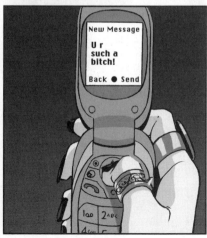

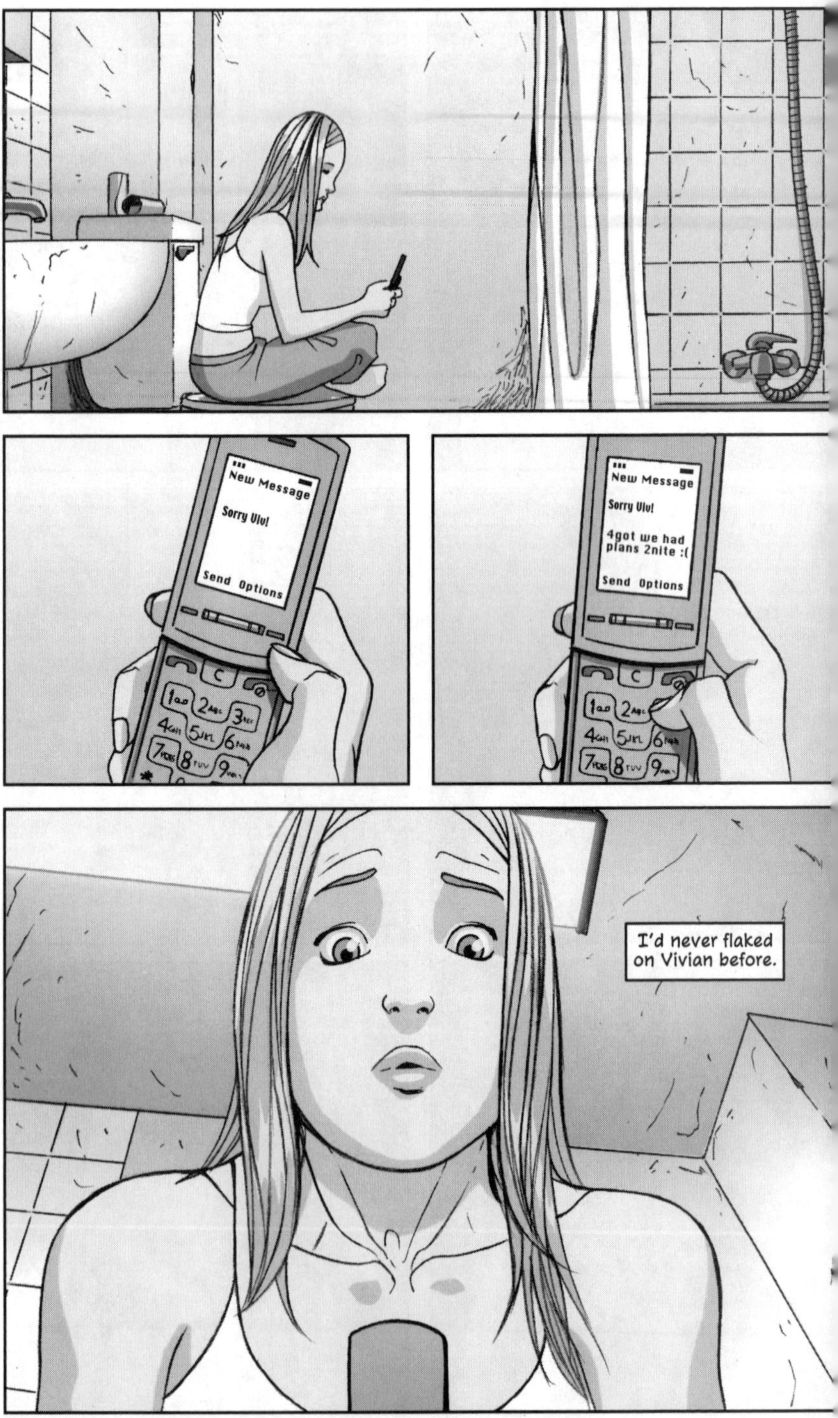
New Message
Sorry Viv!
Send Options
New Message
Sorry Viv!
4got we had plans 2nite :(
Send Options
I'd never flaked on Vivian before.

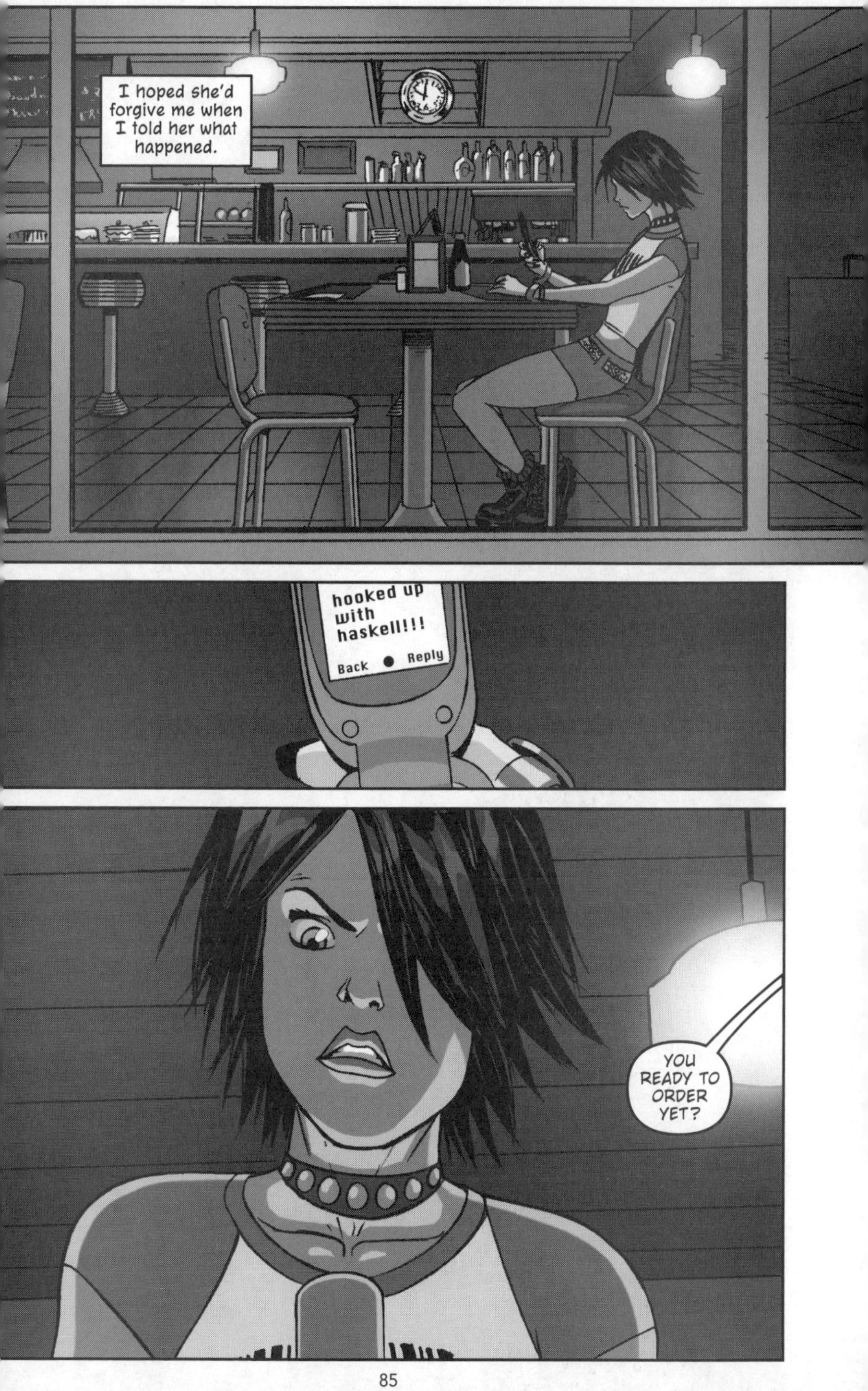
I hoped she'd forgive me when I told her what happened.
hooked up with haskell!!!
Back
Reply
YOU READY TO ORDER YET?

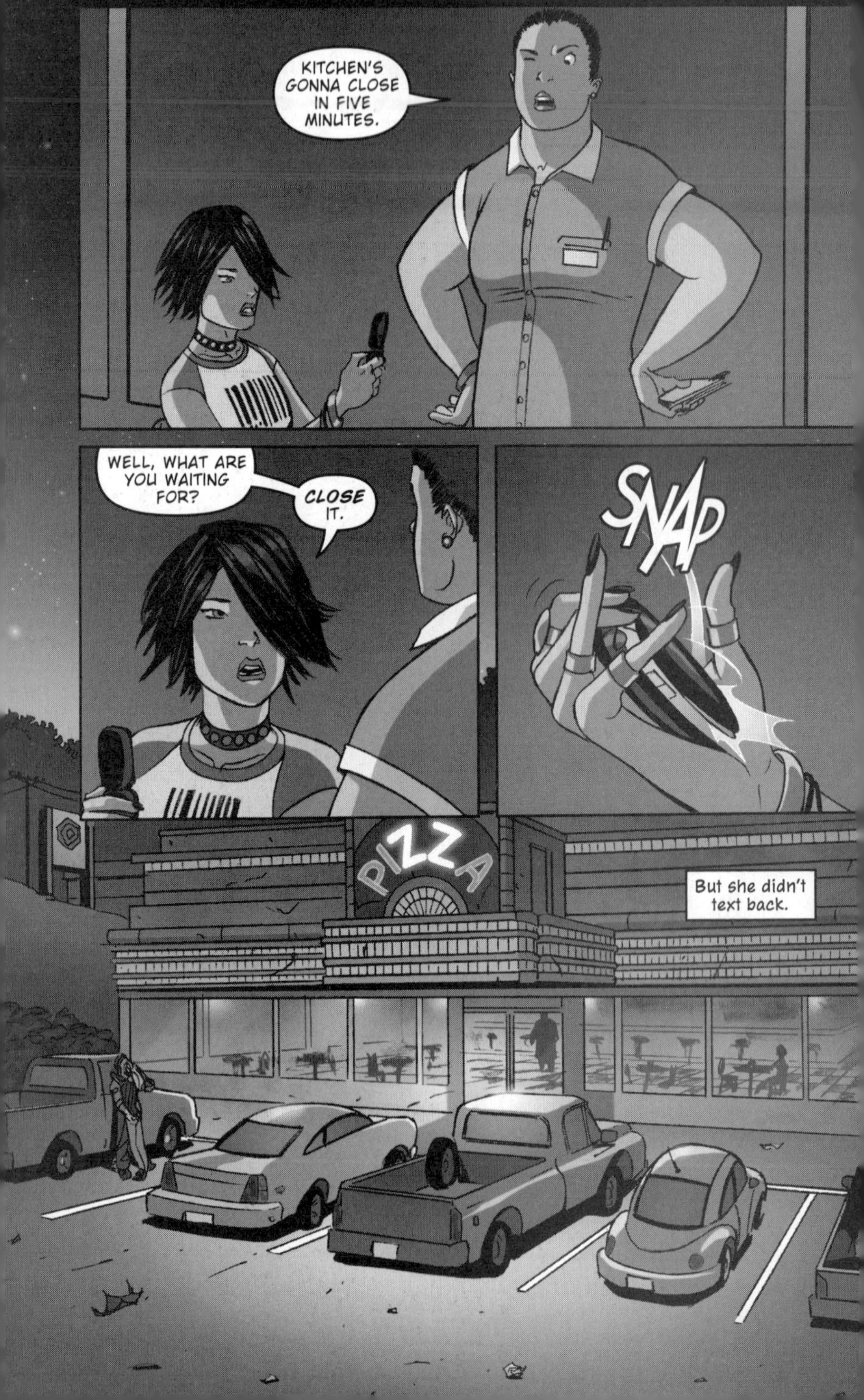
KITCHEN'S GONNA CLOSE IN FIVE MINUTES.
WELL, WHAT ARE YOU WAITING FOR?
CLOSE IT.
SNAP
PIZZA
But she didn't text back.

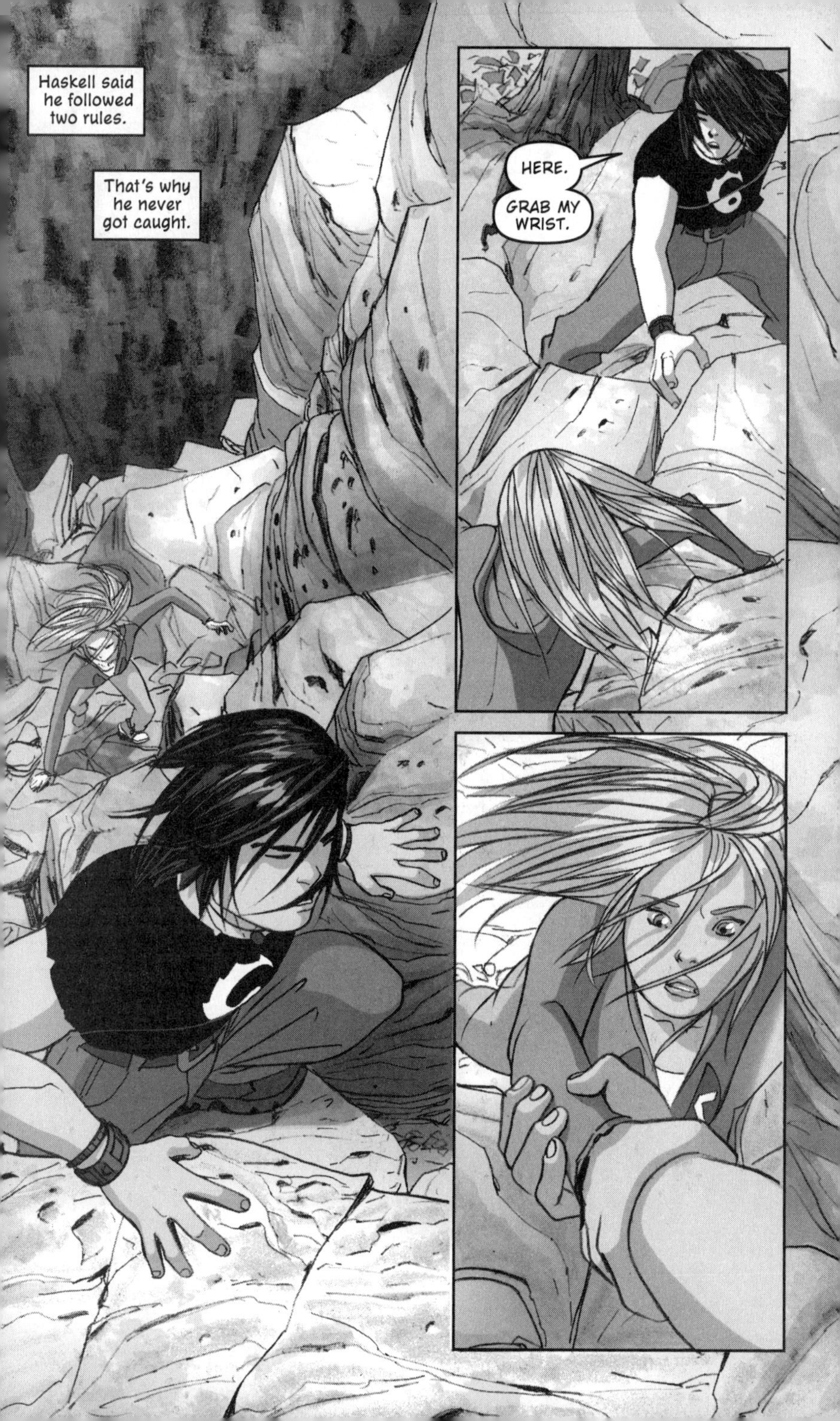
Haskell said he followed two rules.
That's why he never got caught.
HERE.
GRAB MY WRIST.

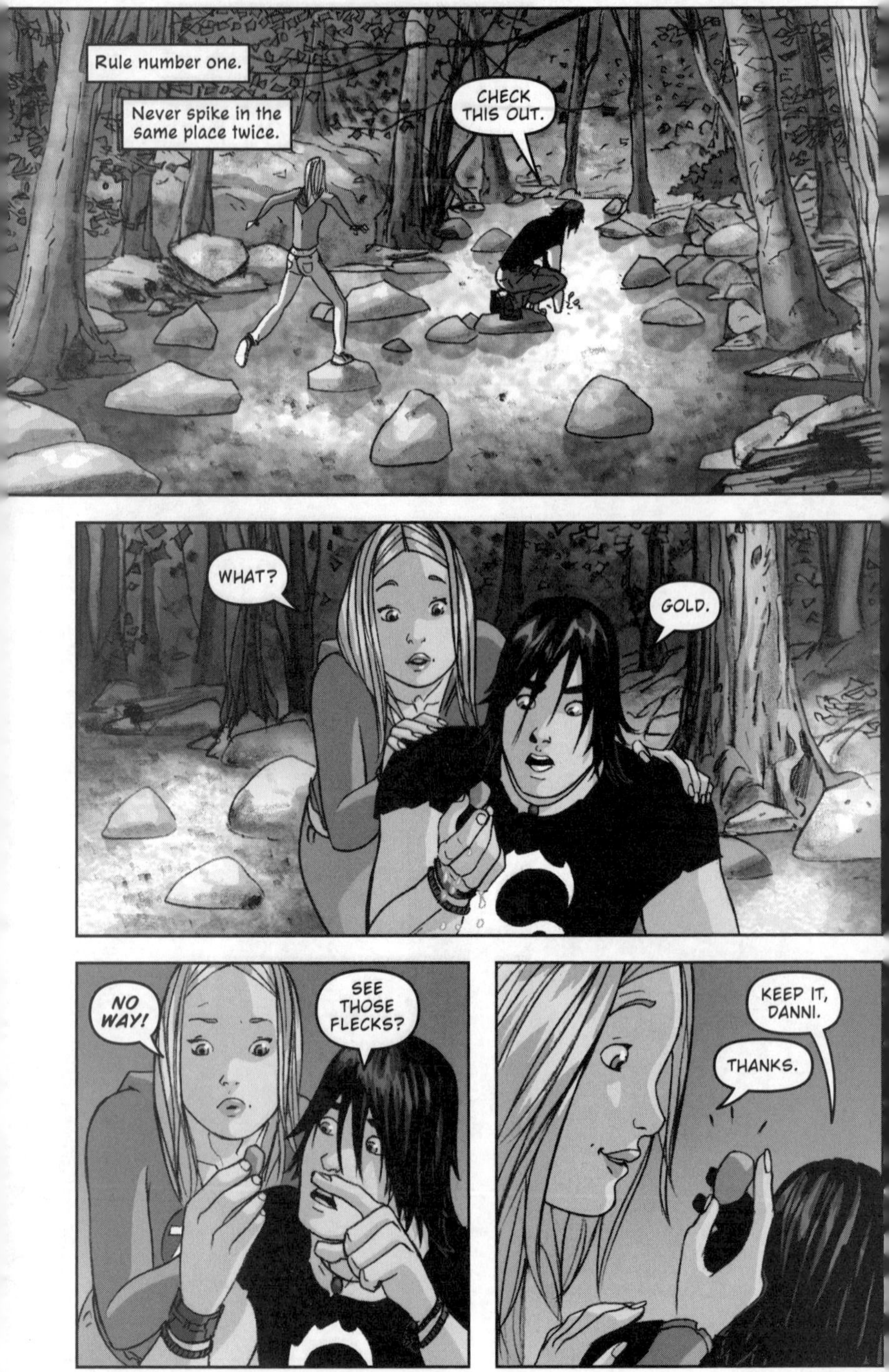
Rule number one.
Never spike in the same place twice.
CHECK THIS OUT.
WHAT?
GOLD.
NO WAY!
SEE THOSE FLECKS?
KEEP IT, DANNI.
THANKS.

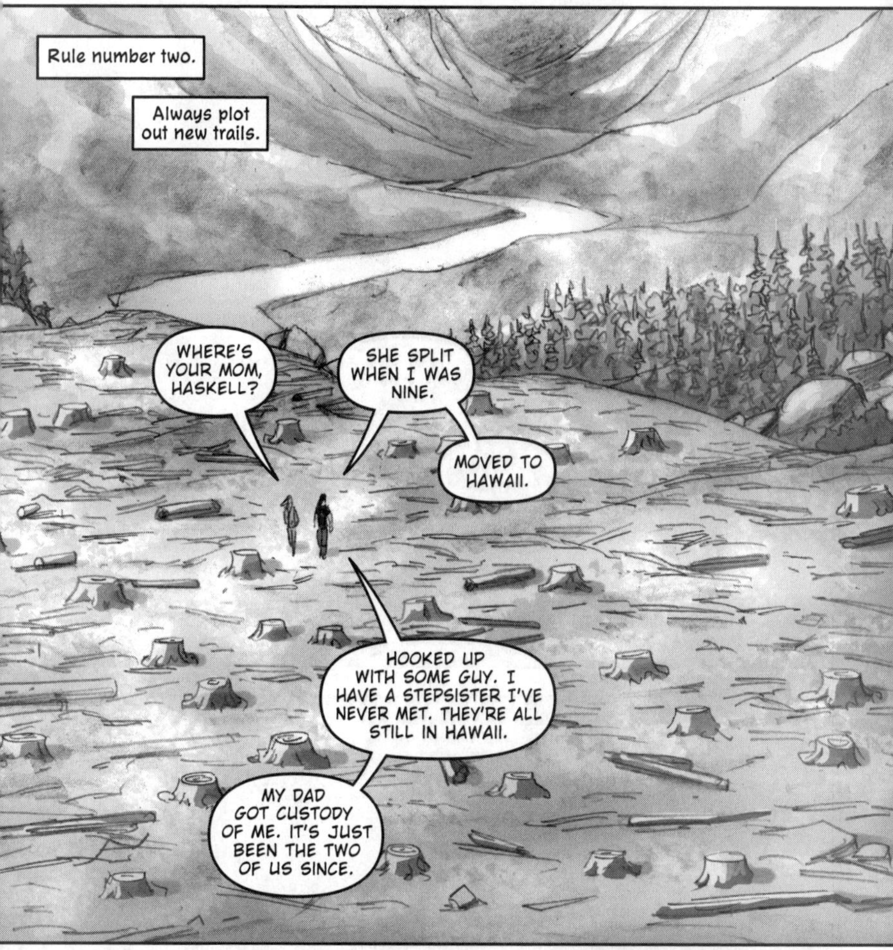
Rule number two.
Always plot out new trails.
WHERE'S YOUR MOM, HASKELL?
SHE SPLIT WHEN I WAS NINE.
MOVED TO HAWAII.
HOOKED UP WITH SOME GUY. I HAVE A STEPSISTER I'VE NEVER MET. THEY'RE ALL STILL IN HAWAII.
MY DAD GOT CUSTODY OF ME. IT'S JUST BEEN THE TWO OF US SINCE.

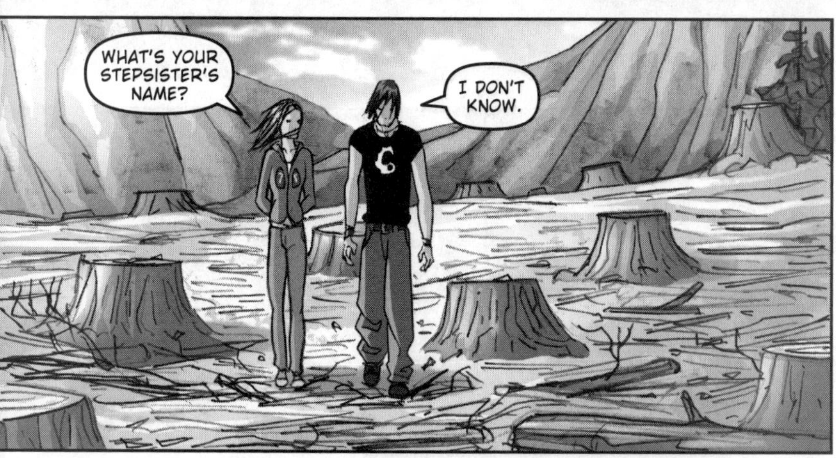
WHAT'S YOUR STEPSISTER'S NAME?
I DON'T KNOW.

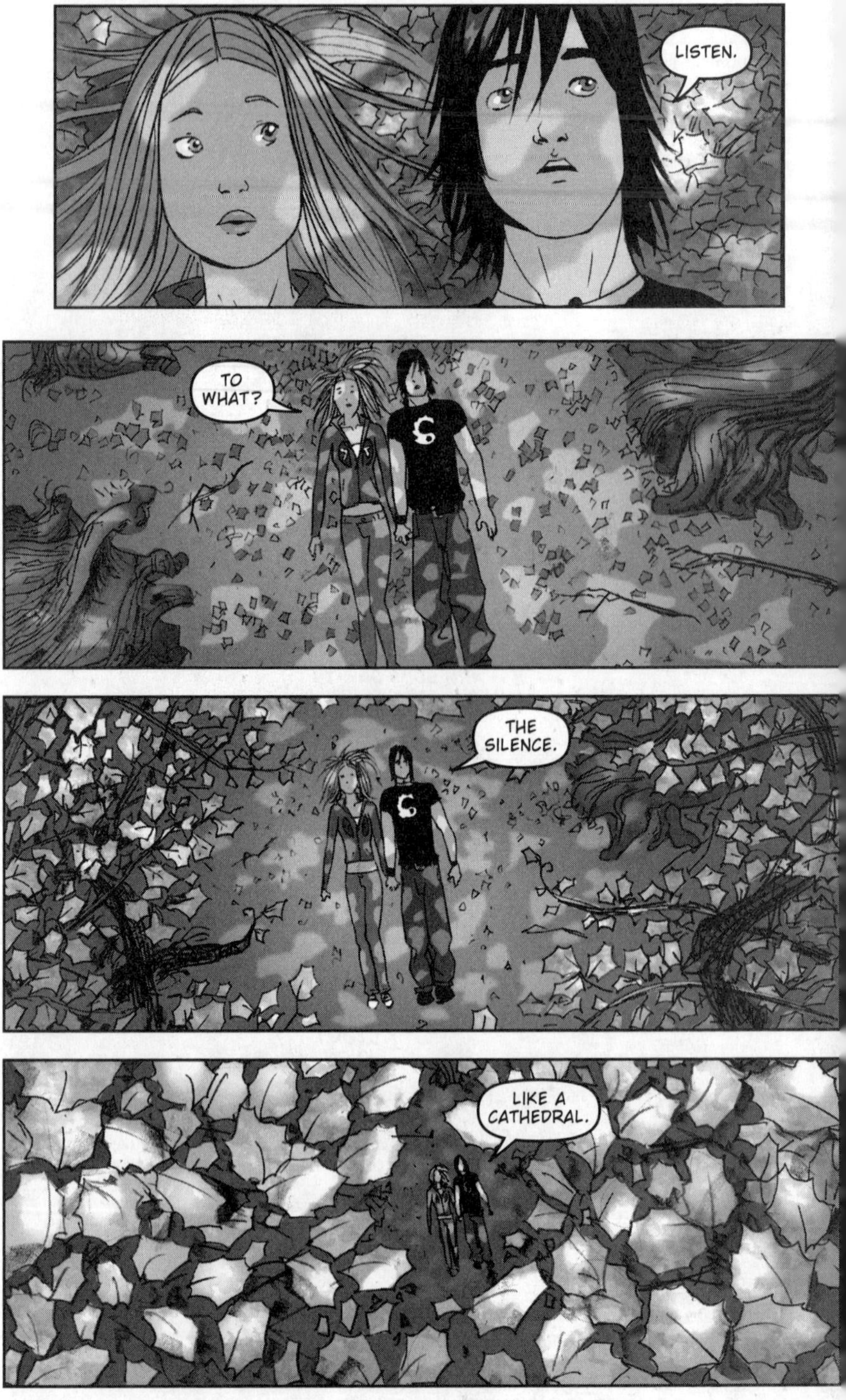
LISTEN.
TO WHAT?
THE SILENCE.
LIKE A CATHEDRAL.

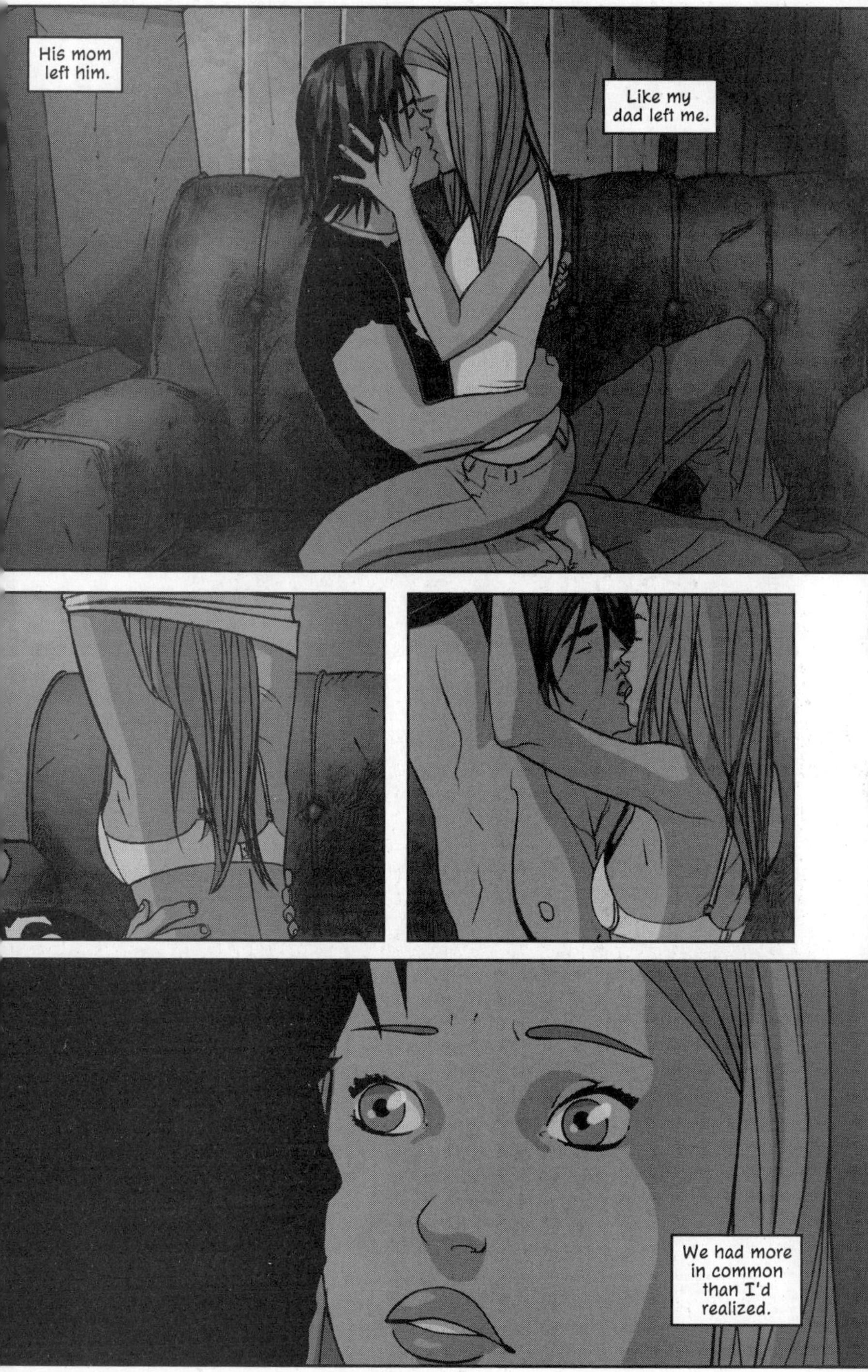
His mom left him.
Like my dad left me.
We had more in common than I'd realized.

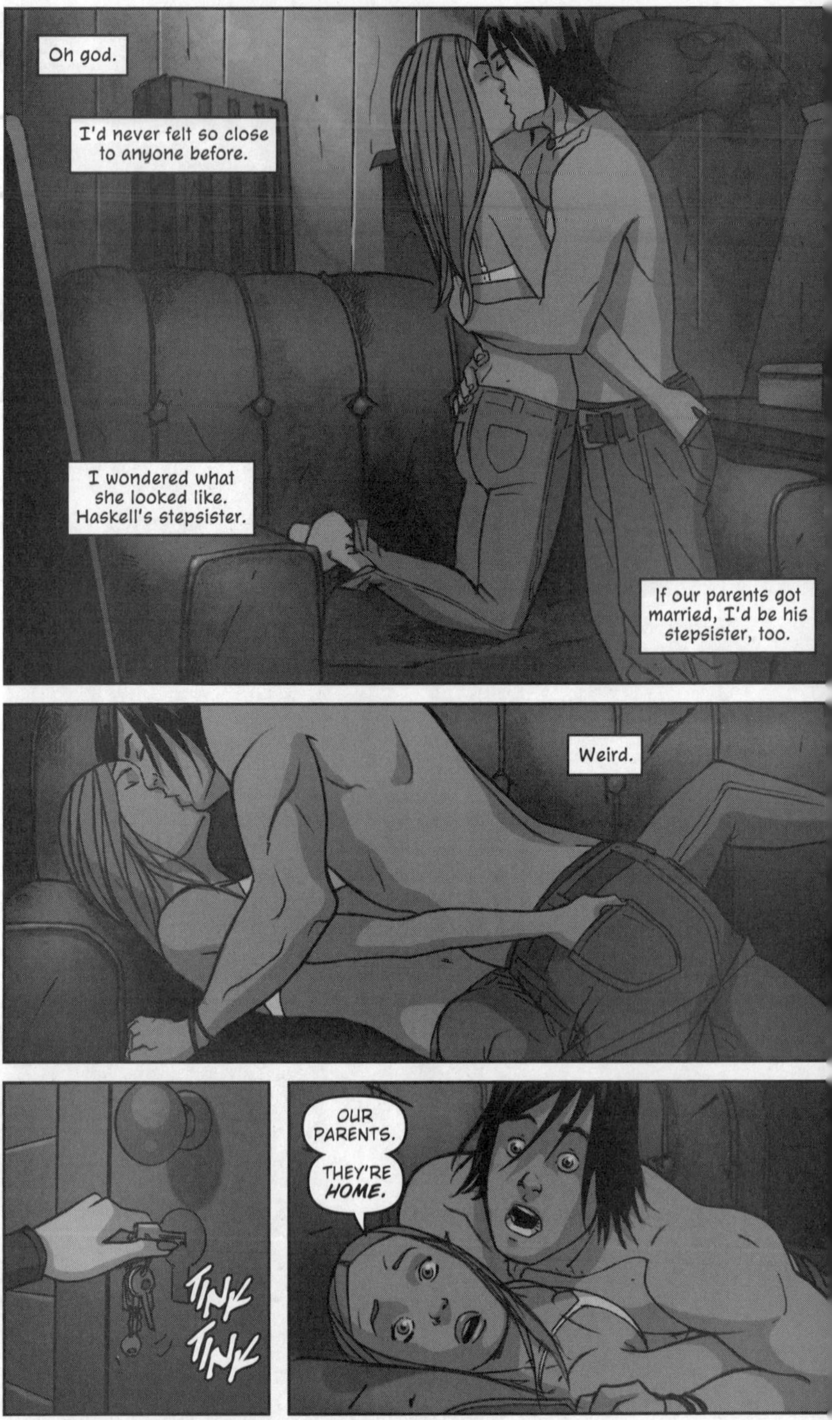
Oh god.
I'd never felt so close to anyone before.
I wondered what she looked like. Haskell's stepsister.
If our parents got married, I'd be his stepsister, too.
Weird.
TINK TINK
OUR PARENTS.
THEY'RE *HOME.*

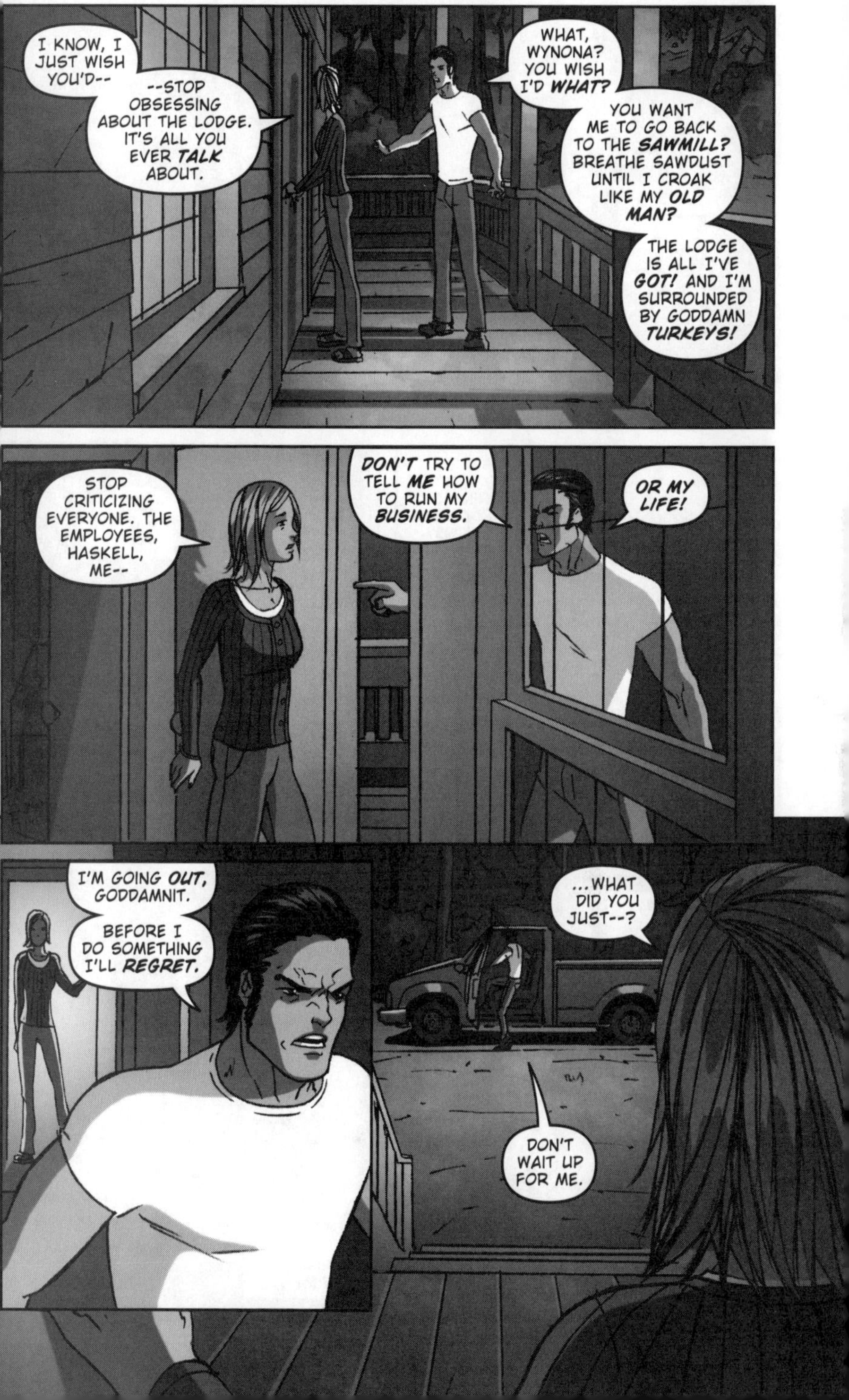
I KNOW, I JUST WISH YOU'D--
--STOP OBSESSING ABOUT THE LODGE. IT'S ALL YOU EVER TALK ABOUT.
WHAT, WYNONA? YOU WISH I'D WHAT?
YOU WANT ME TO GO BACK TO THE SAWMILL? BREATHE SAWDUST UNTIL I CROAK LIKE MY OLD MAN?
THE LODGE IS ALL I'VE GOT! AND I'M SURROUNDED BY GODDAMN TURKEYS!
STOP CRITICIZING EVERYONE. THE EMPLOYEES, HASKELL, ME--
DON'T TRY TO TELL ME HOW TO RUN MY BUSINESS.
OR MY LIFE!
I'M GOING OUT, GODDAMNIT.
BEFORE I DO SOMETHING I'LL REGRET.
...WHAT DID YOU JUST--?
DON'T WAIT UP FOR ME.

OH.

WHAT ARE YOU TWO DOING IN THERE?

HOMEWORK.

SHOOT, I FORGOT ABOUT CLEARING OUT THIS ROOM FOR YOU, HONEY.

I'LL BET YOU'RE PRETTY TIRED OF SHARING A BEDROOM.

UH. IT'S OKAY, MOM.

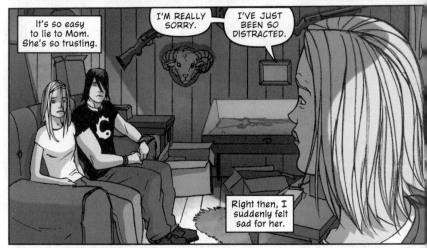

It's so easy to lie to Mom. She's so trusting.

I'M REALLY SORRY.

I'VE JUST BEEN SO DISTRACTED.

Right then, I suddenly felt sad for her.

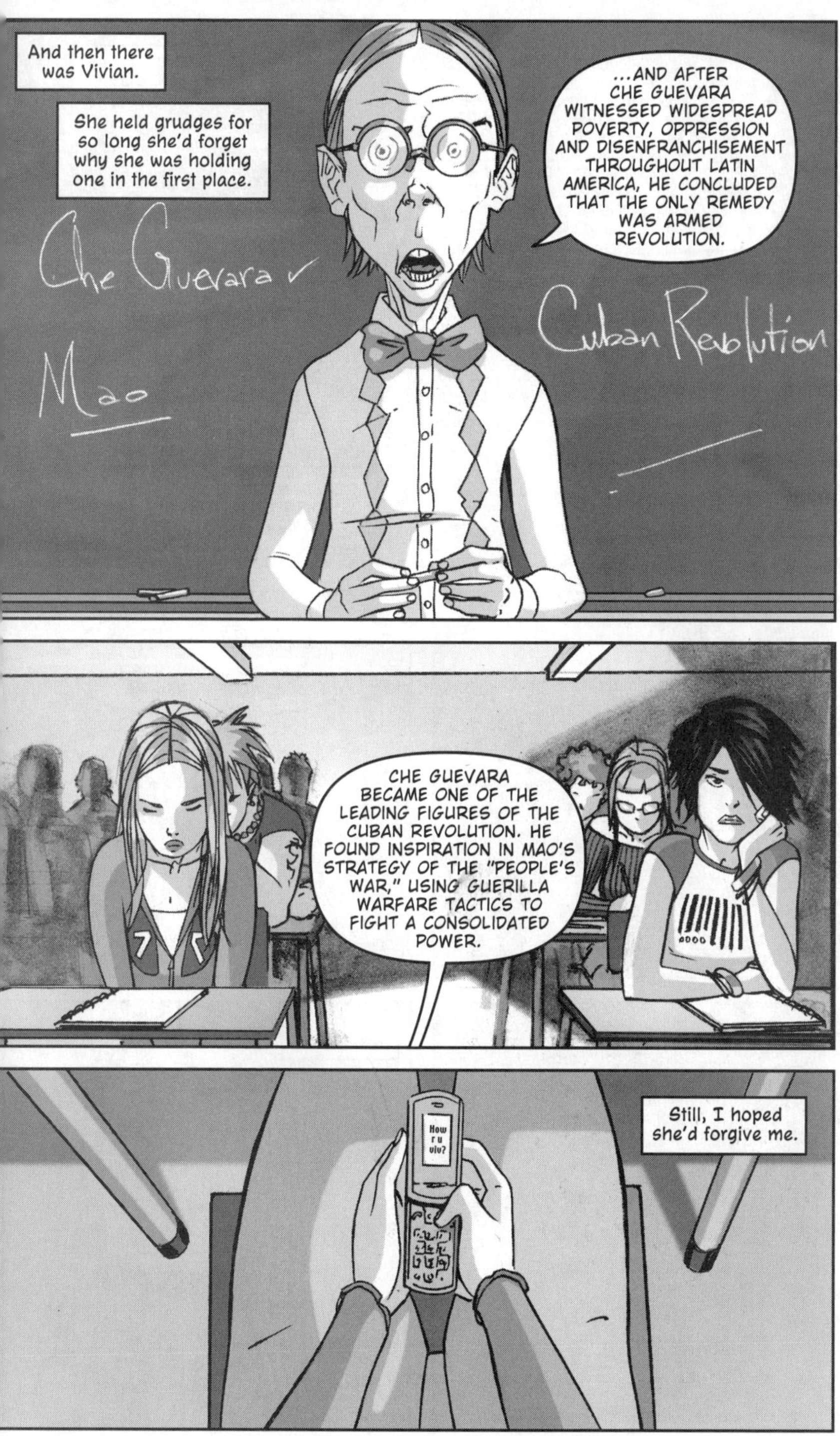
And then there was Vivian.
She held grudges for so long she'd forget why she was holding one in the first place.
...AND AFTER CHE GUEVARA WITNESSED WIDESPREAD POVERTY, OPPRESSION AND DISENFRANCHISEMENT THROUGHOUT LATIN AMERICA, HE CONCLUDED THAT THE ONLY REMEDY WAS ARMED REVOLUTION.
Che Guevara
Cuban Revolution
Mao
CHE GUEVARA BECAME ONE OF THE LEADING FIGURES OF THE CUBAN REVOLUTION. HE FOUND INSPIRATION IN MAO'S STRATEGY OF THE "PEOPLE'S WAR," USING GUERILLA WARFARE TACTICS TO FIGHT A CONSOLIDATED POWER.
How r u viv?
Still, I hoped she'd forgive me.

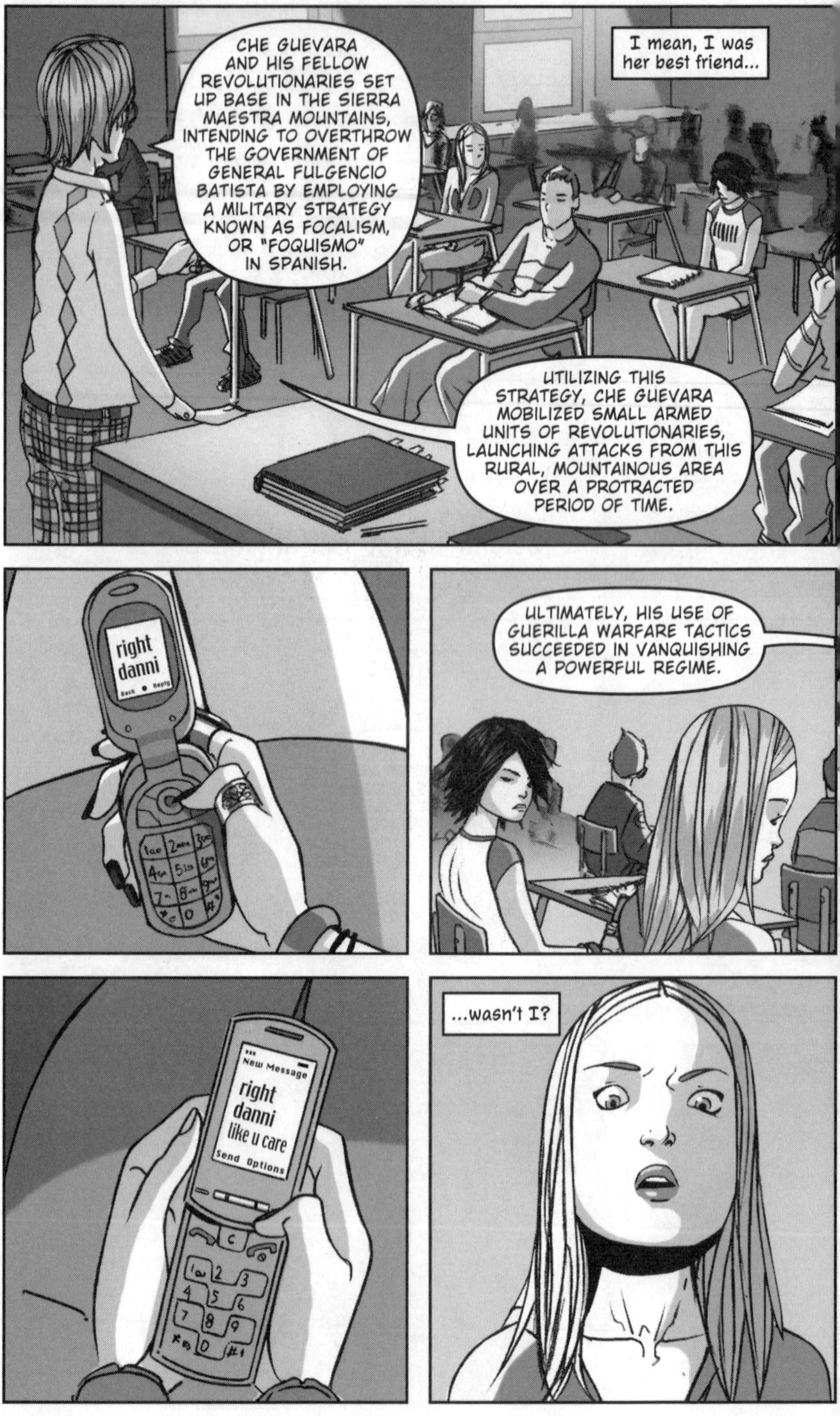

CHE GUEVARA AND HIS FELLOW REVOLUTIONARIES SET UP BASE IN THE SIERRA MAESTRA MOUNTAINS, INTENDING TO OVERTHROW THE GOVERNMENT OF GENERAL FULGENCIO BATISTA BY EMPLOYING A MILITARY STRATEGY KNOWN AS FOCALISM, OR "FOQUISMO" IN SPANISH.
I mean, I was her best friend...
UTILIZING THIS STRATEGY, CHE GUEVARA MOBILIZED SMALL ARMED UNITS OF REVOLUTIONARIES, LAUNCHING ATTACKS FROM THIS RURAL, MOUNTAINOUS AREA OVER A PROTRACTED PERIOD OF TIME.
right danni
Back Reply
ULTIMATELY, HIS USE OF GUERILLA WARFARE TACTICS SUCCEEDED IN VANQUISHING A POWERFUL REGIME.
New Message
right danni like u care
Send Options
...wasn't I?

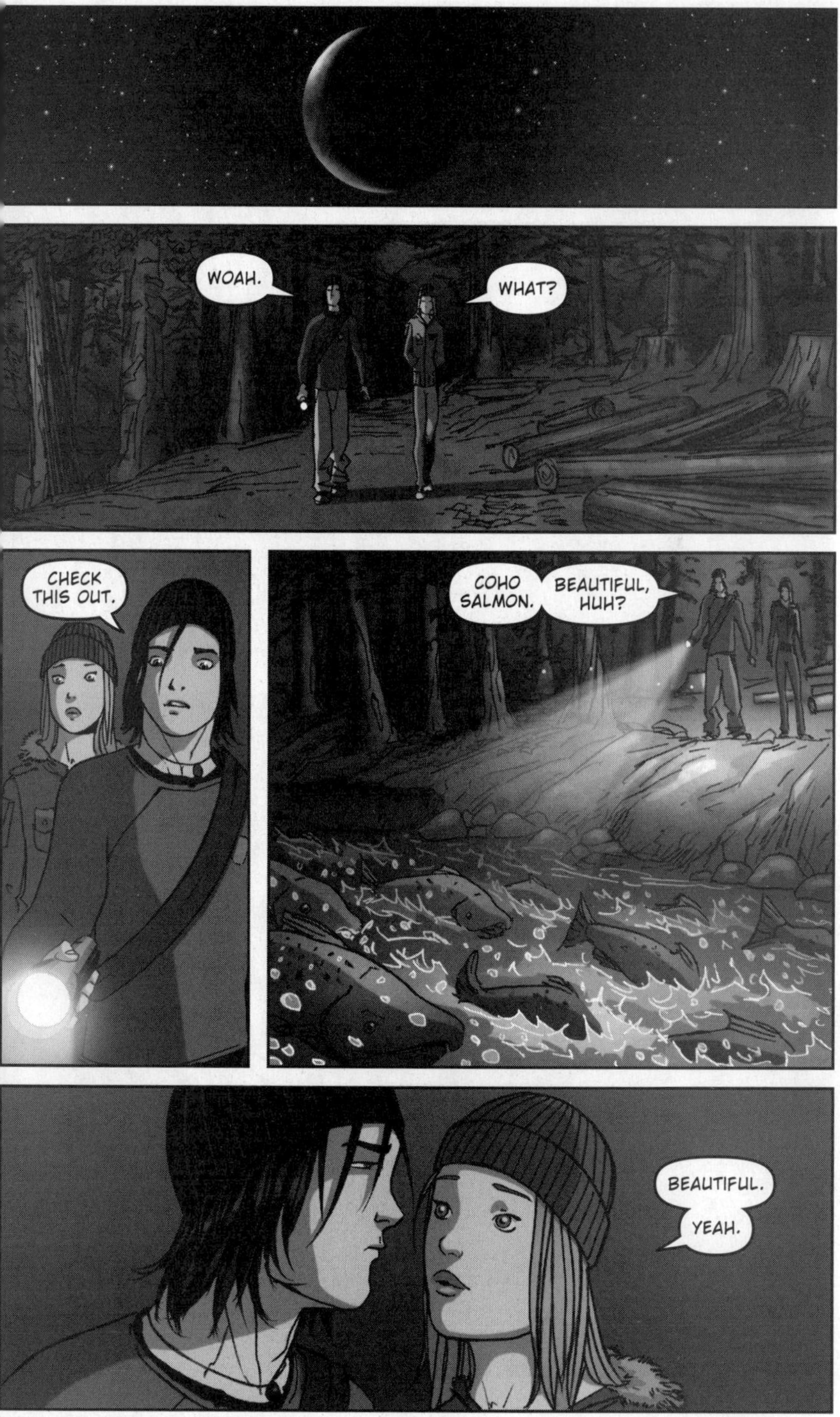
WOAH.
WHAT?
CHECK THIS OUT.
COHO SALMON.
BEAUTIFUL, HUH?
BEAUTIFUL.
YEAH.

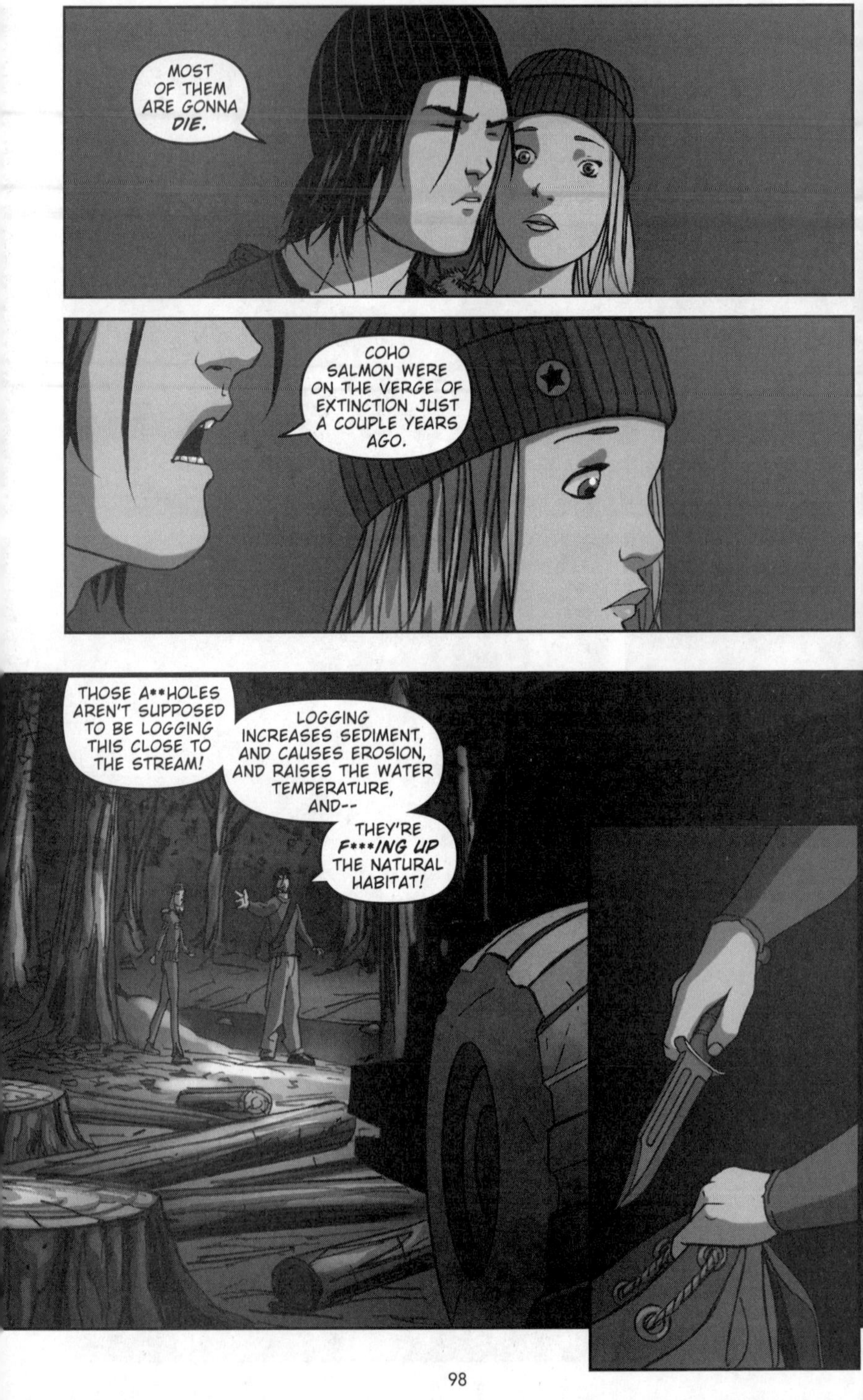
MOST OF THEM ARE GONNA *DIE.*
COHO SALMON WERE ON THE VERGE OF EXTINCTION JUST A COUPLE YEARS AGO.
THOSE A**HOLES AREN'T SUPPOSED TO BE LOGGING THIS CLOSE TO THE STREAM!
LOGGING INCREASES SEDIMENT, AND CAUSES EROSION, AND RAISES THE WATER TEMPERATURE, AND--
THEY'RE ***F***ING UP*** THE NATURAL HABITAT!

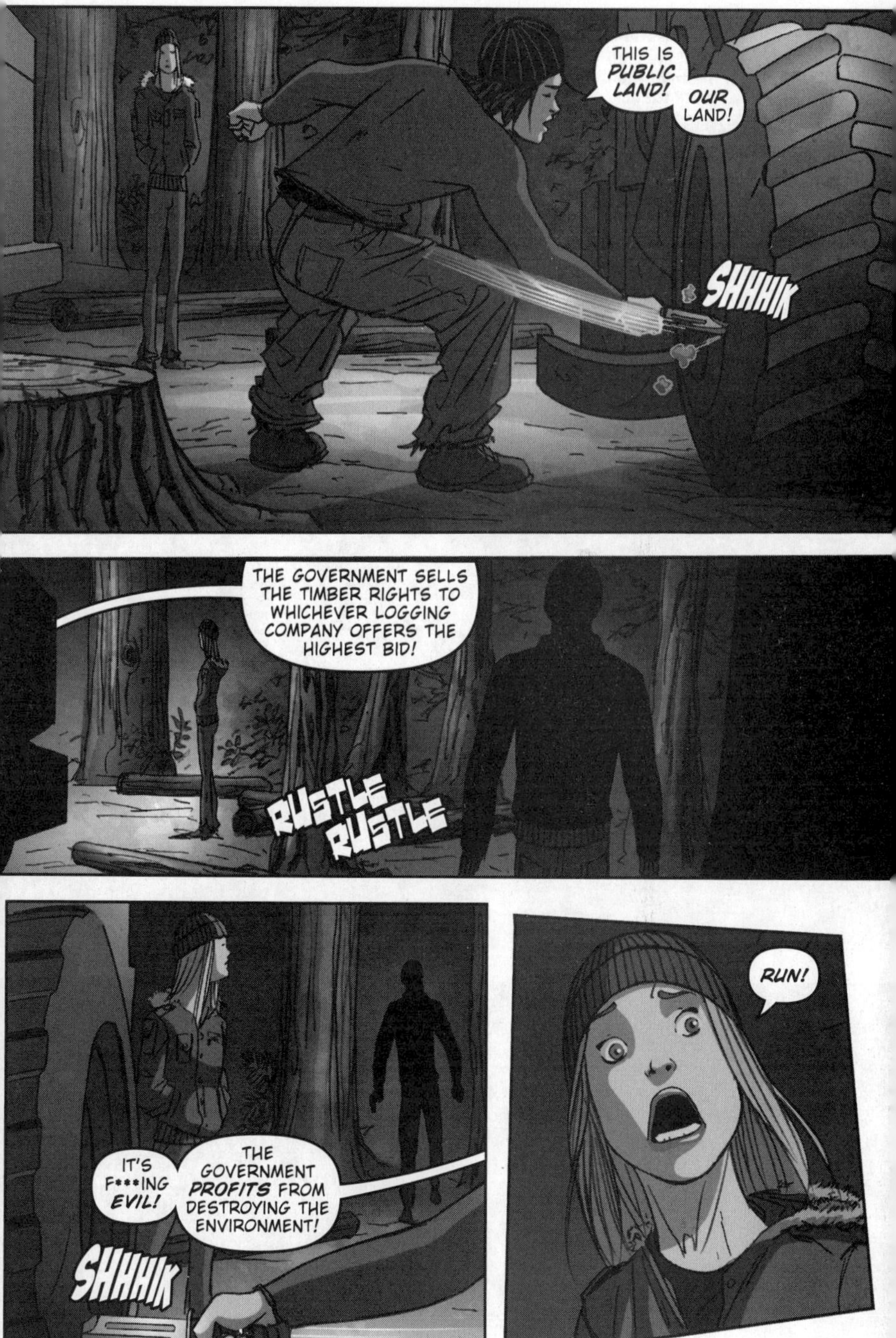
THIS IS PUBLIC LAND!
OUR LAND!
SHHHIK
THE GOVERNMENT SELLS THE TIMBER RIGHTS TO WHICHEVER LOGGING COMPANY OFFERS THE HIGHEST BID!
RUSTLE RUSTLE
THE GOVERNMENT PROFITS FROM DESTROYING THE ENVIRONMENT!
IT'S F***ING EVIL!
SHHHIK
RUN!

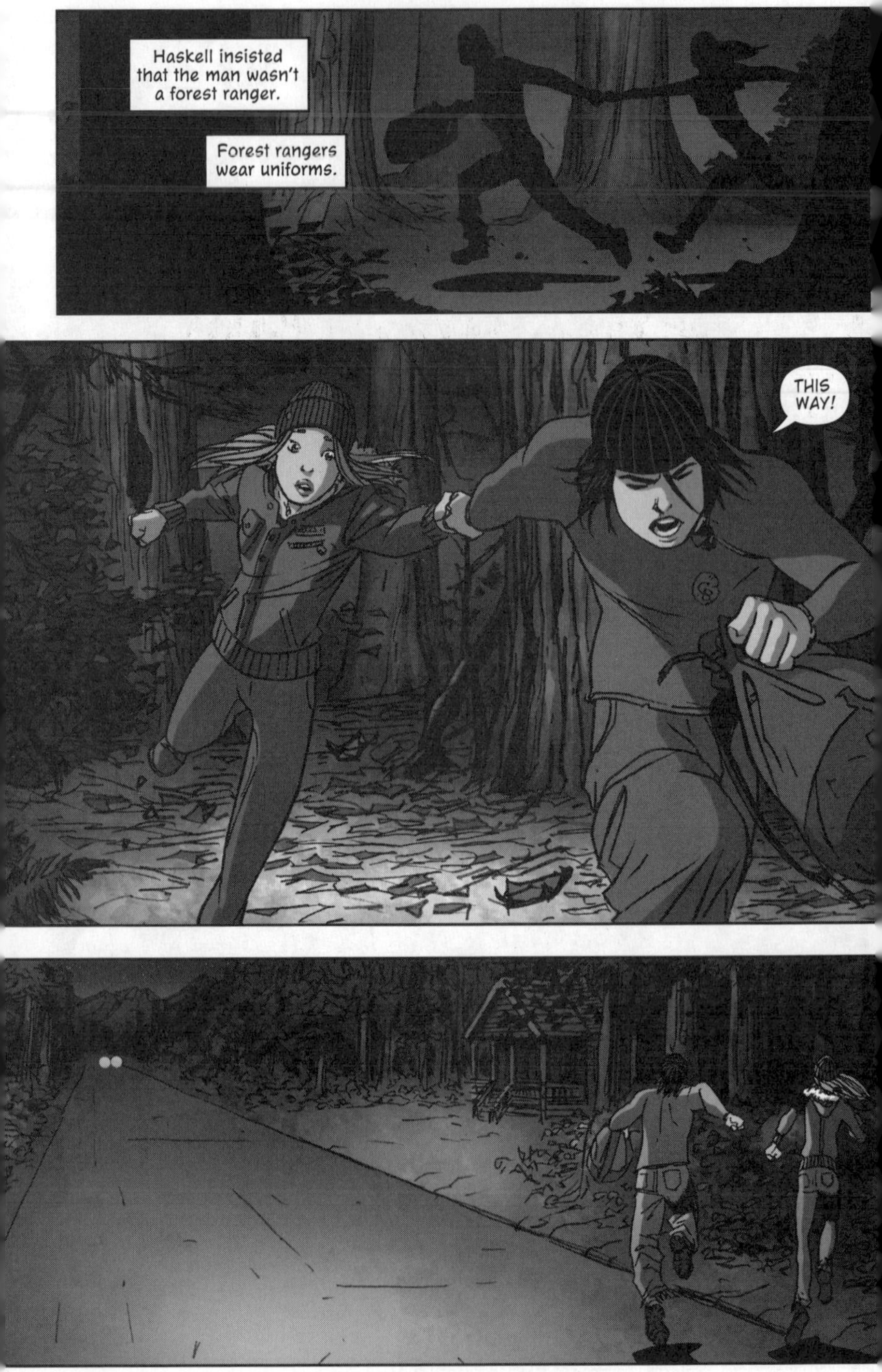
Haskell insisted that the man wasn't a forest ranger.
Forest rangers wear uniforms.
THIS WAY!

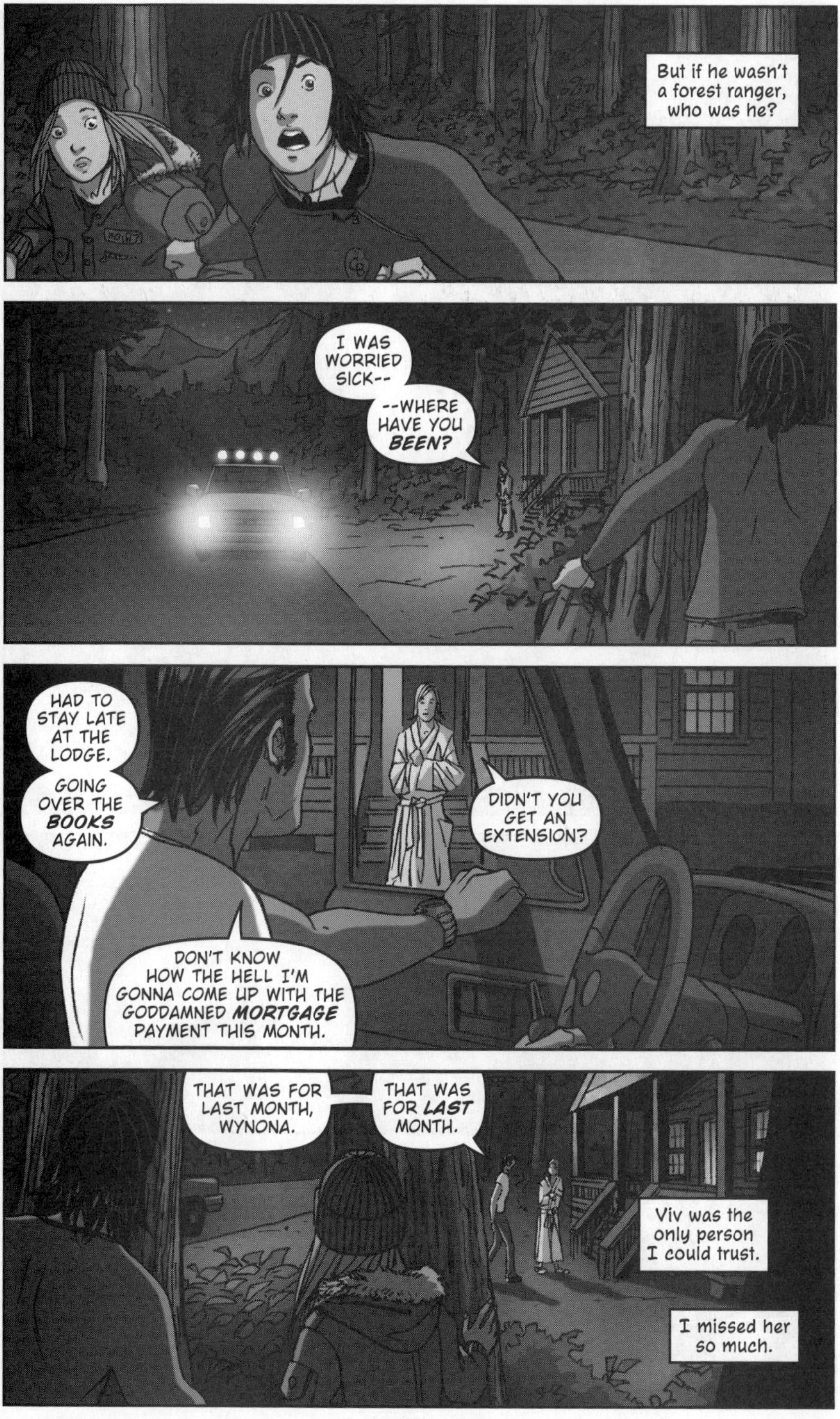
But if he wasn't a forest ranger, who was he?
I WAS WORRIED SICK--
--WHERE HAVE YOU BEEN?
HAD TO STAY LATE AT THE LODGE.
GOING OVER THE BOOKS AGAIN.
DIDN'T YOU GET AN EXTENSION?
DON'T KNOW HOW THE HELL I'M GONNA COME UP WITH THE GODDAMNED MORTGAGE PAYMENT THIS MONTH.
THAT WAS FOR LAST MONTH, WYNONA.
THAT WAS FOR LAST MONTH.
Viv was the only person I could trust.
I missed her so much.

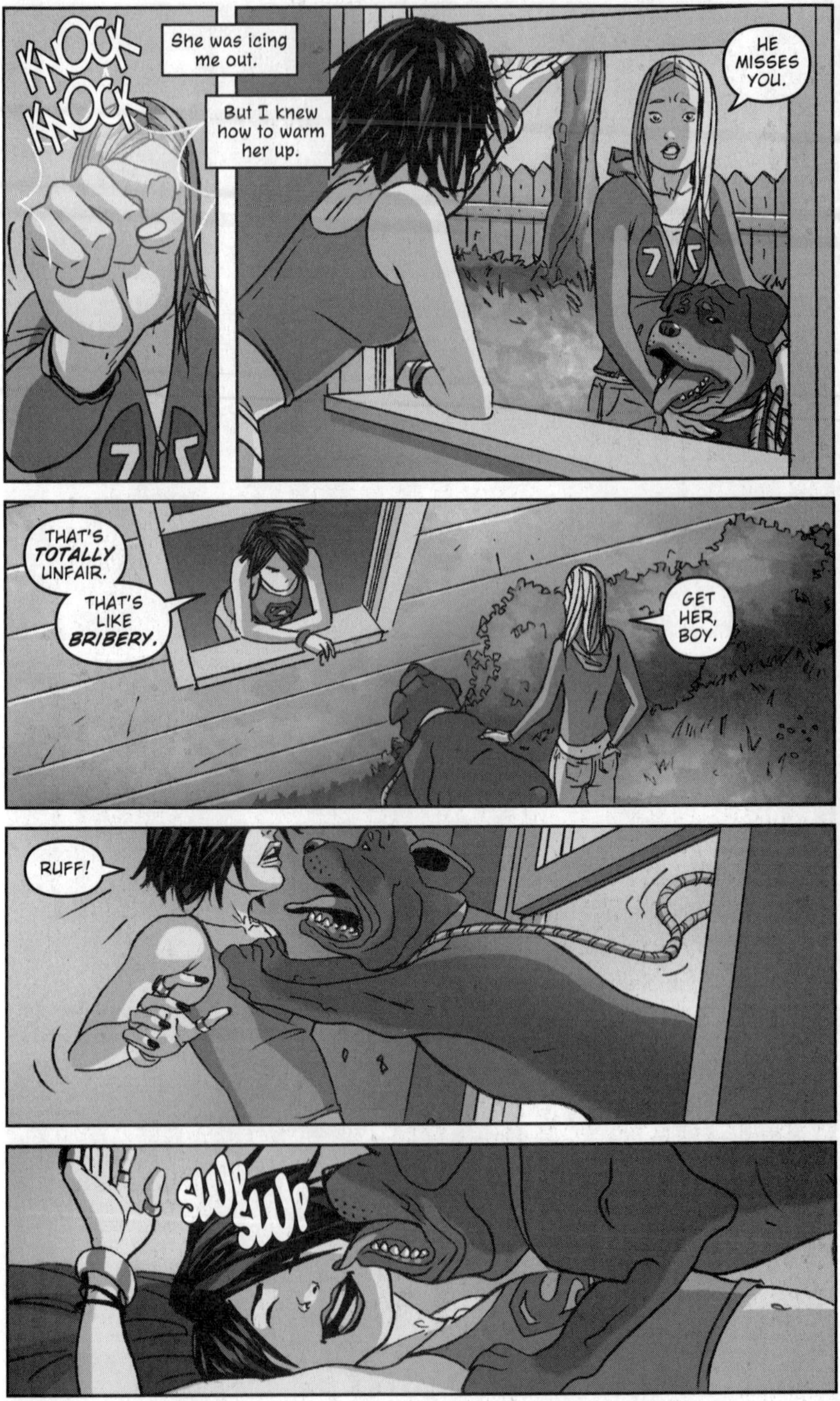
KNOCK
KNOCK
She was icing me out.
But I knew how to warm her up.
HE MISSES YOU.
THAT'S TOTALLY UNFAIR.
THAT'S LIKE BRIBERY.
GET HER, BOY.
RUFF!
SLUP
SLUP

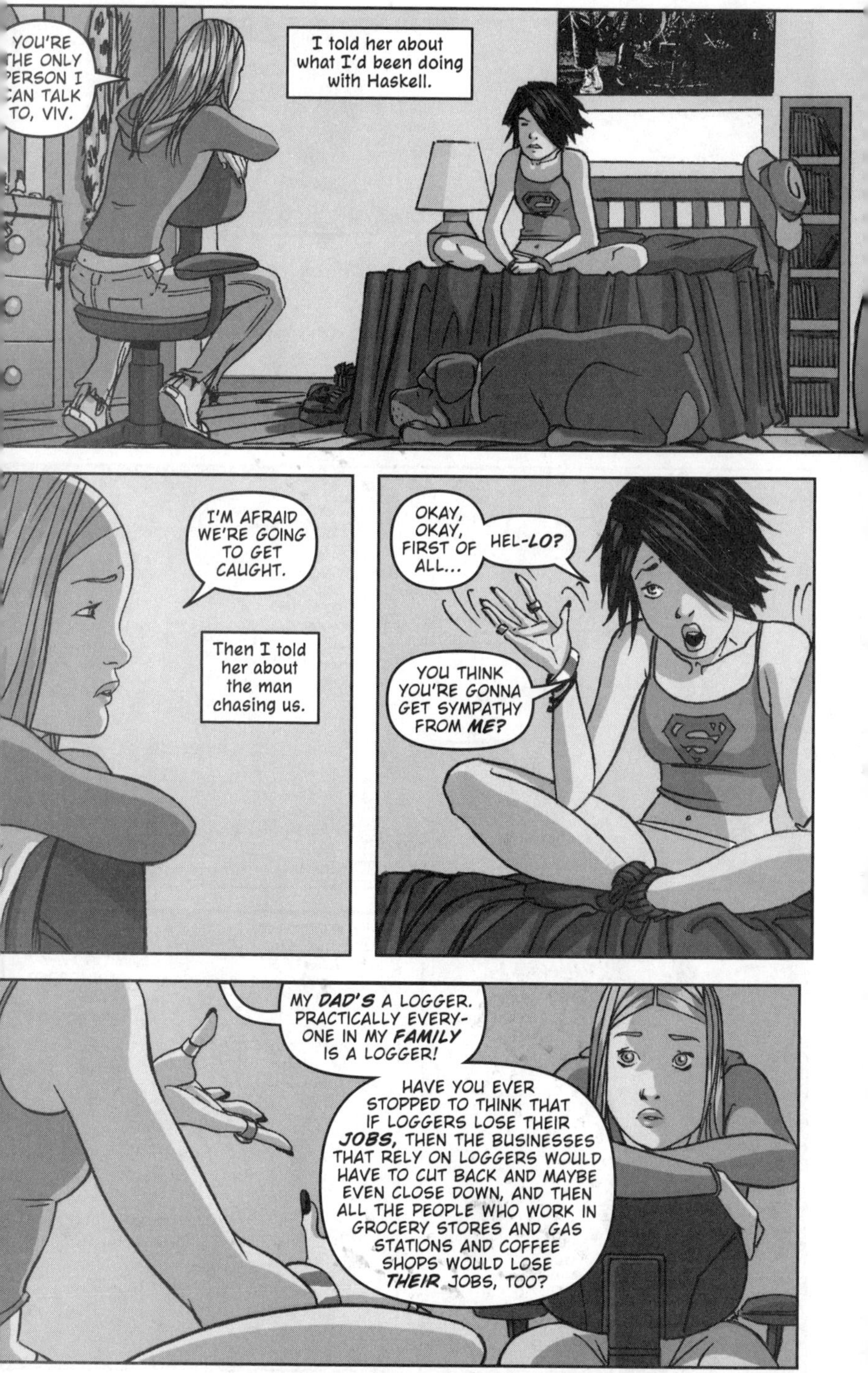
YOU'RE THE ONLY PERSON I CAN TALK TO, VIV.
I told her about what I'd been doing with Haskell.
I'M AFRAID WE'RE GOING TO GET CAUGHT.
Then I told her about the man chasing us.
OKAY, OKAY, FIRST OF ALL...
HEL-LO?
YOU THINK YOU'RE GONNA GET SYMPATHY FROM ME?
MY DAD'S A LOGGER. PRACTICALLY EVERY-ONE IN MY FAMILY IS A LOGGER!
HAVE YOU EVER STOPPED TO THINK THAT IF LOGGERS LOSE THEIR JOBS, THEN THE BUSINESSES THAT RELY ON LOGGERS WOULD HAVE TO CUT BACK AND MAYBE EVEN CLOSE DOWN, AND THEN ALL THE PEOPLE WHO WORK IN GROCERY STORES AND GAS STATIONS AND COFFEE SHOPS WOULD LOSE THEIR JOBS, TOO?

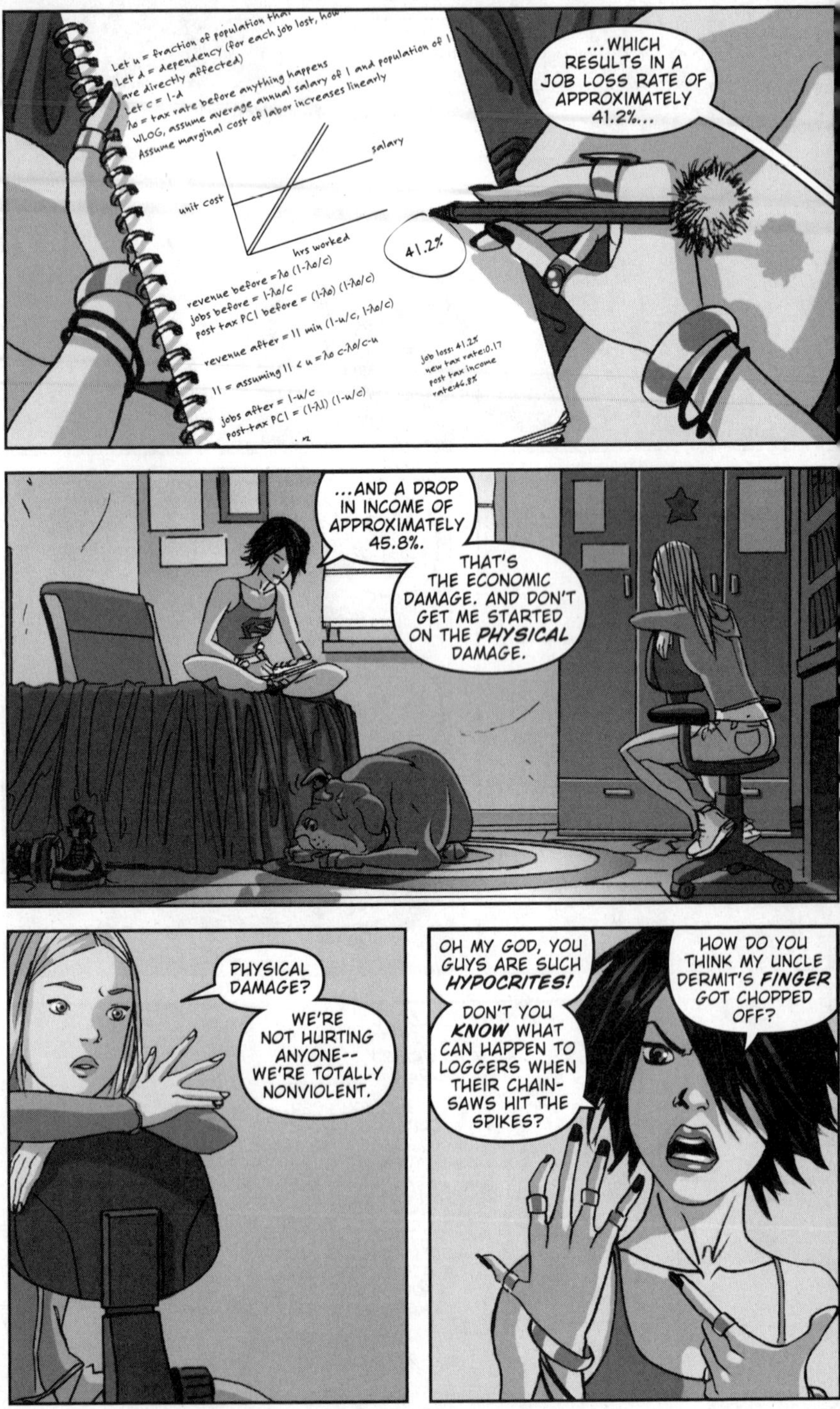
Let u = fraction of population tha
Let d = dependency (for each job lost, how
are directly affected)
Let c = 1-d
λo = tax rate before anything happens
WLOG, assume average annual salary of 1 and population of 1
Assume marginal cost of labor increases linearly
salary
unit cost
hrs worked
41.2%
revenue before = λo (1-λo/c)
jobs before = 1-λo/c
post tax PC1 before = (1-λo) (1-λo/c)
revenue after = l1 min (1-u/c, 1-λo/c)
l1 = assuming l1 < u = λo c-λo/c-u
jobs after = 1-u/c
post-tax PC1 = (1-λ1) (1-u/c)
job loss: 41.2%
new tax rate: 0.17
post tax income
rate: 46.8%
...WHICH RESULTS IN A JOB LOSS RATE OF APPROXIMATELY 41.2%...
...AND A DROP IN INCOME OF APPROXIMATELY 45.8%.
THAT'S THE ECONOMIC DAMAGE. AND DON'T GET ME STARTED ON THE PHYSICAL DAMAGE.
PHYSICAL DAMAGE?
WE'RE NOT HURTING ANYONE-- WE'RE TOTALLY NONVIOLENT.
OH MY GOD, YOU GUYS ARE SUCH HYPOCRITES!
DON'T YOU KNOW WHAT CAN HAPPEN TO LOGGERS WHEN THEIR CHAIN-SAWS HIT THE SPIKES?
HOW DO YOU THINK MY UNCLE DERMIT'S FINGER GOT CHOPPED OFF?

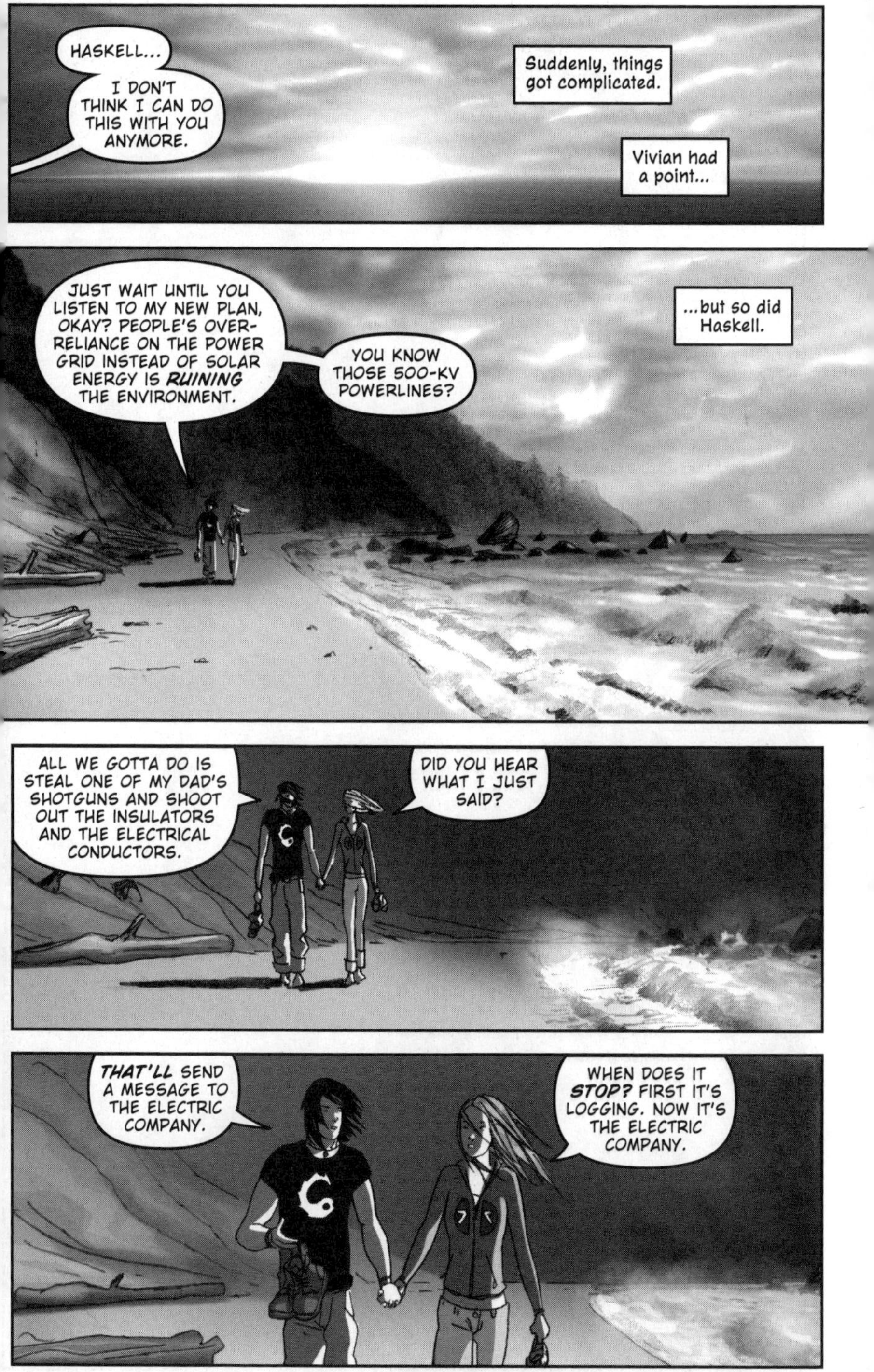
HASKELL...
I DON'T THINK I CAN DO THIS WITH YOU ANYMORE.
Suddenly, things got complicated.
Vivian had a point...
JUST WAIT UNTIL YOU LISTEN TO MY NEW PLAN, OKAY? PEOPLE'S OVER-RELIANCE ON THE POWER GRID INSTEAD OF SOLAR ENERGY IS *RUINING* THE ENVIRONMENT.
YOU KNOW THOSE 500-KV POWERLINES?
...but so did Haskell.
ALL WE GOTTA DO IS STEAL ONE OF MY DAD'S SHOTGUNS AND SHOOT OUT THE INSULATORS AND THE ELECTRICAL CONDUCTORS.
DID YOU HEAR WHAT I JUST SAID?
THAT'LL SEND A MESSAGE TO THE ELECTRIC COMPANY.
WHEN DOES IT *STOP?* FIRST IT'S LOGGING. NOW IT'S THE ELECTRIC COMPANY.

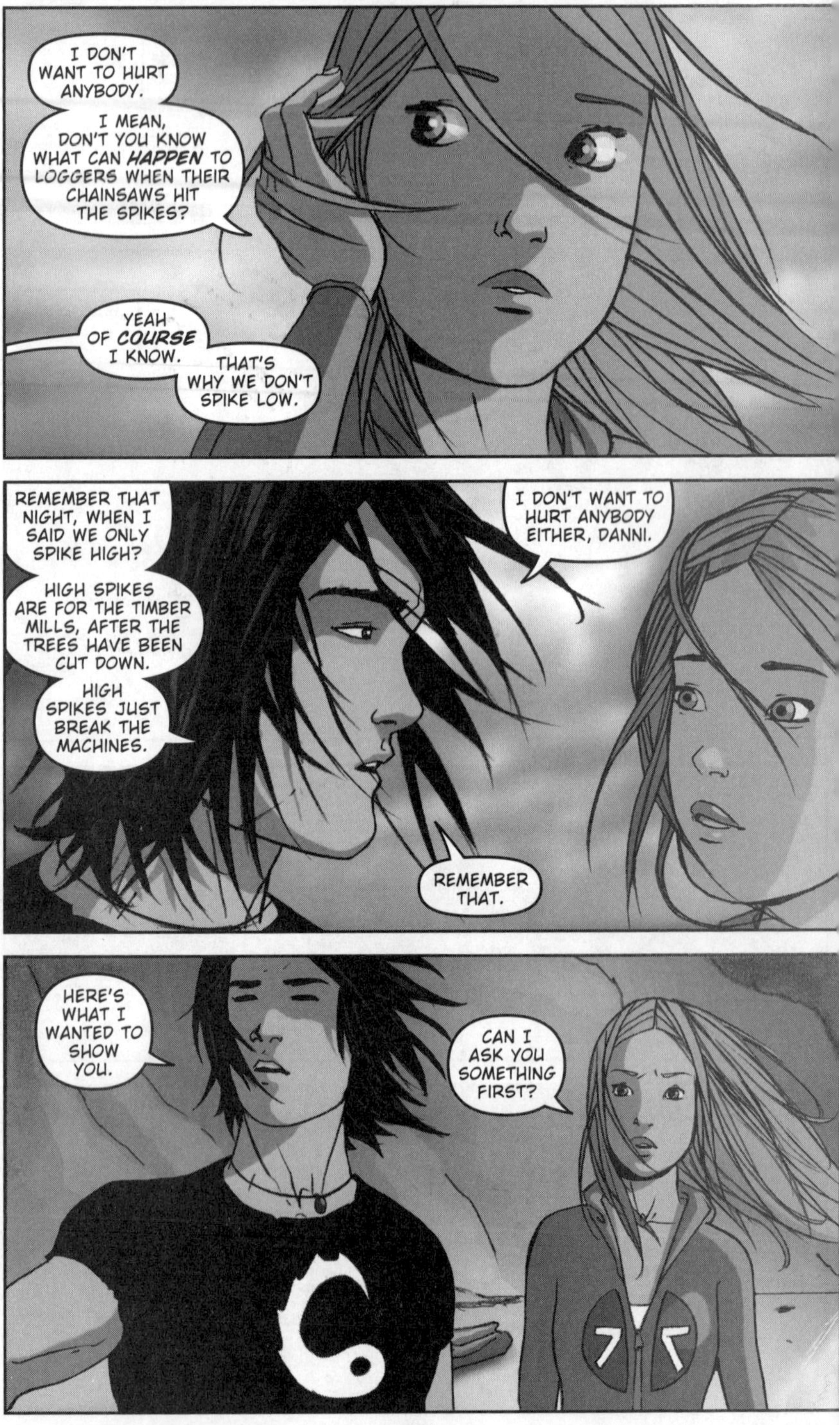
I DON'T WANT TO HURT ANYBODY.
I MEAN, DON'T YOU KNOW WHAT CAN *HAPPEN* TO LOGGERS WHEN THEIR CHAINSAWS HIT THE SPIKES?
YEAH OF *COURSE* I KNOW.
THAT'S WHY WE DON'T SPIKE LOW.
REMEMBER THAT NIGHT, WHEN I SAID WE ONLY SPIKE HIGH?
HIGH SPIKES ARE FOR THE TIMBER MILLS, AFTER THE TREES HAVE BEEN CUT DOWN.
HIGH SPIKES JUST BREAK THE MACHINES.
I DON'T WANT TO HURT ANYBODY EITHER, DANNI.
REMEMBER THAT.
HERE'S WHAT I WANTED TO SHOW YOU.
CAN I ASK YOU SOMETHING FIRST?

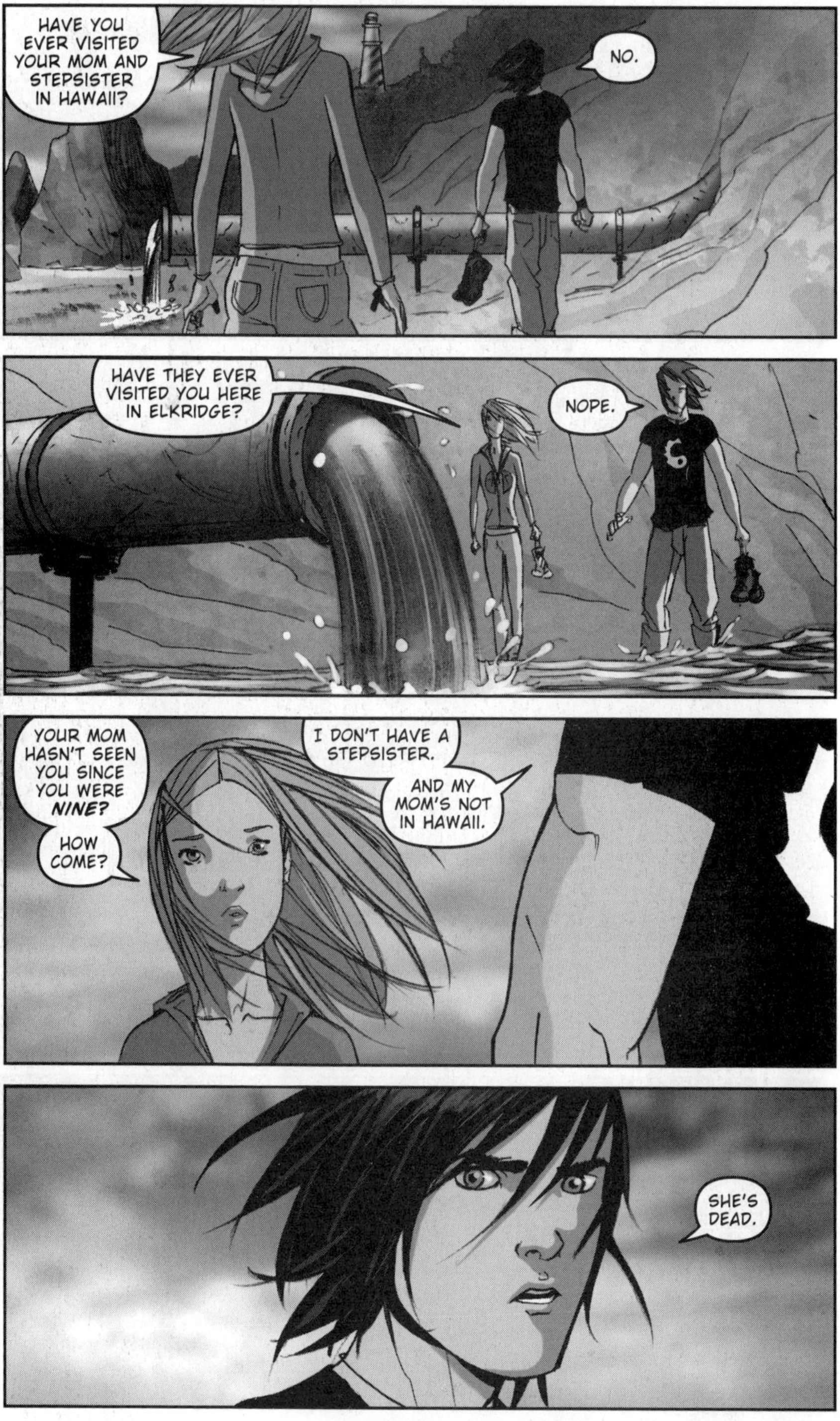
HAVE YOU EVER VISITED YOUR MOM AND STEPSISTER IN HAWAII?
NO.
HAVE THEY EVER VISITED YOU HERE IN ELKRIDGE?
NOPE.
YOUR MOM HASN'T SEEN YOU SINCE YOU WERE *NINE?*
HOW COME?
I DON'T HAVE A STEPSISTER.
AND MY MOM'S NOT IN HAWAII.
SHE'S DEAD.

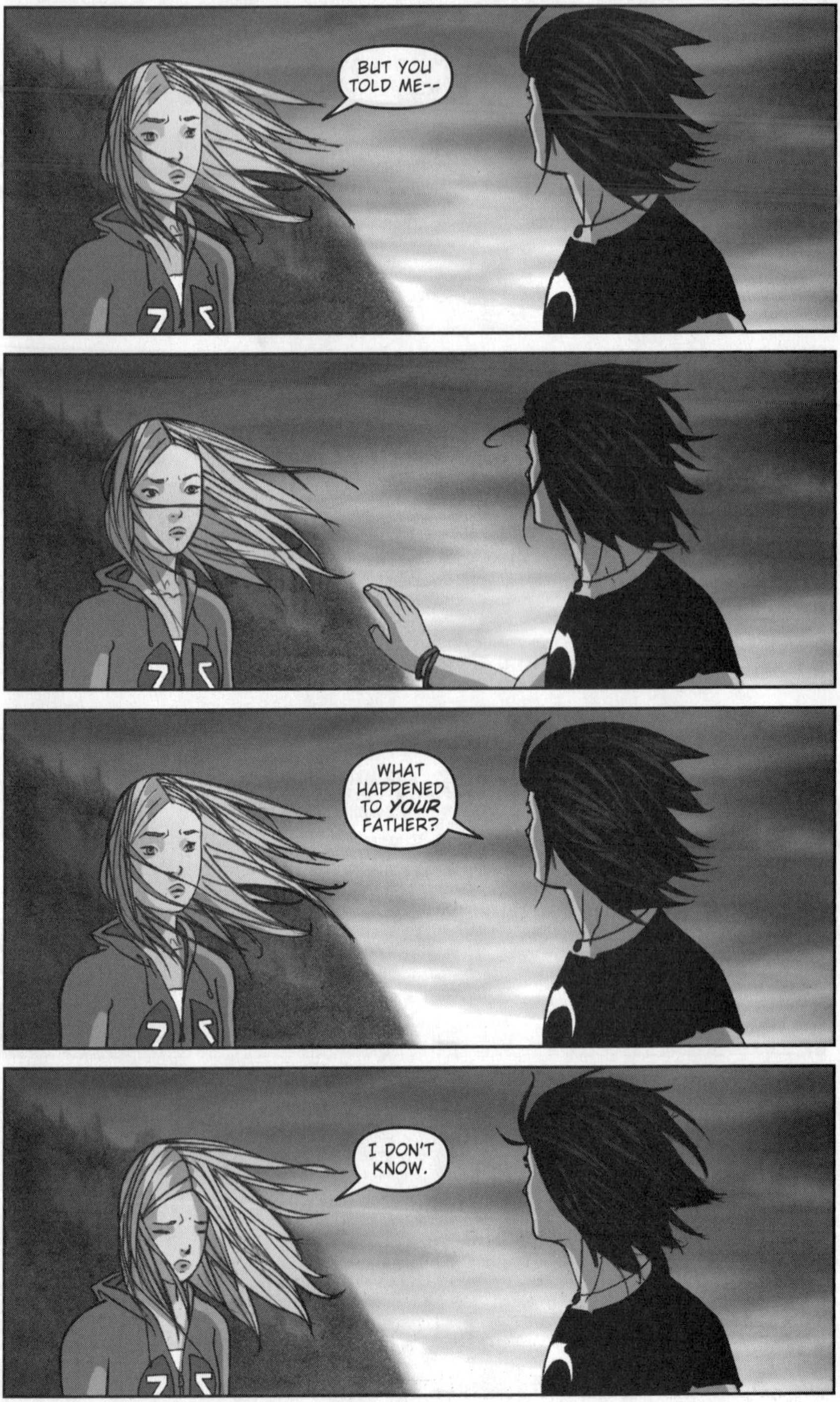
BUT YOU TOLD ME--
WHAT HAPPENED TO *YOUR* FATHER?
I DON'T KNOW.

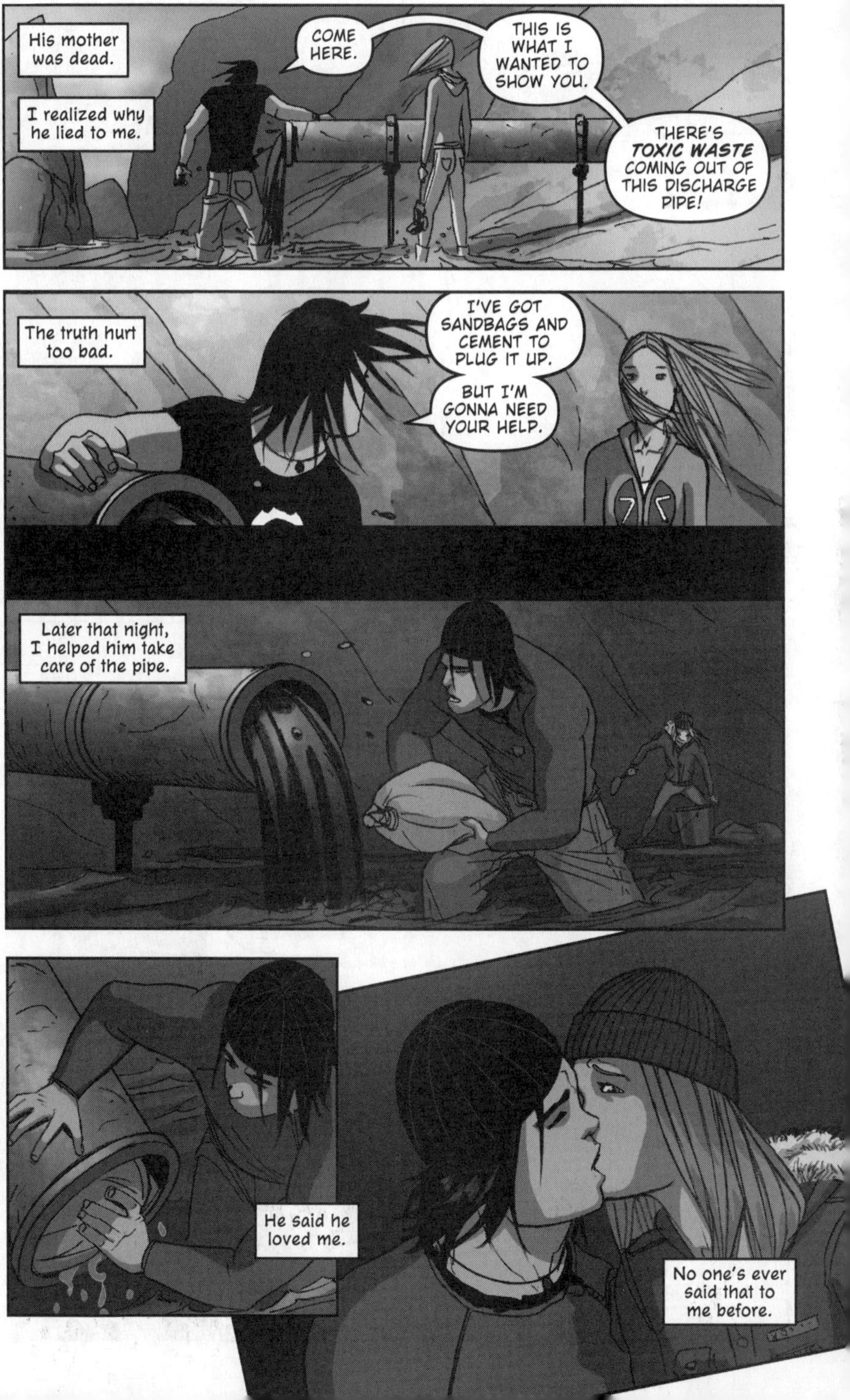

His mother was dead.
I realized why he lied to me.
COME HERE.
THIS IS WHAT I WANTED TO SHOW YOU.
THERE'S *TOXIC WASTE* COMING OUT OF THIS DISCHARGE PIPE!
The truth hurt too bad.
I'VE GOT SANDBAGS AND CEMENT TO PLUG IT UP.
BUT I'M GONNA NEED YOUR HELP.
Later that night, I helped him take care of the pipe.
He said he loved me.
No one's ever said that to me before.

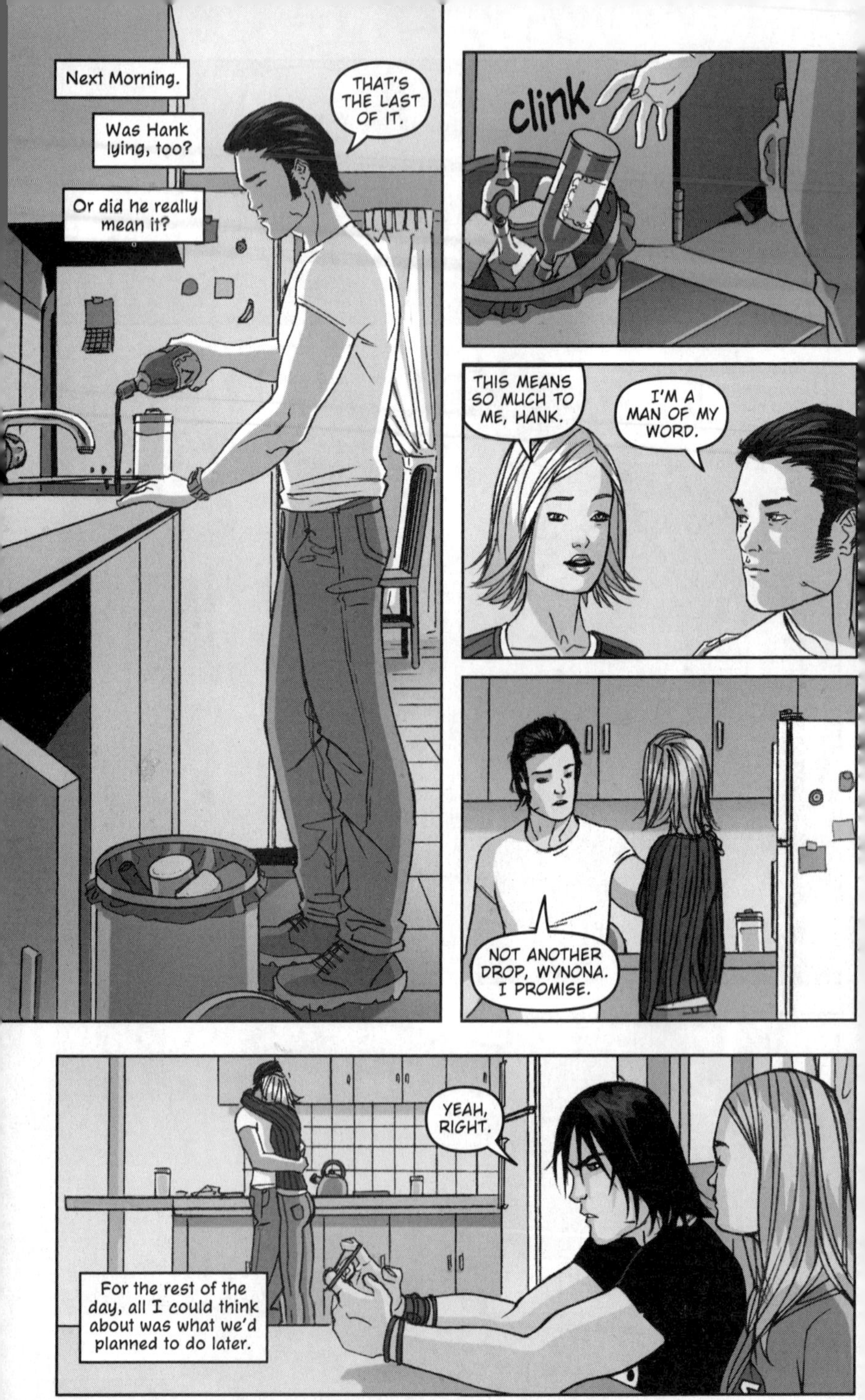

Next Morning.
Was Hank lying, too?
Or did he really mean it?
THAT'S THE LAST OF IT.
clink
THIS MEANS SO MUCH TO ME, HANK.
I'M A MAN OF MY WORD.
NOT ANOTHER DROP, WYNONA. I PROMISE.
YEAH, RIGHT.
For the rest of the day, all I could think about was what we'd planned to do later.

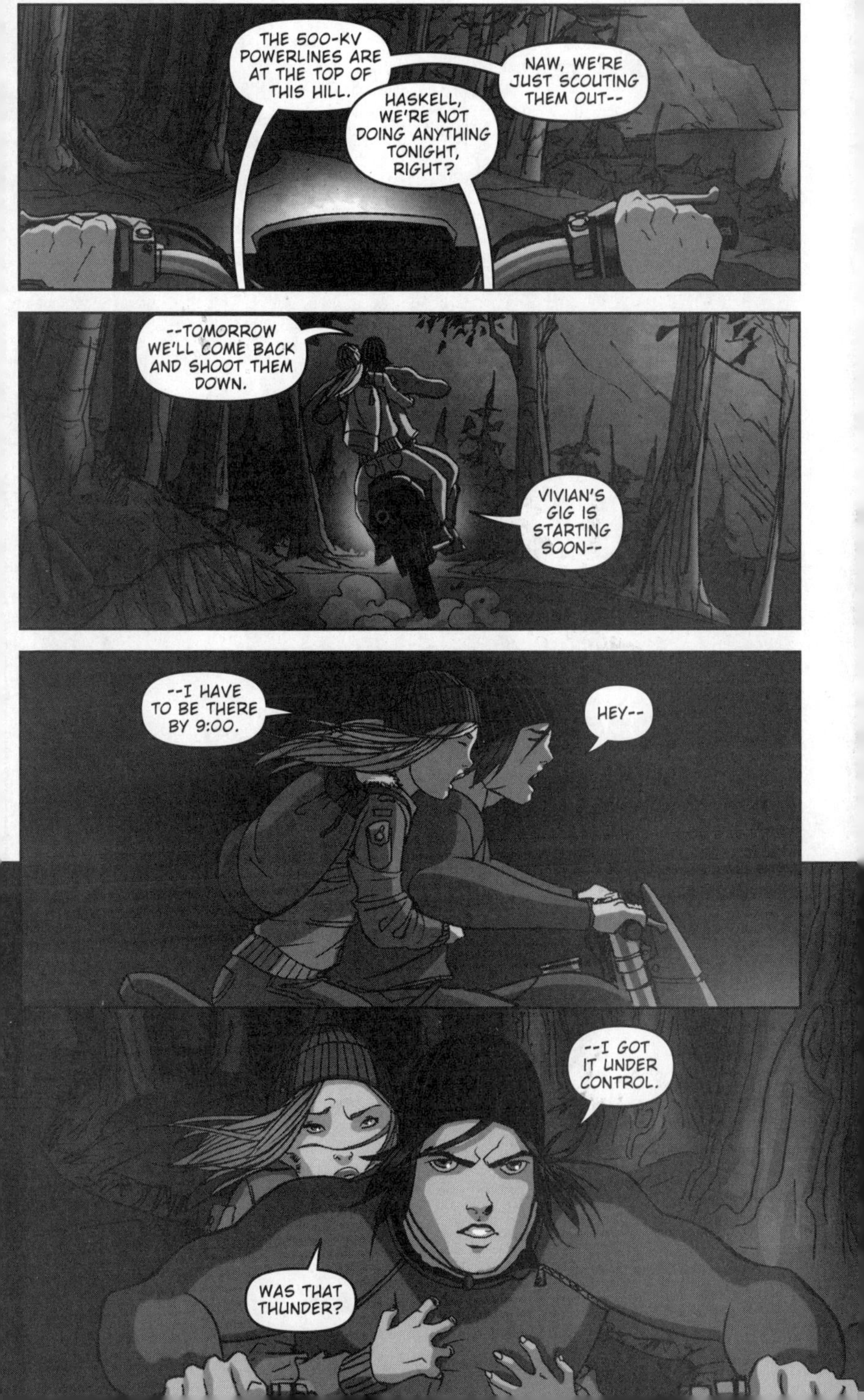
THE 500-KV POWERLINES ARE AT THE TOP OF THIS HILL.
HASKELL, WE'RE NOT DOING ANYTHING TONIGHT, RIGHT?
NAW, WE'RE JUST SCOUTING THEM OUT--
--TOMORROW WE'LL COME BACK AND SHOOT THEM DOWN.
VIVIAN'S GIG IS STARTING SOON--
--I HAVE TO BE THERE BY 9:00.
HEY--
--I GOT IT UNDER CONTROL.
WAS THAT THUNDER?

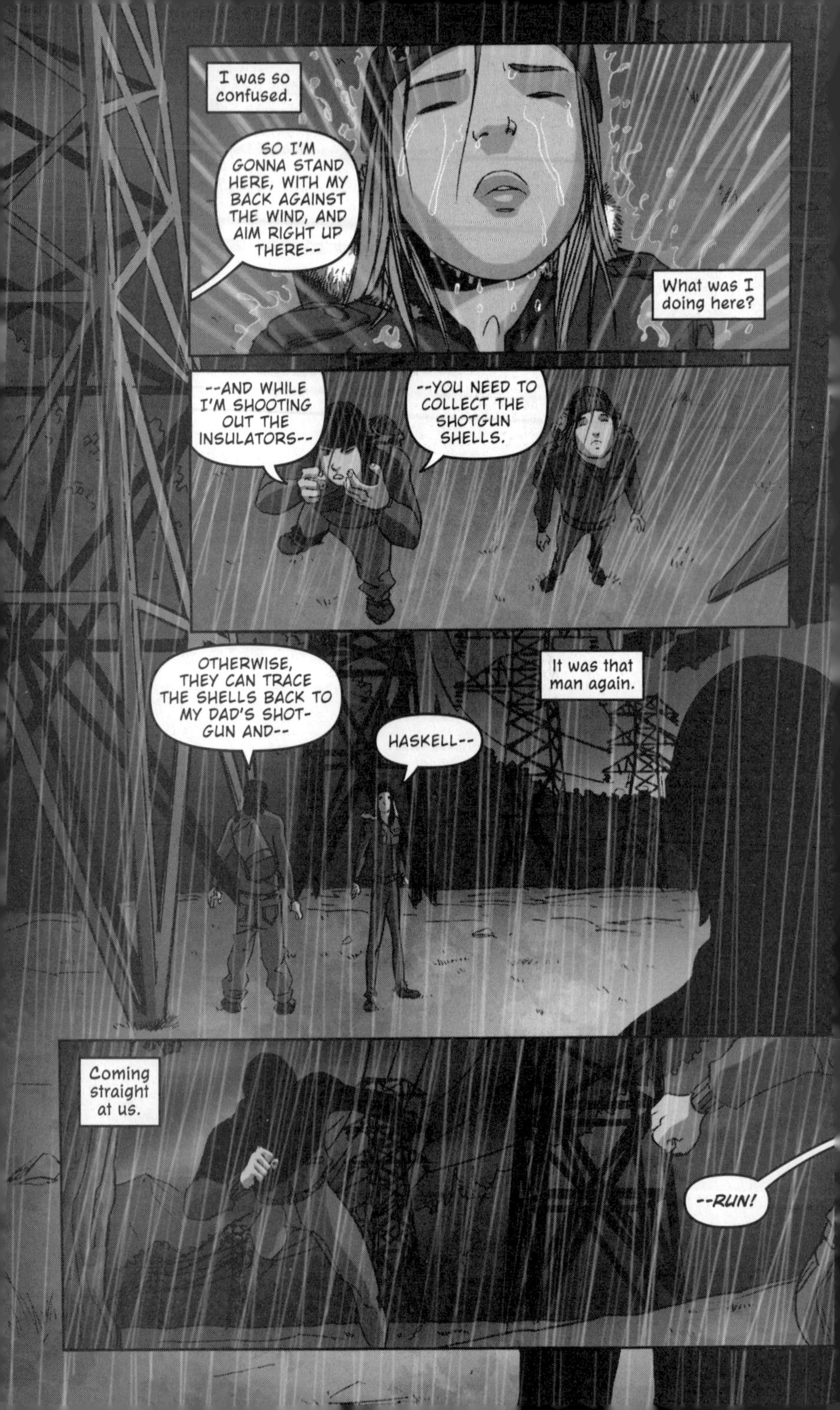
I was so confused.
SO I'M GONNA STAND HERE, WITH MY BACK AGAINST THE WIND, AND AIM RIGHT UP THERE--
What was I doing here?
--AND WHILE I'M SHOOTING OUT THE INSULATORS--
--YOU NEED TO COLLECT THE SHOTGUN SHELLS.
OTHERWISE, THEY CAN TRACE THE SHELLS BACK TO MY DAD'S SHOT-GUN AND--
It was that man again.
HASKELL--
Coming straight at us.
--RUN!

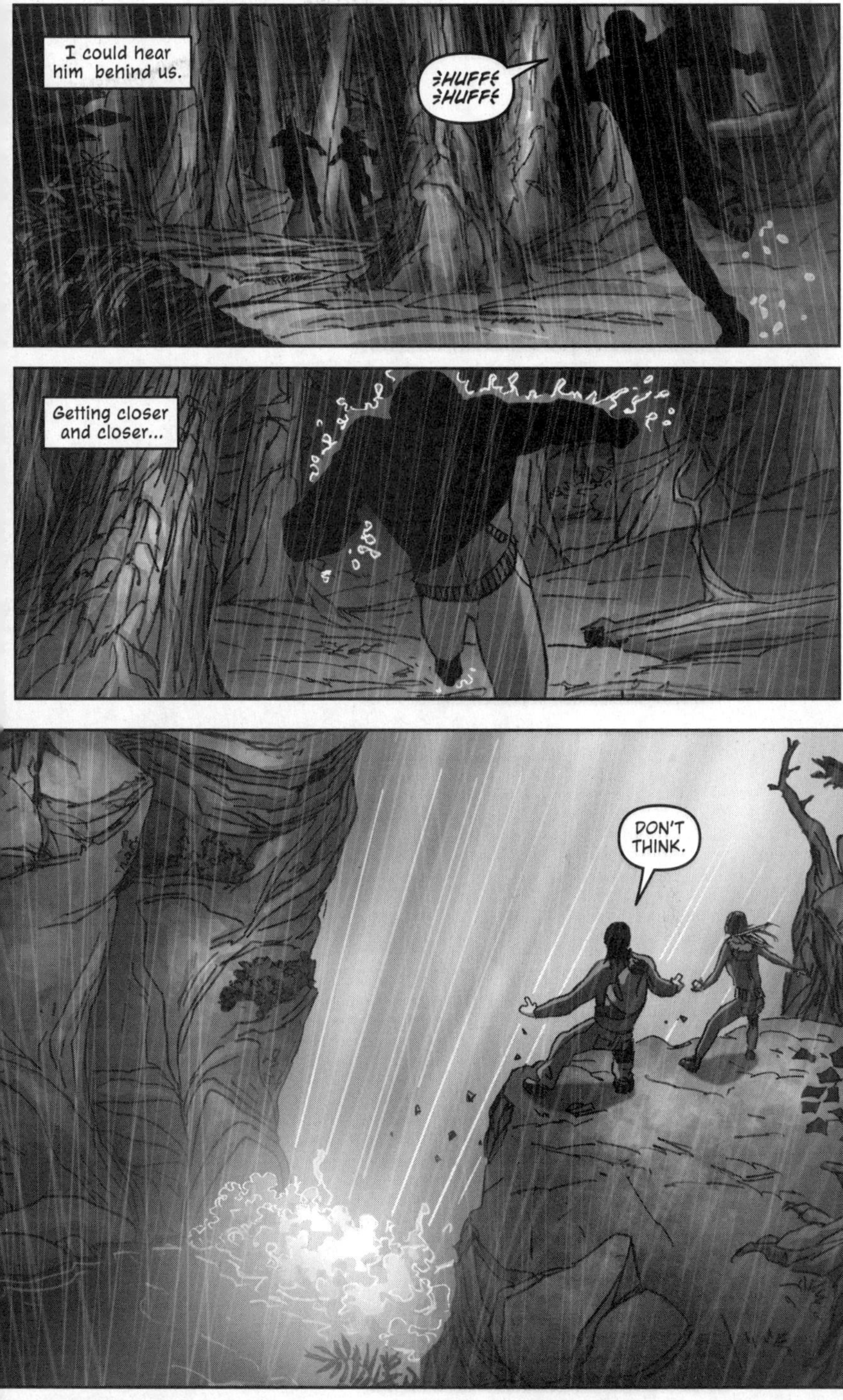

I could hear him behind us.
HUFF HUFF
Getting closer and closer...
DON'T THINK.

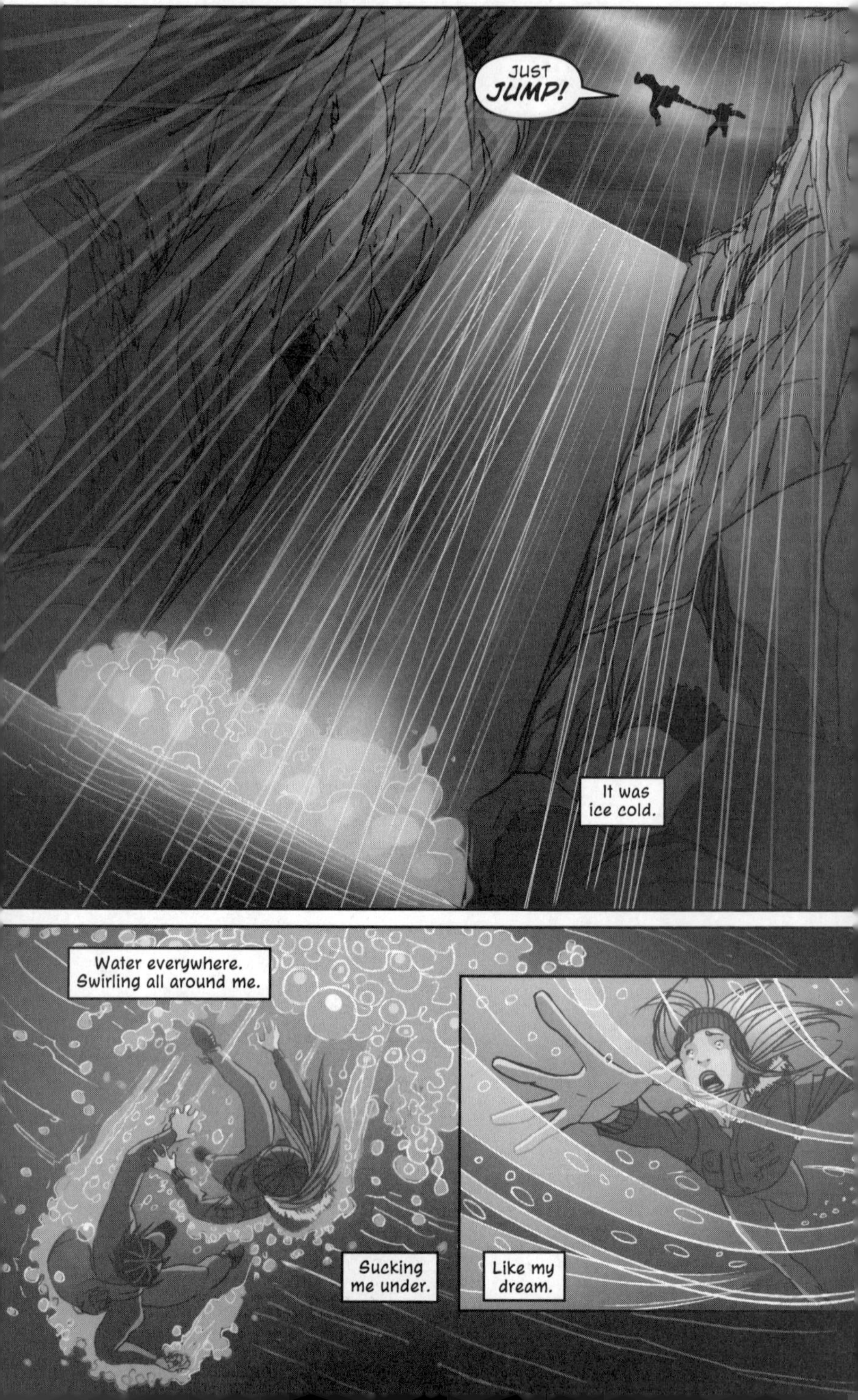

JUST JUMP!
It was ice cold.
Water everywhere. Swirling all around me.
Sucking me under.
Like my dream.

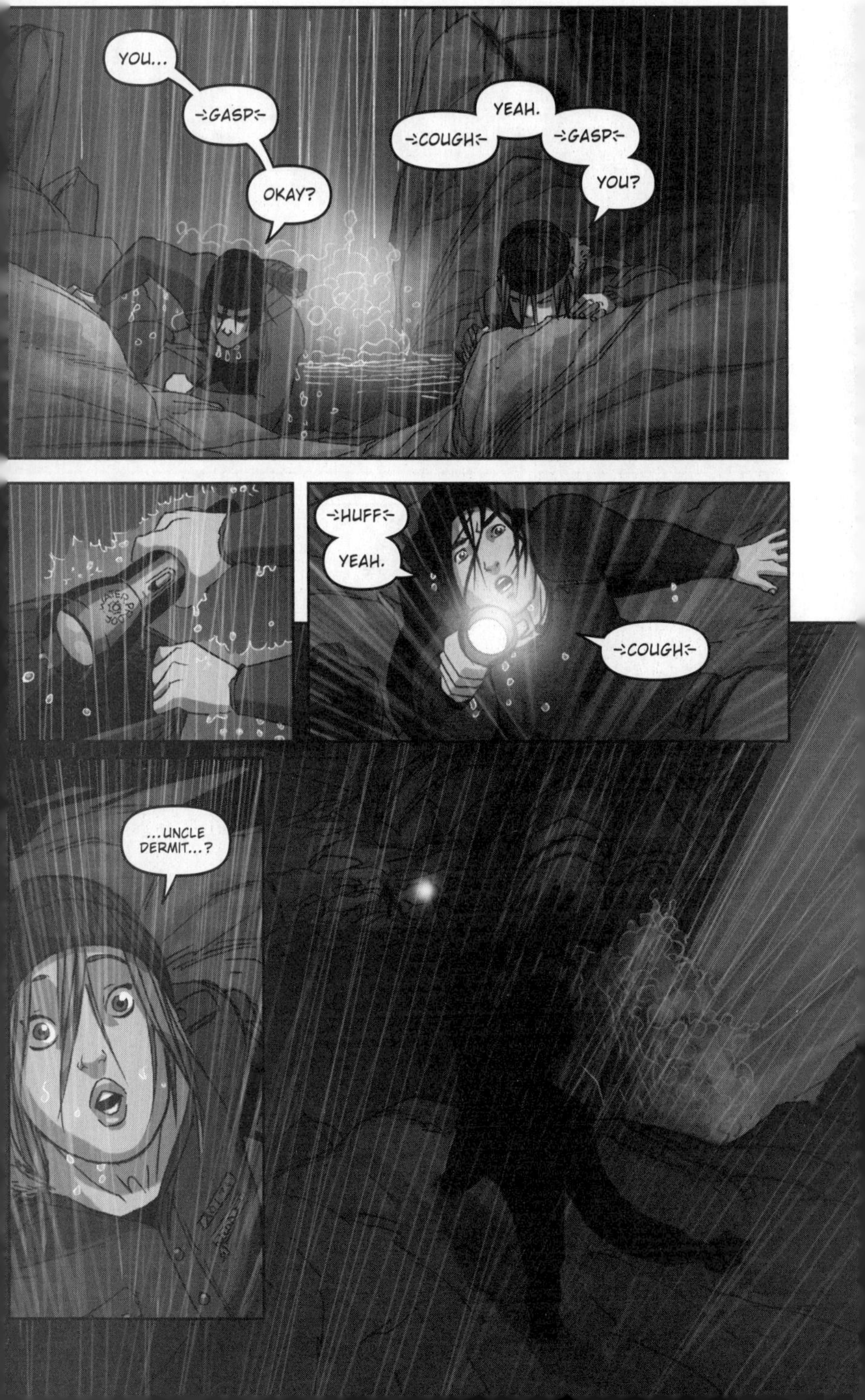
YOU...
-GASP-
OKAY?
-COUGH-
YEAH.
-GASP-
YOU?
-HUFF-
YEAH.
-COUGH-
...UNCLE DERMIT...?

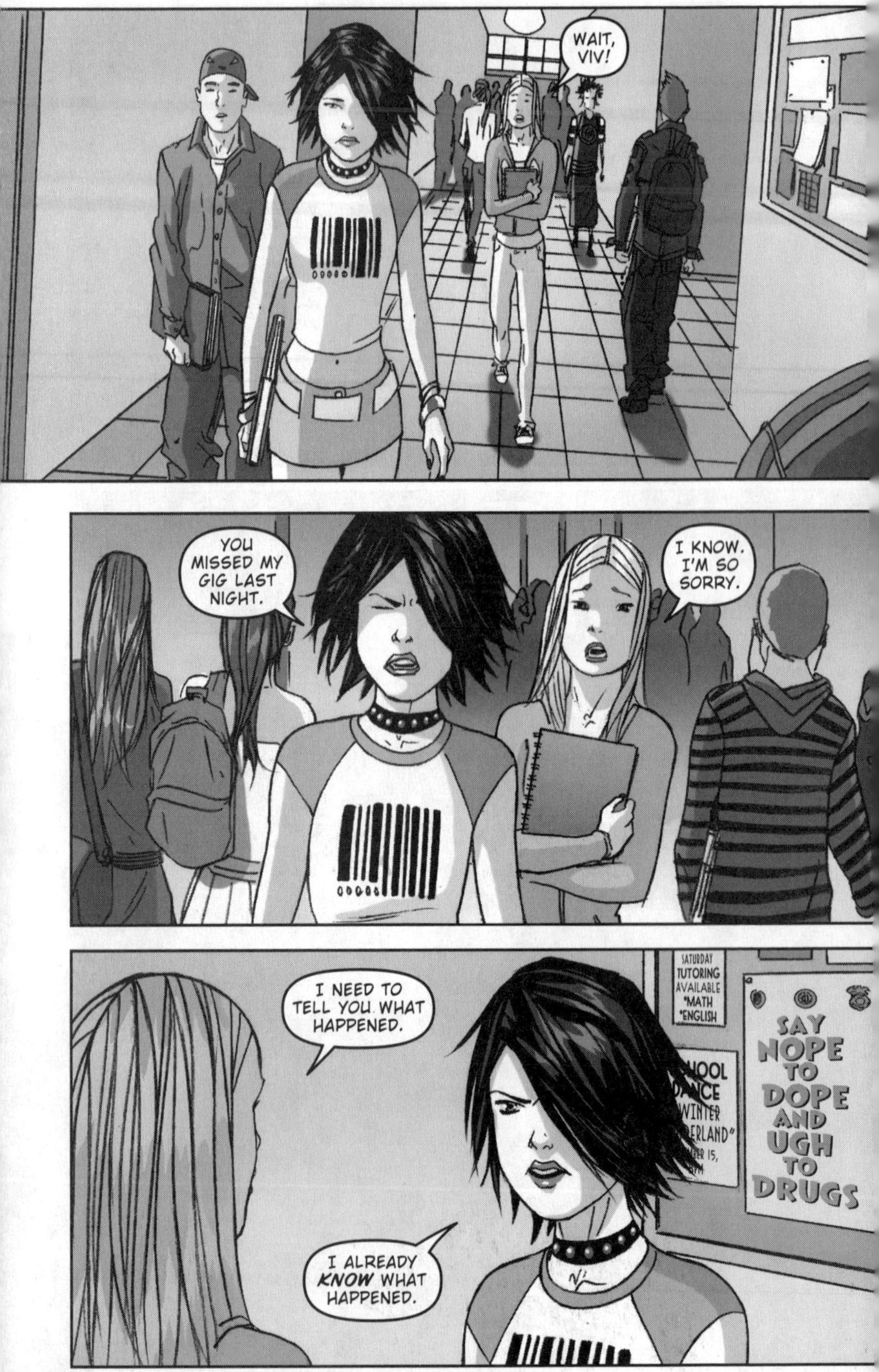
WAIT, VIV!
YOU MISSED MY GIG LAST NIGHT.
I KNOW. I'M SO SORRY.
I NEED TO TELL YOU WHAT HAPPENED.
SATURDAY TUTORING AVAILABLE *MATH *ENGLISH
SAY NOPE TO DOPE AND UGH TO DRUGS
I ALREADY *KNOW* WHAT HAPPENED.

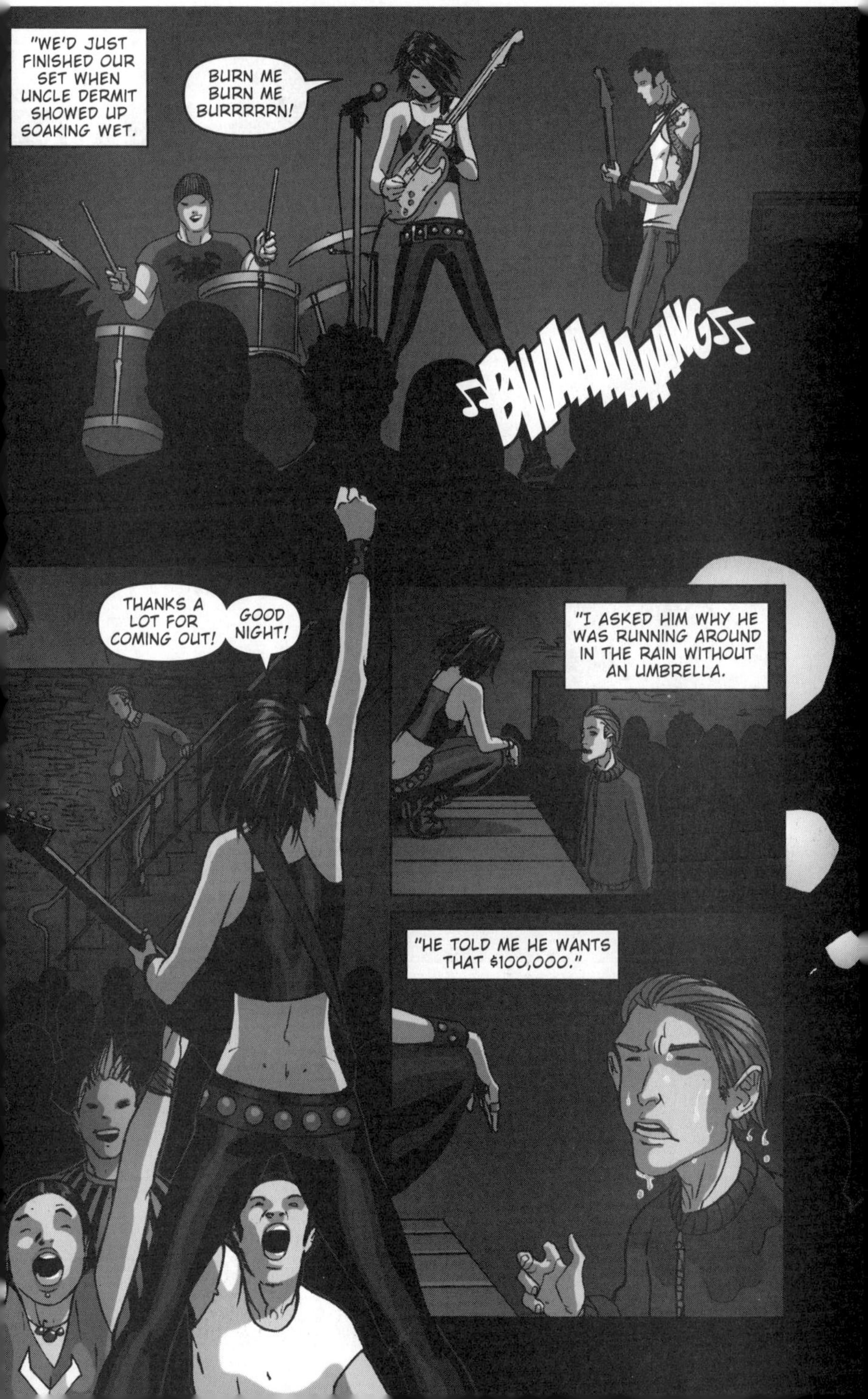
"WE'D JUST FINISHED OUR SET WHEN UNCLE DERMIT SHOWED UP SOAKING WET.
BURN ME BURN ME BURRRRRN!
BWAAAAAAANG
THANKS A LOT FOR COMING OUT!
GOOD NIGHT!
"I ASKED HIM WHY HE WAS RUNNING AROUND IN THE RAIN WITHOUT AN UMBRELLA.
"HE TOLD ME HE WANTS THAT $100,000."

HE HASN'T FIGURED OUT **WHO** YOU ARE YET, BUT HE WILL--

--IT'S JUST A MATTER OF TIME.

FBI $100,000 REWARD For information leading to the arrest of ECO-TERRORISTS

YOU GOTTA STOP NOW.

FBI $100,000 REWARD For information leading to the arrest of ECO-TERRORISTS

YOU'LL GET SO BUSTED IF YOU DON'T.

HEY, DANNI.

I NEED TO TALK TO YOU.

SO DO I.

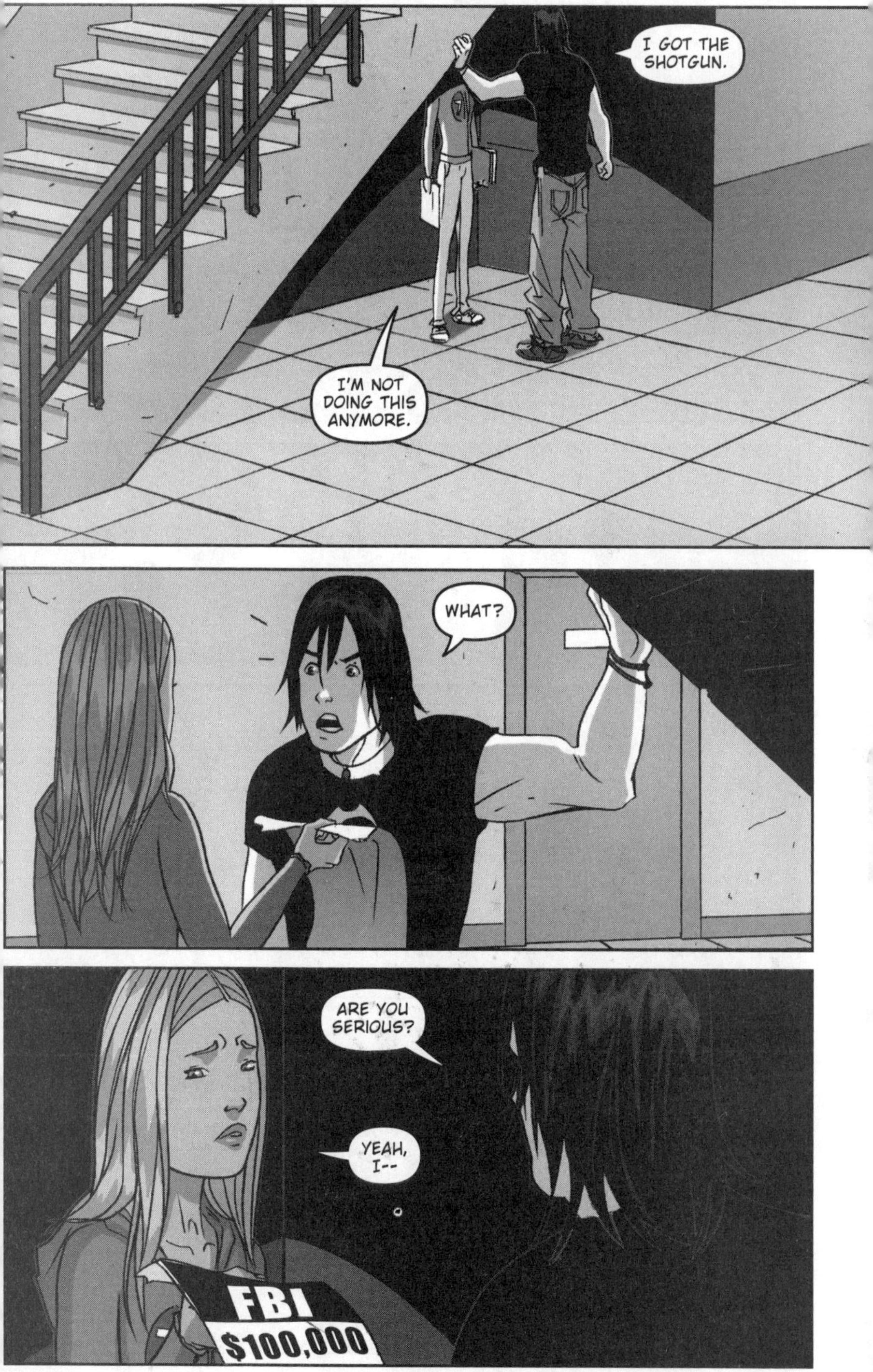
I GOT THE SHOTGUN.
I'M NOT DOING THIS ANYMORE.
WHAT?
ARE YOU SERIOUS?
YEAH, I--
FBI
$100,000

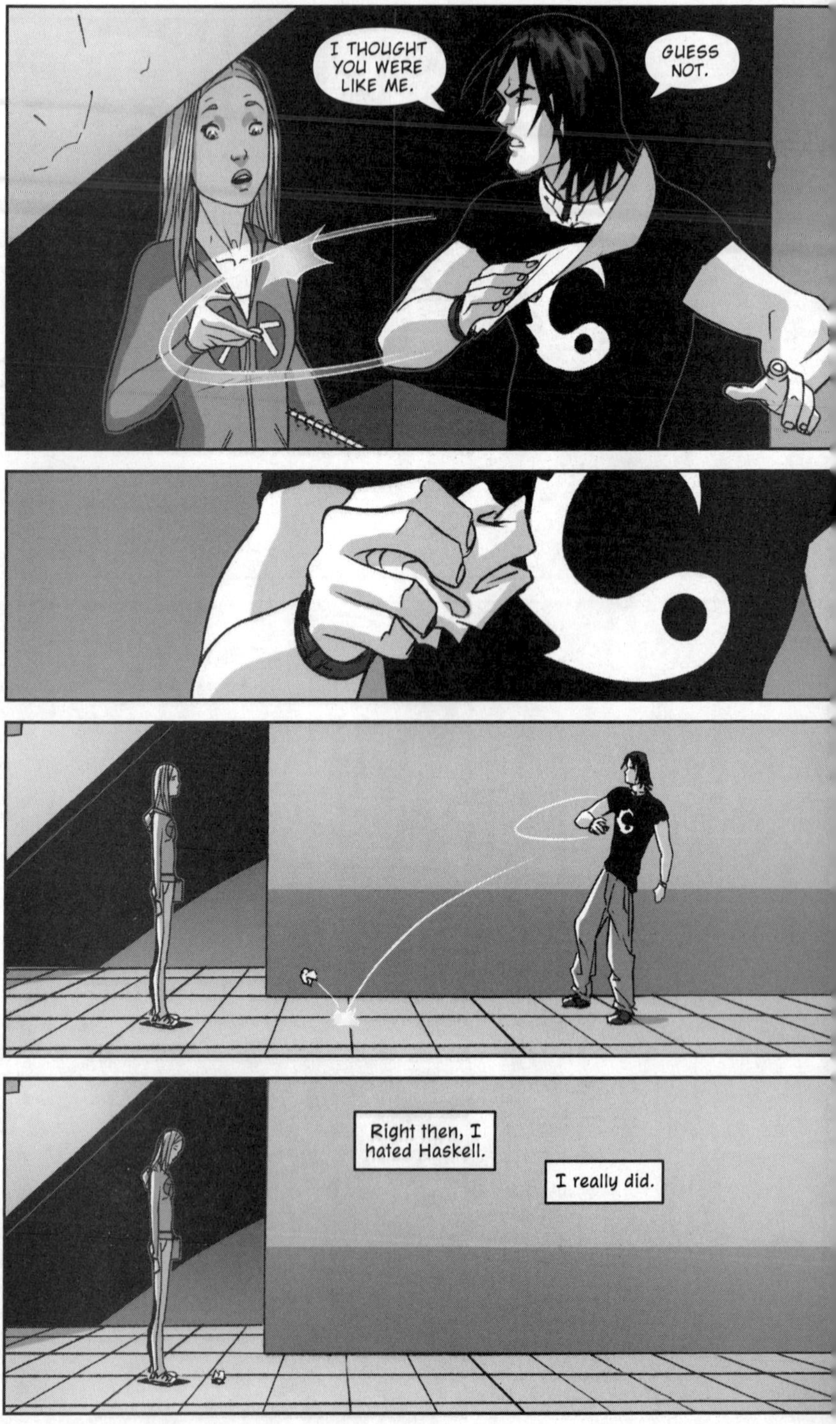
I THOUGHT YOU WERE LIKE ME.
GUESS NOT.
Right then, I hated Haskell.
I really did.

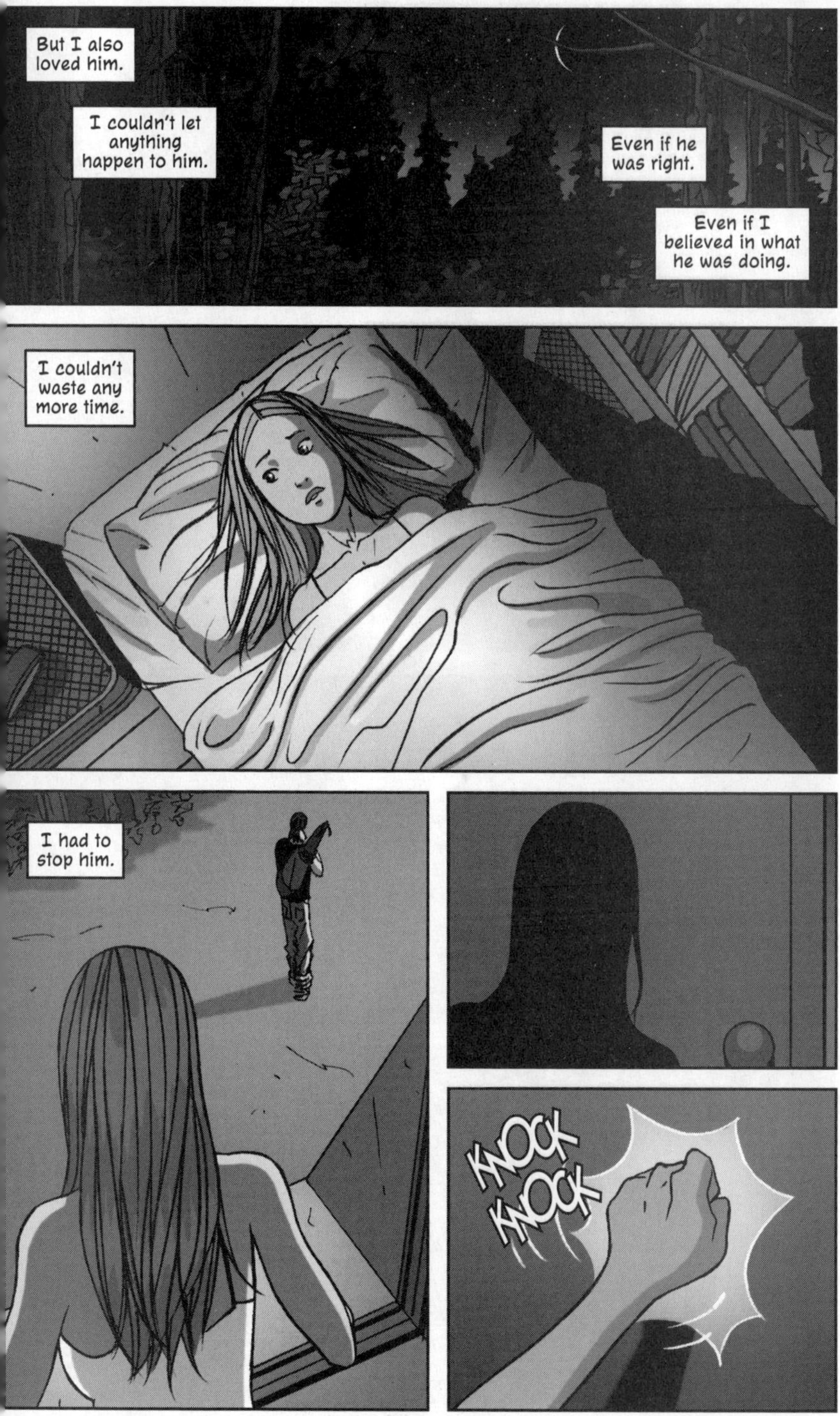
But I also loved him.
I couldn't let anything happen to him.
Even if he was right.
Even if I believed in what he was doing.
I couldn't waste any more time.
I had to stop him.
KNOCK KNOCK

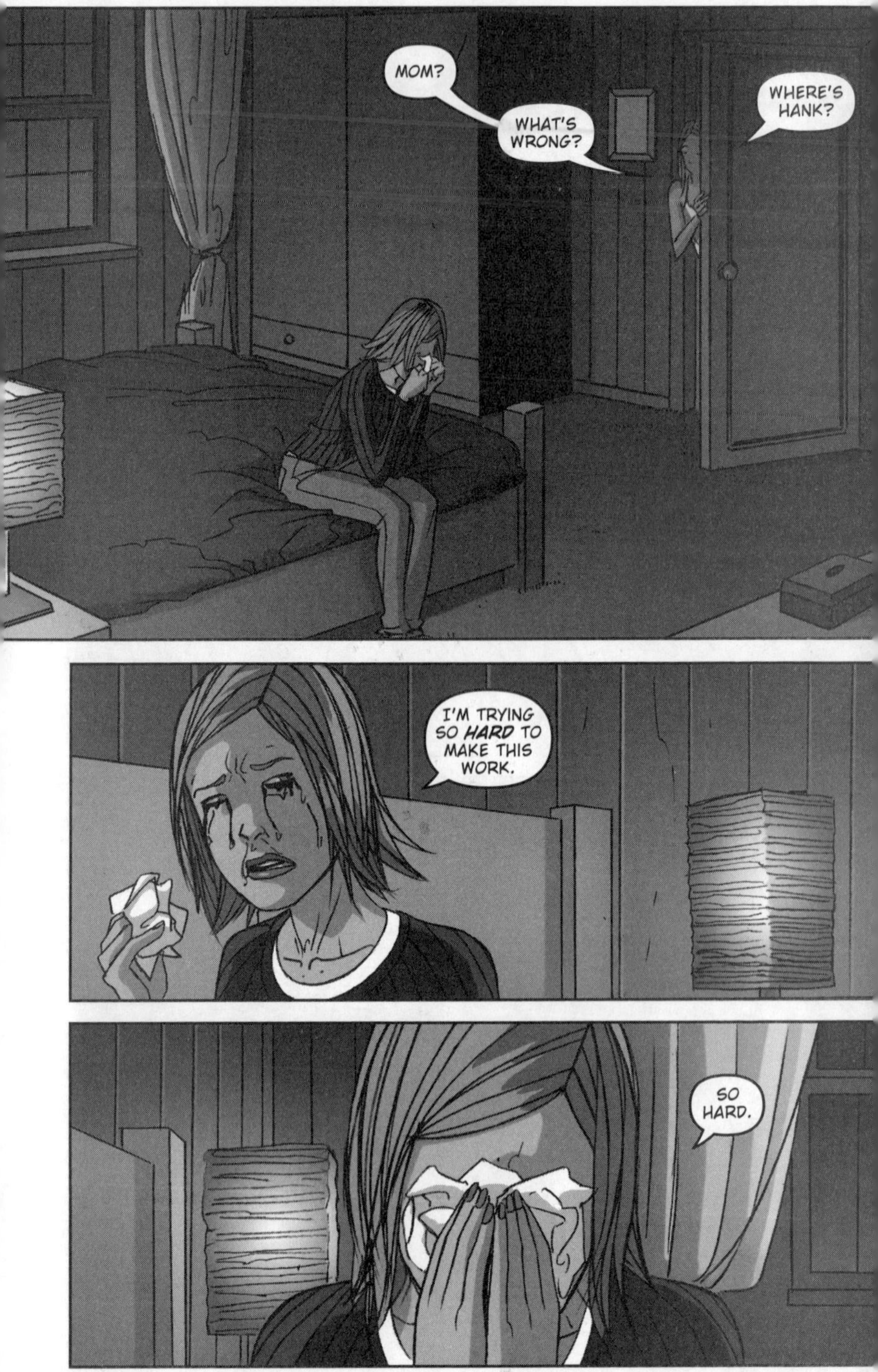
MOM?
WHAT'S WRONG?
WHERE'S HANK?
I'M TRYING SO **HARD** TO MAKE THIS WORK.
SO HARD.

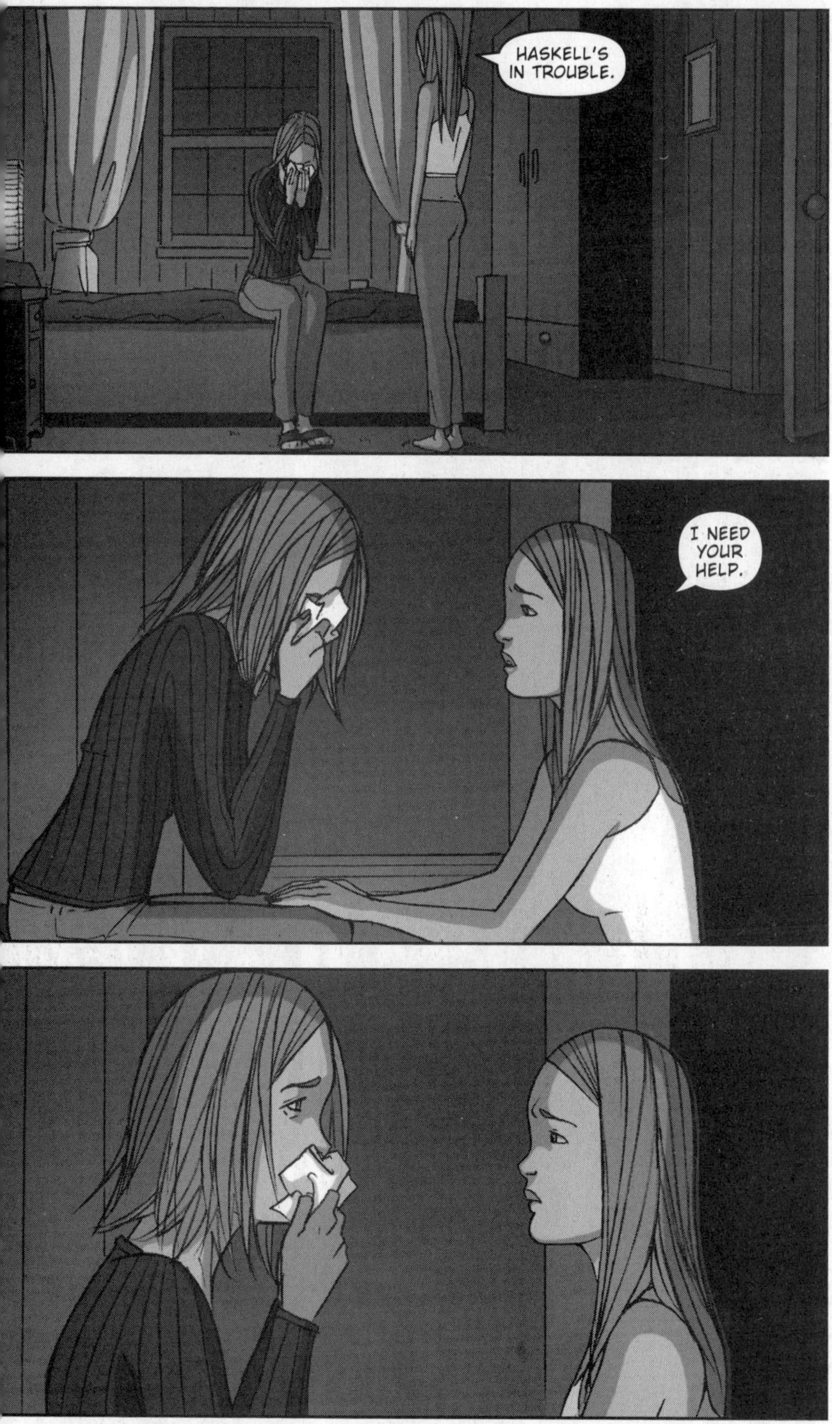
HASKELL'S IN TROUBLE.
I NEED YOUR HELP.

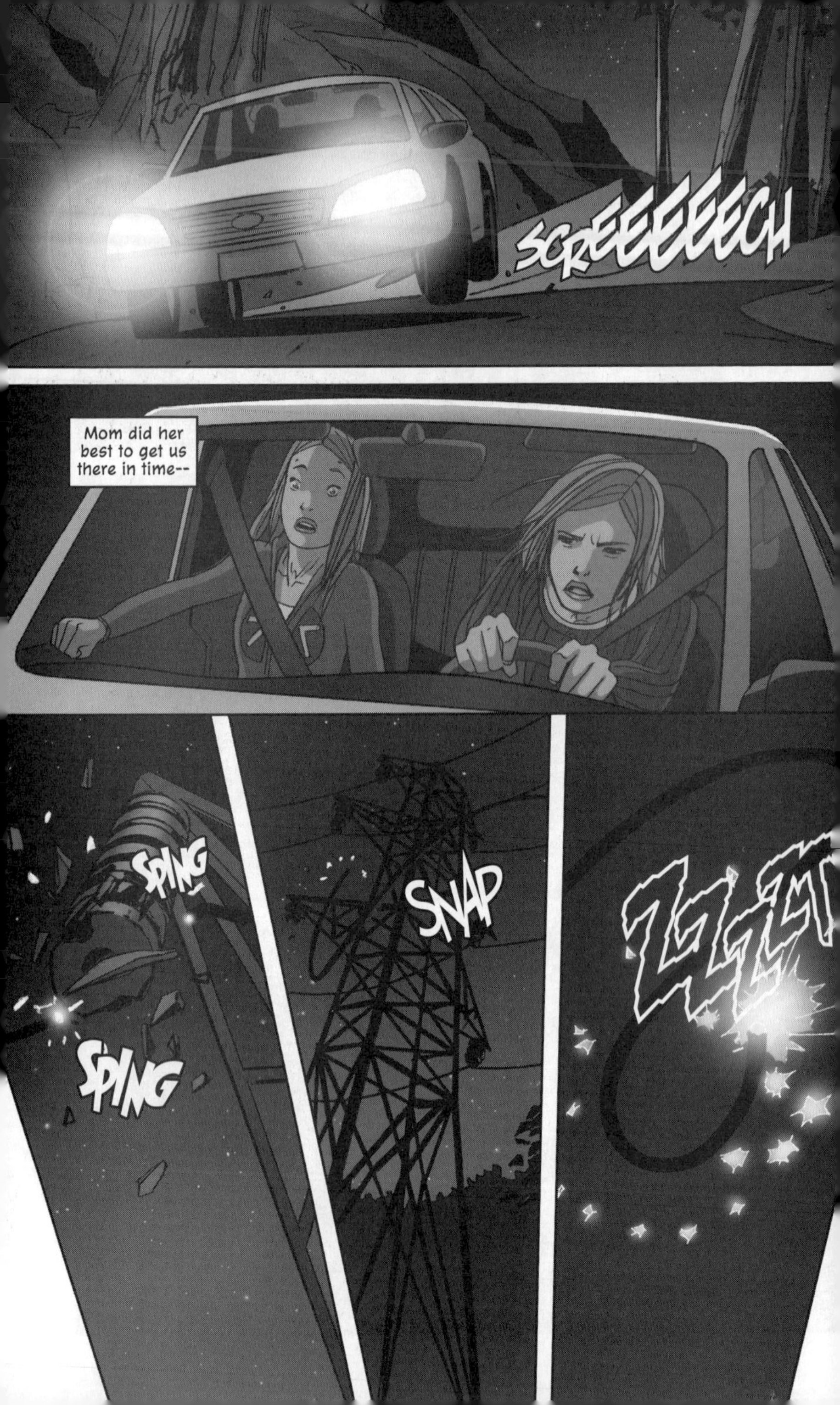
SCREEEEEECH
Mom did her best to get us there in time--
SPING
SPING
SNAP
ZZZZT

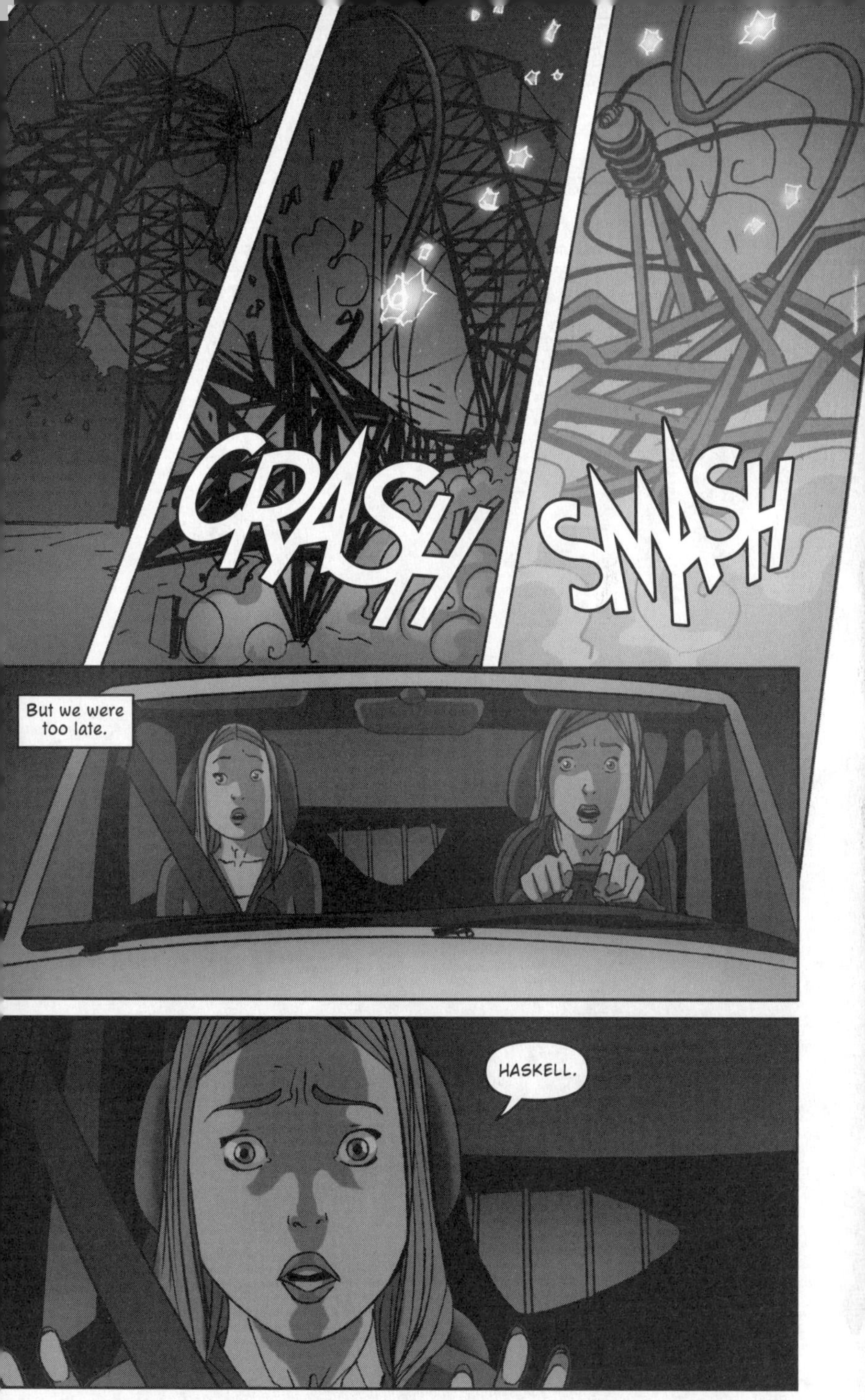
CRASH
SMASH
But we were too late.
HASKELL.

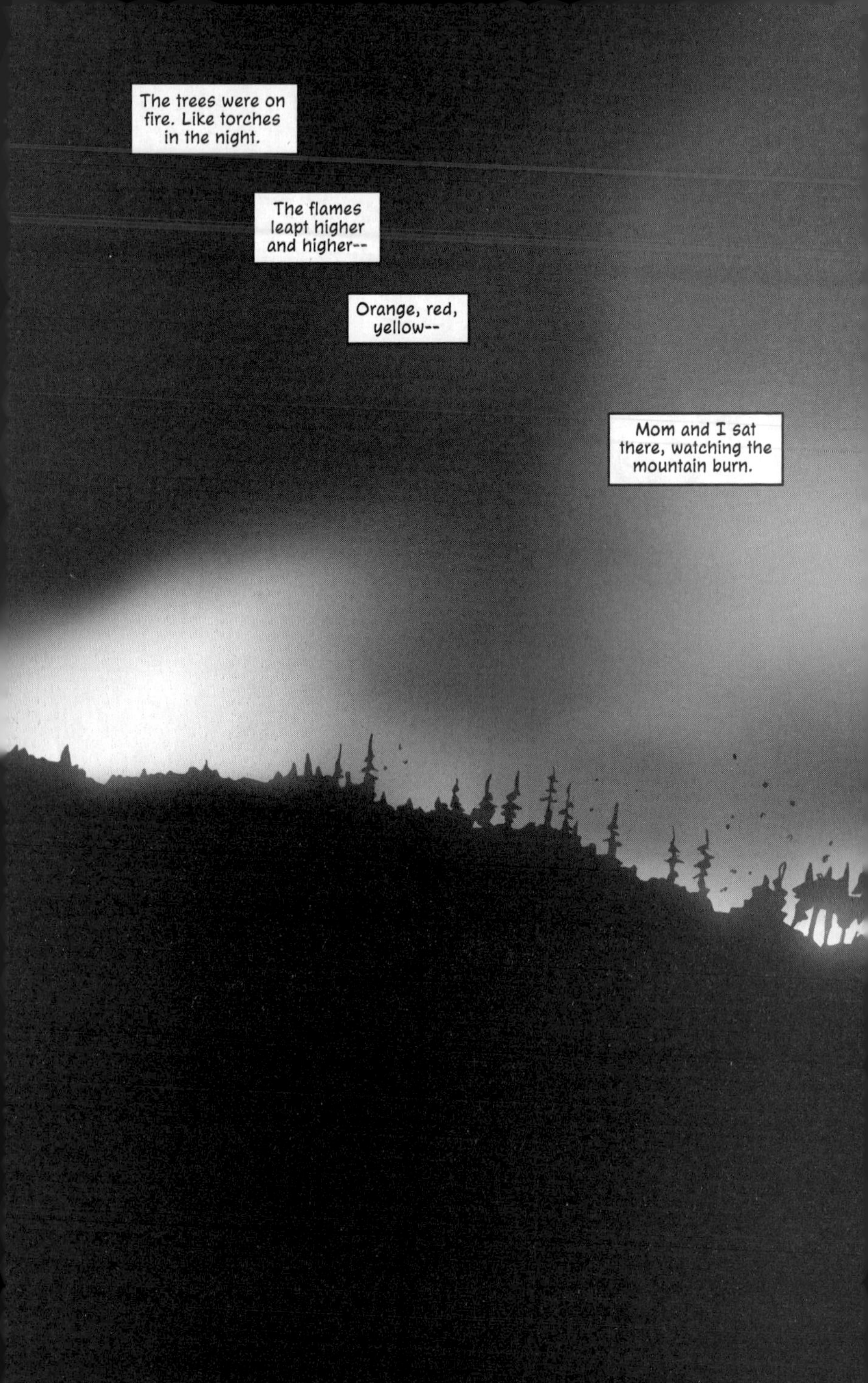
The trees were on fire. Like torches in the night.
The flames leapt higher and higher--
Orange, red, yellow--
Mom and I sat there, watching the mountain burn.

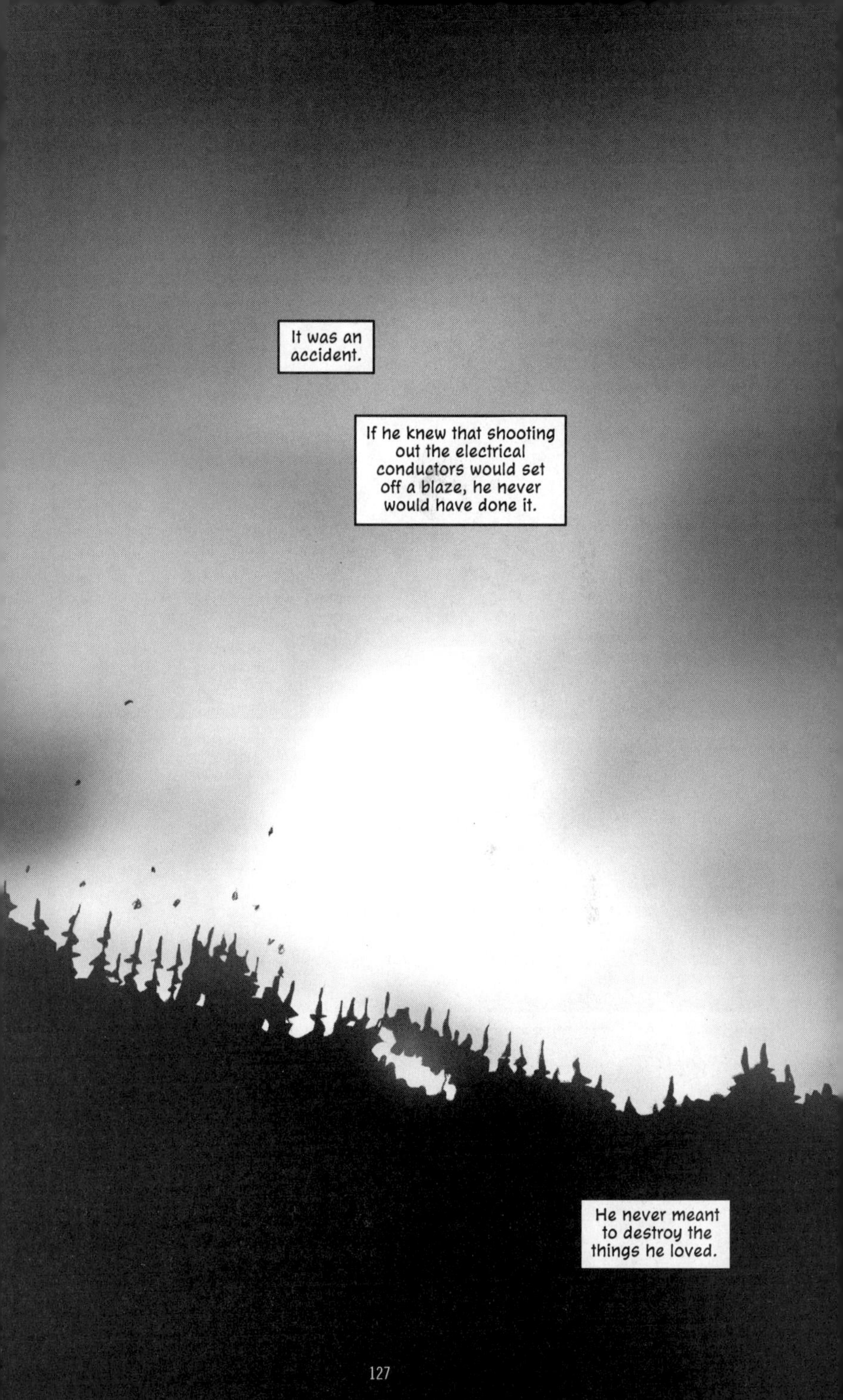
It was an accident.
If he knew that shooting out the electrical conductors would set off a blaze, he never would have done it.
He never meant to destroy the things he loved.

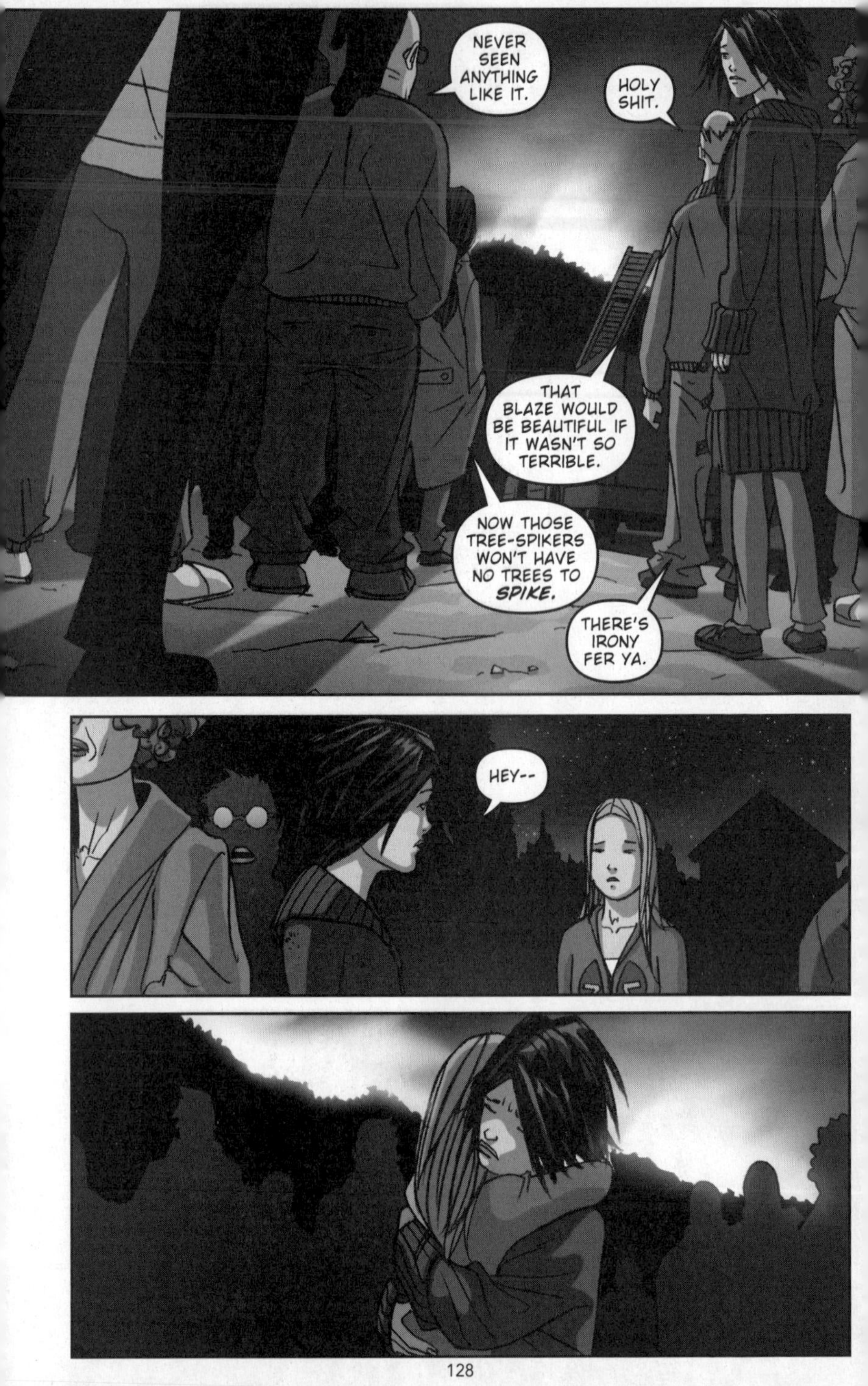
NEVER SEEN ANYTHING LIKE IT.
HOLY SHIT.
THAT BLAZE WOULD BE BEAUTIFUL IF IT WASN'T SO TERRIBLE.
NOW THOSE TREE-SPIKERS WON'T HAVE NO TREES TO *SPIKE.*
THERE'S IRONY FER YA.
HEY--

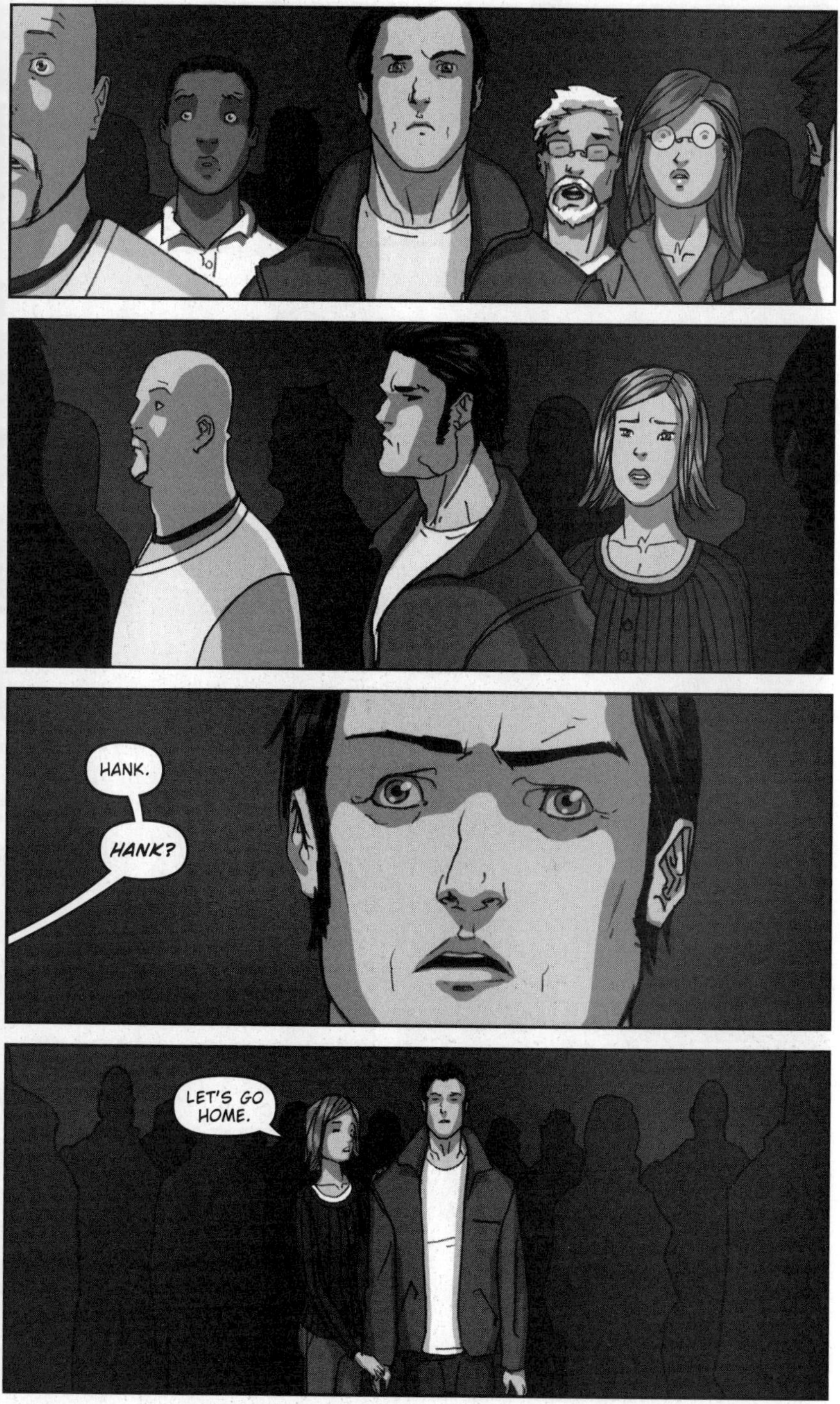
HANK.
HANK?
LET'S GO HOME.

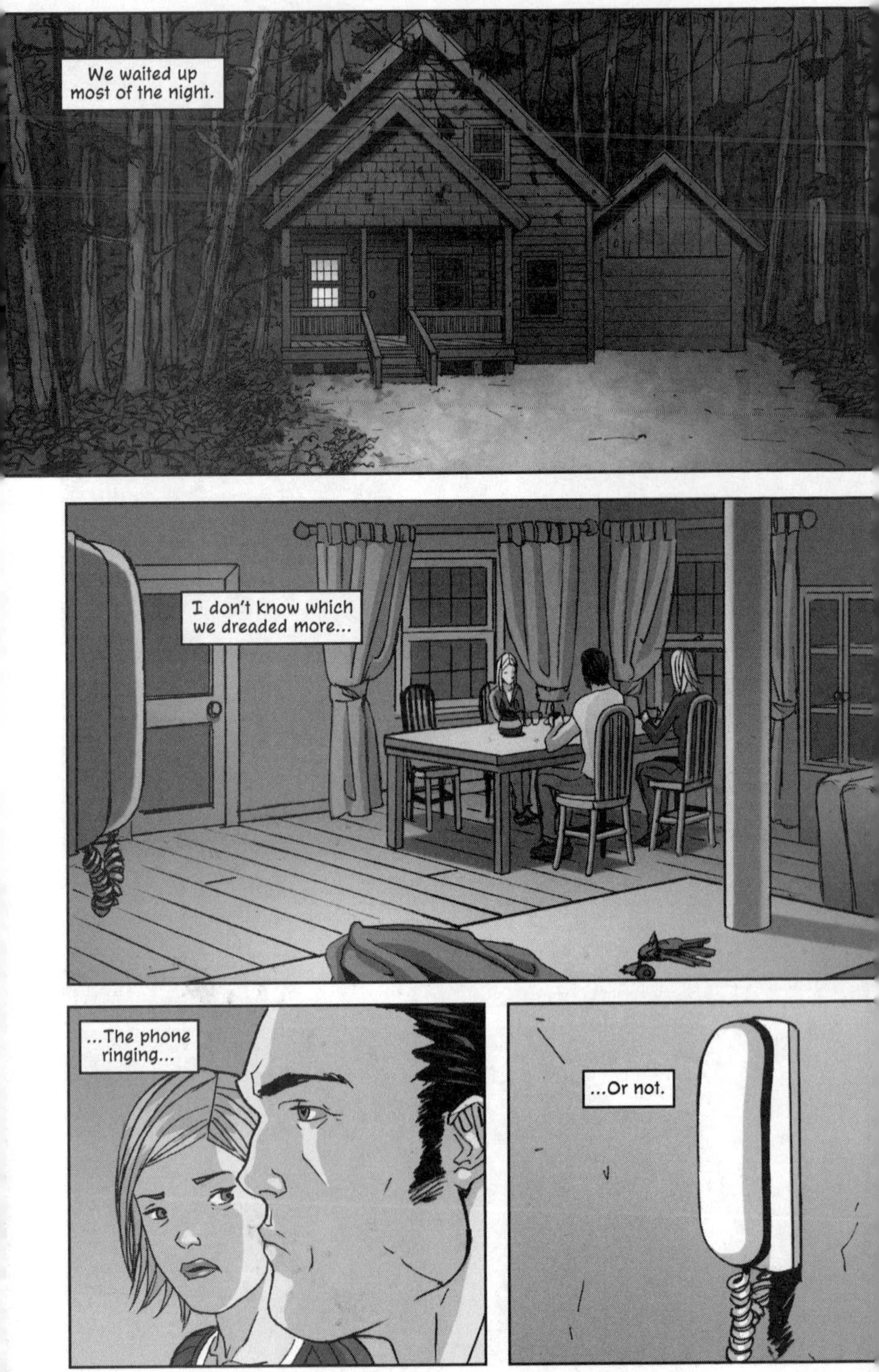
We waited up most of the night.
I don't know which we dreaded more...
...The phone ringing...
...Or not.

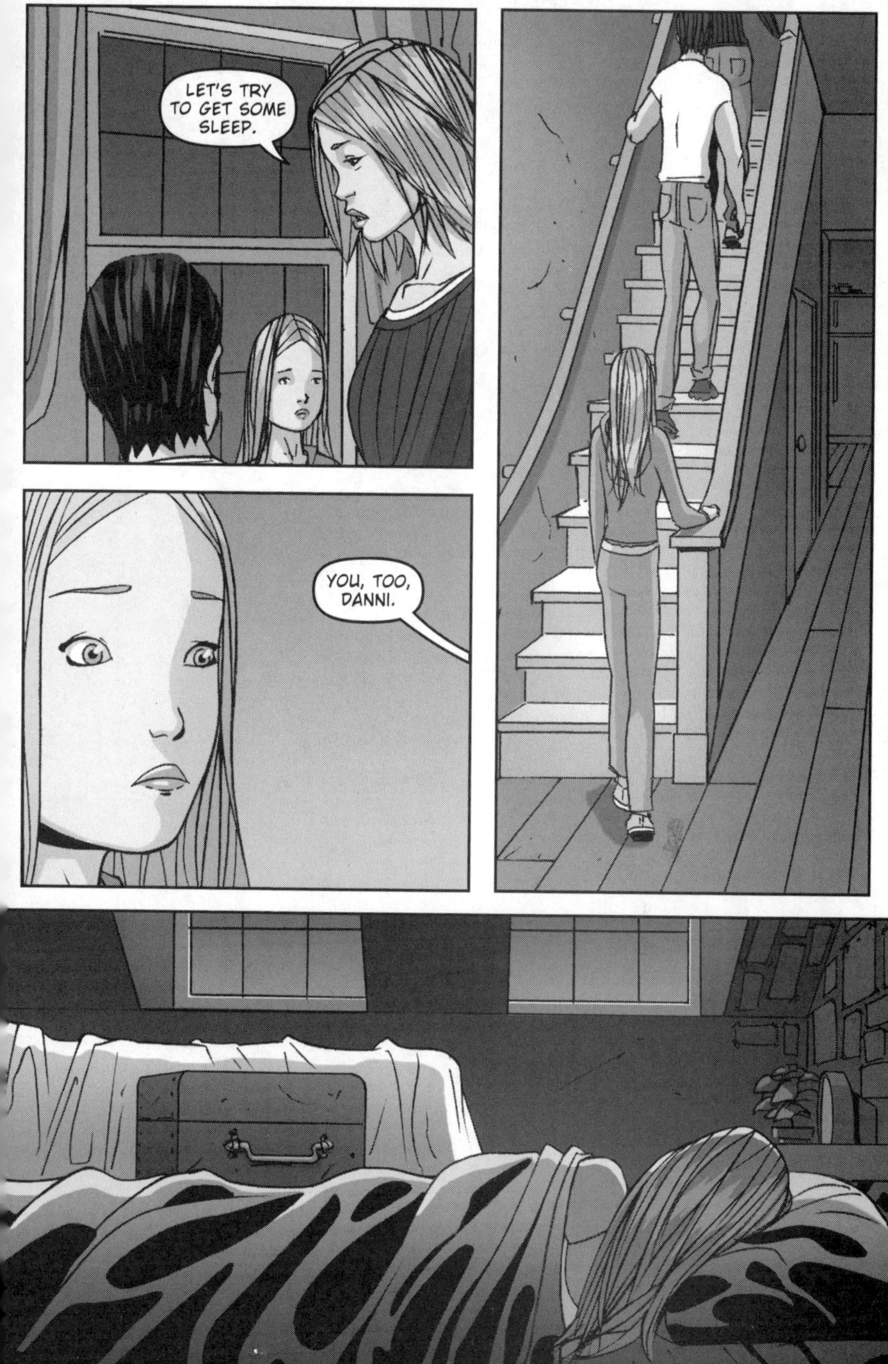
LET'S TRY TO GET SOME SLEEP.
YOU, TOO, DANNI.

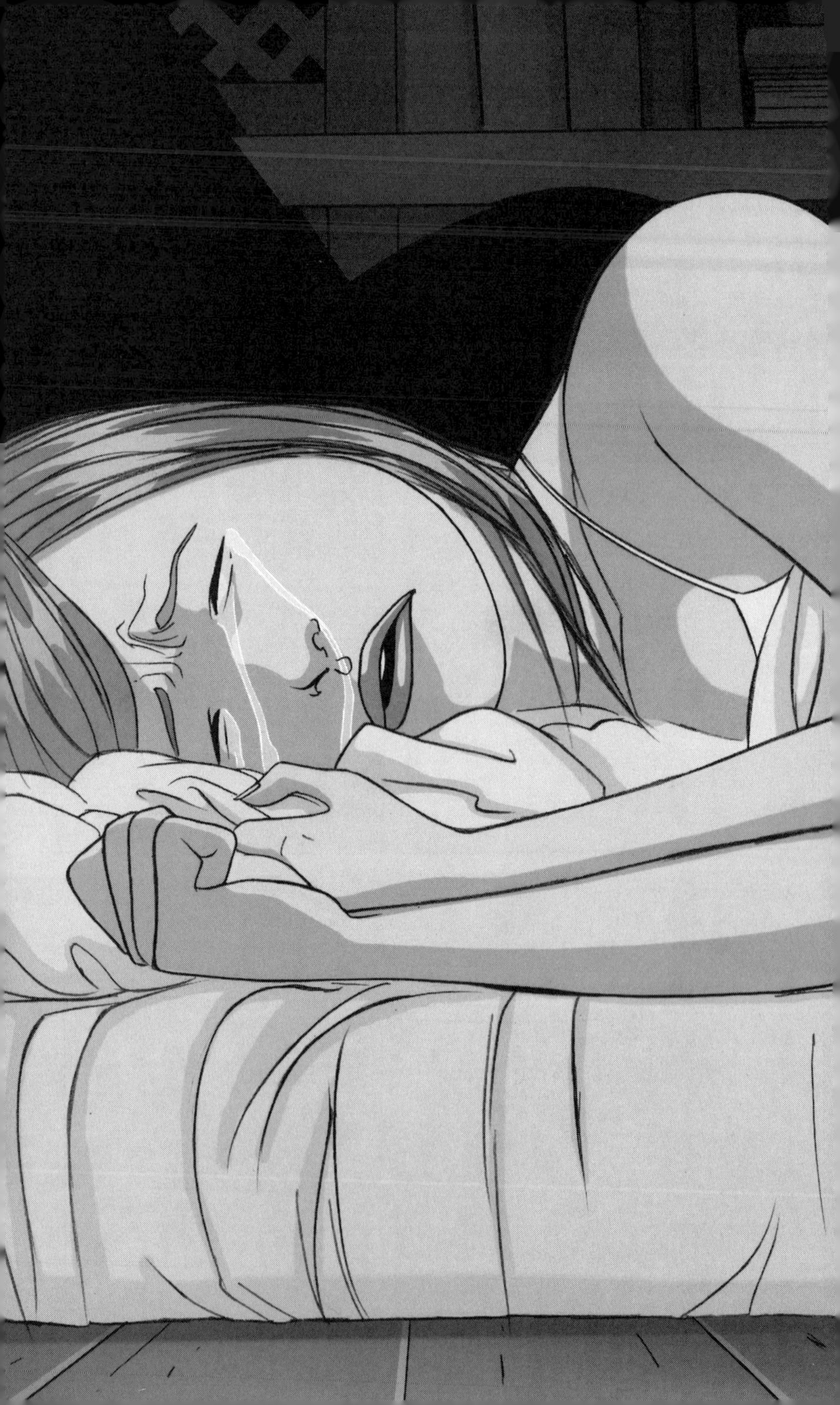

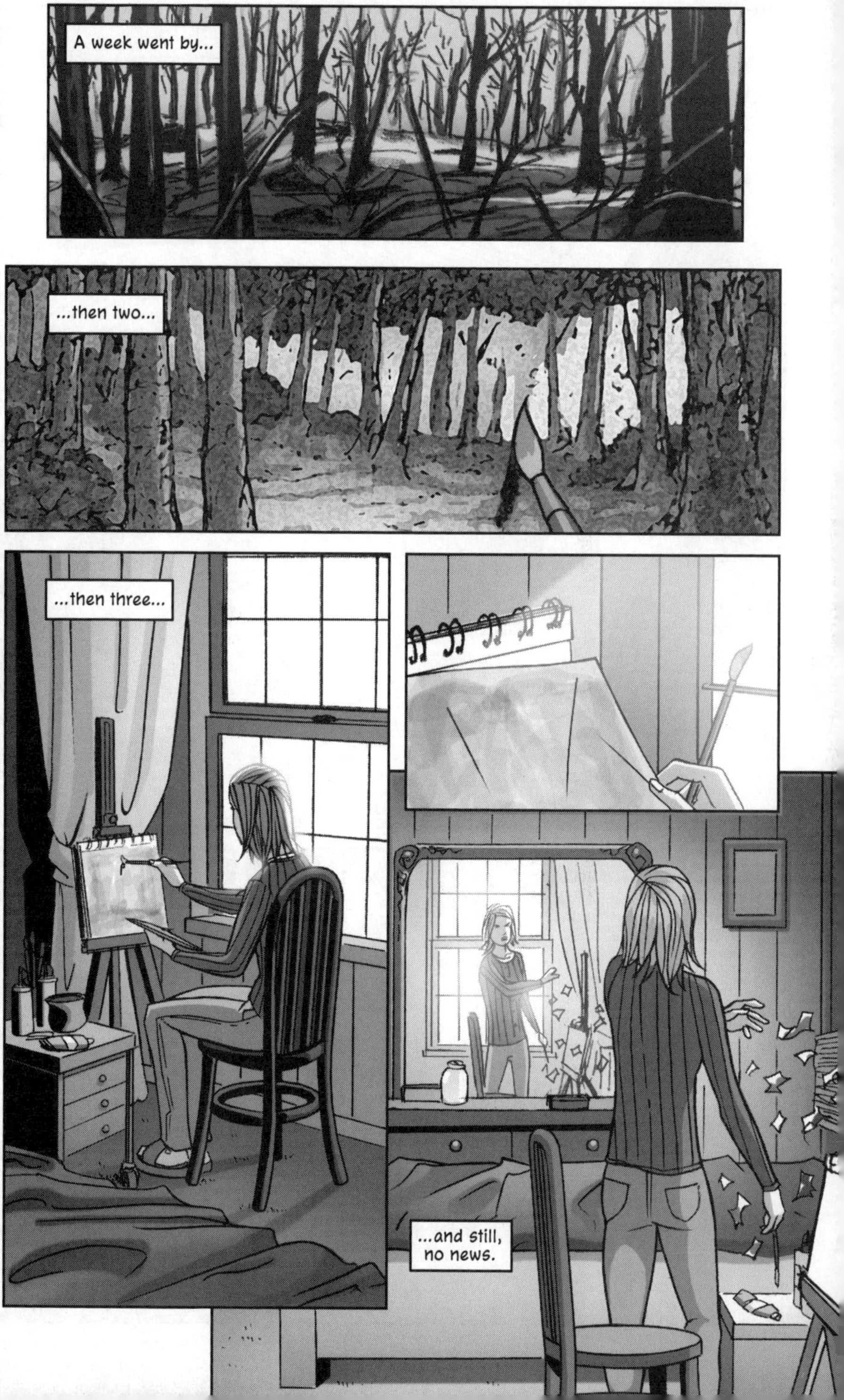
A week went by...
...then two...
...then three...
...and still,
no news.

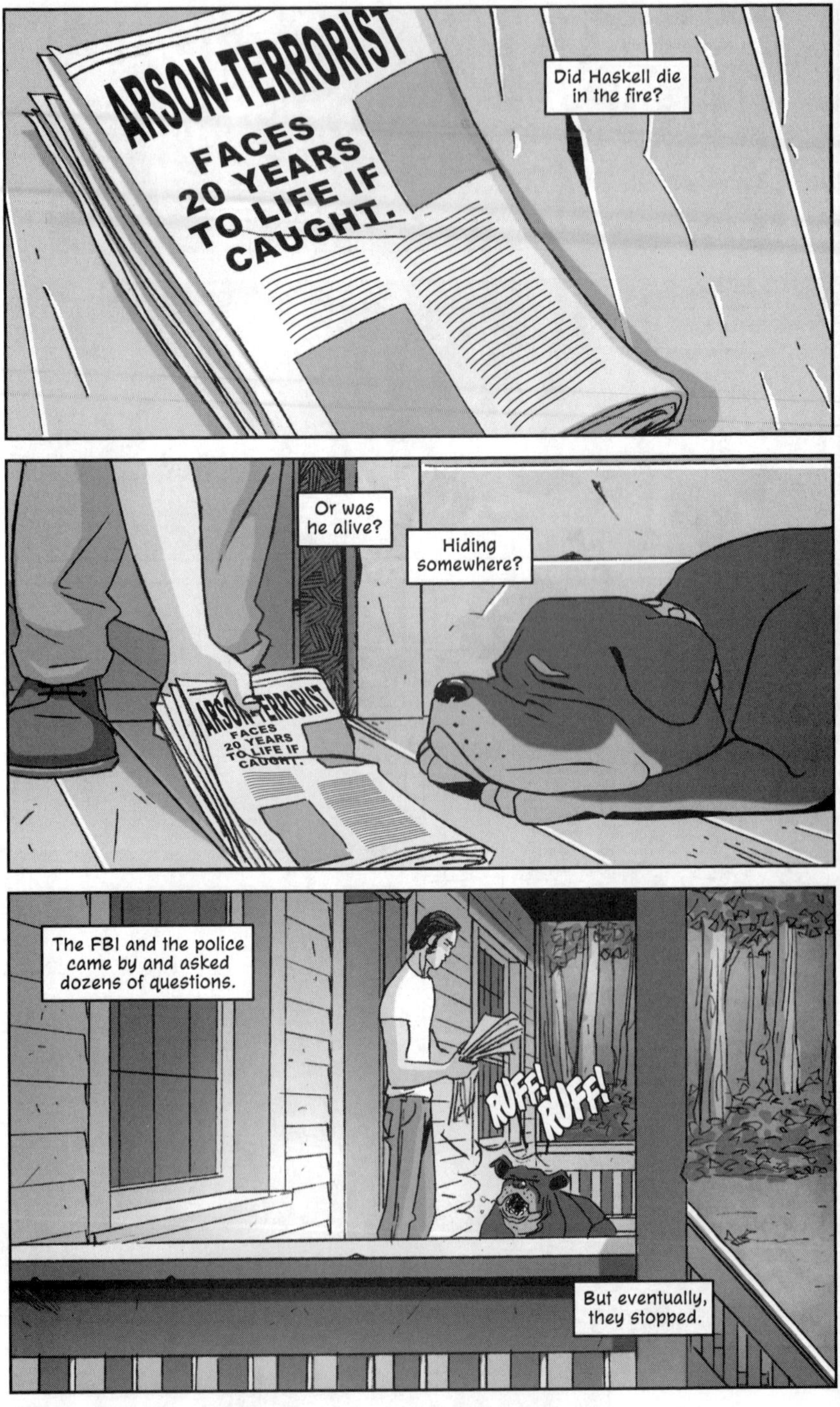
ARSON-TERRORIST
FACES 20 YEARS TO LIFE IF CAUGHT.
Did Haskell die in the fire?
Or was he alive?
Hiding somewhere?
ARSON-TERRORIST
FACES 20 YEARS TO LIFE IF CAUGHT.
The FBI and the police came by and asked dozens of questions.
RUFF! RUFF!
But eventually, they stopped.

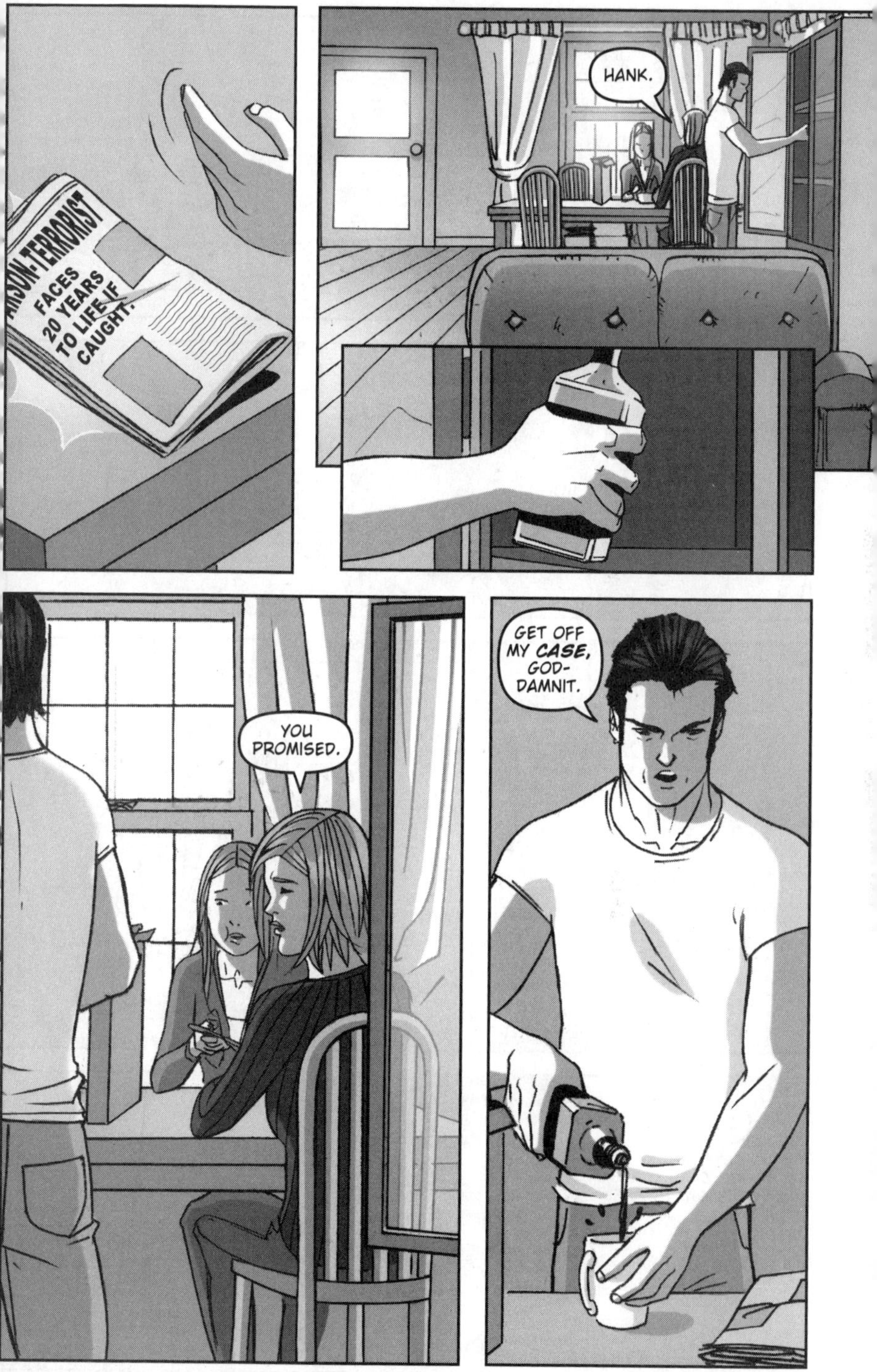
ARSON-TERRORIST
FACES 20 YEARS TO LIFE IF CAUGHT.
HANK.
YOU PROMISED.
GET OFF MY CASE, GOD-DAMNIT.

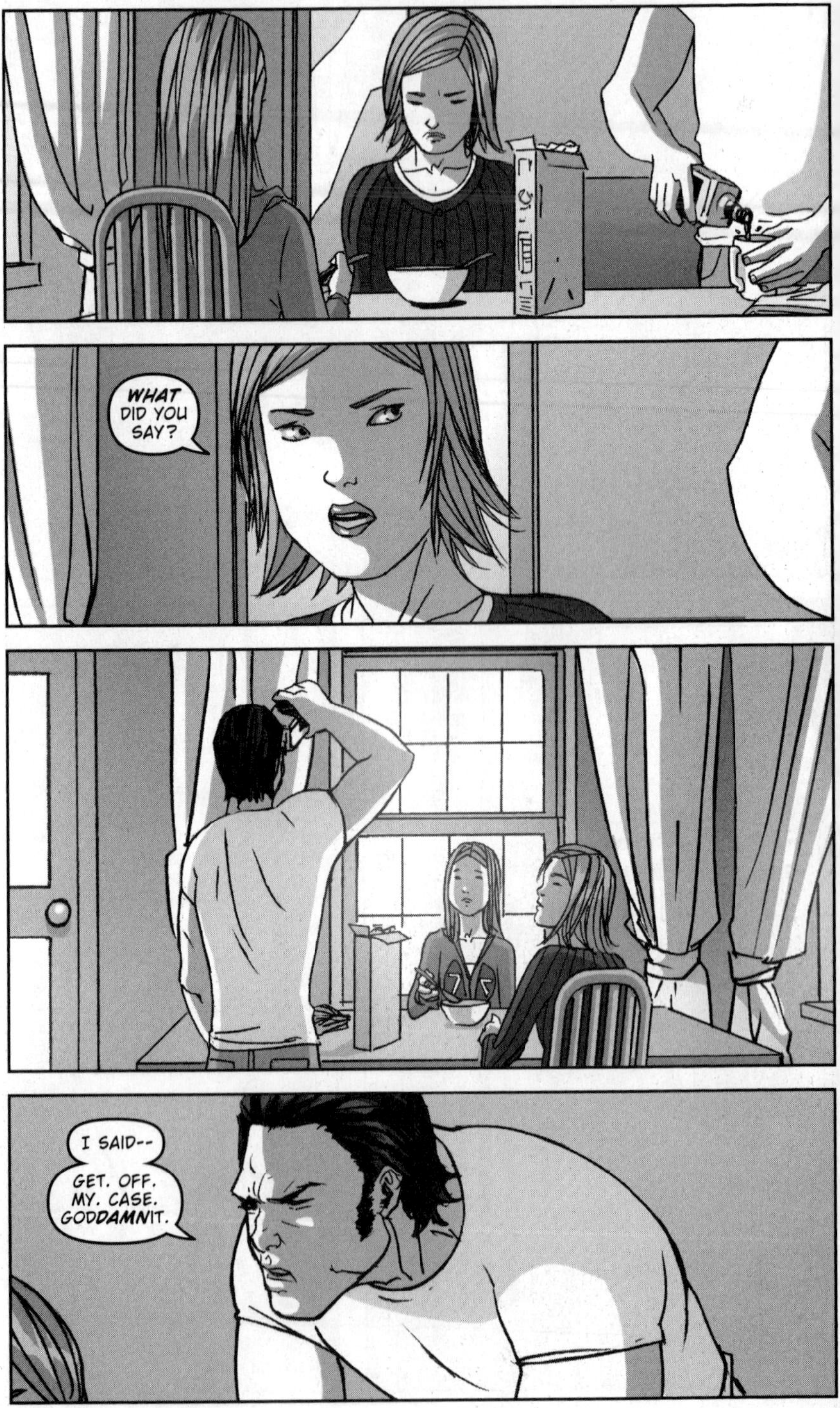
WHAT DID YOU SAY?
I SAID--
GET. OFF. MY. CASE. GODDAMNIT.

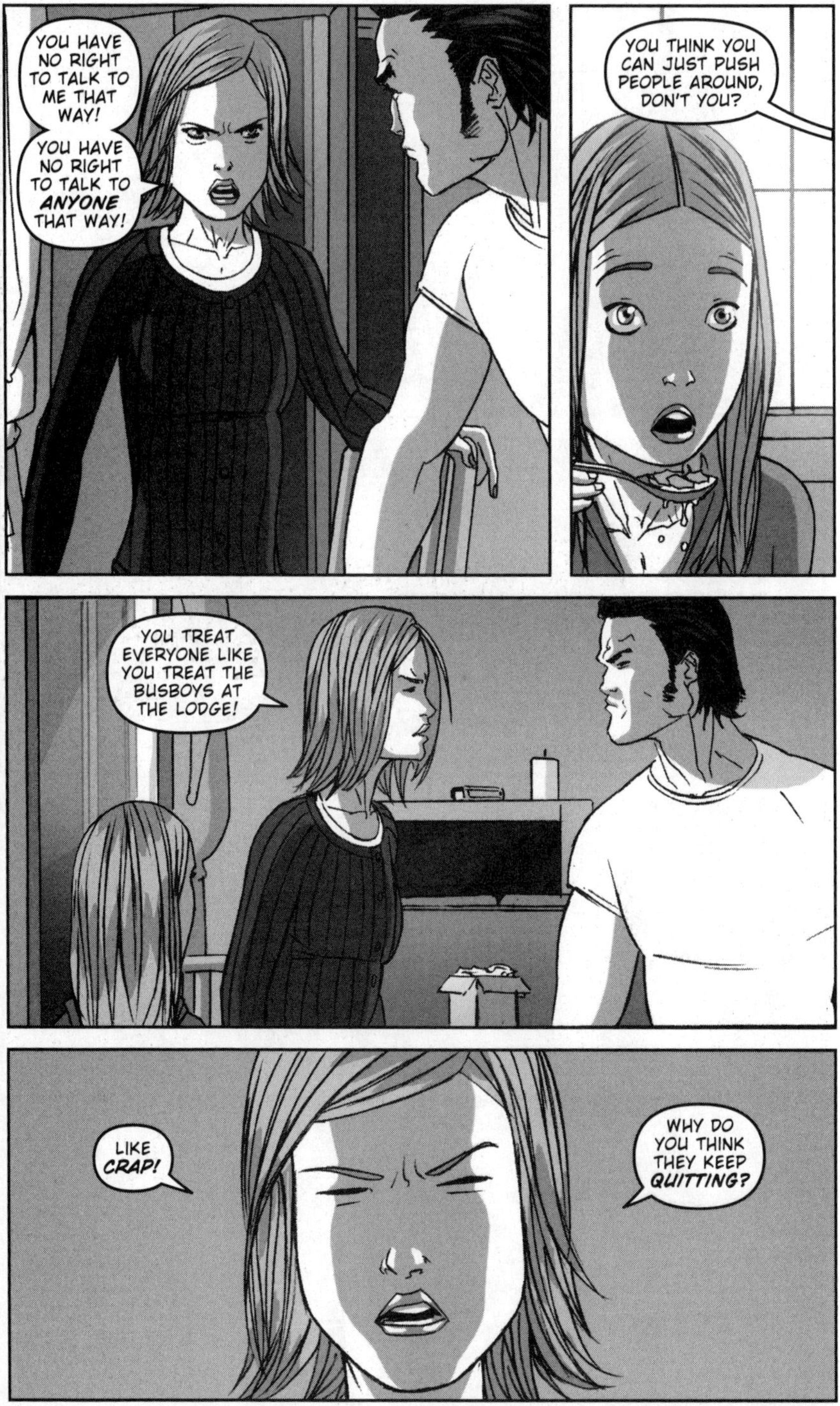
YOU HAVE NO RIGHT TO TALK TO ME THAT WAY!
YOU HAVE NO RIGHT TO TALK TO ANYONE THAT WAY!
YOU THINK YOU CAN JUST PUSH PEOPLE AROUND, DON'T YOU?
YOU TREAT EVERYONE LIKE YOU TREAT THE BUSBOYS AT THE LODGE!
LIKE CRAP!
WHY DO YOU THINK THEY KEEP QUITTING?

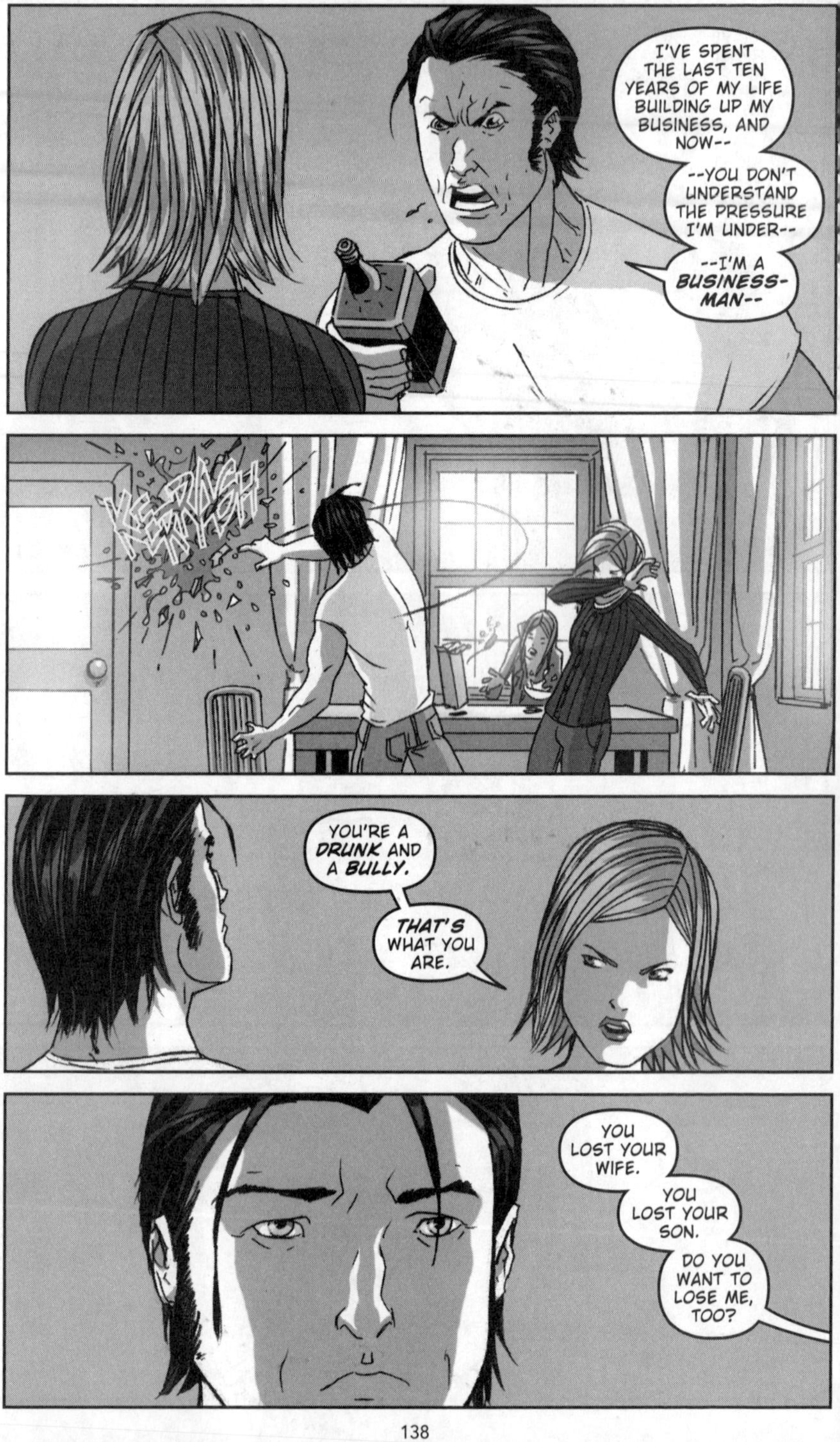

I'VE SPENT THE LAST TEN YEARS OF MY LIFE BUILDING UP MY BUSINESS, AND NOW--
--YOU DON'T UNDERSTAND THE PRESSURE I'M UNDER--
--I'M A *BUSINESS-MAN*--
YOU'RE A *DRUNK* AND A *BULLY.*
THAT'S WHAT YOU ARE.
YOU LOST YOUR WIFE.
YOU LOST YOUR SON.
DO YOU WANT TO LOSE ME, TOO?

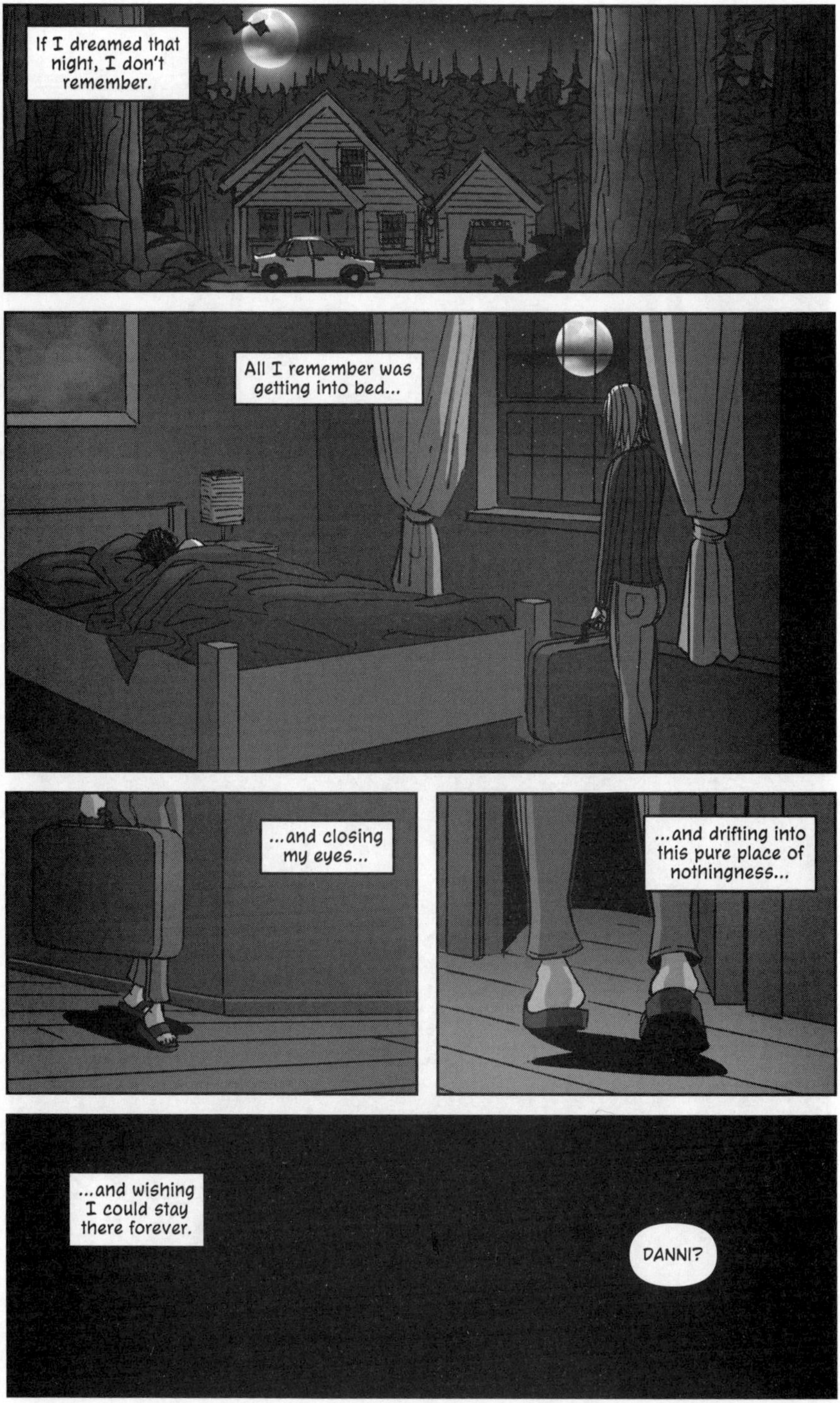
If I dreamed that night, I don't remember.
All I remember was getting into bed...
...and closing my eyes...
...and drifting into this pure place of nothingness...
...and wishing I could stay there forever.
DANNI?

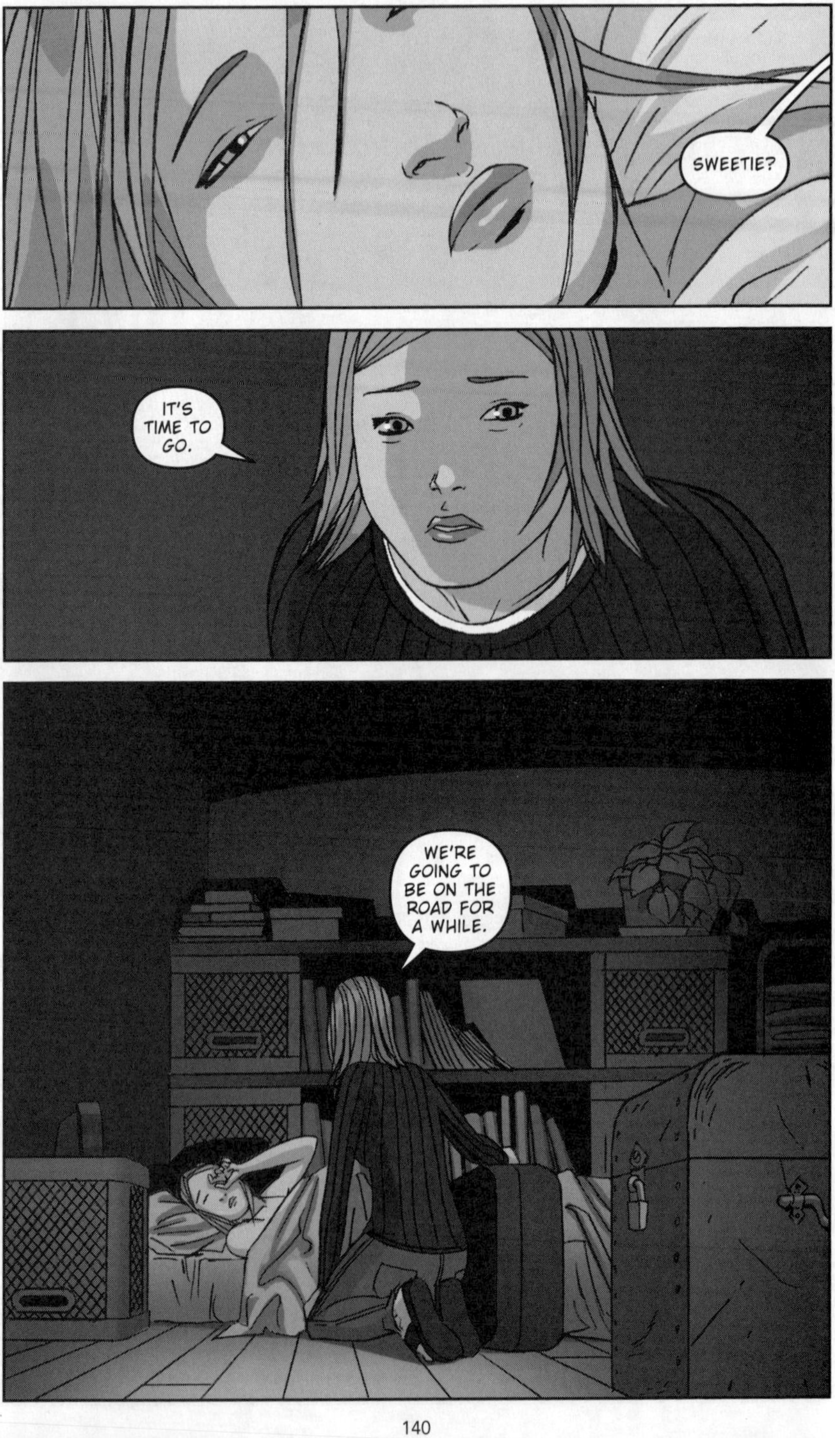
SWEETIE?
IT'S TIME TO GO.
WE'RE GOING TO BE ON THE ROAD FOR A WHILE.

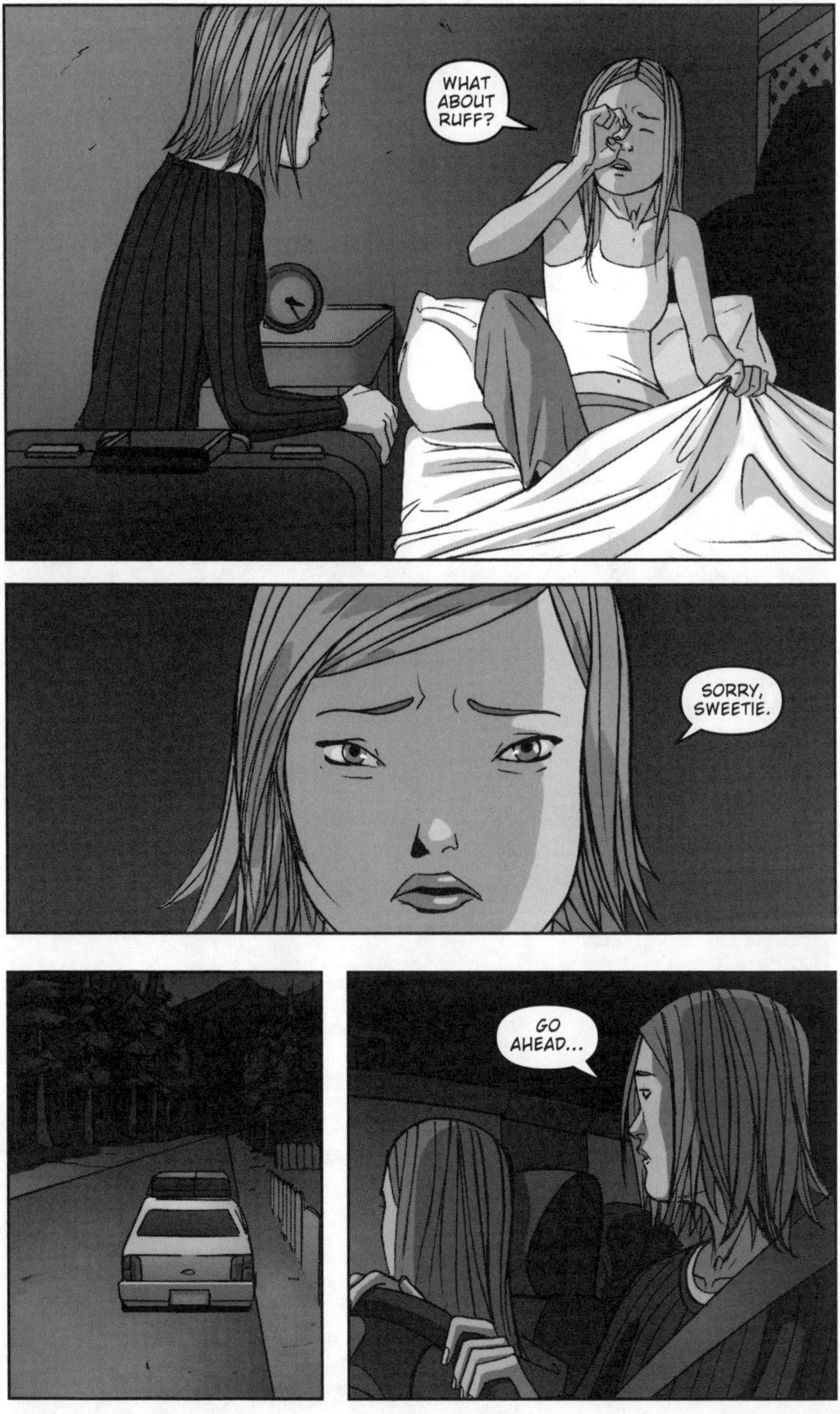
WHAT ABOUT RUFF?
SORRY, SWEETIE.
GO AHEAD...

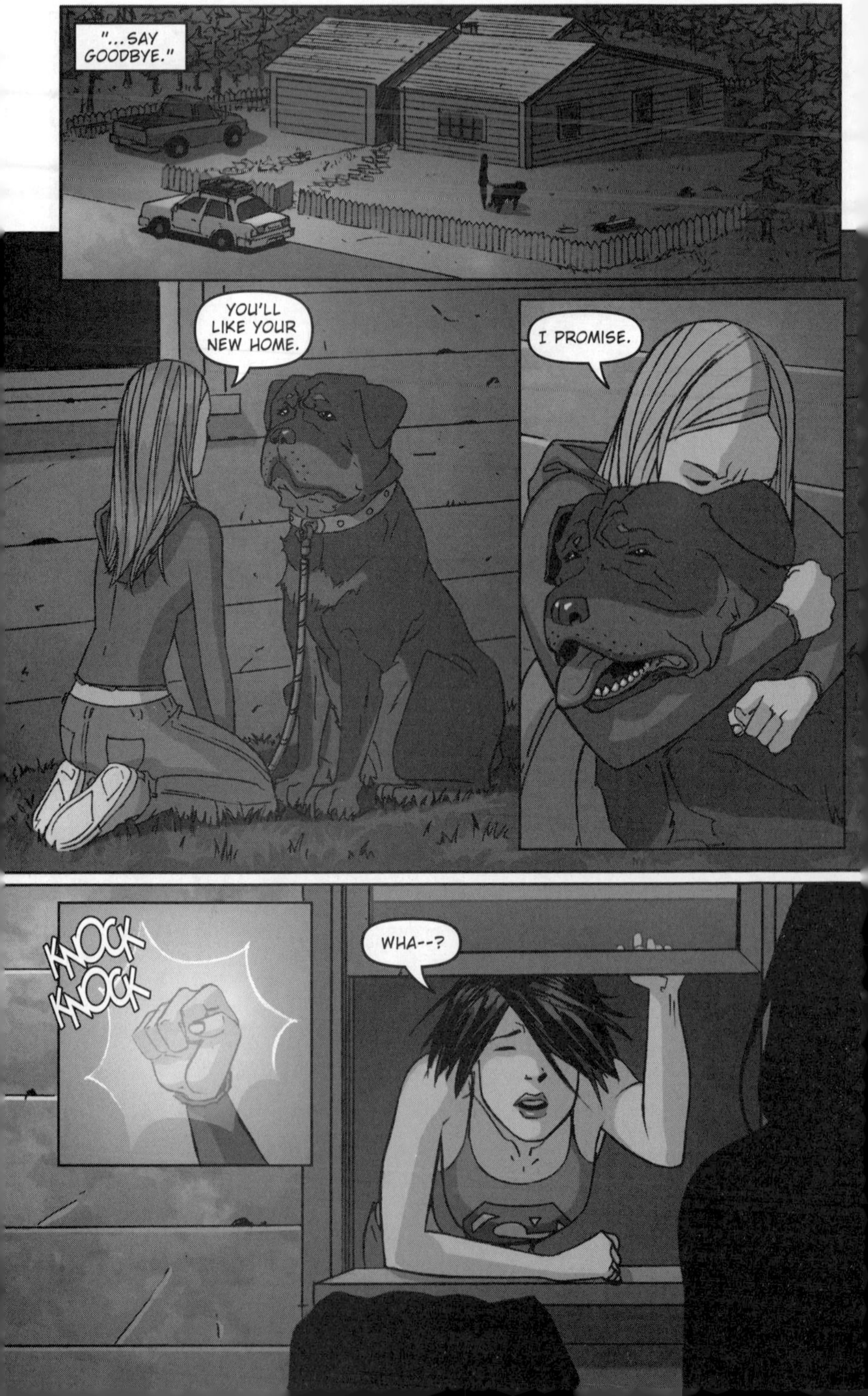
"...SAY GOODBYE."
YOU'LL LIKE YOUR NEW HOME.
I PROMISE.
KNOCK KNOCK
WHA--?

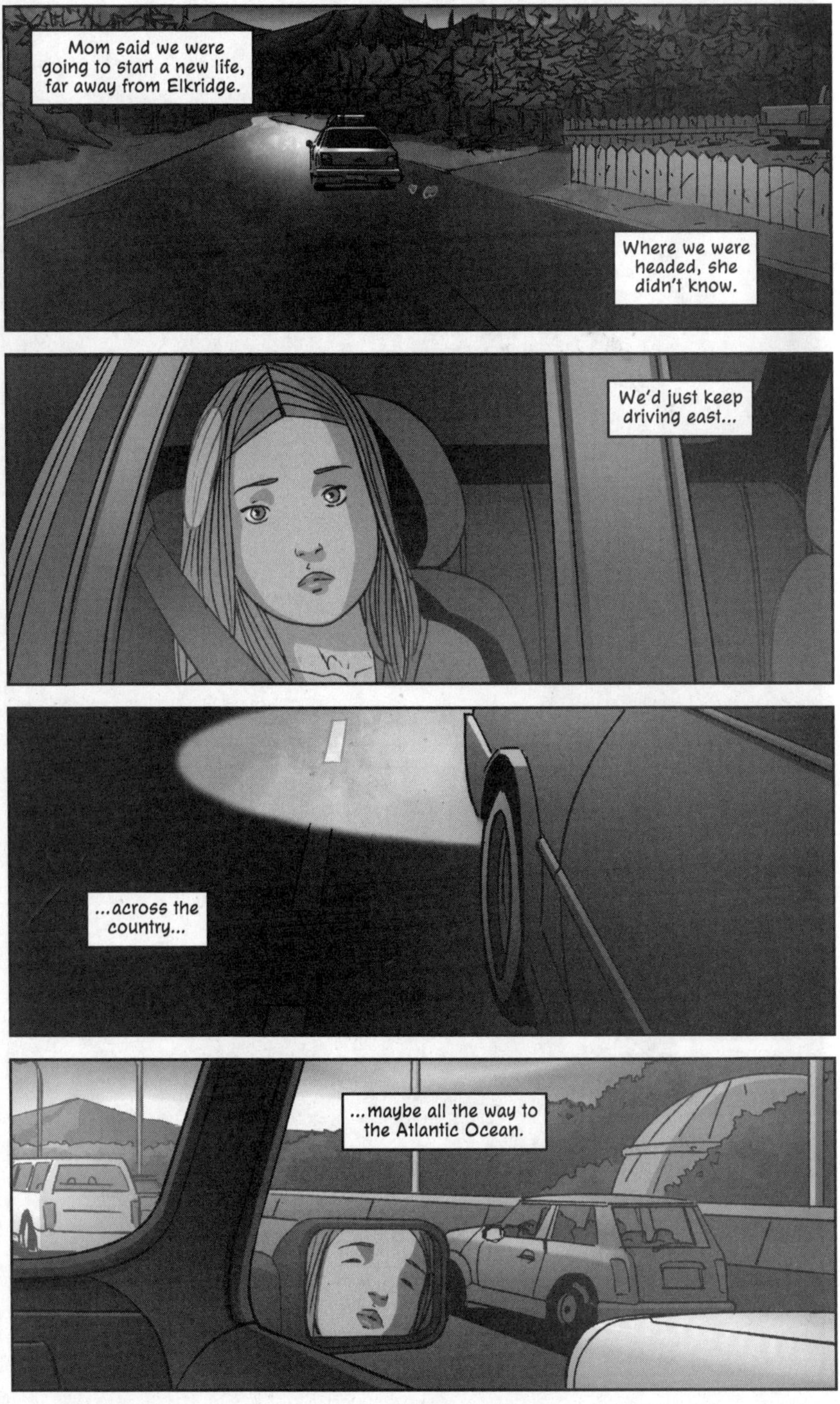
Mom said we were going to start a new life, far away from Elkridge.
Where we were headed, she didn't know.
We'd just keep driving east...
...across the country...
...maybe all the way to the Atlantic Ocean.

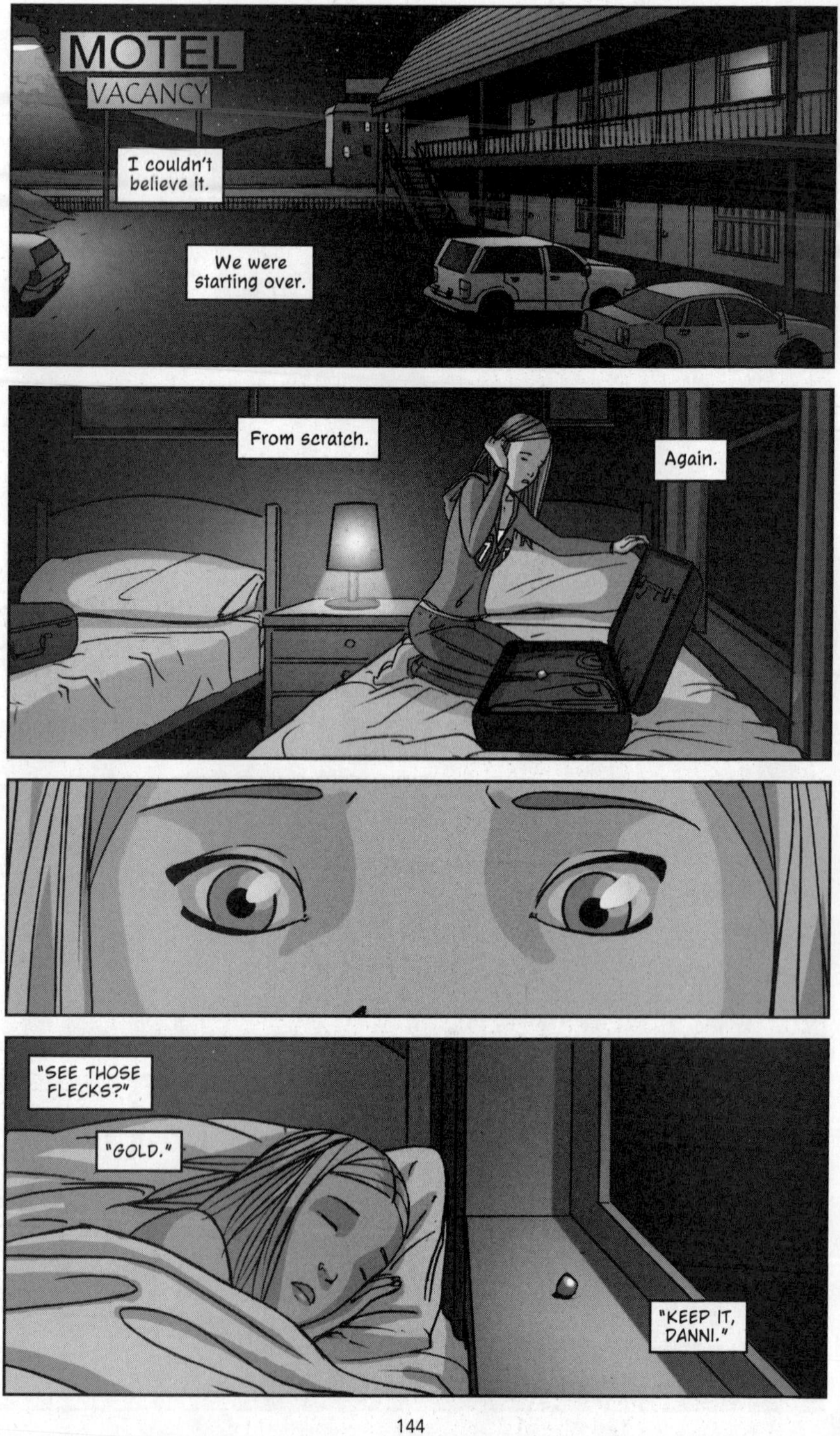
MOTEL
VACANCY
I couldn't believe it.
We were starting over.
From scratch.
Again.
"SEE THOSE FLECKS?"
"GOLD."
"KEEP IT, DANNI."

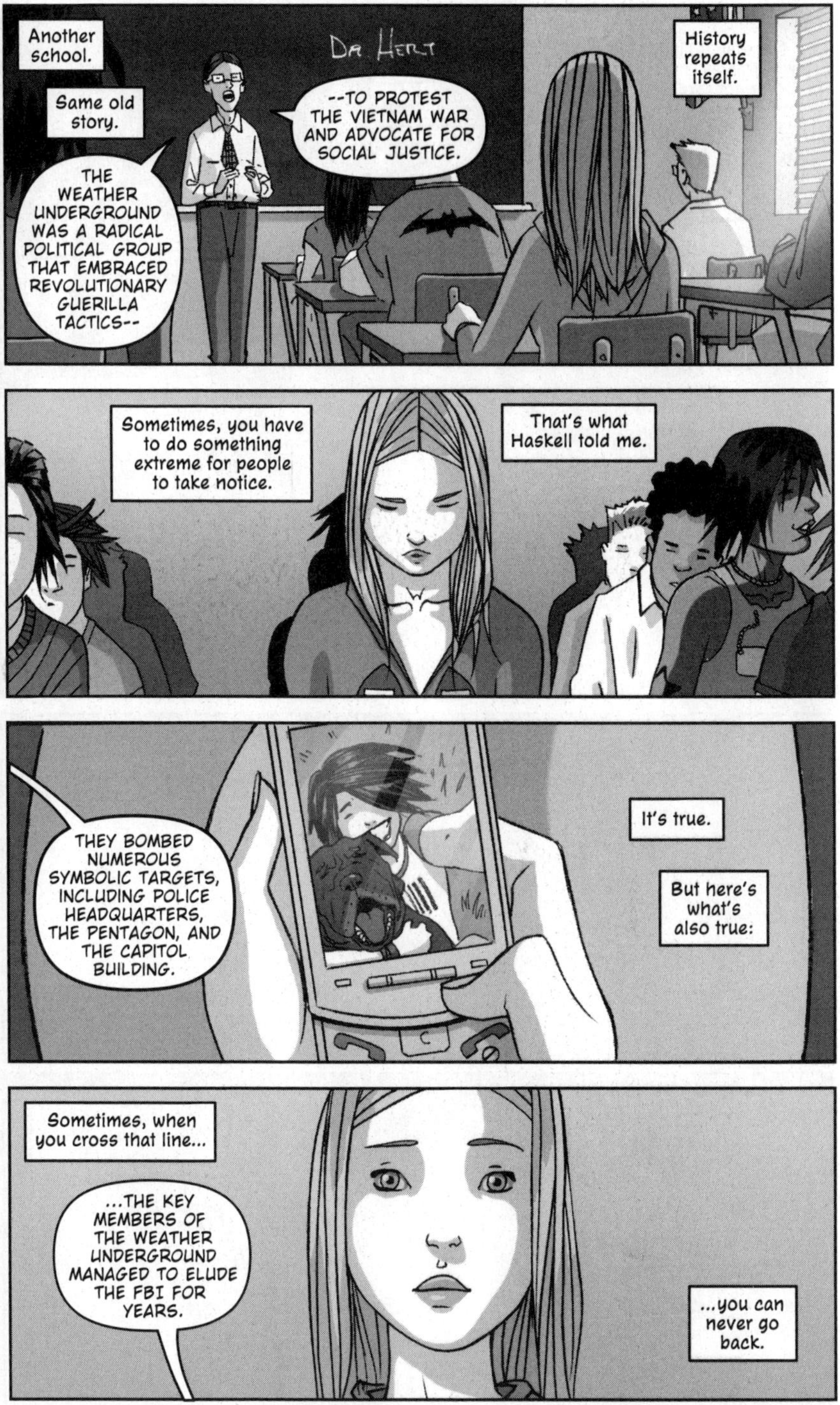

Another school.
Same old story.
DR. HERLT
--TO PROTEST THE VIETNAM WAR AND ADVOCATE FOR SOCIAL JUSTICE.
History repeats itself.
THE WEATHER UNDERGROUND WAS A RADICAL POLITICAL GROUP THAT EMBRACED REVOLUTIONARY GUERILLA TACTICS--
Sometimes, you have to do something extreme for people to take notice.
That's what Haskell told me.
THEY BOMBED NUMEROUS SYMBOLIC TARGETS, INCLUDING POLICE HEADQUARTERS, THE PENTAGON, AND THE CAPITOL BUILDING.
It's true.
But here's what's also true:
Sometimes, when you cross that line...
...THE KEY MEMBERS OF THE WEATHER UNDERGROUND MANAGED TO ELUDE THE FBI FOR YEARS.
...you can never go back.

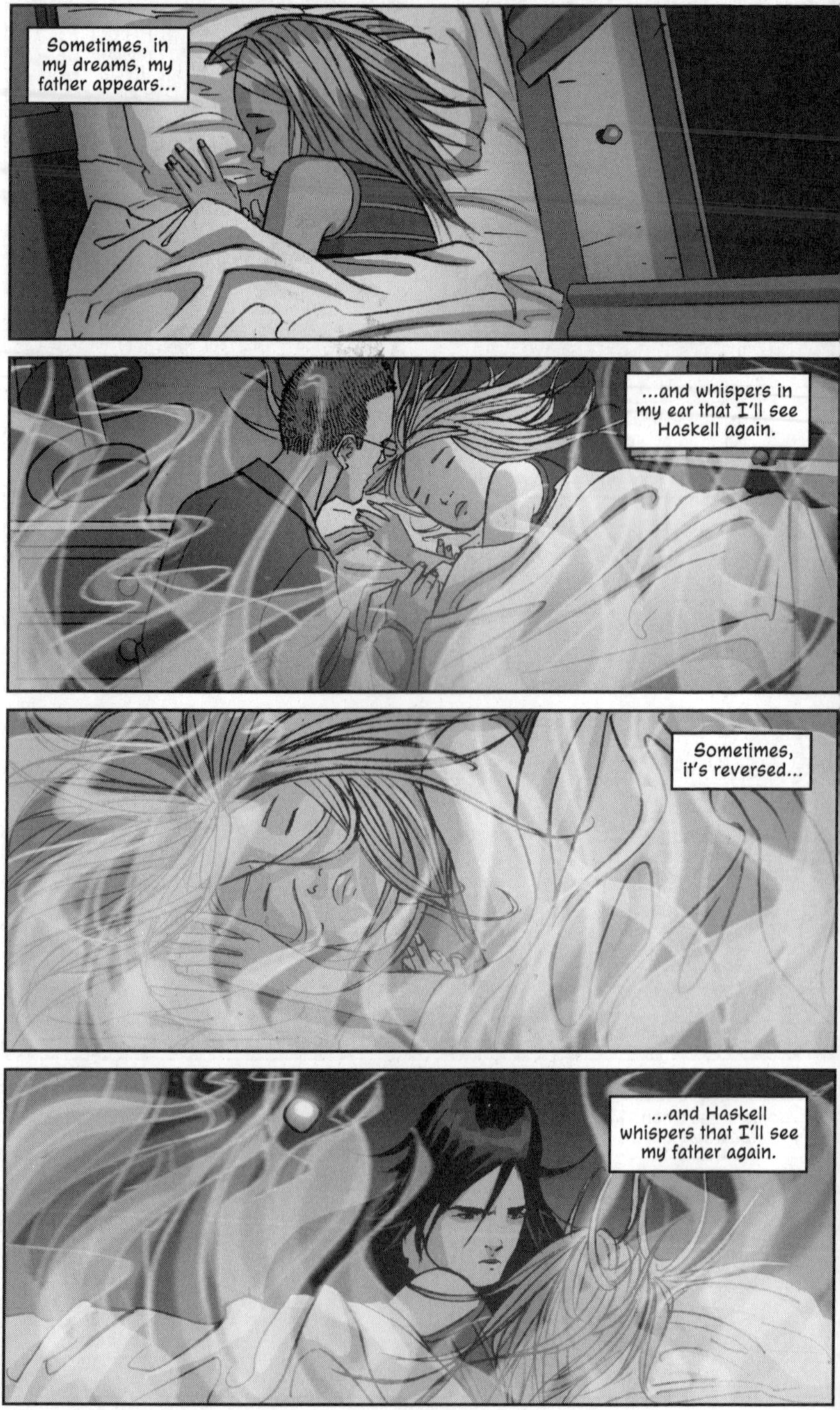

Sometimes, in my dreams, my father appears...
...and whispers in my ear that I'll see Haskell again.
Sometimes, it's reversed...
...and Haskell whispers that I'll see my father again.

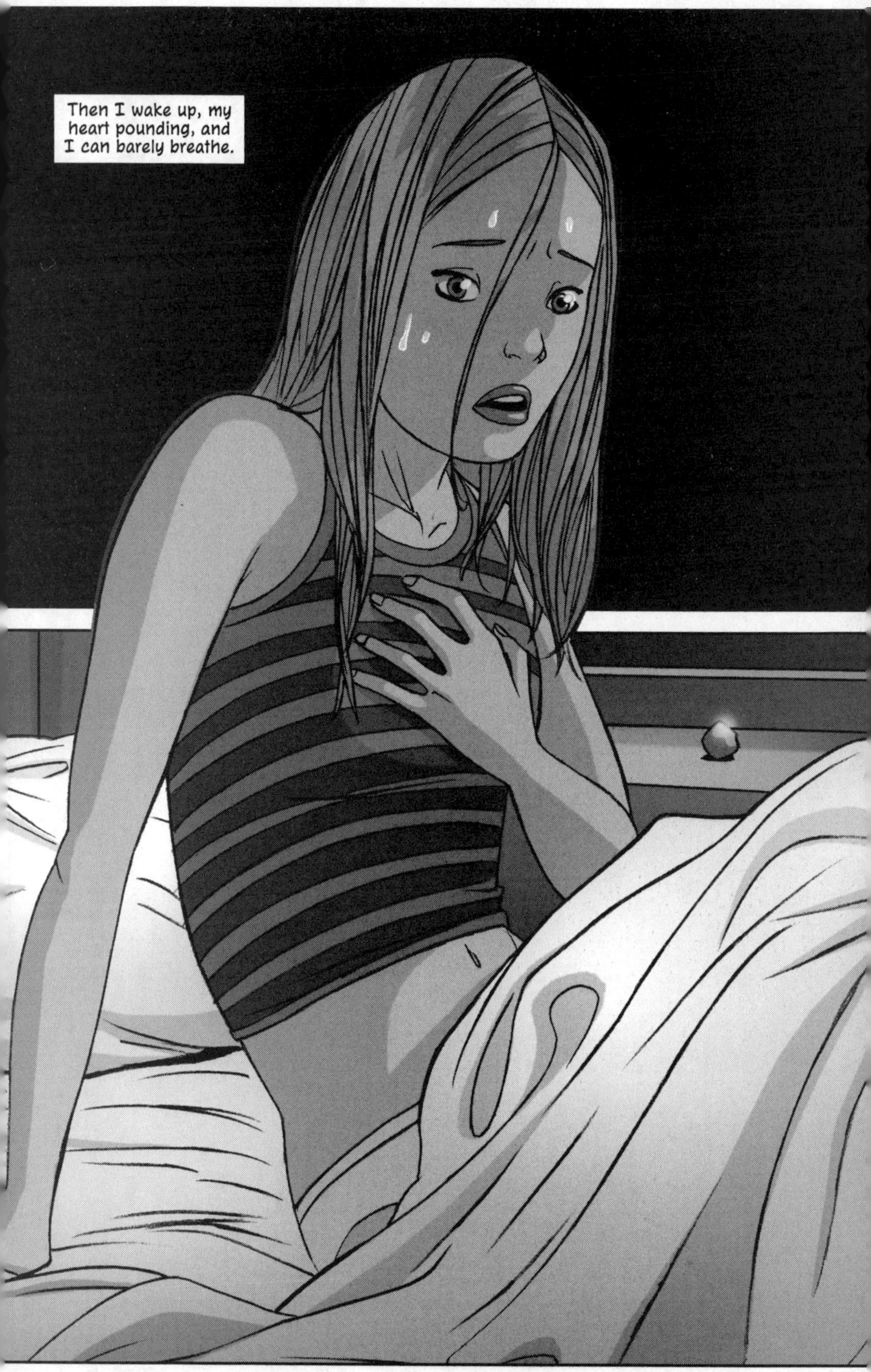
Then I wake up, my heart pounding, and I can barely breathe.

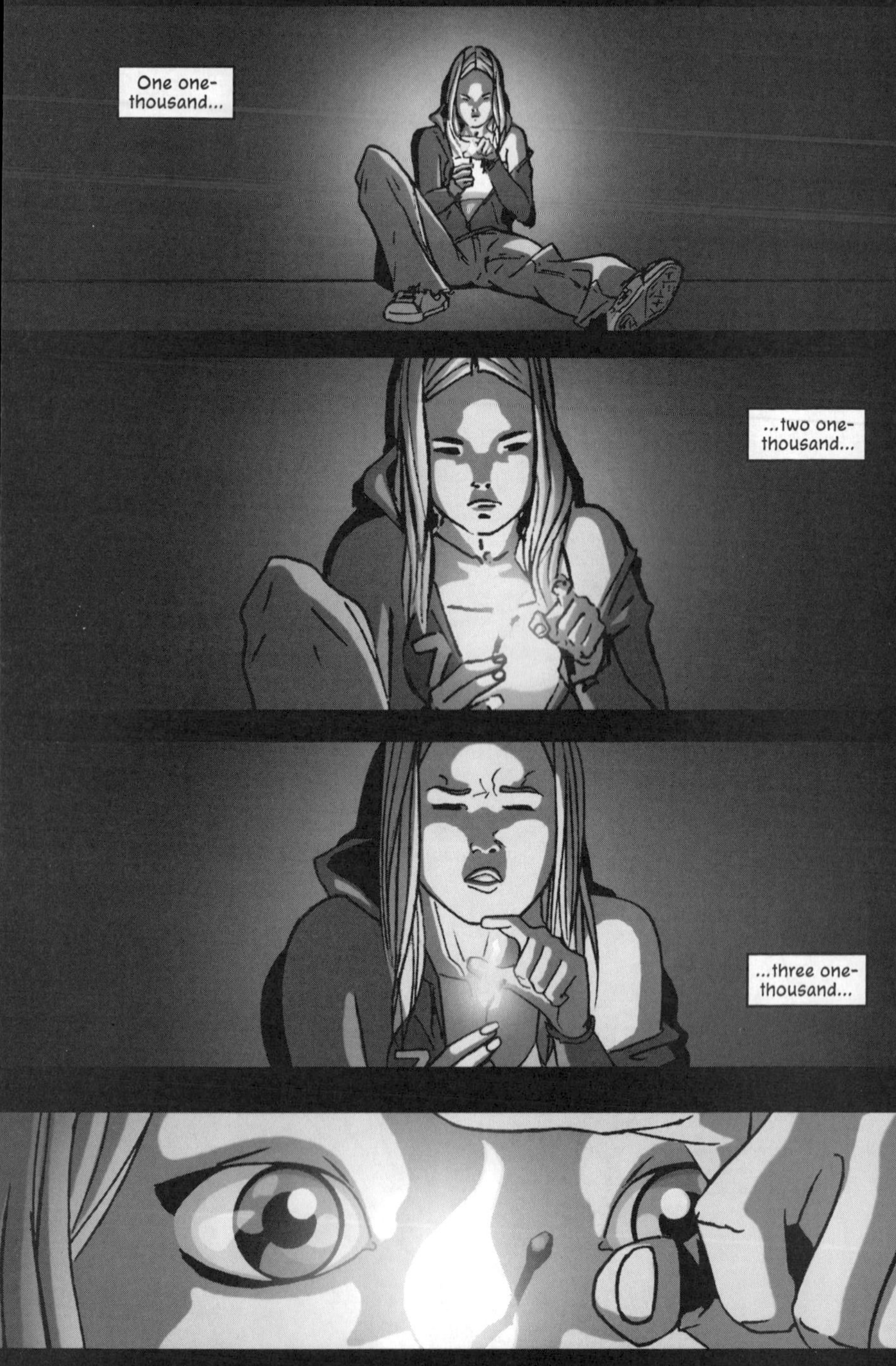
One one-
thousand...
...two one-
thousand...
...three one-
thousand...

REBECCA DONNER

Rebecca was born in Canada but grew up in a Section 8 apartment building in Los Angeles, an experience that inspired her critically acclaimed novel *Sunset Terrace*. Her stories, book reviews, and essays have appeared in numerous publications, and she has taught writing at Wesleyan and Barnard. Rebecca also wrote and directed two short films, wrote three plays that were produced in Los Angeles and New York, sings in a rock band, and is actively resisting the ridiculous notion that you have to focus on one thing in life. She lives in the East Village in New York City and is writing her third novel.

INAKI MIRANDA

Inaki was born in Argentina, spent part of his childhood in California and finally established his bones in Madrid, Spain, where he attended the Complutense University and earned a degree in fine arts. After testing the waters of animation and videogames, he made himself a place in the comics industry by illustrating *2000AD*'s *Judge Dredd*, *The Lexian Chronicles*, *The Chase* and a story in VERTIGO'S multiple Eisner Award-winning series FABLES. He likes long walks in the rain and popping bubble wrap whenever he gets the chance.

EVA DE LA CRUZ

Having acquired experience from working in the animation and videogame industries, Eva made her professional comics debut in the pages of *2000AD* coloring *Judge Dredd*. She also colored a *Judge Dredd* strip which ran for six months in UK's *Metro* newspaper. Eva currently resides in the Spanish capital but would happily renounce the chaotic streets of Madrid for the abundant beauty of the Northern Canadian wilderness.

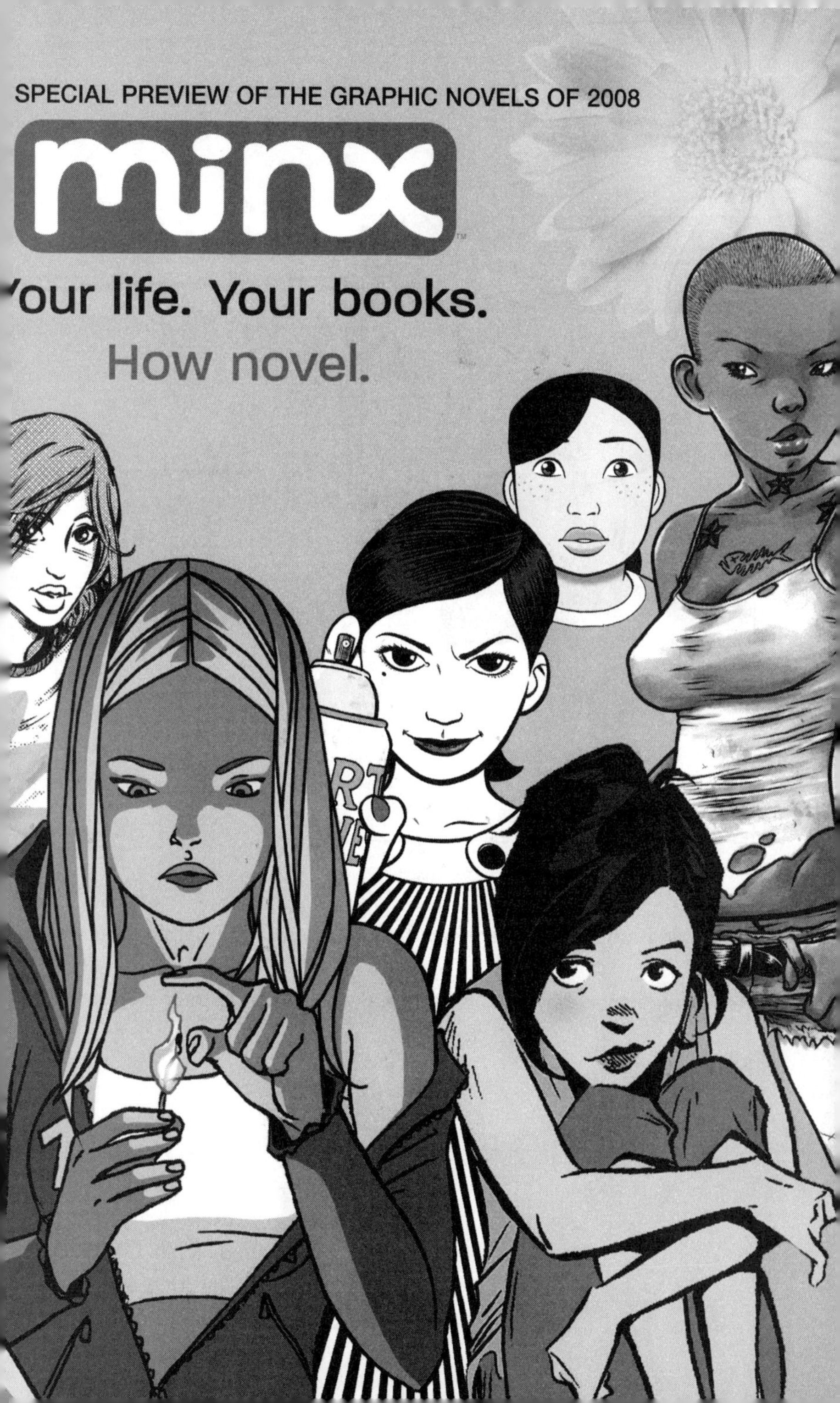
SPECIAL PREVIEW OF THE GRAPHIC NOVELS OF 2008
minx
Your life. Your books.
How novel.

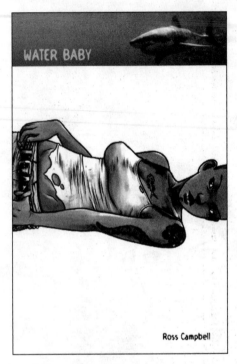

WATER BABY

Ross Campbell

By two-time Eisner Award nominee
ROSS CAMPBELL

Surfer girl Brody just got her leg bitten off by a shark. What's worse?

Her shark of an ex-boyfriend is back, and when it comes to Brody's couch,

he's not budging.

By ROSS CAMPBELL
AVAILABLE IN JUNE ∎ Read on.
But please note: The following pages are not sequential.

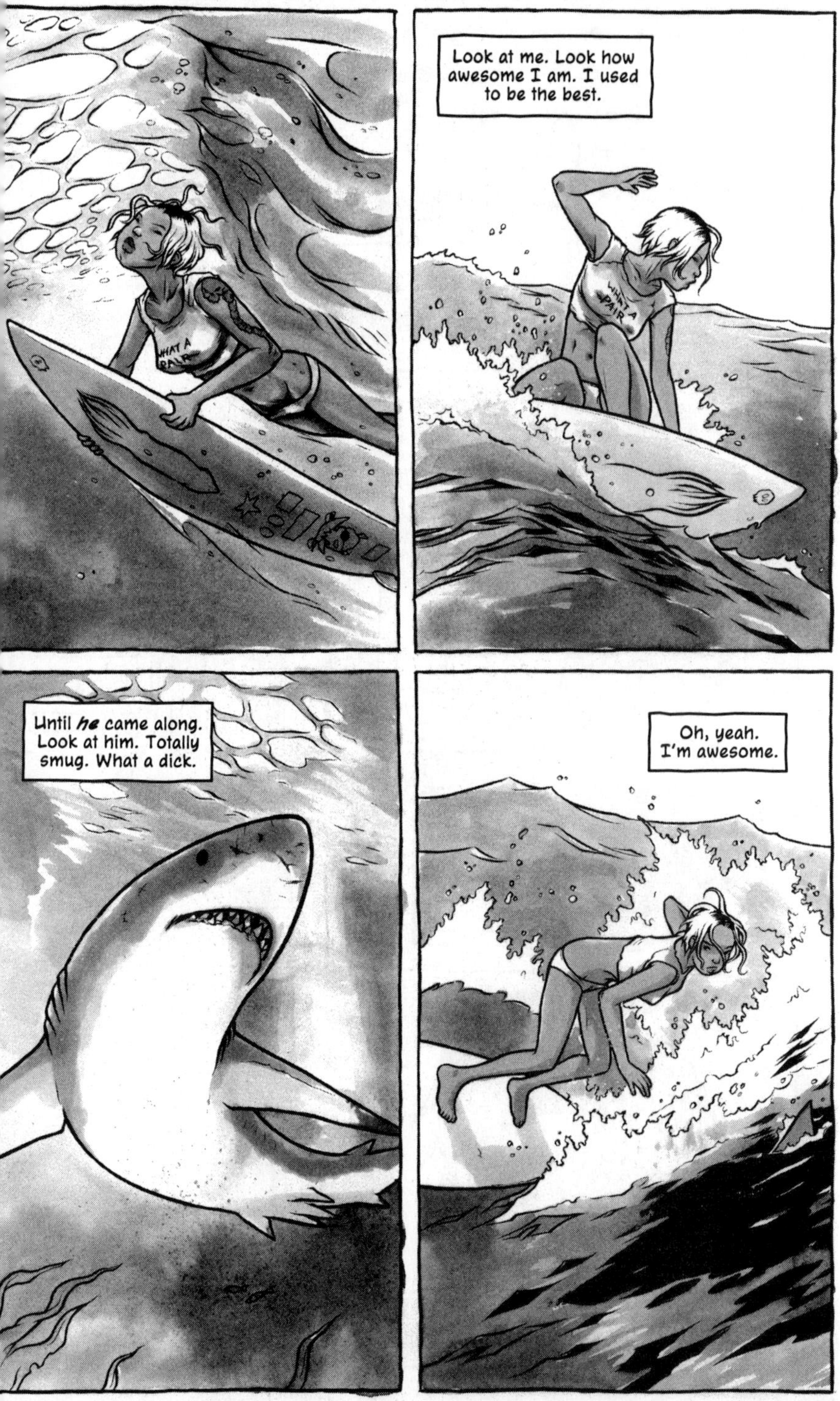
WHAT A PAIR
Look at me. Look how awesome I am. I used to be the best.
WHAT A PAIR
Until *he* came along. Look at him. Totally smug. What a dick.
Oh, yeah. I'm awesome.

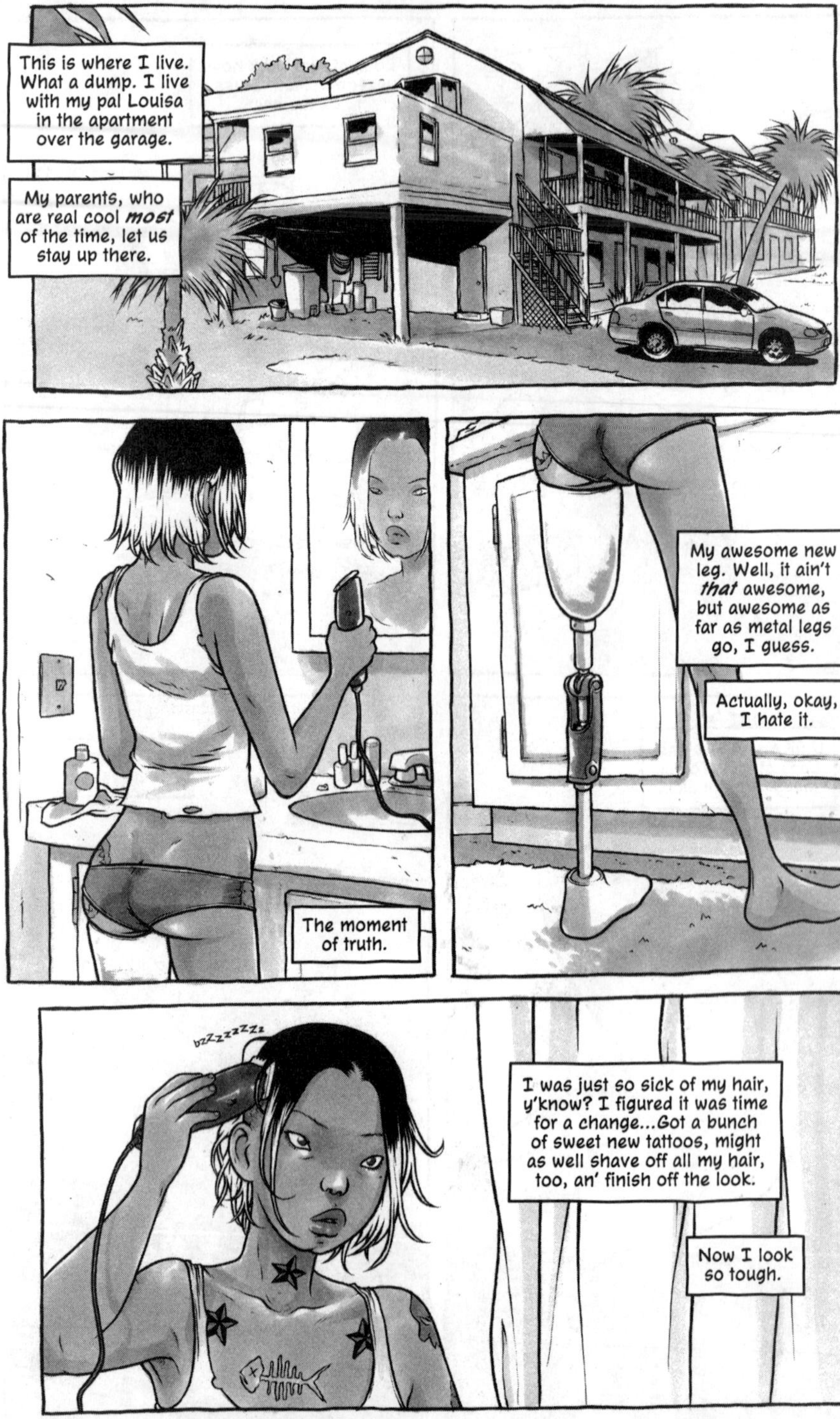
This is where I live. What a dump. I live with my pal Louisa in the apartment over the garage.
My parents, who are real cool *most* of the time, let us stay up there.
The moment of truth.
My awesome new leg. Well, it ain't *that* awesome, but awesome as far as metal legs go, I guess.
Actually, okay, I hate it.
bzzzzzzzz
I was just so sick of my hair, y'know? I figured it was time for a change...Got a bunch of sweet new tattoos, might as well shave off all my hair, too, an' finish off the look.
Now I look so tough.

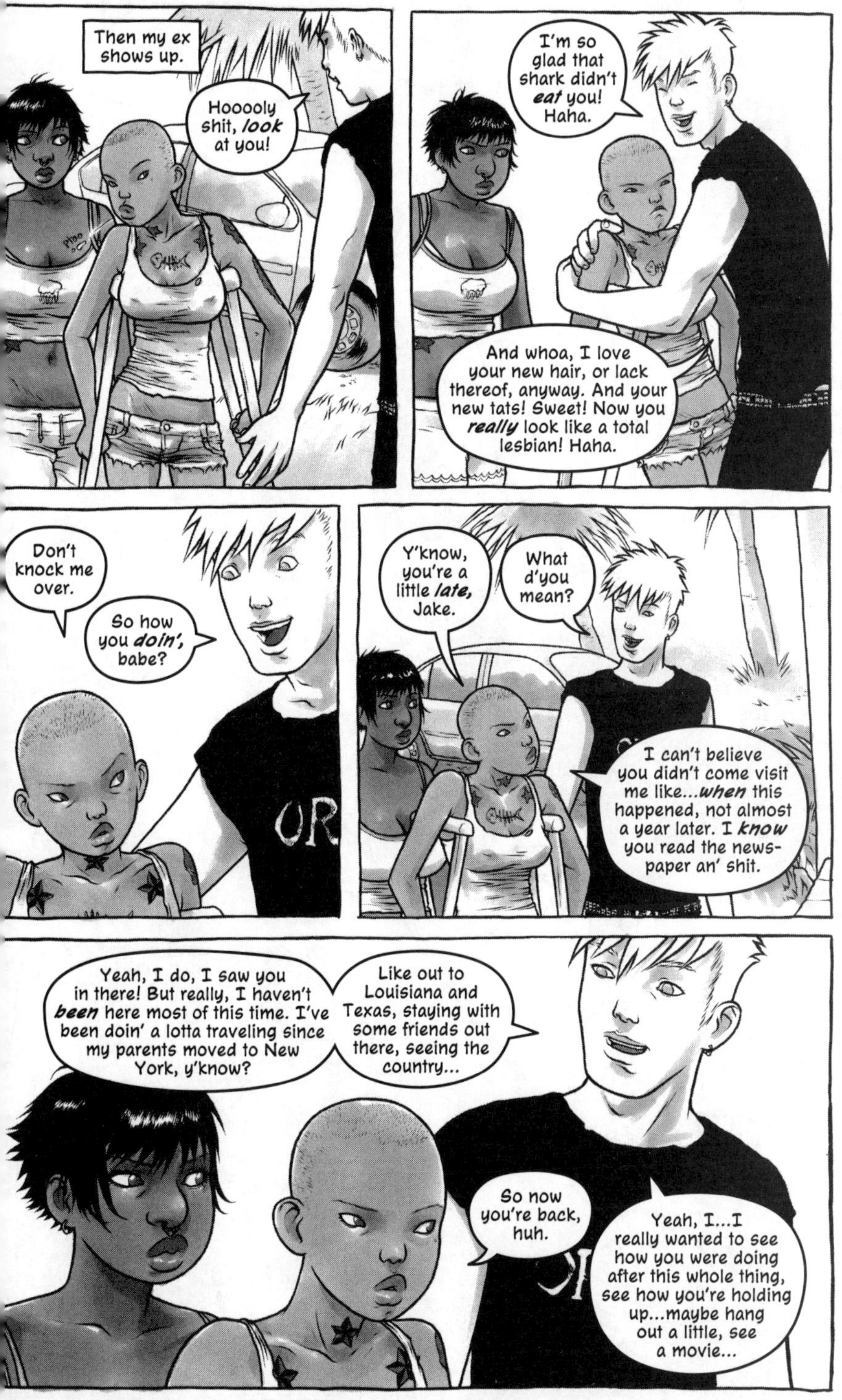
Then my ex shows up.
Hoooooly shit, *look* at you!
I'm so glad that shark didn't *eat* you! Haha.
And whoa, I love your new hair, or lack thereof, anyway. And your new tats! Sweet! Now you *really* look like a total lesbian! Haha.
Don't knock me over.
So how you *doin',* babe?
Y'know, you're a little *late,* Jake.
What d'you mean?
I can't believe you didn't come visit me like...*when* this happened, not almost a year later. I *know* you read the news-paper an' shit.
Yeah, I do, I saw you in there! But really, I haven't *been* here most of this time. I've been doin' a lotta traveling since my parents moved to New York, y'know?
Like out to Louisiana and Texas, staying with some friends out there, seeing the country...
So now you're back, huh.
Yeah, I...I really wanted to see how you were doing after this whole thing, see how you're holding up...maybe hang out a little, see a movie...

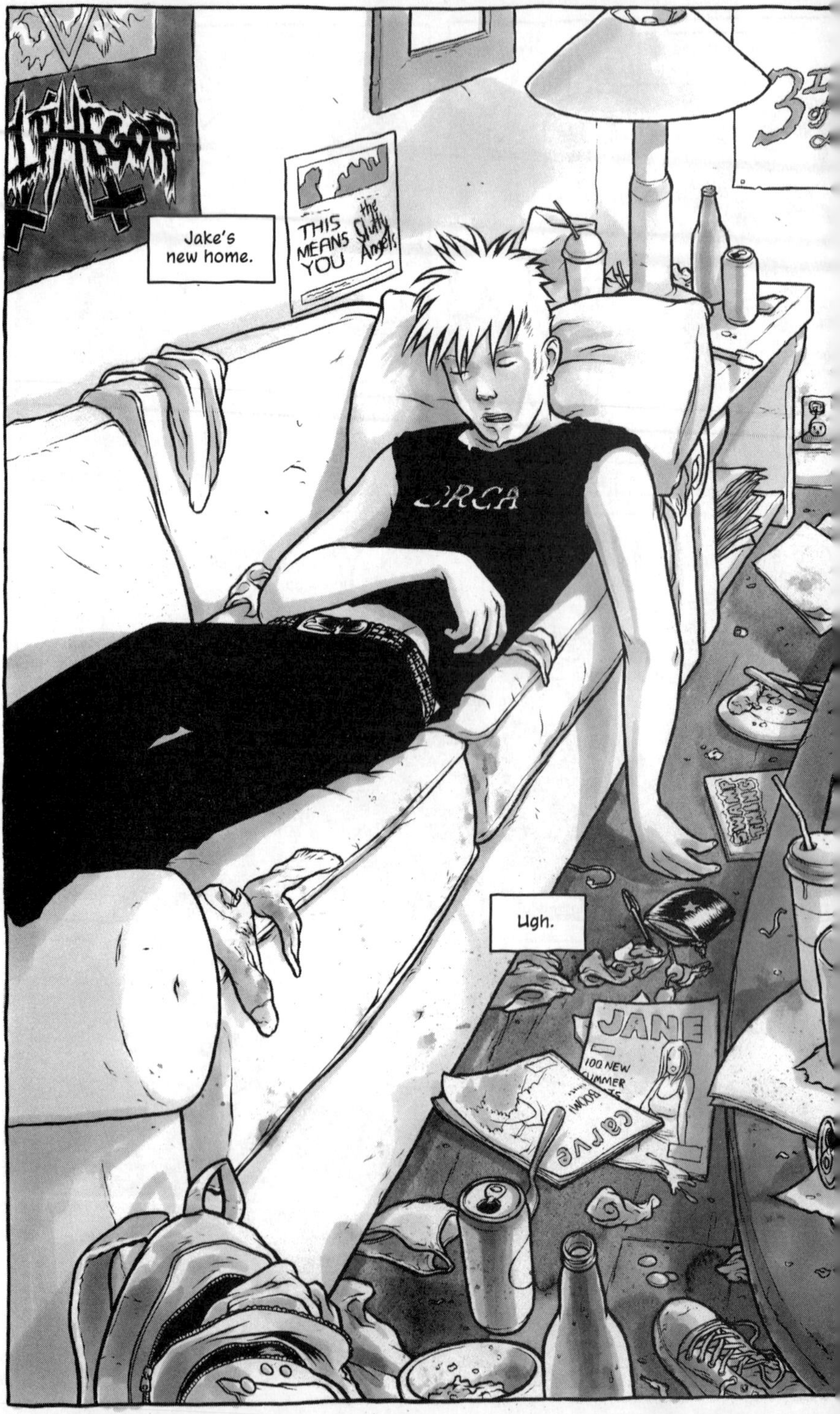
Jake's new home.
THIS MEANS YOU
the Slutty Angels
ORCA
Ugh.
JANE
100 NEW SUMMER
carve

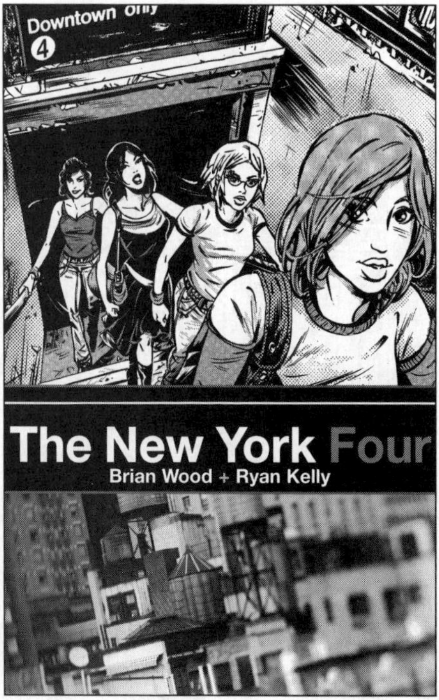
Downtown Only
4
The New York Four
Brian Wood + Ryan Kelly

Written by multiple Eisner Award nominee/Indie icon BRIAN WOOD

Experience New York City through the eyes of Riley, a shy, almost reclusive straight-A student who convinces three other NYU freshmen to join a research group to earn extra money.

As the girls become fast friends, two things complicate what should be the greatest time of Riley's life: connecting with her arty, estranged older sister and having a mysterious online crush on a guy known only as "sneakerfreak."

Will Riley be able to balance new relationships with academics and her stuffy literati parents as the intensity of her secret romance threatens to unravel everything?

By BRIAN WOOD & RYAN KELLY

AVAILABLE IN JULY ■ Read on.

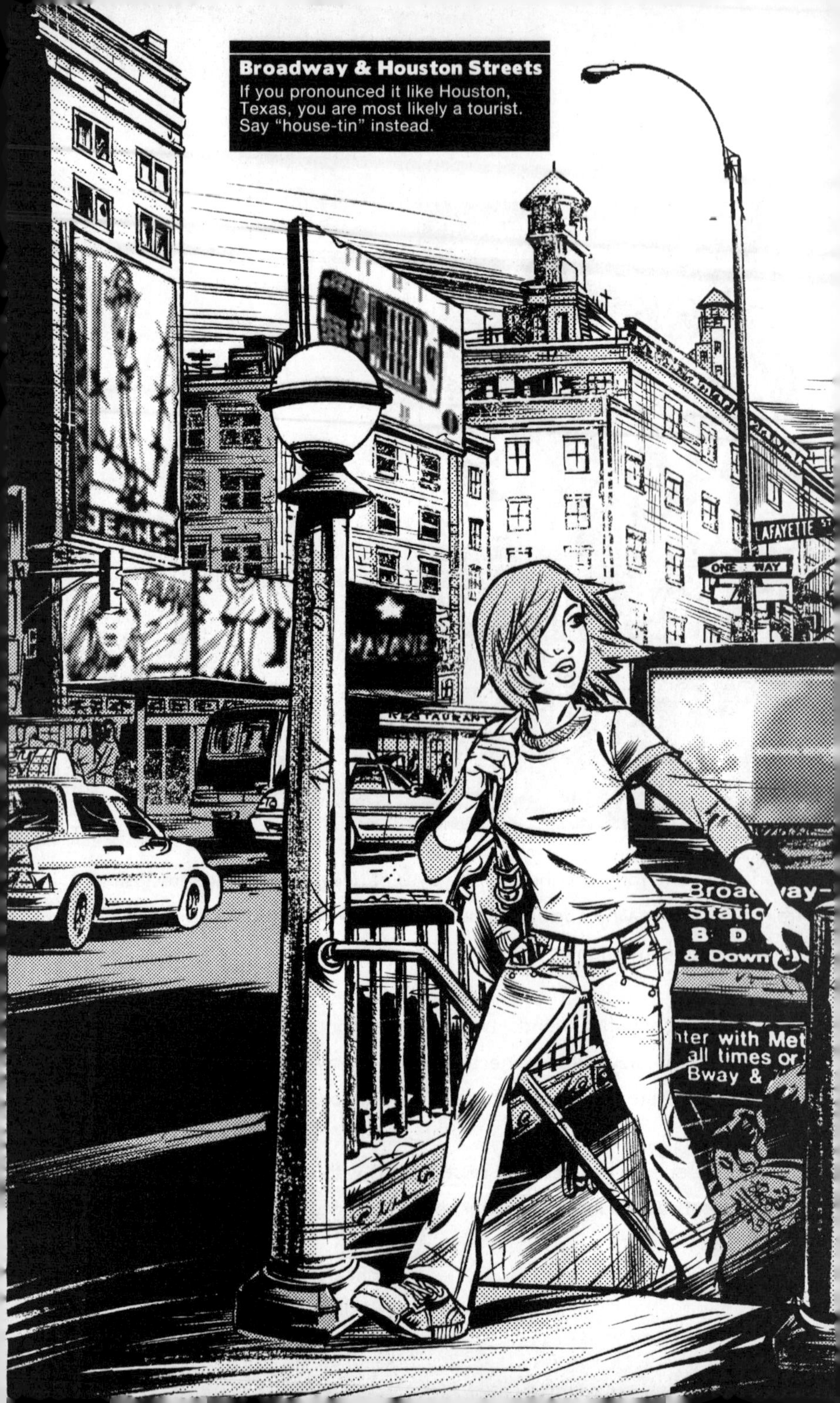
Broadway & Houston Streets
If you pronounced it like Houston, Texas, you are most likely a tourist. Say "house-tin" instead.
JEANS
LAFAYETTE ST
ONE WAY
RESTAURANT
Broadway-
Static
B D
& Down
nter with Met
all times or
Bway &

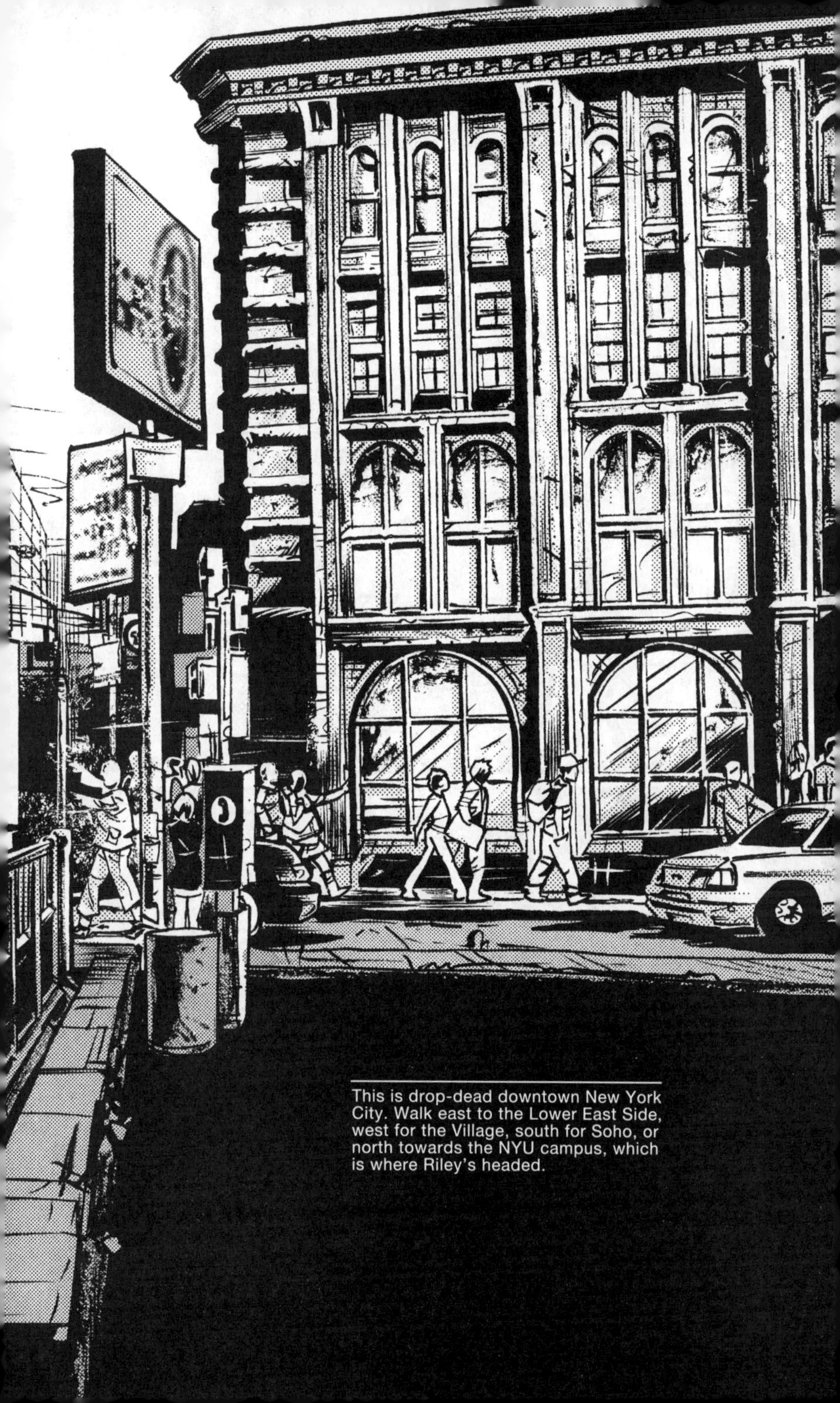
This is drop-dead downtown New York City. Walk east to the Lower East Side, west for the Village, south for Soho, or north towards the NYU campus, which is where Riley's headed.

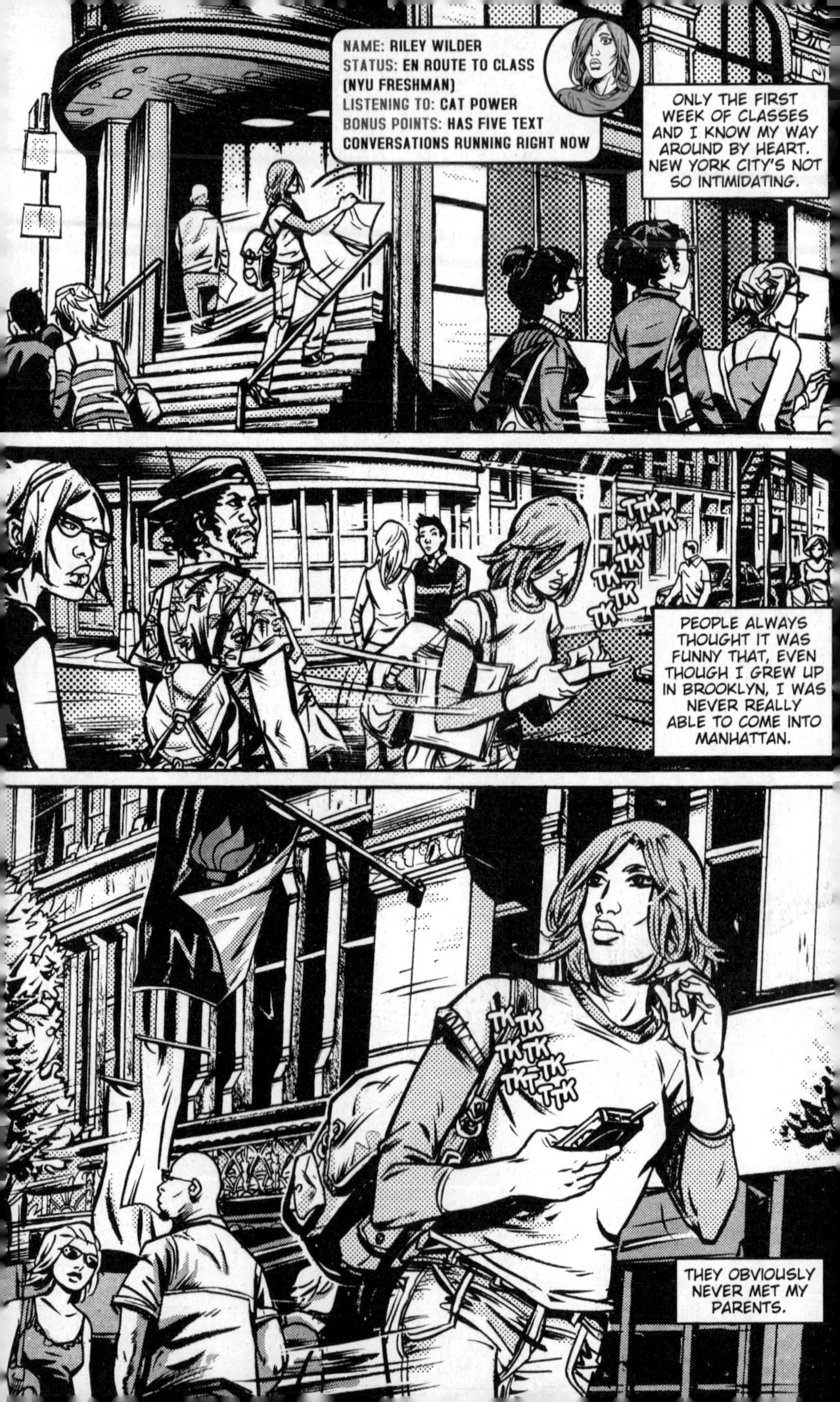
NAME: RILEY WILDER
STATUS: EN ROUTE TO CLASS
(NYU FRESHMAN)
LISTENING TO: CAT POWER
BONUS POINTS: HAS FIVE TEXT
CONVERSATIONS RUNNING RIGHT NOW
ONLY THE FIRST WEEK OF CLASSES AND I KNOW MY WAY AROUND BY HEART. NEW YORK CITY'S NOT SO INTIMIDATING.
TK TK TK TK TK TK TK TK TK
PEOPLE ALWAYS THOUGHT IT WAS FUNNY THAT, EVEN THOUGH I GREW UP IN BROOKLYN, I WAS NEVER REALLY ABLE TO COME INTO MANHATTAN.
TK TK TK TK TK TK TK TK TK
THEY OBVIOUSLY NEVER MET MY PARENTS.

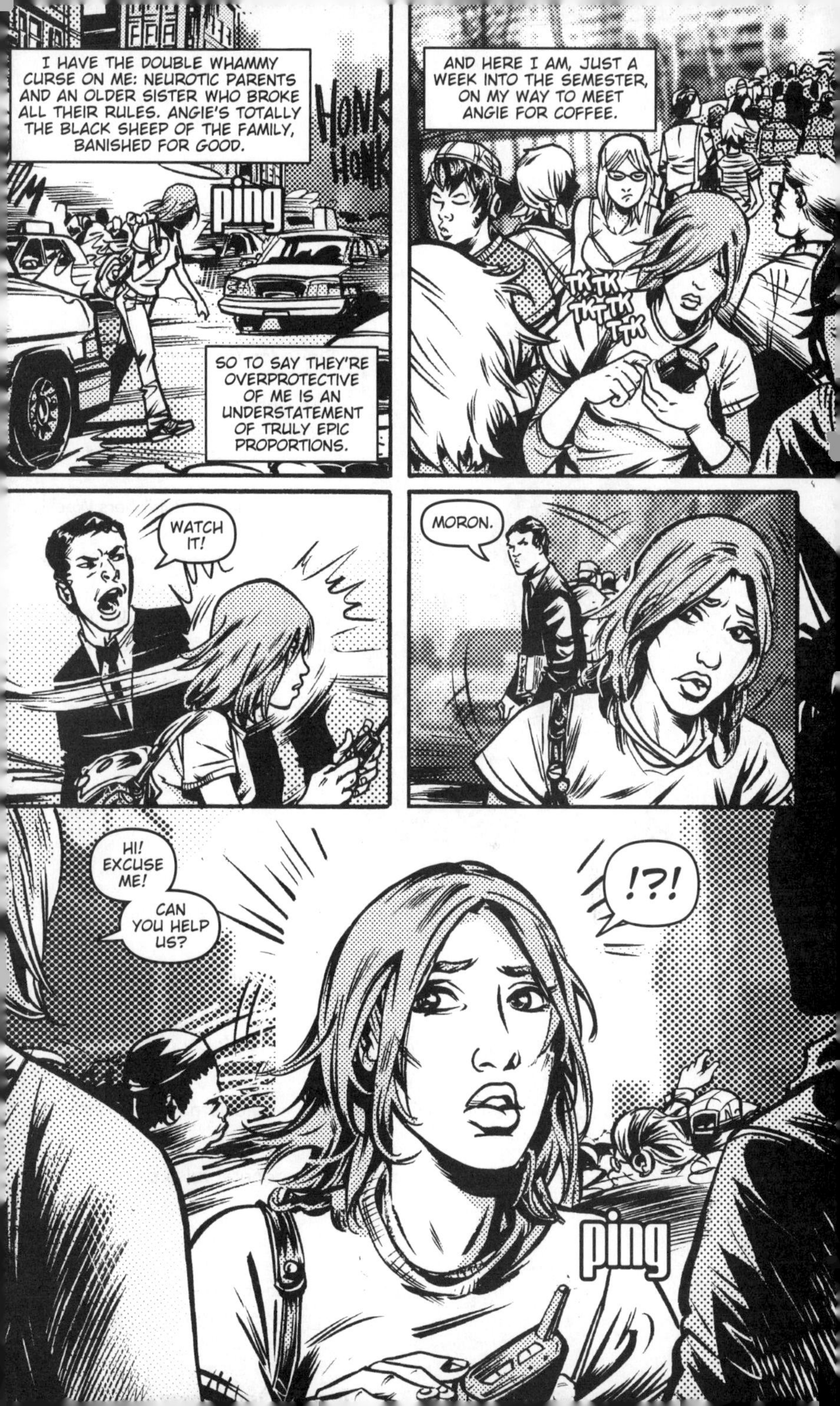
I HAVE THE DOUBLE WHAMMY CURSE ON ME: NEUROTIC PARENTS AND AN OLDER SISTER WHO BROKE ALL THEIR RULES. ANGIE'S TOTALLY THE BLACK SHEEP OF THE FAMILY, BANISHED FOR GOOD.
HONK HONK
ping
SO TO SAY THEY'RE OVERPROTECTIVE OF ME IS AN UNDERSTATEMENT OF TRULY EPIC PROPORTIONS.
AND HERE I AM, JUST A WEEK INTO THE SEMESTER, ON MY WAY TO MEET ANGIE FOR COFFEE.
TK TK TK TK TK
WATCH IT!
MORON.
HI! EXCUSE ME!
CAN YOU HELP US?
!?!
ping

By the highly acclaimed author of *Boy Proof* and *Beige*

JANES ♥ in LOVE
by CECIL CASTELLUCCI and JIM RUGG

Praise for *The Plain Janes*:

"Thought-provoking....absolutely engaging..."
—Booklist, Starred review

Starred review in Publishers Weekly

Washington Post Best of 2007 pick

Included in The New York Public Library's Books for the Teen Age 2008

The second title in the PLAIN JANES series finds the coolest clique of

misfits playing cupid and becoming entangled in the affairs of the heart.

P.L.A.I.N., People Loving Art In Neighborhoods, goes global once the art

gang procures a spot in the Metro City Museum of Modern Art contest.

And the girls will discover that in art and in love, general rules don't

often apply.

By CECIL CASTELLUCCI & JIM RUGG
AVAILABLE IN SEPTEMBER ■ Read on.

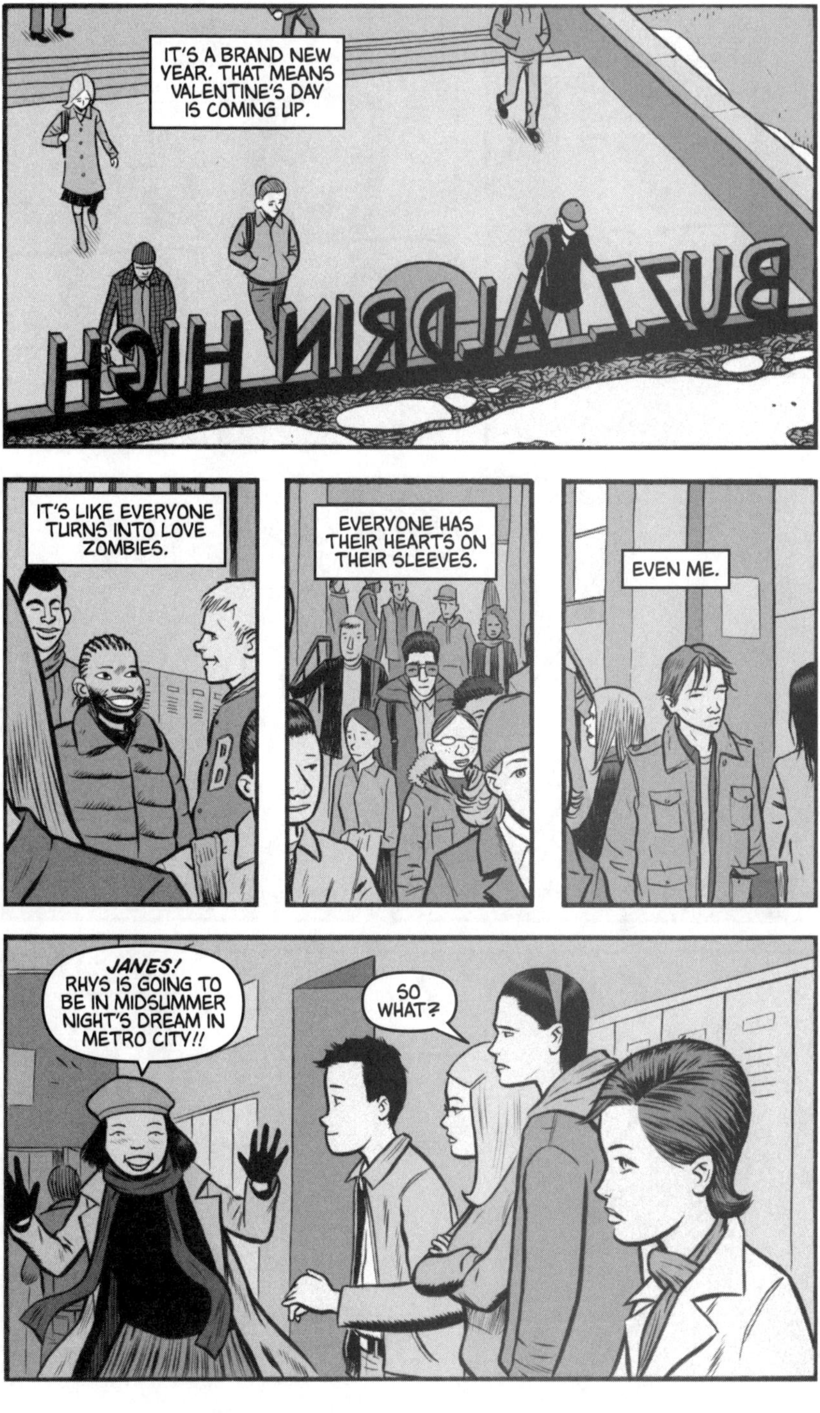
IT'S A BRAND NEW YEAR. THAT MEANS VALENTINE'S DAY IS COMING UP.
BUZZ ALDRIN HIGH
IT'S LIKE EVERYONE TURNS INTO LOVE ZOMBIES.
EVERYONE HAS THEIR HEARTS ON THEIR SLEEVES.
EVEN ME.
JANES! RHYS IS GOING TO BE IN MIDSUMMER NIGHT'S DREAM IN METRO CITY!!
SO WHAT?

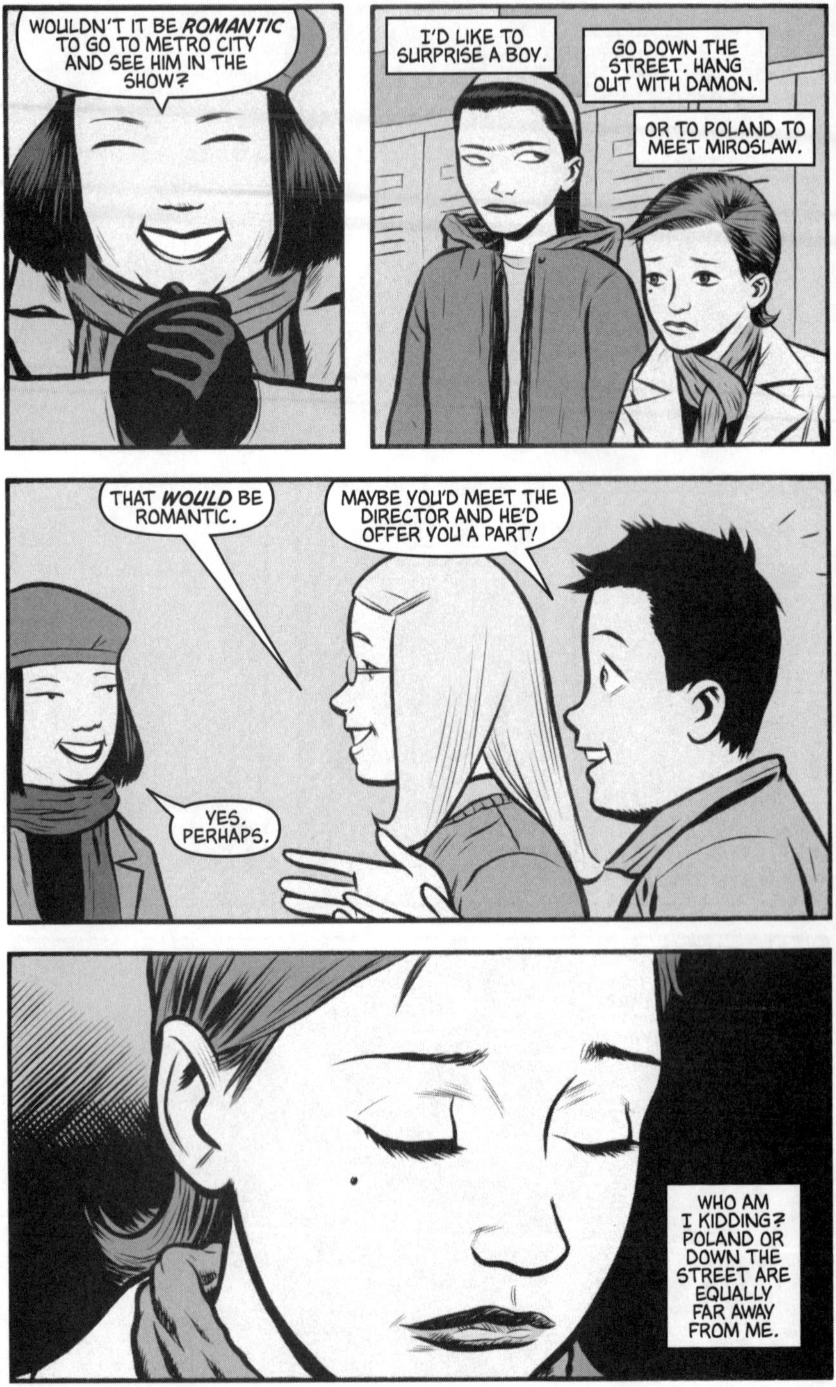

WOULDN'T IT BE ROMANTIC TO GO TO METRO CITY AND SEE HIM IN THE SHOW?
I'D LIKE TO SURPRISE A BOY.
GO DOWN THE STREET. HANG OUT WITH DAMON.
OR TO POLAND TO MEET MIROSLAW.
THAT WOULD BE ROMANTIC.
MAYBE YOU'D MEET THE DIRECTOR AND HE'D OFFER YOU A PART!
YES. PERHAPS.
WHO AM I KIDDING? POLAND OR DOWN THE STREET ARE EQUALLY FAR AWAY FROM ME.

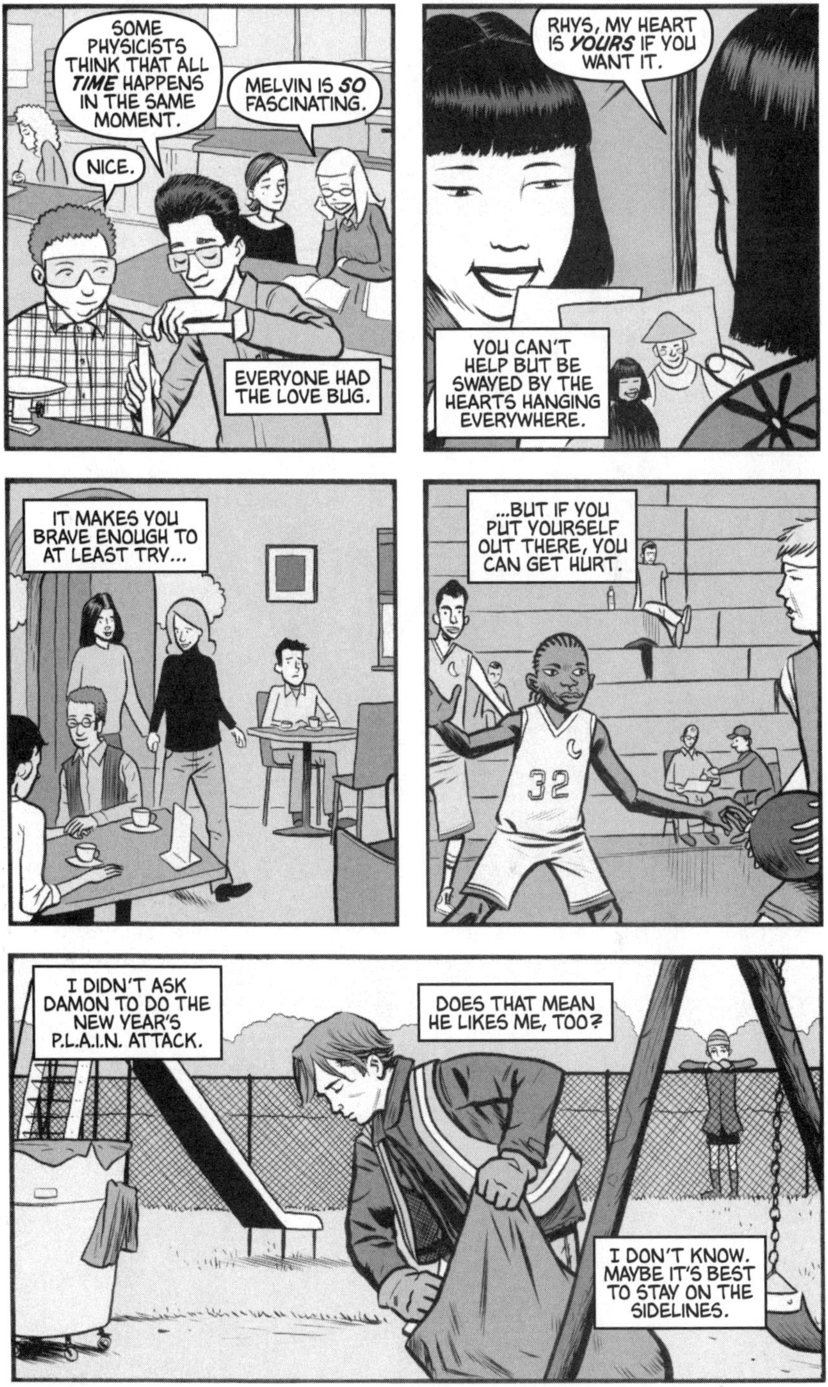
SOME PHYSICISTS THINK THAT ALL *TIME* HAPPENS IN THE SAME MOMENT.
MELVIN IS *SO* FASCINATING.
NICE.
EVERYONE HAD THE LOVE BUG.
RHYS, MY HEART IS *YOURS* IF YOU WANT IT.
YOU CAN'T HELP BUT BE SWAYED BY THE HEARTS HANGING EVERYWHERE.
IT MAKES YOU BRAVE ENOUGH TO AT LEAST TRY...
...BUT IF YOU PUT YOURSELF OUT THERE, YOU CAN GET HURT.
32
I DIDN'T ASK DAMON TO DO THE NEW YEAR'S P.L.A.I.N. ATTACK.
DOES THAT MEAN HE LIKES ME, TOO?
I DON'T KNOW. MAYBE IT'S BEST TO STAY ON THE SIDELINES.

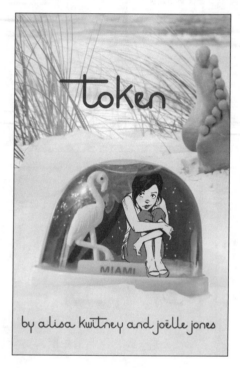

by alisa kwitney and joëlle jones

Written by noted comics author and novelist ALISA KWITNEY

Can a Jewish "girl out of time" and a Spanish old soul survive culture clashes and criminal records to find true love in the sun-drenched, sequined miasma that was South Beach in the Big '80s?

By ALISA KWITNEY & JOËLLE JONES
AVAILABLE IN OCTOBER ■ Read on.

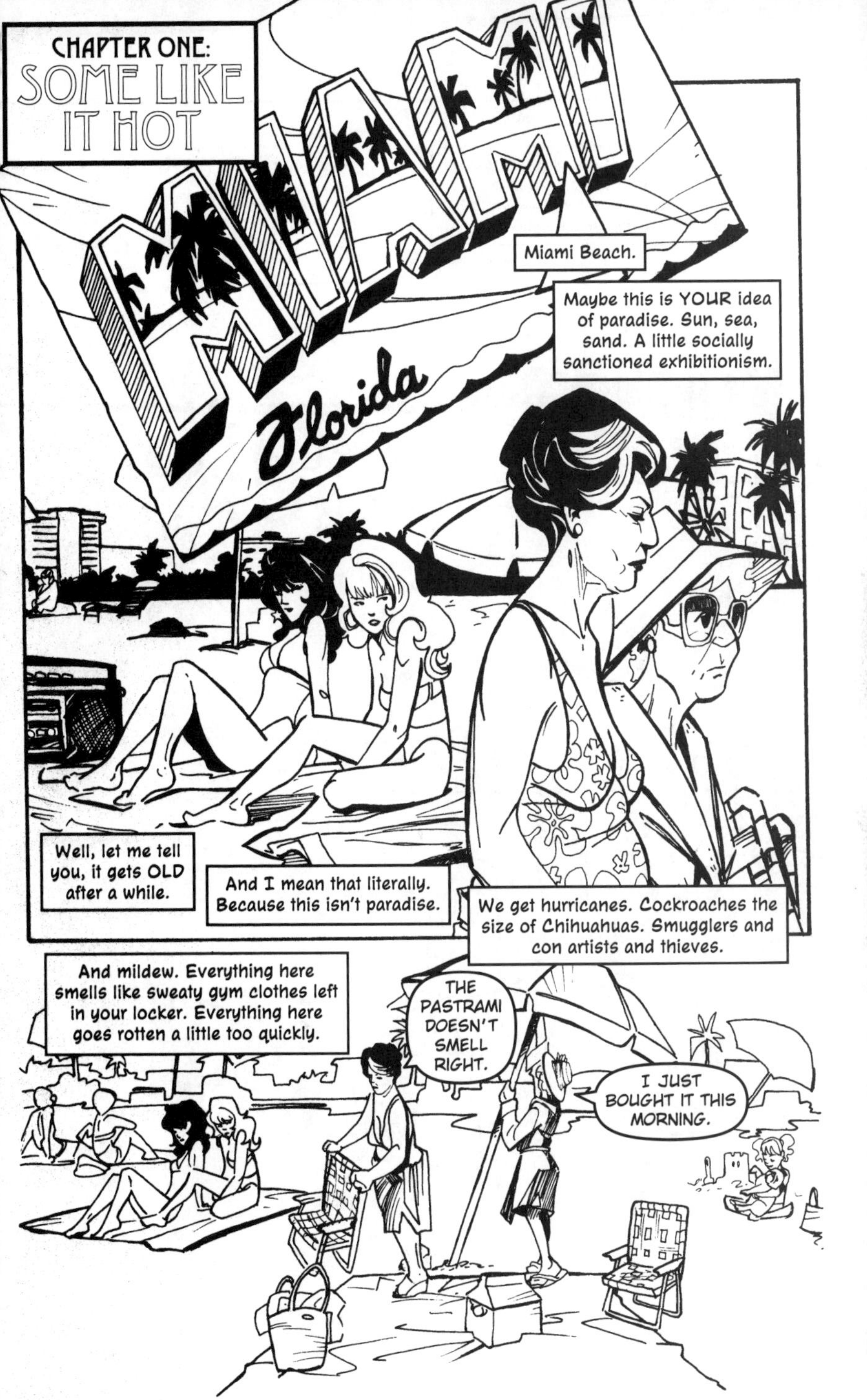

CHAPTER ONE:
SOME LIKE IT HOT
MIAMI
Florida
Miami Beach.
Maybe this is YOUR idea of paradise. Sun, sea, sand. A little socially sanctioned exhibitionism.
Well, let me tell you, it gets OLD after a while.
And I mean that literally. Because this isn't paradise.
We get hurricanes. Cockroaches the size of Chihuahuas. Smugglers and con artists and thieves.
And mildew. Everything here smells like sweaty gym clothes left in your locker. Everything here goes rotten a little too quickly.
THE PASTRAMI DOESN'T SMELL RIGHT.
I JUST BOUGHT IT THIS MORNING.

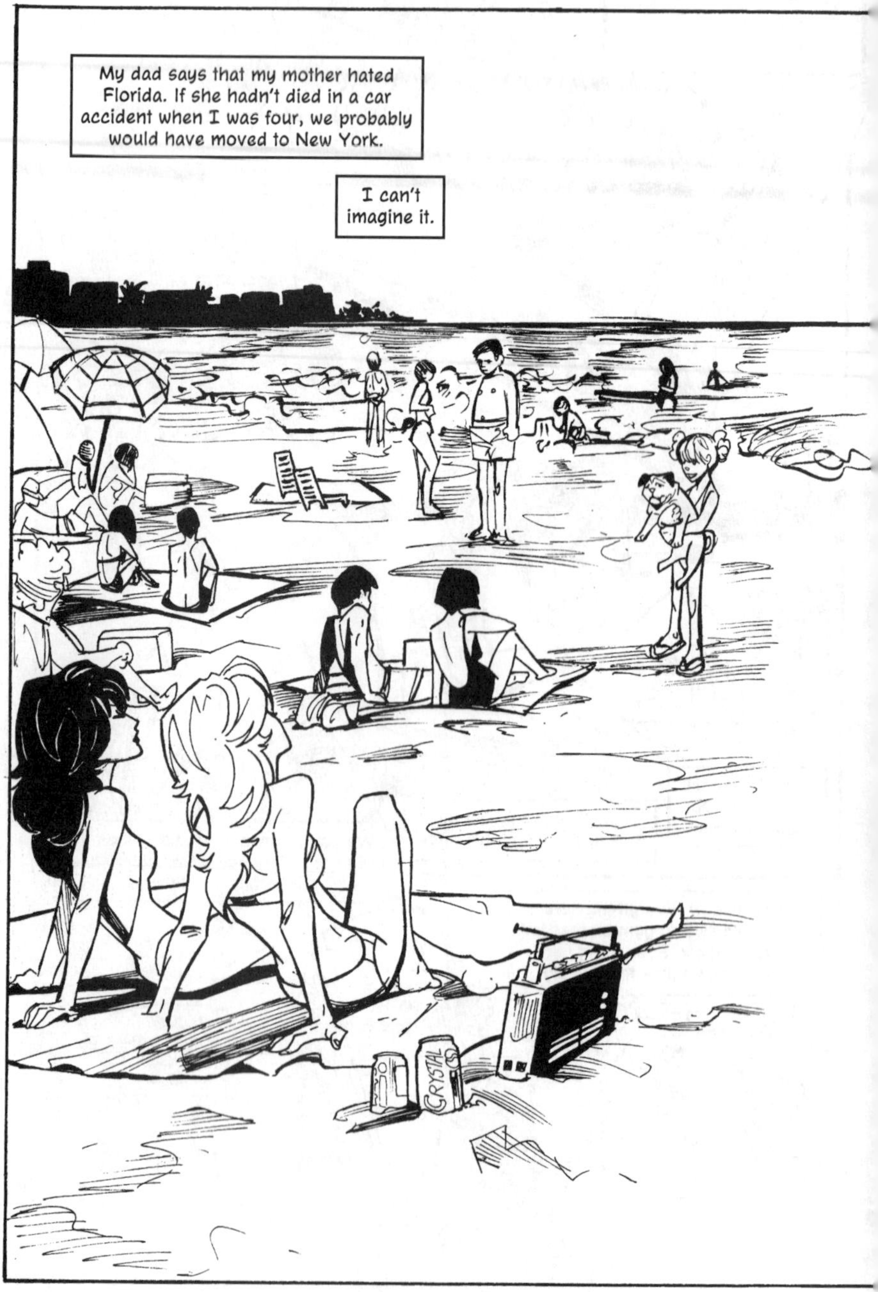
My dad says that my mother hated Florida. If she hadn't died in a car accident when I was four, we probably would have moved to New York.
I can't imagine it.
CRYSTAL

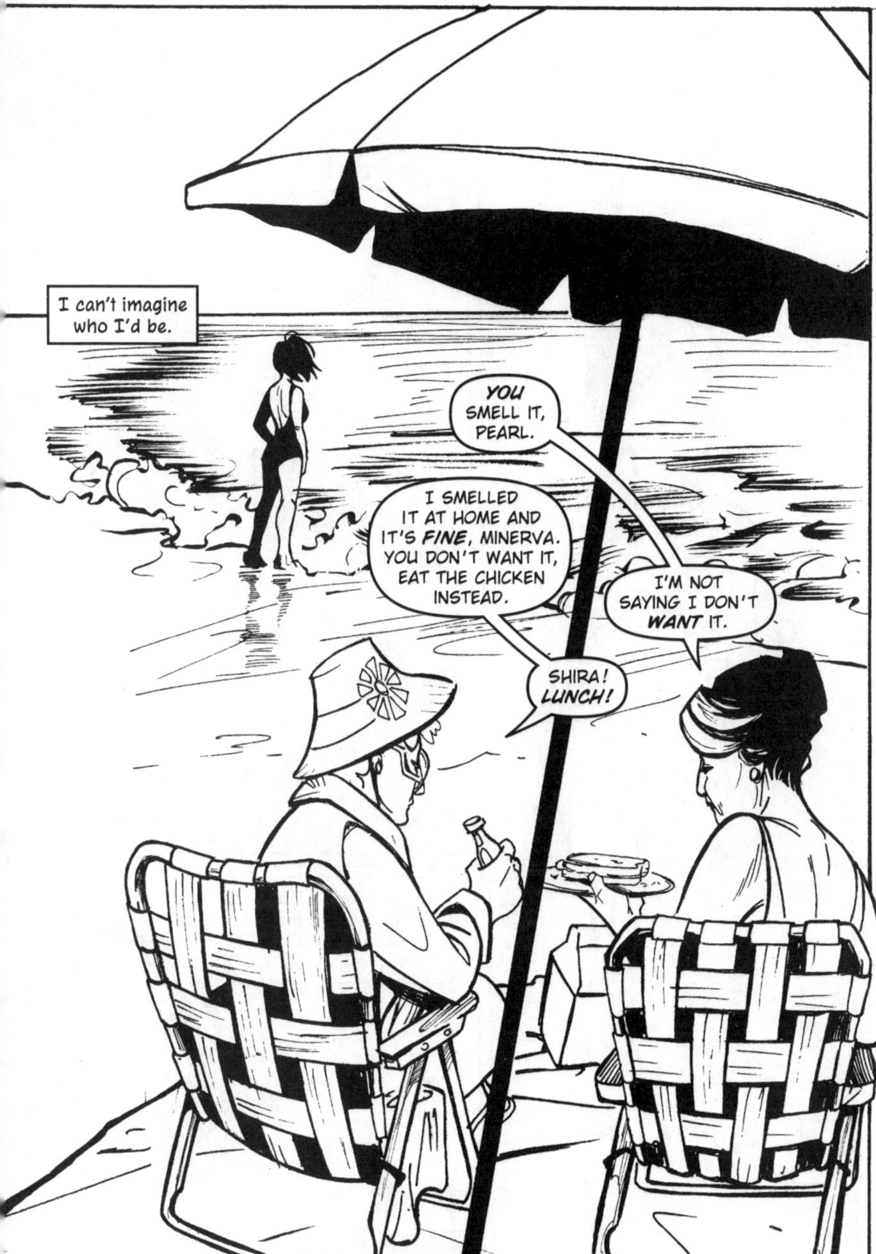
I can't imagine who I'd be.
YOU SMELL IT, PEARL.
I SMELLED IT AT HOME AND IT'S FINE, MINERVA. YOU DON'T WANT IT, EAT THE CHICKEN INSTEAD.
I'M NOT SAYING I DON'T WANT IT.
SHIRA! LUNCH!

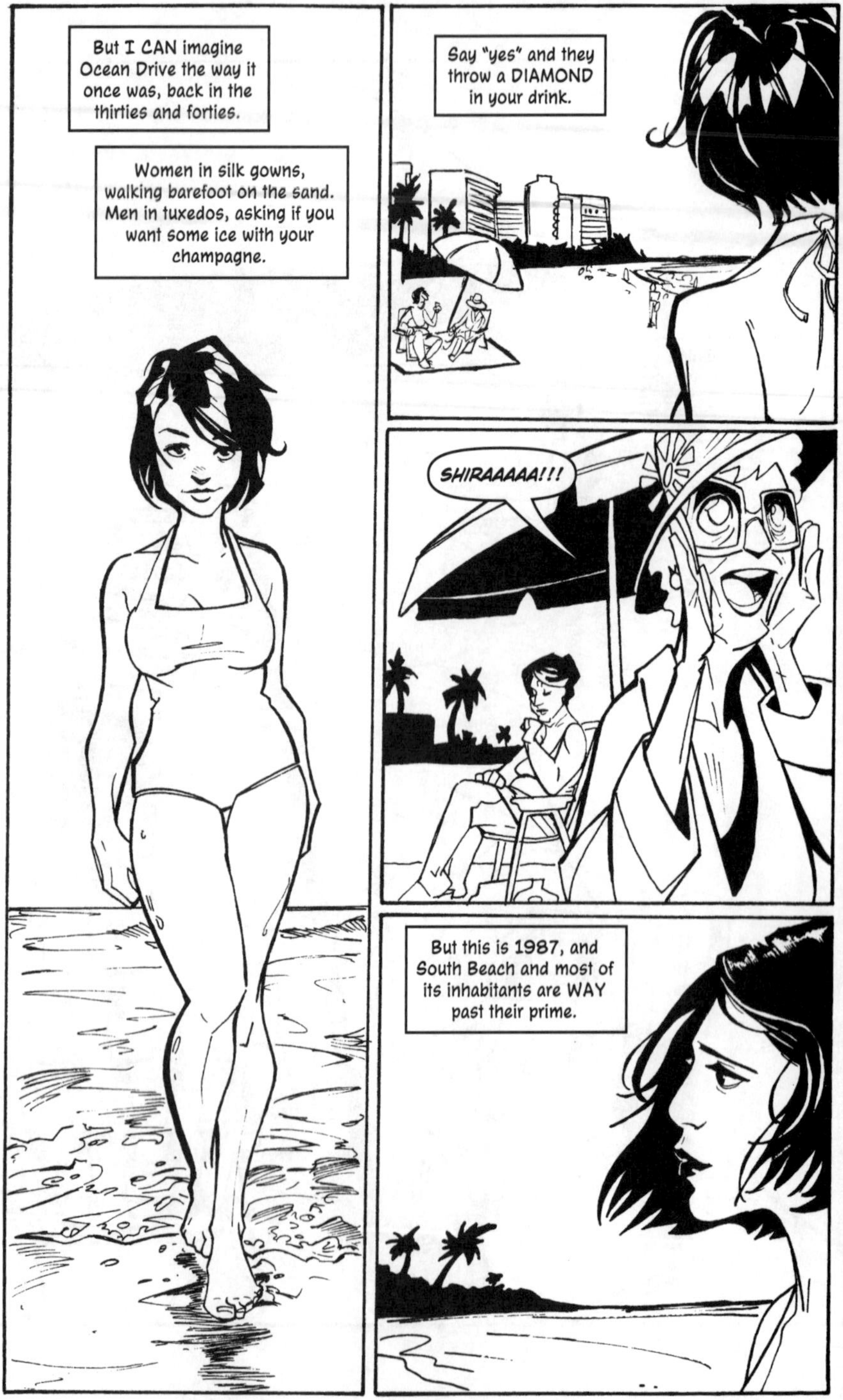
But I CAN imagine Ocean Drive the way it once was, back in the thirties and forties.
Women in silk gowns, walking barefoot on the sand. Men in tuxedos, asking if you want some ice with your champagne.
Say "yes" and they throw a DIAMOND in your drink.
SHIRAAAAA!!!
But this is 1987, and South Beach and most of its inhabitants are WAY past their prime.

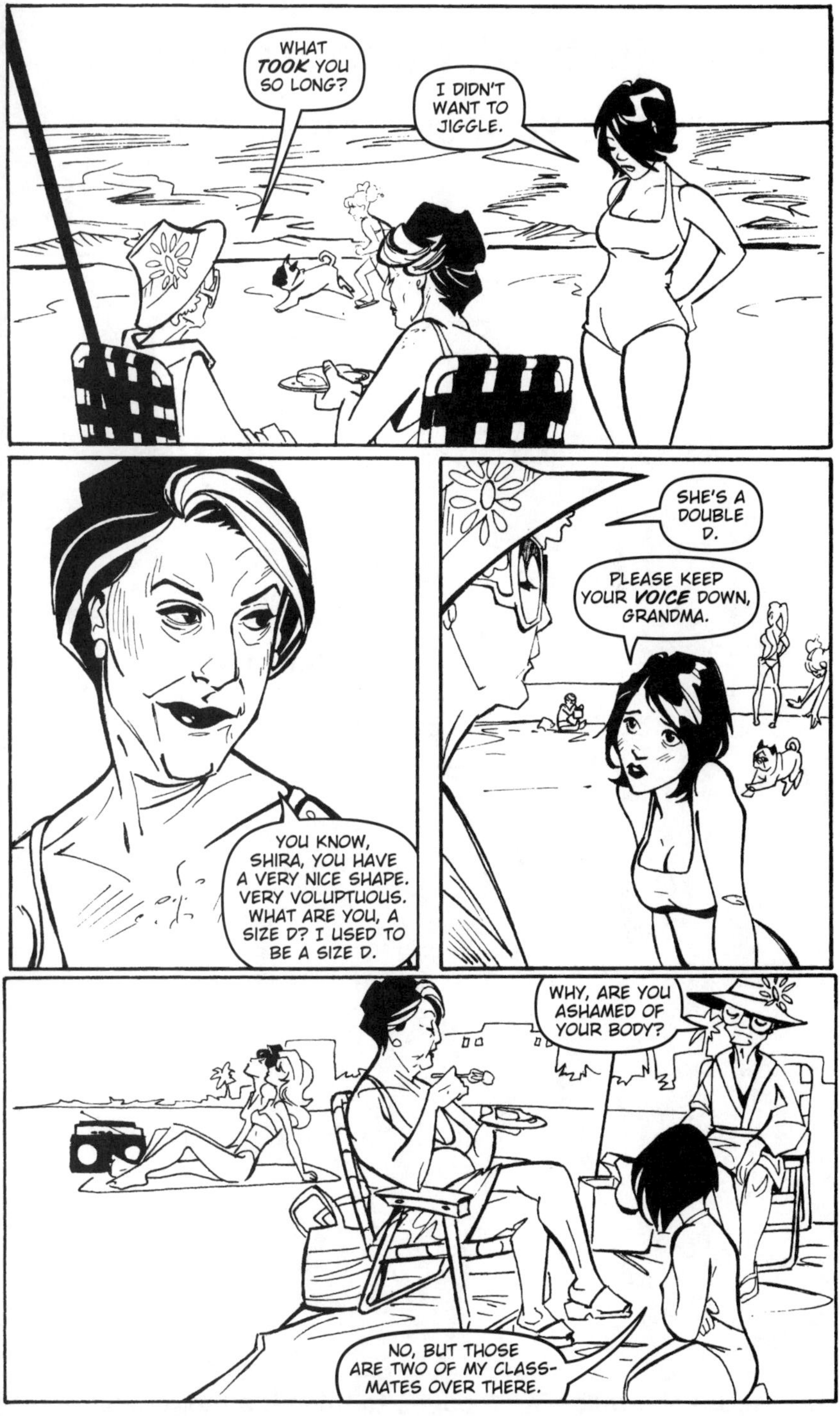

WHAT TOOK YOU SO LONG?
I DIDN'T WANT TO JIGGLE.
YOU KNOW, SHIRA, YOU HAVE A VERY NICE SHAPE. VERY VOLUPTUOUS. WHAT ARE YOU, A SIZE D? I USED TO BE A SIZE D.
SHE'S A DOUBLE D.
PLEASE KEEP YOUR VOICE DOWN, GRANDMA.
WHY, ARE YOU ASHAMED OF YOUR BODY?
NO, BUT THOSE ARE TWO OF MY CLASS-MATES OVER THERE.

Your life in pictures starts here!

~A DO-IT YOURSELF MINI COMIC~

Write your story ideas here:

Draw your main character sketches here:

Use the following 3 pages to bring it all together.

TITLE: BY:

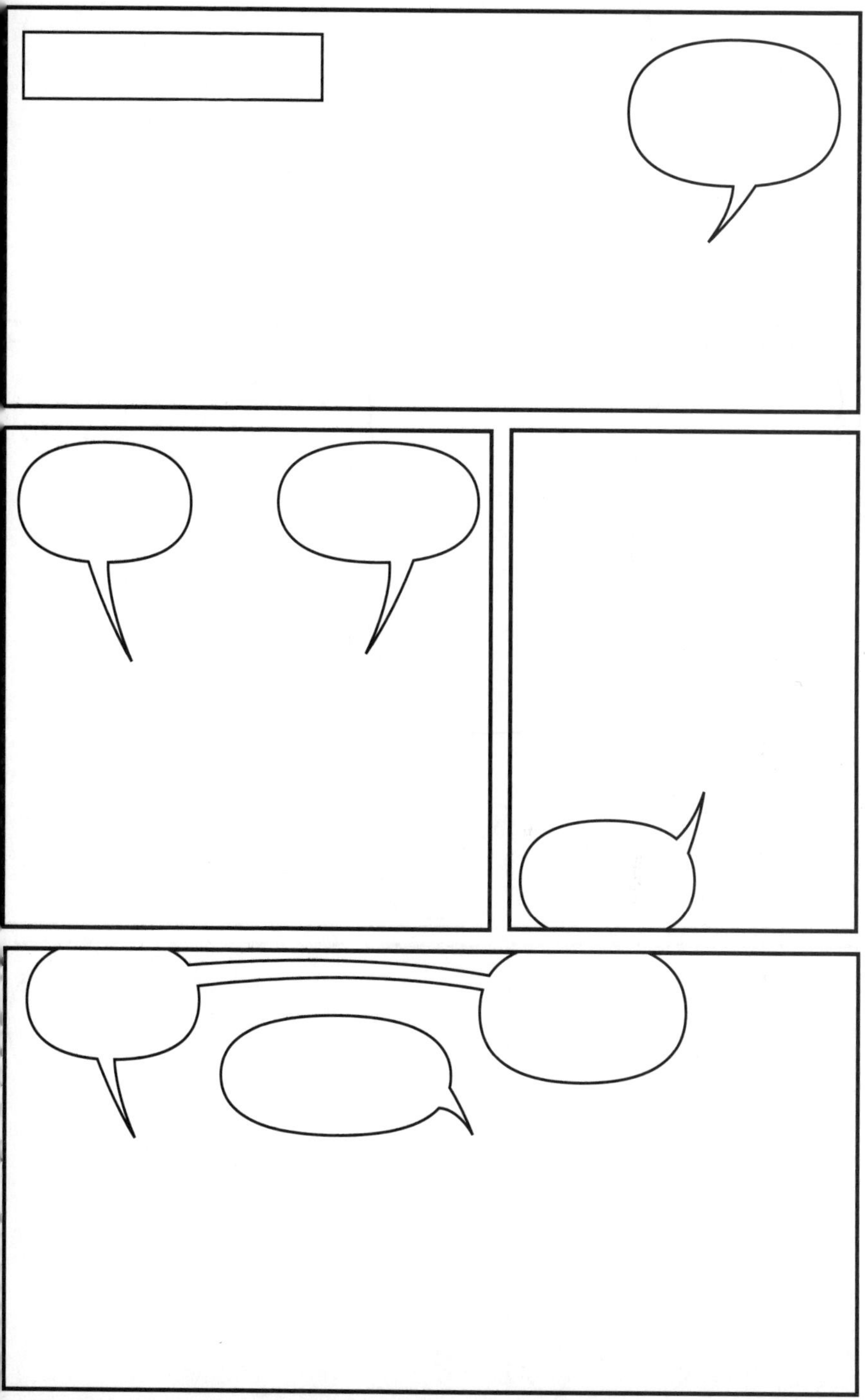

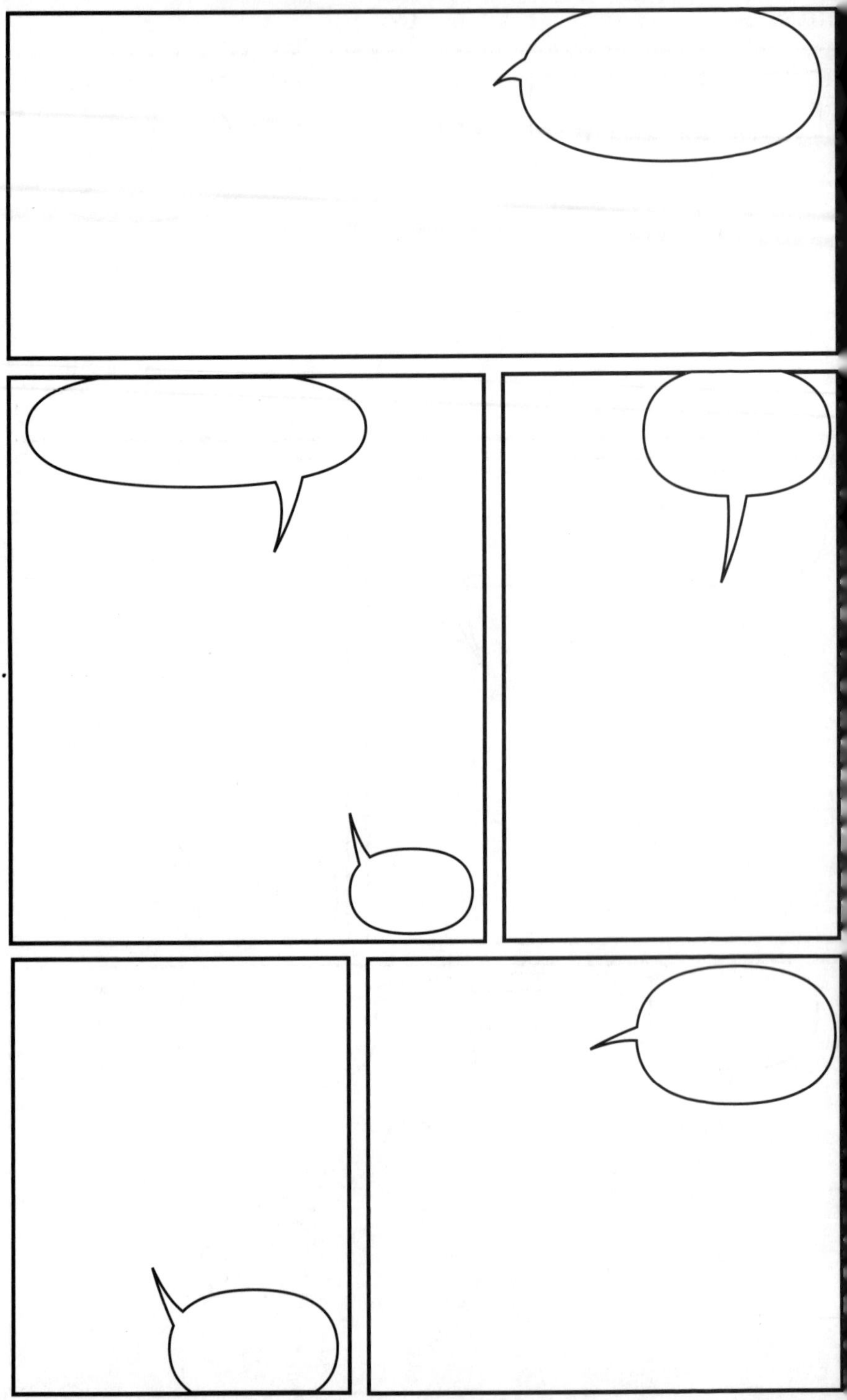

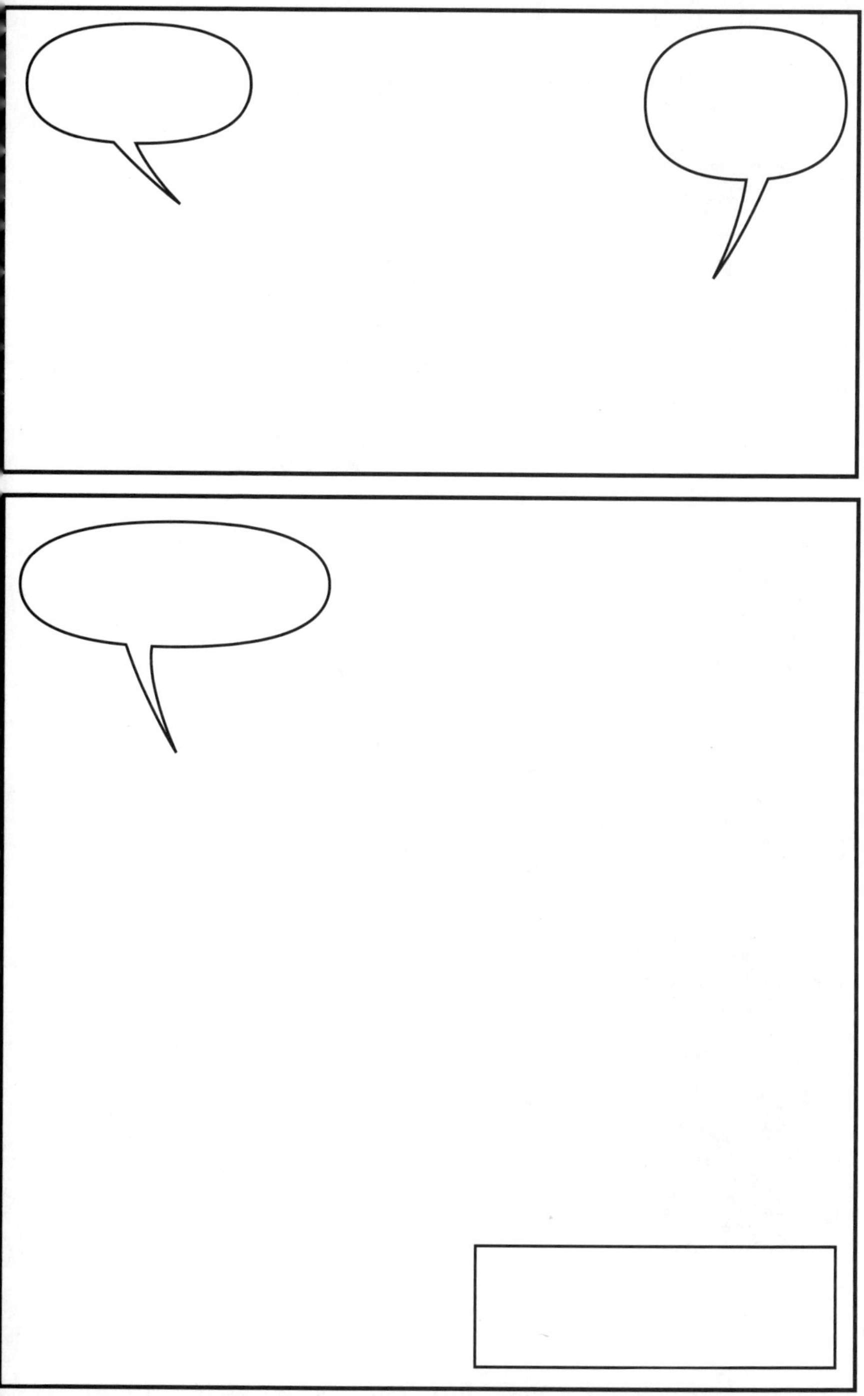

CHECK OUT STORYTELLING TIPS FROM TOP WRITERS AND ARTISTS AT MINXBOOKS.NET

Don't miss any of the minx books:

THE PLAIN JANES
CECIL CASTELLUCCI
and JIM RUGG

THE PLAIN JANES
By Cecil Castellucci
and Jim Rugg

Four girls named Jane are anything but ordinary once they form a secret art gang called P.L.A.I.N. — People Loving Art In Neighborhoods. But can art attacks really save the hell that is high school?

Derek Kirk Kim & Jesse Hamm
Good As Lily

GOOD AS LILY
By Derek Kirk Kim
and Jesse Hamm

What would you do if versions of yourself at 6, 29 and 70 suddenly appear and wreak havoc on your already awkward existence?

Re-Gifters

RE-GIFTERS
By Mike Carey, Sonny Liew
and Marc Hempel

It's love, Korean-American style when a tenacious martial artist falls for a California surfer boy and learns that in romance and recycled gifts, what goes around comes around.

YALSA Winner

confessions of a
blabbermouth
MIKE CAREY LOUISE CAREY AARON ALEXOVICH

CONFESSIONS OF A BLABBERMOUTH
By Mike and Louise Carey
and Aaron Alexovich

When Tasha's mom brings home a creepy boyfriend and his deadpan daughter, a dysfunctional family is headed for a complete meltdown. By the father-daughter writing team.

Included in The New York Public Library's Books for the Teen Age 2008

clubbing

CLUBBING
By Andi Watson
and Josh Howard

A spoiled, rebellious London girl takes on the stuffy English countryside when she solves a murder mystery on the 19th hole of her grandparents' golf course.

kimmie66
AARON ALEXOVICH

KIMMIE66
By Aaron Alexovich

This high-velocity, virtual reality ghost story follows a tech-savvy teenager on a dangerous quest to save her best friend, the world's first all-digital girl.

"Neuromancer for the Hello Kitty crowd."
—*Village Voice*

Your life. Your books. ***How novel.***
minxbooks.net